UNLOCKING

T H E

4th edition

Mark Ryan
with contributions from
Steve Foster

UNLOCKING
THE
LAW

Routledge
Taylor & Francis Group

LONDON AND NEW YORK

Fourth edition published 2019
by Routledge
2 Park Square, Milton Park, Abingdon, Oxon, OX14 4RN

and by Routledge
711 Third Avenue, New York, NY 10017

Routledge is an imprint of the Taylor & Francis Group, an informa business

© 2019 Taylor & Francis

The right of Mark Ryan and Steve Foster to be identified as authors
of this work has been asserted by them in accordance with sections
77 and 78 of the Copyright, Designs and Patents Act 1988.

First edition published by Hodder in 2007
Third edition published by Routledge 2014

Library of Congress Cataloging-in-Publication Data
Names: Ryan, Mark (Law teacher) author. | Foster, Steve,
    1955– author.
Title: Unlocking Constitutional and Administrative Law / by Mark
    Ryan ; with contributions from Steve Foster.
Description: 4th edition. | Milton Park, Abingdon, Oxon ; New York,
    NY : Routledge, 2019. | Series: Unlocking the law | Includes
    bibliographical references and index.
Identifiers: LCCN 2018020861| ISBN 9781138322691 (hbk) | ISBN
    9781138101777 (pbk) | ISBN 9781315652610 (master ebk) | ISBN
    9781317313601 (web pdf) | ISBN 9781317313595 (epub) | ISBN
    9781317313588 (mobipocket)
Subjects: LCSH: Constitutional law—Great Britain. | Great Britain—
    Politics and government.
Classification: LCC KD3989 .R93 2019 | DDC 342.41—dc23
LC record available at https://lccn.loc.gov/2018020861

ISBN: 978–1–138–32269–1 (hbk)
ISBN: 978–1–138–10177–7 (pbk)
ISBN: 978–1–315–65261–0 (ebk)

Typeset in Palatino
by Swales & Willis Ltd, Exeter, Devon, UK

Visit the companion website: www.unlockingthelaw.co.uk

Printed and bound in Great Britain by
TJ International Ltd, Padstow, Cornwall

Contents

3   *THE NATURE OF THE BRITISH CONSTITUTION*

4   *THE SOURCES OF THE BRITISH CONSTITUTION*

5 THE SEPARATION OF POWERS

CONTENTS

11   *THE EXECUTIVE*

12 *EXECUTIVE/PARLIAMENTARY RELATIONS*

13   THE JUDICIARY

14   THE DECENTRALISATION OF PUBLIC POWER

16 THE EUROPEAN CONVENTION ON HUMAN RIGHTS

17 THE HUMAN RIGHTS ACT 1998

18 FREEDOM OF SPEECH

19 JUDICIAL REVIEW I (RATIONALE AND PROCEDURE)

20 JUDICIAL REVIEW II (GROUNDS OF REVIEW AND REMEDIES)

21   *GRIEVANCE MECHANISMS*

Acknowledgements

The books in this series are a departure from traditional law texts and represent one view of a type of learning resource that we feel is particularly useful to students. The series editors would therefore like to thank the publishers for their support in making the project a reality. In particular we would also like to thank Alexia Chan for her continued faith in the project from its first conception.

Jacqueline Martin and Chris Turner

I would like to thank Gibson Fairnie for his support during the writing of this text. I would also like to thank Steve Foster for updating Chapter 18 on freedom of speech.

This book is dedicated to my mother and my siblings (John, PJ, Gerard, Mandy, Caroline and Maureen) and my nieces and nephews (Jamie, Jonathan, Tara, Natacha, Jade, Sebastian, Celia, Bailey, Dulcie, Ned and Theo).

Mark Ryan

Crown copyright material is reproduced under the terms of the Click-Use Licence.

Every effort has been made to trace and acknowledge ownership of copyright. The publishers will be glad to make suitable arrangements with any copyright holders whom it has not been possible to contact.

Preface

The Unlocking the Law series is an entirely new style of undergraduate law textbook. Many student texts are very dense prose and have little in the way of interactive materials to help a student feel his or her way through the course of study on a given module.

The purpose of this series, then, is to try to make learning each subject area more accessible by focusing on actual learning needs, and by providing a range of different supporting materials and features.

All topic areas are broken up into 'bite-size' sections, with a logical progression and extensive use of headings and numerous sub-headings. Each book in the series will also contain a variety of charts, diagrams and key facts summaries to reinforce the information in the body of the text. Diagrams and flow charts are particularly useful because they can provide a quick and easy understanding of the key points, especially when revising for examinations. Key facts charts not only provide a quick visual guide through the subject but are useful for revision purposes also.

Note also that for all incidental references to 'he', 'him', 'his', we invoke the Interpretation Act 1978 and its provisions that 'he' includes 'she' etc.

Chapters 1–15 and 18–21 were written by Mark Ryan, and Chapters 16–17 were written by Steve Foster.

The law is stated as we believe it to be on 1 January 2018, although where space permits some material has been added after this date.

Mark Ryan
Steve Foster

Guide to the book

In the Unlocking the Law books all the essential elements that make up the law are clearly defined to bring the law alive and make it memorable. In addition, the books are enhanced with learning features to reinforce learning and test your knowledge as you study. Follow this guide to make sure you get the most from reading this book.

AIMS AND OBJECTIVES

Defines what you will learn in each chapter.

definition

Find key legal terminology at a glance.

SECTION

Highlights sections from Acts.

ARTICLE

Defines Articles of the EU Treaty or of the European Convention on Human Rights or other Treaty. In this text, this symbol also denotes an aspect of a national constitution.

tutor tip

Provides key ideas from lecturers on how to get ahead.

CLAUSE

Shows a Bill going through Parliament or a draft Bill proposed by the Law Commission.

CASE EXAMPLE

 Illustrates the law in action.

JUDGMENT

 Provides extracts from judgments on cases.

Indicates that you will be able to test yourself further on this topic using the Key Questions and Answers section of this book on www.unlockingthelaw.co.uk.

Student mentor tip

Offers advice from law graduates on the best way to achieve the results you want.

QUOTATION

Encourages you to engage with primary sources.

ACTIVITY

Enables you to test yourself as you progress through the chapter.

SAMPLE ESSAY QUESTIONS

Provide you with real-life sample essays and show you the best way to plan your answer.

SUMMARY

Concludes each chapter to reinforce learning.

Table of cases

TABLE OF CASES

Table of statutes

Table of statutory instruments

Table of international legislation

1

Introductory concepts

public law

the law regulating the powers of the institutions of the state, how they relate to each other and how they relate to individuals

private law

the law regulating the relationship between individuals

AIMS AND OBJECTIVES

At the end of this chapter you should be able to:

- Distinguish between **public law** and **private law**
- Define and distinguish between constitutional and administrative law

1.1 The distinction between public law and private law

In general, the term 'law' can be broadly divided into two branches: public law and private law. Constitutional and administrative law form part of public law.

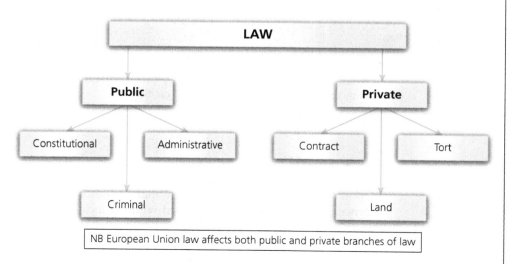

Figure 1.1 The distinction between public law and private law

1.1.1 Private law

In essence, private law is that branch of the law that is concerned with the relationship that individuals have with one another. For example:

- An individual forms a legally binding contract with a work colleague when he agrees to purchase a three-piece suite from him (see further *Unlocking Contract Law*).
- An individual sues a neighbour in the law of defamation for making untrue slanderous accusations about his past (see further *Unlocking Torts*).
- Two adjoining land owners legally dispute the location of a boundary fence between their land (see further *Unlocking Land Law*).
- A pedestrian sues the driver of a car in the law of negligence after being badly injured in an accident caused by his careless driving (see further *Unlocking Torts*).

1.1.2 Private law involving other than private individuals

It is also worth noting at this point that it is possible for individuals to have private law transactions or legal relations with the state (in this context and for present purposes, the state means simply the government, public authorities, local authorities, etc). For example, an individual may form a legally binding contract with a local authority, or indeed may even sue that same body in the law of negligence if it has acted carelessly and caused harm. Although in one sense such relations would appear to form part of contract and tort law respectively (with the defendant in these cases being the state, rather than a private individual), such actions could also have a public law dimension. This is because as these actions in contract and negligence involve the state they will be governed by special rules and principles which have the effect of treating the state differently from an ordinary private individual defendant. This point serves to indicate at this early stage that in the United Kingdom the distinction between private and public law is not absolute and so it is not always easy to draw the line between them with complete precision. For example, in this context Lord Wilberforce in *Davy v Spelthorne Borough Council* [1984] 1 AC 262 commented:

JUDGMENT

'The expressions "private law" and "public law" have recently been imported into the law of England from countries which, unlike our own, have separate systems concerning public law and private law. No doubt they are convenient expressions for descriptive purposes. In this country they must be used with caution.'

For more on public law issues, see section 19.5.

1.1.3 Public law

Public law (which subsumes both constitutional and administrative law – see section 1.2) is that branch of the law that focuses on the power of the state. In essence, public lawyers are concerned with the location of state power, how that power is exercised and controlled, and how it impacts on the individual. At a very basic level, public law is concerned with the following questions:

- Who and what bodies/institutions/individuals exercise state/public power?
- What is the nature and extent of these powers?

- Why do these bodies/institutions exercise power?
- How do these bodies relate to each other?
- How is power used?
- How is the use of power regulated?
- How are these bodies/institutions/individuals made accountable?
- What protection is given to the individual from the power of the state?

In other words, the study of public law is concerned with the identification of public power, the institutions that exercise it and how these institutions relate to one another and to the individual. Most importantly, it is concerned with how the use of public power is regulated and controlled. Thus, the constitutional principle of the accountability of the state (whether in a legal or a political form) is a major theme that underpins the subject of public law and consequently, therefore, this text.

In summary, in contrast to private law, which is concerned essentially with individual/private legal relations, public law focuses on the structure and organisation of the state and how the individual relates to the state.

1.1.4 Public law and criminal law

At this point, it is pertinent to note that the broad term public law also technically embraces criminal law, as crimes are termed as offences against the state, and so punishable by it. Although criminal law clearly has a public law dimension, historically the substantive subject of criminal law (eg offences against the person, theft etc) has nevertheless been taught as a separate subject (see further *Unlocking Criminal Law*). Notwithstanding this, certain aspects of criminal law (for example the breadth and extent of police powers for arresting and detaining individuals) will necessarily be subsumed within the field of public law as they raise issues concerning basic **human rights** and civil liberties. In particular, the substantive criminal law offences which involve restricting **freedom of expression**, for example the laws of obscenity and indecency will be considered as part of Chapter 18.

human rights

rights and freedoms to which every human being is entitled

freedom of expression

a right set out in Article 10 of the European Convention on Human Rights and now part of UK law as a consequence of the Human Rights Act 1998

constitutional convention

a binding political rule of the constitution

1.1.5 Public law and politics

Public law, more so than any other substantive law subject, is intimately and inextricably linked with the disciplines of political science and government. As a consequence, it is an advantage to have a background interest in, and awareness of, general British politics when studying public law as the subject necessarily draws upon some of these principles. In fact, as we will see in Chapter 4, some of the sources of the British constitution are actually political practices (**constitutional conventions**).

For example, in the context of the government's relations with Parliament, government ministers are both collectively and individually responsible to Parliament for their actions and yet this accountability is not legal but political in nature, determined by predominately political factors. Furthermore, the connection and overlap between politics and constitutional law is evident in the context of civil liberties which involves the basic human rights and freedoms of the individual. These rights – which include, for example, the right to free speech – raise the issue of whether such rights should be enjoyed, and whether they are actually political/moral/religious questions which happen to be dressed up as legal questions which are determined by (unelected) judges in a courtroom (whether domestically or in Europe).

Public law is highly topical and an ever-changing and dynamic subject. In studying public law, therefore, it is advisable to keep abreast of recent developments through the daily broadsheet newspapers. Thus, every day there will be, invariably, something with a public law dimension and therefore of interest to public lawyers. Hypothetical examples could include the following:

- A government minister resigns over a scandal.
- A local authority acts illegally by abusing its powers.
- The European Court of Human Rights in Strasbourg makes a judgment against the United Kingdom for breaching the European Convention on Human Rights.
- The Queen approves the appointment of 10 new life peers to sit in the House of Lords.
- Parliament passes a law which restricts freedom of expression.
- The European Court of Justice in Luxembourg (technically called the Court of Justice of the EU) declares that the United Kingdom has failed to follow European Union law.
- The **Administrative Court** declares that the Home Secretary has breached the Human Rights Act 1998.

Administrative Court

that part of the High Court which processes judicial review cases

ACTIVITY

Applying the law

Read one week's issues of a national daily newspaper and try to identify articles which you think have relevance to the study of public law.

1.1.6 Public law and European Union law

As a result of the enactment of the European Communities Act 1972 (see Chapter 15), in recent decades both public law and private law have been significantly affected by, and subject to, European Union (EU) law. Although the main substantive subjects of **EU law** (eg the free movement of goods, workers, services, etc) are studied separately (see further *Unlocking EU Law*), certain aspects of it – such as the primacy of EU law – have had such a profound effect on the constitution of the United Kingdom that they have to be considered in any study of public law. In particular, the reception of EU law (which currently has overriding legal effect) into the United Kingdom has resulted in, *inter alia*, the restriction of the power of the United Kingdom Parliament to pass any law that it chooses (see Chapter 7 in conjunction with section 15.6).

NB. The above notwithstanding, the point must be noted that in 2016 in a national referendum the United Kingdom voted to leave the European Union (ie 'Brexit'). Although the scheduled date of exit is March 2019, at the time of writing the terms of the United Kingdom's exit, together with any transitional arrangements thereafter, had yet to be agreed. In any event, EU law will continue to have overriding legal effect until the United Kingdom exits the European Union. This issue of Brexit is considered further at section 15.6.6.

EU law

law and legal practices emanating from the European Union

KEY FACTS

Public law embraces both constitutional and administrative law and is essentially concerned with the organs of the state, together with how they relate to each other and to individuals.

Public law is concerned with the use and regulation of public power.

1.2 The distinction between constitutional and administrative law

Although both constitutional and administrative law form part of the generic term public law, a distinction, albeit a fine one, can be made between them.

1.2.1 Constitutional law

constitution

the rules which govern the government which can be found in either a codified or uncodified form

At a very basic level, constitutional law can be described simply as the law relating to the **constitution**. Although the term constitution will be considered in Chapter 2, for present purposes a constitution represents a set of basic rules and principles which govern the government/state.

A more detailed definition is provided by Barnett, who defined constitutional law in the following terms:

QUOTATION

'Constitutional law is concerned with the role and powers of the institutions within the state and with the relationship between the citizen and the state.'

H Barnett, *Constitutional and Administrative Law* (12th edn, Routledge/Taylor & Francis Group, 2017), p 4.

Parliament

composed of the House of Commons and the House of Lords

In other words, constitutional law concerns, among others, the following elements (all of which will be considered in this text):

- The principal institutions of the state, *viz*, **Parliament** (see Chapters 8 to 10), the government (see Chapter 11), the courts (see Chapter 13) and devolved/ decentralised state bodies (see Chapter 14).
- The specific roles and functions conferred on these institutions, together with the nature and extent of their powers (for example, see Chapter 11 on the powers of the executive).
- The procedures and mechanisms used to oversee, regulate and check these powers (for example, see Chapter 12 in relation to the parliamentary/political controls over the government and Chapters 19 and 20 for legal controls).
- The ways in which these institutions relate to one another (for example, see Chapter 10 on how the House of Lords and Commons relate to one another).
- The ways in which these institutions relate to the individual (for example, see Chapter 9 on parliamentary elections).
- The basic and fundamental rights of the individual (for example, the right to life and free speech) and how – and to what extent – these rights and freedoms can be protected from infringement by the state (see Chapters 16 and 17 on human rights and Chapter 18 on freedom of speech).

1.2.2 Administrative law

In general terms, administrative law (in contrast to constitutional law above) is concerned with, simply, the law relating to the administration/government. Wade and Forsyth defined it in the following terms:

QUOTATION

'A first approximation to a definition of administrative law is to say that it is the law relating to the control of governmental power . . . As a second approximation to a definition, administrative law may be said to be the body of general principles which govern the exercise of powers and duties by public authorities.'

H Wade and C Forsyth, *Administrative Law*
(11th edn, Oxford University Press, 2014), pp 4–5.

judicial review

the process whereby the courts review the legality of governmental actions

Ombudsman

an officer who investigates complaints of maladministration

The government, its officers and agencies are invested with extensive powers to provide services (eg administering welfare benefits) and to carry out specific government functions (eg making regulations). Administrative law, therefore, is focused specifically on the various powers that the government exercises and how these powers are controlled and regulated to ensure that the administration acts strictly within its limits. This branch of the law is concerned with the control of the government through the mechanisms of **judicial review** (see Chapters 19 and 20), tribunals (see Chapter 21) and inquiries (see Chapter 21). In addition, it also embraces other controls in the form of the Parliamentary **Ombudsman** (see Chapter 21).

It is clear that in the United Kingdom the distinction between administrative law and constitutional law is not easy to draw. At a general level it could be said that, whereas constitutional law tends to consider the whole apparatus of the state, administrative law, in contrast, is more specifically focused on how the executive/administration uses and misuses its powers. For practical purposes, this text considers each branch separately through a collection of various chapters: constitutional law is considered in Chapters 1–14 and 16–18, while administrative law is detailed in Chapters 19–21. In addition, a general introduction to European Union law is covered in Chapter 15. As such, it will be plain that constitutional law will form the major component of this book.

KEY FACTS

Constitutional law is the law relating to the constitution, the state institutions and their powers, together with how they relate to the individual.

Administrative law is concerned specifically with the law relating to the administration/executive/government and its control.

ACTIVITY

Self-test question

How can one define and recognise constitutional law?

2

Constitutions

AIMS AND OBJECTIVES

At the end of this chapter you should be able to:
- Define a constitution
- Appreciate the nature and content of constitutions
- Appreciate the purpose of constitutions
- Distinguish between different types of constitution
- Understand the concept of constitutionalism

2.1 Definition

All organisations – whether a university chess club or a state – have a constitution of some description, as society requires rules in order to function and ensure order. These rules are simply known as the constitution (constitutional rules). Bradley and Ewing (in the 2011 edition of their textbook) noted that a constitution can be defined in two ways: with a narrow or a wide meaning. In a narrow sense they have described a constitution as:

QUOTATION

'. . . a document having a special legal status which sets out the framework and principal functions of the organs of government within the state and declares the principles or rules by which those organs must operate.'

A Bradley and K Ewing, *Constitutional and Administrative Law*
(15th edn, Pearson/Longman, 2011), p 4.

In a broader sense of the term, they referred to, and quoted, Wheare, who had stated that it described:

QUOTATION

'. . . the whole system of government of a country, the collection of rules which establish and regulate or govern the government.'

K Wheare, *Modern Constitutions* (2nd edn, Oxford University Press, 1966), p 1.

In its first report in July 2001, the House of Lords Select Committee on the Constitution recognised the difficulty in defining the term constitution and put forward the following definition:

QUOTATION

'Our working definition of a constitution is that it is the set of laws, rules and practices that create the basic institutions of the state and its component and related parts, and stipulate the powers of those institutions and the relationship between the different institutions and between those institutions and the individual.'

The House of Lords Select Committee on the Constitution, *Reviewing the constitution: Terms of reference and method of working*, HL Paper 11 (2001), p 16.

For present purposes, therefore, we may conclude that a constitution is simply a set of rules and principles that govern the organisation and structure of the state which the governing institutions must, or should, adhere to. As will be indicated below, these constitutional rules almost invariably will be found in a single written document entitled 'The Constitution', although sometimes – as in the United Kingdom – these rules are located other than in a specific constitutional document (see Chapter 4 on the sources of the constitution of the United Kingdom).

ACTIVITY

Self-test question

Using the above definitions, how would you define a constitution in your own words?

2.2 The contents of a constitution

constitution-alism

the principle which requires a constitution to provide sufficient restraints on governmental/state power

What will a constitution contain? The exact contents of a state constitution will differ from state to state. It must be remembered that constitutions exist in both democratic and non-democratic countries, although by their nature, democratic constitutions should follow the principles of **constitutionalism** (see section 2.6.2).

As an introduction or foreword, a preamble is found in many state constitutions. It tends to be declaratory in nature and identifies the people as the constituent (sovereign) power from which the moral authority and legitimacy of the constitution derives. For example, in the Irish Constitution (1937) it is stated at the outset that:

ARTICLE

We the people . . . do hereby adopt, enact and give to ourselves this constitution.

In general, the main text of a constitution will contain the following elements.

2.2.1 The establishment of the institutions of government together with their roles, powers and functions

A constitution will set out the basic ground rules of the state which will include the establishment of its institutions (and so their legitimacy – see section 2.4.2). In short,

Cabinet

the collection of the most senior government ministers

Supreme Court

the highest domestic court

it will establish and detail the principal institutions of the state together with their roles/functions:

- The law-making institution which passes legislation (Parliament/Congress/Assembly).
- The executive/government institution which enforces the law and makes policy decisions (Prime Minister/**Cabinet**/President).
- The judicial institution which interprets and declares the law (the courts/Constitutional Court/**Supreme Court**).

For example, the Constitution of the United States of America (1789) states the following:

ARTICLE

- Art I, s 1. All legislative powers herein granted shall be vested in a Congress of the United States, which shall consist of a Senate and House of Representatives.
- Art II, s 1. The executive power shall be vested in a President of the United States of America.
- Art III, s 1. The judicial power of the United States shall be vested in one Supreme Court and such inferior courts as the Congress may from time to time ordain and establish.

In this way the constitution of the United States sets out the three key institutions of the state.

The constitution will also set out the specific powers of each institution. For example, again with reference to the constitution of the United States, Art II, s 2 states that the President shall have the power (with the consent of the Congress) to make Treaties and to nominate (also with congressional consent) the judges of the Supreme Court. Similarly, Art I, s 8 states that Congress shall have the power to lay and collect taxes and declare war. In short, a constitution will establish the key institutions of the state and allocate them constitutional roles and responsibilities and equip them with public powers.

It is fascinating to point out that in 2014 the Scottish Government, in advance of the impending referendum on Scottish independence (see section 14.3.2) issued a draft Scottish Independence Bill which provided for an interim Constitution for Scotland, which would have taken effect had Scotland voted for independence (*The Scottish Independence Bill: A consultation on an interim Constitution for Scotland* (The Scottish Government, Crown Copyright, 2014)).

2.2.2 The establishment of the relationship between the different institutions of the state

The constitution will also set out the constitutional relationship between the various institutions established under it. In a democracy this relationship will necessarily involve the principle of the system of checks and balances between the institutions (see Chapter 5). For example, as seen above, the constitution of the United States stipulates that Congress is the body responsible for passing legislation; however, Art I, s 7 states that before a Bill becomes law it must be presented to the President for approval. If the latter rejects the Bill, it can still become law providing that Congress reconsiders it and both congressional chambers pass the Bill with a two-thirds majority. This therefore sets out the constitutional relationship between the President and Congress in the context of the passage of legislation.

In the German Constitution (1949), Art 67 states that the Bundestag (the lower House of the German Parliament) can express a lack of confidence in the Federal Chancellor by electing (with a majority of its members) a successor to replace them. Thus, a major theme of public law is how the state institutions relate to and complement one another and, most importantly, how these institutions check and balance one another.

2.2.3 The establishment of the relationship between the state institutions and the individual

As noted above, constitutional law is partly concerned with how the individual relates to the state (ie what powers can the state exert over the individual?). For example, in what circumstances can the individual be arrested and detained or have his freedom of expression interfered with? A democratic constitution, however, will constitutionally ring-fence and safeguard certain basic rights of the individual with which the state institutions cannot interfere (or can only do so with compelling justification). In other words, this means that the rights of the individual are put beyond the reach of the state. In one sense, this can be seen as part of the social contract (see section 2.4.2) which the citizen makes with the state. This in turn confers legitimacy on the state institutions to rule.

Bill of Rights
document containing a list of basic and fundamental human rights

One of the most famous declarations of basic and fundamental human rights is 'the **Bill of Rights**' containing the first ten amendments of the constitution of the United States. As an example, Art IV of the Bill of Rights is set out below:

ARTICLE

The right of the people to be secure in their persons, houses, papers, and effects, against unreasonable searches and seizures, shall not be violated, and no warrants shall issue, but upon probable cause, supported by oath or affirmation, and particularly describing the place to be searched, and the persons or things to be seized.

Similarly, Part III of the Indian Constitution sets out the fundamental rights of the individual which include, among others:

- the right to equality
- the right to freedom of religion
- the right to freedom of speech, assembly, association, etc
- the right against exploitation.

By setting out the basic rights of the individual in the constitution in this way, these fundamental rights and freedoms are accorded special protection from infringement by the state.

2.2.4 The methods and procedures to change the constitution

Although constitutions are (generally) documents which embody the framework of the state, they are not necessarily meant to be documents which are incapable of amendment and improvement. Indeed, the contents of a state constitution which could not be altered in any way in order to adapt to changing times would make the citizens of that state a prisoner of their constitution, as their constitution may have been drafted decades, if not centuries, before. A constitution will typically, therefore, stipulate the method and procedures that must be complied with in order to alter its provisions.

For example, amendments to the constitution of the United States can be made provided two-thirds of both Houses of Congress, together with three-quarters of the state legislatures, approve such changes. In fact, there have been 27 such amendments made in the past two centuries – one notable example was the 22nd Amendment in 1951, when the Constitution was altered to prevent a President being elected to serve more than two terms in office. Similarly, in France under Art 89 of the Constitution of the Fifth Republic (1958), an amendment can be made when a proposal has been passed – in identical terms – by both Houses of the French Parliament and thereafter approved by the people in a referendum. In 2005 the French people, in a referendum, rejected the Treaty Establishing a Constitution for Europe (see section 15.1.2). More recently, in May 2015 the Irish people voting in a referendum approved of legalising same-sex marriages (an issue of equality and human rights) as Art 46 of the Republic of Ireland's constitution requires any constitutional amendment to be submitted to the Irish people for approval.

KEY FACTS

Key facts on the contents of a constitution

A constitution will detail the principal institutions of the state, their functions and powers.

A constitution will establish the relationship between each of the state institutions together with how these institutions relate to the citizen.

A constitution will also indicate how (or if) it can be altered and the process that must be undertaken in order to do so.

2.3 Entrenching constitutional law

Owing to the nature of its subject matter (ie establishing the structure and institutions of the state), a constitution and its laws ideally should be of a higher/fundamental status. In other words the law relating to the constitution (ie 'constitutional law') should, in legal terms, be superior and more fundamental than other 'ordinary' or 'non-constitutional' laws (eg private laws such as contract and land law). Thus, as the constitution represents the basic framework of the government, it should necessarily have a greater legal and moral authority than other 'ordinary' laws in the legal system. This reflects the comparative importance and significance of constitutional law. Indeed, it could be contended that, in a jurisprudential sense, constitutional law is more significant and important than *all* other laws, which of course only exist because of the existence of a constitution and constitutional law.

Typically, therefore, the constitutional document embodying the constitutional law of the state will invariably be a form of law which is superior/higher than other laws in the legal system. For example, s 2 of the South African Constitution of 1997 states that:

ARTICLE

This Constitution is the supreme law of the Republic; law or conduct inconsistent with it is invalid, and the obligations imposed by it must be fulfilled.

Similarly, Art 98 (Chapter X: *Supreme Law*) of the Japanese Constitution (1947) states that:

ARTICLE

This Constitution shall be the supreme law of the nation and no law, ordinance, imperial rescript or other act of government, or part thereof, contrary to the provisions hereof, shall have legal force or validity.

In addition, see Art VI of the Constitution of the United States.

As constitutional law will (typically) be accorded a higher and fundamental legal status, this means that it will be more difficult to alter than other 'ordinary' laws, which can be amended, or even abolished, through the ordinary legislative process (see section 2.2.4 for the special procedures that may be necessary in order to amend a constitution).

The notion of constitutional law having a superior status will be reconsidered in Chapter 3 in the context of the United Kingdom's very unusual constitutional arrangements (see section 3.4.4).

KEY FACTS

Key facts on constitutional law

Constitutional laws are typically given a higher and more fundamental legal status than non-constitutional laws (eg private laws governing the formation and enforcement of contracts made between private individuals – contract law).

2.4 The purpose of a constitution

Why do countries have constitutions? There are many reasons for creating a constitution and these are set out below.

2.4.1 To ensure stability and order

As noted above, all countries (and organisations) have a constitution of some description because all societies require rules and organisation in order to ensure stability. Without a set of basic rules there would be no structure or organisation and chaos would ensue. Constitutions, therefore, provide a set of basic ground rules and principles which establish and regulate the basic framework of the state. A constitution helps ensure that a state – or indeed even a social club – achieves its primary purpose and objectives.

For example, if one object of a people is to safeguard the basic rights of the individual in society (particularly vulnerable minorities), this can be achieved with a constitution setting up a mechanism such as a declaration of human rights, together with a Supreme/Constitutional Court to safeguard and protect such rights from infringement.

2.4.2 To ensure that government operates by consent and has constitutional and moral legitimacy

Thomas Paine, writing in the eighteenth century, stated that:

QUOTATION

What Paine meant was that a constitution ensures that the governing institutions (Congress/Parliament, President/government and courts) should have constitutional legitimacy and so govern with the consent of the people. In other words, by agreeing to and endorsing the constitution, the people confer legitimacy on it and the institutions created under it. For example, this was done in the Republic of Ireland, where the constitution was approved by the people in a national referendum. Art 6, s 1 of the Irish Constitution states specifically that:

ARTICLE

All powers of government, legislative, executive, and judicial, derive, under God, from the people, whose right it is to designate the rulers of the state.

This in turn conferred moral and constitutional authority on those institutions created under the Irish Constitution to govern the state and regulate the lives of Irish citizens. As noted above, this can be likened to a social contract between the governed (the citizens) and the governing institutions (Parliament, government and the courts). As part of this constitutional bargain, the governing institutions are conferred with the constitutional and legal powers to rule and govern the people. In return, these institutions ensure stability and order in the state/society and are (largely) prevented from interfering with the basic human rights of the individual, which are typically enshrined in a Bill/Charter of Rights.

A democratic constitution ensures (at least in theory) that government is with the consent of the people. For example, in Iraq in January 2005, the Iraqi people voted for a transitional National Assembly, which would draft a new constitution. This draft constitution was in turn approved by the people in a national referendum in October 2005, and following this the new democratic Iraqi government was formed. Having said this, the approval of the people can, in practice, be somewhat nominal, as demonstrated by the Indian Constitution. Although it was approved by a constituent assembly (representing the people), the terms of the constitution were not actually directly approved by the Indian people themselves.

In short, if the constitution has the consent of the people (nominal or otherwise), this means that the institutions created under it have the constitutional legitimacy to carry out their prescribed functions and exercise their powers stipulated in the constitution. In other words, the constitution, its institutions and state apparatus have a badge of legitimacy. In this context see Art 1 of the Brazilian Constitution (1988):

ARTICLE

All power emanates from the people, who exercise it by means of elected representatives or directly, as provided by this constitution.

2.4.3 To represent a constitutional watershed

A state constitution is generally founded to represent a break with the past and so represent a watershed in terms of the history, politics and institutional structure of that particular state. For example, the creation of a constitution may well follow:

- a revolution: the United States of America (1789)
- independence following colonial rule: Malawi (1966)
- the removal of a dictatorship: Spain (1978)
- a war: West Germany (1949), Japan (1947).

The creation of a new constitution will enable that country to draw a clear line under its past and give it the opportunity to establish a new state apparatus with new institutions governed by principles which have the clear approval of the people.

2.4.4 A constitutional limit and control on governmental power

As a constitution establishes institutions and invests them with public powers and responsibilities, it is the hallmark of a democratic constitution that these institutions are controlled, regulated and checked by the constitution itself (which, of course, embodies the consent of the people, nominal or otherwise – see section 2.4.2). In other words, a constitution will set out the limitations of governmental power (this can be done in various ways, in particular see section 2.6.2 on the notion of constitutionalism). A constitution must therefore not only allocate and distribute public power but also ensure that the use of that power is checked; otherwise public power will be misused and abused at the expense of the citizen. For example, the Swedish Constitution (the Instrument of Government of 1975 (Ch 1)) states boldly that:

ARTICLE

Public power shall be exercised under law.

2.4.5 To affirm particular values and goals

All constitutions are by their nature man-made and so drafted with certain underlying principles and goals in mind. These could be, for example, the promotion of democratic values, open government, the welfare and public good of the citizen or the attainment of religious aims. For example, the Irish Constitution of 1937 (as originally drafted) made specific reference to the special position of the Roman Catholic Church, thereby reflecting the importance attached to the church in society as a whole. It is of interest to note, however, that as a result of the divisive nature of this provision, in an amendment to the constitution in 1973 (the Fifth Amendment), the special position of the Catholic Church was removed. One goal of the Brazilian Constitution is concerned with economic and social reforms in society as a whole. In particular, Art 3 sets out that one objective of the constitution is to eradicate poverty.

Key facts on the purpose of a constitution

The rationale behind a constitution is to ensure the following:
- order and stability
- the legitimacy of the governmental institutions
- to mark a watershed
- to limit governmental power
- to affirm specific goals considered important for that society.

ACTIVITY

Applying the law

In July 2022, a country obtains its independence after occupation by a foreign power for over 30 years. You are asked to advise the drafters of its new constitution as to how it should be drawn up. In particular,

- What needs to go into the constitution?
- What does not need to go into the constitution?
- How can you ensure that the constitution achieves both what (a) the citizens and (b) the envisaged governing institutions desire from the constitution?

2.5 Different types of constitutions

There are various types of constitutions in existence around the world and noted below are the principal ways in which they can be (very broadly) categorised and classified.

2.5.1 Written and unwritten constitutions/codified and uncodified constitutions

Historically, one major way of classifying and distinguishing between constitutions was through the labels of written and unwritten constitutions. A written constitution was one in which the rules of the constitution were located in a written document entitled 'The Constitution'. For example, the constitution of the United States can be found in the document called the 'United States Constitution', which contains seven articles along with their various amendments. Similarly, the Indian constitution can be found in a document which comprises almost 400 articles and nine accompanying schedules. In contrast, an unwritten constitution would be one in which the major constitutional rules of the state could not be found in a single written document – as in the United Kingdom.

Care, however, has to be taken with this particular method of classifying constitutions:

▪ Firstly, it is clear that not every single principle and rule relating to a constitution will be detailed in one single written constitutional document. For example, as constitutional rules are not necessarily self-explanatory or cover every constitutional eventuality, these rules have to be interpreted by the courts (Supreme or Constitutional Court). As a consequence, these judgments interpreting the constitution will also form part of the constitutional rules which govern the country. In addition, the rules of a written constitution will be invariably supplemented by unwritten political practices and conventions which have grown up around it (on constitutional conventions see section 4.13).

- Secondly, even in the United Kingdom (which has historically been labelled as having an unwritten constitution in the absence of a single constitutional document called 'The United Kingdom Constitution'), it is nevertheless clear that many of its constitutional rules are actually written down, for example in parliamentary legislation.

As a consequence, in recent years it has become fashionable to classify constitutions on the basis of being codified or not, rather than on the basis of the written/unwritten dichotomy. In this way the constitution of the United States would be defined rightly as a codified constitution, with its major rules being codified largely (but not exclusively) in its seven articles and subsequent amendments. In contrast, the constitution of the United Kingdom can be described as uncodified in the sense that its constitutional rules and principles are located in a multitude of different sources which have not been brought together and codified in a single document (see further Chapter 4). It is fascinating to note, however, that recently the House of Commons Political and Constitutional Reform Select Committee's report on possible codification of the United Kingdom's constitution included an illustrative blueprint called a 'written constitution' (see section 3.5).

2.5.2 Rigid and flexible constitutions

Historically, constitutions have also been classified according to whether or not there is a special procedure which must be followed in order to change the constitutional text (and therefore constitutional law). In order to alter the content and provisions of a rigid constitution, a procedure is stipulated which requires specific legal/constitutional obstacles to be overcome. For example, a proposed amendment may require the approval of the people in a national referendum and/or the use of special majorities in the parliament/assembly. By way of illustration, Chapter 8 of the 1901 'Constitution of Australia' stipulates that a proposed amendment to the provisions of the constitution must be initiated and approved in the Australian parliament and thereafter approved by the Australian people in a referendum.

In contrast, a flexible constitution is one in which the content and principles of the constitution can be amended by the ordinary legislative process which is used to alter non-constitutional laws. Flexible constitutions are much less common than rigid constitutions because constitutional rules, by their very nature, are viewed as being fundamental and so *should* be more difficult to change than other laws. Israel, New Zealand and the United Kingdom provide examples of flexible constitutions. An example of a change to the constitutional arrangements of the United Kingdom is illustrated by the enactment of the Constitutional Reform Act 2005, which created a separate Supreme Court, which came into effect in 2009. This legislation was passed by the United Kingdom Parliament through the ordinary channels of the law-making process: the consent of both the House of Commons and the House of Lords, together with the **Royal Assent**. No special majority, or indeed referendum, was required.

It should be noted that, just because a constitution is labelled as rigid (owing to its prescribed method of amendment), it does not necessarily follow that the constitution

CONSTITUTIONS

Royal Assent

the consent conferred on a Bill by the monarch in order to convert it into an Act of Parliament is never amended or that in practice it is *actually* very difficult to alter. In reality, changes to a constitution are driven by, and dependent on, the political will in that particular state. As indicated above, the constitution of the United States has been altered formally on 27 occasions, even though there are significant obstacles to be overcome in order to change it. In contrast, a flexible constitution may not necessarily be changed frequently in practice, even though it is possible to do so. Although the United Kingdom constitution has traditionally been labelled as flexible, there are certain aspects of it which have not actually been altered for generations. Two examples will suffice at this stage:

- In Parliament, the House of Commons (as the elected House) has dominance over the House of Lords (see section 10.10).
- The monarch will always confer her assent to a Bill in order to make it law. This consent has not been refused for centuries (see section 11.9.3).

2.5.3 Federal and unitary constitutions

A federal constitution (such as in the United States, Australia and Germany) is one where the powers and responsibilities of the institutions of the state are constitutionally divided between the centre (federal institutions) and the regions/states/provinces. For example, in the United States the federal (national) Congress has specified powers and responsibilities under the constitution (eg in relation to national and international affairs). In contrast, the legislatures of the various states (eg Florida or California) have powers and responsibilities which relate specifically to the regulation and government of that particular state. In essence the rationale behind a federal constitution is twofold:

- Firstly, to reduce further the power of the state (and so minimise the exercise of arbitrary power) by separating and dividing power and responsibilities between central and local institutions. This is also known as a 'horizontal' type of separation of powers.
- Secondly, to safeguard and constitutionally ring-fence the powers of the local states/provinces/regions to enable them to determine their own local laws which are tailored to local needs.

local authorities

directly elected layer of government which administers functions at a local level and tailored to local needs

In a unitary constitution (found for example in the United Kingdom), power is focused in the main and central law maker (in the United Kingdom this is Parliament). Although, as we shall see in Chapter 14, there exist a number of other decentralised bodies in the United Kingdom, namely **local authorities**, this does not however, make the United Kingdom a federal state, as these bodies are necessarily legally subordinate to, and ultimately dependent on, the United Kingdom Parliament in Westminster. For example, for five decades until the early 1970s Northern Ireland had its own local parliament, but this was abolished by the Westminster Parliament which had established it in the first place. In short, these decentralised institutions do not have express constitutional protection, unlike the state/provincial/regional legislatures in a federal constitution (however, in relation to the Scottish Parliament and the National Assembly for Wales, now see sections 14.3.13 and 14.5.6, respectively).

ACTIVITY

Self-test question

Explain the main ways in which constitutions can be classified. Are these useful or definitive?

2.6 Constitutionalism and acting 'constitutionally'

2.6.1 Introduction

Although commentators generally appear to find it difficult to define the term constitutionalism, in essence it means government (or the institutions of the state) acting in accordance with the rules and principles enshrined in the constitution, thereby resulting in limited constitutional government. Generally speaking, anything allowed by a constitution would be considered 'constitutional' (ie conforming to, and acting strictly within, the parameters permitted by the constitution). In countries which adhere to the ideas of limited government, however, constitutionalism would demand that there is sufficient control on the power of the government. In other words, a constitution should not be merely descriptive – simply describing the powers of the governing institutions – but must also control and check that power. The rationale behind constitutionalism is to prevent an abuse of public power by the state institutions.

Consider the following imaginary constitution which details the following provision:

ARTICLE

Art X

The President may, if in his personal opinion he deems it appropriate to do so, order the arrest, detention, torture and execution of any citizens he considered undesirable. This power, and the exercise of it, cannot be challenged in any court of law under any circumstances.

Suppose a President acted under this provision and used his conferred powers to torture 'undesirable' citizens of this state. In a very technical sense, the President could claim to be acting simply in accordance with what the constitution expressly permits him to do and, therefore, technically he could claim to be acting 'constitutionally' (at least in a bare legal sense). Public lawyers, however, would not regard the exercise of this power, and the content and nature of Art X itself, as following the basic precepts of constitutionalism. In short, this provision gratuitously – and unnecessarily – interferes with the basic and fundamental rights of the citizen. Moreover, Art X (and therefore the constitution) does not permit any effective regulation or legal check on the exercise by the President of this arbitrary and exceptionally wide power which violates the basic human rights of the individual.

A former law lord defined constitutionalism in the following terms:

QUOTATION

'It is neither a rule nor a principle of law. It is a political theory. It holds that the exercise of government power must be controlled in order that it should not be destructive of the very values which it was intended to promote. . . . What matters is that the institutional arrangements must provide for effective control of the abuse of executive power.'

Lord Steyn, *The Constitutionalism of Public Law* (The Constitution Unit, 1999), p 13.

2.6.2 The basic principles of constitutionalism

The principles of constitutionalism (particularly in the context of the constitution of the United Kingdom) will be referred to continuously throughout this text, but for present purposes it should be noted that, in order to comply with constitutionalism, a constitution should control the use of public power in the following ways (as adapted from Barnett, *Constitutional and Administrative Law*, 12th edn, Routledge/Taylor & Francis Group, 2017, p 14):

- The governing institutions should be separated in terms of personnel and functions (see Chapter 5 on the separation of powers).
- The basic rights of the individual should be safeguarded and protected (see Chapters 16 and 17 on human rights).
- In exercising public power, state institutions must act strictly within their legal limits (see Chapter 6 on the rule of law together with Chapters 19 and 20 on judicial review).
- There must exist an independent court system staffed by impartial judges to check the use of public power (see Chapter 13 on the judiciary).
- Basic democratic and other principles and values must be adhered to (eg see Chapter 9 for democratic elections to the House of Commons).

In addition, owing to the unusual constitutional arrangements that exist in the United Kingdom, the terms acting 'constitutionally' and 'unconstitutionally' have specific meanings in our constitution (see section 4.16).

ACTIVITY

Essay writing

What state/government conduct or law would you consider to be (a) constitutional and (b) unconstitutional? Revisit this question after you have completed section 4.16 and again at the end of this text.

KEY FACTS

Key facts on the basic principles of constitutions and constitutionalism

A constitution is a body of rules (usually enshrined in a formal document) which sets out the main framework of the state.

A constitution is 'a set of laws, rules and practices that create the basic institutions of the state and its component and related parts, and stipulate the powers of those institutions and the relationship between the different institutions and between those institutions and the individual' (working definition of the House of Lords Select Committee on the Constitution).

Constitutionalism is concerned with limiting governmental power through the rules and values of the constitution.

Acting constitutionally means acting in accordance with the rules of the constitution, whereas acting unconstitutionally means to breach or infringe these constitutional rules.

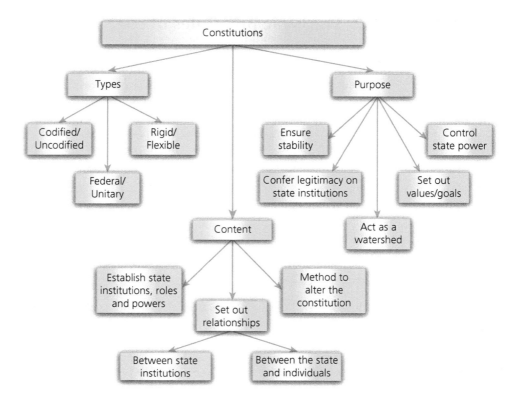

Figure 2.1 Constitutions

SUMMARY

At the end of this chapter you should be able to:

- Understand the nature and typical content of a constitution.
- Appreciate why constitutions are created.
- Identify and distinguish between different types of constitutions.
- Understand the term constitution.

Further reading

Books

Barendt, E, *An Introduction to Constitutional Law* (Oxford University Press, 1998), Chapter 1.

Barnett, H, *Constitutional and Administrative Law* (12th edn, Routledge/Taylor & Francis Group, 2017), Chapter 1.

Bradley, A, Ewing, K and Knight, C, *Constitutional and Administrative Law* (16th edn, Pearson, 2015), Chapter 1.

Finer, S, Bogdanor, V and Rudden, B, *Comparing Constitutions* (Clarendon Press, 1995), Chapters 1 and 2.

Heringa, AW and Kiiver, P, *Constitutions Compared* (2nd edn, Intersentia, 2009).

Maddex, R, *Constitutions of the World* (2nd edn, CQ Press, 2001). This text sets out in very brief terms the main elements of 100 constitutions of the world.

Wheare, K, *Modern Constitutions* (2nd edn, Oxford University Press, 1966), Chapters 1 to 4.

For an interesting examination of how constitutions operate in a non-democratic context see:

Ginsburg,T, and Simpser, A (eds), *Constitutions in Authoritarian Regimes* (Cambridge University Press, 2014).

3

The nature of the British constitution

AIMS AND OBJECTIVES

At the end of this chapter you should be able to:

- Explain what is meant by the term the British constitution
- Identify and explain the main features of the British constitution

3.1 Introduction and terminology

QUOTATION

'The UK does not have a codified constitution. There is no single document that describes, establishes or regulates the structures of the state and the way in which these relate to the people. Instead, the constitutional order has evolved over time and continues to do so.'

The Cabinet Manual – A guide to laws, conventions and rules on the operation of government (Crown Copyright, 2011), p 2.

The aim of this chapter is to provide a general overview of the main characteristics of the United Kingdom constitution. All of the features and themes detailed below will be developed, to a greater or lesser extent, throughout the rest of this text.

At this stage it is important to note that the United Kingdom is an unusual state in international law as it is composed of four distinct countries, namely:

- England
- Scotland
- Wales and
- Northern Ireland.

Moreover, there are three distinct legal jurisdictions and three systems of law, namely:

- England and Wales (as a single jurisdictional entity) – but note section 14.5.1.
- Northern Ireland and
- Scotland.

As there is a constitutional framework which governs the whole of the United Kingdom, strictly speaking it is correct to refer to *the United Kingdom constitution* (however, the exact constitutional arrangements pertaining to each jurisdiction may on occasions differ). In order to illustrate the workings of the constitution, throughout this text examples will be drawn from all three jurisdictions.

Furthermore, for ease of reference, hereafter in the text, the term *the United Kingdom constitution* will be replaced by the term *the British constitution*.

3.2 Does the United Kingdom have a constitution?

3.2.1 The absence of a codified constitutional document

Before considering the nature and sources of the British constitution, we must first consider the question of whether the United Kingdom has a constitution at all. This is because the United Kingdom lacks a formal codified document called 'The British Constitution'. In short, there is no single document which has special legal status and which embodies the principal rules concerning the government of the country. If we refer to the definition of a constitution at section 2.1 it is clear that the United Kingdom does not possess a constitution in terms of the first definition (ie a constitutional document or code setting out the framework of the state with 'special legal status' attached to it) as it lacks a single formal constitutional document. The United Kingdom does, however, have a constitution in the second sense of the term (ie 'a collection of rules' which govern the governing institutions) as it clearly has rules and practices (albeit derived from disparate sources) which govern the state. There are rules, for example, governing:

■ how the various state institutions are composed
■ the scope of the powers exercised by the monarch
■ how the government is legally controlled
■ how legislation is passed.

Wheare has defined the United Kingdom constitution in the following terms:

QUOTATION
....
'The British Constitution is the collection of legal rules and non-legal rules which govern the government in Britain.'

K Wheare, *Modern Constitutions* (2nd edn, Oxford University Press, 1966), p 1.

3.2.2 The factors which indicate a British constitution

It could be argued that the following factors indicate (and presuppose) that the United Kingdom clearly has a constitution of some sort:

■ If the United Kingdom had no constitution there would necessarily be no government, Prime Minister, Parliament or police force. Indeed, there would be no apparatus of the state of any kind.
■ United Kingdom cases and statutes make specific reference to constitutional issues (an example of the latter is the Constitutional Reform Act 2005).
■ Numerous books and papers have been written about 'the British Constitution' and the constitutional law of the United Kingdom.

- British commentators may on occasions speak of a 'constitutional crisis' (for example, commentators spoke of a constitutional crisis with the break-up of the Prince of Wales's first marriage).
- There was (until 2007) a department called the Department for Constitutional Affairs headed by the Lord Chancellor and Secretary of State for Constitutional Affairs. In addition, in 2016 the Cabinet had a sub-committee (a Cabinet committee) called the Constitutional Reform Committee.
- In 2001 the House of Lords established the House of Lords Select Committee on the Constitution with the specific remit to:
  (i) consider the constitutional implications of all public Bills, and
  (ii) to keep under review the operation of the constitution.
- Between 2010 and 2015 the House of Commons had a select committee called the Political and Constitutional Reform Committee, which was created to consider political and constitutional reform issues. Although this committee was not reappointed after 2015, today constitutional issues are examined by the Public Administration and Constitutional Affairs Select Committee.

Although the United Kingdom may lack a single authoritative constitutional document, this does not mean that we do not have a constitution. The United Kingdom has a constitution in the broader sense of the term used above as it has rules and principles that regulate the government of the country. There is a clear framework of rules, both legal and political, from which we can identify:

- the key institutions of the state
- the composition and powers of these institutions
- how these institutions interrelate and check and balance one another
- how these institutions relate to the individual
- how the rights and freedoms enjoyed by the individual are safeguarded.

Finally, it is worth noting the following observation:

QUOTATION

'What Britain lacks is not a written constitution but a *codified* Constitution, a Constitution with a capital "C" . . .'

A King, *The British Constitution* (Oxford University Press, 2007), p 5.

3.2.3 The five tenets of the British constitution

The United Kingdom, therefore, has a constitution, albeit different in form from other states that have a codified written document. It is highly pertinent to note that the House of Lords Select Committee on the Constitution, in setting out its remit, identified five tenets of the British constitution, which are as follows:

ACTIVITY

Applying the law

Can you think of any factors that might suggest that the United Kingdom has a constitution? Revisit this question after you have completed this chapter and again at the end of this text.

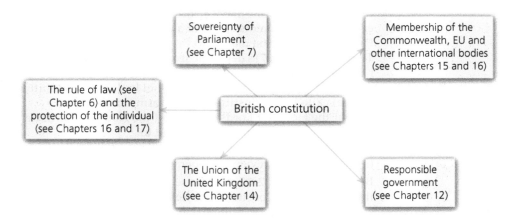

Figure 3.1 The five tenets of the British constitution

3.2.4 A system of government rather than a constitution?

Some commentators such as Ridley, however, have questioned whether the United Kingdom has a constitution in any meaningful sense of the term given that it lacks the key characteristics of a constitution. These essential features as identified by Ridley are as follows:

▪ **'It establishes, or constitutes, the system of government**.' A constitution establishes (and so is necessarily prior to) the system of government and its institutions. In short, the constitution is a constituent act.

  In the United Kingdom the system of government and state institutions have not been specifically created by a single authoritative constitutional document or code; instead, they have developed and evolved over the years. By way of example, the Scottish Parliament, a major institution of the state, was created only in 1998. It is of interest, however, to note that the legislation creating the Scottish Parliament was preceded by a national referendum in Scotland.

▪ **'It therefore involves an authority outside and above the order it establishes**.' A constituent power (namely the people) ratifies the constitution, thereby conferring it and the institutions established under it with constitutional legitimacy (see section 2.4.2).

  In the United Kingdom the people in a referendum have never formally ratified the British 'constitution'. Notwithstanding this, as we have a parliamentary democracy, the people do at least every five years elect the House of Commons, which, in turn, gives democratic legitimacy to the laws that Parliament passes. Furthermore, these elections also confer legitimacy (albeit in an indirect sense) on the government to govern and determine major policy issues (see Chapter 11).

▪ **'It is a form of law superior to other laws.**' The laws of the constitution should be supreme and a higher form of law in relation to other ordinary or non-constitutional laws.

---

parliamentary sovereignty

the legal principle that the Crown in Parliament can pass any law that it chooses

---

In the United Kingdom, historically, the laws of the constitution have not assumed a legal status higher than other 'ordinary' laws. In this context, however, now see the comments of Laws LJ at section 4.4.5.

'It is entrenched.' Owing to their content and importance, constitutional laws should be entrenched, thereby making it difficult (in some cases impossible) to repeal or alter them.

As a consequence of the principle of **parliamentary sovereignty**, historically, laws in the United Kingdom legally could not be entrenched and so protected from subsequent repeal or amendment. In this context, however, now see the comments of Laws LJ at section 4.4.5 and also the current impact of EU law (see section 15.6).

In the absence of these characteristics, Ridley has argued that the United Kingdom does not have a constitution, but instead merely a system of government (F Ridley, 'There is no British constitution: A dangerous case of the Emperor's clothes' (1988) 41 *Parliamentary Affairs* 340).

Similarly, it is worth recording the following comment of the nineteenth-century French commentator Alexis de Tocqueville:

QUOTATION

'In England the constitution may change continually, or rather it does not in reality exist . . .'
Alexis de Tocqueville, *Democracy in America* (Wordsworth, 1998), p 44.

ACTIVITY

Self-test question

Do you agree with Ridley's arguments that the United Kingdom does not have a constitution? Revisit this question after you have completed this chapter and again at the end of this text.

3.3 The nature of the British constitution

3.3.1 An uncodified constitution

As noted above, the United Kingdom lacks a single authoritative constitutional text entitled 'The British Constitution'. Instead, the constitutional rules which regulate the state/government are located elsewhere in a variety of sources which include, *inter alia*, Acts of Parliament, case law and binding political practices (see Chapter 4).

In this sense, therefore, the United Kingdom has an uncodified constitution which sets it apart from most other states which have codified documents (eg the United States, France and the Republic of Ireland). As a result, the British constitution has been described by Finer, Bogdanor and Rudden as indistinct and indeterminate. In short, the exact boundaries of the British constitution are less easy to identify and pinpoint than in a state with a formal codified constitution. Indeed, even within the United Kingdom, academics and commentators may disagree over what is and what is not part of the British constitution and even what is and what is not a constitutional issue (see section 4.2).

3.3.2 Why does the United Kingdom not have a codified constitution?

As noted in section 2.4.3, state constitutions are generally founded to represent a political watershed and a clear break with the past. The catalyst for this watershed could have been, for instance:

- a political upheaval
- an invasion
- a revolution.

In simple terms, the United Kingdom/Great Britain (with the clear exception of the period in England of 1649–60 with Oliver Cromwell as Lord Protector overseeing a non-monarchial government under the 1653 *Instrument of Government*, which *was* a written constitution) has not experienced such momentous events as being invaded or colonised. As a consequence, it has not been felt necessary to create a new codified constitution to mark a watershed. In fact, it has been pointed out by the Institute for Public Policy Research that the reality is that very few constitutions are actually conceived as a result of a sober and measured reflection on the perceived shortcomings of existing, functioning arrangements. Instead, they are drafted in the context of other factors such as political upheaval and independence (R Blackburn (ed), *A Written Constitution for the United Kingdom* (Mansell, 1993) p 5).

It is of interest to mention that in 1991 the Institute for Public Policy Research produced a draft '*Constitution for the United Kingdom*' and, although this constitution has not been implemented, it does serve as a useful blueprint should there come a time when the United Kingdom decided that it required a written codified, entrenched constitution. More recently, in 2014 the House of Commons Political and Constitutional Reform Select Committee set out three possible blueprints for a written/codified constitution for the United Kingdom (see section 3.5). NB: see also R Gordon, *Repairing British Politics: A blueprint for constitutional change* (Hart Publishing, 2010).

3.3.3 The incremental development of the British constitution

QUOTATION

'In a country with a codified constitution, the framework must be visibly and noticeably altered either by an amendment to the constitution or through a decision by judges which in effect re-interprets the constitution. In Britain, by contrast, the framework can be gradually adapted to create a wholly different constitution almost without anyone noticing.'

V Bogdanor, *The New British Constitution* (Oxford, 2009), pp 5–6.

Most countries have a clear date indicating the origin of their constitution; for example, the Indian Constitution was passed in 1949 and came fully into force in January 1950. In contrast, in the absence of a single constitutional text, the British constitution lacks a clear and single identifiable origin. Instead, the constitution has gradually developed over the centuries. In fact, one hallmark of the United Kingdom is that constitutional change has tended traditionally to be somewhat measured and incremental. As the British constitution has developed historically in an *ad hoc* fashion, it is clear that there has been no great and overall grand design behind it. Instead, it has grown organically to meet the needs required at the time and this is particularly the case in respect of, for example, the development of constitutional conventions (see section 4.13).

In recent years, however – and particularly under the government of the last Labour administration (1997–2010) – the form of our constitutional arrangements has been reshaped radically by the passage of a raft of constitutional statutes passed in very quick succession (see section 3.4.5).

KEY FACTS

Key facts on the nature of the British constitution

The United Kingdom, unlike most states, has an uncodified constitution. It lacks a single authoritative constitutional text/document in which the main rules and principles governing the framework and organisation of the state are set out.

Constitutions are established typically, for instance, in the aftermath of a war or gaining independence from a former colonial/foreign power. The United Kingdom historically has not experienced such momentous events, and therefore not found it necessary to mark a political watershed by drafting a written codified document called 'The British Constitution'.

In the absence of a single constitutional text, the British constitution lacks a clear and single identifiable origin, and instead its constitutional rules and principles have developed incrementally over the centuries through, among other things, statute and common law.

3.4 The key features of the British constitution

The key features of the British constitution are set out below. By identifying and highlighting these features at this stage, students will be provided with a snapshot of the essential elements which make up the British constitution.

3.4.1 An unwritten constitution?

As noted at section 2.5.1 above, constitutions historically, have been classified as either written or unwritten, with the United Kingdom traditionally falling within the latter category. Notwithstanding this, it must be remembered that many of the United Kingdom's constitutional rules *are* written down and therefore are found in documentary form. For example, the legal and constitutional principle that parliamentary legislation (Acts of Parliament) can be enacted without the consent of the upper chamber is set out in the Parliament Acts of 1911 and 1949 (see section 10.10.1). The description of the British constitution as unwritten does not therefore appear to be strictly accurate. A more apposite label would be to describe the constitution as uncodified as the constitutional rules have not been brought together in one single authoritative document or constitutional code.

3.4.2 Law and convention as sources

The sources of the British constitution embrace both legal and non-legal sources.

The legal sources include, among others, Acts of Parliament, case law and international Treaties. The non-legal sources include binding political rules known as constitutional conventions. It should be noted that the United Kingdom is not unique in having constitutional rules that are in effect political practices (for example, United Kingdom government ministers are constitutionally responsible to Parliament for their actions). Other countries also have political rules which supplement the legal rules detailed in their constitution. For example, in the United States of America, by convention congressional committees reflect the composition of Congress. What is significant in the United Kingdom, however, is the extent to which these political rules arguably play a more significant role in the context of our constitutional arrangements than they do in countries with a codified constitution.

See also Chapter 4.

3.4.3 The legislative supremacy of Parliament

In essence, the legislative supremacy of Parliament (parliamentary sovereignty) means that, in law, Parliament (technically the Queen in Parliament) can pass any law that it chooses. In short, historically there has been no legal limitation on the legislation that Parliament can pass. This feature is the foundation of, and underpins, the British constitution. This is in contrast to the vast majority of other constitutions. For example, the legislatures of the United States (Congress) and the Republic of Ireland (the Oireachtas) cannot pass any law that they choose. Instead, they are limited legally by their formal codified documentary constitutions.

As parliamentary sovereignty is the cornerstone of the British constitution it is considered in detail in Chapter 7. Moreover, as the United Kingdom's membership of the European Union has challenged the traditional conception of parliamentary sovereignty, the principle will be revisited in Chapter 15 in the context of the study of the European Union.

3.4.4 No special legal and higher status

As noted at section 2.3, constitutional laws (owing to their fundamental character and substance) typically possess a higher and fundamental legal status in relation to other 'ordinary' or 'non-constitutional' laws such as contract or tort. In the United Kingdom, however, historically no clear and sharp distinction has been made between:

- constitutional (or fundamental) laws and
- ordinary (or non-constitutional) laws.

In the United Kingdom, therefore, in historical terms, both constitutional and ordinary laws have had equal legal standing. This point, however, has to be reconsidered in the context of the comments made by Laws LJ in *Thoburn v Sunderland City Council* [2002] EWHC 195 (Admin), where he drew a distinction between constitutional statutes and non-constitutional statutes (see section 4.4.5). In addition, see the current status of EU law in the United Kingdom (see section 15.6).

Historically, therefore, the United Kingdom has been characterised as having no special higher constitutional law and has lacked a clear hierarchy of laws which distinguished constitutional laws from non-constitutional/ordinary laws. As noted above, for commentators such as Ridley, one fundamental prerequisite of a constitution is that its constitutional laws should have a higher and superior legal status *vis-à-vis* other laws. The United Kingdom has historically lacked such a hierarchy of laws.

3.4.5 A flexible constitution

Following on from the fact that the United Kingdom has an uncodified constitution, together with the fact that its main characteristic is that Parliament can pass any law that it chooses, the British constitution is also described as being flexible (see section 2.5.2). For example:

- ▪ **The Constitutional Reform Act 2005**: s 18 of this Act created a separate Supreme Court to replace the Appellate Committee of the House of Lords, which was hitherto the highest domestic court which used to sit within Parliament (see section 5.7.10). The new Supreme Court, in contrast, is legally and constitutionally separate from Parliament.

- ▪ **The House of Lords Act 1999**: this Act reduced the number of hereditary **peers** (these were peers who assumed a place in the House of Lords by virtue of inheriting their seat) from 759 to 92. In effect, at a stroke, this Act reduced the size of the upper chamber by over one-half (see section 10.6.3).

In short, the United Kingdom has been characterised as having a flexible constitution since its constitutional laws and rules can in theory be amended relatively easily (but note the point made at section 2.5.2 and Laws LJ at section 4.4.5). This is in contrast to other countries such as the United States whose constitution (Art V) stipulates a special procedure which must be complied with in order to amend the rules of the codified constitution.

As noted above, the flexibility of our constitution has been demonstrated graphically during the administration of the last Labour government (1997–2010), which radically reshaped the constitutional landscape of the United Kingdom. These changes include, among others:

- ▪ The **Human Rights Act 1998**, which conferred positive human rights on individuals.
- ▪ The Government of Wales Act 1998, which created the National Assembly for Wales.
- ▪ The House of Lords Act 1999, which removed the majority of hereditary peers from the House of Lords.
- ▪ The Freedom of Information Act 2000, which enabled individuals to have access to information held by public authorities. Interestingly, the disclosures made under the Freedom of Information Act as a result of the case of *Corporate Officer of the House of Commons v Information Commissioner* [2008] EWHC 1084 (Admin) led to the controversy over MPs' expenses (see section 8.8.3).
- ▪ The Constitutional Reform Act 2005, which reformed the office of the Lord Chancellor and the system of judicial appointments.
- ▪ The Electoral Administration Act 2006, which reduced the minimum age of candidates to be elected to the House of Commons from 21 to 18 years.
- ▪ The Terrorism Act 2006, which created a criminal offence of encouraging terrorism (including statements which glorify the commission or preparation of acts of terrorism).
- ▪ The Parliamentary Standards Act 2009, which reformed the regulation of the expenses system of MPs.
- ▪ The Constitutional Reform and Governance Act 2010, which, *inter alia*, placed the Civil Service on a statutory footing.

This collective raft of reforms represented arguably the most significant reshaping of the British constitution for centuries and demonstrates the highly flexible nature of our constitution. This legislation, however, was passed through the ordinary parliamentary legislative process without the need for special majorities in either House (in this context see section 4.2.4) or the support of the people in a referendum. Although referendums

---

peer

a person conferred with a peerage and a member of the upper chamber of Parliament, the House of Lords

---

Human Rights Act

legislation enacted in 1998 that brought the European Convention on Human Rights into domestic law for the whole of the UK on 2 October 2000 were held in Scotland, Wales and Northern Ireland prior to the creation of the devolved institutions for these regions, such referendums were not strictly (ie legally) necessary in order to pass the relevant legislation (see Chapter 14).

The Conservative-Liberal Democrat coalition government of 2010–15 also made significant constitutional changes including, for example:

- The Fixed-Term Parliaments Act 2011, which set general elections to the House of Commons at five yearly intervals.
- The European Union Act 2011, which provides that a referendum would have to be held, for example, before the United Kingdom could agree to an amendment to the European Treaties (but now see Brexit at section 15.6.6).

More recently, the Conservative government of 2015–2017 also introduced constitutional changes, including the Scotland Act 2016, which devolved further powers to Scotland. During this period, without doubt the most seismic constitutional, legal and political change to be instituted in modern times followed the Brexit referendum in June 2016 which took place under the aegis of the European Union Referendum Act 2015 (see later at 15.6.6).

It is interesting to record the pertinent words of Lord Norton of Louth in 2010 in a debate in the House of Lords:

QUOTATION

'Changes made to our constitutional framework have been pronounced in recent years. They have been several and substantial. From the perspective of the constitution, they have also been incoherent: that is, they have derived from no clear view of the type of constitution deemed appropriate for the United Kingdom. Each has been justified on its individual merits and not set in a broader, intellectually coherent approach to constitutional change. We are therefore in something of a constitutional wilderness.'

Hansard, HL Vol 716, col 1562.

ACTIVITY

Self-test questions

1. Why were the reforms outlined above implemented?
2. Are you aware of any other constitutional reforms which have been made in recent years?

3.4.6 A unitary constitution

As noted at section 2.5.3, in a federal system of government such as the United States, the federal constitution divides the power of the state horizontally between the centre (federal institutions: Congress, President etc) and the local regions (state institutions: eg the State Legislature of Florida). In contrast, the United Kingdom has a unitary constitution in the sense that ultimate legal and political power is focused centrally on the Westminster Parliament. In essence, Parliament has the legal power in theory to enact laws for all parts and all three legal jurisdictions (ie Scotland, Northern Ireland, England and Wales) that make up the United Kingdom. Under the Westminster Parliament there exist the following layers of decentralised government:

- Local authorities.
- The Scottish Parliament.

- The National Assembly for Wales.
- The London Assembly.
- The Northern Ireland Assembly.

These layers of decentralised government, however, only exist by virtue of Parliament in Westminster. In other words, they are all creatures of statutes passed by the Westminster Parliament and could ultimately be legally abolished by a subsequent Act of Parliament. These tiers of government, therefore, lack the constitutional status and legal/constitutional protection that they would enjoy under a federal constitution. However, s 1 of the Scotland Act 2016 now provides that the Scottish Parliament and Government could only be abolished following a referendum in Scotland (see section 7.10.2) – a similar provision has also been passed in relation to Wales (see section 14.5.6).

3.4.7 A limited monarchy

The head of state in the United Kingdom is the monarch, although her role in the constitution is typically ceremonial. In historic terms, the monarch formerly enjoyed extensive personal legal powers and, even today the Queen, in legal theory, still has considerable legal power vested in her. For example, the monarch can legally:

- dispense the prerogative of mercy
- appoint Supreme Court Justices
- appoint life peers to the House of Lords.

These powers are, however, exercised by the monarch strictly in accordance with constitutional convention: that is, she acts on the advice of her ministers. For example, although the monarch formally and legally appoints government ministers, it is the Prime Minister of the day that will request that she do so. In other words, although these powers continue to be vested legally in the monarch, they are in effect practically exercised by her government ministers. In this sense the powers of the monarchy are constitutionally limited (limited by constitutional convention: see section 4.13) and thus the United Kingdom is characterised as having a limited constitutional monarchy. See also section 11.1.2.

3.4.8 No strict separation of powers

The United Kingdom, historically, has been characterised as failing to adhere to a strict separation of powers whereby the three organs of state, namely the legislature, executive and judiciary, are separate and distinct from each other in terms of their functions and personnel. Instead, owing to the various overlaps of personnel and functions, the United Kingdom has traditionally exhibited a weak separation of powers.

The Constitutional Reform Act 2005, however, provides a recent example of Parliament attempting to realign our constitutional arrangements so as to accord with a stricter concept of the separation of powers. This Act, *inter alia*, constrains the role of the executive in the appointment of the judiciary and created a Supreme Court separate from Parliament. See also Chapter 5.

3.4.9 An independent and impartial judiciary

Although the United Kingdom does not have a strict separation of powers, historically the judicial arm of the state has been largely separate from the other two organs. Indeed, in constitutional terms it is of paramount importance that the judges are independent of both the executive and the legislature and that they are protected from political pressure.

A related characteristic of the British constitution is the limited role of the judiciary. In the United Kingdom the judiciary is constitutionally limited in the sense that it does not exercise the constitutional power enjoyed by many of its judicial counterparts elsewhere in the democratic world. For example, in the United States the Supreme Court has the power to declare Acts of Congress 'unconstitutional', and invalidate them if they contravene the written, entrenched constitution (*Marbury v Madison* (1803) 1 Cranch 137). In international terms, this principle is known as the constitutional or judicial review of legislation. In contrast, in the United Kingdom, historically the judiciary has consistently reiterated that it is not constitutionally empowered to strike down and challenge Acts of Parliament. This point will be revisited in the context of both European Union law (see Chapter 15) and the Human Rights Act 1998 (see Chapter 17).

The judiciary is discussed in more detail in Chapter 13.

3.4.10 A parliamentary executive

The United Kingdom has a **parliamentary executive** whereby the executive (the government) is drawn from the legislature (Parliament). Far from being separated as required by a strict interpretation of the doctrine of the separation of powers (see Chapter 5), the executive and legislature are actually fused. This can be contrasted with the presidential system of government in, for example, the United States, where the executive (President) is constitutionally and legally separate from the legislature (Congress). Parliamentary executives, however, are not uncommon. For example, the Republic of Ireland also has a parliamentary executive, but, unlike the United Kingdom, it has a codified constitution.

See also sections 5.7.1 and 11.6.1.

3.4.11 Responsible and accountable government

A constitutional principle associated with the parliamentary executive is that of responsible government. This principle entails the government being politically and constitutionally accountable to Parliament (and ultimately therefore to the **electorate**) for its actions and decisions. In recent decades, however, there has been concern that the balance between the executive and the legislature has shifted far too much in favour of the former, thereby undermining the principle of accountable government. In short, the modern executive is (typically) in a position to dominate and largely control the legislature amounting to what Lord Hailsham described as an 'elective dictatorship' (see section 9.8 and Chapter 12). However, at the time of writing, see the somewhat difficult position of the 'minority' 2017 Conservative government (see sections 9.5 and 11.6.1).

As an aside, it is worth recording that there is a general academic divide between the idea of a 'legal constitution' (ie a legal control of power) and a 'political constitution' (ie a political control of power).

QUOTATION

'It is commonplace, after all, for textbooks and articles to juxtapose the idea of a political constitution with that of a *legal constitution*, the latter being associated with holding those exercising political power to account, to a substantial and increasing extent, through judicial review. It is also commonplace to suggest that Britain's constitution is slowly evolving away from a political constitution towards something more akin to a legal constitution.'

G Gee, 'What is a Political Constitution?' (2010) 30 OJLS 273.

THE NATURE OF THE BRITISH CONSTITUTION

parliamentary executive

the constitutional arrangement whereby the executive/ government is drawn from, and accountable to, the legislature/ Parliament

electorate

individuals eligible to vote in an election

On a 'political constitution' see, JAG Griffith, 'The Political Constitution' (1979) 42 MLR 1.

3.4.12 A bicameral legislature

Parliament (the legislature) is the principal law-making body within the constitution and is bicameral as it is composed of two Houses:

- the House of Commons.
- the House of Lords.

This is common to many major democracies whose legislatures comprise two chambers (eg the United States, France, Germany and Spain). In contrast, it is generally the case that smaller states have unicameral legislatures with only one chamber (eg Denmark, Sweden and New Zealand – the latter having abolished its second chamber in 1950). In terms of the principle of constitutionalism, bicameral legislatures disperse power, though not necessarily equally, between two competing sources of power (ie chambers/Houses).

See also Chapters 8 –10.

3.4.13 A representative democracy

The United Kingdom has a parliamentary democracy whereby the composition of the legislature (or at least the House of Commons) is determined by the people through periodic and free national elections. See also section 9.4.

3.4.14 An acceptance of the rule of law and respect for human rights

A major characteristic of the British constitution is the acceptance of the rule of law, which is a foundation of any democratic state (see Chapter 6). This is the constitutional principle that all organs, institutions and state officials are under the law. The rule of law is linked inextricably to an independent and impartial judiciary (see Chapter 13) as it is, in effect, the judiciary that legally enforces the principles underpinning it.

The United Kingdom is also hallmarked by its historic general respect for basic human rights and freedoms. In other words, certain underlying democratic values are inherent within our constitutional arrangements such as:

- the freedom of political action (Chapters 16–17).
- the right to vote (see section 9.6).
- freedom of speech (see Chapter 18).

ACTIVITY

Essay writing

Explain the nature of each of the characteristics of the British constitution.

- Which features do you consider to be particularly important?
- Which features set the United Kingdom apart from other countries?
- Revisit this activity at the end of this text.

KEY FACTS

The key features of the British constitution

- An uncodified constitution (although it is largely collected from written sources).
- A largely flexible constitution.
- In legal theory Parliament can pass any law that it chooses (parliamentary sovereignty).
- The sources of the constitution are both legal (eg Acts of Parliament) and non-legal (eg constitutional conventions).
- Historically, constitutional law has not had a fundamental, higher legal status.
- There is no strict separation of powers.
- An acceptance of the rule of law and respect for human rights.

The principles of the constitution which affect particular state institutions	
Parliament	• Parliamentary sovereignty. • A representative democracy. • A bicameral legislature. • A unitary constitution.
The government/executive	• A parliamentary executive. • Responsible and accountable government. • A limited monarchy.
The judiciary	• An independent and impartial judiciary. • Upholds the rule of law and respect for human rights.

3.5 Conclusion

According to Barber:

QUOTATION

'Britain is one of a very few states which lack a written constitution, but this bare accident of history does not provide an argument for us to adopt one. Britain's constitution has, by and large, been a success. It has produced stable government and – in terms of democracy, transparency, human rights and the provision of social welfare – it compares reasonably favourably with many other constitutions.'

N Barber, 'Against a written constitution', [2008] PL 11.

Bogdanor and Vogenauer concluded that, although the enactment of a written constitution was feasible:

QUOTATION

'The problems involved in this enterprise are, however, formidable. Some of the problems are similar to those that have been faced and successfully resolved by other countries seeking to enact a constitution; others, however, are more specific to Britain, in particular, the problems of enacting a constitution that has long been uncodified, and of confronting the doctrine of the Sovereignty of Parliament.'

V Bogdanor and S Vogenauer, 'Enacting a British Constitution: some Problems', [2008] PL 38.

Finally, in 2014 the House of Commons Political and Constitutional Reform Select Committee issued a report (*A New Magna Carta?* HC 463 (The Stationery Office, 2014)) in which it not only detailed the various arguments for and against codifying the British constitution but also set out three possible blueprints for codification. The rationale behind this report was to engender and inform public debate about codification as the United Kingdom approached the 800th anniversary of the signing of the Magna Carta. The three illustrative blueprints were as follows:

- *'Constitutional code'* (11 pages – 95 paragraphs in length) – in essence this option set out the existing principles of the United Kingdom constitution/government (including key constitutional conventions). This Code as a document would not have the status of an Act of Parliament.
- *'Constitutional Consolidation Act'* (239 pages) – this option consolidated existing constitutional laws, the practices within Parliament and the common law. It also codified key constitutional conventions.
- *'Written Constitution'* (74 pages) – this option was the most radical of all three blueprints and depicted one version of a possible codified/written constitution for the United Kingdom.

It is pertinent to set out below some of the arguments as recognised by the select committee as being advanced in favour of, and against, a written/codified constitution for the United Kingdom:

QUOTATION

'The case for a written constitution is that it would enable everyone to know what the rules and institutions were that governed and directed ministers, civil servants and parliamentarians in performing their public duties. The sprawling mass of common law, Acts of Parliament, and European treaty obligations, surrounded by a number of important but sometimes uncertain unwritten conventions, is impenetrable to most people, and needs to be replaced by a single document of basic law dictating the working and operation of government in the United Kingdom easily accessible for all.' . . .

'The case against a written constitution is that it is unnecessary, undesirable and un-British. The fact that the UK system of government has never been reduced to a single document is an indication of the success of the Westminster system of parliamentary democracy and the stability it has brought to the country. This is in contrast to most other countries whose written constitutions were the product of revolution or independence. The unwritten nature of the constitution is something distinctively British, it reminds us of a great history, and is a source of national pride.'

House of Commons Political and Constitutional Reform Select Committee, A *New Magna Carta?* HC 463 (The Stationery Office, 2014), pp 19 and 24.

In 2015 the select committee published its follow-up report in which it set out the overall response to its report above. It is interesting that it pointed out the balance of responses that it had received favoured some form of codification. In an attempt to encourage further debate on the constitution and options for reform, it published a 'Pocket Constitution' as an annex to its report (*Consultation on A New Magna Carta?* HC 599 (The Stationery Office, 2015)). This pocket constitution summarised the current constitutional position, but also included alternative options as well. Although the select committee has undertaken an admirable inquiry into possible codification, it is arguable that its work has been in vain as the current prospect of any form of codification taking place looks very poor to say the least. Indeed, it is rather telling that the select committee itself was not even reappointed after 2015.

Further reading

Books

Barendt, E, *An Introduction to Constitutional Law* (Oxford University Press, 1998), Chapter 2.

Blackburn, R (ed), *A Written Constitution for the United Kingdom* (Mansell, 1993). This book rather usefully sets out a proposed blueprint for a written codified constitution for the United Kingdom.

Bogdanor, V, *The New British Constitution* (Hart Publishing, 2009), Chapters 1 and 9.

Finer, S, Bogdanor, V and Rudden, B, *Comparing Constitutions* (Clarendon Press, 1995), Chapter 3.

Gordon, R, *Repairing British Politics: A blueprint for constitutional change* (Hart Publishing, 2010). Part 2 provides a working draft of a possible model for a written/codified constitution for the United Kingdom.

Leyland, P, *The Constitution of the United Kingdom* (3rd edn, Hart Publishing, 2016).

Munro, C, *Studies in Constitutional Law* (2nd edn, Butterworths, 1999), Chapter 1.

Qvortrup, M (ed), *The British Constitution: continuity and change* (Hart Publishing, 2015).

On the history of the British constitution see Lyon, A, *Constitutional History of the United Kingdom* (2nd edn, Routledge, 2016).

Articles

Barber, N, 'Against a written constitution' [2008] PL 11.

Bindman, G, 'Time to write it all down?' (2009) 159 NLJ 1564.

Bogdanor, V and Vogenauer, S, 'Enacting a British constitution: some problems' [2008] PL 38.

Bogdanor, V, Khaiton, T and Vogenauer, S, 'Should Britain have a written Constitution?' (2007) 78 *Political Quarterly* 499 (see Appendix: The Constitution of the United Kingdom as of 1 Jan 2007).

Feldman, D, 'None, one or several? Perspectives on the UK's constitution(s)' (2005) 64 CLJ 329.

Jones, B, 'Preliminary warnings on "constitutional" idolatry' [2016] PL 74.

Ridley, F, 'There is no British constitution: A dangerous case of the Emperor's clothes' (1988) 41 *Parliamentary Affairs* 340.

Tucker, A, 'Constitutional writing and constitutional rights' [2013] PL 345.

Walker, N, 'Our constitutional unsettlement' [2014] PL 529.

Papers

House of Commons Political and Constitutional Reform Select Committee, *A New Magna Carta?* HC 463 (The Stationery Office, 2014).

House of Commons Political and Constitutional Reform Select Committee, Consultation on *A New Magna Carta?* HC 599 (The Stationery Office, 2015).

Melton, J, Stuart, C and Helen, D, *'To codify or not to codify?'* (The Constitution Unit, 2015).

For a fascinating critique of the British constitution, see the following pamphlet: *The Unspoken Constitution* (Democratic Audit, 2009).

4

The sources of the British constitution

AIMS AND OBJECTIVES

At the end of this chapter you should be able to:

▪ Appreciate the difficulties in ascertaining the sources of the British constitution

▪ Identify and explain the different domestic legal sources that make up the British constitution

▪ Identify and explain the different international legal sources that make up the British constitution

▪ Identify and explain the different domestic non-legal sources that make up the British constitution

4.1 Introduction

QUOTATION

'The UK does not have a codified constitution. There is no single document that describes, establishes or regulates the structures of the state and the way in which these relate to the people. Instead, the constitutional order has evolved over time and continues to do so. It consists of various institutions, statutes, judicial decisions, principles and practices that are commonly understood as "constitutional".'

The Cabinet Manual: A guide to laws, conventions and rules on the operation of government (Cabinet Office, 2011), p 2.

QUOTATION

'It is clear, then, that understanding the constitution well enough to be able to "piece it together" for "ourselves" is an almost impossible task. If the constitution is a jigsaw, then it is a jigsaw where the pieces change in size and shape according to the interpretations and intentions of the narrow band of people who make the pieces and do the piecing. They have made the constitution to be more or less whatever they have wanted it to be.'

R Colls, 'After Bagehot: Rethinking the Constitution,' (2007) 78 *Political Quarterly* 523.

In the overwhelming majority of countries, the laws of the constitution can be found in their respective documentary constitutions. Notwithstanding this, as noted at section 2.5.1, the point needs to be made that, even in countries with a codified constitution, not all aspects of the constitution will be set out explicitly in that constitutional documentary text. The legal rules contained in the documentary constitution will have to be interpreted by a Supreme or Constitutional Court and therefore these judicial interpretations will also form part of the constitutional rules. Furthermore, the legal rules of a constitution will be supplemented to a greater or lesser extent, by binding political rules and practices.

As the United Kingdom has no codified constitutional document entitled 'The British Constitution', this necessarily raises the question of where the laws and rules of the constitution are to be located. The answer is that these rules are gleaned from consulting a wide range of sources. As indicated in Chapter 3, these disparate sources embrace legislation, case law and international Treaties together with constitutional conventions. It is highly pertinent to note that in 2011 the coalition government issued *The Cabinet Manual: A guide to laws, conventions and rules on the operation of government* (quoted above). It set out the internal procedure and rules by which the government operates. More recently, the House of Commons Political and Constitutional Reform Select Committee published in an illustrative blueprint, the *'Constitutional Code'*, which set out the existing principles of the United Kingdom constitution/government (see section 3.5). Both of these documents are descriptive of how the current constitution operates.

4.2 The difficulties associated with the sources of the British constitution

The United Kingdom has a constitution of multiple sources. There are a number of difficulties in locating these sources.

4.2.1 What is a constitutional issue?

In the British constitution it is not necessarily easy to determine what is, and what is not, a constitutional principle, rule or issue. In the Republic of Ireland, for example, the principal constitutional laws and rules are set out in its formal constitutional text. In contrast, in the United Kingdom, in the absence of such a document, the task of identifying a law of (or issue relating to) the constitution is inevitably more difficult. Instead of consulting an authoritative constitutional text, the main rules and laws of the British constitution are found by consulting, *inter alia*, various statutes and case law and deciding whether the statute or case in question encapsulates a constitutional principle or rule.

4.2.2 The lack of a clear demarcation between constitutional and ordinary laws

In the United Kingdom constitutional law has not assumed a legally higher or fundamental status (but see Laws LJ at section 4.4.5). In fact, constitutional law in the United Kingdom is not even clearly segregated so as to demarcate it from other 'ordinary' (ie non-constitutional) law. Dicey noted that:

QUOTATION

'There is under the English constitution no marked or clear distinction between laws which are not fundamental or constitutional and laws which are fundamental or constitutional.' (*Sic*)

A Dicey, *Introduction to the Study of the Law of the Constitution* (10th edn, Macmillan, 1959), p 89.

More recently, Hazell has commented that:

QUOTATION

'There is no clear classification of what is a constitutional Bill and what is not, and with our unwritten constitution it is impossible to devise one.'

R Hazell, 'Time for a New Convention: Parliamentary Scrutiny of Constitutional Bills 1997–2005' [2006] PL 247.

In this way, as indicated earlier, the British constitution is somewhat indeterminate, as its parameters are not necessarily clear. In fact, in giving evidence before the House of Lords Select Committee on the Constitution, Lord Irvine (the then Lord Chancellor) stated not only that the then Labour government did not have a definition of the British constitution, but that it took a pragmatic view as to whether a Bill should be termed a constitutional Bill or not. Indeed, in terms of legislation regulating trade unions, how should that be classified? For example, although the recent Trade Union Act 2016 is clearly in the field of industrial relations and labour/employment law, it nevertheless raises issues concerning the constitutional, political and social rights of individuals (as part of a trade union) to engage in industrial action.

Accordingly, the student of the British constitution needs to consult various statutes and decide on an Act by Act basis whether the legislation expounds a rule of the constitution. Compare for example the following two statutes:

- **The Consumer Rights Act 2015**: this Act regulates the selling of goods, for example their quality and being fit for their purpose, etc.
- **The Scotland Act 1998**: this Act established the Scottish Parliament together with the Scottish Executive (see Chapter 14).

The Consumer Rights Act 2015 is a non-constitutional statute as it is part of the private law of contract and is essentially concerned with contractual relations of consumers (therefore, generally speaking, not of interest to a public/constitutional lawyer). In contrast, the Scotland Act 1998 is clearly a constitutional statute as it created a major institution of the state: the Scottish Parliament, which has the power to pass legislation (Acts of the Scottish Parliament). It is pertinent to note that on odd occasions an Act may actually refer to the constitution in its title, as with the passing of the Constitutional Reform Act 2005.

4.2.3 A possible sub-division of constitutional law?

A proposal was put to the House of Lords Select Committee on the Constitution that in terms of parliamentary scrutiny of constitutional legislation it was possible to divide such Bills into the following:

- Bills of major (first-class) constitutional significance and
- Bills of less than first-class constitutional significance (legislation which represents a minor amendment to the constitution).

The rationale behind the proposal was to enable Bills of first-class constitutional importance to receive greater and more effective scrutiny. The Committee recognised the problems with such a division as, although Bills such as the House of Lords Bill 1999 and European Communities Bill 1972 would clearly fall within the first category, it questioned which category legislation such as the Political Parties, Elections and Referendums Bill 2000 would fall into. As such it would prove impossible to provide a watertight definition of a first-class constitutional Bill (the House of Lords Select Committee on the Constitution, *Changing the constitution: The process of constitutional change*, HL Paper 69 (2002), p 17). Nevertheless, it should be remembered that during the legislative process in the House of Commons it is a constitutional convention that a Bill of *first-class* constitutional importance will be committed to a committee of the whole House (see section 12.7.3).

4.2.4 All statutes passed in essentially the same manner

Constitutional statutes cannot be identified simply by how they were enacted by Parliament. In essence there is a single passage for all primary legislation and therefore constitutional statutes are passed through Parliament in the same way as non-constitutional statutes. In other words, no special majority is needed in the two Houses of Parliament in order to enact a statute that alters an established constitutional principle or which abolishes a previous constitutional statute.

Moreover, in historical terms constitutional statutes (such as the House of Commons Disqualification Act 1975) were viewed as having the same legal standing as ordinary/non-constitutional statutes such as the Sale of Goods Act 1979 (the precursor to the Consumer Rights Act 2015) which do not raise constitutional issues. Even though the House of Commons Disqualification Act 1975 legally prohibits specified elements of the executive from sitting as MPs, historically in law this Act did not have higher legal status than the Sale of Goods Act 1979. In fact, Dicey asserted that Acts such as the Union with Scotland Act 1706 (which established the Parliament of Great Britain) were not supreme over a statute such as the Dentists Act 1878, as both could be repealed in the same way. In other words, the 1975 Act above could be amended or repealed in the same way as the 2015 Consumer Rights Act. No special supermajority of votes (other than a simple majority) in either House is required to repeal either Act, even though the 1975 House of Commons Disqualification Act deals with fundamental constitutional issues of the state.

This general point above, however, now has to be revisited in the light of Laws LJ's comments in the *Thoburn* (2002) case, in which he stated that constitutional statutes, unlike non-constitutional statutes, cannot be impliedly repealed (see section 4.4.5).

In any event, it is worth repeating that, as noted, even though there is a single passage for legislation, a constitutional convention exists in the House of Commons that Bills of first-class constitutional importance (however these are determined) are considered in a committee of the whole of the House, rather than in a general committee (formerly known as a standing committee – see section 12.7.3). A recent example is the Constitutional Reform and Governance Bill in January 2010.

It is significant to point out that in 2011 the House of Lords Select Committee on the Constitution drew attention to the lack of a single agreed process for legislative constitutional change in the United Kingdom: House of Lords Select Committee on the Constitution, *The Process of Constitutional Change*, HL Paper 177 (2011).

4.2.5 No definitive list of statutes of a constitutional nature

What is clear is that there is no exhaustive list of statutes deemed to have constitutional status as stated by the House of Lords Select Committee on the Constitution:

QUOTATION

'The constitution is said to be in flux, and the sense of what it is constantly evolving. The constitution is uncodified and although it is in part written there is no single, accepted and agreed list of statutes which form that part of the constitution which is indeed written down.'

First Report of Session 2001–02 of the House of Lords Select Committee on the Constitution, *Reviewing the constitution: Terms of reference and method of working*, HL Paper 11 (2001), p 8.

4.2.6 No Constitutional or Supreme Court specifically to resolve issues of a constitutional nature

In terms of constitutional case law, the student must consider, on a case by case basis, whether or not it raises a constitutional issue or expounds a particular constitutional rule. The difficulty in the United Kingdom is the lack of a special Constitutional or Supreme Court which has the responsibility to process constitutional cases *per se* as, for example, do the Irish and United States Supreme Courts. Such courts authoritatively and definitively interpret the documentary constitution and will necessarily process cases that raise constitutional issues. Instead, the United Kingdom extracts its constitutional principles from case law drawn from all courts (both criminal and civil jurisdictions). Indeed, a case which *prima facie* appears to deal with a matter of private law (eg the law of trespass) may also have a constitutional dimension to it by raising a constitutional issue. For example:

CASE EXAMPLE

Entick v Carrington *(1765) 19 St Tr 1030 (for details see section 4.8.2)*

At one level this case may appear to deal with the private law of trespass, namely the king's messengers trespassing on Entick's property. In fact, the case has a clear constitutional resonance as it is also concerned with protecting the individual from the state and restricting the powers of the executive.

CASE EXAMPLE

Derbyshire County Council v Times Newspapers Ltd and others *[1993] 1 All ER 1011 (for details see section 4.8.2)*

This case dealt with the private law of defamation, but it necessarily raised the constitutional issues of free expression and the freedom to criticise state/governmental institutions (see also section 18.4.1).

It should be pointed out, however, that, although the United Kingdom lacks a special Constitutional Court which specifically resolves constitutional issues *per se*, cases that form part of the jurisdiction of the Administrative Court (part of the High

Court) will necessarily raise constitutional issues. This court is specifically responsible for applying judicial review principles to public authorities/government bodies so as to ensure that they exercise their legal public powers strictly in accordance with the law (see Chapters 19 and 20).

In contrast, it is pertinent to remember that not all cases coming before the United Kingdom Supreme Court, despite its title, will necessarily be of interest to public/constitutional lawyers. In short, the Supreme Court essentially functions as the Appellate Committee of the House of Lords used to and so it processes appeals concerning all aspects of law including private law cases. In one respect at least, the new court resolves 'specified' constitutional issues as its jurisdiction involves processing 'devolution issues' which concern the actions of the devolved institutions (see Chapter 14).

ACTIVITY

Applying the law

Explain the difficulties in trying to locate the sources of the British constitution. Using your knowledge gained from the first three chapters, how would you decide whether something was a constitutional issue?

4.3 The classification of the sources of the British constitution

4.3.1 The classification of legal and non-legal sources

The aim of this section is to identify the variety of sources that make up the British constitution. A number of examples will be given to illustrate each particular constitutional source.

With the difficulties identified at section 4.2 in mind, set out below are some of the main rules and principles of the constitution extracted from a wide variety of sources. These sources can be demonstrated by the following diagram:

Legal sources:

(a) Domestic primary legislation (see section 4.4)
(b) Domestic delegated legislation (see section 4.5)
(c) Domestic legislation of local authorities and the devolved institutions (see section 4.6)
(d) European Union legislation (see section 4.7)
(e) Domestic case law – the common law (see section 4.8.2)
(f) Domestic case law – interpreting statutes (see sections 4.8.3 and 4.8.4)
(g) Domestic case law – the royal prerogative (see section 4.9)
(h) European Union case law (see section 4.10.1)
(i) European Convention case law (see section 4.10.2)
(j) The law and custom of Parliament (see section 4.11)
(k) Treaties and international law (see section 4.12)

Non-legal sources:

(a) Constitutional conventions (see section 4.13)
(b) Documents relating to the constitution (see section 4.14)
(c) Academic writings (see section 4.15)

Figure 4.1 Sources of the British constitution

4.4 Domestic primary legislation

4.4.1 Acts of Parliament

Domestic primary legislation is legislation passed by the Queen in Parliament. These Acts of Parliament will have passed through both the House of Commons and the House of Lords (unless the Parliament Acts apply – see section 10.10.1) and have received the Royal Assent. It is pertinent to note the suggested list of 'fundamental parts of constitutional law' set out in the Joint Committee on the Draft Civil Contingencies Bill's report: *Draft Civil Contingencies Bill*, HL Paper 184, HC 1074 (The Stationery Office, 2003), para 183.

4.4.2 Acts of Parliament affecting the organs of the state

Primary legislation (as well as domestic delegated legislation) may have constitutional importance if it defines the powers of the state/government organs or regulates the procedure of those organs.

Below is a list of selected (but not exhaustive) statutes which illustrate a particular constitutional principle or rule:

The Magna Carta 1215 (affirmed as a statute in 1297)

This first authority concerned the limitation of an institution of the state, *viz*, the monarch. This historic document is of constitutional significance as it represented a legal limitation and curb on the power of the monarch. It also concerned the constitutional relationship between the individual and the state. In essence, the Magna Carta set out, among other things,

- the church's freedom;
- the protection of the liberties of 'freemen' not to be imprisoned:

'No freeman shall be taken or imprisoned, or be disseised of his freehold, or liberties, or free customs, or be outlawed, or exiled, or any otherwise destroyed; nor will we not pass upon him, nor condemn him, but by lawful judgment of his peers, or by the law of the land' (Sic) (Chapter 29).

In short, this is an embryonic constitutional statement concerning an individual's right to a fair trial. It is apposite to point out that in 2014 the House of Commons Political and Constitutional Reform Select Committee in its report entitled *'A New Magna Carta?'* set out three possible blueprints for a written/codified constitution. This report was timed to coincide with the 800th anniversary of the signing of the Magna Carta (see section 3.5). On the impact of the Magna Carta, see the recent publication of R Hazell and J Melton, *Magna Carta and Its Modern Legacy* (Cambridge University Press, 2015).

The Bill of Rights 1689

This statute concerned the constitutional relationship between two institutions of the state, namely the monarch and Parliament. In brief, in historic terms the Bill of Rights set out the conditions on which William of Orange (William III and Mary II) ascended the throne as joint monarchs. The Act altered the constitutional relationship between Parliament and the monarch, by expanding the power of the former at the expense of the latter. It included, among other things:

- Art 1, prohibiting the monarch from suspending laws without parliamentary consent (a constitutional limitation on the power of the monarch);
- Art 6, prohibiting the monarch from keeping a standing army without parliamentary consent (a constitutional limitation on the power of the monarch);
- Art 9, stating that 'the freedom of speech and debates or proceedings in Parliament ought not to be impeached or questioned in any court or place out of Parliament'. In essence, this meant that parliamentary members enjoyed legal immunity in respect of their words used in Parliament (see section 8.6.1).

The Union with Scotland Act 1706

One function of a constitution is to establish the institutions of the state, as illustrated by this and the following statute directly below. The Union with Scotland Act related directly to the creation of the Parliament of Great Britain (the legislature which existed until 1800). Before this Act, England (together with Wales) and Scotland had separate independent parliaments and the effect of this Union legislation was to dissolve both and replace them with a single Parliament, namely the Parliament of Great Britain.

The Union with Ireland Act 1800

This legislation provided for the unification of Great Britain with Ireland and created the Parliament of the United Kingdom of Great Britain and Ireland (replacing the Parliament of Great Britain above).

Parliament Act 1911 (as amended in 1949)

This Act set out the legal and constitutional relationship between two institutions of the state, namely the House of Commons and the House of Lords. It established the legal domination of the elected House of Commons over the unelected House of Lords. Prior to this Act a Bill required the consent of both Houses in order to become law. Following the passage of the Act, however, certain Bills technically could be passed with the consent of the House of Commons alone as the House of Lords could only delay the enactment of such legislation but not veto it (see section 10.10.1).

The Act is also constitutionally significant as it reduced the maximum length of a parliament from seven to five years. It is of interest to contrast this provision with

THE SOURCES OF THE BRITISH CONSTITUTION

other countries with codified constitutions. For instance, Art I of the United States Constitution states that Senators serve for six years and members in the House of Representatives for two years.

The European Communities Act 1972

This Act is an example of Parliament formally incorporating international legal obligations into the United Kingdom's domestic legal system. It is undoubtedly the most important statute passed in the past few hundred years. This Act legally incorporated European Community law (now called European Union law) and principles into the law and three legal systems within the United Kingdom. European law has had a profound effect on our uncodified constitutional arrangements. In particular, it has affected the classic doctrine of parliamentary sovereignty (as expounded by Dicey) as since 1973 Parliament cannot now simply pass any law that it chooses if that law will violate European Union law. It has affected the constitutional role of the judges in relation to legislation and has conferred European law rights on individuals that they can enforce in the domestic courts (see Chapter 15). It must be remembered, of course, that following the June 2016 referendum vote the United Kingdom is scheduled to exit the European Union. At the time of writing, the European Union (Withdrawal) Bill 2017–19 was proceeding through Parliament. Clause 1 of this Bill provides for the express repeal of the European Communities Act 1972 (see section 15.6.6).

The House of Commons Disqualification Act 1975

This Act limited the power of the executive. It is concerned with the constitutional relationship and balance between the executive and the House of Commons. Section 2 specifies that only 95 government ministers (ministerial offices) can sit in the House of Commons, thereby ensuring (at least in constitutional theory) that the executive ministers, by virtue of their limited numbers, do not dominate the rest of the chamber (see section 11.6.3).

The Government of Wales Act 1998

This Act refers to the establishment of a new state institution. It devolved power to Wales by establishing a National Assembly for Wales. This legislation had been preceded by a referendum in Wales, which, albeit very narrowly, endorsed the creation of this Assembly. This demonstrates participatory democracy whereby the people who would be affected by the legislation were specifically consulted as to whether (or not) they approved of its proposals. Such a referendum (known as a pre-legislative referendum) was not technically legally necessary but was considered politically appropriate (see section 14.5).

The House of Lords Act 1999

This Act altered the composition of an institution of the state, namely the second chamber in Parliament. It removed the vast majority of hereditary peers from the House of Lords. The existence of hereditary peers (members who inherited their seats in the House of Lords) has always marked out the United Kingdom's constitutional arrangements as being very unusual in a democracy. The Act demonstrates graphically the power of Parliament to pass any law that it chooses. In short, the House of Lords Act 1999 effectively halved the size of the House of Lords (see section 10.6.3).

The Constitutional Reform Act 2005

This Act reformed various aspects of the constitution. As its title indicates, it is a quintessential constitutional measure. Its constitutional impact is as follows:

- It made provision for a new Supreme Court (see section 5.7.10).
- It reformed the way in which judges are appointed (see section 13.3.1).
- It remodelled the historic role of the Lord Chancellor, who is a major official of state (see section 5.7.9).

Three recent Acts are also worth noting:

The Fixed-Term Parliaments Act 2011

This Act removed from the Prime Minister the prerogative power to decide the date of a general election. It also set five years in between elections with the result that following the 2017 general election (all things being equal) the next general election to the House of Commons will be in May 2022 (see section 8.1.1).

The Succession to the Crown Act 2013

The Act ended male preference in respect of the line of succession to the throne and also removed the bar on a person who marries a Roman Catholic from succeeding to the Crown.

The Recall of MPs Act 2015

This Act provided for the constituents of an MP to trigger a by-election for that seat (see later at section 9.3.4).

ACTIVITY

Exercise

Select a number of the Acts of Parliament set out above and explain in each case why the statute is considered to be constitutionally significant. Find other Acts which relate to the organs of the state.

4.4.3 Acts of Parliament conferring rights on the individual

Legislation may also have constitutional importance if it contains provisions which directly or indirectly affect the rights and liberties of the individual. A statute may therefore have ramifications for human rights or fundamental freedoms either by conferring special rights on individuals, or by restricting their freedoms.

The following Acts confer rights on individuals:

The Sex Discrimination Act 1975 (historic – but see below)

This Act was an example of Parliament passing a law to protect individuals by providing them with rights and legal redress in the event of discrimination. In short, the Act made it illegal to discriminate against individuals on the grounds of sex in the context of education, work, housing or providing goods or services. If an individual had been discriminated against he or she had the right to seek legal redress.

The Race Relations Act 1976 (historic – but see below)

This Act related to discrimination on the grounds of race (whether this was at work, renting accommodation, etc). If an individual had been racially discriminated against he or she had the right to seek legal redress. In both this statute and the one above, the state had recognised that one function of the state is to ensure that all individuals are treated with equal respect, providing them with a remedy if discrimination occurred.

The Equality Act 2010

This Act repealed and *restated* both the Sex Discrimination Act 1975 and the Race Relations Act 1976.

European Convention on Human Rights

originally formulated in 1950, this document aims to protect the human rights of all people in the member states of the Council of Europe

The Human Rights Act 1998

Along with the European Communities Act 1972, this statute is arguably the most constitutionally significant statute of the twentieth century. The Act gives further effect in domestic law to the fundamental rights and freedoms set out in the **European Convention on Human Rights**. This legislation represents a constitutional sea change in the way in which human rights are protected in the United Kingdom, as with the implementation of this Act individuals are permitted to raise alleged breaches of these rights directly before domestic courts (see Chapter 17).

The Representation of the People Act 1983

This Act consolidated earlier Representation of the People Acts, which conferred the legal right on individuals to vote in elections to the House of Commons. It is of constitutional importance as it relates directly to the foundation of (participatory) democracy and the constitutional relationship between the individual and the state: the right of the people to elect and determine the composition of the legislature and, indirectly, the executive. On voting, see section 9.6.

It should be noted that under the doctrine of parliamentary sovereignty all of the above statutes (even though they detail important principles underpinning our constitution) could be repealed or amended. No special procedure (or special majority in Parliament) is required to alter or repeal them (but see section 4.4.5).

4.4.4 Acts of Parliament restricting the freedoms of the individual

It is important to note that Parliament will also pass statutes that will restrict the actions and freedoms of individuals. The following four Acts illustrate this:

The Perjury Act 1911

Under this Act it is a criminal offence for a person sworn in as a witness in court proceedings to make a statement which he knows to be false or does not believe to be true. This legislation protects the administration of justice.

The Public Order Act 1986

This legislation is concerned, *inter alia*, with the control and limitation of public processions and assemblies in order to protect public order.

The Prevention of Terrorism Act 2005 (historic)

The objective of this Act was to prevent terrorism-related activity. The Act aimed to achieve this by providing for the issuing of two types of 'control orders' which imposed obligations on individuals suspected of being involved in terrorism-related activities. The obligations imposed were tailored to the risk posed by the suspect concerned and could include, for example, restricting movement, prohibiting the possession of specified items or restricting communication and association. Owing to its draconian nature and restriction on human rights, the legislation was highly contentious, but nevertheless passed expeditiously through Parliament. The Act was repealed by the Terrorism Prevention and Investigation Measures Act 2011, which introduced TPIMs instead (see section 6.7.11).

The Investigatory Powers Act 2016

This Act increased state surveillance over individuals, involving the obtaining and retention of their communications data.

ACTIVITY

Exercise

Select a number of the Acts of Parliament set out above and explain in each case what constitutional significance the statute has for the individual and individual rights. Find other Acts which have a constitutional impact on the individual.

4.4.5 Laws LJ and Acts of Parliament with constitutional status

As indicated, historically the United Kingdom has been characterised as not having higher fundamental, entrenched constitutional laws. In recent years this orthodoxy has been questioned. For example, Laws LJ in *Thoburn v Sunderland City Council* [2002] EWHC 195 (Admin) (albeit *obiter)* argued that:

JUDGMENT

'We should recognise a hierarchy of Acts of Parliament: as it were "ordinary" statutes and "constitutional" statutes. The two categories must be distinguished on a principled basis.'

He added that these 'constitutional statutes' should embrace, among others, the following:

- The Magna Carta.
- The Bill of Rights.
- The Act of Union.
- The Human Rights Act.
- The Scotland Act.
- The Government of Wales Act.
- The European Communities Act.

Furthermore, he commented that, whereas ordinary statutes could be impliedly repealed by a later inconsistent Act, constitutional statutes such as the ones listed above are not subject to implied repeal. On implied repeal see section 7.9.3. In relation to the 'constitutional status' of the Government of Wales Act 2006, see Beatson J in *R (Governors of Brynmawr Foundation School) v The Welsh Ministers* [2011] EWHC 519 (Admin). More recently, in the context of 'fundamental principles' found in 'constitutional instruments', see Lords Neuberger and Mance (with the remainder of the Supreme Court in agreement) in *R (HS2 Action Alliance Limited) v Secretary of State for Transport* [2014] UKSC 3, para 207 (for details of this case, see section 8.6.4).

ACTIVITY

Self-test question

What is the significance of Laws LJ's comments for our understanding of the sources of the British constitution?

4.5 Domestic delegated legislation

4.5.1 The nature of delegated legislation

delegated legislation

legislation made by the executive

Delegated legislation can also have constitutional significance. Delegated legislation is subordinate or secondary legislation made under the authority of a primary statute (the enabling Act of Parliament). This legislative power is conferred on the executive, for example a government minister. In doing so, it represents a clear breach of the separation of powers but is justified constitutionally on the basis of practical necessity (see section 5.7.2).

4.5.2 Examples of delegated legislation

An example of the Prime Minister using a delegated legislative power is as follows:

The Secretary of State for Constitutional Affairs Order 2003 (SI 2003/1887)

This order transferred specified functions of the Lord Chancellor (a position which at that point the government anticipated would be abolished under the impending Constitutional Reform Bill) to the newly created post of the Secretary of State for Constitutional Affairs. This order was passed under the aegis of the Ministers of the Crown Act 1975.

A further example of delegated legislation, the Supreme Court Fees (Amendment) Order 1996, is detailed below in *R v Lord Chancellor, ex parte Witham* [1997] 2 All ER 779 (see section 4.8.3). More recently, the Local Authorities (Conduct of Referendums) (England) Regulations 2012 SI 2012/323 provided for the conduct of local referendums under the aegis of the Local Government Act 2000 (as amended) concerning whether existing local governance arrangements should be changed. Finally, in the context of the increase in university tuition fees in 2012, see the Higher Education (Basic Amount) Regulations 2010 (SI 2010/3021) and the Higher Education (Higher Amount) Regulations 2010 (SI 2010/3020) made under the aegis of s 24 Higher Education Act 2004. This increase in tuition fees was unsuccessfully challenged in judicial review proceedings (see section 19.4.1).

4.6 Domestic legislation of local authorities and the devolved institutions

4.6.1 Local authorities and delegated legislation

Local authorities enjoy a delegated legislative power. As local authorities technically form part of the executive, this is also a breach of the separation of powers, although this power is justified on the basis of practical necessity. Two examples of byelaws are set out later at section 14.2.2.

4.6.2 Legislation and the devolved institutions

As a result of **devolution**, the devolved institutions also have the power to pass legislation (both secondary and primary in nature – see Chapter 14). For example, in the case of Scotland, the Scottish Parliament has the power to pass Acts of the Scottish Parliament, as illustrated by the following example:

The Scottish Parliamentary Standards Commissioner Act 2002

This Act established the office of a Parliamentary Standards Commissioner for the Scottish Parliament to investigate complaints concerning Members of the Scottish Parliament (MSPs) as to whether they had breached, for example, parliamentary Standing Orders or the Code of Conduct.

4.7 Legislation of the European Union

As a result of the European Communities Act 1972, European law (both primary and secondary) now forms an ever-burgeoning and important part of the law of the United Kingdom (see Chapter 15). In broad terms there are two types of European Union law:

- primary sources and
- secondary sources.

4.7.1 Primary sources

These include the founding Treaty of Rome 1957, together with its subsequent amendment over the years (eg the Single European Act 1986, which, *inter alia*, extended the powers of the European Parliament).

4.7.2 Secondary sources

European Union legislation is passed by the European Union institutions and comes in a number of forms:

- regulations.
- directives.
- decisions.

Regulations

The constitutional significance of regulations is that they are of general application and are self-executing as they do not require a Member State to formally implement them. In other words, the United Kingdom Parliament (or any other parliament or assembly in the Union) does not need to pass a law to incorporate the regulation as it will automatically form part of domestic law. An example of a regulation is detailed below:

Regulation 1365/75

This created a European Foundation for the improvement of living and working conditions of workers (which relates to individual social and economic rights).

Directives

In contrast to regulations above, directives do not have general application (instead they are addressed to particular Member States) and they require Member States to implement them through the passage of domestic legislation. In the United Kingdom directives can be implemented through either the passage of an Act of Parliament (see directly below) or by means of delegated legislation in the form of a statutory instrument.

Council Directive 95/46/EC

The Data Protection Act 1998 was passed by the United Kingdom Parliament in order to implement the above European directive. This directive was aimed at protecting the rights of individuals in respect of personal data held about them. This issue relates directly to an individual's right to privacy.

Decisions

A decision does not have general application, but is addressed to particular parties (undertakings/companies) or Member States. Decisions can be used to implement a policy as illustrated by the example below:

Council Decision laying down the Procedures for the Exercise of Implementing Powers Conferred on the Commission 99/468 [1999] OJ L184/23

This Council decision, known as the 'Comitology decision', sets out the procedure to be followed when the Council confers a law-making power on the European Commission.

This delegation of legislative power is analogous to the United Kingdom Parliament (as the **legislature**) delegating a law-making power onto the government (the executive) – see section 5.7.2.

----

legislature

the law-making body in a constitution

Non-legally binding secondary sources

Opinions and recommendations are measures which do not have legally binding effect. For example, the European Commission can issue a 'reasoned opinion' in the context of enforcement proceedings against a Member State for violating European

Union law. The opinion would set out the ways in which the Commission considered the Member State to have breached the law, for example by failing to implement a directive.

KEY FACTS

Key facts on legislation as a source of the British constitution

Legislation may have constitutional importance if it:

- establishes a state institution/organ of government;
- defines the powers of a state institution;
- regulates the functions of a state institution;
- regulates the procedure of a state institution;
- regulates the relationship between state institutions;
- regulates how the state relates to the individual by either conferring rights on the individual or by restricting their freedoms.

4.8 Domestic case law

4.8.1 The role of the courts

The courts play an important role in respect of constitutional rules. This is true also in countries where these rules are codified in a documentary constitutional text. This is because all constitutional rules (whether contained in a codified document or not) need to be interpreted and clarified. As noted earlier, even in the United States the rules and principles set out in the codified constitution need to be interpreted, and this is performed by the United States Supreme Court (see *Marbury v Madison* (1803) 1 Cranch 137).

In the United Kingdom, in the absence of a single authoritative constitutional text, the courts play a particularly important role as many of our constitutional rules are to be found in court decisions (ie judicial decisions made in legal disputes brought before them for adjudication). In fact, the most important principle of our constitution, namely the legislative sovereignty of Parliament, is a court-based doctrine. This principle exists because the courts have declared it so in various decisions. Similarly, the rule of law is underpinned by judicial decisions. Indeed, Dicey, writing at the turn of the twentieth century, referred to England as having a court-based constitution (ie common law constitution). More recently it has been suggested that:

QUOTATION

'. . . while other areas of substantive law have become land-masses of statute, our constitutional law remains a common law ocean dotted with islands of statutory provision.'
S Sedley, 'The Sound of Silence, Constitutional Law Without a Constitution' (1994) 110 LQR 270.

NB. It is also worth remembering that judicial review principles are rooted in the common law (see below and Chapters 19 and 20).

It is certainly the case, however, that following the Labour government of 1997–2010 many statutes affecting the constitution have been enacted and this has continued under subsequent administrations. In addition, it must be remembered that the courts are necessarily reactive as they must wait for a legal dispute to be brought before them in order for them to declare the law.

Not every court decision, of course, will illustrate or expound a constitutional principle or clarify a particular constitutional rule. Therefore it is necessary (as in the case of statutes), to examine each court decision on a case by case basis to ascertain whether the ruling has constitutional significance, and consequently whether it forms part of the constitutional law of the United Kingdom.

In the United Kingdom the courts may make decisions of constitutional importance either by:

- declaring the common law; or
- interpreting statutes in the light of certain constitutional principles.

4.8.2 The common law

Many of our constitutional rules are derived from the judiciary declaring the common law.

The following case declares that the government/state must act within the law:

CASE EXAMPLE

Entick v Carrington *(1765) 19 St Tr 1030*

Under a warrant issued by the Secretary of State (the Earl of Halifax), the defendants (Carrington and three other king's messengers) were required to search for John Entick and deliver him together with his papers before the Secretary of State. The allegation against Entick was that he was suspected of seditious libel. As the king's messengers broke into his house and seized his papers, Entick successfully sued them in the tort of trespass. As the trespass had not been justified by any legal authority (in other words by a valid warrant of the Secretary of State to enter Entick's premises), a tort had been commissioned. The case, though superficially concerned with the private law of trespass, has a clear constitutional dimension as it is concerned with the limitation of the power of the state, and protecting the individual from the exercise of arbitrary state power. In other words, in order for the state to enter a person's property, it must have appropriate legal authority or it will be deemed unlawful.

NB. On this case, see R Gordon, 'Entick v Carrington' [1765] revisited: All the king's horse' in S Juss and M Sunkin (eds), *Landmark Cases in Public Law* (Hart Publishing, 2017), p 1.

The following case concerned the disclosure of documents for which Crown privilege had been claimed by the executive:

CASE EXAMPLE

Conway v Rimmer *[1968] AC 910*

Conway (a former probationary police constable) initiated proceedings for malicious prosecution against his former Superintendent. The Home Secretary refused the disclosure of specified documents (which could have been crucial to the proceedings) by claiming Crown privilege as their production would be injurious to the public interest. The House of Lords held that the Home Secretary's certification was not conclusive and ordered the production of these documents for the court to inspect.

The following case concerns the protection of the constitutional principle of free expression and the freedom to express criticism of governmental institutions:

CASE EXAMPLE

Derbyshire County Council v Times Newspapers Ltd and others
[1993] 1 All ER 1011

In this case Derbyshire County Council wished to sue *The Sunday Times*, its editor and two journalists in defamation for articles concerning alleged share dealings of the council. The House of Lords held that, under the common law of defamation (ie tort law), Derbyshire County Council did not have the right to sue for damages as such a right would have been contrary to the public interest.

Although this case is in the context of the private law of defamation, it necessarily raises the constitutional issue of freedom of speech to criticise the government (see section 18.4.1).

The following case indicates that criminal offences (which restrict the freedom of the individual) can originate from the common law:

CASE EXAMPLE

Shaw v DPP *[1962] AC 220*

Shaw had been convicted, *inter alia*, of a common law conspiracy to corrupt public morals as he had conspired with advertisers and others to debauch and corrupt the morals of the youth and other subjects. Shaw had published a 'Ladies Directory' that contained the names and addresses of prostitutes. Shaw appealed and contended, *inter alia*, that there was no such offence. The House of Lords held that the courts had a residual power to supervise such offences that were prejudicial to public welfare. Viscount Simonds stated that:

JUDGMENT

'. . . there remains in the courts of law a residual power to enforce the supreme and fundamental purpose of the law, to conserve not only the safety and order but also the moral welfare of the State.'

The following case reaffirms the fundamental principle of judicial independence:

CASE EXAMPLE

R v Bow Street Metropolitan Stipendiary Magistrate, ex p
Pinochet Ugarte (No 2) *[2000] 1 AC 119 (for details see section 13.4.2)*

In order to reiterate the fundamental importance of the principle of the independence of the judiciary and the right of individuals to a fair trial, the House of Lords set aside their previous decision in relation to a warrant for General Pinochet's extradition. The decision was set aside as one of the judges, Lord Hoffmann, had had a connection with Amnesty International, which was seeking the extradition of Pinochet.

On the common law and the British constitution, see J Laws, *The Common Law Constitution* (Cambridge University Press, 2014). In fact, the common law remedy of judicial review (see Chapters 19 and 20) is the central way in which governmental power is legally controlled.

4.8.3 Statutory interpretation

The courts in interpreting statutes may do so in the light of certain constitutional principles. In particular, as the United Kingdom has historically lacked a Bill of Rights, the courts have used these principles in order to protect the individual. Accordingly, where a statute is unclear or ambiguous the courts can draw upon certain constitutional principles, which include the assumption that surely Parliament would never have intended to:

- legislate contrary to international law and Treaty obligations
- legislate retrospectively
- legislate so as to interfere with a person's right of access to the courts
- create taxes in the absence of clear authority.

The following case illustrates the first two presumptions:

CASE EXAMPLE

Waddington v Miah *[1974] 2 All ER 377*

In this case the House of Lords interpreted the Immigration Act 1971 so that it did not have retrospective criminal effect. Lord Reid stated that 'it is hardly credible that any government department would promote or that Parliament would pass retrospective criminal legislation'. He also noted that Art 7 of the European Convention on Human Rights prohibited the imposition of retrospective criminal offences. In other words, the courts will assume that Parliament intended to legislate in accordance with the United Kingdom's international obligations (ie the European Convention). Today, of course, the Human Rights Act 1998 has been passed (see section 4.8.4 and Chapter 17).

The following case illustrates the third presumption:

CASE EXAMPLE

R v Lord Chancellor, ex parte Witham *[1997] 2 All ER 779*

ultra vires

acting beyond specified legal powers

Under the authority of s 130 of the Supreme Court Act 1981 (now known as the Senior Courts Act 1981) the Lord Chancellor made the following delegated legislative provision: the Supreme Court Fees (Amendment) Order 1996. Art 3 of this Order removed from litigants in person who received income support their (previously enjoyed) exemption from such court fees. Witham, who was unemployed and on income support, was therefore unable to institute proceedings in person for defamation as the exemption from paying fees had been removed by the above 1996 Order. Witham sought judicial review of Art 3 of the Order as **ultra vires** and so beyond the legal powers of the Lord Chancellor.

It was held by the High Court that access to the courts was, in effect, a constitutional right recognised by the common law and that this right could only be restricted by clear and specific statutory authority. The court interpreted s 130 as not empowering the Lord Chancellor to issue Art 3, the effect of which had been to deny Witham access to the courts and legal redress (a common law constitutional right). This case demonstrates the courts protecting the right of individuals to access the courts and thus seek justice.

NB. See also the recent similar case of *R (UNISON) v Lord Chancellor* [2017] UKSC 51 (at section 6.7.5).

The fourth presumption is demonstrated by *Attorney General v Wilts United Dairies Ltd* (1921) 37 TLR 884.

On statutory interpretation, see the following useful text: I Mcleod, *Principles of Legislative and Regulatory Drafting* (Hart Publishing, 2009).

declaration of incompatibility

a declaration by the courts under the Human Rights Act 1998 that legislation is inconsistent with the European Convention

4.8.4 Statutory interpretation and the Human Rights Act 1998

In recent years the role of the courts in interpreting legislation has been heightened by the passage of the Human Rights Act 1998. The Act is in effect an interpretative one in that s 3 requires all courts and tribunals to interpret all legislation in accordance with the rights and freedoms enshrined in the European Convention on Human Rights. If the relevant statute cannot be read in line, the courts cannot strike down the offending primary legislation; instead the higher courts can issue a **declaration of incompatibility** (see section 17.7).

The following case is an example of the operation of the Human Rights Act:

CASE EXAMPLE

Bellinger v Bellinger *[2003] UKHL 21*

Bellinger was a transsexual who had been born male. In 1981 she went through a ceremony of marriage with a man. Section 11 of the Matrimonial Causes Act 1973 states that a marriage is valid only if the parties are male and female. Bellinger sought, and was denied, a declaration that her marriage was valid notwithstanding that she was born male. The House of Lords stated that the terms male and female in the Act were to be given their ordinary meaning and referred to the respective biological gender at birth. Accordingly, within the meaning of s 11, as the parties were not male and female, the marriage was not valid. The court did, however, issue a declaration of incompatibility that s 11 was incompatible with Art 8 of the European Convention on Human Rights (the right to respect for private and family life) and Art 12 (the right to marry). This declaration did not mean that the 1973 Act was invalidated. However, in 2004 Parliament passed the Gender Recognition Act 2004, which recognised the reassigned gender of a person who has undergone gender reassignment.

For further examples see Chapter 17.

4.9 The royal prerogative

The **royal prerogative** is power that derives from the common law. Historically these powers would have resided personally in the monarch/Crown, but today they are effectively exercised in the name of the Crown by the government of the day (see section 11.9).

The following two cases demonstrate the role of the courts in demarcating the legal parameters of the royal prerogative:

CASE EXAMPLE

The case of Proclamations *(1611) 12 Co Rep 74*

In this case the court declared that the king cannot by proclamation create a new criminal offence and that the king only enjoyed the prerogatives that the law of the land permitted him. In other words, the powers under the royal prerogative were limited.

CASE EXAMPLE

Burmah Oil Company Ltd v Lord Advocate *[1965] AC 75*

This case concerned the destruction of the oil installations of Burmah Oil (a group of four companies). During the Second World War these installations were destroyed by the British Army in Burma under the direction of the British government in order to deny industrial resources which could be useful to the advancing Japanese. The House of Lords held that, although the action had been carried out lawfully under the royal prerogative, a payment had to be made for the destruction of the property. The court further held that the Crown would only be immune from such payment if the destruction had been as a result of 'battle damage'. Here the British Army had not actually been fighting the enemy as the Japanese had been advancing. This case demonstrates that the courts will determine the parameters of the Crown's common law powers.

ACTIVITY

Applying the law

Select a number of the domestic case law decisions above and explain in each case why the case is considered to be constitutionally significant. Can you find any more constitutional cases?

The most important case of recent times involving the royal prerogative concerned the issue of triggering Art 50 in relation to exiting the European Union: *R (Miller) v Secretary of State for Exiting the European Union* [2017] UKSC 5 (see section 15.6.6).

4.10 European case law

Decisions made by the courts in Europe (both in Luxembourg and in Strasbourg) have had an impact on our constitution.

4.10.1 The Court of Justice of the EU in Luxembourg

Decisions and rulings made by this European Court can have a significant impact on our law, and its case law and principles are known as a tertiary source of European Union law. The functions of the Court of Justice of the EU are to ensure that Union law is upheld against Member States and the other European institutions (known as direct actions/the contentious jurisdiction) as well as to provide the definitive interpretation of European Union law (indirect actions/the non-contentious jurisdiction).

In terms of the latter jurisdiction, where a court of a Member State is faced with a provision of Union law that is unclear, Art 267 of the TFEU (formerly the Treaty of Rome 1957) allows that court to refer the point directly to the Court of Justice for it to interpret. The interpretation which clarifies the law is known as a preliminary ruling, which, once delivered, is binding (see section 15.4.2). Preliminary rulings can involve either:

- a court/tribunal of another Member State making a reference to the Court of Justice. In the example below, the reference was made by an Italian court:

CASE EXAMPLE

Costa v ENEL Case 6/64 *[1964] ECR 585*

In 1962 Italy nationalised its electricity industry and Costa claimed that this breached the 1957 Treaty of Rome (the founding Treaty of the European Economic Community, as it was known then). The issue in the case was whether national (Italian) domestic legislation took precedence over European law. On an Art 267 reference the Court of Justice affirmed that the creation of the EEC had created a new legal order whereby Member States had restricted their sovereign rights. In short, European law took precedence over inconsistent domestic law, thereby firmly establishing the principle of the primacy of EEC law (now called European Union law). This principle, although in the context of a ruling involving Italy, had a direct impact on all Member States (including the United Kingdom, which joined a decade after this ruling was issued).

■ a United Kingdom court/tribunal making a reference to the European Court:

CASE EXAMPLE

R v Secretary of State for Transport, ex parte Factortame Ltd (No 2) *[1991] 1 AC 603*

This seminal case is of profound constitutional importance and will be considered in detail at section 15.6.4. In brief, the Court of Justice ruled that rights enjoyed under European law must be given full effect in a domestic legal system even whilst a domestic court is waiting for a preliminary ruling to be given by the Court of Justice. In response to this ruling, the House of Lords – for the first time – disapplied an Act of Parliament (the Merchant Shipping Act 1988), thereby compromising the principle of parliamentary sovereignty (see section 15.6.5).

Through preliminary rulings the European Court has developed major principles underpinning European Union law, for example the doctrines of direct effect and the primacy of European Union law.

On European law and Brexit, see section 15.6.6.

4.10.2 The European Court of Human Rights in Strasbourg

Judgments made by the European Court of Human Rights also have an impact on the United Kingdom. The function of the European Court is to provide the authoritative interpretation of the articles of the European Convention. The effects of these judgments are not as immediate as with the judgments and rulings of the Court of Justice of the EU above (see Chapter 16).

CASE EXAMPLE

Dudgeon v United Kingdom *(1981) 4 EHRR 149*

Dudgeon was a homosexual who resided in Northern Ireland, which in the 1970s still criminalised homosexual activity between adult males (ss 61 and 62 of the Offences Against the Person Act 1861). Dudgeon contended that these provisions interfered with Art 8 of the European Convention (the right to respect for private life). The European Court of Human Rights held that this criminal legislation violated Art 8. Under international law the United Kingdom is bound to adhere to the decisions of the European Court of Human Rights, for example where necessary by desisting from a particular practice or by introducing legislation to remove the incompatibility. In response to this judgment, the Homosexual Offences (NI) Order 1982 was passed, which decriminalised homosexual activity between adult males in Northern Ireland.

ACTIVITY

Self-test question

Why do you think decisions in the European Courts (ie the Court of Justice of the EU and the European Court of Human Rights) are relevant to the study of the British constitution? Revisit this activity after completion of Chapters 15 to 17.

4.11 The law and custom of Parliament

Parliament (both the House of Commons and the House of Lords) regulates its own internal proceedings and determines its own standards of behaviour. This is done through laws and rules which are unique to it, known as the law and custom of Parliament (see section 8.5). These privileges (known as parliamentary privileges) are regarded as necessary in order to ensure that parliamentary members can carry out and discharge their constitutional functions. These laws/privileges comprise:

- statutory sources (Art 9 of the Bill of Rights which guarantees freedom of speech in Parliament)
- internal parliamentary sources (standing orders and resolutions)
- judicial sources whereby the courts recognise that, for example, Parliament has the right to determine and regulate its own membership and proceedings. This includes how legislation proceeds through Parliament, as demonstrated in the following case:

CASE EXAMPLE

British Railways Board v Pickin *[1974] AC 765*

Pickin sought to claim that Parliament had been fraudulently misled into passing the British Railways Act 1968. The House of Lords held that the role of the courts was merely to consider and apply enactments of Parliament and not to challenge the British Railways Act 1968. In essence, the courts would not question the internal proceedings within Parliament as to how the Bill came to be on the parliamentary roll (see sections 7.8.1 and 8.7.2).

KEY FACTS

Key facts on the courts as a source of the British constitution

Judicial decisions in case law may have constitutional importance if they:
- define the powers of a state institution (*Burmah Oil Company Ltd v Lord Advocate* (1965));
- regulate the relationship between state institutions (*British Railways Board v Pickin* (1974)); or
- regulate how the state relates to the individual by either conferring rights onto the individual (*Entick v Carrington* (1765)) or restricting their freedoms (*Shaw v DPP* (1962)).

4.12 Treaties and international law

International Treaties such as:

- the Universal Declaration of Human Rights 1948 and
- the International Covenant on Civil and Political Rights 1966

also act as an indirect influence on the British constitution. Moreover, case law from other national Supreme and Constitutional Courts may also prove to indirectly influence and shape our law. For example, in the *Derbyshire County Council* case (see sections 4.8.2 and 18.4.1) in the context of the importance attached to safeguarding freedom of speech, Lord Keith made reference to a decision issued by the United States Supreme Court (*New York Times Co v Sullivan* (1964) 376 US 254). This Supreme Court decision had endorsed the public policy interest in allowing a citizen to criticise an ineffectual or corrupt public official without fear of legal impediment.

4.13 Constitutional conventions

As noted above, the rules of the constitution can be divided into legal rules (above) and political rules, with the latter being constitutional conventions which are effectively politically binding constitutional rules.

4.13.1 Definition of a constitutional convention

Dicey defined conventions in the following terms:

QUOTATION

'Conventions, understandings, habits or practices which, though they may regulate the conduct of the several members of the sovereign power, of the Ministry, or of other officials, are not in reality laws at all since they are not enforced by the courts. This portion of constitutional law may, for the sake of distinction, be termed the "conventions of the constitution", or constitutional morality.' (*Sic*)

A Dicey, *Introduction to the Study of the Law of the Constitution* (10th edn, Macmillan, 1959), p 24.

More recently, Barendt defined them as follows:

QUOTATION

'Constitutional conventions may be defined as principles of political or constitutional morality which are regarded as binding, but which are not legally enforceable.'

E Barendt, 'Fundamental Principles' in D Feldman (ed), *English Public Law* (Oxford University Press, 2004), p 14.

Furthermore, Barnett has provided a fuller definition:

QUOTATION

'A constitutional convention is a non-legal rule which imposes an obligation on those bound by the convention, breach or violation of which will give rise to legitimate criticism; and that criticism will generally take the form of an accusation of "unconstitutional conduct".'

H Barnett, *Constitutional and Administrative Law* (12th edn, Routledge/Taylor & Francis Group, 2017), p 42.

From these definitions we can see that constitutional rules can be distinguished between legal rules, which are enforced in a court of law, and political rules, which are considered simply politically or morally binding. As noted above, Barnett has contended that the breach or blatant disregard of a convention would be considered to be (morally) unconstitutional (see section 4.16.2).

4.13.2 Preliminary points to note about constitutional conventions

It should be noted that:

- Firstly, constitutional conventions are not actually laws and yet they are studied as part of 'constitutional law'. They are a very important part of the constitution and in fact in some cases may actually assume more constitutional significance than the legal rules that they supplement (see for example, the convention that the monarch will give her consent to a Bill presented to her – see section 4.13.6).
- Secondly, constitutional conventions are not confined to the United Kingdom as they are also found in other countries such as the United States and Canada. These countries have codified constitutions and yet their constitutional text is supplemented by political conventional practices. For example, in Canada it is the practice that the federal Cabinet comprises representatives of all the Canadian provinces.
- Thirdly, constitutional conventions regulate key aspects of the British constitution and in particular, the government and the monarch. Some of the most important conventions are detailed below. It should be pointed out, however, that this is not an authoritative list (nor could it be, as inevitably there would be no universal agreement as to what it should include).
- Fourthly, in terms of their nature it should be recognised that constitutional conventions are rules which are not necessarily prescribed with absolute precision (this gives them flexibility to develop and evolve) and there may be disagreement over their exact content and parameters. It is important to remember that, unlike laws which are ultimately clarified in a court, there is no definitive authority or body which rules upon conventions. For example, although we are fairly clear in general terms about the rule governing the granting of the Royal Assent, other constitutional conventions are much less clear. For instance, in terms of ministerial responsibility, is it a modern-day convention that ministers should resign for major mistakes in their government departments, as opposed to resigning for personal misadventures? (See section 12.3.5.)

4.13.3 Constitutional conventions in respect of Parliament

These include, *inter alia*, the following:

- Committees of the House of Commons should reflect the party political representation in the chamber (see section 12.6.4).
- Money Bills originate in the House of Commons.
- Parliament must meet at least once a year. It is of interest to compare this rule with the United States Constitution, Art 1, s 4 of which states that, legally, Congress shall assemble at least once in every year.

THE SOURCES OF THE BRITISH CONSTITUTION

4.13.4 Constitutional conventions in respect of the monarch/executive

These include, *inter alia*, the following:

- The monarch assents to a Bill passed by both Houses of Parliament (see section 11.9.3).
- Following a general election the monarch will appoint as Prime Minister the MP who is the leader of the political party who can command a majority of support in the House of Commons.
- Many of the legal powers formally vested in the monarch are in fact exercised in practice by the government of the day in the name of the Crown (see section 11.9.3 and 11.9.4).
- Government ministers are collectively responsible to Parliament for the overall operation of government policy (see section 12.2).
- Government ministers are individually responsible to Parliament for their actions and the policy and actions of their government department (see section 12.3).
- The Prime Minster should be drawn from, and sit in, the House of Commons (see section 11.2.2).
- Government ministers must sit in one of the Houses of Parliament (see section 11.6.1).
- Cabinet discussions should remain secret (see section 12.2.3).

4.13.5 Constitutional conventions in respect of the judiciary

These include, *inter alia*, the following:

- Retiring full-time judges should not return to private practice.
- The judiciary in general do not involve themselves in overtly party political issues (see section 13.4.4).

Historically, in the United Kingdom's highest court (the Appellate Committee of the House of Lords) at least two of the judges were Scottish and (usually) one was Northern Irish – but now see s 27 (8) of the Constitutional Reform Act 2005, which effectively maintains this convention by requiring that, in making selections, the Supreme Court justices must collectively have knowledge and experience of the law in each part of the United Kingdom (ie its three legal systems).

4.13.6 The significance of constitutional conventions

The importance of constitutional conventions, particularly in the British constitution, cannot be underestimated as these political rules and principles form a major aspect of our constitution. In fact, if we were to view the British constitution by only examining the legal rules, then we would have an unbalanced perception of the constitution. For example, in relation to the Royal Assent, although under the royal prerogative the monarch legally can refuse to give her consent to a Bill, in practice it has become a long-established convention that this assent is always granted on the advice of her ministers. If we were, however, to simply consider the legal rule concerning the Royal Assent in isolation without reference to the convention supplementing it, we would have a much distorted (and in fact inaccurate) view of the realities of the modern monarch's powers and of the constitution.

4.13.7 The purpose of constitutional conventions

Sir Ivor Jennings stated that constitutional conventions:

QUOTATION

'provide the flesh which clothes the dry bones of the law; they make the legal constitution work; they keep it in touch with the growth of ideas.'

I Jennings, *The Law and the Constitution* (5th edn, Hodder and Stoughton, 1959) pp 81–82.

In short, constitutional conventions supplement the legal rules of the constitution. Their purpose is to ensure that the constitution can develop and adapt to ever-changing contemporary principles and values. For example, the constitutional conventions regulating the legal powers of the monarch ensure that these powers are generally exercised by her government ministers on her behalf and in her name. This is consistent with modern democratic values as executive ministers are politically responsible to Parliament (through the convention of ministerial responsibility) whereas the monarch is unelected. It also illustrates the modern nature of the constitutional monarchy whereby the powers of the monarch are limited and controlled by binding political rules.

Constitutional conventions ensure that the constitution can develop on an incremental basis to address contemporary needs. For example, a constitutional convention (the Sewel Convention – named after Lord Sewel) arose as a result of the creation of the Scottish Parliament. In effect it stated that the Westminster Parliament would not normally legislate in respect of 'devolved matters', except with the consent of the Scottish Parliament. This convention, therefore, regulated the constitutional and political relationship between two major institutions of the state viz, the Westminster and Scottish Parliaments (see section 14.3.13). It should be noted that this convention has now been enacted in statutory form by the Scotland Act 2016.

ACTIVITY

Self-test questions

1. How would you define a constitutional convention?
2. What constitutional purpose do they serve?

4.13.8 Why are constitutional conventions followed?

QUOTATION

'Conventions in Parliament are a cornerstone of our Constitution. In part, they oil the hidden moving parts of parliamentary process and keep it all flowing; and in part they are the glue which commits those with differing objectives to act in accordance with agreed practice. They are non-statutory but binding on those who come to agree them. Those of us interested in how Parliament works in practice should only give up on conventions with the heaviest of hearts.'

Lord Strathclyde, December 2015, *Strathclyde Review: Secondary legislation and the primacy of the House of Commons*, Cm 9177 (Crown Copyright, 2015), p 3.

Student mentor tip

....

'Understand the UK constitutional system and conventions: read widely!'

Anthony, London South Bank University

Constitutional conventions affect the main individuals and institutions in our constitution: the monarch, Prime Minister, Cabinet ministers, judges and members of the House of Commons and Lords. Given that they are merely political rules, why are they followed? Indeed, constitutional conventions are not *justiciable* (ie not suitable for resolution before judicial proceedings) and so not enforced in a court. In fact, according to the 2006 Joint Committee on Conventions, constitutional conventions, owing to their nature, are 'unenforceable' (First Report of Session 2005–06 of the Joint Committee on Conventions, *Conventions of the UK Parliament*, HL Paper 265-I, HC 1212-I (2006), para 279).

As political rules, constitutional conventions are considered by those bound by them to be a constitutional and political obligation. In addition, political repercussions would result from their breach, which, as observed by Barnett earlier, would involve allegations of unconstitutional behaviour (ie acting contrary to the spirit and political principles underpinning the constitution – see section 4.16.2). For example, ministers will generally resign for major and embarrassing personal errors and misadventures (but less so for departmental errors) because of the resulting criticism that would follow if they did not (for examples, see section 12.3.4).

4.13.9 The flexibility of constitutional conventions

It should be noted that, on occasions, owing to their flexible and non-legal nature, constitutional conventions can at times be set aside. For example, in the mid-1970s the convention of collective Cabinet responsibility was temporarily set aside in relation to the 1975 EEC national referendum. The Labour Cabinet at the time was divided over the issue of the referendum, which concerned whether the United Kingdom should remain in the EEC (as it was then known). The Labour Prime Minister at the time, Harold Wilson, set aside this convention on this issue. More recently, the Conservative Prime Minister David Cameron also set aside this convention in relation to the 2016 referendum on the question of our continued membership of the European Union.

4.13.10 What are the origins of constitutional conventions?

The origins of the laws and legal rules of the constitution (whether it be in the form of legislation or a constitutional principle extracted from a case) can be located relatively easily by examining the date of the legislation or case in question. In contrast, the point at which a mere accepted practice has crystallised into a political constitutional rule – with an obligation to follow it – is much more problematic. This is because constitutional conventions develop piecemeal over time on an *ad hoc* basis to supplement the legal rules by adjusting and adapting the constitution to reflect contemporary political principles and needs.

In his work *The Law and the Constitution* (London University Press, 1959), Sir Ivor Jennings suggested a three-part test to determine the existence of a constitutional convention:

1. What are the (political) precedents for the convention?
2. Do those connected with this rule believe that they ought to act in a certain constitutional way (ie follow this rule)?
3. Is there a constitutional reason for this rule?

This test was recognised in the Upper Tribunal in *Evans v Information Commissioner* [2012] UKUT 313 (AAC).

It should be noted, however, that sometimes constitutional conventions can be created by agreement. An example of this is the Sewel Convention in respect of the Scottish Parliament (see section 14.3.13).

4.13.11 The distinction between laws and constitutional conventions

What is the difference between laws (legal rules) and constitutional conventions (non-legal/political rules)?

▢ Firstly, in general, laws are enforced in a court, whereas constitutional conventions are not.

▢ Secondly, a constitutional convention depends upon regular and consistent use for its validity:

QUOTATION

'A law does not lapse if it becomes obsolete, yet a convention can disappear if it is not followed for a significant period, or if it is broken without objection.'
J Alder and K Syrett, *Constitutional and Administrative law* (11th edn, Palgrave, 2017), p 64.

4.13.12 The judicial recognition of constitutional conventions

Although the courts do not enforce constitutional conventions, they have at times recognised their existence and made specific reference to them. An illustration of where a court made direct reference to the convention of collective responsibility is in the following case:

CASE EXAMPLE

Attorney General v Jonathan Cape Ltd *[1976] 1 QB 752*

The Attorney General sought an injunction to restrain publication of a book detailing the diaries of the late Richard Crossman, who died in 1974. The diaries detailed discussion in the Cabinet of which he was a member in the 1960s and the legal action was based on an alleged breach of confidence. The law of confidence concerns the situation where an individual has received information in circumstances that the information should remain confidential. Collective ministerial responsibility includes the rule that Cabinet discussions are secret, so as to allow ministers to discuss issues freely before a collective decision is agreed upon and thereafter defended publicly (see section 12.2.3).

The court held that the law of confidence extended to public secrets and that the court had the power to restrain Cabinet material being published where publication would be a breach of confidence and against the public interest (ie prejudicing the maintenance of the convention of collective responsibility). There was however a time limit after which the confidential nature of the information would lapse and on the facts, an injunction to restrain the publication in 1975 of discussion ten years earlier was not justified. The key point to note in this case is that the Attorney General went to court using the legal action of the law of confidence (which would be breached if Cabinet information was published). In other words, the Attorney General did *not* go to court simply on the basis of pleading that publication would breach a constitutional convention (because as a political rule, this would have been unarguable).

Moreover, in the following case in the context of a Canadian constitutional convention, the Canadian Supreme Court recognised and acknowledged the convention's existence, but affirmed that, as political rules, conventions cannot be enforced in a court of law:

CASE EXAMPLE

Reference Re Amendment of the Constitution of Canada
(1982) 125 DLR (3d) 1

This case considered whether the consent of the Canadian provinces was necessary before the Canadian legislature requested the United Kingdom Parliament to amend the Canadian constitution in a way which affected the federal/provincial relationship. At this time, in order for the Canadian constitution to be altered, it required legislation from the Westminster Parliament in London. The Canadian Supreme Court held that, as a matter of constitutional convention, the consent of the Canadian provinces was required, thereby recognising the existence of the convention. As a matter of law, however, such consent was not legally necessary. The court stated that in respect of the Canadian constitution's 'conventional rules':

JUDGMENT

'In contradistinction to the laws of the constitution, they are not enforced by the courts. One reason for this situation is that, unlike common law rules, conventions are not judge-made rules. They are not based on judicial precedents. . . . Nor are they in the nature of statutory commands which it is the function and duty of the courts to obey and enforce. Furthermore, to enforce them would mean to administer some formal sanction when they are breached.'

Indeed, with reference to the *Jonathan Cape* case, Lord Neuberger in *R (Miller) v Secretary of State for Exiting the European Union* [2017] UKSC 5 stated that judges were:

JUDGMENT

'. . . neither the parents nor the guardians of political conventions; they are merely observers. As such, they can recognise the operation of a political convention in the context of deciding a legal question . . . but they cannot give legal rulings on its operation or scope, because those matters are determined within the political world.'

In the following case, the Court of Appeal in determining the legal powers of a government minister made its decision in the context of the fact that the minister (under the convention of ministerial responsibility) was constitutionally, and politically, accountable to Parliament for his actions:

CASE EXAMPLE

Carltona Ltd v Commissioners of Works and others *[1943] 2 All ER 560*

Carltona Ltd challenged the requisition of their factory by the Commissioners of Works. The power to requisition this property was made under the Defence (General) Regulations 1939. Carltona argued that the requisition was invalid as the decision had in practice been taken by a civil servant (an Assistant Secretary) who was not a competent authority, instead of the Commissioners of Works. The Court of Appeal held that the order was valid. It would not be practical for the minister (who held office as the First Commissioner of Works, which exercised the powers of the Commissioners of Works) to take every decision personally; accordingly, an official can make decisions on the authority of the minister so that the official acts in the name of the minister. Strictly speaking, the official becomes the *alter ego* of the minister. Lord Greene MR stated that:

JUDGMENT

'The duties imposed upon ministers and the powers given to ministers are normally exercised under the authority of the ministers by responsible officials of the department. Public business could not be carried on if that were not the case. Constitutionally, the decision of such an official is, of course, the decision of the minister. The minister is responsible. It is he who must answer before Parliament for anything that his officials have done under his authority, and, if for an important matter he selected an official of such junior standing that he could not be expected competently to perform the work, the minister would have to answer for that in Parliament.'

Similarly, in the controversial (albeit historical) case of *Liversidge v Anderson* [1942] AC 206 the court was influenced by the convention of ministerial responsibility in reaching its decision concerning the exercise of the legal powers of a government minister to detain an individual during wartime (see section 6.7.10). For a more recent reference by a court to a convention, see the case of *R (Evans) v Attorney General* [2015] UKSC 21 (for the facts see section 5.7.6). In this case, the certificate/veto issued by the Attorney General under the Freedom of Information Act 2000 was based on the view that the 'education convention' relating to preparation of the heir to the throne, included 'advocacy correspondence' of the Prince of Wales. In the Supreme Court Lord Mance stated that:

JUDGMENT

'The certificate does not engage with, or begin to answer, the problems about this apparently wholesale acceptance . . . of the emergence of a new or highly expanded constitutional convention, which the Upper Tribunal had so forthrightly and on its face cogently rejected.'

Also see: A Perry, 'Constitutional conventions and the Prince of Wales' (2013) 76 MLR 1119.

4.13.13 Converting constitutional conventions into laws

It is of course possible for a constitutional convention to be converted into statutory form, thereby making it a legal rule and so legally enforceable. In fact, this has already been achieved in the British constitution and is illustrated by the following statutes:

▪ **The Parliament Act 1911**: codification may be considered necessary if a constitutional convention is flagrantly breached. Before the Parliament Act 1911, it had been a convention that the House of Commons was the dominant chamber and that the House of Lords would ultimately give way to it. The constitutional convention was that the Lords would not oppose a money Bill passed by the Commons. The House of Commons was of course elected (although at this point it did not involve universal suffrage). In 1909 the Finance Bill containing Lloyd George's Budget was rejected by the House of Lords and this resulted in the passage of the 1911 Act, which effectively placed on a statutory basis the principle that the upper chamber was legally subordinate to the lower House (see section 10.10.1).

- **The Statute of Westminster 1931**: s 4 of this Act codified (ie enacted in statutory form) the constitutional convention that the United Kingdom Parliament would not legislate for a Dominion (eg Canada, New Zealand and Australia) without their consent.
- **The Fixed-Term Parliaments Act 2011**: this Act gave legal effect to the constitutional convention that following a government losing a vote of no confidence in the House of Commons there would either be a dissolution of Parliament leading to a general election or the government would resign and allow an alternative government to be formed (see section 8.1.2).
- **The Constitutional Reform and Governance Act 2010**: this Act put the Ponsonby rule on a statutory footing (see section 11.9.3).
- **The Scotland Act 2016**: this Act codified the Sewel Convention, which had, hitherto, regulated the relationship between the United Kingdom Parliament and the Scottish Parliament. Section 2 amended the Scotland Act of 1988 to provide that:

SECTION

'. . . it is recognised that the Parliament of the United Kingdom will not normally legislate with regard to devolved matters without the consent of the Scottish Parliament.'

Notwithstanding this, according to Elliott and Thomas:

QUOTATION

'. . . the better view is that rather than making the convention into a law, this provision merely signals Parliament's acknowledgement of (what remains) a convention.'

M Elliott and R Thomas, *Public Law* (3rd edn, Oxford University Press, 2017), p 58.

Indeed, in the *Miller* (2017) case (see section 15.6.6) the Supreme Court made reference to the Sewel Convention in the 2016 Act, and held that this was simply a 'legislative recognition' of a convention in order to entrench it as such, and so did not convert it 'into a legal rule justiciable by the courts' (Lord Neuberger).

It is of interest to remember that other countries have also enacted constitutional conventions in a legal form. For example, the 22nd Amendment to the constitution of the United States codified the convention that limited the President to two terms of office.

Although it is possible for constitutional conventions to be converted into legal rules, is this necessarily desirable? At least two basic objections can be raised:

- Firstly, there would inevitably be debate over defining these conventions and their precise ambit.
- Secondly, new constitutional conventions in any event would develop so as to supplement those conventions which had been codified.

Finally, it is pertinent to point out that in 2006 the Joint Committee on Conventions was established to consider the practicality of codifying the constitutional conventions which regulate the relationship between the House of Commons and the House of Lords. Its conclusions are set out at section 10.11, although for present purposes it is worth noting the following passage:

QUOTATION

'In our view the word "codification" is unhelpful, since to most people it implies rule-making, with definitions and enforcement mechanisms. . . . It would raise issues of definition, reduce flexibility, and inhibit the capacity to evolve. It might create a need for adjudication, and the presence of an adjudicator, whether the courts or some new body, is incompatible with parliamentary sovereignty.'

Joint Committee on Conventions, First Report of Session 2005–06, *Conventions of the UK Parliament*, HL Paper 265-I, HC 1212-I (2006), para 279.

The committee observed that codification of conventions in a broad sense could mean an authoritative statement of conventions, or in a narrower sense, the reduction of them 'to a literal code or system'. In any event, the Committee made it very clear that there was universal opposition to legislating on these matters (as this would, for example, affect their flexibility and inhibit their evolution). Furthermore, the courts should have no role in adjudicating on them. On codification, see J Melton, C Stuart and D Helen, *To codify or Not to Codify?* (The Constitution Unit, 2015).

The following two developments are also worth noting:

▪ In the foreword to The *Cabinet Manual* issued in 2011, the Prime Minister stated that:

QUOTATION

'For the first time the conventions determining how the Government operates are transparently set out in one place. Codifying and publishing these sheds welcome light on how the Government interacts with the other parts of our democratic system.'

The Cabinet Manual – A guide to laws, conventions and rules on the operation of government (Crown Copyright, 2011), p iii.

▪ The 2014 *'Constitutional Consolidation Act'* blueprint proposed by the House of Commons Political and Constitutional Reform Select Committee – see earlier at section 3.5.

KEY FACTS

 Key facts on constitutional conventions

- 'Constitutional conventions may be defined as principles of political or constitutional morality which are regarded as binding, but which are not legally enforceable' (Barendt).
- Constitutional conventions regulate key aspects of the British constitution, in particular, the monarch and the government.
- They supplement the legal rules of the constitution and help to ensure that the constitution can develop and adapt to ever-changing contemporary principles and values.
- Political repercussions would result from their breach, which would lead to allegations of unconstitutional behaviour (acting in a morally unconstitutional way).

4.14 Documents relating to the constitution

In recent years a number of documents/codes relating to various aspects of the British constitution have been published. These include, *inter alia*, documents concerning:

▪ Government ministers (*The Ministerial Code* (Cabinet Office, revised January 2018)). This code is issued and revised by the Prime Minister and given to ministers on assuming office and details their responsibilities and expected standard of conduct. *The Ministerial Code* therefore provides ministerial guidelines for behaviour and so forms part of the sources of the British constitution (albeit non-legal).
▪ Judges (*Guide to Judicial Conduct* (Judiciary of England and Wales, 2013)).
▪ Local and central government relations (*The Central–Local Concordat*).

On the above, together with other codes of a constitutional nature, see: A Blick, *The Codes of the Constitution* (Hart Publishing, 2016).

4.15 Authoritative writers

Historic writers on the British constitution include, for example, the works of Blackstone and Dicey. Indeed, Dicey's work (A Dicey, *Introduction to the Study of the Law of the Constitution* (10th edn, Macmillan 1959)) has informed our understanding of the constitutional principles of, *inter alia*:

▪ the rule of law (Chapter 6)
▪ constitutional conventions (see section 4.13)
▪ parliamentary sovereignty (Chapter 7).

Today distinguished contemporary academics (eg the texts of Feldman's *Civil Liberties and Human Rights in England and Wales* (2nd edn, Oxford University Press, 2002), Bradley, Ewing and Knight's *Constitutional and Administrative Law* (16th edn, Pearson, 2015) or Wade and Forsyth's *Administrative Law* (11th edn, Oxford University Press, 2014)) will also be referred to by the courts in order to assist them in applying the constitution.

It should also be remembered that senior judges, serving or otherwise, will write occasionally in legal academic journals and deliver extra-judicial speeches. For instance, in 2004 the then Lord Chief Justice, Lord Woolf, delivered a speech on the rule of law at Cambridge University (Lord Woolf, 'The rule of law and a change in the constitution' (2004) 63 CLJ 317). Also see Lord Bingham's book *The Rule of Law* (Allen Lane, 2010).

4.16 Acting unconstitutionally in the United Kingdom

4.16.1 The difficulties associated with the term unconstitutional in the United Kingdom

As observed at section 2.6, acting unconstitutionally means to act contrary to the constitutional rules, spirit and principles underpinning the constitution. In the United Kingdom, in the absence of a codified document, the use of the term *unconstitutional* is problematic because the rules of the constitution have not been codified. In fact, these rules have not even been universally and definitively agreed upon and consequently, as indicated earlier at section 4.2, there is no universal agreement on what is, and what is not, a constitutional issue. In light of this, it is difficult to gain universal agreement on what is *unconstitutional* in the United Kingdom.

In addition, in the absence of a codified constitutional document which has fundamental status, the courts in the United Kingdom (unlike a number of Supreme or Constitutional Courts in other countries with a codified constitution) cannot declare Acts of Parliament to be legally unconstitutional. In other words, they cannot declare that an Act is invalid as being contrary to the principles underpinning the constitution because there is no fundamental, codified constitutional text. Instead, owing to the principle of parliamentary sovereignty, Parliament legally can pass any law that it chooses as the courts are (traditionally at least) unable to challenge or question it (see Chapter 7). The current impact of European Union law is dealt with at section 15.6.

4.16.2 Examples of acting unconstitutionally in the United Kingdom

In the United Kingdom we would consider the following to be unconstitutional:

- A violation of the rule of law (see Chapter 6).
- The arbitrary use of power without restraint (see Chapters 6 and 20).
- The departure from and interference with fundamental principles including, for example, the right of access to the courts (see *Chester v Bateson* at section 5.7.2) or the presumption of innocence (*ex parte Khawaja* at section 6.7.10).
- A breach or disregard of a constitutional convention (see section 4.13).
- A breach of European Union law (see Chapter 15).
- A breach of the European Convention, either through an adverse ruling of the European Court of Human Rights or in the context of a declaration of incompatibility made by the domestic courts under the Human Rights Act 1998 (see Chapters 16 and 17, respectively).

Some more examples are detailed below.

Firstly, suppose (however unlikely) the monarch refused to give the Royal Assent to a Bill, despite having been specifically requested to do so by her government minsters. It is a constitutional convention that the monarch confers her assent to a Bill and, as indicated above, a breach of a constitutional convention leads to an accusation of unconstitutional conduct. The failure to give assent to the Bill would, however, not be illegal because the disregard of a constitutional convention could not be enforced in a court of law. We could argue, therefore, that although this behaviour was *legally constitutional* (ie lawful), it would, nevertheless, be *morally unconstitutional* (as being contrary to the fundamental political principles underpinning the British constitution).

Secondly, according to the principle of parliamentary sovereignty, Parliament can legally pass any law that it chooses and so the courts are unable to declare an Act of Parliament *legally unconstitutional* as being repugnant to the British constitution (but in this context see section 7.7). In theory, therefore, suppose Parliament chooses to pass the (imaginary) Elections Act 2022, s 1 of which deprives all individuals with an income of less than £5,000 a year of the right to vote in general elections. Commentators would undoubtedly consider this legislation to be unconstitutional, at least from a moral perspective (ie *morally unconstitutional*), as it interferes with basic democratic principles, namely participatory democracy and the right to vote. The Act, however, would in legal theory be technically enforceable and therefore *legally constitutional*, as Parliament under the British constitution can legally pass any Act that it chooses.

CASE EXAMPLE

Madzimbamuto v Lardner-Burke [1969] 1 AC 645

Lord Reid in the Privy Council made the point that, under the principle of parliamentary sovereignty, Parliament can in legal theory pass any law (ie the Southern Rhodesia Act 1965), even if that statute contravened a well-established constitutional principle (ie that the UK Parliament would not legislate for Southern Rhodesia without its consent). In this context he commented that:

JUDGMENT

'It is often said that it would be unconstitutional for the United Kingdom Parliament to do certain things, meaning that the moral, political and other reasons against doing them are so strong that most people would regard it as highly improper if Parliament did these things. But that does not mean that it is beyond the power of Parliament to do such things. If Parliament chose to do any of them the courts could not hold the Act of Parliament invalid.' (See also section 7.6.4.)

Similarly, in the Privy Council case of *Webb v Outrim* [1907] AC 81 the Earl of Halsbury stated that:

JUDGMENT

'. . . in the British Constitution, though sometimes the phrase "unconstitutional" is used to describe a statute which, though within the legal power of the Legislature to enact, is contrary to the tone and spirit of our institutions, and to condemn the statesmanship which has advised the enactment of such a law, still, notwithstanding such condemnation, the statute in question is the law and must be obeyed.'

It is worth pointing out that the (imaginary) Elections Act 2022 would be inevitably challenged by aggrieved individuals under the European Convention on Human Rights:

■ Initially, in the domestic courts under the Human Rights Act 1998 by the seeking of a declaration that the Act contravenes Protocol 1, Art 3 (the right to vote). Notwithstanding this, Parliament and the government could politically ignore any such declaration and the Act would remain in force (see Chapter 17).

■ Thereafter, aggrieved individuals could petition the European Court of Human Rights in Strasbourg. The European Court inevitably would declare that the (imaginary) Elections Act 2022 violated the European Convention and require that the United Kingdom remove this offending legislation. The United Kingdom Parliament could in legal theory domestically ignore such a ruling; however, for political reasons and for the purposes of international law, it would implement the European Court's ruling. As an aside, however, it is interesting to note the reluctant approach of successive British governments to the ruling of the European Court in *Hirst v UK* (2006) concerning the right of prisoners to vote (see section 9.6.3).

Thirdly, an example of Parliament passing a statute which was arguably *morally unconstitutional* (but perfectly legal and enforceable) is the War Damage Act 1965, which, in effect, reversed a ruling of the House of Lords that proved to be financially inexpedient (see sections 4.9, 6.7.9 and 7.5.1). It is, of course, a fundamental principle of a democratic constitution that the role of the courts and the administration of justice is safeguarded. Similarly, it could conceivably be argued that s 20C of the

Taxes Management Act 1970 was *morally unconstitutional* as it conferred exceptionally wide-sweeping powers on the executive at the expense of the individual (see *Rossminster Ltd and others* at sections 6.7.5 and 6.7.9). Both statutes infringed major principles which are fundamental to a democratic constitution.

As the term unconstitutional is necessarily a somewhat indistinct term, commentators inevitably will disagree over whether legislation or government action is *morally unconstitutional*. For example, was the Prevention of Terrorism Act 2005 (see section 4.4.4) *morally unconstitutional* as it interfered with the fundamental liberties of the individual, or was it a necessary legislative response to an emergency, threatening the life and safety of the public? Finally, it is worth recalling the observation of a former Prime Minister, Stanley Baldwin (albeit in his capacity as Lord President of the Council), almost a century ago:

QUOTATION

'. . . we have to devote our minds to the meaning of the word "Constitution" and how far we are deviating in the course we are taking from what is constitutional. I had the pleasure of hearing an impromptu speech by my right hon. Friend the Member for West Birmingham (Sir A. Chamberlain) about a week ago, and he said, in the course of that delightful speech, that "unconstitutional" was a term that you applied in politics to the other fellow when he did something that you did not like, just as the other fellow always defended his conduct on the grounds that he was constitutional. Of course, that was said partly in chaff, but there is some truth in it.'

Hansard, HC Vol 261, col 530.

More recently, Griffith made the following point:

QUOTATION

'The constitution of the United Kingdom lives on, changing from day to day for the constitution is no more and no less than what happens. Everything that happens is constitutional. And if nothing happened that would be constitutional also.'

JAG Griffith, 'The Political Constitution' (1979) 42 MLR 1.

ACTIVITY

Exercise

What is meant by acting unconstitutionally in the British constitution?

KEY FACTS

Key facts on the sources of the British constitution

Legal sources:

Domestic legislation:
- Acts of Parliament.
- Delegated legislation.
- Legislation of local authorities and the devolved institutions.

European Union legislation:
- Primary sources.
- Secondary sources.

Domestic case law:
- The common law.
- Interpreting statutes.
- The royal prerogative.

European case law:
- Court of Justice of the EU.
- European Court of Human Rights.

The law and custom of Parliament:
- Parliamentary privilege.

Treaties and international law:
- Universal Declaration of Human Rights 1948.

Non-legal sources:

Constitutional conventions:
Documents (eg *The Ministerial Code*).
Academic writings.

SAMPLE ESSAY QUESTION

Essay: Where will you find the British constitution and what are the problems in locating its sources?

Introduction
- UK is very unusual in lacking a written codified document setting out the principles of the constitution (contrast USA and Ireland).
- As a result, UK constitutional rules are located in a wide range of different sources.

Problems in ascertaining sources
- Whereas other countries typically distinguish between constitutional (fundamental/higher) law and non-constitutional (ordinary) law, no such formal demarcation in the UK (but see Laws LJ in *Thoburn* (2002)).
- No special UK Constitutional Court.

Domestic legal sources
- Use examples of legislation which have established state institutions (eg Scotland Act 1998) and which have regulated the relationship between institutions (eg Parliament Acts 1911 and 1949).
- Use examples of case law which have: limited the powers of institutions (eg *Proclamations* (1611)), set out the relationship between institutions (eg *Pickin* (1974)), set out the relationship between the individual and the state (eg *Entick* (1765)) and which set out fundamental principles (eg *Pinochet* (2000)).

International sources

- European Union primary legislation (eg Treaty of Rome 1957) and secondary legislation (eg directives) as well as the case law of the Court of Justice of the EU (eg *Costa* (1964)).
- Articles of the European Convention on Human Rights, the international case law of the European Court of Human Rights (eg *Dudgeon* (1981)) and the Convention's impact on domestic law via the Human Rights Act 1998 (eg *Bellinger* (2003)).
- Universal Declaration of Human Rights 1948.

Non-legal sources

- Constitutional conventions are constitutional rules which are politically binding (eg ministerial responsibility) and which allow the constitution to adapt and develop over time (eg historically, the Sewel Convention in relation to the Scottish Parliament).
- Contrast with laws, though the courts can acknowledge them (eg *Carltona* (1943)).
- Note *The Ministerial Code* and authoritative writers such as Dicey.

Conclusion

Further reading

Books

Alder, J, and Syrett, K, *Constitutional and Administrative Law* (11th edn, Palgrave, 2017), Chapter 3.

Barnett, H, *Constitutional and Administrative Law* (12th edn, Routledge/Taylor & Francis Group, 2017), Chapter 2.

Bradley, A, Ewing, K and Knight, C, *Constitutional and Administrative Law* (16th edn, Pearson, 2015), Chapter 1.

Ellis, E, 'Sources of Law and the Hierarchy of Norms' in Feldman, D (ed), *English Public Law* (2nd edn, Oxford University Press, 2009), p 38.

Feldman, D, 'Constitutional conventions' in Qvortrup, M (ed), *The British Constitution: continuity and change* (Hart Publishing, 2015), p 93.

Galligan, B and Brenton, S (eds), *Constitutional Conventions in Westminster systems* (Cambridge University Press, 2015).

Juss, S and Sunkin, M (eds), *Landmark Cases in Public Law* (Hart Publishing, 2017).

Turpin, C, and Tomkins, A, *British Government and the Constitution* (7th edn, Cambridge University Press, 2012), Chapter 3.

Article

Feldman, D, 'Statutory interpretation and constitutional legislation' (2014) 130 LQR 473.

5

The separation of powers

AIMS AND OBJECTIVES

At the end of this chapter you should be able to:

- Explain what is meant by the principle of the separation of powers
- Identify and explain the aspects of the British constitution that violate the separation of powers
- Identify and explain the aspects of the British constitution that accord with the separation of powers
- Assess the overall significance of the separation of powers in the British constitution

5.1 Introduction

In the context of Chapter 2 on constitutions we noted the importance of ensuring that state/governmental power is limited by a constitution. One way in which state power can be controlled is through the principle of the separation of powers. In essence, under this doctrine public/state power is divided and dispersed between separately constituted institutions, each with a distinct function to perform. This is in accord with the principle of constitutionalism, namely that the power of the state should be limited (see section 2.6.2). The aim of this chapter is to consider the constitutional principle of the separation of powers and examine its significance in the context of the British constitution.

5.2 Definition

5.2.1 Introduction

The separation of powers has been described in the following terms:

QUOTATION

....

> 'In a nation which has political liberty as the direct object of its constitution no one person or body of persons ought to be allowed to control the legislative, executive and judicial powers, or any two of them.'
>
> Lord Lester and D Oliver (eds), *Constitutional Law and Human Rights* (Butterworths, 1997), p 21.

The principle of the separation of powers is typically associated with the French judge and commentator Baron de Montesquieu, writing in the mid-eighteenth century. He was concerned with avoiding a concentration of state power and ensuring that this power was limited. Although the principle of dividing the various functions and powers of the state predates Montesquieu, his description of the three branches of government, namely the legislature, executive and judiciary, has a modern resonance.

In very general terms, the separation of powers denotes that in order to avoid an unnecessary concentration of state power, the following three state functions should be separate from one another:

- The legislative function (the law-making function).
- The executive function (the governmental function).
- The judicial function (the adjudicative and interpretative function).

In short, these functions should be separate and be performed by different institutions with no overlap of personnel. The definition of the separation of powers, however, is a somewhat elastic concept which is subject to different interpretations. These range from a very strict separation of powers, through to gradations of the principle, whereby the functions and institutions interrelate and check and balance each other.

5.2.2 A pure separation of powers

A pure separation of powers would insist that the three organs/institutions of government be completely separate and constitutionally isolated from each other. This would entail the three aspects of the state being institutionally separate from each other, with each organ performing a specific and exclusive constitutional function. Furthermore, individuals should only form part of one organ/institution. This therefore prohibits, for instance, a judge from sitting in the legislature as this would represent an overlap in terms of personnel. The three organs should be separated in terms of their functions so that each performs its own constitutional function and does not purport to exercise the specified function of another. This prohibits, for example, the courts making legislation and thereby performing a legislative function. Similarly, the legislature is prohibited from interfering with the courts' adjudicative and interpretative function.

In summary, under a pure separation of powers there should be no overlap in terms of:

- functions (eg the judiciary should not exercise a legislative function or interfere with the executive function)
- personnel (eg a judge should not form part of the executive body)
- institutions (eg the executive body should not form part of another institution such as the legislature).

5.2.3 A less than pure separation of powers

In contrast to a pure separation of powers, there are various gradations of the principle whereby the institutions of government may be largely separate (to varying degrees), but interrelate and check and balance each other (eg the judiciary checks and balances the legislative power). This less than pure separation of powers – a weaker and partial separation – acknowledges the political reality that the machinery and practice of government require that state institutions have to work with one another. In fact, Barnett (at p 81) has argued that a pure separation of powers could prove to be unworkable in practice. In addition, Barber has described it as a 'fantasy' that the branches of government should, and could, avoid interaction with each other (N Barber, 'Expert Commentary' in M Elliott and R Thomas, *Public Law* (3rd edn, Oxford University Press, 2017), p 101). Under a weaker version of the separation of powers, the tensions and checks and balances between the three state institutions aim to ensure that state power is not abused. In other words, it makes it more difficult for each branch of the state to carry out its particular function, as it is being checked and balanced by the other branches.

ACTIVITY

Essay writing

Explain the difference between a pure separation of powers and a less strict version of the principle.

KEY FACTS

Key facts on the separation of powers

The separation of powers is an internal method of institutionally controlling state power.
Under the doctrine of the separation of powers, public/state power is divided and dispersed between separately constituted institutions, each with a distinct function to perform.
The separation of powers is an important aspect of constitutionalism.

5.3 The different powers of the state

The functions/powers of the state can, in effect, be divided into three. It should be noted, however, that this division into three clearly defined state functions is not without controversy. Some commentators have questioned whether it is really possible to definitively and clearly separate these functions/powers in the following way:

Figure 5.1 The different powers of the state

5.3.1 The legislative function

This function is performed by the legislature and it involves the enactment of general laws. In the United Kingdom the Queen in Parliament represents the law maker (ie a Bill passes through both Houses of Parliament and receives Royal Assent in order to become an Act of Parliament). Similarly, in the Republic of Ireland the Oireachtas is the law maker (Art 15.2 of the Irish Constitution) and in the United States it is Congress (Art 1). We will see later, however, that in the United Kingdom (as in a number of other countries) the legislative role is not performed solely by the legislature.

5.3.2 The executive function

The executive (or governmental) function is performed by the government/administration. The executive administrates (carries out) the functions, powers and duties contained in general legislative provisions. The executive is the most difficult of all three organs to define, and it has been described simply as the residual functions/roles of the state that exist once the legislative and judicial functions have been outlined and demarcated (Lord Lester and D Oliver (eds), *Constitutional Law and Human Rights* (Butterworths, 1997), p 22).

In general terms, the executive executes the law as it carries out and implements it. In the United Kingdom not only does the executive initiate policy (including the drafting of parliamentary legislative proposals) but it also implements the resulting legislation. In addition, the executive determines and executes public policy in terms of both domestic and foreign affairs. In the United Kingdom the term executive can include the following bodies:

- The sovereign as the nominal/symbolic head of the executive (see section 11.1.2).
- Her Majesty's Government, comprising the Prime Minister, Cabinet and junior government ministers (in effect the political executive), supported by government departments staffed by civil servants (see Chapter 11).
- Local authorities. It should be noted that it is possible for the two branches of the executive function (ie central and local government) to be of different political colours. For example, in the 1980s, when central government (the political executive) was Conservative and many local authorities were controlled by the Labour Party, this led to friction and litigation between the branches of the executive. This led to what has been described as the *juridification* of their constitutional relationship. This meant that the courts were used in order to demarcate the boundary between central and local government (see section 14.2).
- The armed forces and the police who carry out and implement the law on a practical basis (see section 11.4).

In the United States the political executive is the President together with his ministers and in the Republic of Ireland it is the government (ie Taoiseach and Cabinet).

5.3.3 The judicial function

The judicial function is performed by the judiciary and it involves the determination of the law (laid down in statutes or in the common law) in relation to disputes arising from that law. It is a forum for resolving legal conflicts. The judicial arm of the state, therefore, settles legal disputes by interpreting and applying the law to a particular case before it. In the United Kingdom this function is performed by an array of judges (both senior and junior, full-time and part-time, legally qualified and those lacking formal legal qualifications, ie lay magistrates).

In the United States, Art III of the constitution confers judicial power on the Supreme Court. In the Republic of Ireland, Art 34.1 stipulates that the exclusive responsibility to administer justice is performed by the judiciary (including the Irish Supreme Court).

KEY FACTS

Key facts on the different powers of the state

In general terms:
- The legislative function involves enacting law.
- The executive function involves the implementation of that law as well as making policy decisions.
- The judicial function involves settling legal disputes arising from the law.

5.4 The relationship between the three powers in the United Kingdom

In the United Kingdom the three institutions/functions of the state are not isolated and completely separate from one another. Instead, they interrelate with each other. This is illustrated in the context of the creation and enforcement of primary legislation. Detailed below are three examples of how the various state institutions/functions would combine with each other in the context of (imaginary) legislation.

5.4.1 The (imaginary) Crime Act 2022

The policy behind this legislation was that the government (the political executive) responded to a perceived public need for a new criminal offence to be introduced. After a White Paper on the policy had been issued, the government drafted the proposed new offence in the Crime Bill 2021. This is an example of the executive formulating policy by initiating legislative proposals in order to create a new criminal offence.

As part of the Queen's Speech in May 2021, the government presented the Crime Bill to Parliament for it to approve. Parliament as the legislature is responsible for enacting legislation and both Houses (the House of Commons and the House of Lords) considered the measure, and the Bill was amended to remedy some minor drafting inaccuracies. Once the Crime Bill passed successfully through both Houses of Parliament it received the Royal Assent in March 2022 (as we saw earlier at section 4.13.4, by constitutional convention, such assent is always given by the monarch) and it became the Crime Act 2022.

Once in force, the Crime Act 2022 would be enforced by the police (the executive in practical terms), who would put before the Crown Prosecution Service (a non-ministerial government department which is responsible for the prosecution of offenders) cases of individuals who are alleged to have committed the new criminal offence enshrined in the Act. In court the accused would be tried and the court process would determine whether the offence contained within the Crime Act 2022 had been committed and, if so, decide what punishment would be appropriate (the parameters of the punishment available being stipulated in the Crime Act 2022).

5.4.2 The (imaginary) Tax Act 2022

The government wanted to introduce a new tax and this policy was encapsulated in the Tax Bill 2021. This Bill was then presented to Parliament (with the House of Commons having special responsibility for financial measures) for it to accept or reject. After Parliament approved the Tax Bill it was given the Royal Assent and it became the Tax Act 2022. This Act would then be enforced; in other words, the new tax would be collected by HM Revenue and Customs (a non-ministerial government department). In the event of a dispute arising concerning the interpretation of this Act (ie what payment is due in law), the judicial arm of the state would adjudicate on this (although a tax tribunal – the Tax Chamber – would initially process the issue).

5.4.3 The (imaginary) Public Order Act 2022

In 2022 Parliament passed, and the Royal Assent was given to, the Public Order Bill, making it the Public Order Act 2022. Section 1 of the Act stated that the Home Secretary may pass such regulations (in the form of a statutory instrument) as he thinks fit in order to protect public order. This is an example of Parliament delegating a legislative power to a government minister which would enable him to pass delegated/secondary legislation (see section 5.7.2). In constitutional terms, the reality in this example is that the executive (which typically controls the House of Commons) has drafted a Bill which, after it has been made law, has conferred a legislative power onto itself (ie, in this example, the Home Secretary).

ACTIVITY

Applying the law

Identify an Act of Parliament that has been passed recently by Parliament and consider how the three state institutions have interacted in the context of that legislation.

5.5 What is the rationale behind the separation of powers?

The separation of powers is central to a democratic constitution.

5.5.1 To avoid a concentration of public power in one body/institution

As noted above, Montesquieu argued that state power should be divided and separated in order to avoid a concentration of power, which otherwise could lead to tyranny and oppression:

QUOTATION

'When legislative power is united with executive power in a single person or in a single body of the magistracy, there is no liberty. . . . Nor is there liberty if the power of judging is not separate from legislative power and from executive power. If it were joined to legislative power, the power over the life and liberty of the citizens would be arbitrary, for the judge would be the legislator. If it were joined to executive power, the judge could have the force of an oppressor. All would be lost if the same man or the same body of principal men, either of nobles, or of the people, exercised these three powers: that of making the laws, that of executing public resolutions, and that of judging the crimes or the disputes of individuals.'

C Montesquieu, The Spirit of the Laws 1748, (edited by A Cohler, et al.
(Cambridge University Press, 1989), p 157.

Thus, if one person performed two or more state functions this would inevitably lead to oppression and tyranny. For example, if a person making the laws (a legislative role) also enforced and implemented these legislative provisions (an executive role) and then determined whether an individual had violated that law in a case before them (a judicial role), this person would in effect enjoy excessive and tyrannical powers. If all state power was concentrated in one body, therefore, it would inevitably be abused. After all, it is well known that 'Power tends to corrupt, and absolute power corrupts absolutely' (Lord Action, *Letter to Bishop Mandell Creighton,* April 1887, cited in M Elliott and R Thomas, *Public Law* (3rd edn, Oxford University Press, 2017), p7).

5.5.2 To provide a system of checks and balances between the branches of government

Under a partial separation of powers the objective is to avoid a concentration of power. This is achieved not by an absolute separation and isolation of the three functions, but instead through the creation of a number of checks and balances between them. In other words, one institution may well interfere with the (constitutional) function of another. For example, in the Republic of Ireland, the Oireachtas as the legislature is responsible for enacting laws. Under Art 34 of the Irish Constitution, however, the Irish Supreme Court may declare legislation legally unconstitutional and therefore null and void. Moreover, under Art 26 the President of Ireland (a formal and typically ceremonial aspect of the executive) may refer a Bill that has not yet been signed (and so yet to become an Act) to the Supreme Court in order to determine whether or not it is unconstitutional. If the Bill, or any part of it, is deemed unconstitutional, the Bill cannot become law. This therefore frustrates the legislature in its function of law-making.

Similarly, the doctrine of the separation of powers is clearly evident in the United States Constitution as it is based on a subtle set of checks and balances. For instance, the President (executive) can, initially at least, check the legislature in the context of legislation by vetoing a Bill which has successfully passed through Congress. Ultimately, however, the latter can overturn the presidential veto by a two-thirds majority in each House. In addition, in terms of appointments to the Supreme Court, the Senate (the second chamber of Congress) must confirm a presidential nomination (an executive decision) of a proposed justice of the Supreme Court.

5.5.3 To provide efficient government

At one level the doctrine of the separation of powers helps to achieve efficient government. In short, by specifically allocating definite functions to specific institutions staffed with particular expertise (eg judges who are expert at assessing evidence and judging), this necessarily provides efficient government.

5.5.4 To safeguard the independence of the judiciary

The separation of powers subsumes the fundamental notion that the judiciary should be constitutionally independent. In other words, in a democratic constitution it is of paramount importance that the judges – who form part of the court system – are independent, impartial and free from interference from the other branches of the state (particularly the executive). The principle of the independence of the judiciary embraces, *inter alia*, the notion that the judiciary must be free to determine disputes before them strictly in accordance with the law (see Chapter 13).

KEY FACTS

The rationale behind the separation of powers
• To avoid an abuse of state power by preventing a concentration of public power in one body/institution.
• To provide a system of checks and balances between the branches of government.
• To provide efficient government.
• To safeguard the independence of the judiciary.

5.6 The separation of powers in the United Kingdom

The question as to whether or not the United Kingdom adheres to the principles underpinning the separation of powers is somewhat controversial as there is no clear agreement on this point. It does depend, of course, in which sense the term is being used.

5.6.1 The separation of powers as part of the British constitution

For example, in *R v Her Majesty's Treasury, ex parte Smedley* [1985] 1 QB 657 Sir John Donaldson MR stated that:

JUDGMENT

'Although the United Kingdom has no written constitution, it is a constitutional convention of the highest importance that the legislature and the judicature are separate and independent of one another.'

Similarly, Lord Diplock in *Duport Steels Ltd and others v Sirs and others* [1980] 1 All ER 529 has commented that:

JUDGMENT

'It cannot be too strongly emphasised that the British constitution, though largely unwritten, is firmly based on the separation of powers: Parliament makes the laws, the judiciary interpret them.'

In addition, see Lord Diplock's observation a few years earlier about the separation of powers being implicit within the Westminster system of government (*Hinds v The Queen* [1977] AC 195).

Further, Lord Templeman in *M v Home Office and others* [1994] 1 AC 377 has noted that:

JUDGMENT

'Parliament makes the law, the executive carry the law into effect and the judiciary enforce the law.'

Finally, see the former Lord Chancellor, Lord Irvine, in 'Constitutional Reform and a Bill of Rights' [1997] EHRLR 483.

5.6.2 The separation of powers not being part of the British constitution

In contrast, the academic writer de Smith, writing in 1998, dismissed the separation of powers in the context of the United Kingdom by arguing that:

QUOTATION

'No writer of repute would claim that it is a central feature of the modern British constitution.'
S de Smith and R Brazier, *Constitutional and Administrative Law* (8th edn, Penguin, 1998), p 18.

See also O Hood Phillips, 'A Constitutional Myth: Separation of Powers' (1977) 93 LQR 11.

NB. Now, however, note the recent reforms made under the Constitutional Reform Act 2005 detailed later in this chapter.

5.6.3 Initial observations on the separation of powers and the British constitution

What is clear is that:

- Firstly, the British constitution does not follow a pure separation of powers, with each branch of the state completely separated from each other in terms of functions and personnel. Instead, to the extent that it does adhere to the separation of powers, it follows a partial/modified version involving checks and balances.
- Secondly, even where the United Kingdom does depart from the doctrine of the separation of powers, these departures may well be driven by practical necessity or be governed by constitutional conventions.

The issue of the separation of powers in the British constitution is inevitably less clear-cut than in other countries. This is because in other democracies with a codified constitution the principle of the separation of powers has been specifically written into, and so is structurally part of, the constitutional text (eg France and the United States). In contrast, the British constitution has developed incrementally and organically over hundreds of years. It is perhaps worth remembering that the modern expression of the separation of powers is found in Montesquieu writing in the eighteenth century (and subsequently incorporated into the constitution of the United States). Yet, a number of our constitutional rules and principles predate this; for instance, the office of the Prime Minister dates back to the first part of the eighteenth century, with Sir Robert Walpole being regarded as the first Prime Minister (1721–42). Finally, it is of interest to note that the institutional structure of the European Union does not exhibit a clear separation of powers (see section 15.2.2).

5.7 Aspects of the British constitution not in accord with the separation of powers

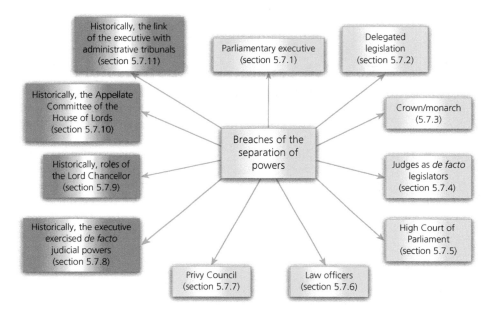

Figure 5.2 Aspects of the British constitution not in accord with the separation of powers

Detailed above are the main ways in which the constitution does not follow the separation of powers. (pure or otherwise). It must be remembered that some of the overlaps (set out on the left of the diagram) are now historical and have been subject to reform in recent years.

5.7.1 The parliamentary executive (an overlap of the legislature and the executive)

One of the main characteristics of the British constitution is that it has a parliamentary executive, as, by constitutional convention, the executive (the political executive) is drawn from the legislature (Parliament). In general, the political executive (ie the government) comprises over 100 members, most of whom are drawn from the elected House of Commons. The remainder are peers in the House of Lords (see section 11.6).

In terms of personnel, therefore, it is clear there is an overlap between members of the executive and the legislature, with members of the government enjoying both executive and legislative functions. Indeed, Bagehot, writing in the nineteenth century, noted that:

QUOTATION

The parliamentary executive and accountable government

One clear advantage of a parliamentary executive is that the government is directly accountable and responsible to Parliament, and in fact this is a core principle of the constitution (see ministerial responsibility at section 12.1). As government ministers are drawn from within Parliament, this provides the opportunity for them to be held accountable on a daily basis through the following parliamentary mechanisms:

- written and oral questions (see section 12.4)
- debates (see section 12.5)
- select committees (see section 12.6.2).

In addition, s 2 of the House of Commons Disqualification Act 1975 specifically limits the number of government ministers (ministerial offices) who can sit in the House of Commons to 95 MPs out of a total of 650 MPs. This, at least in constitutional theory, prevents the government from dominating the House of Commons.

Notwithstanding the above, it is certainly the case that in the last few decades the parliamentary executive has generally ensured dynamic government whereby the government has been able to dominate Parliament. A widely perceived difficulty, however, is that, owing to the current electoral system, the government generally speaking (though not at all times – see the 2010 and 2017 general elections) secures office following a general election with the support of a clear (and sometimes substantial) majority of seats in the House of Commons. This in turn means that the government can dominate the Commons to such an extent that it has led to the suggestion that the balance between the executive and the legislature has swung too heavily in favour of the former. Indeed, Lord Hailsham, writing in the 1970s, suggested that our electoral system produced a government which was akin to an 'elective dictatorship' (see section 9.8).

Although Parliament, in the context of the separation of powers, is the supreme legislative/law-making body, the question has to be asked as to whether in practice Parliament actually legislates or whether it merely legitimises and 'rubber stamps' the Bills initiated by the government of the day. Each year most Bills enacted as Acts of Parliament are government-sponsored Bills. Few Bills which become Acts have been drafted and initiated by Members of Parliament themselves acting as parliamentarians (known as private members' Bills).

The parliamentary executive and the devolved institutions

It is also worth noting that the devolved institutions in Scotland, Wales and Northern Ireland exhibit a form of a parliamentary executive. For example, in Scotland the Scottish Government is drawn from the Scottish Parliament (Members of the Scottish Parliament – MSPs).

The position in other countries

The feature of a parliamentary executive is not, of course, restricted to the United Kingdom. The Republic of Ireland, with its written, entrenched codified constitution, also has a parliamentary executive whereby the Irish government (comprising the Taoiseach and Cabinet ministers) is drawn from, and constitutionally accountable to, the Irish Parliament (the Oireachtas).

In contrast, in the United States the President does not form part of the legislature as it is a presidential system of government with the President sitting separately from Congress. In France, Cabinet ministers do not sit in the French Parliament as Art 23 of the French Constitution (Fifth Republic) states that membership of government is incompatible with that of Parliament. Both the United States and France reflect a greater degree of separation of powers between the executive and legislature than the United Kingdom.

ACTIVITY

Self-test question

What do you think are the dangers of having a parliamentary executive, particularly in the context of the British constitution?

5.7.2 Delegated legislation (an overlap involving the executive performing a legislative function)

Introduction

Under the separation of powers, the constitutional function of the legislature is to enact law, and the role of the executive is to execute and apply it. The practice of delegated legislation, however, entrusts a law-making power onto a member of the executive (ie a government minister or a local authority). The process of delegated legislation involves Parliament passing an Act (the 'enabling' or 'parent' Act), which in turn confers a power onto a minister to make delegated legislation (also known as secondary/subordinate legislation) which generally takes the form of a statutory instrument (see section 12.7.5).

The rationale behind delegated legislation

The rationale behind delegating a legislative power to the executive is partly one of practical necessity. In practice it would be impossible for Parliament to legislate all the details of all the laws that are necessary in a modern society. The general principle governing delegated legislation is that the enabling Act encapsulates the general principles/policies of the legislation, while the secondary legislation – made under the authority of that Act – supplements these general broad principles with detailed provisions. Thus, it fills in the fine details of legislation.

Delegated legislation also has practical uses, as it allows the law to be flexible and responsive, for example updating levels of fines. An example of a local authority enjoying a delegated legislative power to alter local car parking charges is illustrated at section 14.2.2.

Even though there is a widespread view endorsing the necessity of the use of delegated legislation (although not necessarily in the volume in which it is used), it still represents a violation of the separation of powers. It should also be remembered that the vast majority of domestic legislation which is passed each year is delegated, and so *not* primary legislation (ie Acts of Parliament).

There are, however, both political and legal controls over the use of this type of legislation.

Parliamentary/political control of delegated legislation

This is covered at section 12.7.5; however, for present purposes the following extracts from two 2017 House of Lords select committee reports in respect of the legislation required in order to exit the European Union are worth recording:

QUOTATION

'We are concerned about the delegated powers the Government is seeking in the European Union (Withdrawal) Bill. The number, range and overlapping nature of the broad delegated powers would create what is, in effect, an unprecedented and extraordinary portmanteau of effectively unlimited powers upon which the Government could draw. They would fundamentally challenge the constitutional balance of powers between Parliament and Government and would represent a significant – and unacceptable – transfer of legal competence. We stress the need for an appropriate balance between the urgency required to ensure legal continuity and stability, and meaningful parliamentary scrutiny and control of the executive.'

The House of Lords Select Committee on the Constitution, *European Union (Withdrawal) Bill: interim report*, HL Paper 19 (September 2017), para 44.

Shortly after this report, the summary of the report of another House of Lords select committee read as follows:

QUOTATION

'The European Union (Withdrawal) Bill gives excessively wide law-making powers to Ministers, allowing them to make major changes beyond what is necessary to ensure UK law works properly when the UK leaves the EU.'

The House of Lords Delegated Powers and Regulatory Reform Committee, *European Union (Withdrawal) Bill*, HL Paper 22 (September 2017), p 2.

Legal control of delegated legislation

Delegated legislation is also subject to scrutiny and control by the courts. It is a general legal principle that a minister can only pass delegated legislation that is authorised and envisaged by the parent Act. The executive must, therefore, pass legislation which is *intra vires* (within the legal powers conferred by the Act). If the legislation made is outside the powers conferred, and so beyond the purpose for which the delegated power was given, it can be declared *ultra vires* by the courts and invalidated. In this way, the courts mitigate the practice of delegated legislation being a violation of the separation of powers. The courts ensure that the executive uses its conferred delegated legislative powers strictly for its envisaged purpose so that it is not abused. It also ensures that parliamentary sovereignty is upheld by ensuring that Parliament's will is not thwarted, for example by a minister passing legislation which had not been specifically envisaged by Parliament. An example of the legal control exercised by the courts over the use of delegated legislation is illustrated by the following case:

CASE EXAMPLE

Chester v Bateson *[1920] 1 KB 829*

Section 1 of the Defence of the Realm Consolidation Act 1914 conferred a power on the Minister of Munitions to issue regulations (delegated legislation) to prevent the successful prosecution of the war being endangered. Under the aegis of the Act, the minister issued reg 2A(2), which stated that 'no person shall, without the consent of the Minister of Munitions take . . . any proceedings for the purpose of obtaining an order or decree for the recovery of possession of, or for the ejectment of a tenant of, any dwelling house' in which a munitions worker was living.

Chester (a landlord) served on Bateson (a tenant employed in a shell shop) notice of his intention to recover possession of his property as Bateson's tenancy had expired. Bateson challenged this by contending that Chester had not obtained the consent of the minister before commencing proceedings. Chester contended that the Regulation was *ultra vires* the Defence of the Realm Consolidation Act 1914 and the court agreed. The court held that the Regulation effectively prevented the landlord from having access to the courts in order to recover his property without first obtaining the consent of the minister. Avory J stated that:

JUDGMENT

'In my opinion there is not to be found in the statute [ie the 1914 Act] anything to authorise or justify a regulation having that result; and nothing less than express words in the statute taking away the right of the King's subjects of access to the Courts of Justice would authorise or justify it.'

Delegated legislation in other countries

The use of delegated legislation, of course, is not confined to the British constitution. In the Republic of Ireland, for example, although Art 15.2 of the constitution states that only the Oireachtas may create laws, the Irish Parliament does, however, regularly delegate a power onto government ministers to make ministerial orders. Such legislative instruments are supervised by the Irish courts.

5.7.3 The Crown/monarch is formally involved in all three branches of government (an overlap of the legislature, executive and judiciary)

In the United Kingdom the term Crown can denote either the government/executive or the monarch (see section 11.1.2). As noted at section 3.4.7, the United Kingdom has a monarchical constitution and the monarch is constitutionally involved (to a greater or lesser extent) in all three functions of government.

The monarch and the legislative function

The Queen is formally part of the legislature (Parliament) and involved in the legislative process as a Bill requires the granting of the Royal Assent in order for it to become an Act of Parliament. In fact, the supreme legislative power in the United Kingdom is technically known as the 'Queen in Parliament'. The role of the monarch is reflected in the enacting formula of a typical public Bill:

> BE IT ENACTED by the Queen's most Excellent Majesty, by and with the advice and consent of the Lords Spiritual and Temporal, and Commons, in this present Parliament assembled, and by the authority of the same, as follows . . .

A slightly revised version is used when the Parliament Acts of 1911 and 1949 have been used in the absence of the consent of the House of Lords (see section 10.10.1).

In practical reality, the role of the monarch in the legislative process is a purely formal one as by constitutional convention the monarch will grant her assent to a Bill unless her government ministers advise her not to do so. Similarly, in the Republic of Ireland the head of state (the President of Ireland) signs Bills passed by the Oireachtas to give them the force of law. In the United States, the President signs Bills passed by Congress (although he approves them, he can also veto them).

In addition, as part of the legislature, the Queen opens each new parliamentary session and delivers the 'Queen's Speech' which details the government's proposed legislative programme for the ensuing parliamentary session. By constitutional convention, the speech is, of course, written by the government of the day and represents the Bills which it anticipates will become law.

The monarch and the executive function

The monarch is constitutionally part of the executive as she is the head of state and the political executive is known as 'Her Majesty's Government'. The monarch appoints the Prime Minister together with other government ministers, although these appointments are in practice a formal process, as they are governed by constitutional convention. Although the monarch will formally appoint government ministers, this is done on the recommendation of the Prime Minister of the day and so the political reality is that it is the latter that actually chooses which individuals will occupy which particular ministerial office. The monarch is also head of the armed forces and is in fact technically the commander-in-chief of the armed forces (the executive in practical terms).

The monarch and the judicial function

The monarch is also formally part of the judiciary in the sense that she is the source and font of all justice (although she does not actually sit in court as a judge: *Prohibitions del Roy* (1607) 12 Co Rep 63). In fact, judicial appointments are made in the name of the Crown (hence 'Her Majesty's Judges', who operate and dispense justice in the 'Royal Courts of Justice'). Although the monarch formally makes these judicial appointments, by constitutional convention she will act on the basis of ministerial advice. It is of constitutional interest to note that the judicial oath of allegiance sworn by judges is *not* to the British constitution but instead to the Queen/monarch.

5.7.4 Judges as legislators (an overlap involving the judiciary performing a legislative function)

In the British constitution the judicial function involves:

- resolving legal disputes
- determining the law laid down in (a) statutes and (b) the common law and
- providing relevant remedies.

This necessarily raises the question of where the constitutional line exists between the act of interpreting and the act of legislating, and whether the courts ever exercise a *de facto* legislative function.

The interpretation of statutes

In interpreting statutes, the constitutional role of the courts is to ascertain the intention of Parliament when it passes legislation. The obvious difficulty is that words may have a variety of different possible meanings, and in order to circumscribe the role of the judges when determining the meaning of legislative provisions the courts have developed a number of self-limiting principles of statutory interpretation which assist them. For example, the literal rule requires judges to give words their ordinary and natural meaning.

In addition, judges will construe unclear and ambiguous legislation in the light of certain constitutional principles such as the right of access to the courts. These constitutional presumptions are, of course, judicial creations and so determined by the judges themselves. For instance, in *Chester v Bateson* at section 5.7.2, Avory J made it clear that nothing less than express words in the Defence of the Realm Consolidation Act 1914 would justify a regulation passed under it which denied a person access to the courts and the administration of justice.

The common law

The common law involves the courts declaring points of law in the context of cases that come before them for resolution. The gradual development of the common law (which is achieved by the courts making decisions in the context of case law) necessarily permits a degree of flexibility in allowing common law principles to develop and adapt to changing circumstances (social or moral). This is illustrated particularly in the context of the private law of negligence, which progressively developed during the twentieth century; see *Donoghue v Stevenson* [1932] AC 562.

In the context of judges and the legislative function, it is pertinent to repeat the point that Dicey made a century ago:

QUOTATION

'A large proportion of English law is in reality made by our judges . . . the adhesion by our judges to precedent, that is, their habit of deciding one case in accordance with the principle, or supposed principle, which governed a former case, leads inevitably to the gradual formation by the courts of fixed rules for decision, which are in effect laws.'

A Dicey, *Introduction to the Study of the Law of the Constitution* (10th edn, Macmillan, 1959), p 60.

In *Duport Steels Ltd and others v Sirs and others* [1980] 1 All ER 529 Lord Scarman noted that, in the context of the common law and equity, society had permitted the judges 'to formulate and develop the law'. Furthermore, in *Malone v Metropolitan Police Commissioner* [1979] Ch 344 Sir Robert Megarry VC made it clear that at times judges do legislate, albeit only interstitially, and he specifically distinguished between 'The extension of the existing laws and principles' and the creation of wholly new rights, for example in the instant case, a tort of privacy (see section 6.7.9 – but see the *PJS* case below). In short, it is Parliament's role to create such new rights.

Do judges make law?

In general terms as to whether the judges perform a legislative/law-making function, Barnett has argued that:

QUOTATION

'. . . it is artificial to deny that judges "make law". Every new meaning conferred on a word, every application of a rule to a new situation, whether by way of statutory interpretation or under common law, "creates" new law. Judges have themselves abandoned the fiction of the "declaratory theory" which asserts that they do not "make" law but merely discover its true meaning. From the separation of powers perspective, judicial law-making should cause disquiet only if judges display overtly dynamic law-making tendencies.'

H Barnett, *Constitutional and Administrative Law* (12th edn, Routledge/Taylor & Francis Group, 2017), p 90.

In addition, Sir John laws recently made this pertinent observation:

QUOTATION

'Whereas the courts hone and refine principles over time, the legislature creates new regimes at every turn. It may, and often does, reinvent the wheel. The courts do not. Courts and Parliament both make new lamps, but the courts make new lamps from old.'

J Laws, *The Common Law Constitution* (Cambridge University Press, 2014), p 21.

An interesting example of the judiciary effectively 'making' the law is illustrated by the following case.

CASE EXAMPLE

R v R *[1992] 1 AC 599*

In this case the House of Lords set aside the long-standing common law rule that a husband could not rape his wife. Even though this historic rule was viewed as anachronistic, the ruling nevertheless represents a *de facto* use of law-making power. In constitutional terms, this must necessarily be seen as *de facto* legislative, with the courts developing/creating the law.

Lord Reid also made the following observation in an academic article on judges *making* the law:

QUOTATION

'There was a time when it was thought almost indecent to suggest that judges make law—they only declare it. Those with a taste for fairy tales seem to have thought that in some Aladdin's cave there is hidden the Common Law in all its splendour and that on a judge's appointment there descends on him knowledge of the magic words Open Seasame. Bad decisions are given when the judge has muddled the pass word and the wrong door opens. But we do not believe in fairy tales any more.'

Lord Reid, 'The judge as law maker', *Society of Public Teachers of Law* [1972] 22.

Moreover in 1966 Lord Gardiner issued on behalf of the law lords the following seminal practice statement, which enabled the House of Lords to depart from its previous decisions (*Practice Statement* [1966] 1 WLR 1234):

JUDGMENT

'Their Lordships nevertheless recognise that too rigid adherence to precedent may lead to injustice in a particular case and also unduly restrict the proper development of the law. They propose, therefore, to modify their present practice and, while treating former decisions of this House as normally binding, to depart from a previous decision when it appears right to do so.'

See also G Slapper, 'Case law and judicial law-making' (2013) 69 *Student Law Review* 16 as well as the 2016 decision in the Supreme Court concerning a *de facto* privacy law:

CASE EXAMPLE

PJS v News Group Newspapers Ltd [2016] UKSC 26

In this case Lord Neuberger (with whom Lady Hale and Lords Mance and Reed agreed) stated that:

JUDGMENT

'The courts exist to protect legal rights, even when their protection is difficult or unpopular in some quarters. And if Parliament takes the view that the courts have not adapted the law to fit current realities, then, of course, it can change the law . . .'

Judicial law-making outside the United Kingdom

It should be noted that the notion that judges are *de facto* lawmakers is not confined to the British constitution. For example, it is also illustrated in the following judicial decision in the context of the constitution of the United States:

CASE EXAMPLE

Marbury v Madison *(1803) 1 Cranch 137*

In this case, the United States Supreme Court enunciated a major principle underpinning the American constitution by declaring that the Supreme Court had the constitutional power to declare an Act of Congress to be unconstitutional (and so invalid) where it was repugnant to the written constitution. This case illustrates the powerful position of the judiciary in relation to a constitution, as the power to declare Congressional legislation legally unconstitutional had not been specifically and expressly stated in the text of the constitution, but instead had been deemed implicit by the Supreme Court.

Similarly, in the context of the European Union, the Court of Justice of the EU in Luxembourg has developed fundamental principles of European law which have not been expressly or explicitly spelt out in the original 1957 Treaty of Rome. For example, neither of the following principles were expressly written in the text of the Treaty, but were nevertheless deemed implicit:

- The principle of direct effect, which conferred European Union law rights on individuals which could be enforced in the domestic courts of Member States.
- The principle of the primacy of European Union law, which required that, where European law and domestic law are inconsistent, the former must prevail.

ACTIVITY

Essay writing

To what extent do judges ever perform a legislative function and what are the constitutional implications of this?

5.7.5 Parliament exercises functions other than legislative (an overlap involving the legislature performing a judicial function)

The nature of the law and custom of Parliament

Although Parliament is the legislature, it is also responsible for regulating, controlling and disciplining its members, which is effectively a judicial function. These parliamentary privileges are unique to the two Houses of Parliament and its members, and are derived from the law and custom of Parliament.

These privileges are regulated by both Houses of Parliament. Each House exercises its own jurisdiction and can punish those individuals who disregard its rules or who commit a contempt of Parliament, for example obstructing Parliament in its functions.

The High Court of Parliament

MP

a member of Parliament, specifically in the House of Commons

Each House of Parliament acts as a constituent part of the High Court of Parliament, thereby performing a judicial function. In 2003, for instance, the House of Commons temporarily suspended an **MP** for breaching parliamentary rules. In effect, Parliament acts as a self-regulating body and the 'ordinary' courts exercise no jurisdiction over these matters. More recently, in 2009 the House of Lords suspended two peers until the end of that parliamentary session.

Parliamentary law in other countries

The notion that the legislature regulates its own composition and proceedings is not confined to the United Kingdom. For example, in the Republic of Ireland, Art 15.10 of the Irish Constitution expressly authorises the two Houses of the Oireachtas to decide their own rules in terms of the rights of the Houses and their members. Further, if these rules are violated, each House may impose penalties.

5.7.6 The law officers (an overlap involving members of the executive/government sitting in the legislature and performing a quasi-judicial function)

The Attorney General and Solicitor General are members of the government, but not the Cabinet (although the Attorney General can attend the Cabinet when the agenda relates to his responsibilities).

The Solicitor General acts as the deputy to the Attorney General (see s 1 of the Law Officers Act 1997 which enables the Solicitor General to perform any of the functions of the Attorney General). These law officers are chosen from MPs or peers and so are part of the legislature (they therefore form part of the parliamentary executive) and are supported by the Attorney General's Office. The Attorney General has three broad roles. Firstly, as a minister he is responsible for superintending/overseeing the prosecution agencies of the Crown Prosecution Service and Serious Fraud Office. Secondly, he is the legal adviser to the Crown/government and its representative in court. Thirdly, as an independent officer of the Crown the Attorney General has the function of acting as the *guardian of the public interest* (eg granting consent for particular prosecutions, referring sentences which are unduly lenient to the Court of Appeal and bringing legal proceedings for contempt of court). In this context as 'guardian', he should act independently of the government and not take instructions from it. In short, the Attorney General has a number of different responsibilities and as noted by Bradley and Ewing (in the previous edition of their book):

QUOTATION

'The law officers of the Crown (in particular the Attorney General in England and the Lord Advocate in Scotland) have duties of enforcing the criminal law which are sometimes described as 'quasi-judicial'; nonetheless, the law officers are not judges and like all ministers they hold office at the pleasure of the Prime Minister.'

A Bradley and K Ewing, *Constitutional and Administrative Law* (15th edn, Pearson/Longman, 2011), p 85.

In terms of reform of the office of the Attorney General, the previous Labour government consulted on this issue (*A Consultation on the Role of the Attorney General*, Cm 7192 (2007)) and thereafter included some reform proposals as part of Pt 2 of the Draft Constitutional Renewal Bill (Cm 7342-II (2008)). However, in July 2009 the then Lord Chancellor, in a ministerial statement, made the following point:

QUOTATION

'In the event, the significant, necessary reforms to the role of Attorney General are being achieved without the need for legislation. For example, the Attorney has reached a new settlement with the Directors of Public Prosecutions, the Serious Fraud Office and Revenue and Customs Prosecutions to improve relationships, guarantee prosecutorial independence while ensuring an appropriate degree of accountability and to improve transparency about the relationship, as reflected in the new protocol setting out the respective responsibilities of the Attorney and the Directors. This builds on the Prime Minister's statement in July 2007, that the Attorney General has herself decided, except if the law or national security requires it, not to make key prosecution decisions in individual criminal cases. Furthermore, the new protocol makes it clear that the Attorney General will not be consulted in any case which concerns an MP or peer or where there is a personal or professional conflict of interest, other than where her decision is required by law. This protocol will be published by the Attorney very shortly. Furthermore, the Attorney General now only attends Cabinet when matters affecting her responsibilities are on the agenda.'

Hansard, HC Vol 496, col 106 WS.

Now see the *Protocol between the Attorney General and the Prosecuting Departments* (Attorney General's Office, 2009).

Two interesting cases which have involved the Attorney General are *Attorney General v Jonathan Cape* (1976) – see section 4.13.12 and more recently, the following case in the Supreme Court:

CASE EXAMPLE

R (Evans) v Attorney General *[2015] UKSC 21*

This case has particular relevance to the issue of the separation of powers as s 53 of the Freedom of Information Act 2000 empowers an 'accountable person' (ie in this case the Attorney General) to issue a certificate to override the decision of the Upper Tribunal (ie a judicial body). In the case, a journalist (Evans) sought the disclosure under the 2000 Act of communications between the Prince of Wales and government departments between 2004 and 2005. The Information Commissioner upheld the decisions of the departments' refusal to disclose this information. On appeal, the Upper Tribunal ruled that some of the communications should be disclosed and, in response to this, the Attorney General issued a certificate under s 53 of the Act to override this decision. Evans then sought judicial review of the issuing of this certificate, which, although it was dismissed at first instance, was quashed by the Court of Appeal and upheld by the Supreme Court. In brief, the Attorney General could not issue a certificate simply on the basis that he disagreed with the conclusion of an adjudicative tribunal, but instead needed 'reasonable grounds' to do so as required by s 53(2) of the 2000 Act.

However, Lord Wilson (dissenting) made the following point that he would have allowed the appeal from the decision of the Court of Appeal:

JUDGMENT

'For, in reaching its decision, the Court of Appeal did not in my view interpret section 53 of the FOIA. It re-wrote it. It invoked precious constitutional principles but among the most precious is that of parliamentary sovereignty, emblematic of our democracy.'

In addition, the following academic observation has been made:

QUOTATION

'The question with which *Evans* is centrally concerned is the extent to which it is legally and constitutionally legitimate for *a court exercising powers of judicial review* to strike down a *Government Minister's* decision made under powers granted by *Parliament* in order to overturn an *independent judicial tribunal's* judgment. The case thus features four institutional actors drawn from across the three branches of government.'

M Elliott, 'A tangled constitutional web: the black-spider memos and the British constitution's relational architecture' [2015] PL 539. In addition, see C Knight, 'The rule of law, parliamentary sovereignty and the ministerial veto' (2015) 131 LQR 547.

5.7.7 The Privy Council (an overlap involving the executive performing legislative and judicial functions)

The Privy Council (which is part of central government and so part of the executive today) historically acted as the chief advisory body to the monarch. Its importance, in modern times, however, has been superseded by the development of the Cabinet. In fact, the Privy Council:

QUOTATION

'. . . lost most of its advisory and administrative functions and is today little more than an organ for giving formal effect to certain acts done under prerogative or statutory powers'.
O Hood Phillips, P Jackson and P Leopold, *Constitutional and Administrative Law* (8th edn, Sweet & Maxwell, 2001), p 334.

The Privy Council numbers around 650 members (ie Privy Counsellors) who are individuals of high rank. Membership is for life and includes, among others, the following:

- The Prime Minister.
- Cabinet ministers.
- The Leader of the Opposition.
- Senior judges.
- Other senior public figures.

The Lord President of the Council is the ministerial head of the Privy Council Office.

Meetings of the Privy Council comprise:

- Meetings involving the monarch together with (typically) four selected ministers (Her Majesty in Council), at which formal validity will be given to instruments/orders previously agreed to by government.
- Meetings without the monarch (a Committee of the Privy Council).

The role of the Privy Council is to advise the Queen in carrying out her responsibilities as monarch. The Privy Council can make orders, known as Orders in Council, which comprise:

- Statutory Orders in Council (a form of delegated legislation) – where the power to make the order has been delegated by statute onto Her Majesty. By constitutional convention she acts on the advice of her ministers.
- Non-statutory (ie prerogative) Orders in Council – derived from the common law royal prerogative. These orders are, in effect, treated as a form of primary legislation in terms of the Human Rights Act 1998, see further at section 11.9.7.

As pointed out by Hood Phillips et al., the nature of an Order in Council can be legislative (eg a statutory instrument), executive (eg establishing a new government department) or judicial (see directly below).

In addition to the above, one committee of the Privy Council has a judicial function: the Judicial Committee of the Privy Council. This was established under the Judicial Committee Act 1833 and acts as the final court of appeal for various Commonwealth countries (for example, see Saint Lucia directly below), together with a domestic jurisdiction hearing appeals from Guernsey, Jersey and the Isle of Man. In addition, up until 2009 the Privy Council also heard 'internal' devolution cases (for example, whether the Scottish Parliament had exceeded its legal powers under the Scotland Act 1998 – see Chapter 14), but this responsibility has now been passed to the new Supreme Court. The judges staffing the Judicial Committee comprise the justices of the new Supreme Court (although other senior judges may sit as well). It is significant to note that, when acting as a court, the Privy Council may be required to interpret and apply overseas written/codified constitutions, for example the Constitution of Saint Lucia in the case of *Sexius v Attorney General of Saint Lucia* [2017] UKPC 26.

On the Privy Council in general, see M Everett, *The Privy Council* (House of Commons Library, 2016).

5.7.8 Historically, the executive has exercised a judicial function (an overlap involving the executive performing a judicial function)

Ministers have, historically, been given powers which were, in effect, judicial in nature, as illustrated by the following case:

CASE EXAMPLE

R v Secretary of State for the Home Department, ex parte Venables and Thompson *[1997] 3 All ER 97*

Venables and Thompson were convicted of the murder of two-year-old James Bulger. The trial judge stated that in his view the minimum period of detention necessary to satisfy retribution and deterrence was a tariff of eight years. The Lord Chief Justice advised a tariff of ten years, but the Home Secretary, in exercising his powers under s 35 of the Criminal Justice Act 1991, imposed 15 years. The constitutional rationale behind this statutory power was that the Home Secretary had a general responsibility for public order and maintaining public confidence in the criminal justice system. In reaching his decision the Home Secretary indicated that he had had regard for the public concern regarding this case. A public petition including 278,300 signatures, over 5,000 letters and 20,000 'coupons' from a newspaper had demanded that Venables and Thompson should be detained for life.

Venables and Thompson challenged the use of the Home Secretary's discretion and the House of Lords held, *inter alia*, that he had acted unlawfully as he had misdirected himself by giving weight to irrelevant considerations (namely, the public protest directed to the detriment of these two particular individuals). Lord Steyn stated that:

JUDGMENT

'In fixing a tariff the Home Secretary is carrying out, contrary to the constitutional principle of the separation of powers, a classic judicial function . . . the power to fix a tariff is nevertheless equivalent to a judge's sentencing power. Parliament must be assumed to have entrusted the power to the Home Secretary on the supposition that, like a sentencing judge, the Home Secretary would not act contrary to fundamental principles governing the administration of justice.'

Thus, as the Home Secretary was exercising a sentencing power (a judicial function) he was required to remain detached from the pressures of public opinion. As a postscript to the *Venables* case, Venables and Thompson subsequently petitioned the European Court of Human Rights (*V & T v UK* (2000) 30 EHRR 121) and successfully contended that their right to a fair trial under Art 6 had been breached. In brief, the setting of the tariff (which was tantamount to a judicial sentence) had not been performed by an independent and impartial figure, as the

Home Secretary was part of the executive. After this European ruling, Parliament enacted s 60 of the Criminal Justice and Courts Services Act 2000, which now requires that the tariff (now known as the minimum term) to be served by young offenders is to be determined by the trial judge. As a result, this realigned the British constitution more in accord with a stricter separation of powers. Similarly, see also *R (Anderson) v Secretary of State* (2002) at section 13.2.1, which resulted in further reforms of the *de facto* judicial powers of the Home Secretary in relation to adults.

5.7.9 The Lord Chancellor (historically, an overlap of the legislature, executive and judiciary)

The office of the Lord Chancellor has traditionally been cited as *the* classic example of the way in which the United Kingdom violates the separation of powers as he formed part of all three state institutions. His main historical responsibilities in relation to each institution are detailed below:

The legislature

The Lord Chancellor sat in the upper chamber as the impartial *ex officio* Speaker of the House of Lords and presided over the House. This role encompassed a number of ceremonial roles (eg the state opening of Parliament). He also exercised a limited power to keep order within the chamber and represented the House both domestically and internationally.

The executive

As a minister of the Crown, the Lord Chancellor was a senior member of the Cabinet and head of a major government department: the Lord Chancellor's Department. In June 2003 this department was replaced with the Department for Constitutional Affairs, which had responsibility for, *inter alia*, the administration of legal aid. The Lord Chancellor was also a spokesman for the government in the House of Lords.

The judiciary

The Lord Chancellor could sit as a senior judge in the Court of Appeal, the Privy Council or the Appellate Committee of the House of Lords. This judicial function was governed and regulated by a constitutional convention that the Lord Chancellor would not sit in cases involving a clearly political issue or those in which the government was a party. The Lord Chancellor was also head of the judiciary in England and Wales and President of the Supreme Court of Judicature (the historic collective term for the Court of Appeal, High Court and Crown Court and not to be confused with the new Supreme Court under the Constitutional Reform Act 2005, detailed below). In respect of the judiciary, the Lord Chancellor was also involved in the appointment of a wide range of judicial posts. For example, in respect of the law lords, by constitutional convention the Prime Minister would consult him on suitable candidates (these appointments would then be formally appointed by the monarch). Furthermore, the Lord Chancellor was responsible for processing complaints against judges and administering judicial discipline.

ACTIVITY

Changes to the office of the Lord Chancellor made by the Constitutional Reform Act 2005

In June 2003, in pursuance of modernising the constitution and realigning it with the separation of powers, the then Labour government announced the abolition of the office of the Lord Chancellor. Simultaneously, the post of Secretary of State for Constitutional Affairs was established, which the government envisaged would eventually supersede the office of the Lord Chancellor. However, the Constitutional Reform Bill proved to be highly contentious in the House of Lords and was amended so as to retain, and so merely modify, the office of the Lord Chancellor, rather than abolish the post outright. This explained the subsequent adoption of the dual title of *Secretary of State for Constitutional Affairs and Lord Chancellor* (in 2017 now called *the Lord Chancellor and the Secretary of State for Justice*). In essence, the changes effected by the Act in respect of the Lord Chancellor are as follows:

The legislature

▩ The Speaker of the House of Lords

In the context of reforming the office of the Lord Chancellor, it was necessary to reform his position as Speaker of the House of Lords. For one thing, s 2 of the Constitutional Reform Act 2005 made it clear that a future Lord Chancellor need not even be a peer (it had been a long-standing constitutional convention that the office holder sat in the upper chamber). In 2006 the House of Lords agreed to the Report of the Select Committee on the Speakership of the House (First Report, HL Paper 92 (2005)). This report recommended that the House elect a Speaker for five years to replace the Lord Chancellor. In July 2006 the House elected Baroness Hayman as Lord Speaker and in 2016 Lord Fowler was elected Lord Speaker (replacing Baroness D'Souza).

▩ The Lord Chancellor as a peer

One issue raised by the Constitutional Reform Bill was whether a future Lord Chancellor/Secretary of State for Constitutional Affairs should continue to be drawn exclusively from the House of Lords. The House of Lords attempted to amend the Bill by codifying the constitutional convention that the Lord Chancellor should be a peer and therefore be unable to sit in the House of Commons. In the end, a compromise was reached between the Labour government and the House of Lords with the effect that s 2 of the Act states that a person cannot be recommended for appointment by the Prime Minister as Lord Chancellor unless he is qualified by experience. This could include, for example, experience as a member of either House. As a result, a future Lord Chancellor need not necessarily be drawn from the second chamber. Indeed, in June 2007 Jack Straw MP was appointed as Lord Chancellor and Secretary of State for Justice (in late 2017 the Lord Chancellor and Secretary of State for Justice was the Conservative MP David Gauke).

The executive

■ The Lord Chancellor as a government minister

The Lord Chancellor/Secretary of State will continue to act as a minister and head a government department (in 2017 this was the Ministry of Justice, which in 2007 replaced the Department for Constitutional Affairs) with responsibility for, *inter alia*, the justice system. He will inevitably continue to form part of the Cabinet. However, with a dilution of his responsibilities, it remains to be seen how senior a figure he will be considered in the future. His constitutional responsibilities within the Cabinet will continue to include protecting the independence of the judiciary and ensuring that the principles underpinning the rule of law are not infringed by the government's legislative proposals. In this context, s 17 of the Act sets out the oath to be sworn by the Lord Chancellor:

SECTION

'I will respect the rule of law, defend the independence of the judiciary and discharge my duty to ensure the provision of resources for the efficient and effective support of the courts for which I am responsible.'

Indeed, under s 3 of the Act the Lord Chancellor has a statutory obligation to 'uphold the continued independence of the judiciary' (see section 13.4.1). At the time of writing, the House of Lords Select Committee on the Constitution had expressed its concern of unjustified criticism of the judiciary by the media in the context of the *Miller* case in relation to the issue of Brexit (see section 15.6.6). The report identified a difference between criticism and abuse (ie attacking the integrity and character of a judge). In terms of the latter, the constitutional duty of the Lord Chancellor was clear, which was to defend the independence of the judiciary (see *Judicial Appointments: follow-up*, HL Paper 32 (House of Lords, 2017), p 18).

Notwithstanding the reforms of the 2005 Act, the Lord Chancellor/Secretary of State's position as a government minister (and so part of the parliamentary executive) will therefore *still* represent a breach of the separation of powers.

The judiciary

■ The appointment of judges

In the event of a vacancy in England and Wales, since April 2006 a new statutory Judicial Appointments Commission (established under the Act) presents a candidate to the Lord Chancellor for consideration. Although the Act reduced the discretion of the Lord Chancellor (in the form of an executive function) in making judicial appointments, it still retained him as part of the process. On whether the executive should be involved in judicial appointments and for more recent reforms transferring some of his judicial appointment powers to the Lord Chief Justice under the Crime and Courts Act 2013, see later at section 13.3.

■ The Lord Chancellor as a judge

In terms of sitting as a judge, even before the Constitutional Reform Bill had been introduced into Parliament, the then Lord Chancellor, Lord Falconer, had already announced in the government's September 2003 consultation paper on the reform of the Lord Chancellor, that he did not intend to sit as a judge as:

QUOTATION

The Act now prohibits the office holder of the Lord Chancellor from holding judicial office.

The head of the judiciary

The Lord Chief Justice has now assumed the office of the President of the Courts of England and Wales and is the head of the Judiciary of England and Wales.

NB. For two useful reports on the Lord Chancellor, see the House of Lords Select Committee on the Constitution, *The Office of Lord Chancellor*, HL Paper 75 (2014) and A Horne, 'The role of the Lord Chancellor' SN/PC/2015 (House of Commons Library, 2015).

ACTIVITY

Essay writing

Compare and contrast the legislative, executive and judicial roles exercised by the Lord Chancellor before and after the enactment of the Constitutional Reform Act 2005.

5.7.10 The Appellate Committee of the House of Lords (an historical overlap involving the judiciary forming part of the legislature)

The historical constitutional function of the House of Lords

■ Firstly, the House comprises part of the legislature as it is the upper chamber in Parliament (see Chapter 10). Thus, it plays an integral part in the law-making process.
■ Secondly, the House, or more specifically a committee of the House known as the Appellate Committee of the House of Lords, acted historically as the highest domestic court in the United Kingdom. The judges in the Appellate Committee were technically known as the Lords of Appeal in Ordinary (more commonly referred to as the law lords). In legal theory the law lords could perform two different constitutional functions:
(i) A judicial function – they resolved legal disputes as part of the Appellate Committee.
(ii) A legislative function – they could engage in debate and vote on proposed legislation during the passage of a Bill in the second chamber.

A new Supreme Court

Part 3 of the Constitutional Reform Act 2005 established a Supreme Court to replace the Appellate Committee of the House of Lords. The purpose of this Act was to bring the British constitution more into line with a stricter separation of powers as the

Supreme Court is legally, constitutionally and physically separate from Parliament. The new court became operational in October 2009 and the law lords who were judicially active at this time were transferred to the new court and became justices of the Supreme Court. These justices exercise the same powers as the judges of the former Appellate committee, with the exception that they also process 'devolution issues' (see Chapter 14), a function which has been transferred from the Judicial Committee of the Privy Council (see section 5.7.7).

Three additional points should be noted. Firstly, those retired law lords who were not transferred to the new Supreme Court in 2009 remained in the House of Lords and sat as crossbenchers (see section 10.7.3). Secondly, the judges that were transferred to the Supreme Court in 2009 can return to the House of Lords on their retirement from the Court. Thirdly, detailed below are the main arguments that were used for and against the removal of the law lords from Parliament and the setting up of a new Supreme Court:

Student mentor tip

'Try to see the law operating to make it seem less distant: go to the Houses of Parliament; visit courts; speak to Judges. Seeing the practical side of the subject will help bring it to life.'
Pelena, University of Surrey

The arguments for the removal of the law lords from Parliament

- It was part of the government's drive to modernise a constitution which was antiquated in a number of ways.
- It would realign the constitution in accordance with a purer separation of powers. As noted by the Lord Chancellor:

QUOTATION

'The Law Lords are judges and not legislators: the separation between those two roles should be made explicit. That principle of separation is already established in many other democracies.'
House of Lords Select Committee on the Constitutional Reform Bill, Constitutional Reform Bill (HL) Volume 2: Evidence, HL Paper 125-II (2004), p 9.

- In this way, separating the judges from Parliament would enhance their independence.
- As a result of other constitutional reforms (in particular, the Human Rights Act 1998), it was important to clearly separate the law lords from Parliament.
- It would be consistent with Art 6 of the European Convention which prescribes a right to a fair trial.
- The self-denying ordinance of the law lords (whereby they would not participate in relation to matters with a 'strong element of party political controversy', Lord Bingham, *Hansard*, HL Vol 614 col 419) was no longer sustainable. A complete separation from the legislature would avoid law lords having to 'recuse' themselves from court cases relating to legislation which they had previously had a role in scrutinising/passing.
- On a pragmatic and practical level, in terms of accommodation, the law lords could be better catered for in a new Supreme Court building specifically equipped for that purpose.

It should be noted that the proposal for a Supreme Court had significant support, including the then senior law lord (Lord Bingham), the Bar, the Law Society and a number of academics. There were, however, a number of arguments levelled against the creation of a new Supreme Court.

The arguments against removal

- As noted by Lord Norton, the law lords were already considered to be independent, therefore separation could hardly 'enhance' their independence (*Hansard*, HL Vol 657, col 1269).
- If the argument for a Supreme Court was based solely on the principle of the separation of powers, it foundered because according to a former law lord (Lord Lloyd): 'the separation of powers is not part of our constitution' (*Hansard*, HL Vol 665, col 57).
- Article 6 of the European Convention does not always require an institutional separation of powers, as illustrated by the following case:

CASE EXAMPLE

Pabla Ky v Finland *(2006) 42 EHRR 34*

In 1997 an MP of the Finnish Parliament acted as an expert member of a panel of the Finnish Court of Appeal, which rejected Pabla Ky's appeal concerning a rent contract. Pabla Ky contended that the dual constitutional function of the MP (ie as part of the legislature and the Court of Appeal) violated Art 6 of the European Convention protecting the right to a fair trial before an independent and impartial court.

A chamber of the European Court held by a majority that there had been no violation of Art 6 as the MP in the case had not previously participated in the passing of the legislation which was at issue (ie the Act on Commercial Leases 1993) as he had not been part of Parliament at this time.

The court stated that:

JUDGMENT

'The Court is not persuaded that the mere fact that the MP was a member of the legislature at the time when he sat on the applicant's appeal is sufficient to raise doubts as to the independence and impartiality of the Court of Appeal. While the applicant relies on the theory of separation of powers, this principle is not decisive in the abstract.' (*Sic*)

- No practical benefit would result from the separation. Instead, the new Supreme Court justices could become constitutionally isolated without the protection of Parliament. Moreover, not only would the judges lose out on the benefit of working with parliamentarians (eg non-lawyers), but Parliament itself would lose the advantage of the input of their judicial wisdom. It should be noted, however, that both Houses already contain a number of lawyers.
- The cost would not justify the reform.

It is not without significance that at the time of the 2005 Act the law lords themselves were divided on the issue (the then senior law lord, Lord Bingham in favour; the then second senior law lord, Lord Nicholls, against it). On the Supreme Court see: M Ryan, 'The House of Lords and the shaping of the Supreme Court' (2005) 56 NILQ 135 and M Ryan, 'A Supreme Court for the United Kingdom?' (2004) 17 *Talking Politics* 18.

ACTIVITY

Self-test question

From a constitutional perspective, do you think that the new Supreme Court was necessary?

5.7.11 Administrative tribunals (historically having a link with the executive)

Many legal disputes that an individual will have with the state will be resolved not by the ordinary courts of law but instead by an administrative tribunal. These tribunals act in a judicial manner and apply law to the facts before them. Historically, in terms of the principle of the separation of powers, concern was expressed that these bodies were effectively associated with the administration over which they were adjudicating. However, in 2006 the independence of tribunals was enhanced by removing them from their associated and sponsoring parent government department and transferring them to the new Tribunals Service (see section 21.1.3).

KEY FACTS

Aspects of the British constitution which infringe the separation of powers
The following aspects of the British constitution are infringements of the separation of powers: • The parliamentary executive whereby the executive is drawn from the legislature. Although this allows government ministers to be accountable directly to Parliament, there has been concern that this overlap permits the executive to control the legislature. • The practice of delegated legislation entrusts a law-making power onto a member of the executive. In constitutional theory it is controlled by both parliamentary and legal means. • The monarch is constitutionally involved (albeit formally) in all three functions of the state. • Parliament exercises functions other than legislative as it can act as the High Court of Parliament. • The Privy Council is an executive body which has legislative and judicial functions. • The law officers are part of the government (ie the parliamentary executive) and have a quasi-judicial function. • The judges inevitably perform a *de facto* legislative function in interpreting statutory provisions and developing common law principles.
Historically, the following aspects of the British Constitution were violations of the separation of powers, but have now been subject to recent reform: • The Appellate Committee of the House of Lords has been replaced by a new Supreme Court. • Although historically the Home Secretary exercised *de facto* judicial powers in relation to sentencing, legislation has subsequently reformed this overlap. • The Lord Chancellor historically has been involved in all three functions, but the Constitutional Reform Act 2005 reformed this overlap (although the Lord Chancellor *still* forms part of the parliamentary executive – see above). • Historically, concern has been expressed at the link between the executive and administrative tribunals; however, recent reforms have enhanced the independence of tribunals.

5.8 Aspects of the British constitution in accord with the separation of powers

5.8.1 Introduction

Although the above examples indicate the ways in which the United Kingdom infringes the doctrine of the separation of powers, these violations may be driven by practical considerations (eg delegated legislation). In any event, the various breaches of the separation of powers may well be governed by constitutional conventions. For example we have already noted the following:

▪ The parliamentary executive (see section 5.7.1) – although government ministers are drawn from Parliament, they are governed by the conventions of collective and individual ministerial responsibility.

▪ The role of the monarch (see section 5.7.3) – although the monarch is involved in all three state institutions, these are largely formal overlaps as she is governed by convention (eg in respect of the Royal Assent).

The existence of these constitutional conventions, therefore, serves to mitigate the fact that there is a breach of the separation of powers in the United Kingdom.

5.8.2 The existence of three state institutions

It is also clear that (at least descriptively) it is possible to identify the three state institutions in the British constitution as follows:

▪ The legislature (the United Kingdom Parliament).

▪ The executive (the United Kingdom government comprising the Prime Minister, government ministers, government departments, civil servants together with local authorities).

▪ The judiciary (the judges in the various different jurisdictions and courts of the United Kingdom).

It is also worth noting that in terms of sub-dividing state power:

▪ The legislative branch is divided into two chambers (the House of Commons and the House of Lords). Parliament, therefore, does not necessarily act as a single cohesive force (see section 10.12).

▪ The executive branch is divided into central and local government. As indicated earlier at section 5.3.2, there can be tension and conflict between these two branches of the executive.

Both of the above sub-divisions ensure that there are competing power sources within the legislative and executive state institutions.

▪ The judicial branch of state is divided into a formal hierarchical court structure and a system of tribunals.

The following examples illustrate how the British constitution, to varying degrees, respects the doctrine of the separation of powers (whether a pure or weaker version of the principle):

5.8.3 The legislature and judiciary

▪ **Historically there has been no judicial review of parliamentary legislation**
Parliamentary sovereignty is the foundation of the British constitution, with the result that the courts (at least historically) could not strike down an Act of Parliament. This respects the pure doctrine of the separation of powers with

the courts recognising the constitutional function of Parliament, which is to enact primary legislation (Parliament is, of course, democratically elected). The role of the courts, accordingly, is simply to interpret Acts of Parliament and not to question or challenge them (but see the impact of European Union law at section 15.6).

In countries such as the United States and the Republic of Ireland however, their respective Supreme Courts can invalidate legislation passed by their legislatures (as part of the checks and balances of the separation of powers and the constitution). In contrast, France exhibits a purer separation of powers as the French courts lack the constitutional authority to judicially review legislation passed by the French Parliament.

The *sub judice* resolution
Parliament recognises the respective constitutional roles of the judiciary and the legislature through the use of the *sub judice* resolution. This prohibits parliamentary members commenting on 'live' or pending cases before the courts. This rule protects the role of the courts in carrying out its judicial business free from interference (see section 13.4.3). Notwithstanding this traditional 'comity' between parliamentarians and the judiciary whereby the former respect the role of the courts, it is of constitutional significance to refer to the issue of individuals in Parliament (albeit very rarely) using parliamentary immunity to flout a court anonymised injunction. These so-called 'super-injunctions' are themselves controversial as they prohibit the disclosure of the existence of the injunction itself – see section 8.6.1.

Parliamentary criticism of the judiciary
By parliamentary practice, parliamentary members refrain from criticism of individual judges except on a substantive motion supporting an address to remove them. This prevents interference with the judicial function.

Internal parliamentary proceedings
The judiciary will refrain from trespassing upon the constitutional province of Parliament in respect of the law and custom of Parliament. For example, they will refuse to investigate the internal proceedings of Parliament, even if specifically invited to do so in litigation. This is the 'comity' principle between the judges and Parliament. Indeed, as stated by Lord Simon in the *Pickin* case below, '. . . for many years Parliament and the courts have each been astute to respect the sphere of action and the privileges of the other'. In *British Railways Board v Pickin* [1974] AC 765 the House of Lords held that, if it is alleged that Parliament had been 'deceived' into passing a particular piece of legislation, then this is a matter for Parliament to rectify, and not the courts (see sections 7.8.1 and 8.7.2). A more recent case raising the issue of proceedings within Parliament is *R (HS2 Action Alliance Limited) v Secretary of State for Transport* [2014] UKSC 3 – see section 8.6.4.

Judicial appointments
There is a degree of separation between the legislature and the judiciary in that the former has no part to play in the appointment of judges, although Parliament can remove the senior judiciary (see section 13.4.1). In contrast, in the United States putative justices of the Supreme Court have to undergo a congressional hearing before the Senate (the upper chamber in Congress), for approval. For example, in 2017 the Senate confirmed the appointment of Associate Justice Neil Gorsuch.

Judicial disqualification
Section 1 of the House of Commons Disqualification Act 1975 prohibits full-time members of the judiciary from sitting in the House of Commons, thereby achieving a degree of separation between the judiciary and the legislature.

The new Supreme Court

As noted at section 5.7.10, historically the law lords formed part of the legislature. However, the Constitutional Reform Act 2005 transferred the serving law lords in 2009 to a new Supreme Court which is constitutionally, practically and legally separate from Parliament. Section 137 of the Act prohibits serving justices of the Supreme Court from sitting in the House of Lords. This brought the British constitution more into line with a stricter separation of powers.

Statutory interpretation

In terms of interpreting legislation, the courts have consistently reiterated the constitutional role of the judge in relation to statute law. This is illustrated by the House of Lords in the following case, where they effectively rebuked the Court of Appeal in terms of how it had interpreted a statutory provision:

CASE EXAMPLE

Duport Steels Ltd and others v Sirs and others *[1980] 1 All ER 529*

The case concerned the very restrictive interpretation which the Court of Appeal had given to s 13 of the Trade Union Labour Relations Act 1974 (as amended in 1976) which, in effect, conferred an immunity in tort in respect of acts done by a person in contemplation or furtherance of a trade dispute.

On 2 January 1980 the Iron and Steel Trades Confederation (ISTC) called a strike of its members employed by the British Steel Corporation with which it was in dispute concerning wage rates for 1980. In an effort to exert pressure on the government to provide British Steel with extra public funds so that it could make an acceptable offer to ISTC, by 17 January the latter had resolved to extend the strike to its union members in the private sector of the steel industry.

Duport Steels Ltd, together with other private companies, sought injunctions against Sirs (the general secretary of ISTC) and others against inducing private employees to break their contracts of employment and come out on strike. Although at first instance the injunctions were refused, they were granted by the Court of Appeal on the basis that the dispute on 17 January was a second dispute, this time involving the government, and therefore did not fall within a trade dispute (as the government was not an employer). The court also considered the injustice to employers and workers in the private sector and the economic consequences for the country as a whole of the extension of the strike.

The House of Lords, however, reversed this decision and stated that the test was subjective in that, provided Sirs and others honestly believed at the time that their action might help one of the parties to the trade dispute achieve their objectives, then they would be entitled to immunity in tort under s 13. The action of Sirs and others, therefore, had been taken in furtherance of the trade dispute with British Steel. Lord Diplock reaffirmed that the role of the courts in relation to statutory provisions was to give effect to the words that Parliament had approved:

JUDGMENT

'Where the meaning of the statutory words is plain and unambiguous it is not for the judges to invent fancied ambiguities as an excuse for failing to give effect to its plain meaning because they themselves consider that the consequences of doing so would be inexpedient, or even unjust or immoral. In controversial matters such as are involved in industrial relations there is room for differences of opinion as to what is expedient, what is just and what is morally justifiable. Under our Constitution it is Parliament's opinion on these matters that is paramount.'

Similarly, Lord Scarman noted that his criticism of the Court of Appeal was:

JUDGMENT

'. . . that in their desire to do justice the court failed to do justice according to law'.

More recently, the retired senior judge Lord Carswell (sitting in Parliament), commented in general terms that:

QUOTATION

'The judges have had the job of trying to apply legislation conscientiously and, according to my own observations and practice, they have tried to observe that as faithfully as possible. The judges' own opinions of the legislation are irrelevant and are left out of account. They take the law as enacted by Parliament and apply it, whatever they think of it and whether they think it is good or bad.'

Hansard, HL Vol 716, col 1566.

It should also be pointed out that, under s 3 of the Human Rights Act 1998, all courts and tribunals are now required to interpret all legislation in line with the rights detailed in the European Convention on Human Rights where it is possible to do so. It is clearly the case that this statutory obligation has inevitably given the judges a more dynamic approach to statutory interpretation. Nevertheless, Lord Woolf CJ in *Poplar Housing and Regeneration Community Association Ltd v Donoghue* [2001] EWCA Civ 595 made it very clear that the constitutional role of the judiciary in relation to the Human Rights Act 1998 (and the constitution in general) was to interpret legislation and not to legislate:

JUDGMENT

'It is difficult to overestimate the importance of section 3. . . . When the court interprets legislation usually its primary task is to identify the intention of Parliament. Now, when section 3 applies the courts have to adjust their traditional role in relation to interpretation so as to give effect to the direction contained in section 3 [however] section 3 does not entitle the court to *legislate;* its task is still one of *interpretation,* but interpretation in accordance with the direction contained in section 3.'

A case, however, in which the House of Lords arguably crossed the line between interpreting and legislating was in *R v A (Complainant's sexual history)* [2001] UKHL 25 (see section 17.6.1).

KEY FACTS

Aspects of the British constitution in accord with the separation of powers (legislature and judiciary)

The following aspects of the British constitution are in accord with the principles underpinning the separation of powers (a pure version or otherwise) in respect of the legislature and judiciary:

- The *sub judice* resolution ensures that Parliament does not interfere with the constitutional role of the court which is to resolve cases free from influence or interference.
- By parliamentary practice, parliamentary members refrain from criticising individual judges, as this could undermine their perceived independence.
- The courts do not interfere with the internal proceedings of Parliament.
- Parliament is not involved in the appointment of judges.
- Full-time judges are precluded from sitting in the House of Commons.
- In 2009 under the Constitutional Reform Act 2005, the judicially active law lords were removed from Parliament and reconstituted in a separate Supreme Court.
- The judges have consistently reiterated their limited constitutional role in respect of interpreting statutory provisions.

5.8.4 The judiciary and executive

Judicial independence of the executive

judicial independence

the principle that judges are independent of the other arms of the state

It is a fundamental constitutional principle that the judiciary must remain independent of the executive. Indeed, s 3 of the Constitutional Reform Act 2005 specifically requires ministers of the Crown to uphold **judicial independence** and prohibits them from having special access to the judiciary. Moreover, the Act put on a statutory footing the *concordat* which had been agreed between the Lord Chief Justice and the Lord Chancellor. The *concordat* spelt out the constitutional relationship (and demarcated the boundaries) between the executive and judicial arms of the state.

NB. In terms of engagement, see the following recent document: *Guidance to the judiciary on engagement with the Executive* (Judicial Executive Board).

Executive criticism of judges

By parliamentary practice/constitutional convention, members of the executive do not criticise judges. According to Sir Ivor Judge in his evidence to a select committee, in the event of a government minister's department receiving an adverse judgment in the Administrative Court:

QUOTATION

'. . . commenting on the judge seems to me to be completely unacceptable, but of course the Minister is allowed to say "we disagree with the judge's position and we intend to appeal".'
House of Lords Select Committee on the Constitution, *Relations Between the Executive, the Judiciary and Parliament*, HL Paper 115 (The Stationery Office, 2007), Q 284.

The removal of senior judges

Senior judges are not removable by the government of the day, but instead by Parliament. This means that the executive cannot simply remove a senior judge who has proved to be troublesome for the government in court.

Judicial review (adhering to the separation of powers?)

Judicial review involves the courts reviewing the actions of the executive to ensure that ministers/executive officials act lawfully and strictly within their legal powers when they, for example:

- enact delegated legislation.
- make a public law decision.
- exercise a public law discretion.

In constitutional terms, on the one hand, judicial review could be seen as a violation of a pure separation of powers as the judiciary is effectively interfering with the actions of another state institution: the executive. Conversely, on the other hand, the process of judicial review could be viewed as part of a modified version of the separation of powers, with the courts checking and balancing the executive, thereby avoiding an abuse of executive power.

In the United Kingdom, the courts are conscious of their constitutional position in supervising the activities of the executive. For example, in the context of an alleged abuse of power by a local authority in respect of how it exercised a particular public law discretion (eg in terms of the allocation of financial resources), the judges will act with restraint in ensuring that they do not substitute their 'judicial' view of how a particular public law discretion should have been exercised with that of the local authority. Instead, they ensure that the discretion exercised was within the legal limits of the local authority. Judicial review is essentially a procedural mechanism which is aimed at the decision-making process, rather than the decision itself *per se* (see section 19.2.2).

In the context of the relationship between the separation of powers and judicial review, Craig has noted that the concept of the separation of powers:

QUOTATION

'operates as a source of judicial legitimacy, with the courts defending their role as the right-ful interpreters of legislation, and of the legality of executive action. It serves also as the foundation for judicial restraint, with the courts being mindful of not substituting their view on matters of discretion for that of the body to whom Parliament has granted the power.'

P Craig 'Fundamental Principles of Administrative Law in Relation to Basic Principles of Constitutional Law' in D Feldman (ed), *English Public Law* (2nd edn, Oxford University Press, 2009), p 608.

The reform of the Lord Chancellor

As indicated earlier, under the Constitutional Reform Act 2005 the Lord Chancellor is no longer the head of the judiciary in England and Wales and shares the adminis-tering of judicial discipline with the Lord Chief Justice (with the latter able to give, for example, a formal warning to a judicial holder – with the agreement of the Lord Chancellor). Moreover, the Lord Chancellor no longer sits as a judge, thereby mak-ing a clearer separation between the judiciary and the Lord Chancellor (however, he still remains a member of the political executive).

KEY FACTS

Aspects of the British constitution in accord with the separation of powers (executive and judiciary)

The following aspects of the British constitution are in accord with the principles underpinning the separation of powers (a pure version or otherwise) in respect of the executive and judiciary:

- Section 3 of the Constitutional Reform Act 2005 specifically requires ministers of the Crown to uphold judicial independence and prohibits them from having special access to the judiciary.

- By constitutional convention, members of the executive do not criticise judges.
- The senior judiciary are protected from removal by the executive/government.
- The process of judicial review could be viewed as part of a modified version of the separation of powers, with the courts checking and balancing the executive, thereby avoiding an abuse of executive power.
- The Lord Chancellor's historic judicial functions have been reformed under the Constitutional Reform Act 2005. In particular, he is no longer the head of the judiciary in England and Wales nor sits as a judge.

5.8.5 The executive and legislature

The House of Commons Disqualification Act 1975

Section 1 of the House of Commons Disqualification Act 1975 prohibits specified non-elected members of the executive (ie members of the armed forces, civil servants and the police) from sitting in the lower House, thereby achieving a degree of separation between the executive and the House of Commons. In addition, as indicated earlier, the Act specifically limits the number of government ministers who can sit in the House of Commons to 95 MPs thereby, in constitutional theory, preventing the government from dominating the House of Commons.

Lord Chancellor

As the Lord Chancellor is no longer the Speaker in the House of Lords, this has severed the historic connection between the Speaker and the government (although historically the Lord Chancellor, despite being a member of the executive, was of course supposed to act impartially when acting as Speaker). Today the elected Lord Speaker of the House of Lords is not a member of the Cabinet and is politically impartial.

KEY FACTS

Aspects of the British constitution in accord with the separation of powers (executive and legislature)

The following aspects of the British constitution are in accord with the principles underpinning the separation of powers (a pure version or otherwise) in respect of the executive and legislature:

- The House of Commons Disqualification Act 1975 prohibits specified non-elected members of the executive from sitting in the House of Commons.
- The Speaker of the House of Lords is no longer a member of the Cabinet.

5.9 Conclusion

Even before the advent of the Constitutional Reform Act 2005, Munro had made the following concluding observation concerning the separation of powers in the British constitution:

QUOTATION

'In a variety of important ways, ideas of the separation of powers have shaped constitutional arrangements and influenced our constitutional thinking, and continue to do so.

The separation in the British constitution, although not absolute, ought not to be lightly dismissed.'

C Munro, *Studies in Constitutional Law* (2nd edn, Butterworths, 1999), p 332.

Finally, the following two points are worth noting:

QUOTATION

'Constructive relationships between the three arms of government – the executive, the legislature and the judiciary – are essential to the effective maintenance of the Constitution and the rule of law.'

The House of Lords Select Committee on the Constitution, *Relations Between the Executive, the Judiciary and Parliament*, HL Paper 115 (The Stationery Office, 2007), p 7.

JUDGMENT

'In the field of constitutional law the delicate balance between the various institutions whose sound and lasting quality Dicey . . . likened to the work of bees when constructing a honeycomb is maintained to a large degree by the mutual respect which each institution has for the other'.

Lord Hope, *R (Jackson and Others) v Attorney General* [2005] UKHL 56.

The separation of powers in the British constitution in 2017			
	Legislature/ legislative function	**Executive/ executive function**	**Judiciary/ judicial function**
Parliament	**Constitutional function to pass primary legislation**		• The High Court of Parliament – regulates its own proceedings
Executive	• Passes delegated legislation • Forms part of the parliamentary executive	**Constitutional function to determine and initiate policy (carries out the law)**	• (Historically, it was given a *de facto* judicial function in the context of sentencing)
Judiciary	• Develops the common law • Retired judges still sit in Parliament – albeit as crossbenchers – (CRA 2005)		**Constitutional function to resolve legal disputes and interpret the law**

The monarch	• Queen in Parliament • Royal Assent	• Her Majesty's Government ministers	• Her Majesty's judges
The Lord Chancellor	• Part of the parliamentary executive	• Senior Cabinet minister and Head of a government department (Ministry of Justice) • Approves judicial appointments	• The Lord Chief Justice disciplines judicial holders with the agreement of the Lord Chancellor
The Privy Council	• Orders in Council	• Precursor to the Cabinet and advises the monarch	• Judicial Committee of the Privy Council

SUMMARY

▪ The separation of powers is a key concept in any democratic state.
▪ The separation of powers divides state power into the following three functions:
  ● Legislative – enacting law.
  ● Executive – carrying out the law and making policy decisions.
  ● Judicial – interpreting the law and settling legal disputes.
▪ The separation of powers can be interpreted in a very strict sense or in a looser sense involving a system of checks and balances.
▪ The separation of powers avoids a concentration of state power and ensures that the judiciary are independent.
▪ The British constitution is not in accord with the separation of powers in the following ways:
  ● Parliamentary executive (including the Lord Chancellor and law officers).
  ● Delegated legislation.
  ● Crown formally involved in all three bodies.
  ● High Court of Parliament.
  ● Privy Council.
  ● Judges performing a legislative function.
▪ The British constitution is in accord with the separation of powers in the following ways:
  ● Courts do not review legislation passed by Parliament (except in the context of the EU).
  ● *Sub judice* resolution.
  ● Courts refuse to investigate the internal proceedings of Parliament.
  ● Full-time judges and specified non-elected members of the executive are disqualified from the House of Commons.
  ● By constitutional convention members of the executive do not criticise judges.
▪ The Constitutional Reform Act 2005 reformed the role of the Lord Chancellor and removed the law lords from the House of Lords.

SAMPLE ESSAY QUESTION

How does the British constitution violate the principle of the separation of powers?

Introduction:
- Definition of the separation of powers (note the distinction between a pure and less than pure separation of powers). Briefly explain the nature of the British constitution.

The parliamentary executive:
- Executive drawn from Parliament.
- Note the constitutional advantage of this, which enables the government to be held to account to the legislature.
- Consider whether the balance has shifted too much in favour of the executive.
- Note that parliamentary executive includes both the Lord Chancellor and the law officers.

Delegated legislation:
- Executive performing a legislative function in passing delegated/subordinate legislation.
- Note the practical rationale for it, together with the legal/judicial and parliamentary controls over its use.

The Crown:
- Monarch formally forms part of the executive, legislature and judiciary (note, however, this is only a formal overlap in reality).

The High Court of Parliament:
- Legislature performing a judicial function in regulating and disciplining its own membership.

The Privy Council:
- Executive body which has both legislative and judicial functions (on the latter see the Judicial Committee of the Privy Council).

Judges as legislators:
- Judges perform a *de facto* legislative function in developing the common law and in interpreting legislation.

Conclusion

Further reading

Books

Alder, J and Syrett, K, *Constitutional and Administrative Law* (11th edn, Palgrave, 2017), Chapter 7.

Barnett, H, *Constitutional and Administrative Law* (12th edn, Routledge/Taylor & Francis Group, 2017), Chapter 4.

Leyland, P, *The Constitution of the United Kingdom* (3rd edn, Hart Publishing, 2016), pp 71–83.

Munro, C, *Studies in Constitutional Law* (2nd edn, Butterworths, 1999), Chapter 9.

For an historical perspective, see Allison, J, *The English Historical Constitution* (Cambridge University Press, 2007), Chapter 4.

Articles

Barber, N, 'Prelude to the separation of powers' (2001) 61 CLJ 59.

Barendt, E, 'Separation of powers and constitutional government' [1995] PL 599.

Bradley, A, 'Relations between executive, judiciary and parliament: An evolving saga?' [2008] PL 470.

Claus, L, 'Montesquieu's mistakes and the true meaning of separation' (2005) 25 OJLS 419.

Masterman, R and Wheatle, S, 'Unpacking separation of powers: judicial independence, sovereignty and conceptual flexibility in the UK constitution' [2017] PL 469.

Munro, C, 'The separation of powers: Not such a myth' [1981] PL 19.

Ryan, M, 'The House of Lords and the shaping of the Supreme Court' (2005) 56 NILQ 135.

Lord Steyn, 'The weakest and least dangerous department of government' [1997] PL 84.

Papers

Benwell, R and Gay, O, *The Separation of Powers* (House of Commons Library, 2011).

House of Lords Select Committee on the Constitution, *Relations Between the Executive, the Judiciary and Parliament*, HL Paper 115 (The Stationery Office, 2007).

6

The rule of law

AIMS AND OBJECTIVES

At the end of this chapter you should be able to:

- Explain what is meant by the rule of law
- Explain Dicey's conception of the rule of law
- Explain the criticism of Dicey's conception of the rule of law
- Assess the application of the rule of law to the British constitution

6.1 Definition

QUOTATION

'The rule of law is a fundamental tenet of the United Kingdom constitution.'

The House of Lords Select Committee on the Constitution,
The office of Lord Chancellor, HL Paper 75 (2014), p4.

QUOTATION

'A "health warning" is in order for anyone venturing into this area. . . . There is considerable diversity of opinion as to the meaning of the rule of law and the consequences that do and should follow from breach of this concept.'

Professor Craig, Sixth Report of Session 2006–07 of the House of Lords Select
Committee on the Constitution, *Relations between the executive,
the judiciary and parliament*, HL Paper 151 (2007) Appendix 5, p 97.

QUOTATION

'For my part two core meanings of the rule of law are essential to an understanding of our public law. The first is not a legal concept. The rule of law is a term of political philosophy or institutional morality. It conveys the idea of government not under men but under laws. It eschews the instrumentalist conception of law that enables an oppressive regime to attain its aims by the use of law, as happened in South Africa in the apartheid era. It addresses the moral dimension of public power . . .

In its second sense the rule of law is a general principle of constitutional law. Its central focus is to constrain the abuse of official power. It protects a citizen's right to legal certainty in respect of interference with his liberties. It guarantees access to justice. It ensures procedural fairness over much of the range of administrative decision-making by officials.'

Lord Steyn, *The Constitutionalism of Public Law* (The Constitution Unit, 1999), p 4.

In essence, the rule of law means that government and its officials, together with private citizens, must act under the law. The rationale behind it is to control the exercise of public power by the state by ensuring that it is exercised strictly within legal limits. As such, the courts play a central role in upholding the rule of law and therefore, this principle is inextricably linked with the independence of the judiciary (see Chapter 13).

The rule of law does not have one clear fixed meaning, but instead has been subject to a number of different interpretations. It is a key component of the principle of constitutionalism, namely that governmental action must be subject to limitation in order to avoid an abuse of power.

The rule of law is not a modern concept but is of ancient origin, as it was Aristotle (*The Politics* (Penguin, 1962), p 143) who stated that:

QUOTATION

'. . . it is preferable that law should rule rather than any single one of the citizens.' *(Sic)*

In other words, under 'the rule of men', citizens are governed by men (or a group of individuals) who are capable of acting in an irrational, capricious and vindictive manner. In contrast, under the rule of law, citizens are governed by an overarching universal law. Moreover, 'the law', unlike the rule of men, is not applied in a capricious or irrational fashion and governs the actions of private individuals and state officials alike. In short, *all* are under the law. In this context, Lord Denning MR in the Court of Appeal in *Gouriet v Union of Post Office Workers* [1977] 1 QB 729 commented that:

JUDGMENT

'To every subject in this land, no matter how powerful, I would use Thomas Fuller's words over 300 years ago: "Be you ever so high, the law is above you".'

In the United Kingdom, in the absence of a codified constitution legally restraining the actions of the government, the rule of law assumes a particularly important position.

In modern parlance, the rule of law can be interpreted in different ways. For example, Bradley, Ewing and Knight (*Constitutional and Administrative Law* (16th edn, Pearson, 2015), pp 81–86) identified the following three elements of the rule of law today that they consider to be particularly worth noting:

- Law and order are better than anarchy.
- There should be government according to the law.
- 'The rule of law as a broad doctrine' which affects the makers of new law.

It is illuminating to recall that the moribund Draft Constitution for an independent Scotland (see earlier at section 2.2.1) made express reference to the principle of the rule of law, by which laws:

QUOTATION

6.2 The rule of law as a legal principle

6.2.1 A legal principle and procedural mechanism

In this interpretation, the rule of law is seen as a procedural mechanism (Barnett referred to it as 'a procedural device') controlling and limiting the exercise of governmental/public power. In other words, any action of state officials (eg government ministers or police officers) which impact on the individual should have a clear foundation in law. As noted by Bradley, Ewing and Knight, this is the 'principle of legality'.

For example, Art 5(2) of the European Convention on Human Rights states that:

ARTICLE

'Everyone who is arrested shall be informed promptly, in a language which he understands, of the reasons for his arrest and of any charge against him.'

These requirements ensure that an arrested person understands why, and on what grounds (eg legal basis), he has been arrested and detained by the state. It also makes state officials (ie police officers) legally accountable for their actions, as when they interfere with individual freedoms they are required to justify in law their actions. The rule of law in this sense is a procedural mechanism (the principle of legality) which ensures that government and its officials act under the law. An interesting example of the principle of legality is illustrated by the following case.

CASE EXAMPLE

R (Jones) v Chief Constable of Cheshire Police *[2005]*
EWHC 2457 (Admin)

Jones had been issued a pedlar's certificate under the Pedlars Act 1871, and when arrested and interviewed by the police on suspicion in relation to an offence of dishonesty (although he was never charged), his certificate was seized. The court granted a declaration (in judicial review proceedings) that the police had no lawful power to seize or revoke the certificate as the Pedlars Act 1871 had contained no provision to that effect.

See also the case of *Walker v Commissioner of Police of the Metropolis* [2014] EWCA Civ 897 concerning false imprisonment by a police officer.

In other countries, the principle that government action must be in accordance with the law will be specifically set out in the written codified constitutional text. For example, as noted at section 2.4.4, in Sweden Chapter 1 of its 1975 Instrument of Government states that 'Public power shall be exercised under law'. Similarly, Art 20 of the German Constitution states that:

ARTICLE

'The executive and the judiciary are bound by the law.'

Similarly, see Art 40 in respect of the Irish Constitution.

Thus, in the United Kingdom, in the absence of a written codified document legally and constitutionally restraining the power of government, the rule of law is of paramount importance. The judiciary uphold the constitutional principle that all individuals (both private and state officials) are under the law. In particular, they ensure that government and its officials are accountable to the law through the procedural mechanism of judicial review (see Chapters 19 and 20). In brief, the judiciary supervises the actions of the executive to ensure that it acts strictly within its legal powers.

6.2.2 The limitation of the procedural mechanism

As noted by Bradley, Ewing and Knight, the rule of law should not simply be confined to the consideration of the principle of legality. In other words, if the rule of law is viewed exclusively as a procedural mechanism which asks simply (and only) whether a state official possessed, for example, the requisite legal power to arrest an individual (ie had the state official followed the law?), then this in itself does not necessarily fully protect the individual (see the imaginary Detention Act 2022 detailed at section 6.4). This is because it is possible – in the British constitution at least – for exceptionally wide and extensive powers of arrest and detention to be conferred legally on state officials. Such powers could in effect be used almost at will and to the clear detriment of the individual. Notwithstanding their adverse impact on individual freedoms, if these powers had a legal basis to them, under the principle of legality (which requires state action to have a legal foundation), the use of them would be lawful as these powers would be legitimised by law. In strict procedural terms, therefore, these state officials would be acting 'according to the law'. The rule of law, accordingly, may also embrace a broader meaning imbued with a substantive content which would critically evaluate laws in terms of their impact on human rights and other fundamental principles (see section 6.4).

Indeed, Lord Lang of Monkton as Chair of the House of Lords Select Committee on the Constitution has argued that:

QUOTATION

'I suggest that the rule of law requires an independent justice system, free from corruption and outside interference. It requires those in power to comply with the law to ensure a stable and predictable exercise of power, rather than an arbitrary one. But these two elements alone are insufficient. Surely the rule of law goes beyond judicial independence and simple compliance with law, particularly as regards the Government, who can, through Parliament, change the law. We concluded that in the context of government, the rule of law must include the tenet that the Government should seek to govern in accordance with constitutional principles as well as with the letter of the law.'

Hansard, HL Vol 764, col 105.

KEY FACTS

Key facts on the rule of law as a legal principle

The rule of law as a legal principle ensures that government acts under the law.

In this sense it is a procedural mechanism which protects the individual from an unlawful use of state power as it requires state officials to justify their actions.

ACTIVITY

Essay writing

What is the difference between the rule of law and the rule of men?

6.3 The rule of law as a political ideal/theory

6.3.1 A formal view of the rule of law

This interpretation of the rule of law is concerned with the form that the law takes. In other words, once a law has been passed in the requisite constitutional manner (eg in the United Kingdom this would involve the Queen in Parliament passing an Act of Parliament), it should exhibit particular characteristics.

6.3.2 Raz and the rule of law

Raz is a major exponent of a formal conception of the rule of law (J Raz, 'The Rule of Law and its Virtue' (1977) 93 LQR 195). In essence, he stated that the rule of law is a political ideal which means that individuals should be ruled by the law and that the law must be able to guide individuals if they are to obey the law. As a consequence, this allows individuals to plan their lives accordingly.

In particular Raz argued that the making of laws should be guided by, *inter alia*, the following principles:

QUOTATION

'(1) All laws should be prospective, open and clear.'

Prospective laws – Laws should be prospective so that laws look forward rather than punishing behaviour retrospectively. Retrospective laws are objectionable because, of course, an individual has no control over their past conduct. In this context, Willes J in *Phillips v Eyre* (1870–71) LR 6 QB 1 has noted that:

JUDGMENT

'Retrospective laws are, no doubt, *prima facie* of questionable policy, and contrary to the general principle that legislation by which the conduct of mankind is to be regulated ought, when introduced for the first time, to deal with future acts and ought not to change the character of past transactions carried on upon the faith of the then existing law. . . . Accordingly, the Court will not ascribe retrospective force to new laws affecting rights, unless by express words or necessary implication it appears that such was the intention of the legislature.' *(Sic)*

Moreover, Art 7 of the European Convention on Human Rights specifically outlaws retrospective criminal offences:

ARTICLE

'No one shall be held guilty of any criminal offence on account of any act or omission which did not constitute a criminal offence under national or international law at the time when it was committed.'

In terms of the Irish Constitution endorsing the principle that laws should not be retroactive, see Art 15.5.

Open laws – Laws should be open so that individuals are able to access them. Laws should not be secret or difficult to locate as this would not enable an individual to be guided by the law.

One consequence of secret laws is that, as individuals will be unaware of them, they will inevitably be in a state of apprehension. For example, if an individual is unsure as to whether it is a criminal offence (punishable by a term of imprisonment) to hold a political demonstration, in order to err on the side of caution he would in all likelihood not demonstrate in case the demonstration violated the law. Moreover, this demonstration could have been a protest about, for instance, the policies of the incumbent government.

Clear laws – Laws should be clear and intelligible so that the individual can understand them. Ambiguous, imprecise or unclear laws will confuse the individual and prevent the law guiding and influencing their actions.

In the context of open and clear laws, in *Merkur Island Shipping Corporation v Laughton and others* [1983] 2 AC 570 Sir John Donaldson MR in the Court of Appeal stated that:

JUDGMENT

'The efficacy and maintenance of the rule of law, which is the foundation of any parliamentary democracy, has at least two pre-requisites. First, people must understand that it is in their interests as well as in that of the community as a whole, that they should live their lives in accordance with the rules and all the rules. Second, they must know what those rules are. Both are equally important.'

In recent years the following developments have been made to make legislation clearer and thus more accessible:

■ Explanatory notes – these notes which accompany Bills and Acts are prepared to make legislation more intelligible. These explanatory notes have been made available to the public since 1998. Furthermore, in 2006 the *Coroner Reform: The Government's Draft Bill*, Cm 6849 (DCA, 2006) was published which included detailed passages explaining each aspect/clause of the Bill in alternative pages. This was designed specifically to make the draft Bill as intelligible (and so accessible) to the public as possible.

■ Explanatory memorandum – is now available in respect of statutory instruments. Such notes explain the purpose, objective and application of the measure.

Further, Lord Bingham has argued that the volume of modern legislation raises problems of accessibility, but that, in addition:

QUOTATION

'. . . the length, complexity and sometimes prolixity of modern common law judgments, particularly at the highest level, raise problems of their own.'

'The rule of law' (2007) 66 CLJ 67.

QUOTATION

> '(2) Laws should be relatively stable.'
>
> Raz.

Laws should remain relatively stable and not change too frequently as otherwise individuals could be fearful that the law may have changed in the intervening period. As a result, they would be unable to plan their lives effectively for fear that the law had in fact changed and may change again in the near future.

QUOTATION

> '(3) The making of particular laws (particular legal orders) should be guided by open, stable, clear and general rules.'
>
> Raz.

For example, particular laws of an ephemeral status (eg administrative law-making/delegated legislation) should be enacted in the context of 'detailed ground rules laid down in framework laws' (ie parent legislation).

Thus, Raz views the above characteristics as not in themselves concerned with the *substance* of the law itself (see section 6.4), but instead with the *form* of the law. Raz accepts that these characteristics (open, clear, stable, prospective laws) could, of course, be met by a non-democratic state. He also included within the principles underpinning the rule of law that the independence of the judiciary must be guaranteed. It is the courts that apply the law and they should do so free from external interference. The judiciary, in ensuring the correct application of the law, should also apply the principles of **natural justice/the duty to act fairly** (see Chapter 20) and ensure that they are observed. In addition, the courts should be accessible to an aggrieved individual (so that the judiciary can provide an effective remedy) and the judges should have power of review over both primary and subordinate legislation together with administrative action to ensure conformity with the principles underpinning the rule of law.

natural justice/ duty to act fairly

common law rules developed by the judiciary to ensure that public bodies exercise their powers and functions fairly

KEY FACTS

Raz and a formal conception of the rule of law:
Laws should possess the following characteristics in order to conform to a particular standard which should enable them to guide individual behaviour: • Open • Clear • Stable • Prospective.
The following principles concern the legal machinery for enforcing the rule of law: • The independence of the judiciary must be guaranteed as the judges ensure that the law is correctly applied and followed. In ensuring the correct application of the law they will apply the principles of natural justice/the duty to act fairly. • The courts should be accessible to individuals so that the judiciary can provide an effective remedy, and the judges should have power of review over legislation and administrative action to ensure conformity with the principles underpinning the rule of law.

6.4 The rule of law as a substantive concept

QUOTATION

'A state which savagely represses or persecutes sections of its people cannot in my view be regarded as observing the rule of law, even if the transport of the persecuted minority to the concentration camp or the compulsory exposure of female children on the mountainside is the subject of detailed laws duly enacted and scrupulously observed.'

Lord Bingham, *The Rule of Law* (Allen Lane, 2010), p 67.

This interpretation of the rule of law is concerned in particular with the substantive content of laws. In essence, laws should encapsulate and respect certain fundamental values, for example basic constitutional principles and the protection of human rights. In this context, consider the following imaginary statute:

SECTION

The (Imaginary) Detention Act 2022

Section 1 permits a police officer to arrest, and detain for 10 days, any individual who criticises the economic policy of the incumbent government.

In 2023 Emily is arrested and detained for ten days for criticising the Chancellor of the Exchequer's Budget proposals. In relation to the rule of law as a substantive concept, the questions are *not* simply:

▨ Does the state official (ie police officer) possess the legal power to detain Emily? (ie is Emily's detention authorised by law / Act of Parliament?) – see the principle of legality at section 6.2.

and

▨ Has this law (the (Imaginary) Detention Act 2022) been promulgated in the constitutionally correct manner by the appropriate body? In other words, was it passed by the Queen in Parliament?

and

▨ Does this law exhibit certain characteristics? (ie is the (Imaginary) Detention Act 2022 open, clear, stable, general and prospective so as to be capable of guiding Emily's behaviour?) – see the formal conception of the rule of law at section 6.3.2.

Rather, the rule of law as a substantive concept is concerned with the substance and moral character of the law and asks the following question:

▨ *Should* state officials (ie the police) have been conferred with wide and extensive powers of detention in respect of individuals who merely criticise a government's economic policy? In other words, *should* Parliament have passed the (Imaginary) Detention Act 2022 in the first place?

In this sense the rule of law embraces a substantive concept as it evaluates laws made according to a set of fundamental constitutional principles which include the protection of individual freedoms. In this way, this interpretation of the rule of law effectively has a moral dimension to it which would question whether the state really required the (Imaginary) Detention Act 2022. This would be on the basis that the Act is draconian legislation which violates the principles underpinning the rule of law (ie it is an excessive interference with an individual's right to freedom of expression and the right of personal liberty). Ironically, therefore, the (Imaginary) Detention Act 2022 – although *itself* a law – would be considered to be a violation of the rule of law (as a substantive concept). Although such legislation would undoubtedly be considered *morally unconstitutional* (see section 4.16), owing to the doctrine of parliamentary sovereignty it would nevertheless be legally enforceable (though subject to a declaration of incompatibility by the courts under section 4 of the Human Rights Act 1998 – see section 17.7).

The inherent problem with the substantive conception of the rule of law is that the principles which underpin it (including balancing the basic rights of the individual against other competing interests such as public order/safety and national security, etc), are not universally agreed upon. For example, there is no universal agreement on the legitimate scope of police powers. To some extent, therefore, the substantive conception of the rule of law is necessarily subjective and in essence depends upon a personal conception of human rights. In short, it depends to a great extent upon one's personal judgement of what is a 'good law' (morally right because it protects the rights and things *you* favour) and what is a 'bad law' (morally wrong because it infringes the rights and things that *you* favour).

For example, returning to the example given at section 4.16.2, did the Prevention of Terrorism Act 2005 (now repealed) breach the rule of law because it interfered with the fundamental liberties of the individual? Or was it consistent with the rule of law as an unfortunate, but necessary, response to an emergency threatening the life and safety of the nation/public? Indeed, was the Act aimed at actually protecting the rule of law itself by dealing with elements that threaten to undermine the existence of the state itself?

ACTIVITY

Applying the law

Distinguish between the rule of law as:

- A procedural mechanism.
- A political ideal.
- A substantive concept.

6.5 The rule of law as the antithesis of anarchy and chaos

This (rather basic) interpretation of the rule of law emphasises the need for social order within the state, as opposed to anarchy and chaos. In other words, the rule of law requires an ordered state comprising, *inter alia*, a functioning legal system and independent courts in which citizens' disputes can be resolved and settled by peaceful and consensual means, as opposed to individuals having to resort to armed force. This interpretation would be in contrast to a country which was administered by state officials who acted arbitrarily and in a completely unregulated and capricious fashion. In short, a state governed by the rule of men.

An inextricable aspect of an ordered legal system is the principle of the independence of the judiciary and court system. In order to hold the government to account, to ensure that legal disputes are resolved fairly and according to the law and that citizens will have confidence in the administration of justice, judges must be impartial and independent from the government and state officials (see section 13.4).

6.6 The rule of law in international terms

As noted above, the concept of the rule of law is of some antiquity and is also used in an international context, although its meaning may differ.

6.6.1 The rule of law and the Universal Declaration of Human Rights

The preamble to the Universal Declaration of Human Rights (1948) adopted by the General Assembly of the United Nations confirms respect for fundamental human rights and states:

ARTICLE

'whereas it is essential, if man is not to be compelled to have recourse, as a last resort, to rebellion against tyranny and oppression, that human rights should be protected by the rule of law'.

In effect, this emphasises that the state should protect basic individual rights and not undermine them. Implicit within this is that should such rights be infringed by the state, then the individual should have access to legal machinery (ie the courts) in order to challenge it.

6.6.2 The rule of law and the European Convention on Human Rights

The European Convention sets out the basic rights and freedoms of individuals in Europe and seeks to ensure that these rights are protected by their respective state and domestic legal system. The European Court of Human Rights, in interpreting the rights of the Convention, draws upon the concept of the rule of law. In fact, the preamble makes reference to the rule of law as being part of the common heritage of the signatory states.

Most of the rights in the European Convention are conditional rights (eg the right to freedom of expression), rather than being absolute (see Chapter 16). In brief, conditional rights can be legitimately interfered with by the state for specified and limited purposes. For example, Art 10 confers on everyone the right to freedom of expression. This right is, however, conditional and can be legitimately interfered with in order to, *inter alia*, protect health or morals (see section 18.2.4). Moreover, any legitimate interference with the rights of the Convention has overtones of the terminology of the rule of law. This is illustrated by the following case:

CASE EXAMPLE

Handyside v United Kingdom *(1976) 1 EHRR 737*

Handyside was the publisher of The *Little Red Schoolbook* (a reference book aimed at children and adolescents aged 12–18 which had a section concerning sex, including topics on masturbation, contraceptives, pornography etc). He was prosecuted under the Obscene Publications Act 1959 (as amended in 1964), as the book was adjudged to be obscene. Handyside argued (unsuccessfully) in the European Court of Human Rights that this criminal conviction and the destruction of his books violated Art 10 (the right to freedom of expression).

In essence, any interference with Art 10 had to be consistent with the main elements of the rule of law. In other words, the restriction/interference (ie the Obscene Publications Acts 1959/1964) had to have a legitimate aim, be 'prescribed by law' and be legally justified. The reasoning of the court in the case was as follows:

The court noted at the outset that the action taken against Handyside (ie his conviction and destruction of his books) was an interference with his right to freedom of expression under Art 10(1). However, the question was: could it be justified by the state (ie the United Kingdom)?

- Firstly, any interference with Handyside's right had to be 'prescribed by law'. In other words, the interference had to have a clear legal foundation in domestic law so that it was accessible and intelligible to Handyside. The court held that the Obscene Publications Acts 1959/1964 were clearly set out in domestic law.
- Secondly, any interference with Handyside's right to freedom of expression had to have a legitimate aim. Art 10(2) permits interference where the aim is to protect morals. In this case the court held that the interference with Handyside's right was in the interests of the protection of morals (ie the children who would be exposed to the book) and so had a legitimate purpose under Art 10(2).
- Thirdly, any interference with Handyside's right also needed to be proportionate and so not excessive, thereby ensuring that any restriction did not unnecessarily infringe the rights of the Convention. In this case the restriction on Handyside's right to freedom of expression had not been disproportionate and so was necessary in a democratic society.

In short, the European Court of Human Rights held that the interference with Handyside's right to freedom of expression under Art 10 was legitimate, prescribed by law and justified. The reasoning employed by the court clearly draws upon the various principles underpinning the rule of law.

ACTIVITY

Applying the law

Re-read the *Handyside* case example above and link the reasoning and tests employed by the European Court with the principles underpinning the rule of law that you have already covered in this chapter.

6.6.3 The Declaration of Delhi

In 1959 the Declaration of Delhi was issued by the International Commission of Jurists. Although the Declaration is not legally binding, it noted that the obligations imposed by the rule of law included, *inter alia*, the right to a representative government, an independent judiciary and a fair trial (including due process).

6.6.4 The European Union

In the context of the European Union, the 1997 Treaty of Amsterdam made it clear that the Union itself was founded on respect for democratic principles, human rights and the rule of law. Furthermore, in performing its function of interpreting

European Union law, the Court of Justice of the EU uses a number of principles to assist it. One of these principles is that of legal certainty, which is essentially based on the rule of law. For example, in reviewing the Acts/legislation made by the political institutions in the European Union, the Court of Justice in *Commission v France* Case C–30/89 [1990] ECR 1-691 has noted that:

JUDGMENT

'It must be remembered that the Court has repeatedly held that certainty and foreseeability are requirements which must be observed all the more strictly in the case of rules liable to entail financial consequences.'

KEY FACTS

Key facts on the rule of law

- The rule of law is a concept of some antiquity that has been subject to a number of different interpretations and meanings.
- In general terms it means that all are subject to the law, rather than being subject to the whims of man (ie the rule of men).
- It is a key element of constitutionalism which is aimed at ensuring that government and its officials act under the law and strictly within their legal powers.
- It can be interpreted as a principle of legality, a political ideal and as a substantive concept.
- At a basic level it emphasises the need for social order within the state as opposed to anarchy and chaos.
- The principle is also used in an international context.

6.7 The rule of law in the British constitution

6.7.1 Introduction to the rule of law in the United Kingdom

The rule of law is a central aspect of the British constitution. In fact, it assumes a particular significance in the absence of a written codified and entrenched constitution which legally sets out the limits of the government (particularly in relation to human rights). Jowell has noted that, in countries with a 'written' constitution, a Bill of Rights will typically disable the government and elected Parliament from abusing their power, while in the United Kingdom the rule of law as an unwritten principle of the constitution 'performs a similar disabling function' ('The Rule of Law' in J Jowell, D Oliver and C O'Cinneide (eds), *The Changing Constitution* (8th edn, Oxford University Press, 2015), p 27). It should be remembered, however, that the British courts have been traditionally unable to challenge primary legislation (see Chapter 7).

In the United Kingdom, therefore, the rule of law denoting the fundamental principle that government is under the law takes on a particular significance. Indeed, Lord Woolf in a lecture on the rule of law reaffirmed the constitutional significance of this principle:

QUOTATION

'One of the most important of the judiciary's responsibilities is to uphold the rule of law, since it is the rule of law which prevents the Government of the day from abusing its powers.'

Lord Woolf, 'The rule of law and a change in the constitution' (2004) 64 CLJ 317.

In the United Kingdom, the rule of law (at least historically) has been closely associated with Dicey. This classic conception of the rule of law in his book *Introduction to the Study of the Law of the Constitution* represented an early attempt at explaining the rule of law in the context of the 'English' constitution (today Dicey would use the term British constitution). In particular, Dicey argued that the constitution rested upon the twin pillars of parliamentary sovereignty and the rule of law (see further at section 7.13).

Although Dicey's conception has been criticised (and these criticisms are considered below), his principles arguably still have resonance today.

6.7.2 Dicey and the rule of law

Dicey highlighted three aspects (or conceptions as he described them) of the rule of law:

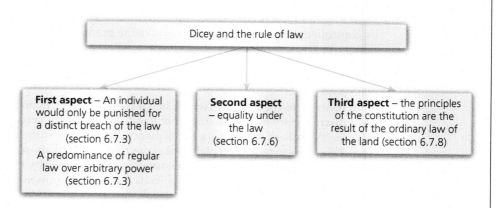

Figure 6.1 Dicey and the rule of law

6.7.3 Dicey's first aspect

Dicey stated that the rule of law meant:

QUOTATION

'that no man is punishable or can be lawfully made to suffer in body or goods except for a distinct breach of law established in the ordinary legal manner before the ordinary courts of the land. In this sense the rule of law is contrasted with every system of government based on the exercise by persons in authority of wide, arbitrary, or discretionary powers of constraint.

'It means, in the first place, the absolute supremacy or predominance of regular law as opposed to the influence of arbitrary power, and excludes the existence of arbitrariness, of prerogative, or even of wide discretionary authority on the part of the government. Englishmen are ruled by the law, and by the law alone; a man may with us be punished for a breach of the law, but he can be punished for nothing else.'

A Dicey, Introduction to the Study of the Law of the Constitution (10th edn, Macmillan, 1959), pp 188 and 202 respectively.

This first aspect can be broadly broken down into two elements:

- An individual is only punished for a breach of the law.
- The predominance of regular law.

Element 1 – An individual is only punished for a breach of the law

In short, Dicey argued that a punishment would only be imposed on an individual if he violated the law as established in ordinary legal proceedings before a court. In other words, the individual was not subject to the whims of a state official.

Element 2 – The predominance of regular law

In essence, Dicey argued that the rule of law denoted the predominance of regular law as opposed to the exercise of arbitrary power. As regular law had a clear legal origin and was reasonably precise in its ambit, the use of regular law could be controlled. Regular law did not involve the granting of arbitrary or wide discretionary powers on state officials as such powers could be used to the detriment of the individual. As Dicey asserted, 'wherever there is discretion there is room for arbitrariness'. Regular law, therefore, necessarily limited and controlled the use of state power.

In contrast to regular law (which had a clear legal origin and clear legal limits), wide discretionary powers on the other hand, lacked clear ascertainable legal parameters (ie 'the rule of men'). As a consequence, it would be difficult for an individual to challenge government officials and claim that they had abused their wide discretionary powers. Arbitrary power, of course, is characterised by the lack of clear legal limits and it in effect permits state officials to act in an unregulated and effectively unchallengeable manner. This in turn makes it difficult to make these bodies legally accountable for their actions which have adversely and unfairly affected the individual. As stated by Lord Bingham:

QUOTATION

'The broader and more loosely-textured a discretion is, whether conferred on an official or a judge, the greater the scope for subjectivity and hence for arbitrariness, which is the antithesis of the rule of law.'

'The rule of law' (2007) 66 CLJ 67.

Legal accountability, therefore, benefits the individual as it gives certainty in terms of the limits and parameters of state power. It has also been argued that, from an administrative/governmental perspective, regular law (with the absence of wide discretionary powers) benefits state officials themselves as it makes the use of their powers more efficient.

6.7.4 Critique of Dicey's first aspect (element 1)

In terms of the first element of Dicey's first aspect, it is worth noting the following examples, which indicate that an individual could 'suffer in body or goods' without having violated a law as established before the ordinary courts.

- **Remand** – under the Bail Act 1976 an *unconvicted* but accused person, can be remanded in custody prior to his criminal trial. There are, of course, sound public policy reasons for the authorisation of the detention of such an individual, for example if the court has substantial grounds that if granted bail the accused would abscond, commit an offence or interfere with witnesses. Nevertheless, in the event of a person denied bail subsequently being found not guilty at trial, he would have suffered in body whilst being remanded in custody waiting for his criminal trial to commence. Moreover, no compensation is awarded for this detention.
- **Search powers** – s 1 of the Police and Criminal Evidence Act 1984 authorises a police officer to stop and search a person or vehicle for stolen or prohibited articles provided the officer has reasonable grounds for suspecting that he will find such articles. The officer may detain the person or vehicle in question for the purpose of the search. Suppose David is detained and searched in the street under this provision: provided the police officer had reasonable grounds for suspecting that he would find stolen/prohibited articles on David's person, the detention and search would be lawful even though no such articles were actually found. David has suffered in body in the absence of a violation of the law.
- **Indefinite detention of suspected international terrorists** – Below is an interesting example of how Parliament can pass a law (albeit now historic) which authorises the indefinite detention of non-United Kingdom nationals suspected of terrorism. In summary, foreign nationals were detained without either charge or trial and so were made to 'suffer in body' even though no charge was brought against them.

CASE EXAMPLE

A and others v Secretary of State for the Home Department *[2004] UKHL 56*

Section 23 (Pt 4) of the Anti-terrorism, Crime and Security Act 2001 authorised the indefinite detention without charge or trial of foreign nationals suspected of being international terrorists, but who could not be deported (whether temporarily or indefinitely). These detainees could not be charged before a court as, *inter alia*, the exposure of the alleged evidence against these individuals could compromise the intelligence services who had gathered it. Further, these individuals could not be deported as, under Art 3 of the European Convention, a state cannot deport an individual to a country where there is a real risk that the deportee will be subjected to torture or inhuman or degrading treatment (see section 16.9.4). As a consequence, the detainees were not prosecuted for any criminal offences, nor were they deported, which left the suspects detained indefinitely without charge or trial. These individuals could, however, leave the United Kingdom voluntarily to go to a country which would accept them.

Under Art 5 of the Convention, deportation proceedings of individuals must be pursued with due diligence (*Chahal v UK* (1997) 23 EHRR 413) and so in 2001 the government made the Human Rights Act 1998 (Designated Derogation) Order in respect of this obligation (ie an official departure from Art 5). Such derogations are permissible under Art

15 in times of war or other public emergency threatening the life of the nation (eg the threat of terrorism).

Detainees held under the Act challenged this terrorism legislation and the derogation order under the Human Rights Act 1998. The House of Lords declared that s 23 of the Act was incompatible with Arts 5 (the right to liberty and security of person) and 14 (the right not to be discriminated against) and the derogation order made by the government was quashed. In brief, the court held that s 23 of the Act was disproportionate and discriminatory against non-UK nationals. Lord Nicholls stated that: 'Indefinite imprisonment without charge or trial is an anathema in any country which observes the rule of law.'

It should be noted, however, that, owing to the doctrine of parliamentary sovereignty, this decision of the court did not disapply the 2001 Act (see section 17.7); instead it merely alerted Parliament and the government that the Act violated the European Convention. In due course, the Prevention of Terrorism Act 2005 replaced the provisions for detention without trial under Pt 4 of the 2001 Act with 'control orders'. These control orders were in turn then replaced by Terrorism Prevention and Investigation Measures (TPIMs) under the Terrorism Prevention and Investigation Measures Act 2011. On powers to deal with terrorism, see section 6.7.11.

As a postscript to this case, in 2009 in *A v UK* (2009) 49 EHRR 29 the European Court of Human Rights held that there had been a violation of Art 5 of the European Convention.

 ▪ **Compulsory purchase powers** – local authorities typically have powers of compulsory purchase, which empower them to compulsorily purchase private property, for example to make way for a new road. In these circumstances, the homeowner will suffer without having breached a law.

6.7.5 Critique of Dicey's first aspect (element 2)

This aspect of Dicey's first conception has been subject to some criticism.

The obvious question to ask is: are there any wide discretionary powers conferred on the state which are open to abuse in the modern British constitution? Although there are laws which are relatively precise, there are also examples where exceptionally wide powers have been conferred on the executive by way of legislation. It should be remembered that, under the principle of parliamentary sovereignty, Parliament can simply pass whichever law it chooses. For instance, the following case is a good example of Parliament passing a law which conferred an exceptionally wide power on state officials:

CASE EXAMPLE

Inland Revenue Commissioners and another v Rossminster Ltd and Others *[1980] AC 952*

Section 20C of the Taxes Management Act 1970 stated that a judicial authority could issue a warrant authorising Inland Revenue officers to enter and search premises if satisfied that 'there is reasonable ground for suspecting that an offence involving any form of fraud in connection with, or in relation to, tax has been committed and that evidence of it is to be found on premises specified in the information'.

A senior revenue officer suspected some tax fraud had been committed and sought (and obtained) a warrant to search the premises of Rossminster Ltd and seize anything the officers had reasonable cause to believe as evidence of a tax fraud. The revenue officers (accompanied by the police) entered Rossminster Ltd's premises and seized anything believed to be evidence of a tax fraud. As Rossminster Ltd had not been informed of the specific offences suspected, or the person suspected of committing them, it sought judicial review to quash the search warrant as illegal.

The Court of Appeal granted such a declaration. In particular Lord Denning MR commented that 'the trouble is that the legislation is drawn so widely that in some hands it might be an instrument of oppression'. He noted further that an offence involving fraud in relation to tax could include a number of different kinds of offences and so in pursuance of the traditional role of the courts to protect the liberty of the individual, the warrant must particularise the specific offence.

The House of Lords, however, reversed the decision of the Court of Appeal and held that the warrants were lawful as they had been issued strictly in accordance with the legal authority of s 20C. Lord Scarman commented regrettably that even though the warrant had not been particularised, the requirements of the Act had nevertheless been complied with. He stated that, although the provision was lawful, it represented 'a breath-taking inroad upon the individual's right of privacy and right of property'.

As an aside, it is of course worth remembering that, as a consequence of the parliamentary executive, it is invariably the case that it is the government of the day which drafts a Bill which, when enacted as law, confers a wide statutory power onto the executive (see sections 5.7.1 and 5.4.3). Indeed, at section 4.16.2 it was suggested that the Taxes Management Act could well have been considered *morally unconstitutional*.

In addition, delegated legislation confers a law-making power onto the executive to enact law, and there is inevitably an element of discretion in carrying out this function. The courts will, however, imply certain limits in respect of the use of this legislative power (see in context of judicial review, Chapters 19 and 20), as illustrated by the following example:

CASE EXAMPLE

Commissioners of Customs and Excise v Cure & Deeley Ltd
[1962] 1 QB 340

Section 33 of the Finance (No 2) Act 1940 conferred a power on the Commissioners of Customs and Excise to 'make regulations providing for any matter for which provision appears to them to be necessary for the purpose of giving effect to the provisions of this Part of this Act and enabling them to discharge their functions'. In pursuance of this power, the Commissioners made reg 12 of the Purchase Tax Regulations 1945 which, in essence, stated that if a person failed to return a tax return – or an incomplete one – the Commissioners may determine the amount of tax appearing to them to be due and demand this payment and that this *shall* be deemed the proper tax due.

The Queen's Bench Division held that reg 12 was *ultra vires* s 33 of the Finance Act. The court held that although s 33 (ie *'appears to them to be necessary'*, emphasis added) appeared to confer a discretion on the Commissioners, it did not necessarily make that body the sole judge of what its powers were, or of to how it could exercise those powers.

The court held that reg 12 purported to confer on the Commissioners the powers of a judge and it tried to oust the jurisdiction of the court. The consequence of the regulation was to substitute the figure which the Commissioners *deemed* to be due, for the figure that was *lawfully* and *actually* due under the law. As Sachs J noted:

JUDGMENT

'In the result this attempt to substitute in one segment of the taxpayer's affairs the rule of tax collectors for the rule of law fails.'

A more recent case concerning the principle of access to the courts is:

CASE EXAMPLE

R (UNISON) v Lord Chancellor [2017] UKSC 51

Under s 42 of the Tribunals, Courts and Enforcement Act 2007, the Lord Chancellor made the Employment Tribunals and the Employment Appeal Tribunals Fees Order 2013 (SI 2013/1893), which imposed fees (when hitherto there had been none) for claims in the Employment Tribunal and Employment Appeal Tribunal. This legislation was challenged by the trade union UNISON in judicial review proceedings. Although this legal challenge was initially dismissed, the Supreme Court unanimously held that the Fees Order was unlawful and quashed it as a breach of a person's access to justice (ie the courts). Lord Reed stated that:

JUDGMENT

'The constitutional right of access to the courts is inherent in the rule of law . . . At the heart of the concept of the rule of law is the idea that society is governed by law . . . Courts exist in order to ensure that the laws made by Parliament, and the common law created by the courts themselves, are applied and enforced. That role includes ensuring that the executive branch of government carries out its functions in accordance with the law. In order for the courts to perform that role, people must in principle have unimpeded access to them. Without such access, laws are liable to become a dead letter . . . That is why the courts do not merely provide a public service like any other.'

An example of Parliament (largely controlled, of course, by the government) proposing to confer wide discretionary powers on the state (in the form of the police) was the Terrorism Bill of 2005 (which became the Terrorism Act 2006). The Terrorism Bill sought to permit the police to detain terrorist suspects for up to a maximum of 90 days without charge. It was argued that such a time period was necessary in order to allow the police the time to acquire and analyse the evidence against those detained under the legislation. In the event, at the report stage of the Bill the House of Commons voted against the detention of up to 90 days and instead voted for the reduced period of 28 days. During the passage of the Bill, a number of commentators argued that the period of 90 days was excessive and contrary to the traditions of the rule of law. It must be remembered that the detention relates to the period before the detainee has even been charged with committing an offence.

Such was the criticism of the draconian and excessive nature of the proposed powers (which would have conferred extensive and wide-ranging powers on the police) that it represented the first defeat in the House of Commons for the Labour government since assuming office in 1997. The Labour government subsequently tried again to extend the detention period as part of its 2008 Counter-Terrorism Bill (see section 6.7.11). In addition, see the stop and search powers authorised under s 44 of the Terrorism Act 2000 in circumstances where it was considered 'expedient for the prevention of acts of terrorism' (but now see *Gillan* (2010) below).

The advantages of state discretion

In terms of discretionary powers, it is clear that, in a complex modern state, discretion is a necessary tool for the modern-day administrator (eg in terms of the areas of welfare benefits and immigration, etc). In fact, far from adversely affecting the individual, discretionary power in the hands of a state official can be used to their advantage and benefit. In other words, if regular, clear and precise laws are applied rigorously to *all* individuals at *all* times and in *all* circumstances, this in itself could cause injustice and unfairness to a particular individual. Accordingly, discretion can be used by an administrator to mitigate the rigidity and harshness of the law.

Thus, far from being a disadvantage, discretion is a necessary and unavoidable tool, as the following examples demonstrate:

- Local authorities (an executive body) with limited and finite financial resources need the power to make decisions as to how best to deploy those limited resources. The use of this discretion is, however, controlled through the process of judicial review, which ensures that its exercise is legal, rational and procedurally fair (see Chapter 20). In this way, the use of the discretion is regulated in order to avoid an abuse of power.
- The Crown Prosecution Service (which takes over prosecutions instigated by the police) has a discretion not to prosecute in an appropriate case. This decision is taken with consideration of *The Code for Crown Prosecutors* in mind.
- The courts, in dispensing punishment to convicted offenders may have a degree of discretion, within specific parameters, as to which sentence to impose. This is determined according to the facts and circumstances of the particular case. In brief, it would be manifestly unfair to stipulate exactly the same penalty on all defendants convicted of the same offence (eg theft under the Theft Act 1968), as the circumstances, nature, impact and significance of the offence (together with the circumstances of the convicted defendant) will necessarily vary. Although judicial discretion is considered to be a central part of the practice of sentencing, there is inevitably a risk of disparity between sentences imposed. In effect, therefore, this discretion is to some extent 'structured' by the establishment of general sentencing principles (ie see the authoritative guidelines produced by the Sentencing Guidelines Council, which aims to encourage consistent sentencing in court).

The control of discretion

If discretion is considered a necessary tool, its use needs to be controlled and circumscribed; otherwise the unregulated use of a discretionary power could be tantamount to the use of an arbitrary power. This regulation can be achieved through the courts via the process of judicial review (see Chapters 19 and 20). For example, a statute may confer a discretionary power on a government minister to:

(i). 'act as he thinks fit'/'act when it appears to him to be necessary',
   or
(ii). 'pass such regulations as he thinks fit', in order to achieve a particular public purpose.

The courts, however, will necessarily imply that the use of such power is not without its legal limits. Even though Parliament has conferred a discretionary power, it is assumed that Parliament envisaged the minister exercising that power/discretion to use it:

- legally
- rationally
- in a procedurally fair manner
- consistently with the rights set out in the European Convention (now required under the Human Rights Act 1998).

In this way the courts can control and 'structure' the use of discretionary power. We saw that in *Cure & Deeley* (and previously in *Witham* at section 4.8.3 and *Chester v Bateson* at section 5.7.2) that the courts will make it plain that, notwithstanding the power to enact delegated legislation which 'appears to them to be necessary', this is not an absolute power. As pointed out by Lord Bingham:

QUOTATION

'There is in truth no such thing as an unfettered discretion, judicial or official, and that is what the rule of law requires.'

'The rule of law' (2007) 66 CLJ 67.

Dicey specifically disapproved of, and referred to, 'wide discretionary authority'. Today, in a modern-day, complex state, discretion is inevitable and practically unavoidable. Moreover, the principle of discretion can benefit the individual by mitigating the harshness of the law, but that discretion must be exercised within clear legal parameters and subject to review by the courts to ensure that it is not abused or misused. Recently, in *Gillan v UK* (2010) 28 BHRC 420 (Application No 4158/05) the European Court of Human Rights held that the wide discretion of the police to stop and search individuals under the Terrorism Act 2000 violated Art 8 of the European Convention. The court stated that:

JUDGMENT

'In matters affecting fundamental rights it would be contrary to the rule of law, one of the basic principles of a democratic society enshrined in the Convention, for a legal discretion granted to the Executive to be expressed in terms of an unfettered power. Consequently, the law must indicate with sufficient clarity the scope of any such discretion conferred on the competent authorities and the manner of its exercise . . .

'In conclusion, the court considers that the powers of authorisation and confirmation as well as those of stop and search under sections 44 and 45 of the TA 2000 are neither sufficiently circumscribed nor subject to adequate legal safeguards against abuse. They are not, therefore, "in accordance with the law".'

It is of interest to point out that in *R (Gillan) v Metropolitan Police Commissioner* [2006] UKHL 12 the House of Lords had earlier held that these provisions did *not* violate the Convention.

NB. Section 59 of the Protection of Freedoms Act 2012 repealed the stop and search powers set out in sections 44 to 47 of the Terrorism Act 2000.

ACTIVITY

Self-test question

What do you think are the advantages and disadvantages of the use of executive or other discretion?

Dicey's first aspect is that a punishment would only be imposed on an individual if he violated the law as established in the ordinary legal proceedings before a court. It also denoted the predominance of regular law, as opposed to the exercise of arbitrary power.

It is clear that at times individuals can suffer without breaking the law (eg remand, stop and search powers of the police etc).

Discretion is inevitable and necessary in a modern state and can be used to the advantage of the individual in order to mitigate the harshness of the 'regular' law. This discretion, however, has to be regulated and controlled by the courts.

6.7.6 Dicey's second aspect

In terms of equality before the law, Dicey stated that:

QUOTATION

'. . . with us no man is above the law, but (what is a different thing) that here every man, whatever be his rank or condition, is subject to the ordinary law of the realm. . . . In England the idea of legal equality, or of the universal subjection of all classes to one law administered by the ordinary courts, has been pushed to its utmost limit. With us every official, from the Prime Minister down to a constable or a collector of taxes, is under the same responsibility for every act done without legal justification as any other citizen.

'. . . equality before the law, or the equal subjection of all classes to the ordinary law of the land administered by the ordinary law courts; the "rule of law" in this sense excludes the idea of any exemption of officials or others from the duty of obedience to the law which governs other citizens or from the jurisdiction of the ordinary tribunals.'

A Dicey, *Introduction to the Study of the Law of the Constitution*
(10th edn, Macmillan, 1959), pp 193 and 202–203 respectively.

Dicey argued that all individuals (both private citizens and state officials) are under the ordinary law. As a consequence, if a state official breached the law, he would be treated in the same way as an ordinary private individual would be if they had violated the same legal provision: the same law would be applied to both before the ordinary courts. In other words, state officials did not enjoy special immunities from the law, nor were they given special protection from the reaches of the 'ordinary' law.

In particular, Dicey contrasted our system with that which existed in France, whereby disputes with the government or state officials were processed in specific courts/tribunals (*tribunaux administratifs*). These tribunals processed administrative law (*droit administratif*), which was distinct from the ordinary court system. This meant that, in France, there was a clear and separate system of administrative law which regulated the constitutional relationship between the individual and the state. Dicey perceived that these tribunals afforded the state and its officials a degree of protection, which meant that these officials were not fully accountable as a private citizen would be before the ordinary French court system. In fact, the *tribunaux administratifs* were staffed by specialists in public administration who were able to determine and assess the liability of public officials and hold them to account for their actions.

Dicey's principle of equality under the law is neatly illustrated by *Entick v Carrington* (1765) (see section 4.8.2). In this case, officials of the state were sued in the law of trespass for unlawfully entering Entick's property and seizing his papers. A private individual would have been sued in the same way had they entered and seized Entick's property. This illustrates the state being held to account by the ordinary law of the land before the ordinary court system.

A further example is demonstrated if the police exceed their legal powers of detention:

SECTION

Section 41 of PACE 1984 requires that a suspect may not be held in police detention beyond 24 hours without being charged (unless this has been extended under s 42 by a superintendent or above). If the police exceed this time limit without lawful authority, then they (typically the Chief Constable) are liable to be sued in the tort of false imprisonment in the same way that an individual would be if they detained another individual without lawful authority.

An important judicial affirmation of the principle that everyone is equal under the law, in particular government ministers, is illustrated by the following case:

CASE EXAMPLE

M v Home Office *[1994] 1 AC 377*

M, a citizen of Zaire, was unsuccessful in seeking political asylum in the United Kingdom. On the day he was to be removed from the country, he applied for leave to move for judicial review of this rejection. The judge in chambers thought M might have an arguable point and therefore required M's deportation to be postponed pending the hearing of his application. The judge thought that counsel for the Secretary of State had, in effect, given an undertaking that M would not be removed pending the hearing of his case. In any event, M was removed from the United Kingdom to Paris bound for Zaire. Later that evening the judge issued a mandatory 'without notice' order which required the Home Secretary to return M to the jurisdiction of the United Kingdom court. The Home Secretary successfully challenged this order on the basis that the judge had had no jurisdiction to make it. Nevertheless, M's lawyers issued contempt proceedings against the Secretary of State for failing to comply with the court order while it was in force.

The House of Lords held, firstly that the court did have the jurisdiction to make coercive orders against ministers of the Crown (while they were acting in their official ministerial capacity). Secondly, if a government minister ignored an injunction made against him in his official capacity as a minister, the court possessed the legal jurisdiction to make a finding of contempt of court against him or his government department. Lord Templeman stated that:

JUDGMENT

'The argument that there is no power to enforce the law by injunction or contempt proceedings against a minister in his official capacity would, if upheld, establish the proposition that the executive obey the law as a matter of grace and not as a matter of necessity, a proposition which would reverse the result of the Civil War.'

NB. Most recently in two conjoined appeals (*Belhaj v Straw* and *Rahmatullah v Ministry of Defence* [2017] UKSC 3), the Supreme Court rejected the defendant/

government's pleas of 'state immunity' and 'foreign act of state' that an English court was barred from determining claims made against it.

6.7.7 Critique of Dicey's second aspect

The rule of law and judicial review

Although Dicey disapproved of the French administrative law system, in the last few decades it is arguable that the United Kingdom has developed a separate form of administrative law which in some ways is akin to the French system. In fact, judicial review proceedings, in which the courts supervise the actions of the executive to ensure that they act lawfully, are hallmarked by special features which are not present in the ordinary court system (see Chapter 19, and in particular section 19.2.5). For example:

- A claimant must seek permission to apply for judicial review (there is no right *per se*).
- A claimant must act promptly and not later than three months (in contrast, litigants suing in tort have six years – three if it involves personal injuries (Limitation Act 1980)).
- The claim must be made against a public body (or a body treated as such).
- The claim must also concern a public law issue (for example, how a public body misused its public law powers).
- The remedies which the court can issue are discretionary and so not automatic and as of right. As a consequence, even if the claimant can demonstrate that a public authority has acted unlawfully by misusing its public law powers, the court may take the view that it is not in the interest of public administration to grant relief.
- Judicial review proceedings are heard before specialist judges in the Administrative Court.
- These judges apply special public law principles (eg the public body must act rationally, in a procedurally fair way and respect the requirements of the European Convention on Human Rights).

In this way the state and its officials are not being treated in the same way as ordinary individuals. Instead, they are subject to a specialist court applying special public law principles. In this sense, in many ways the Administrative Court today is not too dissimilar to the French administrative law system which Dicey disapproved of. In fairness to Dicey, however, the process of judicial review is an area of judicial activity which has only really exploded since the second half of the twentieth century.

The system of tribunals

Today, many disputes between the individual and the state (for example, in relation to the processing of welfare benefits and immigration issues) are resolved not through the ordinary courts but instead by specialist tribunals (see section 21.1).

Main exceptions to the principle of equality

Although there should be general equality under the law, this does not mean that there should be no immunities at all or that everyone should be treated the same in all circumstances. There are a number of exceptions to the general principle of equality before the law and these include:

- Article 9 of the Bill of Rights 1689 states that the freedom of speech, debates or proceedings in Parliament ought not to be questioned in a court. The constitutional rationale behind this legal immunity for parliamentarians is to ensure that they can exercise their functions without fear of litigation. This immunity is regulated by Parliament itself so that if a member abuses this immunity (eg gratuitously defames a constituent) this will be investigated and punished by Parliament. As an aside, it is pertinent to note the so-called 'Wilson doctrine' (named after the Prime Minister Harold Wilson), which was a convention that the communications of MPs should not be intercepted by the security services/police. Today s 26 of the Investigatory Powers Act 2016 provides that the Secretary of State needs the approval of the Prime Minister and Judicial Commissioner prior to issuing a warrant to intercept the communications of parliamentarians, as well as members of the devolved institutions and United Kingdom MEPs. See further, P Strickland, J Dawson and S Godec, *The Wilson Doctrine,* Briefing Paper No 4258 (House of Commons Library, 2017).

- The sovereign, together with foreign heads of state/sovereigns, enjoys legal immunity from criminal liability: s 20 of the State Immunity Act 1978. However, following the passage of the Crown Proceedings Act 1947, Crown government departments could thereafter be sued in private law as of right.

- Diplomatic agents enjoy immunity under s 2(1) of the Diplomatic Privileges Act 1964.

- In relation to the courts, judges are not liable for anything said while carrying out their judicial function (*Anderson v Gorries* [1895] 1 QB 668 and the Courts Act 2003, see section 13.4.2). This is justified on the basis of the protection of judicial independence and the administration of justice so that judges can perform their constitutional functions of adjudication and applying the law independently, without fear of litigation. This benefits the wider public whose cases will be processed by the courts.

- For public policy reasons, specified classes of individuals are treated differently. For example, employers and employees as a group or class of individuals have different obligations imposed upon them by the law, which reflect the imbalance of power in their relationship. This is also the case in respect of landlords and tenants.

- In respect of equality, it should be remembered that public authorities exercise particular functions that individuals do not. The exercise of these powers, therefore, have no real parallel in the private world of individuals. As a result, it is argued that these public bodies should be subject to *additional* legal controls. Indeed, the consequence of treating 'unequal' entities (ie state officials and private individuals) equally is that it can give rise to constitutional difficulties, as illustrated in *Malone v Metropolitan Police Commissioner* [1979] Ch 344. In brief, Malone alleged that the tapping of his telephone conversations in order to obtain evidence against him in criminal proceedings was unlawful. The court held, however, that there was no law against it. Sir Robert Megarry VC stated that:

JUDGMENT

'England, it may be said, is not a country where everything is forbidden except what is expressly permitted; it is a country where everything is permitted except what is expressly forbidden . . . if such tapping can be carried out without committing any breach of the law; it requires no authorisation by statute or common law; it can lawfully be done simply because there is nothing to make it unlawful.'

In this case the tapping of Malone's telephone took place on the premises of the Post Office and so no breach of the law of trespass had taken place (contrast *Entick* – see section 4.8.2). This case demonstrated the danger in treating constitutional unequals (here the police and a private individual – the latter would not have had access to Post Office premises) equally. In other words, in these circumstances, in pursuance of protecting the individual, it could be argued that the actions of the police should be subject to *extra* controls and regulation. In any event, Fenwick, Phillipson and Williams have made the following point that the High Court judgment:

QUOTATION

'. . . arguably missed the basic point that this freedom to do that which the law does not forbid should apply to *citizens*, who have a right to liberty, but not to *government*, which does not have such a general liberty of action, but only duties . . .'

H Fenwick, G Phillipson and A Williams, *Text, Cases and Materials on Public Law and Human Rights* (4th edn, Routledge/Taylor & Francis Group, 2017), p 78.

ACTIVITY

Applying the law

Should the government be bound by the law? Can you think of reasons why the government should (a) be immune under the law and (b) have more duties under the law?

KEY FACTS

Key facts on Dicey's second aspect of the rule of law

Dicey contended that all individuals (both private individuals and state officials) are equal under the ordinary law. This meant that if a state official breached the law, he would be treated in the same way as an ordinary private individual. Under the principle of equality, state officials do not enjoy special immunities from the law.

It is clear that there are a number of exceptions to the principle of equality before the law:
- The sovereign, foreign heads of state, diplomats and parliamentarians enjoy immunity from the law.
- Judges are not liable for anything said while carrying out their judicial function.
- In terms of their rights and responsibilities, certain classes of people, for instance landlords and tenants, will be treated differently under the law.

6.7.8 Dicey's third aspect

Dicey stated that:

QUOTATION

'We may say that the constitution is pervaded by the rule of law on the ground that the general principles of the constitution (as for example the right to personal liberty, or the right of public meeting) are with us the result of judicial decisions determining the rights of private persons in particular cases brought before the courts . . . with us the law of the constitution, the rules which in foreign countries naturally form part of a constitutional code, are not the source but the consequence of the rights of individuals, as defined and enforced by the courts.' (*Sic*)

A Dicey, *Introduction to the Study of the Law of the Constitution* (10th edn, Macmillan, 1959), pp 195 and 203.

Dicey was making the point that Britain had a court-based constitution (ie a common law constitution) in the sense that the principles of the constitution, concerning the rights of the individual, were the direct consequence of decisions made by judges. In this way, Dicey contrasted the English (British) constitution with constitutional arrangements pertaining elsewhere, in which the rights and freedoms of the individual were found in a Bill or Charter of Rights as part of a written codified document.

For example, Entick (see section 4.8.2) successfully sued the king's messengers (state officials) in the ordinary law of trespass. Entick did not need to rely on a constitutional guarantee set out in a Bill of Rights. Instead, Entick relied on the common law to equip him with a practical remedy which could be enforced in the ordinary courts. For Dicey, these practical remedies gave the individual better protection than guarantees enshrined in a written constitution (typically in a Bill of Rights). As pointed out by Craig:

QUOTATION

'Dicey dealt in detail with the precarious protection of rights on the continent, where constitutions enshrining rights would often be abrogated at the stroke of the pen or the point of a sword. He felt that in the UK, where individual rights were the result of numerous judicial decisions indicating when the individual was at liberty to speak freely etc, it would be considerably more difficult for an authoritarian regime to sweep these rights aside.'

Sixth Report of Session 2006–07, *Relations between the executive, the judiciary and the Parliament*, HL Paper 151 (2007), Appendix 5, p 98.

ACTIVITY

Self-test questions

1. How did Dicey think that liberty should be protected?
2. Do you agree with him?

6.7.9 Critique of Dicey's third aspect

The courts have clearly fashioned a number of common law remedies for the individual, which include the following:

- Trespass to person.
- Trespass to land.
- Trespass to property.
- False imprisonment.
- Assault.
- Battery.

These remedies, accordingly, can be used against state officials, as well as other individuals. For example, if an individual is unlawfully detained by the police they can sue in an action for false imprisonment. These remedies are in addition to any statutory rights and remedies which have been specifically conferred by an Act of Parliament (eg the right not to be discriminated against on the grounds of sex under the Equality Act 2010). The courts, however, can only protect the individual if in fact a particular right has been recognised either by the common law or enacted in statute.

This point was neatly illustrated in the *Malone* (1979) case at section 6.7.7, as one of Malone's submissions against the Metropolitan Police Commissioner in respect of the tapping of his telephone was that it violated his right to privacy. Sir Robert Megarry VC dismissed this by indicating that no tort of privacy existed as Parliament had not legislated to create one and the courts in developing the common law had not fashioned one. In fact, in terms of the separation of powers, he noted that it was not the constitutional function of the judiciary to 'legislate in a new field' and create this new right of privacy:

JUDGMENT

'No new right in the law, fully-fledged with all the appropriate safeguards, can spring from the head of a judge deciding a particular case: only Parliament can create such a right.'

The courts, therefore, have been selective as to which remedies an aggrieved individual can employ.

In any event, the capacity of the courts to protect the individual from the actions of the state are necessarily curtailed by the central element of the British constitution, namely parliamentary sovereignty. Although Parliament can pass legislation conferring legal remedies on an individual (eg in the context of sexual and racial discrimination), conversely, it can pass laws which interfere excessively with the liberties and freedoms of the individual as well. In these circumstances, the courts are effectively rendered powerless if this excessive interference is expressly authorised and legitimised in the provisions of an Act of Parliament.

For instance, it is worth recalling Lord Scarman's comments in *Rossminster Ltd* (1980) in relation to s 20C of the Taxes Management Act 1970, which conferred sweeping powers on Inland Revenue officers (see section 6.7.5). According to Lord Scarman, the Act represented 'a breath-taking inroad' into the right of individual privacy and property. It was not, however, the constitutional responsibility of the courts to set it aside.

In fact, Parliament has on occasions passed retrospective law to negate and reverse the ruling of the courts, the most famous example being the enactment of the War Damage Act 1965, which in effect overruled the decision in the *Burmah Oil* case (see sections 4.9 and 7.5.1). This legislation was arguably *morally unconstitutional* (see section 4.16.2) as it interfered with the ruling of the highest court on the grounds of financial expediency. More recently, see the retrospective Terrorist Asset-Freezing (Temporary Provisions) Act 2010 at section 20.2.2. The following year the Police (Detention and Bail) Act 2011 was fast-tracked through Parliament. It reversed a decision of the High Court (*R (Chief Constable of Greater Manchester Police) v Salford Magistrates' Court* [2011] EWHC 1578 (Admin)) concerning the calculation of the 'detention clock' under the Police and Criminal Evidence Act 1984. The court had held that this clock was *not* paused when the individual was released on police bail. In addition, the Jobseekers (Back to Work Schemes) Act 2013 was enacted, which, in effect, retrospectively validated the Jobseeker's Allowance (Employment, Skills and Enterprise Scheme) Regulations 2011, which had been quashed by the Court of Appeal as *ultra vires* s 17A of the Jobseekers Act 1995 in (*R (Reilly) v Secretary of State for Work and Pensions* [2013] EWCA Civ 66). Section 1 of the 2013 Act states that 'The 2011 Regulations are to be treated for all purposes as regulations that were made under section 17A of the Jobseekers Act 1995'. In *R (Reilly) v Secretary of State for Work and Pensions* (No 2) [2016] EWCA Civ 413, the Court of Appeal affirmed a declaration of incompatibility that the 2013 Act was incompatible with Art 6 of the European Convention in that it interfered with the administration of justice (ie interferes with a pending appeal).

In short, the courts:

- can develop the common law so as to provide (selected) practical remedies if an individual's freedoms have been violated, and
- will also interpret unclear legislative provisions in the light of constitutional principles which protect the individual (eg the presumption that Parliament did not intend to interfere with a person's right of access to the courts – see section 4.8.3).

Ultimately, however, Parliament can simply override the protection provided by the judges by passing legislation which clearly and explicitly authorises an interference with the freedoms of the individual. In contrast, under a codified constitution with an entrenched Bill of Rights, such legislation – all things being equal – would be rendered legally (and morally) unconstitutional and declared invalid by a Constitutional/Supreme Court.

For Dicey, however, as Parliament is elected by the people (or at least the dominant House of Commons is) it is answerable to the electorate and so this restrains Parliament from passing draconian laws. In short, the constitutional theory is that parliamentarians will not pass laws which would unnecessarily and gratuitously infringe individual rights and freedoms, as the electorate have political sovereignty (see section 7.2.2). In other words, MPs must face the public at the time of re-election at a general election and so are ultimately answerable to the people for the laws (ie Acts) that they have passed. The problem with this, of course, is that draconian legislation which only affects a certain (unpopular) section of society (eg prisoners, terrorist suspects and paedophiles) may in reality be popular with the public at large. This serves to illustrate that democracy should not be equated simply with majority rule as it may be necessary to ring-fence the rights of 'unpopular' individuals and protect them from the 'tyranny of the majority' (the relationship between the rule of law and parliamentary sovereignty will be considered further at section 7.13).

Another point to note is that this element of Dicey's conception of the rule of law is now subject to the passage of the Human Rights Act 1998. This Act, in effect, gives further effect in the law of the United Kingdom to the rights enshrined in the European Convention on Human Rights. Under s 3 of the Act all courts and tribunals have the responsibility to interpret all legislation 'so far as it is possible to do so' in line with the rights of the European Convention. The effect of s 6 of the Act is that, whenever the courts apply or develop the common law, they constitute a public authority for the purposes of the Act and so must act consistently with the European Convention. The Human Rights Act represents a significant shift in terms of 'rights protection' in the British constitution, and in some ways is akin to a Bill or Charter of positive rights (albeit a weak one) whereby positive and lawful justification is now needed by the state to interfere with the rights of the individual.

Although the Human Rights Act would appear to be at odds with Dicey's suspicion of written constitutional guarantees of rights, the articles of the Convention are enforced by individuals before the courts (in fact, any court or tribunal and not necessarily the Administrative Court). The role of the courts, therefore, will continue to remain central to the protection of individual rights. Under the Human Rights Act 1998 the function of the court is to uphold the protection afforded by these rights by construing all legislation in line with the European Convention and ensuring that public authorities fully respect these rights and freedoms.

ACTIVITY

Self-test question

What impact do you think that the Human Rights Act 1998 has had on Dicey's third aspect of his conception of the rule of law?

KEY FACTS

Key facts on Dicey's third aspect of the rule of law

Dicey contended that our constitution was in effect a court-based constitution in the sense that the rights and freedoms of the individual were the direct consequence of decisions made by judges.
In this way, Dicey contrasted the English (British) constitution with the constitutional arrangements elsewhere, in which the rights and freedoms of the individual were derived from a written Bill or Charter of Rights embedded in a written/codified constitutional document.
Dicey's third aspect now has to be re-evaluated in the light of the passage of the Human Rights Act 1998 which, in effect, represents a list of basic positive rights of individuals which can be enforced by them in the domestic courts.

6.7.10 The role of the United Kingdom courts and the rule of law

The following cases are examples where the principles underpinning the rule of law have been invoked in the domestic courts.

The rule of law as a basis for the control of de facto arbitrary powers

In *Entick v Carrington* (see section 4.8.2), one of the arguments used by the defendants (ie the state) as a justification for the use of its warrant was that this power was essential to 'government and state necessity' and moreover that such warrants had been issued before and had not been questioned. In response, Lord Camden CJ stated that:

JUDGMENT

'This power, so claimed by the secretary of state, is not supported by one single citation from any law book extant. . . . According to this reasoning, it is now incumbent upon the defendants to shew the law, by which this seizure is warranted. If that cannot be done, it is a trespass.' (*Sic*)

The court also rejected the argument that this power was essential to government. In short, this case tells us that it is not the constitutional function of the judiciary to equip the government with new powers. If the government required such powers, then Parliament would need to pass the requisite legislation. In fact, the *Entick* case neatly demonstrates all three of Dicey's propositions:

- **The government/state must act within the law and not exercise arbitrary powers** – The state tried (unsuccessfully) to use a power in the form of a warrant which had no legal foundation or lawful origin. As a result, the state could not 'trump' or lawfully negate the common law right of Entick (as expressed in the law of trespass) not to be trespassed against without lawful justification.
- **Equality under the law** – The state was held to account according to the ordinary law (trespass) before the ordinary courts.
- **A court-based constitution** – The ordinary courts provided Entick with a practical remedy against the state in the law of trespass. In other words, he did not need to rely on a Bill or Charter of Rights in a codified constitution.

More recently, in *Webb v Chief Constable of Merseyside Police* [2000] 1 All ER 209, the Court of Appeal reiterated the principle that government is under the law. In this case the court made it clear that it was unlawful for a public authority (ie the police) to expropriate money or property from an individual without authorisation in a statute.

The House of Lords also reiterated the rule of law in the following ruling by refusing to countenance an abuse of public power by the executive:

CASE EXAMPLE

R v Secretary of State for the Home Department, ex parte Fire Brigades Union *[1995] 2 All ER 244*

The Criminal Injuries Compensation Scheme was established in 1964 under the royal prerogative to provide compensation to victims of crimes. In 1988 the Criminal Justice Act codified the scheme, but under s 171 it would not come into force until a day to be determined by the Secretary of State. This section therefore conferred a power on the minister to decide exactly when the statutory scheme should come into force. In December 1993 a government White Paper indicated that the compensation provisions of the Act would not be implemented, but would in due course be repealed. Instead, in March 1994 the government announced - under the royal prerogative – that a new tariff scheme would take effect from April 1994 (this flat-rate tariff scheme was in effect a cheaper scheme as it would compensate victims on the basis of the category that they fell into, rather than on an individual basis).

Trade unions (whose members were susceptible to violent crime in their work) sought judicial review of the decision and sought a declaration, *inter alia*, that the Secretary of State had acted unlawfully by failing to bring into force the above provisions of the 1988 Act.

The House of Lords held that the Home Secretary had a power to act (as he had been conferred with a discretion as to when it was appropriate to bring the scheme into force) and that this was a matter for him to decide. Accordingly, it would not be constitutionally appropriate for the courts to interfere and require the Home Secretary to bring those provisions of the Act into effect. This statutory discretion, however, was not unlimited and the Home Secretary was required (while the sections were not in force) to keep under review the question of whether these provisions should be brought into force. It was, therefore, unlawful and an abuse of power to use royal prerogative power inconsistently with that responsibility. As a result, the Home Secretary's decision not to implement the provisions of the Act and instead impose a tariff scheme in its place, was unlawful. Lord Browne-Wilkinson stated that:

JUDGMENT

'It does not follow that, because the Secretary of State is not under any duty to bring the section into effect, he has an absolute and unfettered discretion whether or not to do so . . . the

Secretary of State comes under a clear duty to keep under consideration from time to time the question whether or not to bring the section (and therefore the statutory scheme) into force. In my judgment he cannot lawfully surrender or release the power contained in section 171(1) so as to purport to exclude its future exercise either by himself or by his successors.'

Similarly, in *Cure & Deeley* (1962) (see section 6.7.5) the courts demonstrated that they will limit the scope of wide discretionary powers conferred on executive authorities. The case below also demonstrates the courts invoking the rule of law in overseeing executive action:

CASE EXAMPLE

R v Horseferry Road Magistrates' Court, ex parte Bennett *[1994] 1 AC 42*

Bennett was a New Zealand citizen who claimed that he had been kidnapped from South Africa and brought to England, where he was arrested to face criminal charges. The Magistrates' Court refused his request to adjourn the committal of his case to the Crown Court. Bennett sought judicial review of the decision, but the High Court refused his application.

The House of Lords held that the courts should take cognisance of the circumstances which led a defendant to appear before the court. In this case, Bennett had been brought back to the United Kingdom without regard to the available extradition process and in violation of international law. The High Court could therefore inquire into the circumstances that led an individual to be brought before the court and could stay the prosecution (as an abuse of process) if it was satisfied that extradition proceedings had been disregarded. Lord Griffiths stated that:

JUDGMENT

'The judiciary accept a responsibility for the maintenance of the rule of law that embraces a willingness to oversee executive action and to refuse to countenance behaviour that threatens either basic human rights or the rule of law.'

Judicial deference

In contrast to the cases above, on occasions the courts have (albeit historically) adopted a 'hands-off approach' in order to avoid trespassing on the constitutional role of the executive (ie to determine public policy or to make politically sensitive decisions). In this way, judicial deference to executive decision-making avoids infringing the principle of the separation of powers as the executive has been charged with making these decisions. This in turn, however, gave the individual little legal protection from the exercise of state power, as illustrated in the following infamous and historic case:

CASE EXAMPLE

Liversidge v Anderson *[1942] AC 206*

Under reg 18B of the Defence (General) Regulations 1939, the Secretary of State could make an order to detain a person if *he had reasonable cause* to believe that the person was of hostile origin or associations.

The House of Lords held that under this emergency legislation (in the context of the Second World War) a court could not inquire as to whether in fact the minister had reasonable grounds for his belief that the person be of hostile associations. In other words, this was an issue of executive discretion for the minister concerned and the court could not require the minister to give the particulars of the grounds on which he had had reasonable cause to believe the detainee to be of hostile associations.

This is a highly controversial case as it effectively conferred a considerable power onto the executive. Indeed, as Lord Atkin said in his dissenting opinion, 'I protest, even if I do it alone, against a strained construction put on words with the effect of giving an uncontrolled power of imprisonment to the minister'.

In this case the court was aware that the minister was politically accountable for his actions to Parliament under the constitutional convention of ministerial responsibility (see section 4.13.12).

The controversial majority decision in this case was rejected in subsequent case law: see Lords Diplock and Scarman in *Inland Revenue Commissioners and another v Rossminster Ltd and Others* [1980] AC 952.

A more recent example than *Liversidge* of the courts adopting a 'hands-off approach' (where the source/nature of information against the individual was highly confidential) is the following case:

CASE EXAMPLE

R v Secretary of State for Home Affairs, ex parte Hosenball *[1977] 1 WLR 766*

Hosenball was an American journalist and in the interests of national security the Home Secretary had decided to make a deportation order against him under s 3 of the Immigration Act 1971. It was alleged that Hosenball had obtained for publication information harmful to the security of the United Kingdom. He was informed that he could make representations to an individual panel in respect of his deportation, but could not appeal. Despite a request by Hosenball's solicitors, the Secretary of State declined to provide further information (ie the relevant particulars of what was alleged against him).

The panel subsequently conducted a hearing at which Hosenball called witnesses and made representations. Shortly afterwards the Secretary of State made the deportation order which Hosenball sought to quash on the grounds that the rules of natural justice had been violated as he had been denied the particulars of the allegations made against him.

The Court of Appeal held that the principles underpinning natural justice were modified when issues of national security were involved. Here public policy necessitated the protection of the confidentiality of security information. On the facts of the case, the Secretary of State had considered personally Hosenball's request for further particulars of the allegations (but that this had been refused as it was not in the interests of national security to provide further information) and there was nothing to suggest that he had acted unfairly. The court also noted that under the convention of ministerial responsibility the Secretary of State was politically answerable to Parliament for his decision. Lord Denning MR observed that:

JUDGMENT

'There is a conflict here between the interests of national security on the one hand and the freedom of the individual on the other. The balance between these two is not for a court of law. It is for the Home Secretary, he is the person entrusted by Parliament with the task. In some parts of the world National Security has on occasions been used as an excuse for all kinds of infringements of individual liberties. But not in England.'

More recently, however, see *Secretary of State for the Home Department v AF* (2009) at section 6.8.

A somewhat controversial case involving issues concerning the rule of law was the case of *R (Corner House Research) v Director of the Serious Fraud Office* [2008] UKHL 60. In this case the House of Lords held that the Director of the Serious Fraud Office had acted lawfully and within the lawful bounds of his statutory discretion when he discontinued a criminal investigation, as to continue it would not have been in the public interest (ie to protect the British public). On this case see, J Cooper QC, 'The Day We Sold the Rule of Law' in I McDougall (ed), *Cases That Changed Our Lives* (LexisNexis, 2010), p 207.

NB. For judicial criticism of the use of the term/description judicial 'deference', see Lord Hoffmann in *R (ProLife Alliance) v BBC* [2003] UKHL 23.

ACTIVITY

Self-test question

What is wrong with the (albeit rather historical) approach taken by the majority in *Liversidge* (1942)?

The rule of law in the defence of fundamental constitutional principles

As noted at section 4.8.3, in construing legislative provisions, the courts will do so in the light of certain constitutional principles and presumptions. In this way, the courts recognise and uphold the principles which underpin the rule of law.

Retrospective legislation

One constitutional principle is the presumption against retrospective legislation (see sections 4.8.3 and 6.3.2). In *Waddington v Miah* [1974] 2 All ER 377 the House of Lords construed the Immigration Act 1971 so as not to have retrospective criminal effect. Lord Reid drew upon the presumptions that surely Parliament would never pass retrospective criminal legislation or knowingly legislate contrary to international law/Treaties as he stated that:

JUDGMENT

'There has for a very long time been a strong feeling against making legislation, and particularly criminal legislation, retrospective.'

Lord Reid then referred to Art 11 of the Universal Declaration of Human Rights and Art 7 of the European Convention. In this light, he argued:

JUDGMENT

'So it is hardly credible that any government department would promote or that Parliament would pass retrospective criminal legislation.'

Similarly, the House of Lords in *R v Secretary of State for the Home Department, ex parte Pierson* [1998] AC 539 ensured that the Home Secretary's powers of reviewing a tariff to be served by a mandatory life sentence prisoner (s 35 of the Criminal Justice Act 1991), did not, in effect, retrospectively increase his sentence. Lord Steyn noted that:

JUDGMENT

'Unless there is the clearest provision to the contrary, Parliament must be presumed not to legislate contrary to the rule of law. And the rule of law enforces minimum standards of fairness, both substantive and procedural.'

These cases, of course, do not mean that Parliament cannot explicitly pass laws which are retrospective or even contrary to the European Convention. In terms of the former, in 1991 Parliament passed the War Crimes Act, which is retrospective legislation as it relates to atrocities committed during the Second World War in Germany or territories occupied by Germany. Moreover, it is of interest to note that this Act was enacted under the Parliament Acts of 1911 and 1949, as the House of Lords refused to pass it and therefore it was passed without their consent (see section 10.10.2). More recently, see the retrospective effect of s 58 of the Finance Act 2008, which was held to be compatible with Art 1 of the First Protocol of the European Convention (*R (Huitson) v HM Revenue & Customs* [2010] EWHC 97 (Admin)).

The principle of legality

In order to protect the individual, the courts use the doctrine of legality. This precludes legislative interference with the rights/freedoms of citizens unless this is expressly provided for with specific words (this means that general words will be insufficient to achieve this aim). This is illustrated in the following case:

CASE EXAMPLE

R v Secretary of State for the Home Department, ex parte Simms and another *[1999] 3 All ER 400*

O'Brien and Simms had been convicted of murder and claimed to have been the victims of a miscarriage of justice and they sought to reopen their cases through oral interviews with journalists. Under paras 37 and 37A of the Prison Service Standing Order 5A (made under s 47(1) of the Prison Act 1952 and r 33 of the Prison Rules 1964), the prison authorities refused to permit these interviews unless the journalists concerned signed an undertaking not to publish any part of the resulting interviews. The journalists refused to do so and O'Brien and Simms challenged the lawfulness of this prison policy.

The House of Lords held that a blanket ban on interviews of prisoners by journalists was unlawful. The purpose of the interviews was, in effect, to enlist the investigative resources of the journalists to help the prisoners gain access to justice, with the eventual aim of demonstrating that there had been a miscarriage of justice. The court held that a blanket ban, therefore, deprived a prisoner of a basic and fundamental right, that of gaining access to justice. Paragraphs 37 and 37A were to be interpreted in line with the principle of legality, which meant that ambiguous or general words did not override fundamental rights such as the right to gain access to justice (which was in effect a constitutional right). Although the paragraphs themselves were not *ultra vires*, the above policy was unlawful. Lord Steyn stated that:

JUDGMENT

'The starting point is the right of freedom of expression. In a democracy it is the primary right: without it an effective rule of law is not possible. . . . They wish to challenge the safety of their convictions. In principle it is not easy to conceive of a more important function which free speech might fulfil.'

The presumption of innocence

One constitutional principle underpinning the rule of law is the presumption of innocence (ie the burden of proof). In *R v Secretary of State for the Home Department, ex parte Khawaja* [1984] 1 AC 74, the House of Lords stated that, in relation to an application for judicial review of an order detaining an individual under the Immigration Act 1971, it was for the executive/state to prove to the court (on the balance of probabilities) the facts relied upon by an immigration officer as justifying a determination that the person *was* an illegal entrant.

KEY FACTS

Key facts on the British courts and the rule of law

The constitutional function of the judiciary is to uphold the principles underpinning the rule of law.

The courts control the *de facto* use of arbitrary powers by the state (*ex parte Fire Brigades Union* (1995) and *ex parte Bennett* (1994)).

The courts also interpret law in light of certain constitutional principles:
- That legislation should be prospective (*Waddington v Miah* (1974)).
- The principle of legality (*ex parte Simms and another* (1999)).
- The presumption of innocence/burden of proof (*ex parte Khawaja* (1984)).

6.7.11 State power

The past two decades have been punctuated by the successive passage of legislation designed to counter terrorism. These Acts have cumulatively increased the power of the state to interfere with the rights of the individual with the public policy intention of combating terrorism. For example:

- The Terrorism Act 2000 – this Act, in effect, placed counter terrorist powers on a permanent basis (ie not annually reviewed by Parliament as before). In *Beghal v DPP* [2015] UKSC 49 the Supreme Court confirmed that the power under Sch 7 of the 2000 Act to detain and question individuals at ports/border areas for the purposes of determining whether they might be concerned with the commission, preparation or instigation of acts of terrorism, was not incompatible with Art 8 of the European Convention. In contrast, in *R (Miranda) v Secretary of State for the Home Department* [2016] EWCA Civ 6, the Court of Appeal held that the stop power under Sch 7 was incompatible with Art 10 (the right to freedom of expression) in relation to journalistic material/information.
- The Anti-terrorism, Crime and Security Act 2001 (passed in the aftermath of the terrorist attacks of 9/11) – this Act authorised the indefinite detention of non-United Kingdom nationals suspected of being international terrorists. This legislation was successfully challenged in the House of Lords in *A and others v Secretary of State* (2004) (see section 6.7.4), which in turn led to the following Act:
- The Prevention of Terrorism Act 2005 – this Act authorised control orders on individuals which could be used, for example, to restrict their movements (eg a curfew). These control orders were introduced as a result of the successful challenge (above) to the indefinite detention of suspects. The breadth of control orders made under the 2005 Act was then challenged successfully in *Secretary of State for the Home Department v JJ and others* (2007) – see section 13.6.2. In addition,

the failure to disclose sufficient evidence against an individual detained under a control order was challenged successfully in *Secretary of State for the Home Department v AF* (2009) – see section 6.8.

- The Terrorism Act 2006 (passed in the aftermath of the 2005 bombings in London) – this Act extended the length of time that terrorist suspects could be held without charge from 14 to 28 days. As indicated earlier (see section 6.7.5), the Labour government had originally sought a period of detention of 90 days, but the House of Commons refused to accept this. The Act also created an offence of encouraging terrorism (s 1) and one relating to the dissemination of terrorist publications (s 2).
- The Counter-Terrorism Act 2008 – this Act provided for the post-charge questioning of terrorist suspects. The Bill had originally sought powers to allow the detention and questioning of suspects for up to 42 days without charge, but this was abandoned after defeat in the House of Lords (see later at section 10.12).
- The Terrorist Asset-Freezing (Temporary Provisions) Act 2010 – this Act was passed in the context of the decision of the Supreme Court in *HM Treasury v Ahmed* (2010) – see section 20.2.2. This area of law is now covered by the Terrorist Asset-Freezing etc Act 2010, which repealed the earlier temporary Act.
- The Terrorism Prevention and Investigation Measures Act 2011 – this Act abolished the control orders established under the Prevention of Terrorism Act 2005 (s 1 repealed the 2005 Act) and replaced them with Terrorism Prevention and Investigation Measures (TPIMs).
- The Protection of Freedoms Act 2012 – under this Act the maximum period of pre-charge detention for terrorist suspects was reduced to 14 days.
- The Counter-Terrorism and Security Act 2015 – this Act contains a number of elements concerning the government's general strategy for countering terrorism. For example, it includes seizing the passports at the border of individuals suspected of travelling for the purpose of terrorism outside the United Kingdom (Pt 1). Part 5 places the 'Prevent' strategy (ie preventing people from being drawn into terrorist activity) on a statutory basis and it imposes duties on bodies specified in the Act (eg schools).

The following three Acts are also worth noting:

- The Justice and Security Act 2013 – this Act provides for a 'closed material procedure' in civil proceedings whereby sensitive evidence can be heard in closed legal proceedings (ie where the evidence, if publicly disclosed, would damage national security). The Act followed on from the decision in *Al Rawi v Security Service* [2011] UKSC 34 in which the Supreme Court had held that in a civil claim for damages a court could not use a closed material procedure and further that the use of such a procedure would require parliamentary legislation.
- The Data Retention and Investigatory Powers Act 2014 – this legislation was fast-tracked through Parliament and concerned the retention of communications data. The Act had a 'sunset' provision (s 8) providing for the repeal of the Act on 31 December 2016.
- The Investigatory Powers Act 2016 – this Act (originally published in draft form) follows on from the expiry of the above 2014 Act and modernises and reforms the use of surveillance powers by the state (ie the police and security and intelligence agencies). It has been considered somewhat controversial given the wide-ranging nature of its provisions and their impact on the right to privacy.

NB. The preliminary ruling of the Court of Justice of the EU in Case C-203/15 and C-698/15 (Swedish and British joined cases) has raised issues concerning the retention and accessing of communications data.

Finally, according to LIBERTY (an organisation dedicated to the protection of human rights), although a government has a public responsibility to take steps to protect individuals from terrorism, this does not justify encroaching unnecessarily on individual rights and freedoms. The concern of LIBERTY is that legislative measures which confer excessive powers on the state are counterproductive as they risk alienating individuals (thereby acting as a 'recruiting sergeant' for terrorism) and in fact threaten the democratic values which we should be striving as a society to protect.

6.8 Conclusion

The rule of law is a central aspect of the British constitution as it is an essential element of constitutionalism, namely the principle that government and state power must be limited, regulated and controlled. The rule of law is also inextricably linked with the independence of the judiciary as one of the constitutional responsibilities of the judiciary is to uphold the various principles underpinning the rule of law. In particular, a practical demonstration of the rule of law is illustrated every time a judge in judicial review proceedings in the Administrative Court holds the executive and public bodies legally to account for the misuse of their public law powers. This reaffirms the principle that all bodies, and in particular the government, are under the law.

In fact, the importance attached to the principle of the rule of law was recently given statutory recognition in s 1 of the Constitutional Reform Act 2005:

SECTION

1. This Act does not adversely affect –
   (a) the existing constitutional principle of the rule of law, or
   (b) the Lord Chancellor's existing constitutional role in relation to that principle.

NB. In *FP (Iran) v Secretary of State for the Home Department* [2007] EWCA Civ 13 the Court of Appeal recognised that the 2005 Act had not defined the rule of law (Arden, LJ).

For example, traditionally the Lord Chancellor would try to ensure that the principles underpinning the rule of law (eg safeguarding the rights of the individual) were respected when, for example, draft legislative measures were being considered in Cabinet. In addition, s 17 of the Act details the oath to be taken by the Lord Chancellor, which specifies that the incumbent must respect the rule of law (see section 5.7.9). More recently, para 6.4 of *The Cabinet Manual* makes it plain that part of the core function of the law officers (see earlier at section 5.7.6) is to help ministers act in accordance with the rule of law.

In 'The rule of law' (2007) 66 CLJ 67, Lord Bingham rather usefully identified the following eight principles/rules:

- The law must be accessible, intelligible, clear and predictable.
- Questions of legal right and liability should be resolved (ordinarily) by the application of the law and not by the exercise of discretion.
- Laws should apply equally.
- Law should afford adequate protection of (fundamental) human rights.
- Means should be provided for resolving civil disputes.
- Public officers and ministers must exercise their powers reasonably, in good faith, for their proper purpose and without exceeding their limits.
- State adjudicative proceedings should be fair.
- The state must comply with its obligations in international law.

The following is an interesting case in which the rule of law was invoked:

CASE EXAMPLE

Secretary of State for the Home Department v AF *[2009] UKHL 28*

Under s 2 of the Prevention of Terrorism Act 2005 the Secretary of State made a non-derogating control order against AF (and others). The House of Lords held that in terms of Art 6 (the right to a fair trial) the 'controlled' individual had to be given sufficient information about the case/allegations against him.

Lord Hope said:

JUDGMENT

'If the rule of law is to mean anything, it is in cases such as these that the court must stand by principle. It must insist that the person affected be told what is alleged against him.'

As a postscript to the case, in *Secretary of State for the Home Department v AF* [2010] EWHC 42 (Admin) the Administrative Court quashed AF's control order (with retrospective effect).

See also, *R (Mohamed) v Secretary of State for Foreign and Commonwealth Affairs* [2010] EWCA Civ 65 (for the facts, see section 13.6.2).

In conclusion, in considering the rule of law, the following two comments are worth recording:

QUOTATION

'The rule of law may not be, as a former President of the Supreme Court told us, readily defined or readily understood. It remains, as the committee has previously stated, a complex and in some respects uncertain concept. Yet it is also perhaps the single most important characteristic of a democratic nation.'

Lord Lang of Monkton (Chair of the House of Lords Select Committee on the Constitution), *Hansard*, HL Vol 764, col 105.

QUOTATION

'Ultimately, it is the rule of law which stops a democracy descending into an elected dictatorship.'

Lord Woolf, 'The rule of law and a change in the constitution' (2004) 63 CLJ 317.

SUMMARY

- The rule of law is a concept of some antiquity.
- The rule of law has been subject to a number of different interpretations ranging from a legal principle which ensures that government acts under the law to a political ideal/theory which focuses on a formal conception of the principle and the form that laws should take (Raz). The rule of law can be also viewed as a substantive concept as well as being used in an international context.
- The rule of law is a key element of constitutionalism ensuring that government officials act strictly within their powers and the courts play a crucial role in holding the executive to account.

- The rule of law in the United Kingdom is closely associated with Dicey, who expounded the following principles:
  - That no man was punishable except for a distinct breach of the law as established in ordinary legal proceedings before a court.
  - The predominance of regular law over the exercise of arbitrary power (including wide discretionary power).
  - No man is above the law – equality before the law.
  - The United Kingdom has a court-based constitution in that the freedoms of the individual were the direct consequences of the decisions made by the judiciary.
- Dicey's principles, though persuasive, have been subject to criticism:
  - Individuals can suffer without violating the law.
  - Discretion is necessary in a modern state (although it is regulated by the courts).
  - There are exceptions to the principle of equality (eg parliamentarians) and the development of judicial review is akin to the French *tribunaux administratifs*.
  - The Human Rights Act 1998 has created positive rights (albeit they are enforced before the courts).

SAMPLE ESSAY QUESTION

What is meant by the rule of law in the context of constitutional law?

Introduction:
- Note the rule of law as a concept with different meanings.
- In essence, it means government acting under the law and that all are subject to the law.
- The rule of law also ensures social order.

The rule of law as a legal principle:
- The principle is seen as a procedural mechanism checking the executive/state, whereby the actions of public officials should have a foundation in law (*Jones* (2005)).
- Note the limitation of this principle (link to the substantive concept of the principle below).

A formal view of the rule of law:
- Raz's formal conception concerning the form that laws should take (prospective, clear, open, stable etc).

The rule of law as a substantive concept:
- Link the rule of law with certain fundamental values and human rights (eg the presumption of innocence).

> **The international dimension of the rule of law:**
> - Universal Declaration of Human Rights and the European Convention (on the latter see, *Gillan* (2010)).

> **The rule of law in the UK:**
> Dicey's three principles:
> 1. Individuals only punished for a distinct breach of the law and the predominance of regular law as opposed to arbitrary power (*A and Others* (2004)).
> 2. Equality under the law (*M v Home Office* (1994)).
> 3. The rights of individuals are the consequence of judicial decisions (*Entick* (1765)) but now see the Human Rights Act 1998.
>
> Note the criticism of Dicey and the application/relevance of his principles today.

> **The courts and the rule of law:**
> - Note the constitutional role of the judiciary to uphold the rule of law and limit executive power (*Bennett* (1994) and *Fire Brigades Union* (1995)).
> - Also see the cases involving the powers of the state under terrorism legislation (*JJ* (2007) and *AF* (2009)).

> **Conclusion**

Further reading

Books

Allison, J, *The English historical constitution* (Cambridge University Press, 2007), Chapters 7 and 8.

Barnett, H, *Constitutional and Administrative Law* (12th edn, Routledge/Taylor & Francis Group, 2017), Chapter 3.

Lord Bingham, *The Rule of Law* (Allen Lane, 2010).

Bradley, A, Ewing, K and Knight, C, *Constitutional and Administrative Law* (16th edn, Pearson, 2015), Chapter 4.

Craig, P, 'Fundamental principles of administrative law in relation to basic principles of constitutional law' in Feldman, D (ed), *English Public Law* (2nd edn, Oxford University Press, 2009), p 600.

Jowell, J, 'The Rule of Law' in Jowell, J, Oliver, D and O'Cinneide, C (eds), *The Changing Constitution* (8th edn, Oxford University Press, 2015), p 13.

Waldron, J, 'The rule of law in public law' in Elliott, M and Feldman, D (eds), *Public law* (Cambridge University Press, 2015), p 56.

For a more comparative perspective, see Krygier, M, 'Rule of law' in Rosenfeld, M and Sajo, A (eds), *The Oxford Handbook of Comparative Constitutional Law* (Oxford University Press, 2013), p 233.

Articles
Lord Bingham, 'Dicey revisited' [2002] PL 39.
Lord Bingham, 'The rule of law' (2007) 66 CLJ 67.
Foster, S, 'The fight against terrorism, detention without trial and human rights' (2009) 14 *Coventry Law Journal*, 3.
Majid, A, 'Do we care about the rule of law?' (2005) 155 NLJ 1561.
Raz, J, 'The rule of law and its virtue' (1977) 93 LQR 195.
Lord Steyn, 'Democracy, the rule of law and the role of judges' [2006] EHRLR 243.
Lord Woolf, 'Droit public-English style' [1995] PL 57.

Paper
Kassamali, A, *Judges Keep Out: Off-the-Bench Influence on the UK's Anti-terror Regime* (Constitution Unit, 2016).

7

Parliamentary sovereignty

AIMS AND OBJECTIVES

At the end of this chapter you should be able to:

- Define the term parliamentary sovereignty
- Identify and explain Dicey's conception of parliamentary sovereignty
- Identify and explain the different aspects of parliamentary sovereignty
- Explain how parliamentary sovereignty relates to other aspects of the British constitution
- Explain the constitutional importance of parliamentary sovereignty

7.1 Introduction

Parliamentary sovereignty is the central element of the British constitution and it is impossible to understand the nature and mechanics of the constitution without an appreciation of this principle. In fact, this doctrine sets the British constitution apart from the vast majority of other democratic states. For example, although the legislative bodies of the United States (the Congress) and the Republic of Ireland (the Oireachtas) are law-making bodies which pass primary legislation, these legislatures do not have unlimited law-making powers as they are constitutionally and legally constrained by their respective written codified constitutions. For example, Art 15.4 of the Irish Constitution states that the Oireachtas shall not enact legislation 'which is in any respect repugnant' to the constitution. In other words, if either of these two legislatures were to pass legislation which was inconsistent with the rules laid down in their respective codified constitutions, it would be subject to judicial review (constitutional review) by their Supreme Courts. That is to say, the legislation would be declared to be legally unconstitutional (in contrast, see section 4.16) and so invalid.

By contrast, in the United Kingdom the Queen in Parliament (or Crown in Parliament) can in legal theory pass any law and the legislation which is enacted is not subject to judicial review by the courts. This is because – in historic terms – Parliament has not been constrained by a higher set of legal rules enshrined in a written British constitution. In other words, Acts of Parliament (unlike Acts of the United States Congress or the Irish Oireachtas) could not be tested or questioned against an overriding codified constitution (however, the position in relation to European Union law will be considered at section 15.6). Indeed, as Bogdanor has observed:

QUOTATION

'The British Constitution could thus be summed up in just eight words: "What the Queen in Parliament enacts is law".'

The New British Constitution (Hart Publishing, 2009), p 13.

Although in the United Kingdom the courts, historically, have not subjected Acts of Parliament to judicial review, they do review and invalidate delegated legislation made by the executive. This is because this type of legislation (eg statutory instruments) does not enjoy the sovereign status of primary legislation as it has not been passed by the legislature, but rather by the executive (see section 5.7.2). Finally, although the principle of a legislature with the legal power to make any law that it chooses is very unusual, it is not unique. New Zealand also has an uncodified constitution, which comprises a Parliament (a unicameral legislature called the House of Representatives) which possesses the constitutional characteristic of sovereignty. As in the United Kingdom, it too is able to pass any law that it chooses.

7.2 Terminology

The term parliamentary sovereignty (which denotes that the Queen in Parliament has unlimited legislative power) is arguably apt to mislead, because the term 'sovereignty' can have another meaning. Sovereignty is also used in the context of international law, relations and politics to indicate that a state is independent and sovereign (for example, France or Italy). As a consequence, a number of legal academics prefer to use the term the legislative supremacy of Parliament. Notwithstanding this, as parliamentary sovereignty (at least in historic terms) is closely associated with Dicey, and as he used this term, this book will do likewise. This should not be problematic providing we understand the sense in which the term is being used, namely to denote the legal and constitutional principle that Parliament can in theory pass any law that it chooses.

As indicated earlier, Dicey argued that the constitution was founded on the following twin pillars:

- The rule of law and
- Parliamentary sovereignty.

In respect of the term sovereignty, he specifically differentiated between:

- Legal sovereignty and
- Political sovereignty.

7.2.1 Legal sovereignty

In essence, legal sovereignty is concerned with the legislative power of the Queen in Parliament (the principle that any legislation can be made on any subject). Legal sovereignty is concerned with the constitutional relationship between the courts and the legislature (hence it is therefore necessarily an issue of constitutional significance). It is with legal sovereignty that this chapter is specifically concerned. Legal sovereignty relates to Bills which have been consented to (and therefore have become Acts of Parliament) by the following three constitutional elements:

- The House of Commons.
- The House of Lords (providing the Parliament Acts of 1911 and 1949 do not apply – see section 10.10.1).
- The monarch (the Royal Assent).

Legal sovereignty is not concerned with the political machinations within Parliament which led to the passing of an Act. It is not therefore concerned with the scenario, for example, whereby a highly controversial Bill only narrowly passed through both Houses.

7.2.2 Political sovereignty

In contrast, political sovereignty rests with the people (the electorate), for, as Dicey noted, the electorate can 'always enforce their will'. By this he meant that, politically, Parliament (or more specifically the House of Commons and so, by extension, the government) is accountable directly to the people at every general election. In a sense, therefore, this is analogous to a social contract between the governed (specifically the electorate) and the state, whereby the people at a general election confer power and constitutional legitimacy on Parliament to legislate.

Logically therefore, as Parliament can legally pass any law it chooses, this could include a draconian law breaching the basic rights and freedoms of the individual. Such legislation would, however, be unlikely to be passed as, ultimately, parliamentarians serving in the House of Commons would have to face the electorate at the next general election. Political sovereignty, therefore, places external, political restraints on the legislation that the Queen in Parliament will actually enact in practice.

As a fascinating aside, it should be pointed out that, although Dicey is closely associated with parliamentary sovereignty, he also approved of selective referendums in order to give effect to the will of the people, albeit as a negative device (ie a 'bridle'). He recognised that, on occasions, the House of Commons may not be in line with the general views of the public (A V Dicey, 'Ought the referendum to be introduced into England?' (1890) 57 *Contemporary Review* 489 and 'The referendum and its critics' (1910) 212 *Quarterly Review* 538).

KEY FACTS

Key facts on the definition of sovereignty

- Legal sovereignty is concerned with the legal relationship between Parliament and the courts.

- Political sovereignty is concerned with the political relationship between Parliament (specifically the House of Commons and by extension the government) and the people (the electorate).

7.3 The meaning and scope of legal sovereignty

7.3.1 Introduction

Parliamentary sovereignty means simply that the Queen in Parliament legally can pass any law as the courts do not have the constitutional power to invalidate Acts and declare them to be legally unconstitutional (see section 4.16) or even illegal (but now see in the context of European Union law at section 15.6).

In essence, as made clear by Lord Diplock in *Duport Steels Ltd and others v Sirs and others* [1980] 1 All ER 529, 'Parliament makes the laws, the judiciary interpret them'. In fact, this constitutional interaction between the two arms of the state has been described by Lord Bridge in *X Ltd v Morgan-Grampian (Publishers) Ltd* [1991] 1 AC 1 in terms of a 'twin sovereignty':

JUDGMENT

'In our society the rule of law rests upon twin foundations: the sovereignty of the Queen in Parliament in making the law and the sovereignty of the Queen's courts in interpreting and applying the law.'

7.3.2 The origins of parliamentary sovereignty

In other countries, citizens can date accurately the origin and promulgation of their written codified constitution (eg the Indian Constitution was declared passed in November 1949 and came into force on 26 January 1950). In contrast, in view of the fact that parliamentary sovereignty is the central element of the British constitution, it is perhaps surprising that the exact origin of this principle is not only not clear, but actively contested. For many, parliamentary sovereignty is simply a common law doctrine. For example, in terms of the origin of the principle, Lord Steyn in *R (Jackson) v Attorney General* [2005] UKHL 56 argued that:

JUDGMENT

'It is a construct of the common law. The judges created this principle.' (See his further comments at section 7.7.)

In the same case, Lord Hope stated that 'in the absence of higher authority' the common law had created the principle of parliamentary sovereignty.

However, Lord Bingham, writing extra-judicially a few years later, commentated that:

QUOTATION

'I cannot for my part accept that my colleagues' observations are correct. It is true of course that the principle of parliamentary sovereignty cannot without circularity be ascribed to statute, and the historical record in any event reveals no such statute. But it does not follow that the principle must be a creature of the judge-made common law which the judges can alter; if it were, the rule could be altered by statute, since the prime characteristic of any common law rule is that it yields to a contrary provision of statute. To my mind, it has been convincingly shown that the principle of parliamentary sovereignty has been recognized as fundamental in this country not because the judges invented it but because it has for centuries been accepted as such by judges and others officially concerned in the operation of our constitutional system. The judges did not by themselves establish the principle and they cannot, by themselves, change it.'

Lord Bingham, The Rule of Law (Allen Lane, 2010), p 167.

Finally, some 60 years ago Wade made the following point:

QUOTATION

'The rule of judicial obedience is in one sense a rule of common law, but in another sense – which applies to no other rule of common law – it is the ultimate *political* fact upon which the whole system of legislation hangs. Legislation owes its authority to the rule: the rule does not owe its authority to legislation. To say that Parliament can change the rule, merely because it can change any other rule, is to put the cart before the horse.'

H Wade, 'The basis of legal sovereignty' [1955] CLJ 172.

What is clear is that, whatever the provenance of the principle of parliamentary sovereignty, its origins are not democratic as they clearly predate any notion of representative democracy and universal suffrage/voting.

The following case neatly illustrates the principle of parliamentary sovereignty:

CASE EXAMPLE

Cheney v Conn *[1968] 1 WLR 242*

Cheney was assessed for tax under the Finance Act 1964. Cheney challenged his tax assessments on the basis that part of the allocated use of these taxes (ie the construction of nuclear weapons with the intention to use them if necessary) was contrary to international law.

The High Court (Chancery Division) held that the charge to tax under the Act and the tax assessments were not invalidated. Even if there was a conflict between international law and statute, where the latter's provisions were clear and unambiguous, it would prevail. Ungoed-Thomas J stated that:

JUDGMENT

'If the purpose for which a statute may be used is an invalid purpose, then such remedy as there may be must be directed to dealing with that purpose and not to invalidating the statute itself. What the statute itself enacts cannot be unlawful, because what the statute says and provides is itself the law, and the highest form of law that is known to this country. It is the law which prevails over every other form of law, and it is not for the court to say that a parliamentary enactment, the highest law in this country, is illegal.'

ACTIVITY

Applying the law

Do you think that it is logically impossible for the principle of parliamentary sovereignty to have been established in an Act of Parliament?

7.3.3 What constitutes an Act of Parliament?

As the principle of parliamentary sovereignty necessitates that the courts obey and apply Acts of Parliament, this in turn begs the question as to what exactly is an Act of Parliament.

In identifying what constitutes an Act of Parliament, historically the courts have applied the 'enrolled Bill rule' as stated by Lord Campbell in the following case:

CASE EXAMPLE

Edinburgh and Dalkeith Railway Co v Wauchope *(1842) 8 C1 & F 710*

Wauchope unsuccessfully argued that a statute (a private Act of Parliament) should be disapplied because the standing orders of the House of Commons had not been complied with. These orders had required that individuals affected by the proposed legislation were to be consulted. In terms of a Bill's passage through Parliament, Lord Campbell in the House of Lords noted (albeit *obiter*) that:

JUDGMENT

'All that a court of justice can look to is the parliamentary roll; they see that an Act has passed both Houses of Parliament, and that it has received the Royal Assent, and no court of justice can inquire into the manner in which it was introduced into Parliament, what was done previously to its being introduced, or what passed in Parliament during the various stages of its progress through both Houses of Parliament.'

Thus, the judges will simply look to the 'parliamentary roll' to ascertain whether or not a Bill has become an Act of Parliament. The judiciary will not be concerned with the internal process and passage of that Bill within Parliament as that would inevitably contravene parliamentary privilege, which dictates that Parliament has the constitutional right to determine and monitor its own proceedings (see section 8.7.2). In referring to the parliamentary roll, the procedure adopted by the courts would be as follows:

The enrolled Bill rule

- Has the Bill received the consent of the House of Commons?
- Has the Bill received the consent of the House of Lords?
- Has the Bill been granted the Royal Assent?

If the answer to all three questions is yes, the Bill is treated as an Act of Parliament. The courts, therefore, are not concerned with how (or more pertinently, why) the Bill came to be on the parliamentary roll (on this point, see also *Pickin* at section 7.8.1). As noted by Bradley, however, today the courts do not need to consult the parliamentary roll as the words of enactment at the beginning of a statute will indicate this information (House of Lords Select Committee on the Constitution, Seventh Report of Session 2005–06, *Constitutional aspects of the challenge to the Hunting Act 2004*, HL 141 (2006), Appendix 3).

ACTIVITY

Self-test question

What constitutional problems (if any) would arise if the courts were to investigate how a Bill proceeded through Parliament? Revisit your answer after reading Chapter 8.

As it is the Queen in Parliament who makes Acts of Parliament, it is clear that a 'mere' resolution of the House of Commons is not an Act of Parliament as it does not alter the law nor does it have sovereign status (*Stockdale v Hansard* (1839) 9 Ad & El 1; *Bowles v Bank of England* [1913] 1 Ch 57). Thus, it should be remembered that technically it is an Act of Parliament enacted by Parliament which is sovereign, rather than Parliament itself. In the context of what constitutes an Act of Parliament, see also the *Jackson* case at sections 7.10.3 and 10.10.3.

KEY FACTS

Key facts on parliamentary sovereignty

- Parliamentary sovereignty means that in legal theory the Queen in Parliament can legally pass any law.

- One (albeit contested) view of parliamentary sovereignty is that it is a construct of the common law.

- In determining what constitutes an Act of Parliament, historically the judges would look to the 'parliamentary roll' to ascertain whether or not a Bill had become an Act of Parliament. The judiciary would not be concerned with the internal process of the Bill through Parliament (*Edinburgh and Dalkeith Railway v Wauchope* (1842)).

7.4 Dicey and parliamentary sovereignty

Dicey viewed the principle of parliamentary sovereignty as the cornerstone of the constitution and described it in the following terms:

QUOTATION

'The principle of Parliamentary sovereignty means neither more nor less than this, namely, that Parliament thus defined has, under the English constitution, the right to make or unmake any law whatever; and, further, that no person or body is recognised by the law of England as having a right to override or set aside the legislation of Parliament.'

A Dicey, *Introduction to the Study of the Law of the Constitution* (10th edn, Macmillan, 1959), pp 39–40.

Dicey viewed parliamentary sovereignty as having both positive and negative elements.

- The positive aspect was that the Crown/Queen in Parliament can legally pass any law that it chooses (with one exception – see principle 3 below).
- The negative aspect was that no court or other body can question a statute.

Dicey's conception is considered below in the following three interconnected elements/principles:

Figure 7.1 Dicey and parliamentary sovereignty

7.5 Principle 1: The Queen in Parliament can legally pass any law

This in essence embodies the positive element of parliamentary sovereignty, namely that the Queen in Parliament can, in legal theory, pass any law (including the repeal or modification of any existing primary legislation). Parliament can pass any law it considers necessary because under the British constitution there is, legally, nothing (ie a codified constitution) to stop Parliament from doing so.

7.5.1 Parliamentary sovereignty and the common law

In the United Kingdom's three legal systems (see section 3.1) there is a hierarchy of laws with Acts of Parliament (statutory sources) being higher in legal status than the common law. In short, where the content of the common law and a statute are inconsistent, the latter will prevail. This means that, should Parliament decide to do so, it can legislate to override (or codify) the common law, as illustrated in the context of the law of tort, when in 1987 Parliament passed the Consumer Protection Act. In fact, this Act was passed in order to comply with a European Union directive, thereby also demonstrating the influence European law has had on the British constitution (see Chapter 15).

Similarly, in the context of the royal prerogative (a power which the government derives from the common law – see section 11.9), Parliament can, if it chooses to do so, legislate in an area already covered by the royal prerogative. In these circumstances, the resulting statutory provisions will take precedence over the royal prerogative and thereafter the government would be required to act in accordance with the new statutory provision rather than the pre-existing royal prerogative. As Lord Dunedin stated in *Attorney-General v De Keyser's Royal Hotel Ltd* [1920] AC 508 (see section 11.9.5):

JUDGMENT

'If the whole ground of something which could be done by the prerogative is covered by the statute, it is the statute that rules.'

In addition, as noted at section 4.9, in *Burmah Oil Company Ltd* (1965) the House of Lords had determined that, although the destruction of the oil installations in Burma during the Second World War was permissible under the royal prerogative, it nevertheless necessitated compensation for the damage caused. In direct response to this judgment, Parliament in 1965 passed the War Damage Act, which in effect nullified the above decision of the House of Lords. More recently, the Criminal Evidence (Witness Anonymity) Act 2008 abolished the restrictive common law rules on witness anonymity during a criminal trial as set out in the judgment of the House of Lords in *R v Davies* [2008] UKHL 36. In 2013 s 33 of the Crime and Courts Act 2013 abolished the common law offence of scandalising the judiciary/court. In short, therefore, the common law can be overridden by an Act of Parliament at any time. This in itself raises an interesting constitutional question: if the principle of parliamentary sovereignty is a 'construct' and rule of the common law, can Parliament legislate to change this common law rule espousing parliamentary sovereignty? (see section 7.10 and Lord Bingham earlier at section 7.3.2).

7.5.2 Parliamentary sovereignty and the law-making process

Parliament has legislated to alter the law-making process for passing primary legislation. In so doing, it has changed the legal and constitutional relationship between the two Houses of Parliament. As will be explored in more detail at section 10.10.1, the combined effect of the Parliament Acts of 1911 and 1949 is that the House of Lords can delay the enactment of a Bill for approximately one year. As a result, after 1911 a Bill could become an Act of Parliament without the consent of one of the constituent elements of the 'Crown in Parliament': the House of Lords. The Parliament Acts, therefore, have altered the passage of primary legislation within Parliament and rendered the consent of the House of Lords theoretically unnecessary in respect of those Bills passed under its provisions.

In addition, through the Parliament Acts, Parliament has altered the judicial perception of what amounts to an Act of Parliament. When the Parliament Acts are involved (which in itself is rare), the consent that the courts require in order to be satisfied that a Bill has become an Act is simply that it has received the consent of the following two elements:

- The House of Commons.
- The monarch (via the granting of the Royal Assent).

7.5.3 Parliamentary sovereignty and the interpretation of legislation

One constitutional role of the judiciary is to interpret Acts of Parliament with a view to ascertaining the intention of Parliament. Over time the judges have developed certain judicial guidelines for construing legislative provisions. In addition,

Parliament has provided express statutory guidance to the courts as to how to construe legislation. For example, s 6(a) of the Interpretation Act 1978 states that unless the contrary intention is indicated in a statute: 'words importing the masculine gender include the feminine'.

More recently Parliament passed the Human Rights Act 1998 which, in effect, is an interpretation Act governing how all legislation (pre and post 1998) should be interpreted. It expressly directs the judiciary to interpret wherever possible all legislation in line with the articles of the European Convention on Human Rights:

SECTION

Interpretation of legislation

s 3(1)

So far as it is possible to do so, primary legislation and subordinate legislation must be read and given effect in a way which is compatible with the Convention rights.

This mandatory provision imposes a new statutory obligation on the judiciary instructing them how to interpret legislation affecting human rights. In effect, it requires the judiciary to ensure that the interpretation of the legislative provision before them is consistent and compatible with the articles of the European Convention (unless the words of the legislation cannot bear such a meaning and instead a declaration of incompatibility may be given under s 4 (see section 17.7)).

This raises the extent to which s 3 has affected the constitutional role of the judiciary, whereby judges have construed legislation in such a way as to blur the constitutional line between interpretation and legislation. For a case in which it is arguable that the judges may well have crossed this boundary and *de facto* legislated, see s 41 of the Youth Justice and Criminal Evidence Act 1999 in *R v A (Complainant's sexual history)* [2001] UKHL 25 (see section 17.6.1).

Moreover, s 2 of the Human Rights Act 1998 states that a court in the context of applying a Convention right must take into account, *inter alia*, any judgment of the European Court of Human Rights. This provision, therefore, specifically directs the judiciary to consider the jurisprudence of the European Convention in Strasbourg when interpreting legislation.

The Human Rights Act 1998 has clearly altered the way in which the judiciary interprets United Kingdom legislation. Indeed, in *R v A* Lord Hope has described s 3 as:

JUDGMENT

'quite unlike any previous rule of statutory interpretation. There is no need to identify an ambiguity or absurdity. Compatibility with convention rights is the sole guiding principle . . . But the rule is only a rule of interpretation. It does not entitle the judges to act as legislators.'

Parliament could, of course, legally repeal this Act, thereby relieving the judiciary of this statutory interpretative obligation. As indicated at section 7.12, however, it would appear that the Act could only be repealed on an express basis, and not on an implied one.

7.5.4 Parliamentary sovereignty and the constitution

As Parliament can, in law, pass any primary legislation that it chooses, this necessarily means that it can pass any law which alters, whether incrementally or radically, the nature of the United Kingdom's uncodified constitution. As noted earlier at section 3.4.5, the United Kingdom has a flexible constitution. In other countries with a codified rigid constitution (eg the United States), in order for the constitution to be altered, a special procedure – stipulated in the constitutional document – has to be complied with (see section 2.5.2).

In contrast, in the United Kingdom the rules of the constitution do not have special or entrenched legal status and can therefore be altered by Parliament at will. As a consequence, Parliament can simply amend the British constitution by passing a Bill through the ordinary parliamentary legislative process like any non-constitutional Bill (although, by constitutional convention, first-class constitutional Bills in the House of Commons are considered on the Floor of the House – see section 12.7.3). Even though a Bill may have profound, far-reaching constitutional implications, no special majority is needed within Parliament (nor does it need to be supported by the people in a referendum) for the Bill to become an Act. Moreover, even though the resulting Act may radically reshape the United Kingdom's constitutional arrangements, and no matter how politically controversial it is, the courts are, legally, disabled from challenging or invalidating the Act. In legal theory, therefore, Parliament can reform the constitution in any way it sees fit.

A few examples will suffice to demonstrate the principle that Parliament can alter any aspect of the British constitution and it is pertinent to note the comments in 2000 of the Royal Commission on the reform of the House of Lords which stated that, in relation to the then 1997 Labour government's initial batch of constitutional reforms, such measures:

QUOTATION

'would have been impossible under the laborious systems required to amend the written constitutions of many other countries'.

A House for the Future Cm 4534
(The Stationery Office, 2000), para 5.2.

Detailed below are some key constitutional changes since 1997:

- **The Scotland Act 1998** (this Act devolved power to Scotland – see section 14.3).
- **The House of Lords Act 1999** (this Act removed most of the hereditary peers from the House of Lords – see section 10.6.3).
- **The European Parliamentary Elections Act 1999** (this Act altered the electoral system used to elect MEPs to the European Parliament from the **'first past the post'** system to one in which elections took place on the basis of a proportional party list system).
- **The Constitutional Reform Act 2005** (this Act created a Supreme Court for the United Kingdom – see section 5.7.10).
- **The Constitutional Reform and Governance Act 2010** (this Act placed the Civil Service on a statutory basis – see section 11.3.1).
- **The Recall of MPs Act 2015** (this Act made provision for constituents to trigger a by-election for the seat of their local MP).

'first past the post'

the electoral system used to elect representatives in which the candidate with the most votes in a constituency wins the seat

In effect, therefore, no aspect of the constitution is technically unalterable by Parliament (but see section 7.7). In fact, in 1996 Parliament (rather controversially) amended Art 9 of the Bill of Rights Act 1689 with the enactment of s 13 of the Defamation Act 1996 (see section 8.6.2). A further example of a major constitutional change being effected by statute is the Local Government Act 1985, which abolished the Greater London Council (the GLC) and metropolitan councils in London. It demonstrated graphically that local government in the context of the British constitution does not enjoy 'constitutional status' in the sense that it does not have any special constitutional or legal protection from the legislature (see section 14.2.5).

In addition, Parliament can choose to lengthen or shorten the life of a Parliament. For example, the Septennial Act 1715 stipulated that the maximum length of a parliamentary term was seven years (it had previously been three years under the Triennial Act 1694). At the beginning of the twentieth century, s 7 of the Parliament Act 1911 reduced this period to five years. Today the Fixed-Term Parliaments Act 2011 provides that there will be five years in between general elections.

Thus, as Parliament can (at least in legal theory) seemingly alter any aspect of the British constitution, this begs the question as to whether parliamentary sovereignty is consistent with constitutionalism (see sections 2.6, 7.6 and 7.13). Also see Ridley's criticism at section 3.2.4.

ACTIVITY

Self-test question

What are the advantages and disadvantages of Parliament being able to reform the constitution through the passage of a simple Act of Parliament?

7.5.5 Parliamentary sovereignty and international law

Parliament can pass legislation which breaches international law. This was illustrated earlier in *Cheney v Conn* (1968) (see section 7.3.2) and the following case, which demonstrates the same point:

CASE EXAMPLE

Mortensen v Peters *(1906) 14 SLT 227*

A byelaw was passed (by the Fishery Board for Scotland) under s 7 of the Herring Fishery (Scotland) Act 1889 which prohibited trawling within the Moray Firth (part of the Moray Firth is an area beyond British territorial waters). Mortensen (a Danish captain of a Norwegian trawler) was convicted in a Scottish Sheriff Court for violating the above byelaw. Mortensen's appeal was based, *inter alia*, on international law, which permits a state to regulate fishing within its territorial waters; however, Mortensen had been arrested in that part of the Moray Firth which was outside British territorial waters.

The High Court of Justiciary held that the intention of Parliament in the 1889 Act was to allow byelaws to be passed covering the Moray Firth, even if this was contrary to the rules of international law as part of the Moray Firth is in international waters.

JUDGMENT

'For us an Act of Parliament duly passed by Lords and Commons and assented to by the King, is supreme, and we are bound to give effect to its terms.'

The Lord Justice-General.

Even in the context of the European Convention on Human Rights, and irrespective of the Human Rights Act 1998, Parliament can in legal theory if it chooses to do so (though politically unlikely), legislate contrary to the articles enshrined in the European Convention (see later at section 7.12).

Notwithstanding the general rule above, Parliament is constrained in the context of international law by the international Treaties which the United Kingdom has signed. For example, in respect of the European Convention, Art 1 states that:

ARTICLE

'The High Contracting Parties shall secure to everyone within their jurisdiction the rights and freedoms defined in Section I of this Convention.'

As a result, Parliament has tried to avoid passing legislation which violates the rights set out in the Convention, thereby honouring (in international law) the United Kingdom's international obligations in respect of this Treaty. Although in strict legal theory Parliament could deliberately and flagrantly legislate contrary to these articles (irrespective of its obligations in international law to protect such rights), the consequences of such legislation would involve criticism of the United Kingdom in the Council of Europe together with possible expulsion from it (see section 4.16.2).

In addition, whilst the United Kingdom is still a member of the European Union, Parliament could still (in strict legal theory) pass legislation which expressly contravenes and repudiates European Union law principles (see section 15.6.5).

It is worth noting that, although Parliament passes laws on its own volition (albeit invariably under the impetus and direction of the government of the day), it will also pass legislation in order to fulfil its international obligations. For example, when the European Court of Human Rights has declared that a law in the United Kingdom is inconsistent with the Convention, Parliament will invariably introduce legislation in order to remedy this defect, as in international law it is required to fulfil the requirements set out by the court in Strasbourg. The Contempt of Court Act 1981 is an example of this. This legislation regulates freedom of expression (eg of the press) pending and during a court hearing. It was passed in response to a ruling of the European Court that the common law of contempt of court had unnecessarily infringed freedom of speech (*Sunday Times v UK* (1979) 2 EHRR 245). In short, Parliament passed this legislation as a direct result of external pressure, namely the United Kingdom's international obligation to comply with a ruling of the European Court of Human Rights. Similarly, in the context of European Union law, Parliament will pass laws in response to European directives. For example, the Data Protection Act 1998 was enacted as a result of a directive.

7.5.6 Parliamentary sovereignty and extra-territorial jurisdiction

In legal theory, Parliament can enact legislation which purports to have extra-territorial effect. In other words, it could legislate for outside the legal jurisdiction of the United Kingdom (see *Mortensen* (1906) at section 7.5.5). The classic example to illustrate this has been put forward by Sir Ivor Jennings (*The Law and the Constitution* (5th edn, Hodder and Stoughton, 1959), pp 170–171). He theorised that Parliament could, in legal theory, pass legislation banning smoking on the streets of Paris (as an aside, in the Health Act 2006 Parliament did legislate to ban smoking in public places and shared work places in the United Kingdom). In fact, Parliament has legislated for territory outside of the United Kingdom: The War Crimes Act 1991. This Act has extra-territorial effect as it concerns murder, manslaughter or culpable homicide committed by a British citizen (or resident in the United Kingdom) in Germany or an area under German occupation between 1939–45. The Act was passed under the Parliament Acts 1911 and 1949 as the House of Lords refused to pass it. In particular, peers were concerned that the Act had criminal retrospective effect (on retrospective laws, see section 6.3.2) and there were reservations about the reliability of evidence dating back 50 years. In addition, s 134 of the Criminal Justice Act 1988 provides that a public official can commit the offence of torture 'in the United Kingdom or *elsewhere*' (emphasis added).

ACTIVITY

Self-test question

Could the United Kingdom Parliament legislate for the Republic of Ireland?

7.5.7 Parliamentary sovereignty and the conferring of powers onto the executive

Parliament can legislate to confer wide discretionary powers on the executive. As noted earlier in *Inland Revenue Commissioners and another v Rossminster Ltd and Others* [1980] AC 952 (see section 6.7.5), s 20C of the Taxes Management Act 1970 conferred very wide powers on Inland Revenue officers to search premises. In this case Lord Scarman lamented that, as the Act had been complied with:

JUDGMENT

'It is therefore with regret that I have to accept that, if the requirements of section 20C of the Taxes Management Act 1970 . . . are met, the power exists to enter, and search premises, and seize and remove things there found and that the prospect of an immediate judicial review of the exercise of the power is dim.'

Today such a provision could be challenged under the Human Rights Act 1998 (see Chapter 17).

In fact, Parliament often confers law-making powers on the executive in the form of an enabling Act. For example, s 1 of the Export Control Act 2002 conferred a power on the Secretary of State to make an order (delegated legislation in the form of a statutory instrument) in connection with imposing export controls in respect of goods. As indicated earlier (see section 5.7.2), therefore, Parliament can legislate to violate the separation of powers by conferring a law-making power onto the executive.

Under s 1 of this Act a government minister is empowered to legislate by making an order, known as a Legislative Reform Order, to remove unnecessary red tape and regulation. The practical advantage levelled in favour of this Act is that legislative provisions which are a burden can be efficiently amended without following the alternative long-winded route of passing a Bill. The constitutional disadvantage is that this measure permits primary legislation to be altered by means of secondary legislation known as a 'Henry VIII power/clause' (see s 1 (6) (a) of the Act).

In the context of Parliament conferring duties and powers on the executive, it is pertinent to note that, at least in recent decades, the executive has to a large extent typically dominated the House of Commons (see section 9.8). By extension, therefore, the executive has largely controlled Parliament as a whole and determined the legislation that it has passed.

7.6 Non-legal restraints on Parliament

7.6.1 Political restraints

Although Parliament can, in legal theory, pass any law that it chooses, this does not mean that Parliament *will* pass any such law. This is because, although there may be an absence of legal limitations on Parliament, there are, of course, political restraints on it. As indicated earlier, political sovereignty rests with the people as the people elect Parliament. The electorate, therefore, acts as a political restraint on the laws that Parliament passes. In other words, if Parliament passed a highly controversial, objectionable and draconian law, at the following general election these parliamentarians (specifically the elected MPs) would have to face the wrath of the electorate as they sought to be re-elected. In short, as Dicey noted: 'The electors can in the long run always enforce their will' (A Dicey, *Introduction to the Study of the Law of the Constitution* (10th edn, Macmillan, 1959), p 73). As such, Parliament is limited politically as it will inevitably refrain from passing legislation which the electorate would find unacceptable.

One obvious difficulty with this analysis, of course, is that the draconian legislation in question may only affect, or be directed at, a minority of the population who are not popular (eg prisoners or terrorist suspects). As a result, such legislation may in fact be acceptable to (and indeed popular with) the majority of the population who would be unaffected by its consequences. As Bogdanor has observed:

QUOTATION

'New threats, and, in particular, the growth of terrorism, mean that neither public opinion nor Parliament can any longer necessarily be relied upon to protect the rights of unpopular minorities. The progress through Parliament of the 2001 Anti-terrorism, Crime and Security Act and of the 2005 Prevention of Terrorism Act shows that parliamentary scrutiny of legislation bearing on human rights can be somewhat perfunctory during a period of moral panic.'

V Bogdanor, *The New British Constitution* (Hart Publishing, 2009), pp 55–56.

That said, at least since the operation of the Human Rights Act 1998, all legislation must now be interpreted in light of the articles of the European Convention (see Chapter 17).

ACTIVITY

Self-test question

How effective do you think political sovereignty is as a political restraint on the laws that Parliament passes?

7.6.2 Political entrenchment

According to Dicey, legislation cannot be *legally entrenched* and protected from repeal. Nevertheless, it may well be the case that certain Acts of Parliament (owing to their content and political importance) can become *politically entrenched* in the sense that Parliament may lack the political will (ie the support of the electorate) to repeal them.

One example could be the Human Rights Act 1998. In strict legal terms, Parliament could expressly repeal this legislation (on implied repeal of this Act see sections 4.4.5 and 7.12). Politically, however, it might be difficult for Parliament to muster the support from the electorate to repeal this legislation. In other words, once the Human Rights Act conferred positive rights on individuals which they could enforce against the state in a court, it may prove to be difficult *politically* (and *internationally*) to revoke them. In other countries the rights of the individual are contained in a Bill or Charter of Rights which will, typically, form part of a legally entrenched constitution. These rights, therefore, will be difficult to alter or abolish as they are legally entrenched in a codified constitution.

7.6.3 Practical restraints

In respect of parliamentary sovereignty, it is important to distinguish between what is legally possible (which in legal theory is limitless) and what is *actually* possible in practice. For example, in 1931 Parliament passed the Statute of Westminster, which stated in s 4 that no United Kingdom statute passed after the commencement of this Act shall extend to the law of a dominion (in 1931 these dominions included Australia, Canada, New Zealand, the Irish Free State and Newfoundland), unless the dominion in question requested and consented to that legislation.

In strict legal theory, however, the United Kingdom Parliament could simply repeal this provision and proceed to legislate for a Dominion without its consent. This point was made by Viscount Sankey LC in the Privy Council in *British Coal Corporation v The King* [1935] AC 500, who stated that:

JUDGMENT

'It is doubtless true that the power of the Imperial Parliament to pass on its own initiative any legislation that it thought fit extending to Canada remains in theory unimpaired: indeed, the Imperial Parliament could, as a matter of abstract law, repeal or disregard s 4 of the Statute. But that is theory and has no relation to realities.'

In addition, should Parliament legislate to repeal the grants of independence to former dependent territories (eg the Nigeria Independence Act 1960) with the intention of revoking their independent status, the mere legal passage of such legislation would not, of course, affect the *actual* independence of that particular state.

As Lord Denning MR in *Blackburn v Attorney General* [1971] 2 All ER 1380, commented:

JUDGMENT

'Take the Statute of Westminster 1931, which takes away the power of Parliament to legislate for the dominions. Can anyone imagine that Parliament could or would reverse that statute? Take the Acts which have granted independence to the dominions and territories overseas. Can anyone imagine that Parliament could or would reverse those laws and take away their independence? Most clearly not. Freedom once given cannot be taken away. Legal theory must give way to practical politics.'

Moreover, to take the example used above concerning Parliament legislating to ban smoking on the streets of Paris (see section 7.5.6), Jennings pointed out that such a law would not be effective within Paris itself as it is outside the jurisdiction of the United Kingdom courts. In strict legal theory the legislation in question would be legally valid, but not practically enforceable in France.

7.6.4 Constitutional conventions

Parliament can choose to legislate contrary to a constitutional convention. For example, since the establishment of the Scotland Act 1998 a convention has been established to the effect that the United Kingdom Parliament would not legislate in the area of a devolved matter for Scotland without the consent of the Scottish Parliament (the Sewel Convention). As a constitutional convention, it was simply a political rule of the constitution and as such, in legal theory, Parliament could have chosen to ignore it and proceed to pass legislation for Scotland in the absence of consent from the Scottish Parliament. The political ramifications of such action, however, would have prevented Parliament from passing such legislation. As an aside, s 2 of the Scotland Act 2016 has now placed the Sewel Convention on a statutory footing.

Constitutional conventions, therefore, do not legally bind Parliament and this point was reiterated by Lord Reid in the Privy Council in the following case:

CASE EXAMPLE

Madzimbamuto v Lardner-Burke *[1969] 1 AC 645*

In 1965 it was a well-established constitutional convention that the United Kingdom Parliament did not legislate for Southern Rhodesia (now Zimbabwe) without the consent of the government of the legislative Assembly of Southern Rhodesia. In 1965, however, the Prime Minister of Southern Rhodesia issued a declaration of independence to the effect that Southern Rhodesia had become an independent sovereign state and so no longer a Crown colony. In response, the United Kingdom nevertheless passed legislation (the Southern Rhodesia Act 1965) purporting to apply to Southern Rhodesia in contravention of the above convention.

Lord Reid noted that although the constitutional convention was an important principle, it had no legal effect which limited the legal powers of the United Kingdom Parliament to pass legislation (see the full quotation at section 4.16.2). In fact, in reality the legislation in question did not have any impact on Southern Rhodesia and illustrates the practical limitations on Parliament (analogous to legislating to ban smoking on the streets of Paris).

ACTIVITY

Applying the law

Can the Queen in Parliament legally pass the following laws and, if so, what would be their effect?

- The House of Lords Bill (which proposes to reinstate the expelled hereditary peers).
- The Mexico Bill (which proposes to make it a criminal offence for anyone to eat chewing gum on the streets of Mexico City).
- The Elections Bill (which proposes to abolish elections to the House of Commons).
- The Local Government Elections Bill (which proposes to exclude anyone earning less than £25,000 a year from voting in local government elections).
- The Prime Minister Bill (which proposes to override the constitutional convention that the Prime Minister must be drawn from within Parliament).
- The Courts Bill (which proposes to abolish jury trial for all criminal offences).
- Revisit your answers after reading section 7.7.

7.7 Is there a limitation on the laws that Parliament can pass?

Dicey noted that there was one clear limitation on Parliament, namely that Parliament cannot bind its successor, or be bound by its predecessor (see section 7.9). In addition, a number of judges (both in a judicial and an extra-judicial context) have suggested that there are in fact limits to Parliament's legislative power. Lord Woolf, writing extra-judicially in 1995, commented that there might be limits on Parliament's legislative powers as enforced by the courts if Parliament were to pass legislation which fundamentally undermined the rule of law (in particular, by removing or substantially impairing the constitutional role of the courts in the context of judicial review):

QUOTATION

'If Parliament did the unthinkable, then I would say that the courts would also be required to act in a manner which would be without precedent. Some judges might choose to do so by saying that it was an unrebuttable presumption that Parliament could never intend such a result. I myself would consider there were advantages in making it clear that ultimately there are even limits on the supremacy of Parliament which it is the courts' inalienable responsibility to identify and uphold. They are limits of the most modest dimensions which I believe any democrat would accept. They are no more than are necessary to enable the rule of law to be preserved.'

Lord Woolf, 'Droit public-English style' [1995] PL 57.

More recently, in the House of Lords Lord Steyn made the following (albeit *obiter*) observation in *R (Jackson) v Attorney General* [2005] UKHL 56 (for the facts see section 10.10.3):

JUDGMENT

'If the Attorney General is right the 1949 Act could also be used to introduce oppressive and wholly undemocratic legislation. For example, it could theoretically be used to abolish judicial review of flagrant abuse of power by a government or even the role of the ordinary courts in standing between the executive and citizens. This is where we may have to come back to the point about the supremacy of Parliament. We do not in the United Kingdom have an uncontrolled constitution as the Attorney General implausibly asserts . . . The classic account given by Dicey of the doctrine of the supremacy of Parliament, pure and absolute as it was, can now be seen to be out of place in the modern United Kingdom. Nevertheless, the supremacy of Parliament is still the *general* principle of our constitution. It is a construct of the common law. The judges created this principle. If that is so, it is not unthinkable that circumstances could arise where the courts may have to qualify a principle established on a different hypothesis of constitutionalism.

'In exceptional circumstances involving an attempt to abolish judicial review or the ordinary role of the courts, the Appellate Committee of the House of Lords or a new Supreme Court may have to consider whether this is a constitutional fundamental which even a sovereign Parliament acting at the behest of a complaisant House of Commons cannot abolish.'

In other words, if Parliament passed legislation which abrogated certain fundamental principles of the constitution, then the courts, in applying the common law principle of parliamentary sovereignty, may decide that *even* Parliament (notwithstanding the sovereignty of Parliament) could not make such legislation. It is of interest to note that in his evidence to the House of Lords Select Committee on the Constitution in November 2005, the then Lord Chancellor disagreed with Lord Steyn's comments that, aside from Europe, Parliament was prevented from legislating in respect of certain principles of the constitution. The Lord Chancellor considered himself to 'be on the side of the conventional constitutional thinkers' on this issue (Sixth Report of the House of Lords Select Committee on the Constitution, *Meeting with the Lord Chancellor*, HL Paper 84 (2005), Q15).

The above examples of Lords Woolf and Steyn are, of course, highly unlikely to occur in practice and so these potential limitations are somewhat theoretical. In addition in this context, more recently see M Fordham, *Judicial Review Handbook* (6th edn, Hart, 2012), p 1.3:

QUOTATION

'**Judicial review's constitutional inalienability.** It is no heresy to suggest that the Courts could properly choose to disapply as unconstitutional primary legislation which purported, even by the plainest of words, to exclude the right of access to justice by judicial review.'

ACTIVITY

Self-test question

What do the above comments tell us about the constitutional relationship between the judiciary and the legislature?

Key facts on the law-making power of Parliament

Parliament can in legal theory pass a law which:

- Abolishes or alters the common law.
- Infringes international law.
- Alters (either marginally or radically) the uncodified constitution.
- Has extra-territorial jurisdiction.
- Alters the law-making process or the judicial rules of statutory interpretation.
- Is retrospective in nature.
- Abrogates a constitutional convention.
- Confers wide discretionary powers on the executive.

There are, however, political and practical restraints on parliamentary sovereignty.

7.8 Principle 2: The courts cannot challenge the authority of an Act of Parliament

7.8.1 Introduction
Dicey stated that:

QUOTATION

'No person or body is recognised by the law of England as having a right to override or set aside the legislation of Parliament.'

A Dicey, *Introduction to the Study of the Law of the Constitution*
(10th edn, Macmillan, 1959), p 40.

This principle represents the negative side of parliamentary sovereignty, namely that no body (court or otherwise) can challenge an Act of Parliament. This is, of course, inextricably linked to the first principle that the Crown in Parliament can legally pass any law that it chooses because, once primary legislation is enacted, no court can invalidate it. In essence, therefore, parliamentary sovereignty concerns the constitutional relationship between the United Kingdom's courts and the United Kingdom Parliament, with the former being legally subordinate to the latter. Thus, irrespective of the content of the statute, the constitutional responsibility of the courts is simply to interpret and apply the legislation passed by Parliament.

CASE EXAMPLE

R v Jordan *[1967] Crim LR 483*

Jordan had been convicted and sentenced to imprisonment for offences committed under the Race Relations Act 1965. He contended that the Act was invalid on the basis that it curtailed freedom of expression and sought legal aid to apply for a writ of *habeas corpus* on this ground.

The Queen's Bench Division of the High Court held that the courts did not have the power to question the validity of primary legislation. Jordan's claim was dismissed as completely unarguable.

Similarly, in *Duport Steels Ltd and others v Sirs and others* [1980] 1 All ER 529 (for the facts, see section 5.8.3) Lord Scarman reiterated that the constitutional relationship between the judge and parliamentary legislation was that the former:

JUDGMENT

'must not deny the statute. Unpalatable statute law may not be disregarded or rejected, merely because it is unpalatable.'

The following case illustrates a number of principles relating to sovereignty and the constitutional relationship between the courts and Parliament:

CASE EXAMPLE

British Railways Board v Pickin *[1974] AC 765*

In 1968 a private Act of Parliament (The British Railways Act 1968) was passed with the effect of nullifying the effect of an earlier private Act of 1836. The latter had established a railway line and provided that, if the line should be abandoned, the lands on which the line was built should vest in the owners of the adjoining lands. Instead, under s 18 of the later 1968 Act, such land would now vest in the British Railways Board.

Pickin owned land adjoining a track and instituted an action against the British Railways Board claiming ownership of the adjoining land to the centre line of the track. The Board argued that under the 1968 Act the land vested in the Board. In reply, Pickin alleged that the Board (in promoting the British Railways Bill) had misled Parliament by a false recital in the preamble to the 1968 legislation. It was argued accordingly that the Board could not rely on the 1968 Act to deprive Pickin of title to this land. The Court of Appeal reversed a decision to strike out Pickin's above argument and the Board appealed to the House of Lords which allowed its appeal.

The House of Lords held that the function of the court was to apply Acts of Parliament. It was not lawful to impugn the validity of legislation by seeking to establish that Parliament in passing such legislation had been misled by fraud. Lord Reid said that:

JUDGMENT

'The idea that a court is entitled to disregard a provision in an Act of Parliament on any ground must seem strange and startling to anyone with any knowledge of the history and law of our constitution.'

Further, Lord Morris noted:

JUDGMENT

'When an enactment is passed there is finality unless and until it is amended or repealed by Parliament. In the courts there may be argument as to the correct interpretation of the enactment: there must be none as to whether it should be on the Statute Book at all.'

The *Pickin* case illustrates the following principles concerning our constitution:

- Firstly, the House of Lords reiterated that the courts do not have the constitutional authority to impugn or challenge the validity of an Act. This applied whether the statute was a public or private Act of Parliament (this case concerned a private Act).

Secondly, Lord Reid dismissed the notion that the modern courts could disregard an Act of Parliament on the basis that: 'it was contrary to the law of God or the law of nature or natural justice' as 'since the supremacy of Parliament was finally demonstrated by the revolution of 1688 any such idea has become obsolete'(*Sic*). This was a clear reference to, and repudiation of, the earlier historic case of *Dr Bonham's Case* (1610) 8 Co Rep 114, in which Coke CJ had stated that the common law would control and adjudge to be void an Act of Parliament which was 'against common right and reason, or repugnant, or impossible to be performed'.

It should be remembered that, although the courts will not impugn the validity of an Act of Parliament, this does not preclude them from questioning and invalidating secondary legislation. In fact, the courts regularly judicially review the content and exercise of delegated legislation made by the executive and other bodies (see Chapters 19 and 20). Although the term judicial review is used in the British constitution, this is in relation to delegated, rather than primary, legislation (but in the context of European Union law see section 15.6.4).

ACTIVITY

Applying the law

Can you envisage any circumstances in which Parliament passed an Act where you think it would be (a) morally or (b) constitutionally appropriate for the courts to question it?

7.8.2 The courts may assume that Parliament did not intend to act unconstitutionally

Although the courts do not question an Act of Parliament, it is pertinent to remember that it is in fact the judiciary who interpret statutes and extract and apply their meaning. As Dicey noted:

QUOTATION

'Parliament is supreme legislator, but from the moment Parliament has uttered its will as lawgiver, that will becomes subject to the interpretation put upon it by the judges of the land.' (*Sic*)

A Dicey, *Introduction to the Study of the Law of the Constitution*
(10th edn, Macmillan, 1959), p 413.

Moreover, as indicated earlier at section 4.8.3, in construing legislation the courts have developed a number of principles as aids to their construction. For example, one historic constitutional role of the judiciary is to safeguard the freedom of the individual. As a result, where legislation appears to be ambiguous or capable of a number of interpretations, the courts will apply certain constitutional fundamentals in interpreting that legislation.

These 'constitutional presumptions' include, *inter alia*, that surely Parliament would *never* have intended the following results:

- An interference with the human rights and liberties of the individual.
- A restriction of an individual's access to the courts.
- To legislate contrary to an international Treaty or international obligations.

These presumptions are justified on the constitutional basis that, if Parliament had intended to achieve any of the outcomes indicated above, it would have made this very clear in the relevant statutory provision. As pointed out at section 4.8.3, the last presumption was demonstrated in *Waddington v Miah* [1974] 2 All ER 377, where the House of Lords interpreted the Immigration Act 1971 in line with Art 7 of the European Convention (which outlaws the imposition of retrospective criminal legislation). In other words, the courts assume that Parliament intends to legislate consistently with its international obligations, unless the statute clearly indicates this not to be the case (in the context of European Union law see section 15.6.5).

In the Republic of Ireland, the Irish Constitution also uses an analogous presumption, namely the *'presumption of constitutionality'*. Article 15.4 of the Irish Constitution states that the Oireachtas shall not pass legislation inconsistent with the written codified constitution (see M Forde and D Leonard, *Constitutional Law of Ireland* (3rd edn, Bloomsbury, 2013), 2.17). As a result of this, unless the contrary is proved, the courts will assume that legislation passed by the Oireachtas is 'constitutional', and so in accordance with the constitution.

Dicey summarised the first two principles underpinning parliamentary sovereignty in the following way:

QUOTATION

'Parliamentary sovereignty is therefore an undoubted legal fact. It is complete both on its positive and on its negative side. Parliament can legally legislate on any topic whatever which, in the judgment of Parliament, is a fit subject for legislation. There is no power which, under the English constitution, can come into rivalry with the legislative sovereignty of Parliament.'

A Dicey, *Introduction to the Study of the Law of the Constitution* (10th edn, Macmillan, 1959), pp 68–70.

7.8.3 The surrender of parliamentary sovereignty?

Although there are no legal limits on the laws that Parliament can pass, this does not mean that it cannot, ultimately, surrender its sovereignty forever. In other words, Parliament could in legal theory simply dissolve itself. On this point Dicey has argued that Parliament:

QUOTATION

'may simply put an end to its own existence. Parliament could extinguish itself by legally dissolving itself and leaving no means whereby a subsequent parliament could be legally summoned.'

A Dicey, *Introduction to the Study of the Law of the Constitution* (10th edn, Macmillan, 1959), p 69.

In this sense, Parliament could legally terminate itself – which is likened to suicide, which is, of course, irreversible.

In the albeit unlikely event of the United Kingdom in the future adopting a codified, entrenched constitution which contained constitutional law which had a higher special legal status, Parliament would need to divest itself of the principle of parliamentary sovereignty. This is because the United Kingdom could not have a legally entrenched codified constitution (which would legally control the laws which the new legislature could pass) whilst simultaneously retaining the principle of parliamentary sovereignty.

Key facts on the relationship of the courts with Acts of Parliament

- Historically, the courts cannot question Acts of Parliament (*R v Jordan* (1967), *British Railways Board v Pickin* (1974)). This is in contrast, for example, to the Supreme Court in the United States or the Republic of Ireland.

- The constitutional function of the judiciary is limited simply to interpreting and ascertaining the meaning of an Act of Parliament. In construing legislation, however, the courts will apply certain constitutional fundamentals (*Waddington v Miah* (1974)) and assume that Parliament did not intend to legislate 'unconstitutionally'.

7.9 Principle 3: Parliament cannot bind its successors

7.9.1 Introduction

The third aspect of parliamentary sovereignty involves the following two inter-related principles:

- Parliament cannot bind its successors. In other words, the Parliament in 2020 cannot restrict the laws that could be passed by a future Parliament in 2021.
- Parliament cannot be bound by its predecessor. In other words, the Parliament of 2021 cannot be bound or restricted by the previous 2020 Parliament.

In summary, traditionally it has been argued that Parliament cannot entrench legislation. Dicey stated that, on the occasions that language had been used in an Act of Parliament purporting to imply that a particular statute could not be altered or repealed by a later Parliament, 'the endeavour has always ended in failure'. Thus, one Parliament cannot bind its successor.

This principle ensures that each new Parliament retains its sovereign power to pass whatever legislation is deemed necessary at the time. If one Parliament could tie the hands of its successor, the later Parliament would not enjoy full legislative power to pass any legislation that it chooses, as it would be restrained by this former Parliament. Today this principle can be justified on the basis that each new Parliament should enjoy full sovereign legislative power as each new Parliament represents the latest will of the people as reflected in the latest general election (see political sovereignty at section 7.2.2). It also means that laws can adapt to new developments and that one Parliament does not become a prisoner of the views (as embodied in legislation) of a previous Parliament (perhaps of centuries before).

In short, in the United Kingdom Acts of Parliament cannot be legally (as opposed to being politically) entrenched – that is to say that Acts cannot in law be prevented from being repealed by a future Parliament at a later date. As Herbert CJ noted centuries ago in *Godden v Hales* (1686) 11 St Tr 1165:

JUDGMENT

'If an Act of Parliament had a clause in it that it should never be repealed, yet without question, the same power that made it may repeal it.'

Indeed, this would even apply to two Acts passed within the same parliamentary term, whereby an Act passed in the first session of a Parliament could be repealed by a later Act in the second session of the same Parliament, although this would be highly unlikely to happen in practice. However, note the changes made by the Constitutional Reform and Governance Act 2010 to the Parliamentary Standards Act 2009 – see later at section 8.8.3).

ACTIVITY

Self-test question

How would you distinguish between the legal and political entrenchment of legislation?

The principle that Parliament cannot bind its successors is achieved through the twin doctrines of:

- Express repeal.
- Implied repeal.

7.9.2 Express repeal

This is the principle that a later Act of Parliament expressly and explicitly repeals an earlier inconsistent Act (or section of it). As Dicey stated, Parliament can *unmake* any law that it chooses. For example, s 49(1) of the Inquiries Act 2005 expressly repealed the Tribunals of Inquiry (Evidence) Act 1921 and s 49(2) made reference to Sch 3, which detailed the extent of other provisions of other statutes which were repealed or revoked. The doctrine of express repeal means that even if, as Herbert CJ indicated above, an Act stated that it was exempt from repeal, it could nevertheless be expressly repealed by a later Act (see further section 7.10.1).

NB. For the most seminal express repeal of legislation for decades, see Brexit at section 15.6.6.

7.9.3 Implied repeal

The doctrine of implied repeal comes into operation when two Acts of Parliament dealing with the same subject matter are inconsistent with each other but the later Act does *not* expressly repeal the earlier one. In these circumstances the doctrine of implied repeal would ensure that the provisions of the later Act prevailed, by impliedly repealing the earlier Act to the extent that it was inconsistent. In short, this means that two inconsistent Acts stating two different things on the same subject-matter cannot stand together. In this way, the courts give effect to the latest will of Parliament (as reflected at the last general election). The doctrine is illustrated by the following two cases:

CASE EXAMPLE

Vauxhall Estates Limited v Liverpool Corporation *[1932] 1 KB 733*

Section 2 of the Acquisition of Land (Assessment of Compensation) Act 1919 provided for the assessment of compensation in respect of land acquired compulsorily by a government department or local authority. Section 7 of the Act provided that: 'The provisions of the Act or order by which the land is authorised to be acquired, or of any Act incorporated therewith, shall, in relation to the matters dealt with in this Act, have effect subject to this Act, and so far as inconsistent with this Act those provisions shall cease to have or shall not have effect'.

In 1925 s 46 of the Housing Act provided for the assessment of such compensation for land acquired compulsorily on a less generous basis. The Corporation of Liverpool proposed a scheme under the 1925 Act for the improvement of Liverpool which included lands owned by Vauxhall Estates Ltd who contended that the amount of compensation should be assessed under s 2 of the 1919 Act. This was on the basis that the assessment of compensation under the 1925 Act differed materially from the 1919 Act and that s 7 of this earlier Act had rendered the later 1925 Act of no effect. Counsel for Vauxhall had argued that s 7 of the 1919 Act purported, in effect, to prevent the implied repeal of its provisions (thereby purporting to tie the hands of a successor Parliament).

The Divisional Court held that the 1925 Act repealed by implication (ie impliedly repealed) the earlier Act of 1919, to the extent that it was inconsistent. The court held that, even if the 1919 Act had purported to apply to future Acts, s 46 of the 1925 Act would still prevail. On the facts, Avory J concluded that on its true construction, s 7 applied only to existing Acts in 1919 and not to future Acts (the other two judges did not decide this issue).

JUDGMENT

'Speaking for myself, I should certainly hold, until the contrary were decided, that no Act of Parliament can effectively provide that no future Act shall interfere with its provisions.'

Avory J.

CASE EXAMPLE

Ellen Street Estates Limited v Minister of Health *[1934] 1 KB 590*

In this case the Court of Appeal approved of, and followed, the decision in *Vauxhall Estates* (see above). It is of interest to note that counsel for Vauxhall appeared for Ellen Street Estates and submitted that the Divisional Court decision in *Vauxhall Estates* had been wrongly decided and that it was possible for Parliament to state that an Act could be repealed in express terms only, and not by implication. Since therefore s 46 of the 1925 Act was inconsistent with the 1919 Act, and the 1925 Act had not expressly repealed it, accordingly, this later provision (ie s 46 of the 1925 Act) should have no legal effect. The Court of Appeal rejected this contention in the following terms by Maugham LJ:

JUDGMENT

'The Legislature cannot, according to our constitution, bind itself as to the form of subsequent legislation, and it is impossible for Parliament to enact that in a subsequent statute dealing with the same subject-matter there can be no implied repeal. If in a subsequent Act Parliament chooses to make it plain that the earlier statute is being to some extent repealed, effect must be given to that intention just because it is the will of the Legislature.'

Thus, even if a Parliament in 2020 stated in an Act that it could not be repealed, according to the above two doctrines a later Parliament in 2021 could either:

- expressly repeal the 2020 Act by passing an Act of Parliament specifically stating this (express repeal); or
- impliedly repeal the 2020 Act by passing an Act of Parliament which was plainly inconsistent with the provisions of the earlier 2020 Act (implied repeal), but without expressly stating that it was repealing it.

Notwithstanding the points made above, the doctrine of implied repeal needs to be reconsidered in the context of the following:

- European Union law (see section 15.6).
- The Human Rights Act 1998 (see section 7.12).
- Other constitutional statutes (see Laws LJ at section 4.4.5).

KEY FACTS

Key facts on Parliament being unable to bind its successors

Parliament cannot bind its successors or be bound by its predecessors. This is achieved through the following doctrines:

- Express repeal is the principle that a later Act of Parliament expressly and explicitly repeals an earlier Act (or section of it).
- Implied repeal is the principle that when two Acts of Parliament dealing with the same subject matter are inconsistent with each other (but the later Act does not expressly repeal the earlier one), the later Act impliedly repeals the earlier one to the extent that it is inconsistent (*Vauxhall Estates Limited v Liverpool Corporation* (1932) and *Ellen Street Estates Limited v Minister of Health* (1934)).

These doctrines taken together indicate that Parliament cannot entrench legislation against subsequent repeal by a later Parliament.

7.10 Is legal entrenchment possible?

Notwithstanding the above, is it still possible for Parliament to bind its successors and legally entrench legislation?

In essence, academic commentators traditionally have distinguished between two types of entrenchment:

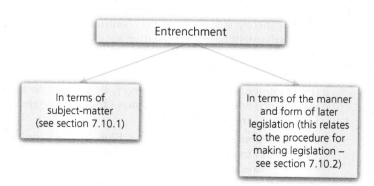

Figure 7.2 Legal entrenchment

One argument typically levelled in favour of entrenchment is that, *if* the principle of parliamentary sovereignty is a common law rule, and since statutes have a superior status to the common law, logically therefore, why cannot Parliament simply legislate to alter this common law rule relating to sovereignty and entrenchment? According to Wade, however, as indicated at section 7.3.2 although the rule of judicial obedience to statutes is in one sense a rule of the common law, in another sense it is a political fact:

QUOTATION

'What Salmond calls the "ultimate legal principle" is therefore a rule which is unique in being unchangeable by Parliament – it is changed by revolution, not by legislation; it lies in the keeping of the courts, and no Act of Parliament can take it from them.'

H Wade, 'The basis of legal sovereignty' [1955] CLJ 172.

(On such a 'revolution' see the impact of European Union law at section 15.6.5).

7.10.1 Entrenchment in terms of subject matter

Democratic constitutions generally protect certain subject matter (such as fundamental basic human rights or other fundamental principles) from legal infringement or revocation by later legislation. Thus, human rights are typically 'constitutionally ring-fenced' in a Bill or Charter of Rights and thereby placed out of the reach of the legislature and the 'ordinary' legislative process.

In contrast, in the United Kingdom as a consequence of parliamentary sovereignty, even if such basic rights were embodied in statutory form with a legal declaration that they could never be repealed owing to their important nature (eg an entrenched British Charter of Rights), a future Parliament could simply legislate to revoke them at a later date (on the Human Rights Act 1998 see later at section 7.12). Indeed, Lord Scarman in 1974 commented that:

QUOTATION

'It is the helplessness of the law in face of the legislative sovereignty of Parliament which makes it difficult for the legal system to accommodate the concept of fundamental and inviolable human rights.'

Lord Scarman, *English Law: The New Dimension* (1974), p 15.

Dicey's theory is known as the 'continuing theory of sovereignty', whereby each new Parliament has full legislative sovereignty.

Acts of Union

It is commonly suggested, however, that owing to their content and fundamental importance one category of statutes – the Union Acts – cannot be repealed. The two Union Acts are:

■ The Union with Scotland Act 1706 – which united England and Wales with Scotland to form the Parliament of Great Britain; and

■ The Union with Ireland Act 1800 – which united England, Wales and Scotland with Ireland to form the Parliament of the United Kingdom.

The argument is that these Acts have a special legal status. In other words, they are legally entrenched against repeal and the Acts themselves indicate as much. In fact, Dicey made specific reference to the Union Acts. In respect of the 1706 Act, which had enacted, *inter alia,* that Scottish university professors should acknowledge, profess and subscribe to the Confession of Faith (a Protestant doctrine), he noted that the Act 'in substance enacts that this provision shall be a fundamental and essential condition of the treaty of union in all time coming'. Notwithstanding this, as he pointed out, this provision was later partly repealed by the Universities (Scotland) Act 1853. Furthermore, more recently, s 37 of the Scotland Act 1998 states that the Union with Scotland Act 1706 has effect subject to this later Act (ie the Scotland Act 1998).

Similarly, Art 5 of the Union with Ireland Act 1800 stated:

SECTION

'that the Doctrine, Worship, Discipline, and Government of the said United Church (United Church of England and Ireland) shall be, and shall remain in full force for ever . . . [and] . . . that the Continuance and Preservation of the said United Church, as the established Church of England and Ireland, shall be deemed and taken to be an essential and fundamental Part of the Union.'

The Irish Church Act 1869, however, subsequently disestablished the Irish Church. In summary, Dicey stated that:

QUOTATION

'The history of legislation in respect of these very Acts affords the strongest proof of the futility inherent in every attempt of one sovereign legislature to restrain the action of another equally sovereign body.'

A Dicey, Introduction to the Study of the Law of the Constitution
(10th edn, Macmillan, 1959), p 65.

These examples indicate, therefore, that even if an Act stated that because of its subject matter, its provisions were 'fundamental and unalterable', they could, nevertheless, be repealed by a subsequent Parliament. More recently, Lord Hope made the following *obiter* point:

JUDGMENT

'. . . it is a fundamental aspect of the rule of sovereignty that no Parliament can bind its successors. There are no means by whereby, even with the assistance of the most skillful draftsman, it can entrench an Act of Parliament. It is impossible for Parliament to enact something which a subsequent statute dealing with the same subject matter cannot repeal.'

R (Jackson and others) v Attorney General [2005] UKHL 56.

However, in the context of the Act of Union with Scotland, see the *obiter* comments of Lord Cooper in *MacCormick v Lord Advocate* (1953) SC 396 and Lord Keith in *Gibson v Lord Advocate* [1975] 1 CMLR 563.

ACTIVITY

Self-test question

What would be the constitutional advantages and disadvantages of Parliament being able to entrench the subject matter of legislation against subsequent repeal by a later Parliament?

7.10.2 Entrenchment in terms of the manner and form of later legislation

This type of entrenchment refers to entrenching legislation in terms of the manner and form of later legislation (that is to say the procedure for making legislation). In other words, it is concerned with the following type of scenario:

The (imaginary) British Charter of Rights Act 2020

Section 1: the human rights detailed in this Act can *only* be repealed by a future Parliament with the support of 80 per cent of both Houses of Parliament.

The above Act purports to entrench the human rights detailed in it by providing that these rights cannot be repealed by a later Parliament unless it has the support of 80 per cent of both Houses of Parliament. Unlike the first type of entrenchment (see section 7.10.1), this Act is not stating that its provisions can *never* be repealed under any circumstances in the future. Rather, by stipulating that 80 per cent support of both Houses is required, it is purporting to make it *difficult* for a subsequent Parliament to repeal its provisions. In other words, it is purporting to entrench those human rights by requiring a specified 'manner and form' of later legislation in order to repeal them (the manner and form here being the support of 80 per cent of both Houses of Parliament).

The question is what would happen if a Parliament in 2021 passed an Act repealing the human rights enshrined in the British Charter of Rights Act 2020, but did so through the ordinary parliamentary process (ie the 2021 Bill passed with a simple majority vote in both chambers and *not* the 80 per cent as stipulated in the 2020 Act). Would the 2021 Act be legal?

There is no absolute answer to this question. Under the traditional conception of parliamentary sovereignty the 2021 Act would prevail, notwithstanding that it had not complied with the manner and form provision stipulated in s 1 of the 2020 Act. Indeed, if we recall the enrolled Bill rule (see section 7.3.3), the judges would simply look to see if the 2021 Bill was on the parliamentary roll and, as stated in *Pickin* (1974) at section 5.8.3, they would not investigate the internal proceedings of Parliament (as this risks breaching the separation of powers). On this traditional basis, therefore, it could be argued that, provided the 2021 Bill was on the parliamentary roll having obtained the consent of both Houses, the courts would not investigate further as to whether the Bill had obtained the support of 80 per cent of both Houses.

There is, however, some support for the proposition that the 2021 Act would not be enforced – or even constitute an Act – where the previous 2020 Act had, in effect, entrenched its provisions by specifically stipulating the 'manner and form' that had to be followed by later legislation in order to repeal them. The following standard cases are used to support this argument (the so-called 'self-embracing theory of sovereignty'):

CASE EXAMPLE

Attorney General for New South Wales v Trethowan *[1932] AC 526*

The Colonial Laws Validity Act 1865 (a United Kingdom statute) conferred power on the New South Wales legislature to make laws in respect of the constitution of that state. Section 5 of the Act stated that every representative legislature shall have full power to make laws respecting the constitution providing such laws 'shall have been passed in such manner and form as may from time to time be required by any Act of Parliament'.

The Constitution Act 1902 as amended in 1929 (s 7A) stated that no Bill abolishing the Legislative Council of New South Wales (the upper chamber) should be presented to the Governor (for royal consent) until it had been approved by a majority of the electors. The same procedure was needed to repeal s 7A.

In 1930 both Houses of the New South Wales legislature passed two Bills (to abolish the Legislative Council and repeal s 7A); however, neither Bill had been approved by the electorate. Two members of the Legislative Council (which was purportedly being abolished) sought a declaration that the two Bills could not be presented to the Governor for assent until approved by the electors, together with an injunction to prevent the Bills being presented for assent.

The Privy Council (on an appeal from the High Court of Australia) confirmed that the Bills needed to comply with the 'manner and form' as stipulated in s 7A. Thus the Bills required the support of the electors before they could lawfully be presented to the Governor.

CASE EXAMPLE

Harris v The Minister of the Interior *(1952) (2) SA 428*

Section 152 of the South Africa Act 1909 stipulated that a Bill which amended section 35 of the Act (concerning the deregistering of individuals for voting purposes on the basis of their colour), required the consent of two-thirds of both Houses (sitting together) of the South African Parliament.

The Supreme Court of South Africa held that in order to pass the 1951 Separate Representation of Voters Act (which had been passed by the two Houses separately and so *not* sitting together), the 'manner and form' stipulated by s 152 of the South Africa Act 1909 had to be followed. As a consequence the 1951 Act was null and void.

CASE EXAMPLE

The Bribery Commissioner v Pedrick Ranasinghe *[1965] AC 172*

Section 29(4) of the Ceylon (Constitution) Order in Council 1946 stated that the Ceylon Parliament may amend or repeal any of the provisions in this Order, but that no Bill be presented for Royal Assent unless it had endorsed on it a certificate stating that it had been passed by not less than two-thirds of the House of Representatives.

The Privy Council affirmed the judgment of the Supreme Court of Ceylon that as the Bribery Amendment Act 1958 (which in effect altered the constitution) had no such certificate, the orders made by the Bribery Tribunal (under the 1958 Act) against Ranasinghe were null and inoperative. In short, in amending the Ceylon constitution, the Speaker's certificate was a necessary part of the legislative process and so any Bill not complying with s 29(4) was invalid and *ultra vires*. The Bribery Amendment Bill, therefore had to follow the 'manner and form' set out in s 29(4).

Although these cases demonstrate that in each case the legislature was required to follow the stipulated 'manner and form' for later legislation, as Commonwealth authorities they are not strictly analogous with the sovereign United Kingdom Parliament. As Barnett has commented, the cases indicate that:

QUOTATION

'. . . legislative bodies do not necessarily enjoy full sovereign power, and that some form of "higher law" may control their powers. In each of these cases, the powers of the legislatures of New South Wales, South Africa and Ceylon (as it then was) had been established under an Act of the sovereign United Kingdom Parliament. That being so, the legislative bodies had to comply with the constitutional laws in force . . .'

H Barnett, *Constitutional and Administrative Law*
(12th edn, Routledge/Taylor & Francis Group, 2017), p 136.

In fact, Dicey clearly distinguished between sovereign legislatures (eg the United Kingdom Parliament) and non-sovereign law-making bodies (ie subordinate legislatures). According to him, judicial persons would have the 'authority to pronounce upon the validity or constitutionality of laws' which had been passed by *non-sovereign law-making bodies*. What is clear, therefore, is that, although as a constitutional principle, all legislatures pass laws, it does not follow that they are all sovereign. For example, the Scottish Parliament is a legislature with the power to pass Acts of the Scottish Parliament (see section 14.3); however, it is necessarily a limited legislature with limited law-making powers as it is governed, and legally controlled, by the legislation which established it: the Scotland Act 1998. In this way the 'non-sovereign' Scottish Parliament should be contrasted with the 'sovereign' United Kingdom Parliament at Westminster which has neither been established, nor had its powers delegated from or controlled, by a prior constitutional document.

The redefinition theory

A variant of the manner and form argument in favour of entrenching legislation is the so-called 'redefinition theory of sovereignty'. In general, an Act of Parliament is passed by a combination of all of the following:

- The House of Commons.
- The House of Lords.
- The monarch (in the form of the Royal Assent).

Under the redefinition theory it is possible for legal entrenchment to take place by the specification of an additional element to the above constituent parts in order to amend or repeal specified (important) legislation. In this way Parliament is *redefining* itself in relation to certain legislation thereby making it more difficult to repeal, as an *extra* element has been added to the legislative process (see the *Trethowan* case above). This extra element will typically be the support of the people in a referendum.

Consider the following provision of the Northern Ireland Act 1998, which states that:

SECTION

s 1
It is hereby declared that Northern Ireland in its entirety remains part of the United Kingdom and shall not cease to be so without the consent of a majority of the people of Northern Ireland voting in a poll held for the purposes of this section.

What is the legal meaning of this provision? Could a later Parliament simply legislate to sever Northern Ireland from the rest of the United Kingdom without the consent of the people in the province? A traditional view of sovereignty would be that a later Act, following the enrolled Bill principle, could sever Northern Ireland without the consent of the people as required by s 1 of the 1998 Act. In other words, the courts would not look beyond the parliamentary roll in order to ascertain whether an additional element had been satisfied (ie the consent of the people of Northern Ireland).

In contrast, the redefinition theory would provide that s 1 of the 1998 Act has redefined Parliament for the purposes of the future status of Northern Ireland. In other words, any Bill attempting to sever the province would require the consent of the following elements in order to be a valid Act:

- The House of Commons.
- The House of Lords (though technically not needed if the Parliament Acts of 1911 and 1949 are used).
- The monarch (in the form of the Royal Assent).
- *The consent of a majority of the people of Northern Ireland voting in a poll.*

It is certainly true that Parliament has already redefined how it passes legislation which is accepted and recognised by the courts. As we shall see (section 10.10.1), under the Parliament Acts of 1911 and 1949 the consent of the House of Lords is no longer needed – all that is required is for the Speaker of the Commons to indicate that a Bill has passed under the Parliament Acts. Accordingly, why is it not possible to add an extra element (eg the consent of the people in a referendum) to the specified legislative process? In this context, consider the following case:

CASE EXAMPLE

Manuel v Attorney General *[1983] 1 Ch 77*

Canadian Indian chiefs sought a declaration that the Canada Act 1982 was *ultra vires* as it was inconsistent with the safeguards provided by the Statute of Westminster Act 1931. Section 4 of the 1931 Act stated that no statute shall extend to a Dominion, eg Canada, without its express consent (the argument here was that the Indian peoples had not given *their* consent). The Court of Appeal refused the declaration on the basis that the Canada Act 1982 was valid as its preamble stated that Canada had expressly requested and consented to this legislation, thereby satisfying s 4 of the 1931 Act.

The court did, however, state *obiter* (making it clear that they were *not* purporting to decide the issue) that it was content to assume that the following proposition was correct: 'that Parliament can effectively tie the hands of its successors, if it passes a statute which provides that any future legislation on a specified subject shall be enacted only with certain specified consents' (Slade LJ).

According to Ellis this case:

QUOTATION

'contains a tiny judicial hint that English courts might consider a future UK Parliament bound by a stipulation as to manner and form, although under what conditions this might be so it is difficult to predict.'
'The Legislative Supremacy of Parliament and its Limits' in D Feldman (ed), *English Public Law* (2nd edn, Oxford University Press, 2009), p 132.

In addition, in the *Jackson* case (see directly below) Lord Steyn and Baroness Hale gave (albeit *obiter*) support for the 'manner and form' argument:

JUDGMENT

'. . . Parliament acting as ordinarily constituted may functionally redistribute legislative power in different ways. For example, Parliament could for specific purposes provide for a two-thirds majority in the House of Commons and the House of Lords. This would involve a redefinition of Parliament for a specific purpose. Such redefinition could not be disregarded.'

Lord Steyn.

JUDGMENT

'. . . if the sovereign Parliament can redefine itself downwards, to remove or modify the requirement for the consent of the Upper House, it may very well be that it can also redefine itself upwards, to require a particular Parliamentary majority or a popular referendum for particular types of measure. In each case, the courts would be respecting the will of the sovereign Parliament as constituted when that will had been expressed. But that is for another day.'

Baroness Hale.

NB. s 1 of the Scotland Act 2016 (amending the 1998 Act) refers to the Scottish Parliament and Government as being a permanent part of the constitutional arrangements of the United Kingdom. It declared that they 'are not to be abolished except on the basis of a decision of the people of Scotland voting in a referendum' (new s 63A of the Scotland Act 1998) – a parallel provision in relation to Wales is found in s 1 of the Wales Act 2017. On the issue of the permanence (in constitutional terms) of the Scottish institutions and parliamentary sovereignty, see the House of Commons Political and Constitutional Reform Committee, *Constitutional Implications of the Government's Draft Scotland Clauses*, HC 1022 (The Stationery Office, 2015).

7.10.3 The *Jackson* case

It is worth noting the recent House of Lords decision in *R (Jackson and others) v Attorney General* [2005] UKHL 56 – for the facts of this case see section 10.10.3. For present purposes, the case concerned the 1911 Parliament Act (as amended in 1949), which allows legislation to be passed without the consent of the House of Lords. Section 2(1) of the 1911 Act, however, expressly excludes from its ambit a Bill purporting to extend the life of Parliament. According to the Act, therefore, legislation proposing to extend the life of Parliament required the express consent of the House of Lords.

According to Young:

- Seven of their Lordships held that were future legislation to be passed extending the maximum duration of Parliament beyond five years – but without the consent of the Upper House – the courts would not recognise this legislation as a valid Act of Parliament. In other words, a future Parliament (consisting *only* of the House of Commons and the Monarch) could not legislate contrary to s 2(1) (ie extend the life of Parliament without the consent of the Lords).
- By a majority, five of their Lordships considered that the Parliament Acts *themselves* could not be used to delete the exception set out in s 2(1). In other words, they were of the opinion that a Bill purporting to delete the requirement

in s 2(1) (ie that a Bill to extend the life of Parliament was excluded from the Parliament Acts) could not *itself* be pushed through under the Parliament Acts. Instead, it would need the express consent of the House of Lords. Conversely, it is noteworthy that the then senior law lord, Lord Bingham, indicated that the special procedure under the Act theoretically *could* be used to delete this exception in s 2(1). See A Young, 'Hunting sovereignty: *Jackson v Her Majesty's Attorney-General*' [2006] PL 187.

Finally in relation to this case, Turpin and Tomkins have noted that:

QUOTATION

'The comments made in *Jackson* about the sovereignty of Parliament were *obiter* and, moreover, they were uttered in the context of litigation concerning statutes passed without the consent of the House of Lords. It may be, for that reason, that they prove to be of little precedential value.'

C Turpin and A Tomkins, *British Government and the Constitution* (7th edn, Cambridge University Press, 2012), p 91.

Conclusion

Notwithstanding the continuing debate concerning *legal entrenchment*, it is arguably the case that a number of legislative enactments (eg the Freedom of Information Act 2000) are in fact *politically entrenched* in the sense that, although legally these Acts could be repealed, the practical reality is that the political will to do so would be lacking. As a result, even if the traditional and orthodox view of parliamentary sovereignty is taken that legal entrenchment is not possible, political entrenchment of certain legislation is possible. Thus, the practical distinction between legal and political entrenchment becomes less important.

ACTIVITY

Exercise

Do you think that Parliament can entrench legislation in terms of the manner and form of later legislation? What would be the constitutional advantages and disadvantages of being able to do so?

KEY FACTS

Key facts on entrenchment

It is traditionally stated that in terms of subject matter (ie content) Parliament cannot entrench legislation against subsequent repeal.

There is, however, disagreement over whether Parliament can entrench itself in terms of the manner and form of later legislation:

- The orthodox view (Dicey's continuing theory of sovereignty) is that one Parliament cannot bind another in terms of the manner and form of later legislation.
- A more modern view is that it is possible for one Parliament to bind itself in this way.

- A variant of the manner and form argument is the redefinition theory of sovereignty which states that Parliament can redefine its constituent elements to include an extra element such as the consent of the people (or a section of it) in a referendum.
- The majority (*obiter*) view in *Jackson* (2005) was that s 2(1) of the Parliament Act 1911 could not be removed without the consent of the House of Lords.

7.11 Parliamentary sovereignty and devolution

In 1998 Parliament passed three devolution Acts which delegated powers to devolved institutions in the following regions:

- Scotland (Scotland Act 1998).
- Wales (Government of Wales Act 1998).
- Northern Ireland (Northern Ireland Act 1998).

As these bodies were established by the Westminster Parliament, they are legally subordinate to it. For example, s 28(7) of the Scotland Act 1998 states that the Westminster Parliament can still legislate for Scotland:

SECTION

28(7)
This section does not affect the power of the Parliament of the United Kingdom to make laws for Scotland.

Strictly speaking, of course, in legal theory such a provision was not necessary as Parliament can pass *any* law that it chooses, including legislating for Scotland. In addition, in strict legal theory, historically these devolved bodies could be simply extinguished by the Westminster Parliament passing legislation expressly repealing the above devolution Acts. Indeed, in 1973 Parliament revoked the then Northern Irish Parliament, which had operated for 50 years (see section 14.4.1). In terms of implied repeal, however, Laws LJ in *Thoburn v Sunderland City Council* (2002) indicated that the devolution Acts (he specifically identified both the Scottish and Welsh statutes) fell within the definition of 'constitutional statutes', and as such would not be susceptible to implied repeal (see section 4.4.5). As noted above, however, today in relation to Scotland now see s 1 of the Scotland Act 2016, which declares that the Scottish Parliament and Government are permanent and can only be abolished with the consent of the Scottish people voting in a referendum (a similar provision applies in relation to Wales as a result of s 1 of the Wales Act 2017).

7.12 Parliamentary sovereignty and the Human Rights Act 1998

In terms of the link between parliamentary sovereignty and the Human Rights Act, two points need to be made.

Firstly, the Human Rights Act 1998 does not enable the courts to invalidate Acts of Parliament which are plainly inconsistent with articles of the European Convention. Although s 4 of the 1998 Act enables the higher courts to issue a declaration of incompatibility, such a declaration *in itself* does not invalidate the offending legislation. The Act, therefore, maintains parliamentary sovereignty. The then Labour government's 1997 White Paper – which preceded the Human Rights Act – made it plain that under the Act the judiciary would not have the power to strike down Acts of Parliament as this would be likely to bring the courts into constitutional conflict with the legislature. Furthermore, it was noted that there was no evidence that such constitutional power was sought either by the judges themselves or by the public (*Rights Brought Home: The Human Rights Bill*, Cm 3782, Home Office (1997), para 2.13).

In short, as noted by Lord Steyn in *R v DPP ex p Kebilene and others* [1999] 3 WLR 972:

JUDGMENT

'It is crystal clear that the carefully and subtly drafted Human Rights Act 1998 preserves the principle of Parliamentary sovereignty.'

The Human Rights Act, therefore, is unlike Charters or Bills of Rights in other countries which typically have fundamental legal status. Indeed, the Act was passed through the ordinary parliamentary legislative process and could in fact be expressly repealed at any time by a future Parliament. Up until the last few years, it could certainly have been argued that the Act was politically entrenched as it would have been politically difficult to remove these rights; however, in recent years there have been proposals to replace the Act with an indigenous British Bill of Rights.

Secondly, the Human Rights Act in one respect is not an 'ordinary statute' as it is, in effect, an 'interpretative Act' setting out how the judiciary is to interpret legislation. As such, it is clear that the rule of implied repeal does not apply to the Act in the sense that:

- The Human Rights Act 1998 does *not* impliedly repeal any Act (or provision of it) passed before 1998 which is inconsistent with one of the articles of the European Convention (given further effect by the 1998 Act). On this point the 1997 White Paper stated that the Act was 'intended to provide a new basis for judicial interpretation of all legislation, not a basis for striking down any part of it' (para 2.14).
- The Human Rights Act 1998 itself is not *impliedly* repealed by legislation passed after 1998 which is inconsistent with the articles of the European Convention. During the parliamentary passage of the Bill the then Lord Chancellor – who introduced the Bill – made it clear that the doctrine of implied repeal could have no application to the Act (*Hansard*, HL Vol 583, col 509). In addition, Laws LJ has argued that the Human Rights Act, as a constitutional statute, is not subject to implied repeal (see earlier at section 4.4.5).

Finally, it is of interest to have regard to the observations of Ellis, who has suggested that, although the consequences of the Human Rights Act will take some years to pan out:

QUOTATION

'If the invariable reaction to a declaration of incompatibility proves to be an immediate remedial order, it might be concluded that the authority of Parliament has in fact been considerably diminished and its supremacy relinquished to the Convention and the courts. The effect of such a position would, in practice, be only slightly different from a power of judicial review over primary legislation.'

'The Legislative Supremacy of Parliament and its Limits', in D Feldman (ed), *English Public Law* (2nd edn, Oxford University Press, 2009), p 134.

NB. For a comprehensive examination of sovereignty and the 1998 Act, see A Young, *Parliamentary Sovereignty and the Human Rights Act* (Hart Publishing, 2009).

7.13 Parliamentary sovereignty and the rule of law

Figure 7.3 Dicey and the British Constitution

Dicey viewed the British constitution as resting on the twin pillars of parliamentary sovereignty and the rule of law. He argued that these pillars pervaded the whole of the constitution, and that parliamentary sovereignty favoured the supremacy of the law of the land. He also pointed out that the independent position of the judges under the constitution (who, of course, uphold the rule of law) was secured by Parliament (it should be remembered that the senior judiciary are not removable by the executive – see section 13.4.1).

Although Parliament can pass any law it chooses, the courts will construe legislation in the light of the political/moral precepts underpinning the rule of law which respect basic constitutional principles (the protection of rights, access to the courts, etc). Writing extra-judicially, Lord Woolf noted that our parliamentary democracy is based on the rule of law:

QUOTATION

'As both Parliament and the courts derive their authority from the rule of law so both are subject to it and cannot act in a manner which involves its repudiation. The respective roles do not give rise to conflict because the courts and Parliament each respects the role of the other.'

Lord Woolf, 'Droit public-English style' [1995] PL 57.

More recently, Baroness Hale made the following *obiter* comment:

JUDGMENT

'The courts will, of course, decline to hold that Parliament has interfered with fundamental rights unless it has made its intentions crystal clear. The courts will treat with particular suspicion (and might even reject) any attempt to subvert the rule of law by removing governmental action affecting the rights of the individual from all judicial scrutiny.'

R (Jackson and others) v Attorney General [2005] UKHL 56 – however, see Lord Bingham quoted earlier at section 7.3.2. On the so-called 'myth' of common law constitutionalism, see J Goldsworthy, *Parliamentary Sovereignty* (Cambridge University Press, 2010), Chapter 2.

In any event, the traditional view of parliamentary sovereignty certainly raises issues concerning constitutionalism. As defined earlier (see section 2.6), constitutionalism is the principle that state power is effectively limited by constitutional rules (typically contained in a written codified constitutional document). Under the principle of parliamentary sovereignty, however, there are no legal limits restraining the laws that Parliament can pass, as there is no codified constitution constraining it as in other countries. Is parliamentary sovereignty, therefore, consistent with constitutionalism?

One response to this is that, although in legal theory Parliament can pass any law that it chooses, in reality it does not. It is an unwritten maxim of the British constitution generally that those in power (parliamentarians and ministers) do not use their full powers to the maximum. In other words, Parliament is restrained politically and morally by the precepts underpinning the rule of law, and generally does not legislate contrary to them.

This is not to say that Parliament has not legislated in breach of the rule of law, as demonstrated by the War Damage Act 1965, which overruled a judicial ruling of the House of Lords for economic expediency (see sections 4.9, 6.7.9 and 7.5.1). Although the British constitution is based on the twin pillars of parliamentary sovereignty and the rule of law, morally, the latter will typically restrain the former. In legal terms, however, ultimately, they are unequal pillars as Parliament can (if it so chooses) legislate to undermine the principles underpinning the rule of law. It is also pertinent to remember that, owing to the electoral system, as the government of the day typically has dominance over the House of Commons, this has led to the argument that in practice we have 'executive sovereignty' rather than parliamentary sovereignty (see section 9.8). In the final analysis, it is instructive to note that in 2005 the then Lord Chancellor commented that we must trust Parliament to understand the basis of our constitution so as not to violate the rule of law (the House of Lords Select Committee on the Constitution, *Meeting with the Lord Chancellor*, HL Paper 84 (2005), Q 20).

In conclusion, given all the debate surrounding parliamentary sovereignty, perhaps Lord Hope summed it up best:

JUDGMENT

'The question whether the principle of the sovereignty of the United Kingdom Parliament is absolute or may be subject to limitation in exceptional circumstances is still under discussion.'

AXA General Insurance Ltd v Lord Advocate [2011] UKSC 46.

ACTIVITY

Exercise

Revisit Chapter 6 and explain how the rule of law relates to, and restrains, parliamentary sovereignty.

SUMMARY

- Parliamentary sovereignty is the key principle which underpins the British constitution.
- Parliamentary sovereignty is concerned with the legal relationship between the courts and the legislature/Parliament.
- Parliamentary sovereignty has been closely associated with Dicey, who viewed it as having both positive and negative elements.

- The positive element was that the Crown/Queen in Parliament can legally pass any law. This is because in the British constitution (unlike in other countries) there is no codified document to stop it from doing so. Parliament can therefore alter any aspect of the constitution or alter any law that it chooses.
- Dicey identified one legal exception to the above which was that Parliament could not bind its successors. This is achieved through the twin doctrines of express and implied repeal.
- Although there may be an absence of legal limitations on Parliament, there are nevertheless political and practical restraints on the laws that Parliament can pass.
- The negative element of parliamentary sovereignty was that no court/body can question a statute. This means that the courts obey and apply Acts of Parliament (historically applying the 'enrolled Bill rule' to ascertain whether a Bill had become an Act).
- In recent years Dicey's principle that Parliament cannot bind its successors has been questioned.
- Today the principle of parliamentary sovereignty must be considered and revisited in the context of EU law (Chapter 15).

SAMPLE ESSAY QUESTION

What is meant by the term parliamentary sovereignty?

Introduction:
- Definition: Crown in Parliament can pass any law.
- Distinguish between legal and political sovereignty.
- Parliamentary sovereignty is central to the British constitution in the absence of a codified constitutional document (Dicey's conception of the principle is highly influential).

Crown in Parliament can pass any law:
- To alter the common law (War Damage Act 1965), to change the constitution (House of Lords Act 1999), to legislate extra-territorially (War Crimes Act 1991) and to interfere with human rights (Anti-terrorism, Crime and Security Act 2001).
- Notwithstanding the above, note the practical restraints on Parliament (Denning MR in *Blackburn* (1971)) and those imposed by constitutional convention (historically the Sewel Convention).
- Note the recent comments of Lord Steyn in *Jackson* (2005).

No court can question an Act of Parliament:
- See *Jordan* (1967) and *Pickin* (1974).

Parliament cannot bind its successors:

- See the traditional Diceyan view in *Vauxhall* (1932) and *Ellen Street Estates* (1934).
- Other views on binding Parliament in terms of 'manner and form' *Minister of the Interior* (1952), *Bribery Commissioner* (1965) and *Manuel* (1983). Also see the *obiter* comments in *Jackson* (2005).

The relevance of parliamentary sovereignty today:

- Since 1973 subject to European Union law – see European Communities Act 1972 and *Factortame* (1991) - but now see Brexit, Chapter 15.

Conclusion

Further reading

Books

Barnett, H, *Constitutional and Administrative Law* (12th edn, Routledge/Taylor & Francis Group, 2017), Chapter 6.

Bradley, A, 'The Sovereignty of Parliament – Form or Substance?' in Jowell, J and Oliver, D (eds), *The Changing Constitution* (7th edn, Oxford University Press, 2011), p 35.

Elliott, M, 'Legislative Supremacy in a Multidimensional Constitution' in Elliott, M and Feldman, D (eds), *The Cambridge Companion to Public Law* (Cambridge University Press, 2015), p 73.

Elliott, M, 'The Principle of Parliamentary Sovereignty in Legal, Constitutional and Political Perspective' in Jowell, J, Oliver, D and O'Cinneide, C (eds), *The Changing Constitution* (8th edn, Oxford University Press, 2015), p 38.

Goldsworthy, J, *Parliamentary Sovereignty* (Cambridge University Press, 2010).

Gordon, R, 'Constitutional Change and Parliamentary Sovereignty – the Impossible Dialectic' in Qvortrup, M (ed), *The British Constitution: Continuity and change* (Hart Publishing, 2015), p 153.

Leyland, P, *The Constitution of the United Kingdom* (3rd edn, Hart Publishing, 2016), pp 47–65.

Articles

Allan, T, 'Parliamentary sovereignty: law, politics, and revolution' (1997) 113 LQR 443.

Lord Bingham, 'Dicey revisited' [2002] PL 39.

Bogdanor, V, 'Imprisoned by a doctrine: The modern defence of parliamentary sovereignty' (2012) 32 OJLS 179.

Burns, S, 'When is an Act of Parliament not an Act of Parliament?' (2006) 156 NLJ 191.

Gordon, M, 'The conceptional foundations of parliamentary sovereignty: Reconsidering Jennings and Wade' [2009] PL 519.

Jowell, J, 'Parliamentary sovereignty under the new constitutional hypothesis' [2006] PL 562.

McGarry, J, 'The principle of parliamentary sovereignty' (2012) 32 LS 577.

Mullen, T, 'Reflections on Jackson v Attorney General: questioning sovereignty' (2007) 27 LS 1.

Pannick, D, 'Securing political success by repetition (F.E. Smith): Can the Parliament Act 1911 be used by the House of Commons to insist on reform of the House of Lords?' [2012] PL 230.

Wade, HWR, 'The basis of legal sovereignty' [1955] CLJ 172.

Young, A, 'Hunting sovereignty: *Jackson v Her Majesty's Attorney-General*' [2006] PL 187.

8

Parliament I: Nature, functions and privilege

AIMS AND OBJECTIVES

At the end of this chapter you should be able to:

▪ Identify and explain the different functions of Parliament

▪ Explain the nature and significance of parliamentary privilege

8.1 Introduction and terminology

The United Kingdom Westminster Parliament is bicameral as it is composed of two Houses. It is also tripartite as it is composed of three constituent elements. These elements are as follows:

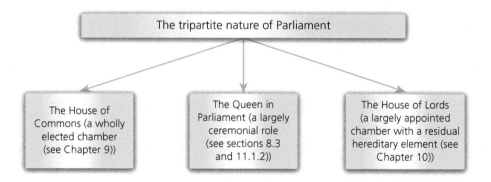

Figure 8.1 The tripartite nature of Parliament

8.1.1 Parliamentary terms

A parliamentary term is the period which exists between national general elections. Each Parliament lasts for a term, which is divided up into a number of sessions. Under the Fixed-Term Parliaments Act 2011, there is a five-year maximum length of a parliamentary term. This Act was a welcome (though not by all) constitutional reform which reduced the power of the Prime Minister as it replaced the historical position whereby the executive (specifically the Prime Minister) determined the length of a parliamentary term by deciding when to call a national general election for the House of Commons. It should be noted that under s 1 of the Act a general election can be delayed by the Prime Minister (via a statutory instrument approved by Parliament) by up to two months. This provision provides for an emergency situation where it would be inappropriate to hold an election (eg in the event of a major national disaster).

8.1.2 A vote of no confidence

Whilst in office, historically a government could lose the support of MPs in the House of Commons via a vote of no confidence being carried against it. The loss of such a vote was rare, although in 1979 the Labour government lost a confidence motion by one vote. As a result, the Labour Prime Minister (James Callaghan) requested a dissolution of Parliament and Mrs Thatcher won the resulting general election and became Conservative Prime Minister in May 1979 (see further section 12.2.1). Today the Fixed-Term Parliaments Act 2011 provides for five yearly terms, but it also allows an early election to be triggered in one of two ways:

- Firstly, section 2(3) gives legal effect to the loss of a vote of no confidence by an incumbent government. Prior to the Act the convention in the event of a loss of a vote of no confidence was either for a dissolution of Parliament, leading to a general election (eg Callaghan in 1979), or for the government to resign to allow an alternative government to be formed (eg Baldwin in 1924). Section 2(3) states that an early election will take place if the House of Commons passed the following motion: 'That this House has no confidence in Her Majesty's Government' (s 2(4)). In addition, thereafter 14 days must also have passed without the House passing the following motion: 'That this House has confidence in Her Majesty's Government' (s 2(5)). This latter provision allows for the creation of an alternative government or even possibly allows the defeated government to reconstitute itself as a credible government.
- Secondly, section 2(1) provides that an early election will take place if the House of Commons passes the following motion: 'That there shall be an early parliamentary general election' (s 2(2)) and, if passed on a division, must be supported by at least two-thirds of the number of seats in the Commons. In effect, this confers a new constitutional power on MPs to precipitate a general election which is in addition to the provision concerning a vote of no confidence set out above. In fact, in April 2017 the House carried this motion by 522 to 13 votes, thereby triggering the 'snap' election of 2017 (*Hansard*, HC Vol 624, col 708).

On the Act, see M Ryan, 'The Fixed-Term Parliaments Act 2011' [2012] PL 213. NB: it is of interest to note that the 2017 Conservative Party general election manifesto stated that it would repeal the 2011 Act (*The Conservative and Unionist Party Manifesto 2017* (Conservative Party, 2017), p 43) – although at the time of going to print it would appear that this would not happen.

8.1.3 A new Parliament

After a general election a new Parliament will be installed. For example, following the general election of 2017 a new Parliament was summoned and it became the 57th Parliament (each Parliament is numbered). Directly after a general election the monarch will appoint the Prime Minister and by constitutional convention she will appoint the person who commands the support of the majority of MPs in the House of Commons. As a consequence of our electoral system, this is typically a mere formality. When a Prime Minister has won a second or third successive general election victory (as with Tony Blair in 2001 and 2005), the monarch does not appoint the Prime Minister as they are *already* the Prime Minister and by constitutional convention will be asked to form the next government. Most recently, after the general election of 2017, Theresa May continued in office as Prime Minister.

Under the Meeting of Parliament Act 1694, Parliament, by law, must be summoned to meet at least once in every three years. The practical reality is that after a general election the next Parliament will be summoned quickly. This is because, in practice, Parliament operates on an annual basis as the machinery of government necessitates this (for example, income tax for the following year needs to be authorised by Parliament). As a result of the 'snap' 2017 general election, the next election scheduled under the Fixed-Term Parliaments Act 2011 will be in 2022.

8.1.4 Parliamentary sessions

Every parliamentary term is subdivided into parliamentary sessions consisting of approximately one year each. Each parliamentary session (which as a consequence of the Fixed-Term Parliaments Act 2011 typically begins in spring and ends the following spring) will be opened by the State Opening of Parliament and the Queen's Speech. The Queen's Speech is written by the government of the day and outlines the proposed legislative programme for the ensuing session. Following the enactment of the Fixed-Term Parliaments Act 2011, each Parliament will consist (ordinarily) of five sessions. However, in order to accommodate the watershed legislation required for Brexit (see section 15.6.6), the first session of the 2017–2022 Parliament was extended to two years (ie 2017–19).

8.1.5 Prorogation

At the end of each parliamentary session Parliament is prorogued (ie suspended). The effect of this is that, if a Bill introduced in one parliamentary session has not passed through Parliament and received the Royal Assent by the end of that session, it is lost and the Bill would have to be reintroduced (as a new Bill) the following session. In recent years, however, it has been possible to 'carry over' Bills from one parliamentary session to the next. For example, the Constitutional Reform Bill 2003–04 was carried over in the House of Lords (where it had not completed its stages owing partly to the fact that, very unusually, it was sent to a select committee for detailed consideration) to the 2004–05 parliamentary session. During the prorogation of Parliament all business in both Houses ceases (including work in parliamentary committees).

KEY FACTS

Parliamentary terminology
• The period between parliaments is known as a term and each term is subdivided into a maximum of five sessions.
• Each session is approximately one year and at the end of each session, Parliament is suspended (prorogued).
• A new parliament is installed following a general election.

8.2 A bicameral legislature

8.2.1 Bicameralism

bicameralism

a legislature composed of two chambers

The United Kingdom Parliament is **bicameral**, consisting of two chambers (namely the elected House of Commons and the non-elected House of Lords). The majority of legislatures/assemblies in the world are, however, unicameral, consisting of only one chamber. For example:

- New Zealand (House of Representatives).
- Denmark (Folketing).
- Sweden (Riksdag).

Unicameral legislatures tend to be found in smaller states (with one clear exception being China) with relatively homogeneous populations. In contrast, the United Kingdom, together with most large democracies such as the United States, Canada, France, Italy and Spain, has two chambers. In fact, a bicameral system tends to be found particularly in federal states (eg Australia and the USA), where the upper house can represent the interests of the various different regions and peoples. Lower chambers tend to be more powerful than their corresponding upper Houses.

8.2.2 Arguments in favour of bicameralism

- Two chambers disperse the power to make law between two (rival) power centres. By dispersing and dividing the power to make legislation, it is necessarily constitutionally limited.
- Two chambers can ensure that legislative proposals are examined and scrutinised more effectively than in a unicameral legislature, as legislation must (generally speaking) pass through both chambers in order to become law. In particular, a second chamber can look afresh at, and revise, legislative proposals which have passed through the lower House.
- A second chamber can act as a constitutional safeguard and protector of the constitution from the wishes of the (generally more powerful) lower chamber.
- A second chamber can represent regional or sectional interests.

8.2.3 Arguments in favour of unicameralism

- Unicameral legislatures tend to be more decisive.
- Unicameral systems avoid inter-chamber constitutional conflict, which is necessarily inherent in a bicameral system where two chambers compete with each other.

In any event, in respect of recent attempts at reforming the House of Lords (see section 10.13), in March 2007 the House of Commons voted to retain a bicameral system by 416 votes to 163. It is clear that any future reform of the House of Lords will necessarily involve retaining the second chamber. Historically, some countries such as Denmark and New Zealand have abolished their second chambers (1953 and 1950 respectively), although in both cases the populations are comparatively small (5 and 4 million, respectively).

ACTIVITY

Self-test question

Do you think that the United Kingdom should have a bicameral legislature? Revisit this question after you have completed Chapter 10 (the House of Lords).

8.3 The Queen in Parliament

It is the Queen in Parliament (Crown in Parliament) which passes primary legislation, and so the monarch is a constituent element of Parliament. Her main constitutional roles include:

- Proroguing Parliament at the end of a parliamentary session.
- Opening each parliamentary session with the state opening and the delivery of the Queen's Speech.
- Granting assent to a Bill in order for it to become an Act of Parliament.
- Appointing the Prime Minister, who is drawn from Parliament.
- Appointing government ministers, who are drawn from Parliament.

The above constitutional duties are performed by the monarch, but in accordance with constitutional convention she acts on the advice of her government ministers.

The monarch is not allowed in the House of Commons to observe debates (a consequence of the English Civil War), which is why Members of Parliament (MPs) go to the House of Lords to hear the delivery of the Queen's Speech. The monarch is, however, permitted to listen to debates in the Lords. The monarch will be considered again at section 11.1.2.

8.4 The functions of Parliament

The principal functions of Parliament are set out below, but they do blend with the individual constitutional functions of the two Houses. Although Parliament is the legislature, it will be noted that its constitutional responsibilities are not confined to simply passing legislation. In 2006 the parliamentary website (www.parliament.uk) identified the following functions of Parliament:

8.4.1 A legislative function (examining and passing proposals for law)

The passing of legislation is the principal constitutional function of a legislature. In the United Kingdom the Queen in Parliament is the supreme domestic law-making body. As Parliament is elected by the people and composed of elected representatives (at least in terms of the House of Commons), the resulting laws made, represent the will of the people.

Although in constitutional theory it is the Queen in Parliament which passes the law, the practical reality is that Parliament to a large extent passes laws which have been drafted and initiated by the government of the day. Indeed, such is this dominance that, it could be argued that, generally speaking, Parliament merely rubberstamps or legitimises the legislative proposals sought by the government. One of the constitutional functions of the executive in the British constitution is that of developing policy and initiating proposed legislation (eg the recent Fixed-Term Parliaments Bill).

Notwithstanding the above, some legislative proposals are initiated by parliamentary members in the form of Private Members' Bills. These can be initiated by members in either House, but the likely success of these measures becoming law are, to a large extent, dependent on support from the incumbent government, as it dominates the parliamentary timetable. For a useful report by the House of Commons Procedure Committee on Private Members' Bills and how to improve their procedures see *Private Members' Bills*, HC 188-I (The Stationery Office, 2013). An example of a recent successful Bill in the field of constitutional law is the House of Lords Reform Act 2014 (see later at section 10.13), which was introduced by Dan Byles MP. In addition to the above public Bills, Parliament also processes private Bills (sponsored by, for example, local authorities) and hybrid Bills (a mixture of both public and private elements).

In general terms, Bills require the consent of both Houses of Parliament in order to become law. In exceptional cases, however, only the consent of the House of Commons is necessary in the event of the Parliament Acts 1911 and 1949 being used (see section 10.10.1).

8.4.2 A deliberative function (the scrutiny of executive policy and administration)

Parliament acts as a constitutional check on the exercise of executive power. In short, Parliament scrutinises executive policy, administration and actions, thereby ensuring that the government of the day is constitutionally accountable and responsible to Parliament (which, of course, represents the people). In constitutional theory, accountability is secured through the following parliamentary mechanisms:

- The scrutiny of legislative proposals.
- Debates.
- Questions.
- Select committees.

For a detailed consideration of the nature and effectiveness of these mechanisms, see Chapter 12. As the legal philosopher John Stuart Mill noted in the nineteenth century:

QUOTATION

'Instead of the function of governing, for which it is radically unfit, the proper office of a representative assembly is to watch and control the government; to throw the light of publicity on its acts; to compel a full exposition and justification of all of them which any one considers questionable; to censure them if found condemnable, and, if the men who compose the government abuse their trust, or fulfil it in a manner which conflicts with the deliberate sense of the nation, to expel them from office. . . '

J S Mill, *On Liberty and Considerations on Representative Government* (Basil Blackwell Oxford, 1946), p 172.

The constitutional function of Parliament (particularly in the context of a parliamentary executive), therefore, is to hold the government to account, ie make it explain and justify its policies and actions/decisions. In doing so, Parliament acts as a constitutional restraint on the executive and acts as a forum for influencing executive policy. By scrutinising – and then endorsing – the actions of the executive, Parliament confers constitutional legitimacy on executive actions.

Both Houses scrutinise the actions of the executive, and it is particularly important in the absence of a written entrenched codified constitution that the executive is effectively scrutinised by Parliament. Effective and meaningful scrutiny, of course, necessarily depends upon the government providing accurate and full information.

8.4.3 A forum for debate (debating the major issues of the day)

Both Houses of Parliament act as forums for debate on matters of public importance and interest (see sections 12.5 and 10.9.2). One interesting development which has taken place in recent years is the use of a parallel chamber known as Westminster Hall. Due to the congested nature of the timetable in the House of Commons, debates can now take place in this 'parallel' chamber. Such debates might otherwise have found little space on the Floor of the House of Commons.

8.4.4 To provide for taxation/finance

By voting for taxation, Parliament enables the administration of government to be carried out. In order for the government of the day to raise money it must have the express permission of Parliament. In particular, it is the House of Commons (which is directly elected by the people) which has control over such financial matters (ie scrutinising expenditure and authorising taxation). On taxation, see the annual Budget – the Finance Bill at section 12.8.

8.4.5 To safeguard the rights of individuals

This is a function performed by both Houses. In particular, every MP in the House of Commons has a specific constituency with a responsibility to help redress the grievances of their constituents (see section 9.3.1). In terms of protecting the rights of the individual, the House of Lords has a specific role to act as a constitutional safe-guard and watchdog of civil liberties when considering legislative proposals which threaten to undermine the basic rights of the individual (see section 10.9.9). In addition, Parliament has established the Joint Committee on Human Rights to consider matters relating to human rights and to consider remedial orders made under the Human Rights Act 1998 (see Chapter 17).

8.4.6 The examination of proposed European legislation

As a member of the European Union, laws can be made in Europe which directly affect the United Kingdom. In fact, these laws can override the domestic law (including Acts of Parliament) of the United Kingdom (see section 15.6). Parliament, through committees in both Houses, supervises proposed European legislative measures (see section 12.9).

8.4.7 A judicial function

Although in 2006 the parliamentary website listed the hearing of judicial appeals by the Appellate Committee as a function, in October 2009 this function was transferred to the new Supreme Court. Notwithstanding this, both Houses perform a judicial function in the context of enforcing parliamentary privilege and disciplining their members (see section 8.5).

In addition to those already mentioned, the following functions could be added:

The recruitment of the government

As the United Kingdom has a parliamentary executive, the executive is necessarily drawn from Parliament. By constitutional convention, members of the government must sit in either House of Parliament (except the Prime Minster, who must sit in the

Commons). Parliament, therefore, provides the pool from which the government is drawn. Although ministers are drawn from both Houses, they predominately come from the House of Commons (see section 11.6.1).

■ **The removal of specified personnel**

Both Houses of Parliament acting in concert with each other are constitutionally responsible for removing key personnel, for example senior judges (see section 13.4.1) and the Parliamentary Commissioner for Administration (see section 21.3.6).

KEY FACTS

The functions of Parliament	Performed by
Legislative	Both Houses, although ultimately the House of Commons is dominant.
The control of finance	The House of Commons (exclusively).
Safeguarding rights	Both Houses, although the House of Lords has a particular responsibility for this.
Scrutiny of the executive	Both Houses, although the House of Commons is typically dominated by the government of the day.
Scrutiny of European legislation	Both Houses.
Debate	Both Houses.
Recruitment of the government	Both Houses, though largely from the House of Commons.
Representative	The House of Commons as it is elected, although life peers in the Lords can to some extent reflect society at large.
Judicial	Both Houses enforce parliamentary privilege.

8.5 Parliamentary privilege

8.5.1 Definition and types of privilege

QUOTATION

'Parliamentary privilege is an essential part of our parliamentary democracy. It ensures that Members of Parliament are able to speak freely in debates, and protects Parliament's internal affairs from interference from the courts.'

Parliamentary Privilege, Cm 8318 (Crown Copyright, 2012), para 1.

Erskine May defined the privileges of Parliament in the following way:

QUOTATION

> 'Parliamentary privilege is the sum of certain rights enjoyed by each House collectively as a constituent part of the High Court of Parliament; and by Members of each House individually, without which they could not discharge their functions, and which exceed those possessed by other bodies or individuals.'
>
> E May, *Parliamentary Practice* (24th edn, LexisNexis Butterworths, 2011), p 203.

According to Erskine May, at the commencement of each new Parliament, the Speaker of the House of Commons lays claim to the following rights/privileges known as the four petitions (it is taken that similar privileges also apply in the Lords):

- **Freedom of speech**
  (see section 8.6).
- **Freedom from arrest**
  The freedom of members not to be arrested within Parliament was established at a very early date and the constitutional rationale behind it was to enable members to attend the chamber so that they could perform their constitutional functions as part of Parliament. This privilege was confined to arrest in the context of civil matters (not criminal ones). As noted by the 1999 Joint Committee on Parliamentary Privilege (see below), since the almost practical abolition of imprisonment for debt (Debtors Act 1869), it seems to have little modern relevance (with the exception of an immunity from arrest for disobeying a court order in civil proceedings – *Stourton v Stourton* [1963] 1 All ER 606). In 1999 the Joint Committee recommended its abolition (Joint Committee on Parliamentary Privilege, *Report, Volume 1 – Report and Proceedings of the Committee*, HL Paper 43-I HC 214-I (1999), p 85). More recently, the 2013 Joint Committee on Parliamentary Privilege (which reported on the coalition government's 2012 Green Paper on parliamentary privilege) also agreed that freedom from arrest in civil matters should be abolished (*Parliamentary Privilege*, Report of Session 2013–14, HL Paper 30, HC 100 (The Stationery Office, 2013), para 257).
- **Free access to the monarch**
  Both Houses have access to the sovereign (although peers have access as individuals) and MPs attend the House of Lords to hear the Queen's Speech.
- **The most favourable construction be placed upon the proceedings in the House**
  According to Erskine May, today this is simply 'a formal courtesy'.

In addition to the above, Parliament also enjoys, *inter alia*:

- the right to determine and regulate its own membership and internal proceedings (see sections 8.7.1 and 8.7.2)
- the right to administer punishments in the event of a privilege being breached (see section 8.7.3).

NB. Following the search in November 2008 of the MP Damian Green's parliamentary office by the police, the Committee on Issue of Privilege (*Police Searches on the Parliamentary Estate*) was established by the House of Commons. Its remit was to 'review the internal processes of the House administration for granting permission for such action, to consider any matter relating to privilege arising from the police operation, and to make recommendations for the future'. In 2010 the committee issued its report (*Police Searches on the Parliamentary Estate*, First Report, HC 62 (The Stationery Office, 2010)). In terms of the issue of privilege, in its report it stated that the committee did not consider that the actions of the police were a breach of privilege or a contempt of the House of Commons (para 140).

8.5.2 The origins, sources and constitutional rationale of parliamentary privilege

Parliamentary privilege forms part of the law and custom of Parliament. The sources of privilege are found in Acts of Parliament (eg Art 9 of the Bill of Rights 1689), practices within Parliament and court decisions which have identified the existence of privileges and rights. Parliament, through the enactment of a statute can:

- Create new privileges.
- Amend or modify an existing privilege. For example, see s 13 of the Defamation Act 1996 (see section 8.6.2).
- Abolish a privilege. For example, the Criminal Justice Act 2003 abolished the immunity and privilege of members to be excused *as of right* from jury service.

The constitutional reason that parliamentary members enjoy these privileges, immunities and rights is to ensure that they can carry out their constitutional functions as parliamentarians. Members need to be able to air grievances and call to account the government. Moreover, Parliament itself must be able to regulate its own composition and affairs without interference from either the ordinary courts or the government of the day (albeit that the latter sits in Parliament). In this way, Parliament enjoys independence. As noted by the 2013 Joint Committee:

QUOTATION

'The corollary of Parliament's immunity from outside interference is that those matters subject to parliamentary privilege fall to be regulated by Parliament alone. Parliament enjoys sole jurisdiction – normally described by the archaic term "exclusive cognisance" – over all matters subject to parliamentary privilege.'

Parliamentary Privilege, HL Paper 30, HC 100 (The Stationery Office, 2013), p 7.

Parliamentary privileges and immunities (in particular freedom of speech), are not unique to the United Kingdom. For example, Art 15.10 of the Republic of Ireland's Constitution permits both chambers of the Oireachtas to make their own internal rules and standing orders regulating each House. These internal rules and procedures cannot be challenged by the Irish courts. In addition, see New Zealand in the context of the *Prebble v Television New Zealand Ltd* (1995) below at section 8.6.2.

8.6 Freedom of speech

8.6.1 Article 9 of the Bill of Rights 1689

Members of Parliament in both Houses enjoy an absolute immunity in respect of freedom of speech within Parliament:

SECTION

Article 9, the Bill of Rights 1689

'The freedom of speech and debates or proceedings in Parliament ought not to be impeached or questioned in any court or place out of Parliament.'

The constitutional rationale behind this is to enable parliamentary members to have freedom of speech so as to be able to discuss whatever subject they choose ('freedom of speech and debates'). This legal immunity is absolute and includes immunity from both civil and criminal liability as anything said during parliamentary proceedings 'ought not to be impeached or questioned'. This enables members to freely perform their parliamentary functions and duties (raising issues of public concern, etc) without the fear of legal repercussions. In *A v United Kingdom* (2003) (see below) the European Court of Human Rights accepted that the justification for this absolute immunity was twofold:

- Firstly, it permitted free debate.
- Secondly, it ensured a constitutional separation between the judiciary and the legislature, as the former could not interfere with debates and speeches in the latter.

Similarly, in the Republic of Ireland, Art 15.12 of the Irish Constitution protects members of both Houses of the Oireachtas in respect of what they say in the legislature, with all official reports and 'utterances' being privileged.

As Art 9 confers an absolute immunity on members this would appear to contravene one of the principles underpinning the rule of law, namely equality under the law with no immunities from its ambit (see section 6.7.6). As a result, it is imperative that parliamentary members use this right/immunity in a responsible way and do not abuse it. In the event of abuse, as recognised by the European Court in *A v United Kingdom* (2003), one safeguard is that internal parliamentary disciplinary proceedings can be taken against the parliamentarian involved (see section 8.7.3).

CASE EXAMPLE

A v United Kingdom *(2003) 36 EHRR 51*

In a parliamentary debate, an MP referred specifically to A and her family in the context of anti-social behaviour as 'neighbours from hell'. A denied the truth of these allegations, but she was prohibited from suing the MP in defamation owing to Art 9 of the Bill of Rights 1689. She petitioned the European Court of Human Rights and argued that this immunity violated, *inter alia*, Art 6 (the right of access to a court) and Art 8 (the right to respect for private life).

The European Court held that there had been no violation as the immunity pursued the legitimate aims of protecting free speech and maintaining a separation of powers. It noted that all Contracting States had some system of parliamentary immunity. In fact, the court pointed out that the immunity in the United Kingdom was narrower than in some countries, as for example the immunity did not extend to an MP's statement made outside Parliament (see section 8.6.3).

In May 2010 at the beginning of the 55th Parliament, the Speaker of the House of Commons made the following speech concerning freedom of speech which:

QUOTATION

'. . . allows us to conduct our debates without fear of outside interference, but it is a freedom that we need to exercise responsibly in the public interest, and taking into account the interests of others outside this House.'

Hansard, HC Vol 510, col 301.

In respect of the 'comity' between Parliament and the courts, in March 2012 the Joint Committee on Privacy and Injunctions made the following recommendation concerning revelations (during proceedings in Parliament) of information which had been protected by 'anonymised injunctions' issued by the courts:

QUOTATION

'If the revelation of injuncted information becomes more commonplace, if injunctions are being breached gratuitously, or if there is evidence that parliamentarians are routinely being "fed" injuncted material with the intention of it being revealed in Parliament, then we recommend that the Procedure Committees in each House should examine the proposals made to us for new restrictions with a view to implementing them.'

Privacy and injunctions, Session 2010–12, HL Paper 273, HC 1443
(The Stationery Office, 2012), para 231.

ACTIVITY

Self-test question

Do you think that from a constitutional perspective parliamentary members should enjoy immunity from the law with respect to free speech?

8.6.2 Section 13 of the Defamation Act 1996

Before 1996, one consequence of Art 9 of the Bill of Rights for MPs was that they were prevented from suing in defamation if the defendant wished to adduce in their defence evidence of an MP's behaviour in Parliament (thereby 'questioning' parliamentary proceedings). In two separate actions initiated by MPs in the mid-1990s (*Allason v Haines, The Times*, 25 July 1995, and the *Hamilton* case, where Neil Hamilton had wanted to sue the *Guardian*), both cases were stayed by the courts as the respective defendants wished to rely, in effect, on proceedings in Parliament in their defence. It was held that it would have been unjust to permit these actions to continue if the defendants could not raise this information to defend their case. The following Privy Council decision influenced these two cases:

CASE EXAMPLE

Prebble v Television New Zealand Ltd *[1995] 1 AC 321*

Prebble instituted defamatory proceedings against Television New Zealand Ltd which wished to rely on statements made by him in the New Zealand Parliament. The Privy Council held that it was an infringement of parliamentary privilege (and contrary to the Bill of Rights 1689) for a party in legal proceedings to question words spoken in Parliament (ie suggesting that they were untrue, misleading or instigated for improper motives) and, therefore, those particulars of the defence which infringed parliamentary privilege had rightly been struck out. Notwithstanding the exclusion of these particulars, the action should not have been stayed, however, as the defendant could still allege the majority of matters on which it wished to rely in order to justify the alleged libel.

The effect of Art 9 meant that, although on the one hand an MP could not be sued in respect of his comments made in Parliament, on the other, it meant that an MP could not sue in defamation to clear his name if the defendant wished to use that MP's words in Parliament to justify his defence. As a result of this type of scenario, s 13 of the Defamation Act 1996 was (rather controversially) passed. This provision permitted a member of either House to waive his right to parliamentary privilege if he was instituting an action for defamation and the defendant wished to raise evidence of parliamentary statements/questions of that MP or peer in their defence. This provision was criticised by the 1999 Joint Committee on Parliamentary Privilege:

QUOTATION

'A fundamental flaw is that it undermines the basis of privilege: freedom of speech is the privilege of the House as a whole and not of the individual member in his own right, although an individual member can assert and rely on it.'

Joint Committee on Parliamentary Privilege, *Report, Volume 1 – Report and Proceedings of the Committee*, HL Paper 43-I HC 214-I (1999), para 68.

Instead, it recommended its replacement with a provision whereby each House could collectively waive privilege. More recently, the 2013 Joint Committee on Parliamentary Privilege recommended repealing s 13 of the Defamation Act 1996 as 'The anomalies it creates are more damaging than the mischief it was intended to cure.' (p 44).

NB. two years later, s 13 was repealed by the Deregulation Act 2015 (Sch 23, Pt 8) so that a person can no longer waive parliamentary privilege.

ACTIVITY

Self-test question

What were the advantages and disadvantages of s 13 of the Defamation Act 1996?

8.6.3 What are 'proceedings' in Parliament?

As noted by the 1999 Joint Committee on Parliamentary Privilege, unfortunately no comprehensive definition has been provided by either Parliament or the courts as to the meaning of proceedings in Parliament. According to the 1999 Joint Committee, 'proceedings' would include, *inter alia*:

- Debates and proceedings on Bills.
- Questions.
- Proceedings within committees (this could include a select committee sitting outside Parliament).
- Parliamentary votes.

The following examples illustrate what is meant by proceedings in Parliament:

CASE EXAMPLE

Dillon v Balfour *(1887) 20 LR Ir 600*

Dillon wished to sue Balfour (a government minister) in defamation for comments made by him about her during the course of the passage of a Bill through the House of Commons (she contended that the comments undermined her professional reputation as a midwife). The action was struck out because the comments were part of the proceedings in Parliament and so the court had no constitutional jurisdiction in respect of the matter.

CASE STUDY

George Strauss *HC Vol 568, Col 814*

This case concerned an allegedly defamatory letter sent by George Strauss MP to a government minister concerning the London Electricity Board (which then threatened to sue Strauss for libel). Strauss argued in Parliament that this legal action would represent a breach of parliamentary privilege. However, a resolution of the House of Commons decided that this letter was not a 'proceeding in Parliament'. In doing so they rejected a recommendation of the Committee of Privileges that it should be covered by parliamentary privilege.

Parliamentary privilege historically did not apply where an MP repeated outside Parliament words which he had used in a speech made earlier in the House of Commons. This explains why parliamentarians may be willing to make comments within Parliament which they would not repeat outside the chamber for fear of legal repercussions. On the issue of 'effective repetition' see para 197ffs of the 2013 Joint Committee on Parliamentary Privilege. In terms of repetition, however, now see the case of *Makudi v Baron Triesman* [2014] EWCA Civ 179, which extended - in very specific circumstances concerning the public interest – the protection provided by Art 9 of the Bill of Rights 1689 to extra-parliamentary speech (which has a close nexus to the original parliamentary speech).

NB. In *R v Chaytor and Others* [2010] UKSC 52 the Supreme Court held that the submitting of allowances/expenses were not part of the proceedings in Parliament. Lord Phillips stated that:

JUDGMENT

'Submitting claims for allowances and expenses does not form part of, nor is it incidental to, the core or essential business of Parliament, which consists of collective deliberation and decision-making. The submission of claims is an activity which is an incident of the administration of Parliament; it is not part of the proceedings in Parliament.'

8.6.4 'Proceedings in Parliament ought not to be impeached or questioned in any court'

As a result of the Bill of Rights the courts cannot question proceedings in Parliament. However, since the *Pepper v Hart* (1993) decision (below) the courts can make reference to parliamentary materials as an aid to the construction of legislation.

CASE EXAMPLE

Pepper v Hart *[1993] 1 All ER 42*

The House of Lords held that, in order to give effect to the true intention of Parliament in interpreting legislation, the court could refer to parliamentary materials where:

- the legislation in question was ambiguous, obscure or absurd;
- the material relied on consisted of statements made by the minister or promoter of the Bill, together (if needed) with other such parliamentary material necessary to understand these statements, and that these statements were clear.

The court made it clear that this reference to parliamentary material would not infringe Art 9 of the Bill of Rights as it was not 'questioning' the freedom of speech within Parliament, rather the court was merely trying to give effect to the intention of Parliament.

In the context of the Human Rights Act 1998 the House of Lords has held that in evaluating the compatibility of Acts of Parliament with European Convention rights, the court if necessary could have regard to relevant background material (ie explanatory departmental notes and ministerial statements when the Bill was progressing through its parliamentary stages), but not to debates in order to identify the policy objective behind the legislation (*Wilson v First County Trust Ltd (No 2)* [2003] UKHL 40). It is interesting to note that the Court of Appeal in *R (Reilly) v Secretary of State for Work and Pensions (No 2)* [2016] EWCA Civ 413 made specific reference to the earlier Administrative Court decision, in which Lang J had criticised the terms of the ministerial statement concerning the compatibility of the Jobseekers (Back to Work Schemes) Act 2013 with the European Convention:

JUDGMENT

'By doing so, she is said to have contravened the provision of article 9 of the Bill of Rights that "proceedings in Parliament ought not to be impeached or questioned in any court". It was accepted before us that in places in her judgment the judge does appear to have transgressed that rule. Our own reasoning does not involve any "questioning" of the kind which Mr Eadie criticises, and we do not see any advantage in lengthening this judgment still further by examining in detail at what point or to what extent the judge crossed the relevant line. '

It should be pointed out that s 1 of the Parliamentary Standards Act 2009 (see later at section 8.8.3) makes it plain that nothing in the Act affected Art 9 of the Bill of Rights 1689. Clause 10 of the original Bill had provided that parliamentary privilege would be set aside to enable evidence to be adduced in court against an MP in relation to a criminal offence under the original incarnation of the Bill (eg the offence of paid advocacy).

Finally, the following case concerned Art 9 and EU law:

CASE EXAMPLE

R (HS2 Action Alliance Limited) v Secretary of State for Transport
[2014] UKSC 3

In 2012 the coalition government published a command paper promoting a high speed rail link (known as HS2) from London to the North. Although the government's decision was challenged in judicial review proceedings, the Supreme Court held, *inter alia*, that the hybrid Bill procedure envisaged by the government to authorise and implement this project was compliant with the Environmental Impact Assessment (EIA) European Union Directive (2011/92). Lord Reed stated that:

JUDGMENT

'The argument presented on behalf of the appellants as to the implications of the EIA Directive, if well founded, impinges upon long-established constitutional principles governing the relationship between Parliament and the courts, as reflected for example in article 9 of the Bill of Rights 1689 . . .there is nothing either in the text of article 1(4) of the EIA Directive, or in the exegesis of that text by the Court of Justice to suggest that national courts are required not only to confirm that there has been a substantive legislative process and that the appropriate information was made available to the members of the legislature, but must in addition review the adequacy of the legislature's consideration of that information, for example by assessing the quality of the debate and examining the extent to which members participated in it. These are not matters which are apt for judicial supervision. . . There is a further difficulty with the contention that EU law requires the internal proceedings of national legislatures to be subject to judicial oversight of this nature. The separation of powers is a fundamental aspect of most if not all of the constitutions of the member states.. . . .Against this background, it appears unlikely that the Court of Justice intended to require national courts to exercise a supervisory jurisdiction over the internal proceedings of national legislatures of the nature for which the appellants contend.'

Publication of proceedings outside Parliament

Section 1 of the Parliamentary Papers Act 1840 conferred an absolute privilege on a person who publishes a paper/report printed by order, or under the authority, of Parliament (correct copies were covered by s 2). This Act had been passed in the context of (and in response to) litigation involving Stockdale suing Hansard for defamation for publishing a report ordered by the House of Commons (*Stockdale v Hansard* (1839) 9 Ad & E1). In this case, although Lord Chief Justice Denman accepted that the House had exclusive jurisdiction over its proceedings, it could not by resolution simply declare material to be privileged.

Under s 3 of the 1840 Act, extracts from, or abstracts of, the above parliamentary papers attract qualified privilege, and in terms of broadcasting s 3 was subsequently amended by the:

- Defamation Act 1952 (in respect of radio).
- Broadcasting Act 1990 (in respect of television).

In terms of reporting parliamentary proceedings, s 15 of the Defamation Act 1996 gives qualified privilege to a fair and accurate report of proceedings of any legislature in the world (as amended by s 7 of the Defamation Act 2013).

KEY FACTS

Art 9 of the Bill of Rights 1689
Article 9 of the Bill of Rights 1689 protects parliamentary members from civil and criminal liability from things said in Parliament.
It protects proceedings in Parliament which would include, *inter alia*: • Debates and proceedings on Bills. • Questions. • Proceedings within committees. • Parliamentary votes.
From a constitutional perspective, Art 9: • Permits free debate and enables parliamentary members to discuss whatever subject they choose without the fear of legal ramifications. • Ensures a clear constitutional separation between the judiciary and the legislature.

8.7 Other privileges

Other privileges enjoyed by both Houses are:

- The right to determine their own composition.
- The right to regulate their own internal proceedings.
- The right to punish individuals for contempt or breach of privilege.

by-election

an election which
takes place in
a constituency
when an MP's seat
becomes vacant

8.7.1 The right to determine their own composition

The House of Commons will, for example, determine who is qualified to be a member of the House and decide if a person is unfit to serve. The House will also determine the timing of **by-elections**. Similarly, the House of Lords will determine whether a peer is entitled by virtue of a writ of summons to sit in the Upper House (*Baron of Mereworthy v Ministry of Justice* [2011] EWHC 1589 (Ch)).

8.7.2 The right to regulate their own internal proceedings

As pointed out by Evans (*Handbook of House of Commons Procedure* (8th edn, Dods, 2011), p 32), this is known as the 'exclusive cognisance' of its proceedings. Each House will make standing orders to regulate its proceedings including in relation to the passage of legislation. A recent example of this is in relation to EVEL *'English Votes for English Laws'* (see section 12.7.3). As indicated earlier (see section 7.3.3), the courts will not look beyond the parliamentary roll and question the manner of parliamentary proceedings as this would violate the separation of powers between the judiciary and the legislature. As a consequence, Parliament will determine its own internal proceedings and decide if these proceedings have been interfered with. As pointed out by Lord Reid:

JUDGMENT

'The court has no concern with the manner in which Parliament or its officers carrying out its Standing Orders perform these functions. Any attempt to prove that they were misled by fraud or otherwise would necessarily involve an inquiry into the manner in which they had performed their functions in dealing with the Bill which became the British Railways Act 1968.'

British Railways Board v Pickin [1974] AC 765.

In this case, Lord Morris added that it would be both undesirable and impracticable for the courts to embark upon such an inquiry (also see, Willis J in *Lee v The Bude and Torrington Junction Railway Company* (1870–71) LR 6 CP 576). In fact, as illustrated by the following two cases, the courts have made it very clear that the internal administration of the House of Commons is not subject to supervision by the courts.

CASE EXAMPLE

Bradlaugh v Gossett *(1884) 12 QBD 271*

The House of Commons passed a resolution excluding Bradlaugh from the chamber (even though he had been elected to the House of Commons) 'until he shall engage not further to disturb the proceedings of the House'. Bradlaugh unsuccessfully sought a declaration that this order was void together with an order to restrain the Serjeant-at-Arms from preventing him from entering the House. The court held that it could not inquire into the propriety of a resolution of the House (this was a matter relating to the internal proceedings of the House).

CASE EXAMPLE

Chaffers v Goldsmid *[1894] 1 QB 186*

The court stated that no action would lie in the event of a member of the House of Commons refusing to present a petition (to redress certain grievances) to the chamber presented to him by a constituent.

More recently the Court of Appeal made it clear that the activities of the Parliamentary Commissioner for Standards (see section 8.8.2) are, in essence, concerned with the proceedings of the House. As such, what the officer did in relation to an investigation was beyond the supervisory powers of the courts (ie judicial review): *R v Parliamentary Commissioner for Standards, ex parte Al Fayed* [1998] 1 All ER 93.

In regulating its own proceedings, the Houses can, for example:

- Exclude disorderly strangers.
- Resolve to sit in a secret session.
- Debate any matter it chooses (subject to the *sub judice* resolution – see section 13.4.3).

8.7.3 The right to punish individuals for contempt

Erskine May defined contempt of Parliament as:

QUOTATION

'Generally speaking, any act or omission which obstructs or impedes either House of Parliament in the performance of its functions, or which obstructs or impedes any Member or officer of such House in the discharge of his duty, or which has a tendency, directly or indirectly, to produce such results.'

E May, *Parliamentary Practice* (24th edn, LexisNexis Butterworths, 2011), p 251.

May points out that contempt covers, *inter alia*, the following:

- Misconduct in the presence of the House or a committee.
- Disobeying a rule or an order.
- Misconduct of members (eg an MP accepting a bribe).
- Premature disclosure of committee proceedings.
- Obstructing or molesting members.
- Obstructing officers of the House or witnesses.

As noted by Evans (above), 'Contempts are often conflated with breaches of privilege. Any breach of the privileges of the House is a contempt' (p 33). However, he added that a contempt can be an action (eg disobedience to the House's commands) which is not a breach of one of the privileges of the House.

The procedure in respect of contempt or a breach of privilege (by a member)

In the House of Commons a member will raise the issue with the Speaker who will decide if it takes precedence over business. If so, the member can table a motion for the next day proposing that the matter is referred to the Select Committee of

Privileges (formerly known until 2013 as the Select Committee on Standards and Privileges). The committee in considering the matter has the power to send for persons, records and papers. Unlike in ordinary legal cases, the accused member is (generally) not allowed representation by counsel. If the committee decides that a breach has occurred, a debate on the committee's report will ensue in the Commons. The House then decides whether or not to accept the report and recommendations of the committee (on occasions it may not) and will determine the punishment. In the upper chamber, the House of Lords Committee for Privileges and Conduct investigates whether a breach of privilege or contempt has taken place and reports to the House, which, in turn, will determine what action (if any) to take.

Both Houses have their own penal jurisdiction and punishments which are separate from the ordinary courts. These are as follows:

- Imprisonment (although this has not been used for some time).
- Fines (seemingly lapsed in the House of Commons, although an MP's salary can be suspended).
- Suspension/expulsion (although historically the House of Lords did not have the power to permanently expel a member, but only suspend them, today legislation provides that members can now be expelled – see section 10.13).
- A formal reprimand/admonishment.

In this context, it is pertinent to note that Parliament is specifically excluded from the ambit of the Human Rights Act 1998 as under s 6 (3) of the Act Parliament is expressly excluded from being classed as a public authority. Parliament, therefore, does not have to legally follow the requirements of the European Convention (including Art 6 – the right to a fair trial). Notwithstanding this, as pointed out by the 1999 Joint Committee on Parliamentary Privilege, Parliament in exercising its internal disciplinary powers could theoretically be challenged under Art 6 of the Convention before the European Court of Human Rights in Strasbourg if its proceedings are not fair. As a result, it indicated that Parliament should adopt (at least) minimum requirements of fairness in its internal disciplinary procedures (Joint Committee on Parliamentary Privilege, *Report, Volume 1 – Report and Proceedings of the Committee*, HL Paper 43-I, HC 214-I (1999), para 284).

Finally, the 1999 Joint Committee recommended the enactment of a Parliamentary Privilege Act which would codify parliamentary privileges. In contrast, neither the coalition government's 2012 Green Paper (para 38) nor the 2013 Joint Committee supported 'comprehensive codification' of parliamentary privilege (p 14). This would not, however, preclude individual legislative measures to address specific issues (eg repealing s 13 of the Defamation Act 1996 or replacing the Parliamentary Papers Act 1840 – see para 280 of the 2013 Joint Committee report). As already noted, the former has now been achieved by the Deregulation Act 2015.

ACTIVITY

Self-test question

Do you think that the way in which Parliament disciplines those who commit contempt or a breach of privilege is consistent with the right to a fair trial under Art 6 of the European Convention? Revisit this question after having completed Chapter 16 on the European Convention.

The main privileges of Parliament
• Freedom of speech. • Freedom from arrest. • Free access to the monarch. • The most favourable construction to be placed upon the proceedings in the House. • The right to determine and regulate its own membership. • The right to determine its internal proceedings. • The right to administer punishments for contempt or breach of privilege.

8.8 Members' interests and standards

8.8.1 The Register of Members' Financial Interests

In the mid-1970s, the House of Commons established a compulsory Register of Members' Interests (renamed in 2009 as the Register of Members' Financial Interests), which required MPs to declare their financial interests with the outside world (ie payments, remunerated directorships or trades, etc). In addition, MPs should declare interests when participating in debates. The House of Lords also has a Register of Lords' Interests in respect of consultancies, remunerated directorships etc.

8.8.2 Standards in Public Life

As a result of the 'cash for questions' affair in 1994, the then Prime Minister established the Committee on Standards in Public Life 'To examine current concerns about standards of conduct of all holders of public office'. This committee (the Nolan Committee) issued its report in 1995 (First Report of the Committee on Standards in Public Life, *Standards in Public Life, Volume 1: Report*, Cm 2850-I (1995)) and led to:

▪ **The creation of the Select Committee on Standards and Privileges** (to replace the then Committee of Privileges). From 2013 this committee was replaced and divided into a Committee on Standards (including three lay members) and a Committee of Privileges (see section 8.7.3). The responsibilities of the Committee on Standards involve overseeing the Parliamentary Commissioner for Standards (see below) and considering breaches of the Code of Conduct and Guide to the Rules (see below).

▪ **The establishment of a Parliamentary Commissioner for Standards**
The functions of this officer, *inter alia*, are to:

○ Oversee the Register of Members' Financial Interests.
○ Advise as to the interpretation of the Code of Conduct and Guide to the Rules (see below) and monitor its operation.
○ Provide MPs with guidance on matters of conduct or propriety.
○ Investigate complaints against MPs alleged to be in breach of the Code and Guide to the Rules and, when appropriate, report the conclusions to the Committee on Standards (which produces its own report). It is the House of Commons, however, which will decide any penalty to be imposed.
○ Oversee other registers (eg the Register of All-Party Groups).

However, the remit of the Commissioner was complicated by the arrangements set out in the Parliamentary Standards Act 2009 (see section 8.8.3).

◼ The establishment of the Code of Conduct for Members of Parliament

Note: the Code and Guide to the Rules have been periodically amended over time and below is the latest version:

QUOTATION

'I. Purpose of the code

1. The purpose of this Code of Conduct is to assist all Members in the discharge of their obligations to the House, their constituents and the public at large by:

(a) establishing the standards and principles of conduct expected of all Members in undertaking their duties;

(b) setting the rules of conduct which underpin these standards and principles and to which all Members must adhere; and in so doing

(c) ensuring public confidence in the standards expected of all Members and in the commitment of the House to upholding these rules.

II. Scope of the Code

2. The Code applies to Members in all aspects of their public life

IV. General Principles of Conduct

8. In carrying out their parliamentary and public duties, Members will be expected to observe the following general principles of conduct identified by the Committee on Standards in Public Life in its First Report as applying to holders of public office.'

The Code of Conduct together with The Guide to the Rules relating to the conduct of Members 2015, HC 1076 (The Stationery Office, 2015), pp 3–4.

QUOTATION

'The seven principles of conduct

- Selflessness
- Integrity
- Objectivity
- Accountability
- Openness
- Honesty
- Leadership.'

First Report of the Committee on Standards in Public Life, *Standards in Public Life, Volume 1: Report*, Cm 2850-I (1995), p 14.

Among other things, the Code of Conduct states that:

◼ Members shall not act as paid advocates (para 11).

◼ Members should not accept a bribe to influence their conduct – as being contrary to the law of Parliament (para 12).

◼ 'Members shall fulfil conscientiously' the requirements in relation to the registration of their interests (para 13).

The House of Lords, by way of a resolution in 2001, also adopted a Code of Conduct, which has been periodically revised: *Code of Conduct for Members of the House of Lords, Guide to the Code of Conduct: 2017*, HL Paper 157 (The Stationery Office, 2017). It should be made clear that the Parliamentary Commissioner for Standards does not operate in the House of Lords. However, in 2010 a House of Lords Commissioner for Standards was appointed to investigate alleged breaches of the House of Lords Code of Conduct. The Commissioner reports to the Sub-Committee on Lords' Conduct, which in turn presents a report to the House of Lords Committee for Privileges and Conduct. This committee then reports to the House of Lords for the final decision.

8.8.3 The Parliamentary Standards Act 2009

QUOTATION

'The public are sullen, some even mutinous.'

(Sir Robert Worcester, June 2009)

'1. We have been set up at a time when the House of Commons is going through a crisis of confidence not experienced in our lifetimes. This is largely, but not exclusively, because of the revelations about Members' expenses, bringing with it a storm of public disapproval and contempt. Public confidence in the House and in Members as a whole has been low for some time, but not as low as now. It is not too much to say that the institution is in crisis.'

House of Commons Reform Committee, *Rebuilding the House*, First Report of Session 2008–09, HC 1117 (The Stationery Office, 2009), para 1.

In response to the furore over MPs' claims and expenses the Parliamentary Standards Act 2009 was passed (rather expeditiously). The Act does not apply to the House of Lords (s 2). Section 3 of the Act established the following:

- The Independent Parliamentary Standards Authority (IPSA), which represented a move away from self-regulation to an independent regulator.
- The Commissioner for Parliamentary Investigations (but now see recent reforms below).
- The Speaker's Committee for the IPSA.

The Act stated that the IPSA was to pay the salaries of MPs (s 4) and their allowances (in accordance with the MPs' allowances scheme to be prepared by the IPSA (s 5)).

Under s 6 MPs would submit their allowances claim to the IPSA, which would determine whether or not to allow it. The IPSA was required by s 8 to produce an MPs' code of conduct relating to financial interests, which 'must require members to register specified information about specified financial interests in a register maintained by the IPSA' (s 8(7)). However, now see the recent reforms detailed below.

Under s 9, the Commissioner for Parliamentary Investigations could undertake an investigation if he had reason to believe that an MP may have been paid an allowance which he should not have been allowed or may have failed to comply with the requirement concerning the registering of information about specified financial interests (see above).

Finally, s 10 made it a criminal offence to make an allowance claim with information which the MP knows to be false or misleading.

In this context, see also the following:

- In November 2009 the Committee on Standards in Public Life (then chaired by Sir Christopher Kelly) published its report on its review of MPs' expenses (*MPs' Expenses and Allowances*, 12th Report of the Committee on Standards in Public

Life, Cm 7724 (Crown Copyright, 2009)). It made a number of recommendations (eg rec 3 stated that 'MPs should no longer be reimbursed for the cost of mortgage interest payments or any other costs associated with the purchase of a property.').

- In December 2009 the then Leader of the House set out the changes that would be made in view of the various recommendations made in the report above. In particular, these included:

  - 'Responsibility for maintaining the register of financial interests and the associated code of conduct should be removed from the independent regulator and returned to the House of Commons' (Kelly's rec 42). The then Labour government, therefore, proposed to repeal s 8 of the 2009 Act.
  - The independent regulator should be given statutory responsibility for setting the level of pay for MPs (Kelly's rec 43). The government proposed to bring forward legislation to enable the IPSA to set the pay system of MPs.
  - The independent regulator should have responsibility for investigating allegations concerning breaches of the rules on expenses and appoint its own compliance officer (Kelly's rec 44). The government proposed to amend the 2009 Act to provide for a compliance officer to be appointed by the IPSA (in other words, to replace the Commissioner under the Act).
  - The enforcement regime of the regulator should be strengthened (Kelly's rec 45). The government proposed to provide the new compliance officer with the power to impose sanctions.

- In January 2010 the IPSA launched a consultation on MPs' expenses in order to inform the content of the MPs' expenses scheme from 2010 onwards.

In February 2010 Sir Thomas Legg published his report on payments of the ACA (Additional Costs Allowance – ie the second home allowance) made to MPs between 2004 and 2009, together with any recommended repayments that individual MPs should make (House of Commons Estimate Committee, *Review of Past ACA Payments*, First Report of Session 2009–10, HC 348 (The Stationery Office, 2010)).

Just before the 2010 general election, the Constitutional Reform and Governance Act 2010 was passed, which made the following changes to the Parliamentary Standards Act 2009:

- It replaced the Commissioner for Parliamentary Investigations with a Compliance Officer for the IPSA (s 26) and appointed by it (Sch 3).
- It added three lay members to the Speaker's Committee for the IPSA (s 27).
- It provided for the IPSA to determine the level of MPs' salaries (s 29) (under the 2009 Act, this was to be determined in accordance with House of Commons' resolutions).
- Section 32 repealed s 8 of the 2009 Act which required the IPSA to produce a MPs' Code of conduct in relation to financial interests.
- Section 33 replaced s 9 of the 2009 Act (which concerned investigations by the Commissioner) with provisions concerning an investigation by a compliance officer and s 34 and Sch 4 concern this compliance officer's enforcement powers. In essence, the compliance officer (who is an independent office holder) investigates a complaint that an MP may have been wrongfully paid expenses/costs and, in addition, reviews an IPSA decision not to pay an MP's claim for expenses/costs – see *Procedures for Investigations of the Compliance Officer for IPSA* (IPSA, 2nd edition, 2012).

SUMMARY

- The United Kingdom has a bicameral legislature which disperses power between two chambers.
- The functions of Parliament involve:
  - A legislative function – passing law as the legislature.
  - A forum for debate.
  - Representing the will of the people and safeguarding the rights of individuals.
  - Disciplining and regulating its membership.
- Parliamentary privilege are those rights and immunities enjoyed by each House.
- Under Art 9 Bill of Rights 1689 parliamentary members enjoy the protection from legal liability for things said in Parliament as proceedings in Parliament should not be questioned in any court.
- Parliamentary privilege also embraces:
  - The right to determine composition.
  - The right to regulate internal proceedings.
  - The right to punish individuals for contempt or breach of privilege.
- Each House has a Code of Conduct which governs its members. Each House has a Commissioner for Standards who investigates complaints against breaches of their respective code.
- As a consequence of the controversy over MPs' claims and expenses, major reforms have taken place, with a move away from self-regulation to an independent regulator (the Independent Parliamentary Standards Authority – IPSA).

Further reading

Books

Alder, J and Syrett, K, *Constitutional and Administrative Law* (11th edn, Palgrave, 2017), Chapter 11.

Carroll, A, *Constitutional and Administrative Law* (9th edn, Pearson/Longman, 2017), Chapter 10.

Leopold, P, 'Standards of Conduct in Public Life' in Jowell, J and Oliver, D (eds), *The Changing Constitution* (7th edn, Oxford University Press, 2011), p 394.

Loveland, I, *Constitutional Law, Administrative Law, and Human Rights* (7th edn, Oxford University Press, 2015), Chapter 8.

Oliver, D, 'The Powers and Privileges of Parliament' in Feldman, D (ed), *English Public Law* (2nd edn, Oxford University Press, 2009).

Articles

Leyland, P, 'Freedom of information and the 2009 parliamentary expenses scandal' [2009] PL 675.

Lord Lisvane, 'The courts and parliament' [2016] PL 272.

Parpworth, N, 'Nothing to declare?' (2009) 159 NLJ 1236.

Ryan, M, 'The Fixed-Term Parliaments Act 2011' [2012] PL 213.

Papers

First Report of the Committee on Standards in Public Life, *Standards in Public Life, Volume 1: Report*, Cm 2850-I (1995).

Joint Committee on Parliamentary Privilege, *Parliamentary Privilege*, HL Paper 30, HC 100 (The Stationery Office, 2013).

Joint Committee on Parliamentary Privilege, *Report Volume I – Report and Proceedings of the Committee*, HL Paper 43-I, HC 214-I (1999).

Kelly, R and Gay, O, '*The Establishment of the Independent Parliamentary Standards Authority* SN/PC/05167 (House of Commons, 2009).

Parliamentary Privilege, Cm 8318 (Crown Copyright, 2012).

Internet link

www.parliament.uk

9

Parliament II: The House of Commons

AIMS AND OBJECTIVES

At the end of this chapter you should be able to:

▪ Identify and explain the different functions of the House of Commons

▪ Explain the composition of the House of Commons

▪ Explain the nature and significance of the electoral system

9.1 The functions of the House of Commons

The House of Commons is the lower but pre-eminent chamber of Parliament. This is in common with other bicameral legislatures where the lower chamber is dominant (a clear exception to this is the House of Representatives in the United States, which in some respects is not as powerful as the upper chamber, the Senate).

9.1.1 Bagehot and the functions of the House of Commons

The specific functions of the House of Commons overlap and blend with those of Parliament as a whole (see section 8.4), and these are considered in brief below. Before considering them, it is of interest to set out the functions of the Commons as identified by Bagehot in the nineteenth century (W Bagehot, *The English Constitution* (Oxford University Press, 2001), Chapter 6). He set out the following five roles:

▪ An elective function (the electoral chamber).

▪ An expressive function.

▪ A teaching function.

▪ An informing function.

▪ A legislative function.

These will be referred to in the context of a modern formulation of the functions of the House of Commons below.

9.1.2 Modern functions of the House of Commons

Today the functions of the House of Commons can be defined as follows:

A representative role to represent and reflect the will of the people

As each MP is directly elected by his own constituents, the House of Commons performs a representative function reflecting the will of the people. How accurately that will is reflected is determined by the electoral system (see section 9.4). In the context of the representative function, in 2004 the Select Committee on Modernisation of the House of Commons issued a report entitled: 'Connecting Parliament with the Public'. It opened its report in the following manner:

QUOTATION

'The legitimacy of the House of Commons, as the principal representative body in British democracy, rests upon the support and engagement of the electorate. The decline in political participation and engagement in recent years, as well as in levels of trust in politicians, political parties and the institutions of State should be of concern to every citizen. But it should be of particular concern to the House of Commons.'

First Report of Session 2003–04, *Connecting Parliament with the Public*, HC 368 (2004), p 9.

In particular, the report set out recommendations to:

- Make the building more accessible to people.
- Make greater effort to engage young people.
- Encourage better use of information and communication technology, in order to re-connect the public with Parliament.

For a recent publication on political disengagement in general, see E Uberoi, *Political Disengagement in the UK: Who is disengaged?* Briefing Paper CBP7501 (House of Commons Library, 2016).

As part of their role, MPs also try to resolve the grievances of their constituents. In addition, people can present written petitions to their constituency MP.

Bagehot commented that the House of Commons can 'express the mind' of the people on issues before it (the expressive function). In other words, the chamber reflects and expresses the will of the people and is the sounding board of the nation.

To make laws

In particular, the House of Commons has a dominant role in the passage of legislation as the most important Bills are usually commenced there and the consent of the House of Lords is not always necessary (see section 10.10.1). Bagehot subsumed within the legislative function the financial function (ie the authorisation of finance).

To provide the personnel of the government

It is the House of Commons that is largely responsible for providing government ministers. In fact, in a technical sense it is the House of Commons which chooses the government as it is periodically elected and represents the will of the people. In effect, the government is determined by the outcome of the general election, as the leader of the political party that secures the majority of seats in the House of Commons will, by constitutional convention, be appointed Prime Minister by the monarch. For example, in May 1997 Tony Blair's Labour Party secured the majority of seats in the House of Commons and he was appointed Prime Minister. Bagehot described this function as the elective function with the House of Commons as the 'electoral chamber'.

To provide the Official Opposition

The House of Commons also (largely) provides the opposition to the government (known as Her Majesty's Official Opposition). The main Official Opposition in the 2017 Parliament was Labour. As the Official Opposition, it acts as the 'government in waiting' and its responsibility is to scrutinise and examine government actions and policy.

To scrutinise the executive

In constitutional terms, a major role of the House of Commons is to hold the government to account to the elected representatives of the people.

To maintain the government

As noted at section 5.3.2, it is the constitutional function of the government to govern. The role of the House of Commons is somewhat contradictory as it should constitutionally sustain the government (while the government has the support and confidence of the lower House), allowing it to govern and carry on the business of government. At the same time, however, the House must simultaneously scrutinise the actions and policy of the government and withdraw support from it if it loses confidence in it (in other words, if the government has lost the confidence of the people). On rare occasions, such as in 1979, the government has lost a vote of no confidence in it, thereby symbolically losing the support of the people as represented in the House of Commons (see section 12.2.1).

To legitimise government actions

The actions of government are legitimised by the House of Commons if they pass scrutiny by MPs. This could be in the form of a particular government policy or in a Bill drafted by the government. In this context it is important to bear in mind the political composition of the House of Commons, which is dictated by the nature of the electoral system (see section 9.5).

A judicial function

The House of Commons also performs, in effect, a judicial function when it enforces parliamentary privilege (see section 8.7.3).

In addition, according to Bagehot, the teaching function of the House of Commons involved it teaching 'the nation what it does not know' (arguably this could occur, for example, in the context of a debate). Finally, the informing function involved the House making 'us hear what otherwise we should not' (it could be argued that this function would be performed in the context of the answers provided by government ministers to questions and also in the course of debates).

KEY FACTS

The key functions of the House of Commons
Representative
Each MP is elected and collectively they express the will of the nation.
Recruitment of government
The government is drawn largely from the lower chamber.
To maintain the government and legitimise its actions
The chamber sustains and maintains the government. The latter needs the continuous support of the chamber to survive.
To redress grievances and scrutinise the executive
Individual MPs try to resolve the grievances of their constituents and the chamber as a whole holds the government to account (which can include passing a vote of no confidence in it).
Legislative
Bills pass through both chambers with the most important Bills usually beginning in the lower chamber.
Judicial
The House enforces parliamentary privilege and disciplines members.

9.2 The size and composition of the House of Commons

9.2.1 The number of seats in the House of Commons

The size of the last seven House of Commons is set out below:

- 1992/1997 – 651 MPs
- 1997/2001 – 659 MPs
- 2001/2005 – 659 MPs
- 2005/2010 – 646 MPs
- 2010/2015 – 650 MPs
- 2015/2017 – 650 MPs
- 2017/2022 – 650 MPs

> Source: drawn from L Audickas, O Hawkins and R Cracknell,
> *UK Election Statistics: 1918–2017*, Briefing Paper CBP7529
> (House of Commons Library, 2017), Table 1b.

Under the Fixed-Term Parliaments Act 2011, the next scheduled election is 2022.

In comparison to other democracies, with 650 MPs the House of Commons is a large lower chamber in relation to its population. In contrast, for example, the United States has 435 members in its lower House (the House of Representatives).

As an aside, although the Parliamentary Voting System and Constituencies Act 2011 provided for a reduction of MPs to 600, this has been delayed by s 6 of the Electoral Registration and Administration Act 2013 (see later at section 9.4.5).

9.2.2 The House of Commons as a representative body?

The regions
The House of Commons is part of the United Kingdom Parliament and so MPs represent all parts of the state as indicated below:

The 2017–2022 Parliament
England	–	533 MPs
Wales	–	40 MPs
Scotland	–	59 MPs
Northern Ireland	–	18 MPs
		650 MPs

Source: V Apostolova, L Audickas, C Baker, A Bate, R Cracknell, N Dempsey, R McInnes, T Rutherford and E Uberoi, *General Election 2017: Results and Analysis*, Briefing Paper CBP7979 (House of Commons Library, 2017), p 8.

Ethnic minorities
In the 2005 general election 15 black and minority ethnic MPs (standing for mainstream political parties) were elected. At the time, the Electoral Commission pointed out that, proportionately:

QUOTATION

'While this figure still falls well short of the total required for the House of Commons to mirror the UK population (51), it is more than twice that in 1992 and nearly four times that in 1987.'

Election 2005: turnout. How many, who and why? (Electoral Commission, 2005), p 18.

More recently, at the 2015 and 2017 general elections, 41 and 52 non-white MPs (respectively) were elected (C Barton and L Audickas, *Social Background of MPs 1979–2017*, Briefing Paper CBP7483 (House of Commons Library, 2017), p 6).

Women
The number of female MPs in the past seven parliaments is as follows:

Women MPs
1992 Parliament – 60 MPs (9 per cent of all MPs)
1997 Parliament – 120 MPs (18 per cent)
2001 Parliament – 118 MPs (18 per cent)
2005 Parliament – 128 MPs (20 per cent)
2010 Parliament – 143 MPs (22 per cent)
2015 Parliament – 191 MPs (29 per cent)
2017 Parliament – 208 MPs (32 per cent)

Source: R Kelly and M Everett, *Women in the House of Commons*, Briefing Paper 06651 (House of Commons Library, 2017), Table 2.

Even though 208 female MPs were returned in 2017, proportionately this is still only 32 per cent of all MPs in the House of Commons. In fact, in January 2017 the United Kingdom was ranked at forty-seventh in the World in terms of women in a national Parliament (see V Apostolova, *Women Around the World: International Women's Day 2017*, Briefing Paper CBP7910 (House of Commons Library, 2017), Table 3). The long-standing concern about the under-representation of women in the House of Commons led to the passage of the Sex Discrimination (Election Candidates) Act 2002. This Act enabled political parties to take positive action to encourage the election of female MPs by permitting political parties to draw up an 'all-female shortlist' for the selection of their official parliamentary constituency candidate for a general election. This legislation amended the Sex Discrimination Act 1975 as detailed in the following case:

CASE EXAMPLE

Jepson and Dyas-Elliott (applicants) v The Labour Party *[1996] IRLR 116*

Jepson and Dyas-Elliott were not considered for selection as Labour Party candidates in parliamentary constituencies because these particular constituencies were required to have 'all-women shortlists'. The policy behind this was to increase the number of women elected to Parliament.

Jepson and Dyas-Elliott contended that they had been unlawfully discriminated against on the grounds of their sex (they were male and so prevented from forming part of the shortlist) contrary to s 13 of the Sex Discrimination Act 1975.

The tribunal upheld their complaints that the policy of all-women shortlists contravened the Sex Discrimination Act. This was because the endorsement of a prospective parliamentary candidate was an 'authorisation' under the Act, which facilitated 'engagement in a particular profession', that is, the public office of an MP.

Part 7 of the Equality Act 2010 (which brought together and restated the various laws on discrimination) extended the use of women-only shortlists until 2030.

Age

MPs tend to be middle-aged, as demonstrated by the fact that between 1979 and 2017 the average age of an MP was 49–51 years of age (source: see p 5 of the Barton and Audickas Briefing Paper below). It should be pointed out that, although individuals can vote at 18, until the passing of the Electoral Administration Act 2006 they could not become MPs until 21 years of age, to ensure that MPs had a minimum of experience. The 2006 Act reduced the minimum age to 18. In 2015, Mhairi Black was elected at the age of 20 years and seven months for the seat of Paisley and Renfrewshire South (source: J Brown, *Youngest Members of Parliament since 1979*, Parliamentary Information List 04416 (House of Commons Library, 2016), p 4).

On the age, gender, occupation, ethnicity, education and parliamentary experience of MPs, see C Barton and L Audickas, *Social Background of MPs 1979–2017*, Briefing Paper CBP7483 (House of Commons Library, 2017).

ACTIVITY

Exercise

Do you think that the House of Commons is sufficiently representative of the population? In terms of its constitutional legitimacy, does this matter?

9.3 The Member of Parliament

9.3.1 The role of a Member of Parliament (MP)

The United Kingdom has a representative democracy. Although MPs are elected representatives of the people, this does not mean that they are simply their delegates who mechanically act on instructions from the electorate. MPs clearly serve their constituents, represent their concerns and redress their grievances, but they also exercise independent mature judgement by themselves.

Carroll (*Constitutional and Administrative Law* (9th edn, Pearson/Longman, 2017) p 145) has identified five factors ('constituencies') which a modern MP has to consider, namely:

■ **The political party**

The overwhelming majority of MPs are members of an organised political party with official policies. Political parties ensure discipline through a 'whip' system which compels MPs within that party to vote for the official party line. As a consequence, MPs can ultimately be deselected as the parliamentary candidate for their constituency in a future general election if they behave (and vote) in a way which is detrimental to the official party line and interests.

■ **The constituency**

As a constituency MP, an MP has to be sensitive to the needs of his constituents (indeed para 6 of the Code of Conduct for Members of Parliament – see section 8.8.2 – states that MPs have 'a special duty to their constituents'). MPs will typically have surgeries to meet constituents and will also receive written correspondence from them. The Recall of MPs Act 2015 now enables constituents to sign a 'recall petition' which, if successful, provides that the seat of their local MP becomes vacant and a by-election is triggered (see further section 9.3.4).

In fact, an MP may have a constituency which has particular circumstances (eg a government proposal to site a chemical plant there), which will require the MP to articulate and raise in Parliament in the interests of his constituents (whether or not this happens to be against the official party political line).

■ **An MP's own conscience**

As indicated by Edmund Burke MP, writing in the eighteenth century, MPs are not mere delegates of the people but are also charged with exercising their personal judgement on a matter. On his famous address to his electorate in Bristol, he said:

QUOTATION

'Your representative owes you, not his industry only, but his judgement; and he betrays instead of serving you, if he sacrifices it to your opinion.'

Quoted in J Norman, *Edmund Burke* (William Collins, 2014), p 77.

Indeed, some issues which come before Parliament are defined as 'free vote issues' which are above party political divisions. These will, typically, be on moral issues such as the death penalty. Interestingly, the debate and votes in February 2003 and March 2007 on the future reform of the House of Lords were officially on the basis of a free vote, free from party political pressure (see section 10.13). More recently, there was a free vote in 2011 on the issue of prisoners voting (see section 9.6.3).

■ **An interest group**

An MP may have a close relationship with certain interest groups, for example a trade union or a charity/business organisation. Under the Register of Members'

Financial Interests (see section 8.8.1), MPs have to declare their financial interests with the outside world.

Acting in the public interest

An MP is a parliamentarian and as such one of his constitutional roles is to hold the government to account. It would appear that MPs perform this role most effectively when they sit in select committees scrutinising government departments. Select committee reports tend to produce a cross-party consensus (see section 12.6.6) and it seems that MPs in this context act in a less partisan way than they do on the Floor of the House. Moreover, para 6 of the Code of Conduct for Members of Parliament states that 'Members have a general duty to act in the interests of the nation as a whole. . .'.

On MPs see the following informative article: R Campbell and J Lovenduski, 'What should MPs do? Public and Parliamentarians' views compared' (2015) 68 *Parliamentary Affairs* 690.

9.3.2 The qualifications required to be an MP

In essence any individual is eligible to become an MP provided:

- they are 18 years of age or older; and
- are a citizen of the United Kingdom, the Commonwealth or the Irish Republic.

The vast majority of MPs belong to a recognised political party, with very few independent MPs being elected. Accordingly, the practical reality is that in order to become an MP a person will need to be selected by a political party as its prospective parliamentary candidate for a constituency.

Prospective parliamentary candidates need to provide a deposit of £500 in order to take part in an election, which is lost in the event of a candidate securing less than 5 per cent of the total votes cast in a constituency. The rationale behind the deposit is to prevent frivolous candidates standing for election. From a constitutional perspective, however, it could be argued that the use of the deposit actively discourages individuals from standing for election (putting oneself up for election is part of a participatory democracy). It may also impact adversely on smaller parties who may wish to field candidates in all or most constituencies across the United Kingdom.

9.3.3 The factors which disqualify a person from becoming an MP

Erskine May (*Parliamentary Practice* (24th edn, LexisNexis Butterworths, 2011), Chapter 3) identified, *inter alia*, the following factors which disqualify a person from becoming an MP and sitting in the House of Commons:

Under age

Although individuals can vote at 18 years of age (see section 9.6.2), historically they could not stand for parliamentary elections until they were 21 (Parliamentary Elections Act 1695). Under the Electoral Administration Act 2006, the age has now been reduced to 18. In contrast, in the House of Lords, peers must be at least 21 years of age to take their seat (see section 10.8).

Aliens

Aliens are disqualified from membership under the Act of Settlement 1700. The British Nationality Act 1981 states that this does not apply to individuals who are Commonwealth citizens or from the Republic of Ireland. However, s 18 of the Electoral Administration Act 2006 limited the rights of the former to stand for election to those with a right of abode or indefinite leave to remain.

Peers

Members cannot sit in both parliamentary chambers. It is pertinent to point out, however, that those hereditary peers removed from the House of Lords under the House of Lords Act 1999 (see section 10.6.3) are eligible to be elected as MPs. Indeed, in 2001 one hereditary peer (Viscount Thurso), who formerly sat in the House of Lords until 1999, was elected as an MP (John Thurso) – see further at section 10.6.3.

Those suffering from mental disorder (now historic)

Those detained under mental health legislation (ie Mental Health Act 1983) would have historically been disqualified. Under s 141 of the 1983 Act there was a procedure to vacate the seat of an MP who was suffering from mental disorder. Section 1 of the Mental Health (Discrimination) Act 2013 repealed s 141 of the Mental Health Act 1983, together with the abolition of any common law rule which disqualified membership of the Commons on the grounds of mental illness.

Treason

Those convicted of treason under the Forfeiture Act 1870 are disqualified until pardoned or the term of imprisonment has expired.

Bankruptcy

In relation to England, Wales and Northern Ireland, an individual who has a bankruptcy restrictions order in effect against them is disqualified (s 266 of the Enterprise Act 2002). In Scotland it is where a sequestration of estate is awarded (s 427 of the Insolvency Act 1986).

Those sentenced to imprisonment

Under the Representation of the People Act 1981 (as amended), an individual sentenced to be imprisoned for more than one year for any offence is disqualified. This was passed in the context of the election of Bobby Sands as a Westminster MP (who at the time was a prisoner on hunger strike in Northern Ireland).

Corrupt/illegal practices

Under the Representation of the People Act 1983 (as amended) an individual convicted of a corrupt practice at an election is disqualified for five years. Those convicted of illegal practices are disqualified for three years.

Religious representation

In recent years a disqualification in relation to the clergy has been removed. The House of Commons (Removal of Clergy Disqualification) Act 2001 provides that no ministers of any religious denomination are disqualified from membership of the House of Commons. The exceptions to this are the archbishops and bishops sitting in the House of Lords (see section 10.3).

The House of Commons Disqualification Act 1975

This Act constitutionally and legally prohibits certain elements of the executive (civil servants, police officers etc) from sitting in the House of Commons as part of the legislature (see section 11.6.3). It is interesting to note that s 1(1) (a) of the Act prevents full-time-judges from sitting in the House of Commons (including now of course the serving Supreme Court justices). This preserves a degree of separation between the judiciary and the legislature; however, MPs can sit as (part-time) Justices of the Peace/lay magistrates.

Other legislatures

In addition, s 1(1) (e) of the House of Commons Disqualification Act 1975 disqualifies members of other legislatures outside the Commonwealth (except the Republic of Ireland). It should be noted that in terms of a 'dual mandate' MPs cannot also hold a seat in any of the following elected legislatures:

- European Parliament (this followed a decision of the European Council in 2002, but will clearly not be relevant once the United Kingdom leaves the EU – see Brexit at section 15.6.6).
- National Assembly for Wales (by virtue of s 3 of the Wales Act 2014).
- Northern Ireland Assembly (by virtue of s 3 of the Northern Ireland (Miscellaneous Provisions) Act 2014).

At the time of writing, however, there was no legal restriction on MPs having a dual mandate with the Scottish Parliament.

9.3.4 By-elections

In the event of an MP dying, resigning or being disqualified, his seat becomes vacant and a by-election will ensue. For example, when the Labour MP Robin Cook died in August 2005, a by-election was held in that constituency in September 2005. On this occasion, another Labour MP was elected in his place, although it is not always the case that the same political party will win back the seat. For example, when Rachel Squire, a Labour MP, died in January 2006, at the ensuing by-election in February 2006 her seat was taken by a Liberal Democrat candidate.

As a result of the enactment of the Recall of MPs Act 2015, an MP can become subject to a recall petition calling for a by-election to be held. An MP becomes subject to such a petition process if any of the following three 'recall' conditions have been met:

- s 1 (3) the MP has been convicted of a criminal offence in the United Kingdom and given a custodial sentence.
- s 1 (4) the House of Commons, following a report from the Committee on Standards, has ordered the suspension of the MP from the service of the House for a 'specified period'.
- s 1 (9) the MP has been convicted of an offence under s 10 of the Parliamentary Standards Act 2009.

Under s 5 of the Act, once one of these recall conditions has been met, the Speaker of the House of Commons must notify the constituency petition officer of the MP concerned. Thereafter, the petition officer will then arrange for a recall petition to be made available to sign in that constituency. Under s 9 if 10 per cent or more of the eligible registered electors sign the recall petition, the MP loses his seat and a by-election will be held for that constituency. Section s 9 (4) provides that the MP subject to the recall petition may, nevertheless, stand in the resulting by-election.

KEY FACTS

The Role of the MP

An MP has to consider the following competing interests:
- party political pressure from the political party to which he belongs;
- his constituents who elect (and re-elect) him into office as a constituency MP;
- his own conscience on moral matters (eg on the death penalty);
- an interest group with which he has a close relationship (eg a trade union);
- acting as a parliamentarian in the public interest.

9.4 The electoral system

9.4.1 The system of voting

The United Kingdom uses a single-member constituency, simple majority system. It is commonly referred to as the 'first past the post' system. The mechanics of the system are detailed below:

- The whole of the United Kingdom is divided up into single-member constituencies (for the 2017 general election there were 650 parliamentary constituencies).
- In each constituency political parties will put forward one candidate as a prospective MP. Political parties do not, however, have to contest each seat. For example, in Northern Ireland the main political parties have not traditionally put up candidates owing to the historically idiosyncratic political make up of the province.
- Each registered voter who chooses to vote (many choose not to vote) puts a cross on the ballot paper next to their chosen candidate.
- Once polling has closed, all the votes cast will be counted. The winning candidate (and so the elected Member of Parliament for that constituency) will be the person who has secured more votes than any other candidate. For example:

Constituency of Bracknell – general election 2017		
Electorate 79,199 – 71 per cent turnout (55,892 voted)		
Party candidate	**Votes cast in a favour**	**per cent of vote**
Conservative (elected as MP)	32,882	58.8 per cent
Labour	16,866	30.1 per cent
Liberal Democrat	4,186	7.4 per cent
UKIP	1,521	2.7 per cent
Independent	437	0.7 per cent

Table 9.1

Source: *The Times*, Election 2017 (10 June 2017), pp 6–7.

It is imperative to point out that this does not mean that the winning candidate has to obtain 51 per cent of all the votes cast. In fact, in many cases the winning candidate will not do so (eg see Table 9.3 below). Indeed, in 2010 67 per cent of seats were won on a minority of the votes cast (C Rallings and M Thrasher (eds), *British Electoral Facts 1832–2012* (Biteback Publishing, 2012), Table 2.17).

It is in this way that the United Kingdom's electoral system has been described as the 'first past the post' system, as it has been likened to a horse race. In short, the horse that crosses the line first – irrespective of how wide or narrow the margin – is declared the winner. In this sense, the only horse (or candidate) that matters is the winner.

▨ As the United Kingdom Parliament has single-member constituencies, each constituency returns only one MP. In some other countries, constituencies are multi-member whereby a number of representatives are returned for a particular constituency. This scenario is not totally unfamiliar to the United Kingdom as, for example, large multi-member constituencies are used when electing United Kingdom Members of the European Parliament under the European Parliamentary Elections Act 1999 (but now see Brexit at section 15.6.6). On the different voting systems introduced into the United Kingdom since 1997, see N Johnston, *Voting Systems in the UK*, Briefing Paper 04458 (House of Commons Library, 2017).

Although only one MP is returned for each constituency, that MP represents the whole of the constituency irrespective of whether a particular constituent voted for them or not (or even if that constituent was ineligible to vote, eg he was under 18 years of age at the time of the election). Moreover, by constitutional convention one MP will not act for the constituent of another MP unless the latter is unwilling or unable to act.

▨ All constituencies return their MP (either a newly elected MP or an MP who has been re-elected) to the House of Commons. By constitutional convention, the leader of the political party with the majority of seats in the House of Commons will be formally appointed Prime Minister by the monarch and asked to form Her Majesty's Government.

9.4.2 Election turnouts

The turnout of the population eligible to vote at the elections between 1987 and 2005 is indicated below:

Election turnouts 1987–2005
1987 – 75.3 per cent (of those registered to vote)
1992 – 77.7 per cent
1997 – 71.4 per cent
2001 – 59.4 per cent
2005 – 61.4 per cent

Table 9.2

Source: *Election 2005: turnout. How many, who and why?* (Electoral Commission, 2005), p 20.

It is in this context that the 2004 report of the Select Committee on Modernisation of the House of Commons (see section 9.1.2) should be seen. In short, the 2001 general election turnout (ie 59.4 per cent) of those registered to vote was the lowest since 1918. The general decline in voting necessarily means a diminution in participatory democracy, whereby voters are disconnected from the electoral and parliamentary process. Although the percentage of voters who voted in the 2005 election was a marginal improvement on the 2001 election, the Electoral Commission indicated that 17 million people who were registered to vote did not cast a vote. It identified the following factors which contributed to people not voting in the 2005 general election:

- A general disillusionment with politics.
- An ignorance about politics.
- A perception that voting made no real difference.
- The difficulty in deciding which political party to vote for.
- The nature of the election campaign.

In terms of the constitutional and political significance of elections, the Commission made the following comment:

QUOTATION

'Elections underpin our democracy, ensuring that our representative institutions are both accountable to public opinion and legitimised by it. They provide an opportunity for politicians and political parties to outline their ideas and to defend their performance. Elections can interest, inform and empower people and, by doing so, can help to build political engagement.'
Election 2005: turnout. How many, who and why? (Electoral Commission, 2005), p 53.

In respect of the turnout for the two most recent general elections, the figures are as follows:

- 2015 – 66.2 per cent
- 2017 – 68.8 per cent

Source: N Dempsey, *Turnout at Elections*, Briefing Paper CBP8060 (House of Commons Library, 2017), Appendix 1.

In recent years, in order to address voter apathy in general, there have been attempts to engage with voters by using different forms of voting methods. For example, local government elections have experimented with polling booths located in supermarkets as well as universal postal votes. The Electoral Administration Act 2006 is particularly concerned with increasing the highest possible turnout at elections. For example, in order to encourage public participation in elections, s 69 requires that:

SECTION

'A local electoral officer must take such steps as he thinks appropriate to encourage the participation by electors in the electoral process in the area for which he acts.'

On voters engaging in the electoral process, see the following report: the House of Commons Political and Constitutional Reform Committee, *Voter Engagement in the UK*, HC 232 (2014).

ACTIVITY

Self-test questions

Why do you think there is a relatively poor turnout for general elections? In terms of the legitimacy of the House of Commons, does this matter?

9.4.3 The advantages of the 'first past the post' electoral system

The United Kingdom's electoral system is somewhat controversial in certain aspects (see section 9.4.4), but it has a number of distinct advantages:

▨ **Simplicity**

In contrast to other systems available, the current electoral system is comparatively simple. It is relatively easy for the public to understand as only one box on the ballot paper needs to be crossed. In contrast, in some other systems such as the single transferable vote, candidates are ranked in order of preference. The 'first past the post' system is also straightforward to administer and provides an efficient method of voting and of forming a parliamentary chamber. It is also a comparatively inexpensive system of voting because it is easy to administer. It should be remembered that, in a national referendum in 2011, the public decisively rejected the proposal to replace it with the alternative vote (see section 9.10.1).

▨ **Single-member constituencies**

The system uses single- member constituencies, which has the advantage that every constituency in the United Kingdom has one single, identifiable Member of Parliament who represents the interests of that particular constituency. In this way the electoral system constitutionally links each MP with one specific geographical area of the state.

▨ **Produces strong government (historically)**

In general terms – and certainly up until recently – the electoral system has produced an electoral result which has conferred one political party (historically either Labour or Conservative) with a majority of seats in the House of Commons. In fact, in six out of the seven general elections held between 1979 and 2005 (the exception being 1992), the electoral system produced a single-party government with a substantial working majority of seats. For example, in 1983 the Conservative government had a majority of 144 seats, while in 1997 the Labour government enjoyed a majority of 179 seats. It is argued that such majorities allow the government to be decisive and to govern by translating its legislative programme outlined in its general election manifesto, into laws. Moreover, a strong decisive government is an advantage in a crisis (international or domestic) and is generally regarded as preferable to an inherently weaker government typically found in coalition governments consisting of a combination of rival and competing political parties.

NB: Although historically the 'first past the post' system has produced a government with the support of a majority of seats in the House of Commons, in recent years the United Kingdom has experienced hung parliaments, with no one political party with a majority of seats. Indeed, two out of the last three general elections have resulted in an indecisive result (2010 and most recently in 2017). The 2010 election resulted in a coalition government comprising the Conservative and Liberal Democrat parties, whereas in 2017 the minority (single- party) Conservative government was supported by a 'confidence and supply' agreement with the Democratic Unionist Party (DUP).

9.4.4 The disadvantages of the 'first past the post' electoral system

There are at least four major problems with the system as detailed below:

▨ **A disproportionate system**

One clear difficulty with the electoral system is that it is possible for an MP to be elected on a minority of the votes cast in that constituency. The following example from the 2017 general election makes this point:

Constituency of Gordon – general election 2017	
Electorate 78,531 – 68 per cent turnout (53,685 voted)	
Party candidate	**Votes cast in favour**
Conservative	21,861 (40.7 per cent of the votes cast).
SNP (Scottish National Party)	19,254 (35.8 per cent).
Labour	6,340 (11.8 per cent).
Liberal Democrat	6,230 (11.6 per cent).

Table 9.3

Source: *The Times*, Election 2017 (June 10, 2017), p 12.

This example shows that the Conservative candidate who won this constituency to become its MP did so with less than 50 per cent of the total votes cast (in fact, on the basis of only 41 per cent). Indeed, more people voted against the Conservative candidate than in favour of him. This illustrates the nature of the 'first past the post' system: in order to become an MP, all that has to be achieved is to secure more votes than any other candidate. In fact, in 2017 in the constituency of North East Fife the SNP candidate won by only two votes over the nearest rival, making it the most marginal constituency in the United Kingdom (source: N Dempsey, *Marginal Seats*, Briefing Paper CBP8067 (House of Commons Library, 2017), p 4).

If the scenario in Table 9.3 were replicated in many constituencies across the United Kingdom, then it is possible to see how a government can become elected with a majority of seats in the House of Commons but with only a minority of the votes cast nationwide in its favour. For example, at the 2005 general election the Labour Party secured 55 per cent of the seats in the House of Commons (ie 355) and yet secured only 35.2 per cent of the total votes cast nationwide. In contrast, the Conservative Party polled 32.4 per cent of the votes cast and secured only 198 seats, representing just over 30 per cent of the House of Commons (source: figures extrapolated from F McGuinness, *UK Election Statistics: 1918–2012* Research Paper 12/43 (House of Commons Library, 2012), p 7). This in turn raises the question of whether *any* government elected on this basis of a minority of the votes cast has political legitimacy. Indeed, in the second half of the twentieth century, no government (Labour or Conservative) assumed office with over 50 per cent of all votes cast.

Voter apathy

One possible reason for poor turnouts at general elections (as pointed out by the Electoral Commission earlier at section 9.4.2) is the perception that voting *makes no difference*. In fact, a number of constituencies in the United Kingdom are considered 'safe seats' in the sense that one particular political party traditionally has always won the seat. As a result of this, voting for a candidate of a different political party in such a 'safe' constituency would appear to be fruitless. It must be remembered that under the electoral system the 'winner takes all' and the votes cast for the losing candidates are disregarded. These losing votes are, in effect therefore, wasted.

Variations in constituencies

As the United Kingdom uses the single-member constituency system, this inevitably results in some regional variations. Some constituencies such as the Isle of Wight had an electorate of 110,697 at the 2017 general election, whereas, in contrast, the constituency of Na H-Eileanan An Iar in Scotland had an electorate of only 21,301 (source: *The Times* Election 2017 (10 June 2017), pp 13 and 18). In short, the value of a vote cast in the latter constituency will have more significance (in terms of determining who wins the seat) than in the former, much larger constituency. In other words, a vote in a smaller constituency – in proportionate terms – is more significant than a vote in a larger constituency. This necessarily raises the issue of whether all votes have equal value. Section 11 of the Parliamentary Voting System and Constituencies Act 2011 provides for less variation, with each constituency electorate required to be within the parameters of 5 per cent of the United Kingdom electoral quota (but see later at section 9.4.5).

Third parties

One clear disadvantage of the 'first past the post' system is that it is essentially designed to accommodate a two-party system and so smaller third parties are penalised. For example, at the 2017 general election the Liberal Democrats secured only 12 seats (representing 1.8 per cent of MPs) with 7.4 per cent of the United Kingdom vote. In contrast, the Conservative Party obtained 48.8 per cent of the seats (ie 317) with 42.3 per cent of the national vote (source: V Apostolova, L Audickas, C Baker, A Bate, R Cracknell, N Dempsey, R McInnes, T Rutherford and E Uberoi, *General Election 2017: Results and Analysis*, Briefing Paper CBP7979 (House of Commons Library, 2017), pp 10 and 16).

9.4.5 Parliamentary constituency boundaries

The review of constituency boundaries due to population movement is carried out by four independent Boundary Commissions, one for each of the countries of the United Kingdom, and they are governed by the Parliamentary Constituencies Act 1986 (as amended by the Boundary Commissions Act 1992 and the Parliamentary Voting System and Constituencies Act 2011). On receipt of a report of a Boundary Commission, a government minister would lay a draft order before Parliament for it to approve, giving effect to the Commission's recommendations.

The redrawing of constituency boundaries inevitably has an impact on one or more political parties (ie they either gain or lose potential seats). The redrawing of such constituencies can, therefore, be controversial and in the early 1980s the then leader of the Labour Party sought to challenge one of these proposed changes:

CASE EXAMPLE

R v Boundary Commission for England, ex parte Foot *[1983] 1 QB 600*

Michael Foot, the leader of the Labour Party and Leader of the Opposition, unsuccessfully sought in judicial review to prohibit the Boundary Commission for England from submitting to the Home Secretary its revised parliamentary constituencies. The Court of Appeal noted that the Commission's duty did include giving effect to, *inter alia*, r 5 (Sch 2 to the House of Commons (Redistribution of Seats) Act 1949), which provided that 'The electorate of any constituency shall be as near the electoral quota as is practicable' (this was designed to ensure the principle of equal representation for electors). It was held, however, that the rule (as a result of s 2 of the House of Commons (Redistribution of Seats) Act 1958), had the status of a guideline and that Foot had failed to discharge the heavy onus of showing that the recommendations of the Boundary Commission were conclusions which no reasonable Commission could have come to.

Constituency boundaries are reviewed and readjusted periodically (now every five years under s 10 of the Parliamentary Voting System and Constituencies Act 2011).

As a consequence of the Electoral Registration and Administration Act 2013, the seventh general review (ie the '2018 review') is due to be completed by the Boundary Commissions by 1 October 2018, paving the way for a reduction to 600 seats at the next general election under Pt 2 of the Parliamentary Voting System and Constituencies Act 2011. Following the 'snap' 2017 general election, the next scheduled election under the Fixed-Term Parliaments Act 2011 is May 2022.

KEY FACTS

Key facts on the electoral system

- The United Kingdom uses the 'first past the post' system, which comprises 650 single-member constituencies.
- Political parties put forward one candidate as a prospective MP for each constituency.
- The elected Member of Parliament for each constituency will be the person who has secured more votes than any other candidate.
- The leader of the political party that gains the majority of seats in the House of Commons will become Prime Minister.

9.5 The current political composition of the House of Commons

The political breakdown of the House of Commons immediately following the 2017 general election was as follows:

2017 general election	
Party	**Seats**
Conservative	317
Labour	262
Liberal Democrat	12
Scottish National Party	35
Democratic Unionist Party	10
Sinn Fein (historically do not take their seats for political reasons)	7
Plaid Cymru	4
Green	1
Independent	1
Speaker	1
TOTAL	650 MPs

Table 9.4

Source: V Apostolova, L Audickas, C Baker, A Bate, R Cracknell, N Dempsey, R McInnes, T Rutherford and E Uberoi, *General Election 2017: Results and Analysis*, Briefing Paper CBP7979 (House of Commons Library, 2017), p 5.

The results of the 2017 general election (like those in 2010) resulted in a hung Parliament, in which no single party had a majority of seats. In 2017 the Conservative government agreed a 'confidence and supply' arrangement in which the DUP would support the government in critical votes.

Three points are worth remembering about the political composition of the House of Commons.

■ Firstly, the House of Commons is not one single entity that acts as a unified, cohesive unit. Instead, it is composed of a variety of different political parties vying with each other (although it tends to be dominated by one political party, which forms the government of the day).

■ Secondly, the overwhelming majority of MPs are members of political parties and therefore very few independent MPs are elected. In 2017, excluding the Speaker of the House, only one independent MP was elected. In this way the House of Commons differs from the House of Lords, which is composed of a sizeable number of independent peers known as crossbenchers (see section 10.7.3).

■ Thirdly, the political composition of the House of Commons will change (albeit marginally) over the course of a parliamentary term. This necessarily has an impact on a government's majority (which may be highly significant if its majority is slim). There are two main reasons for this:

(i) By-elections are not rare events. For example, there were 21 by-elections held during the 2010–15 Parliament (see S Ayres and O Hawkins, *By-elections 2010–15* Standard Note SN/SG/5833 (House of Commons Library, 2015)).

(ii) Change of allegiance – it is possible for an MP to change political party. For example, in 1999 Shaun Woodward changed parties from Conservative to Labour. This is known as 'Crossing the Floor' of the Commons.

9.6 The electorate

9.6.1 The constitutional significance of voting

In a representative democracy it is a prerequisite that democracy involves 'participatory' democracy. This means that citizens should regularly determine who represents them in Parliament and who should govern the country. In the United Kingdom the people do not *directly* elect the government/executive, rather they elect representatives (MPs) from whom the government is drawn (see Bagehot's elective function, see section 9.1.2).

The constitutional significance of the electorate voting in elections has been clearly recognised by Art 3, Protocol No 1 of the European Convention:

ARTICLE

'The High Contracting Parties undertake to hold free elections at reasonable intervals by secret ballot, under conditions which will ensure the free expression of the opinion of the people in the choice of the legislature.'

The European Court of Human Rights in *Mathieu-Mohin and Clerfayt v Belgium* (1988) 10 EHRR 1 regarded this provision as a very important free-standing right as well as a prerequisite for the enjoyment and protection of other European Convention rights:

'Since it enshrines a characteristic principle of democracy, Article 3 of Protocol No. 1 is accordingly of prime importance in the Convention system.'

9.6.2 Who can vote in parliamentary elections?

This is set out in the Representation of the People Act 1983 (as amended). At a general election a person can vote who is:

 Of voting age: 18 years or over on polling day (s 1 of the Representation of the People Act 1969 reduced the voting age from 21 years of age to 18).

 Registered in the register of parliamentary elections for that particular constituency. Electoral registration officers have a responsibility to produce an electoral register and historically this was compiled on the basis of returns made by householders (ie household registration). However, the Political Parties and Elections Act 2009 provided instead for the introduction of individual electoral registration. More recently, the Electoral Registration and Administration Act 2013 was passed to speed up the process for implementing individual registration. The Act modernised the electoral registration system and was an attempt to tackle the issue of electoral fraud.

 Not disqualified from voting (see below at section 9.6.3).

 A British, Irish or qualifying Commonwealth citizen who is resident in the United Kingdom (the latter two are explained by historical ties).

 A person who is a British citizen resident outside the United Kingdom and qualified as an overseas elector (Representation of the People Act 1985 as amended).

A general election will be held on one day. An individual can vote only once in one single constituency and so cannot vote in more than one constituency in a parliamentary election. It is possible to vote by post (eg if a voter is overseas) or proxy (eg if the voter has a physical disability). Voting is by secret ballot, but voting is not compulsory, as in some countries such as Australia. Compulsory voting would, however, automatically have an impact on electorate turnouts at general elections and in 2005 the then Leader of the House of Commons put forward the suggestion of introducing compulsory voting in order to increase turnout. On the franchise in the United Kingdom, see N Johnston, *The History of the Parliamentary Franchise* Research Paper 13/14 (House of Commons Library, 2013).

9.6.3 Who is disqualified from voting?

The following factors disenfranchise a person from voting at a general election:

 Peers sitting in the House of Lords – see s 3 of the House of Lords Act 1999 (however, members of the House of Lords who were removed under the House of Lords Act 1999 are eligible to vote). NB: bishops are not peers and so can vote.

 Persons under the age of 18 years on the day of the poll.

 Historically there was a common law rule of incapacity to vote by reason of a person's mental state; however, s 73 of the Electoral Administration Act 2006 abolished any common law rule which provided that a person was subject to a legal incapacity to vote by reason of his mental state (thus illustrating how Parliament can override common law – see section 7.5.1).

- Persons guilty of corrupt or illegal practices at elections within the past five and three years, respectively – ss 160 and 173 of the Representation of the People Act 1983.
- Aliens/citizens of the European Union and other countries (except resident citizens from the Republic of Ireland or those qualifying from the Commonwealth).
- Those detained in mental hospitals (as a result of criminal activity) as authorised by statute – s 3A of the Representation of the People Act 1983. It should be noted that the consultation process which followed the *Hirst* case (see below) also embraced the position of certain people detained in mental hospitals.
- Convicted prisoners during the term of their detention. Section 3 of the Representation of the People Act 1983 states that:

SECTION

A convicted person during the time that he is detained in a penal institution in pursuance of his sentence . . . is legally incapable of voting at any parliamentary or local government election.

This is a blanket exclusion on prisoners from voting, which means that even if the prisoner were scheduled for release one week after polling day at a general election, legally they would still be precluded from voting at it. The Act, however, does not apply to:

- persons imprisoned for contempt of court, s 3(2)
- those imprisoned for default in paying a fine, s 3(2)
- prisoners on remand and unconvicted mental patients (as amended by the Representation of the People Act 2000).

In the *Hirst* case (below) in the European Court of Human Rights, the United Kingdom government tried to justify the disenfranchisement of prisoners on the basis that it pursued the following legitimate aims, namely 'of preventing crime and punishing offenders and enhancing civic responsibility and respect for the rule of law, by depriving those who have breached the basic rules of society of the right to have a say in the way such rules are made for the duration of their sentence' (para 33). The blanket disenfranchisement of United Kingdom prisoners to vote was tested in this case.

CASE EXAMPLE

Hirst v United Kingdom (No 2) *(2004) 38 EHRR 40*

Hirst had been serving a sentence of life imprisonment and as a convicted prisoner was legally disqualified from voting (s 3 Representation of the People Act 1983). In the United Kingdom domestic courts he unsuccessfully sought a declaration under the Human Rights Act 1998 that this provision violated Art 3 of Protocol No 1 (the right to free elections). He subsequently petitioned the European Court of Human Rights.

A chamber of the European Court held that there had been a breach of Art 3 of Protocol No 1. The court reaffirmed that elections were the foundation of an effective democracy. Although the right to vote was not absolute, any limitations had to be proportionate. The court held that, as the ban applied automatically to convicted prisoners while in prison and irrespective of the length of sentence or the offence committed, it amounted to a disproportionate restriction of Art 3 of Protocol No 1.

'The applicant in the present case lost his right to vote as the result of the imposition of an automatic and blanket restriction on convicted prisoners' franchise and may therefore claim to be a victim of the measure.'

This decision was subsequently upheld by the Grand Chamber (by 12 to five votes) (*Hirst v United Kingdom (No 2)* (2006) 42 EHRR 41).

The United Kingdom was left to decide on the choice of means for securing the right to vote which had been infringed and in December 2006 the then Labour government initiated a consultation process on the issue. The second stage of this process took place in 2009 (*Voting Rights of Convicted Prisoners Detained within the United Kingdom* CP 6/09 (Ministry of Justice, 2009)). As the Labour government had not introduced legislation to implement the *Hirst* judgment by the time of the 2010 general election, addressing this issue became the responsibility of the incoming coalition government. In addition, in February 2011 a backbench debate took place in the House of Commons which comprehensively agreed by 234 votes to 22 that the House supported the current domestic legal prohibition on prisoners voting and 'that legislative decisions of this nature should be a matter for democratically elected lawmakers' (*Hansard*, HC Vol 523, col 586).

As a result of the *Scoppola v Italy (No 3)* (2012) Application No 126/05 case in the Grand Chamber of the European Court of Human Rights which reaffirmed the principles set out in the *Hirst* case, the United Kingdom had six months to propose legislation to change the law in relation to the voting rights of prisoners. In November 2012 the coalition government issued the Voting Eligibility (Prisoners) Draft Bill, which contained the following three options:

- Retaining the existing position.
- A ban on voting in respect of prisoners sentenced to four years or more.
- A ban on voting in respect of prisoners sentenced to more than six months.

In due course, a Joint Committee of both Houses of Parliament was established to provide the draft Bill with pre-legislative scrutiny and it issued its report in December 2013 (Joint Committee on the Draft Voting Eligibility (Prisoners) Bill, *Draft Voting Eligibility (Prisoners) Bill*, HL Paper 103, HC 924 (The Stationery Office, 2013)). In essence, the report recommended that the government should introduce a Bill to enable all prisoners serving a sentence of 12 months or less to vote in parliamentary (together with local and European) elections (para 239). Notwithstanding this report, no Bill was forthcoming and in 2015 the Council of Europe's Committee of Ministers adopted a resolution which expressed its 'profound concern' that the United Kingdom's blanket ban on prisoners voting still remained in place. Similarly, in *Millbank and Others v UK* (2016) App No 44473/14 the European Court of Human Rights reaffirmed that the United Kingdom's blanket ban was a violation of the European Convention.

At the time of writing, the Lord Chancellor and Secretary for State for Justice made a statement in November 2017 (see below) in which he announced firstly, that in order to ensure clarity for offenders, the government would work with the judiciary to ensure that it is made clear to individuals when they are sentenced that they will lose their right to vote whilst in prison. Secondly, the government would amend guidance (Prison Service Guidance) to allow those offenders in the community released on a temporary licence to vote:

QUOTATION

'We believe the changes address the points raised in the 2005 judgment in a way that respects the clear direction of successive Parliaments and the strong views of the British public.'

Hansard, HC Vol 630, col 1007.

KEY FACTS

Voting at general elections

Voters must be:
- 18 years or over at the date of the poll.
- Registered in the register of parliamentary elections for that particular constituency.
- A British, Irish or qualifying Commonwealth citizen (the latter two must be resident in the United Kingdom). Note: a person who is a British citizen resident outside the United Kingdom can qualify as an overseas elector (Representation of the People Act 1985 as amended).

Those currently disqualified from voting at general elections are:
- Peers in the House of Lords.
- Persons under the age of 18 years.
- Persons guilty of corrupt or illegal practices at elections.
- Aliens/citizens of the European Union and other countries (except resident citizens from the Republic of Ireland or those qualifying from the Commonwealth).
- Those detained in mental hospitals (owing to criminal activity) as authorised by statute.
- Convicted prisoners during the term of their detention (but see recent developments).

ACTIVITY

Self-test question

What is the democratic importance of elections? In particular, do you think that prisoners should vote in elections?

9.7 The supervision and conduct of elections and political parties

9.7.1 The Electoral Commission

The Electoral Commission is an independent body established under the Political Parties, Elections and Referendums Act 2000. The purpose and aim of the Commission is set out below:

QUOTATION

'We work to support a healthy democracy, where elections and referendums are based on our principles of trust, participation, and no undue influence.

We:
- register political parties
- make sure people understand and follow the rules on party and election finance
- publish details of where parties and candidates get money from and how they spend it
- set the standards for electoral administration and running elections and report on how well this is done
- make sure people understand it is important to register to vote, and know how to vote
- run any referendums held in accordance with the Political Parties, Elections and Referendums Act 2000.'

The Electoral Commission: Who we are and what we do, putting voters first (The Electoral Commission, 2012).

Under the 2000 Act the Electoral Commission has the following wide-ranging functions:

- It is required to report on the administration of elections (Parliamentary, European and devolved) and referendums.
- It keeps under review and reports on various electoral and political issues.
- It is empowered to provide assistance and advice.
- It provides advice to broadcasters on political broadcasts.
- It supervises the registration of political parties.
- It supervises the finances of political parties including the publication of financial information (ie statements of accounts). In short, political parties are subject to audit requirements and they must record donations received and campaign expenditure incurred. The Electoral Administration Act 2006 now provides for the regulation of loans and credit facilities.

The Political Parties and Elections Act 2009 made further changes. For example, the regulatory role of the Electoral Commission was enhanced by conferring on it a broader range of investigatory powers, together with new 'civil sanctions' (eg to impose a monetary penalty). In relation to donations to political parties, the Act set out new arrangements in order to improve transparency. The 2009 Act followed on from the then Labour government's White Paper (*Party Finance and Expenditure in the United Kingdom, the Government's Proposals*, Cm 7329 (The Stationery Limited, 2008)).

For its most recent annual report, see *Annual Report and Accounts 2016–17*, HC 223 (The Electoral Commission, July 2017).

9.7.2 Election broadcasts

During general elections registered political parties are able to broadcast party political broadcasts in pursuance of persuading the electorate to vote for their prospective parliamentary candidates. This does not mean that all broadcasts will be screened, as illustrated by the following case.

CASE EXAMPLE

R (ProLife Alliance) v British Broadcasting Corporation *[2003] UKHL 23*

The ProLife Alliance was a political party (opposed to abortion) which was entitled to a party election television broadcast at the 2001 general election. The BBC had a duty under its Charter to preserve good taste and decency and refused to transmit ProLife

Alliance's election broadcast video as it depicted the abortion process (although the video had been an honest and unsensationalised account). ProLife Alliance sought judicial review of this decision.

The House of Lords held that the principles underpinning freedom of speech under Art 10 of the European Convention on Human Rights required that access to a public medium of communication (ie a television broadcast) should not be refused on an unreasonable, arbitrary or discriminatory basis. The BBC had to justify restricting the content of a programme produced by a political party promoting its aims, but it was for the broadcasters and not the court to apply the appropriate standard. The court held that there was nothing in the reasoning or the overall decision of the BBC to suggest that it had used an inappropriate standard in determining whether the transmitting of ProLife's pictures was likely to be offensive to public opinion. It is of interest to note that in the Court of Appeal (the decision of which was reversed in the House of Lords) Laws LJ had particularly emphasised the constitutional importance of free speech at election times.

9.8 The constitutional significance of the electoral system

The 'first past the post' electoral system has had a profound impact on the British constitution. As noted earlier, the system has, historically at least, typically resulted in one political party having a clear majority of seats in the House of Commons, thereby allowing it to form a government. This occurred most recently in 2015, when the Conservative government secured a small but working majority of seats. On some occasions, it has equipped a party with an overwhelming and almost insuperable majority; for example, after the 1997 general election the Labour government enjoyed a commanding majority of 179 seats. It must be reiterated that most of the dominant political party's MPs will *not* formally be part of the government, but through a combination of party loyalty and the whip system they will generally support its policies and legislative proposals.

The constitutional consequences of the electoral system include the following:

- It alters the constitutional balance between the executive and the House of Commons in favour of the former at the expense of the latter. In particular, with a commanding majority of seats in its favour, it would be very unlikely for a government to be defeated on its proposed legislation.
- Similarly, it would be very unlikely that a government would suffer a defeat on a vote of no confidence. Although in constitutional theory the motion of no confidence is the key parliamentary mechanism to remove a government during a parliamentary term, it has rarely been successful. The last occasion when it was successful was in 1979, which triggered the 1979 general election (see section 12.2.1).
- It affects the composition of committees in the House of Commons as, by constitutional convention, such committees reflect the party composition of the chamber. As a result, a majority of the MPs serving on these committees will necessarily be of the same political persuasion as the governing party (see section 12.6).
- Lord Hailsham has argued that our electoral system results in what he termed 'an elective dictatorship' (Elective dictatorship, *Listener*, 21 October 1976, pp 496–500). In short, a government with the comfortable support of a majority of MPs in the House of Commons can, in effect, push through whatever legislation it deems necessary. In this way the House of Commons merely legitimises and 'rubber stamps' the wishes of the government, which in turn has generally been elected on the basis of a minority of the nationwide votes cast. According to Bogdanor:

QUOTATION

'The legal doctrine of the sovereignty of Parliament has thus come to legitimize a political doctrine, the doctrine that a government enjoying an overall majority in the House of Commons should enjoy virtually unlimited power. What the governing party enacts thus becomes, *ipso facto*, constitutional.'

V Bogdanor, *The New British Constitution* (Hart Publishing, 2009), p 15.

In addition, in a debate in the House of Lords in 2004 Lord Desai stated that:

QUOTATION

'We now have an effectively unicameral legislature. A majority in the House of Commons gives any Prime Minister enormous powers.'

Hansard, HL Vol 664, col 1249.

■ Finally, as an adjunct to the above point made by Lord Hailsham, it raises the issue of whether such a government is truly politically legitimate with the moral right to carry out its electoral mandate. Indeed, in the second half of the twentieth century and the first part of the twenty-first, no government has secured more than half of the votes cast in a general election (although in 1955 Anthony Eden's Conservative Party did secure 49.7 per cent of the votes cast). All of these administrations, therefore, were acting on the basis of the wishes of a minority of the electorate (that had chosen to vote). In this sense it could be argued that the electoral system – to some extent – distorts the will of the electorate by, generally speaking, conferring an inordinate amount of power on one political party that (typically) forms the government. NB: the combined votes cast for the *two* parties in the 2010 coalition government *did* exceed 50 per cent – although, of course, the electorate had not expressly voted for a coalition government and its *Coalition Agreement* proposals.

9.9 An overview of the main elements of the House of Commons – a snapshot at November 2017

In brief, the House of Commons in November 2017 contained the following elements:

■ **Her Majesty's Government**

This consisted officially of 93 Conservative MPs. A minority of these MPs sat in the Cabinet (22), as most ministers were outside it. These ministers were also supplemented by a number of unpaid members. All of Her Majesty's Government ministers were supported (at least in theory) by the remainder of the Conservative MPs (ie government backbenchers). NB: the Conservative government had a 'confidence and supply' arrangement with the DUP.

■ **Her Majesty's Official Opposition**

The main Official Opposition was the Labour Party (the second largest party), headed by the Leader of the Opposition.

■ **Government front and backbenchers**

The Conservative frontbenchers were government ministers, whereas their backbenchers (known as government backbenchers) were not technically in the government *per se*, but, being of the same political party as the government, generally speaking, supported the Conservative government.

▪ The Official Opposition's frontbenchers

These were composed of shadow spokespersons of government departments collectively known as the shadow Cabinet. For example, the Labour Shadow Home Secretary shadowed and opposed the Home Secretary. The Labour Party's backbenchers were Labour MPs who were not in the shadow Cabinet.

▪ Party whips

Each political party had party whips to ensure discipline within the ranks of their party and ensure that MPs voted in accordance with official party allegiance and interests. Party whips also helped to keep their respective MPs informed about the parliamentary timetable and business.

▪ The Speaker of the House of Commons

His constitutional roles included, among others:

- To chair debates and proceedings (including calling members to speak).
- To deal with the administration of the House.
- To call members to order and keep order within the chamber.
- To act as the representative of the House of Commons in state events.

The Speaker was assisted by three Deputy Speakers.

▪ The Leader of the House of Commons

This was a member of the government who attended the Cabinet. The responsibilities of this post included arranging and supervising government business in the chamber (in particular, the legislative programme).

9.10 Reform

9.10.1 The electoral system

The 1997 Labour Party manifesto committed the incoming government to establish an independent commission on the voting system for the House of Commons and thereafter to hold a referendum on the system. As indicated earlier, one of the perceived difficulties with the present 'first past the post' system (see section 9.4.4) is that it can distort the wishes of the electorate. In 1998 the Jenkins Commission delivered its report (*The Report of the Independent Commission on the Voting System*, Cm 4090-I (1998)), which recommended a highly convoluted system.

More recently the 2005 Labour Party manifesto proposed to review 'the experience of the new electoral systems' introduced since 1997. In 2008 the then Labour government issued its review (*Review of Voting Systems: the Experience of New Voting Systems in the United Kingdom Since 1997*, Cm 7304 (The Stationery Office, 2008)). This review was designed to inform the debate on electoral reform for Parliament. In February 2010 the Constitutional Reform and Governance Bill was amended in the Commons to provide for a national referendum on the electoral system (*Hansard*, HC, Vol 505, col 790ff). This amendment provided that 'A referendum is to be held, not later than 31 October 2011, on the voting system for Parliamentary elections'. The question to be asked would have involved a choice between the existing 'first past the post' system and the alternative vote system. This provision was removed from the Bill in the 'wash-up' process prior to the 2010 general election.

Following the 2010 election, the new coalition government issued its *Coalition Agreement* in May 2010 which pledged a referendum on the alternative vote. This national referendum took place in May 2011 under the aegis of Part 1 of the Parliamentary Voting System and Constituencies Act 2011. In the event, the public rejected the alternative vote in favour of retaining the existing system (67.9 per cent voted No to using the alternative vote instead – albeit on a 42 per cent turnout (source: C Rallings and M Thrasher (eds), *British Electoral Facts 1832–2012* (Biteback Publishing, 2012), Table 22.02)).

NB: At the time of writing, following an e-petition (number 168657) Westminster Hall debated the issue of proportional representation (*Hansard*, HC Vol 630, col 237 WH).

SUMMARY

- The House of Commons is the lower chamber of Parliament and is wholly elected with 650 MPs. Its functions are as follows:
  - Legislative – to pass legislation as part of the legislature.
  - Representative – to reflect the will of the people at the latest general election and help resolve their grievances.
  - To recruit, maintain and hold to account the government.
  - To discipline its members.
- An MP has a number of competing factors to consider, ranging from, following his political party to acting in the public interest.
- There are a number of factors which disqualify a person from, becoming an MP (eg serving a prison sentence of more than one year).
- In terms of composition, concern has been expressed as to the extent to which the House of Commons accurately reflects society as a whole.
- The electoral system used to elect MPs is the 'first past the post' system using 650 single-member constituencies.
- There are a number of factors which disqualify a person from voting at a general election (eg convicted prisoners during their term of detention).
- In terms of political composition, very few independent MPs are elected and so the main political parties dominate the composition of the House.
- The leader of the political party who secures the overall majority of seats after a general election will become the Prime Minister.
- The Electoral Commission oversees the electoral process.

SAMPLE ESSAY QUESTION

Explain the electoral system used for electing MPs and consider whether the system should be reformed.

Introduction:
- The House of Commons uses the 'first past the post' electoral system.

'First past the post system':
- Simple majority system.
- UK divided into 650 single member constituencies.
- Winning candidate needs to obtain the most votes (i.e one more vote than their rivals).
- Following an election, the leader of the party with an overall majority of seats becomes Prime Minister.

Arguments for reform:
- A disproportionate system which distorts the wishes of the electorate.
- Candidates can become MPs with less than 51 per cent of the votes cast in a constituency.
- Governments can be formed with less than 51 per cent of the votes cast nationwide.
- Disadvantages smaller third parties.
- Only the votes cast for the winning candidate count.
- Problem of safe seats.

Arguments for retaining the system:
- Simple system to operate (which encourages people to participate).
- Produces (historically) a clear-cut election result.
- Produces (historically) strong government – which can act decisively.
- Single member constituencies ensure a direct link between MP and constituents.

Recent events:
- The Jenkins Commission.
- The 2008 Ministry of Justice paper *(Review of Voting Systems)*.
- The 2010 and 2017 general elections produced hung parliaments
- In a 2011 national referendum the public rejected the alternative vote system as a replacement for the existing system.

Conclusion

Further reading

Books

Barnett, H, *Constitutional and Administrative Law* (12th edn, Routledge/Taylor & Francis Group, 2017), Chapters 12 and 13.

Carroll, A, *Constitutional and Administrative Law* (9th edn, Pearson/Longman, 2017), Chapters 6 to 8.

Loveland, I, *Constitutional Law, Administrative Law, and Human Rights* (7th edn, Oxford University Press, 2015), Chapters 5 and 7.

Morris, C, *Parliamentary Elections, Representation and the Law* (Hart Publishing, 2012).

Papers

See the wide range of papers in the House of Commons Library.

Internet links

www.parliament.uk
www.electoralcommission.org.uk

10

Parliament III: The House of Lords

AIMS AND OBJECTIVES

At the end of this chapter you should be able to:

- Identify and explain the different types of membership of the House of Lords
- Explain the political composition of the chamber
- Identify and explain the various different functions of the House of Lords
- Identify and explain the legal and political powers of the House of Lords
- Appreciate the attempts at reform of the House of Lords

10.1 Introduction and size of the House of Lords

The House of Lords has evolved over many hundreds of years and, in fact, predates the House of Commons. It is the second chamber of Parliament and is, by both law and constitutional convention, subordinate to the House of Commons. The House of Lords is an unusual and distinctive House in a number of ways. For example:

- There is no legal or constitutional cap on the size of its membership. In fact, the size of the House is ultimately in the hands of the executive (specifically the Prime Minister).
- The composition of the House is very different to that of the House of Commons, as not only do a significant number of independent members sit in the Upper House but, uniquely in a democracy, it comprises a number of individuals who have inherited their seat.

The House of Lords, historically, has been an exceptionally large house in comparison with other upper chambers. Indeed, before it was reformed in 1999, its membership was almost twice the size of the House of Commons. It is generally the case that, where states have bicameral legislatures, the Upper House will be smaller than the lower chamber. According to research undertaken by Russell, the second chamber of other states tends on average to be 60 per cent of the size of the lower one (M Russell, *Second Chambers Overseas: A Summary* (The Constitution Unit, 1999), p 3). Before the enactment of the House of Lords Act 1999, the House of Lords comprised almost 1,300 members, although not all regularly attended. In contrast, the House of Commons had 659 MPs (the 1997–2001 Parliament).

The size of upper chambers in other democracies is comparatively smaller. For example, the United States Senate has 100 members and Canada's Senate has 104. Moreover, there is no legal cap on the size of the House of Lords (although there is a statutory cap in respect of the House of Commons, this can be altered). This is not unique for upper chambers, however, as there is no fixed number of members in respect of, for example, Spain's Senato or Belgium's Sénat. In this respect, therefore, the size of the House of Lords constantly fluctuates as peers die and new **life peers** are created.

10.2 The composition of the House of Lords

The following diagram indicates the composition of the House of Lords in November 2017:

Figure 10.1 The composition of the House of Lords (it excludes ineligible members).

Source: Parliament website www.parliament.uk

The House of Lords and gender

In November 2017, 209 members of the House of Lords were female (source: see above). The overwhelming majority of female members have been appointed there as life peers. As around one-quarter of the House is female this is roughly comparable to the elected House of Commons, where, after the 2017 general election, 208 female MPs were elected, representing 32 per cent of the House (see section 9.2.2). On women in the Lords, see D Hughes, *Women in the House of Lords*, LLN 2015/017 (House of Lords Library Note, 2017).

In broad terms, members of the House can be divided into Lords Spiritual and Lords Temporal.

10.3 Lords Spiritual

The Lords Spiritual are, technically speaking, not peers at all but Lords of Parliament. They are further subdivided into bishops and two archbishops of the established church: the Church of England. They represent the link between the church and state – the sovereign is, of course, the Supreme Governor of the Church of England and swears an oath on coronation as monarch to preserve the church. The spiritual members sit as 'independents' as they are independent of any political party (they sit on the *Bishops' Benches*). They are *ex officio* members of the House and when they retire from their religious office they leave the House (although it is possible for them subsequently to be appointed as life peers). The United Kingdom is in fact the only democracy in Europe that specifically reserves spiritual seats in its law-making body. Nevertheless, the 2000 Royal Commission on the Reform of the House of Lords (*A House for the Future*, Cm 4534 (The Stationery Office, 2000), Ch 15) specifically recommended the retention of such explicit religious representation. It further recommended that the designated religious element of any reformed Upper House in the future should be broadened to include other Christian denominations, together with other non-Christian faiths (eg Islam, Judaism etc). In particular, the Royal Commission noted the contribution that the Spiritual Lords made in the House. In addition to the bishops, a number of members of both parliamentary chambers have a religious affiliation to various different faiths and are therefore able to contribute to debates with a religious dimension. In terms of gender, historically all of the bishops have been male. However, following the passage of the Lords Spiritual (Women) Act 2015, until 2025 any vacancy is to be filled by a female bishop. In September 2017 there were two female bishops sitting in the House of Lords (see further, S White, *House of Lords: Lords Spiritual*, Library Briefing (House of Lords, 2017).

ACTIVITY

Self-test question

What are the advantages and disadvantages of having religious representation in the legislature?

As indicated by the diagram at section 10.2, the Lords Temporal are subdivided into the following elements:

- Judicial life peers.
- 'Ordinary' life peers.
- Hereditary peers.

10.4 The judicial life peers

Until October 2009, the Appellate Committee of the House of Lords was the highest domestic court in the United Kingdom (except for Scottish criminal matters). The court was staffed by the Lords of Appeal in Ordinary (more commonly known as the law lords). When the law lords retired from judicial office, they remained in the House as crossbench members (see section 10.7.3). As indicated at section 5.7.10, under Pt 3 of the Constitutional Reform Act 2005, the Appellate Committee was replaced by a new Supreme Court outside and independent of the legislature. In October 2009 when the Supreme Court became operational the existing judicially active law lords (eg Lord Mance) were transferred to the new court to act as justices of the Supreme Court. Those law lords who had already retired from judicial office remained in the House (eg Lord Carswell) and continued to sit as crossbench members.

In short, in 2017, despite the existence of the Supreme Court, which is separate from Parliament, the House of Lords *still* contains some judicial peers (albeit retired judges), who sit as crossbench members and can engage in the proceedings of the chamber. For example, see the following point made by Lord Carswell in the context of a debate on constitutional reform in 2010:

QUOTATION

'My Lords, I have had the privilege of being a Member of this House for a little over six years, but I have not until now had occasion to address your Lordships in debate. The reason is simple: I was, until my fairly recent retirement, a member of the Appellate Committee and sat as a Lord of Appeal in Ordinary. We all observed, rightly or wrongly, the self-imposed abstinence from participation in debates. But I am now released from that Trappist-type vow of silence and I hope to be able to make a modest contribution from time to time to the proceedings of the House.'

Hansard, HL Vol 716, col 1565.

ACTIVITY

Self-test question

What are the advantages and disadvantages of having retired judges in the legislature?

10.5 'Ordinary' life peers

10.5.1 The Life Peerages Act 1958

Under the Life Peerages Act 1958, the Crown (for practical purposes, the Prime Minister) is conferred with the power to award life peerages to individuals so that they can sit in the House of Lords. They now represent the largest single category of peers. There are at least three clear advantages to the creation of life peerages:

- Firstly, it means that distinguished individuals in different fields (such as medicine, commerce, academia, journalism etc) can bring their particular skills, expertise and experience to bear in the workings of the House. This is particularly useful in the context of a debate or when scrutinising legislative proposals in these fields.

  The 2000 Royal Commission recognised the importance of this experience in respect of the workings of the House as 'Many can offer expertise and experience outside politics. Many are men and women of distinction in their own right' (para 14.3). In fact, the Royal Commission noted that these characteristics were ones which they envisaged should ideally exist in any reformed second chamber.

- Secondly, as life peerages by their nature only exist for the life of the recipient, this means that the awarding of life peerages does not permanently enlarge the size of the chamber.

- Thirdly, the creation of life peerages ensures that the House can be more representative of society. In particular, it allows women and individuals from ethnic minorities to be specifically appointed to the House. Indeed, the vast majority of women sitting in the House of Lords have been appointed there under the Life Peerages Act 1958.

10.5.2 The creation of life peerages

The Life Peerages Act 1958 permits the Prime Minister of the day to create new life peers and is therefore a form of patronage. In legal theory, under the Act the Prime Minister could technically recommend to the monarch that hundreds of new life peers of the same political colour as the governing party be appointed. This scenario raises an interesting issue as to whether it would be constitutional for the monarch to refuse to approve these peerages (see section 4.16). In any event, it is the Prime Minister who determines the size of the upper chamber as they decide how many life peerages to create. By constitutional convention, however, this power of the Prime Minister is not abused. The then Labour government's justification for creating a significant number of Labour life peers after 1997 was on the basis of ensuring a level of parity with the Conservative Party in the chamber.

10.5.3 The appointment of party political peers

The position is that the Prime Minister will determine the overall number of life peerages that are to be created and how many each party should receive, for example:

- 10 for Party A,
- 12 for Party B,
- four for Party C, etc.

Although the Prime Minister will determine the list of names for his own political party, the respective leaders of the other parties will compile their own list of names. These names would in due course be placed before the monarch to approve, and, by constitutional convention she would act on the advice of the Prime Minister.

10.5.4 The appointment of non-party political peers (independent peers)

In terms of the appointment of non-party political peers (ie independent peers who sit as crossbenchers – see 10.7.3), it is the Prime Minister who will determine how many crossbench peers should be created. In 1999, the then Labour government announced in its White Paper (*Modernising Parliament, Reforming the House of Lords*, Cm 1183 (1999)) that in the transitional phase of reforming the House it would establish a non-statutory body to make these non-party political appointments. In essence, this body would determine the *names* of the non-party political peers. The Prime Minister would, however, still determine the *number* of crossbench peers required.

The House of Lords Appointments Commission

The House of Lords Appointments Commission is an independent, non-statutory public body and was established in 2000. In 2017 it comprised the following:

- a chairperson
- three non-party political members
- three members who have been nominated from the main political parties (Labour, Conservative and Liberal Democrats).

The Appointments Commission has two principal functions:

- Firstly, it determines the individuals who are to be recommended for nomination as non-party political life peers. The Commission submits the required number of peers sought by the Prime Minister. On receipt of the nominations from the Appointments Commission, the Prime Minister will then put forward these recommendations to the monarch for approval.

- Secondly, it vets the propriety of nominations for life peerages before they are appointed. This applies to both non-party political peers as well as to the party political peers submitted by the leaders of the political parties through the conduit of the Prime Minister.

The Appointments Commission set out the assessment criteria that it would use in selecting non-party political peers to be as follows:

- Ability to make a significant and effective contribution to the work of the chamber.
- A record of achievement in a person's chosen field.
- A willingness to commit the necessary time to the chamber.
- Some understanding of the framework of the constitution.
- Independence and integrity.
- A commitment to the highest standards of public life.
- Independent of a political party.
- Resident for tax purposes in the United Kingdom.

Criteria Guiding the Assessment of Nominations for Non-Party Political Life Peers (lordsappointments.independent.gov.uk)

The Commission stated that all appointments would be on the basis of individual merit and no other basis.

In total, according to figures derived from the Appointments Commission, between 2001 and 2015 it had appointed 67 life peers, which hitherto would have been effectively within the power of the Prime Minister.

ACTIVITY

Essay writing

What are the advantages and disadvantages of having appointed life peers in the legislature? How do they differ from elected MPs in the House of Commons?

10.6 Hereditary peers

10.6.1 The position before the House of Lords Act 1999

Prior to the enactment of the House of Lords Act 1999, there were 759 hereditary peers and peeresses who inherited their seat in the Lords. This did not, however, mean that they all necessarily attended (the same point could also have been made in respect of the appointed life peers).

10.6.2 The arguments for the removal of the hereditary peers

In 1997 the then Labour government was elected on a manifesto commitment to remove the right of hereditary peers to sit and vote in the House of Lords. In its subsequent White Paper of 1999 the government asserted that:

QUOTATION

'The right of hereditary peers to sit and vote in the House of Lords is a significant factor in the lack of political effectiveness and balance of the House. We believe no individuals should have the right to be Members of Parliament solely on the basis of the actions or position of their ancestors. A place in the legislature should be reserved for those who achieve it on their own merits. The continuing right of the whole hereditary peerage to sit and vote has been accepted as an anomaly for most of this century.'

Modernising Parliament, Reforming the House of Lords, Cm 4183
(The Stationery Office, 1999), p 8.

The government, in the above White Paper, identified the following reasons for their removal:

- Hereditary membership of a legislature was an anachronism – especially in a democracy. It is of interest to note that, according to Russell (*Second Chambers Overseas: A Summary*, p 5), only one country in the world, Lesotho, in Africa, uses the hereditary principle as the main basis for determining the composition of its second chamber.
- The hereditary element was unrepresentative of society (for example, only 16 of the hereditaries were female).
- Almost half of the hereditary peers (excluding those on leave or without a writ of summons to enter the House) were identified with the Conservative Party. The result of this was that – as a whole – the Conservative Party had an 'in-built party bias in the House of Lords'.

In due course the Labour government introduced legislation to remove the hereditary element from the House: The House of Lords Bill (which became the House of Lords Act 1999).

ACTIVITY

Self-test question

Can you think of any arguments in favour of retaining the hereditary principle in the House of Lords?

10.6.3 The House of Lords Act 1999

This legislation ended the right of most of the hereditary peers to sit and vote in the House of Lords.

SECTION

s 1 of the House of Lords Act 1999

'No-one shall be a member of the House of Lords by virtue of a hereditary peerage.'

While the House of Lords Bill was being considered in the upper chamber, an amendment was made to it (the Weatherill amendment, named after Lord Weatherill) which enabled 92 of the then existing hereditary peers to remain in the chamber.

The government was prepared to accede to this compromise for two main reasons:

- Firstly, it meant that the Bill would pass through the House of Lords and that at least the majority of hereditary peers would be removed. These individuals would thereafter be entitled to become MPs. In fact, in 2001 an ex-peer, Viscount Thurso (Liberal Democrat), was elected as an MP (but now see below).
- Secondly, the retention of a rump of hereditary peers was only ever meant to be a temporary arrangement pending long-term full reform of the House, at which point they would finally be removed.

The removal of the remaining hereditary peers?

In 2017 the hereditary element was *still* present in the House. This is because there is no universal agreement on the composition of a fully reformed Upper House and so the hereditary element still remains pending the realisation of long-term reform.

It is inevitable that full reform of the Lords will continue to be a protracted business. Indeed, although the House of Lords Act 1999 was supposed to be an interim measure pending long-term reform of the House, it is also worth remembering that the 1911 Parliament Act was only ever supposed to be a temporary measure pending future reform being implemented. It is pertinent to note that in March 2007 the House of Commons voted in principle to remove the remaining hereditary peers by 391 votes to 111. In addition, in July 2012 the Commons gave a second reading to the coalition government's House of Lords Reform Bill, which, among other things, would have removed the remaining hereditary peers. However, the Bill was abandoned – see section 10.13.

The remaining hereditary peers

Section 2 of the House of Lords Act 1999 retained 92 hereditary peers as follows:

- Two holding hereditary Great Offices of State (Lord Great Chamberlain – the Queen's representative, and the Earl Marshal – responsible for ceremonies).
- 75 (in total) elected by each respective political party or group. The number of peers each party received was in direct proportion to the number of hereditary peers each party had at the time of the Act. As the Conservatives had the most hereditaries, they elected the most hereditary peers. The results were as follows:
  42 Conservative
  2 Labour
  3 Liberal Democrat
  28 crossbenchers (independent peers)
- 15 office holders (for example, Deputy Speakers and Committee Chairs) elected by the whole of the House of Lords.

> Source: House of Lords Briefing, *Reform and Proposals for Reform since 1900* (Parliamentary Copyright, House of Lords, 2006), p 8.

Overall, 92 hereditary peers were retained, three of whom were female. As a result of the House of Lords Act 1999 we now have the rather paradoxical situation in which the remaining hereditary peers – by virtue of their election – could in one sense claim to be more constitutionally legitimate than their appointed life peer counterparts. The point must be made, however, that the electorate was very limited: the 15 office holders were elected by the whole House and the 75 party and crossbench peers were elected by their respective members. In any event, none were voted for by the electorate outside of the House.

The death of an (elected) hereditary peer

The House of Lords Act 1999 was meant to represent a staging post on the way to full long-term reform of the chamber. Full reform of the House has to date not been realised and consequently the 'transitional' House has had to deal with the situation when one of the retained hereditary peers has died. From the end of the 2001–02 parliamentary session, vacancies due to death (and latterly following resignation or expulsion under the House of Lords Reform Act 2014) have been filled by a by-election. Candidates for the by-election are filled, in essence, by peers expelled in 1999 (Standing Order No 10). It should be pointed out that the 2010 Constitutional Reform and Governance Bill proposed to abolish these by-elections in order to allow the hereditary element to eventually die out (see section 10.13). However, by the time this measure became the Constitutional Reform and Governance Act 2010, the above provision had been removed. It should also be noted that Lord Steel of Aikwood has (albeit unsuccessfully) on a number of occasions in the last decade or so, tried to pilot a Private Members' Bill through Parliament which would have abolished by-elections for hereditary peers.

In terms of hereditary peers, the following two points are worth making. Firstly, from 2002 to July 2017, 30 hereditary by-elections have taken place (figures extrapolated from: E Scott, *Hereditary By-elections: Results* (House of Lords Library Briefing, 2017)). Secondly, Viscount Thurso has enjoyed a fascinating (and unique) parliamentary career. He joined the House of Lords as a hereditary peer in 1995, before leaving the chamber as part of the 1999 reforms and becoming an MP in 2001 until 2015. Thereafter, he won the April 2016 (Liberal Democrat) hereditary by-election on the death of Lord Avebury and so returned to the House of Lords.

ACTIVITY

Self-test question

What are the advantages and disadvantages of having 'elected' hereditary peers in the House of Lords?

10.6.4 Renouncing a peerage

Since the Peerage Act 1963 it has been possible for hereditary peers to renounce their peerages. This represented an irrevocable renunciation for the duration of their lifetime, although their successors would not be affected by it. Under this legislation two major political figures renounced their hereditary peerages:

- In October 1963 Harold Macmillan resigned as Prime Minister. This resulted in the Earl of Home disclaiming his hereditary peerage under the 1963 Act in order to succeed Macmillan as Prime Minister (as Sir Alec Douglas-Home). This was necessary as by constitutional convention a Prime Minister must be a member of the House of Commons (see section 4.13.4), thereby being directly accountable to the elected representatives of the people.
- Tony Benn – on the death of his father in 1960, he automatically succeeded to the hereditary peerage of the Viscountcy of Stansgate, with an entitlement to sit in the House of Lords. At the time he was an MP and he wanted to renounce

this peerage and continue to serve in the House of Commons. As an individual cannot sit in both Houses, his Bristol constituency seat became vacant and a by-election was held. Although Benn won the by-election, the Election Court disbarred him from assuming his seat in the House of Commons. After the passing of the Peerage Act 1963, Benn renounced his peerage and was thereafter elected as an MP.

ACTIVITY

Essay writing

Compare and contrast the different types of members in the House of Lords.

KEY FACTS

Key facts on hereditary peers

Spiritual Lords	**Archbishops and bishops –** they represent the link between the established church and the state. They provide a religious/moral dimension to the chamber. A very unusual category of members in a democratic legislature.
Temporal Lords	**Hereditary peers –** originally they inherited their seat in the chamber, although after the 1999 reforms they were 'elected' by their counterparts. A unique category of members in a democratic legislature.
	Life peers: • **Judicial life peers –** members of the judiciary who have retired from judicial office. • **'Ordinary' life peers –** appointed under the Life Peerages Act 1958. They provide the chamber with expertise and specialism. A number of legislatures, including Canada, have appointed members.

10.7 The party political composition of the House

10.7.1 Political breakdown of the composition of the House of Lords

In common with the House of Commons, members of the House of Lords are organised into political parties and take a party whip. The House of Lords, however, is a less partisan chamber and members are more likely to defy their party whips and official party line largely based on the fact that they are not subject to re-election. The main political parties are, therefore, represented in the Lords, although, in contrast to the Commons, they are supplemented by a significant independent element. Moreover, no single political party controls the chamber.

In November 2017 the political breakdown of the House was as follows:

Political composition of the House of Lords in 2017	
Party	**Number of peers**
Conservative	252
Labour	199
Liberal Democrat	100
Crossbenchers	181
Others	14

Table 10.1

These figures exclude bishops, non-affiliated and ineligible members.
Source: Parliament website: www.parliament.uk.

On the regional background of members, see C Coleman, *Regional Representation in the House of Lords*, LLN 2016/038 (House of Lords Library Note, 2017).

ACTIVITY

Problem-solving

Compare and contrast the party political composition in the two Houses of Parliament.

10.7.2 Government ministers in the House of Lords

As will be considered at section 11.6.2, a number of government ministers, including a few Cabinet ministers, sit in the House of Lords. The most prominent figure historically was of course the Lord Chancellor; however, as stated in s 2 of the Constitutional Reform Act 2005, a future Lord Chancellor may be drawn from either chamber. Until the passage of this Act, by constitutional convention the Lord Chancellor had traditionally resided in the upper chamber. In late 2017 David Gauke MP was Lord Chancellor.

The constitutional advantage of ministers sitting in the House of Lords is that it ensures that the government has representatives in the upper chamber to act as spokespersons and to pilot Bills through it.

10.7.3 Independent/crossbench peers

The House of Lords is hallmarked in terms of its composition by virtue of the fact that a significant number of its members are classed as independents (crossbenchers – they sit on the crossbenches in the chamber between the benches of the government and the Opposition). In essence, crossbenchers can be defined as those peers who do not take a party political whip and have no specific allegiance to one of the main political parties. Crossbenchers sit as individual members and do not constitute a party. They do, however, regularly meet under the aegis of the Convener of crossbench peers, where issues of common interest are raised and discussed. Crossbenchers are noted for their independent, non-party political stance on matters.

The importance of having an independent (non-politically aligned) element in the second chamber was emphasised strongly by the 2000 Royal Commission. In particular, it recommended that a fully reformed House should contain a strong crossbench element amounting to around 20 per cent of the total membership of the House. In terms of House of Lords reform, therefore, one of the inevitable consequences of the widely supported proposal of a wholly elected chamber would be the loss of this independent element. In short, elected members will invariably always be associated with one of the major political parties. As we saw in respect of the House of Commons, very few politicians are elected as an 'Independent'.

In 2002 the Joint Committee on House of Lords Reform underlined the importance of the existing independent element of the House:

QUOTATION

'The role of Crossbenchers is often particularly significant in relation to participation in debates and committees and the quality they bring to these deliberations.'

House of Lords Reform: First Report, HL Paper 17, HC 171 (2002), p 17.

The other advantage of having a sizeable independent, non-party political element is that it helps to ensure that, in terms of numbers, no one political party dominates the second chamber (see the following table). Indeed, it now seems that a constitutional convention has developed in relation to the House that it should not be dominated by one political party.

Breakdown of the composition of the political and non-political elements in November 2017				
	Conservative	Labour	Liberal Democrats	Crossbencher
Life peers	203	195	96	149
Hereditary peers	49	4	4	32
Total	252	199	100	181

Table 10.2

These figures exclude the bishops and non-affiliated, other-party and ineligible members.
Source: Parliament website www.parliament.uk.

10.7.4 Other key personnel of the House

The Speaker of the House

Traditionally the Speaker of the House of Lords had been the Lord Chancellor; however, following the Constitutional Reform Act 2005, which reformed the nature of this office, the House had to make alternative arrangements in respect of the post of Speaker. Under s 2 of the Act a future Lord Chancellor may sit in either House and so therefore may not necessarily be a peer. As indicated at section 5.7.9, it is in this context that the chamber resolved to elect a Speaker for five years. They would be known as the Lord Speaker and would be expected to give up party politics and occupy the Woolsack (the seat on which, historically, the Speaker of the House sat). In 2016 Lord Fowler was elected as Lord Speaker.

The office of Lord Speaker is not an exact parallel of the Speaker of the House of Commons, as the former has fewer responsibilities and is less powerful than his counterpart in the Commons. In fact, although he presides over proceedings, his role is in practice a symbolic one:

- As the House of Lords is a self-regulating body (by virtue of its unelected status, the atmosphere is less partisan or politically charged), the responsibility for maintaining order rests not with the Speaker but with the House collectively.
- The Speaker does not call members to speak and neither does he curtail debate in the chamber.

In common with the House of Commons, however, the Lord Speaker is assisted by a number of Deputy Speakers. The Speakers in both Houses represent each respective House abroad and on ceremonial occasions.

The Leader of the House

The Leader of the House is a member of the Cabinet and is responsible for the conduct of government business in the chamber – this is a similar function to the Leader of the House of Commons.

10.8 Disqualification of membership of the House of Lords

There are a number of factors which disqualify individuals from membership of the House of Lords and to some extent these parallel those relating to the House of Commons (see section 9.3.3). According to Erskine May (*Parliamentary Practice* (24th edn, LexisNexis Butterworths, 2011), Chapter 3), the following are disqualified from membership:

Individuals under 21 years

See Standing Order No 2, 1685. This partly explains why historically some hereditary peers were absent from the chamber, as when they inherited their seat they may have been too young to enter the House.

Aliens

See the Act of Settlement 1700 (as amended by the British Nationality Act 1981 which excludes Commonwealth and Republic of Ireland citizens from the 1700 Act). In addition, s 41 of the Constitutional Reform and Governance Act 2010 states that for the purposes of tax members of the House of Lords are treated as resident and domiciled in the United Kingdom.

Bankrupts

In England and Wales disqualification will apply if a member has been adjudged bankrupt (the Insolvency Act 1986, as amended by the Enterprise Act 2002). In Scotland it applies where the member's estate is sequestered.

Treason

Those convicted of treason under the Forfeiture Act 1870 (until pardoned or the term of imprisonment has expired) are disqualified.

Mental health

Unlike the House of Commons, the Mental Health Act 1983 did not specifically apply to the Lords. The House of Lords Committee for Privileges (HL 254, 1983–84) had recommended that in order to resolve this issue, future legislation should make it clear that such mental health provisions applied to members of the House. In any case, now see section 9.3.3 and the repeal of this statutory provision in relation to MPs.

Judicial office

Under s 137 of the Constitutional Reform Act 2005 peers sitting as Supreme Court justices are prevented from sitting and voting in the House.

Members of the European Parliament

See the European Parliament (House of Lords Disqualification) Regulations 2008 SI 2008/1647.

10.9 The functions of the House of Lords

In the absence of a written codified constitutional text there is no authoritative and constitutionally definitive statement setting out the powers of the House of Lords (or, for that matter, the House of Commons). In 1968, however, the then Labour government's White Paper on House of Lords reform identified the following functions:

QUOTATION

'Functions of the House of Lords
Apart from providing the Supreme Court of Appeal, the House of Lords at present performs the following main functions:
(a) the provision of a forum for full and free debate on matters of public interest;
(b) the revision of public Bills brought from the House of Commons;
(c) the initiation of public legislation, including in particular those government Bills which are less controversial in party political terms and private members' Bills;
(d) the consideration of subordinate legislation;
(e) the scrutiny of the activities of the executive; and
(f) the scrutiny of private legislation.'

House of Lords Reform, Cm 3799 (1968), para 8.

The House of Lords information publication (*Work of the House of Lords 2015–16* (Parliamentary Copyright, House of Lords, 2016), p 39) provided a useful breakdown of the time typically spent by the House of Lords on its various functions:

- 57 per cent on legislation (Bills and statutory instruments)
- 30 per cent on debates on policy issues
- 6 per cent on questions
- 4 per cent on statements
- 3 per cent on 'other'.

Also see, *Guide to Work in the Chamber* (Parliamentary Copyright, House of Lords, 2017).

10.9.1 The judicial role of the House

It should be remembered that in a very general sense the House – as a whole – performs a judicial function when it regulates and enforces the internal rules of parliamentary privilege (see Chapter 8). For example, in terms of self-regulation, in 2009 the House of Lords suspended two peers until the end of the parliamentary session.

In addition, as indicated earlier at section 10.4, historically until 2009 the Appellate Committee of the House of Lords was the highest domestic court. As a result, the law lords formed part of both the legislature and the judiciary and so violated a pure interpretation of the separation of powers (see sections 5.2.2 and 5.7.10). The Constitutional Reform Act 2005, however, created a new separate free-standing Supreme Court, which became operational in October 2009.

10.9.2 A forum for debate

The House of Lords is a debating chamber in which matters of public interest are examined and considered. As in the House of Commons, debates can take place either:

■ in the context of the passage of legislation by debating the principles and details of a Bill; or

■ as free-standing general debates.

Although both parliamentary chambers hold debates, it is generally argued that debates in the House of Lords are qualitatively better than in the House of Commons for three reasons:

■ Firstly, there is a broader range of experience and expertise in the upper chamber, which arguably allows debates to be richer and more informed than in the Commons. Much of this experience and knowledge has been appointed under the Life Peerages Act 1958, but some of it is drawn from the ranks of the hereditaries. It must also be remembered that peers are unsalaried and (if working) can continue with their careers in parallel with their duties in the House. Writing in 2015 Rogers and Walters noted that: 'It is a knowledgeable place in a way that distinguishes it from most other parliamentary assemblies in the world' (R Rogers and R Walters, *How Parliament Works* (7th edn, Routledge, 2015), p 271).

■ Secondly, the atmosphere of the chamber is less partisan. The 2000 Royal Commission made particular reference to the non-polemic style of the House.

■ Thirdly, as an adjunct to the point above, a significant number of peers are crossbenchers in any event, and so are not aligned to the major political parties.

NB. On the wide range of backgrounds of members, see T Brown, *House of Lords: Backgrounds in Public Life*, LLN 2017/019 (House of Lords Library Note, 2017).

10.9.3 The revision of public Bills brought from the House of Commons

The House of Lords spends over half of its time examining legislative proposals. This indicates that a major constitutional function of the House of Lords is to act as a 'revising chamber'. Most important Bills, as well as controversial ones, tend to begin in the House of Commons, where the government is dominant.

In considering and scrutinising public Bills which have passed through the Commons, the House of Lords can revise, propose and make amendments (with the exception of money/financial Bills – see section 10.10.1). Such amendments can be:

■ technical drafting amendments to remedy unclear, imprecise or sloppily drafted provisions, or

■ policy amendments based on aspects or provisions of the Bill considered objectionable, unsatisfactory, unnecessary etc. For example, the detention of terrorist suspects for up to 28 days under the Terrorism Act 2006 had the safeguard that it was subject to periodic review by Parliament (this was added in the House of Lords).

Although the procedure and nature of passing legislation is largely similar for both Houses, there are some key differences and these are considered at section 12.7.4.

10.9.4 The initiation of public legislation

In order to spread the legislative workload between the two parliamentary chambers, Bills can begin in either House. In fact, this practice is consistent with other countries such as France and the Republic of Ireland. Two examples of highly significant constitutional Bills which commenced in the House of Lords are as follows:

- The Human Rights Bill (introduced in 1997).
- The Constitutional Reform Bill (introduced in 2003).

In each case the then Lord Chancellor, as a government minister and a peer, was responsible for piloting the Bill through the House.

In contrast to the above, money Bills must begin in the House of Commons as it is the pre-eminent chamber. Similarly, in Australia financial legislation must also be introduced in the lower House (the House of Representatives).

10.9.5 The consideration of subordinate legislation

As indicated at section 5.7.2, subordinate legislation is a clear violation of the separation of powers as it involves the executive performing a legislative function: making legislation (albeit subordinate legislation). In view of this breach, from a constitutional perspective it is imperative that subordinate legislation is subject to adequate scrutiny. As we shall see at section 12.7.5, it is generally agreed that parliamentary supervision of this type of legislation is inadequate; however, the House of Lords performs a useful role in providing some supervision of it. It does so through the following committees:

- The Delegated Powers and Regulatory Reform Committee.
- As part of the Joint Committee on Statutory Instruments.
- The Secondary Legislation Scrutiny Committee.

10.9.6 The scrutiny of the activities of the executive

As Parliament as a whole is constitutionally responsible for supervising the actions of the executive, this means that it is the responsibility of both the House of Commons and the House of Lords to hold the government to account (this is considered further in Chapter 12). It should be remembered that the House of Lords contains a number of ministers who can be directly questioned and scrutinised by peers. However, as Russell (*Second Chambers Overseas: A Summary* (The Constitution Unit, 1999), p 11) has noted, it is generally the case that upper chambers have less power in holding the government to account than lower Houses.

In essence, the House of Lords will scrutinise the actions and policy of the executive in the following ways:

- in general debates
- in debates on legislative proposals
- through questions
- in debates on government statements
- through the committee system.

The 2000 Royal Commission argued that the second chamber needed to be authoritative because, together with the Commons, it must scrutinise effectively the work of the government. After all, a 'more accountable Government is better Government' (*A House for the Future*, Cm 4534 (The Stationery Office, 2000), p 80).

The importance of the House of Lords supervising and checking the actions of the government has been heightened in recent decades in light of the executive's general dominance in, and control over, the lower chamber (see section 9.8).

10.9.7 The scrutiny of private legislation

Private Bills affect particular groups or individuals, rather than having general application as do public Bills. Both Houses scrutinise and process private legislation.

In addition to the functions listed above, two other functions should be mentioned – the scrutiny of proposed European legislation and the role of guardian and protector of the constitution.

10.9.8 The scrutiny of proposed European legislation

One function not referred to in the 1968 White Paper (owing to the fact that the United Kingdom did not join the EEC – now called the EU – until 1973) is the useful role that the modern House plays in respect of proposed European Union legislation. This consists of the House of Lords European Union Select Committee examining EU documents/matters before decisions are taken on them by the British government in Europe (see section 12.9). However, on Brexit and leaving the EU, see section 15.6.6.

10.9.9 A guardian of the constitution and watchdog of civil liberties and human rights

One function commonly attributed to the House of Lords is that of the guardian and protector of the constitution. In other words, it acts as a constitutional longstop. It has been commented that this is a classic function performed by second chambers:

QUOTATION

'The origins of second chambers, either as a representative of "establishment" interests or as a representative of regional territories in a federal system, has made them natural bulwarks against impulsive or politically-motivated action taken by the lower house.'
A Reidy and M Russell, *Second Chambers as Constitutional Guardians & Protectors of Human Rights* (The Constitution Unit, 1999), p 2.

Such a role (ie acting as a 'natural bulwark') is particularly important in the context of the United Kingdom, which lacks an entrenched codified constitution which would act as a legal restraint on the government. As specifically pointed out by the 2000 Royal Commission:

QUOTATION

'The risk, however, is that a Government with a secure majority in the House of Commons, even if based on the votes of a minority of the electorate, could in principle bring about controversial and ill-considered changes to the constitution without the need to secure consensus support for them.'
A House for the Future, Cm 4534 (The Stationery Office, 2000), p 48.

In other constitutions, the upper house will typically have special legal powers in respect of legislation proposing to alter the constitution. In France, for example, the upper chamber (Sénat) has a veto over constitutional amendments as they must pass both Houses. It is interesting to point out that the 2000 Royal Commission specifically refused to recommend that a reformed second chamber should have extra powers over 'constitutional legislation'. For one thing, it would be very difficult to definitively identify a 'constitutional Bill' (as noted at section 4.2).

In the following circumstances, however, various statutes have specifically recognised the constitutional role of the House of Lords as a 'constitutional longstop'. The consent of the House is expressly required in order to:

■ Extend the life of Parliament (Parliament Act 1911).
■ Remove senior judges (Act of Settlement 1700 as amended by the Senior Courts Act 1981 and the Constitutional Reform Act 2005).
■ Remove the Parliamentary Ombudsman – see section 21.3.6 (The Parliamentary Commissioner Act 1967).

In addition, the House of Lords Select Committee on the Constitution has the following remit:

QUOTATION

'To examine the constitutional implications of all public bills coming before the House; and to keep under review the operation of the constitution.'
The House of Lords Select Committee on the Constitution, *Reviewing the Constitution: Terms of reference and method of working*, HL Paper 11 (2001), p 5.

For the most recent summary of the committee's work, see the House of Lords Select Committee on the Constitution, *Sessional report 2016–17*, HL Paper 6 (2017).

KEY FACTS

	Functions
Judicial	• The House as a whole enforces parliamentary privilege.
Legislative	• Can initiate and revise private Bills. • Can initiate and revise public Bills – except money Bills. • Examines subordinate legislation. • Examines proposed European legislation.
Scrutiny of the executive	• Debates. • Questions. • Committee work. • Legislation.
Debating chamber	• General forum for debate on matters of public interest (see also in the context of the scrutiny of the executive).
Protector of the uncodified constitution	• Acts as a constitutional longstop and watchdog of civil liberties.

10.10 The legal powers of the House of Lords

The powers of the upper chamber are limited by both:

- law (ie the Parliament Acts – see section 10.10.1) and
- constitutional convention (see section 10.11).

10.10.1 Legal limitations

Before the Parliament Act 1911, historically the two Houses of Parliament had equal legal power over legislation. In essence, the House of Lords could block/veto Bills passed by the Commons. A constitutional convention, however, had developed to the effect that on financial matters (ie money Bills) the Upper House would not oppose such Bills passed by the Commons. Notwithstanding this, in 1909 the House of Lords rejected the then Liberal government's finance Bill (the Budget), which the House had the power to do in law but not by constitutional convention. This eventually led to the passage of the Parliament Act 1911, which legally limited the powers of the House of Lords.

The Parliament Act 1911 achieved the following things:

- The House of Lords lost the legal power to reject money Bills (as certified by the Speaker in the House of Commons) which have passed through the Commons. After no more than a month in the Lords, if a money Bill has not been approved (ie passed) it proceeds to the Royal Assent without the consent of the Upper House (s 1).
- Any public Bill passed by the House of Commons in three successive parliamentary sessions with at least two years between the second reading in the Commons in the first session and the third reading in the Commons in the third session, could become law without the consent of the Lords (s 2). In short, this meant that, in future, the House of Lords could only delay legislation (effectively for two years). It thereafter had a temporary 'suspensive veto' over proposed legislation. In summary, although it could reject and oppose legislation, *ultimately* it could not stop it from becoming law.

The following were excluded from the ambit of the Parliament Act 1911:

- A Bill proposing to extend the life of Parliament beyond five years. NB: as the 2011 Fixed-Term Parliaments Bill proposed to extend the parliamentary term beyond five years (ie the Prime Minister would be allowed to delay an election beyond five years by up to *two months*) this meant that the Parliament Acts did not apply to it – see section 8.1.1.
- A public Bill commenced in the House of Lords.
- A public Bill sent to the House of Lords less than a month before the end of the session.
- A private Bill.

  In addition, the Parliament Act does not apply to statutory instruments (ie delegated legislation).

Source: House of Lords Briefing: Work, Role, Function and Powers
(Parliamentary Copyright, House of Lords, 2009), p 5.

Although legally the House of Lords could have refused to pass the 1911 Parliament Bill, it seems clear that if it had done so the Prime Minister would have (in effect via the monarch) created sufficient new hereditary peers in order to ensure its passage. Moreover, in 1949 the 1911 Parliament Act was amended so as to reduce further the delaying power of the House of Lords. In fact, the Labour government of the day used the Parliament Act of 1911 itself to force through the Parliament Bill of 1949 against the wishes of the House of Lords (see the challenge to this in *Jackson* (2005) at section 10.10.3). The change introduced by the Parliament Act 1949, in effect, reduced the delaying power of the Lords to one year (ie the three successive sessions were reduced to two and the minimum period in the Commons reduced from two years to one).

As Russell has commented, it is relatively common for upper chambers to have the constitutional and legal power to delay legislation passed by the lower House (the 'suspensive veto') although, ultimately, the lower chamber generally speaking has the final say (M Russell, *Resolving Disputes between the Chambers* (The Constitution Unit, 1999), p 3).

10.10.2 The use of the Parliament Acts

The Parliament Acts, historically, have been invoked rarely; however, the last Labour government used them three times. In total the use of the Acts has been as follows:

- Welsh Church Act 1914 (disestablishment of the Church in Wales).
- The Government of Ireland Act 1914 (Irish home rule).
- Parliament Act 1949 (to reduce further the legal powers of the House of Lords).
- War Crimes Act 1991 (concerned with atrocities committed in Germany and German-occupied territories during the Second World War).
- European Parliamentary Elections Act 1999 (established a 'closed party' list system for candidates for elections to the European Parliament).
- Sexual Offences (Amendment) Act 2000 (reduced the homosexual age of consent to 16).
- Hunting Act 2004 (banned fox hunting – see section 10.10.3).

The provisions in relation to money Bills have not been invoked.

10.10.3 Is the Parliament Act 1949 legal?

In one of the most important constitutional cases of recent times, in 2005 the Appellate Committee of the House of Lords had to determine whether the Hunting Act 2004 and the Parliament Act 1949 had been lawfully passed as Acts of Parliament.

CASE EXAMPLE

R (Jackson and others) v Attorney General *[2005] UKHL 56*

The Hunting Act 2004 made the hunting of wild animals with dogs (ie fox hunting) illegal. This Act had been passed without the consent of the House of Lords under the Parliament Acts of 1911 and 1949. Jackson sought, unsuccessfully (in both the Divisional Court and the Court of Appeal), a declaration that:

- the Parliament Act 1949 was of no legal effect as it had been passed without the consent of the House of Lords; and
- as a consequence, the Hunting Act 2004 was of no legal effect either, and so not an Act of Parliament.

The House of Lords dismissed Jackson's appeal and affirmed that the Parliament Act 1949 had been lawfully passed under the Parliament Act 1911 (notwithstanding the lack of consent from the Lords). As a consequence, the Hunting Act 2004 was a lawful Act of Parliament with full legal effect.

The House of Lords noted that after 1911 there were two routes to passing legislation:

- *with* the consent of the House of Lords; and
- *without* the consent of the House of Lords (ie under the Parliament Acts).

As a matter of statutory construction, the 1911 Act did not preclude the use of the s 2 procedure (ie rendering the consent of the Upper House unnecessary) to amend itself (ie to create the 1949 Act). Logically, therefore, on the basis of this judgment, it would appear that the Parliament Acts could be amended to reduce further the power of the House to delay legislation, for example to only six months.

One of the arguments advanced in favour of Jackson was that the 1949 and 2004 Acts were, in effect, *delegated legislation* as they were derivative of the 1911 Act. In short, they owed their validity to a prior enactment (the 1911 Act) and consequently with the status of delegated, rather than primary legislation, they could be reviewed by the court. The court dismissed this argument. As pointed out by Lord Bingham, the 1911 Act referred to legislation complying with the provisions of this Act becoming 'an Act of Parliament on the Royal Assent being signified thereto' (s 2(1)). This clearly denoted primary (and not delegated) legislation. As Lord Bingham stated:

JUDGMENT

'The 1911 Act did, of course, effect an important constitutional change, but the change lay not in authorising a new form of sub-primary parliamentary legislation but in creating a new way of enacting primary legislation.'

NB. Also on the *Jackson* case, see earlier at section 7.10.3.

As a postscript to this case, in *R (Countryside Alliance and Others) v Attorney General and Another* [2007] UKHL 52, the House of Lords dismissed an appeal by the claimants who had argued that the Hunting Act breached both European Union and European Convention law. The latter was upheld by the European Court of Human Rights in *Countryside Alliance v UK* (2010) 50 EHRR S E6.

10.11 Limitations imposed by constitutional convention

Quite apart from the legal limitations outlined above, the House of Lords traditionally has recognised that the House of Commons, as the elected House to which the government is directly accountable, is the pre-eminent chamber in Parliament. As a consequence, it adheres to the following three constitutional conventions in its dealings with the House of Commons. By convention the House of Lords:

■ Should accord a second reading (and not table wrecking amendments) to a government Bill which has passed through the House of Commons and which has been foreshadowed in the governing party's most recent general election manifesto (the Salisbury–Addison Convention). This is on the basis that, if a government has been elected on specified manifesto commitments, it would be constitutionally inappropriate and essentially undemocratic for the Lords to thwart the most recent will of the people as expressed and represented in the House of Commons. There is some argument, however, as to whether the convention applies – strictly or otherwise – to either a coalition (eg the 2010 Conservative and Liberal Democrat) or a minority (eg the 2017 Conservative) government (see the recent report of the House of Lords Select Committee on the Constitution, *The Salisbury-Addison Convention*, HL Paper 28 (2017)).

- Should consider government business within a reasonable time (see above in relation to manifesto Bills).
- Does not reject statutory instruments – although in law it is entitled to. Russell and Sciara (*The House of Lords in 2005: A More Representative and Assertive Chamber?* (The Constitution Unit, 2006), p 14) have pointed out, however, that in 2005 there was considerable tension between the then Labour government and the House of Lords over two delegated orders under the aegis of:
  - (i) The Licensing Act 2003 (the Lords voted on a motion to condemn an order expanding drinking hours, though they did not defeat the order itself).
  - (ii) The Criminal Justice Act 2003 (an order – subsequently dropped – to restrict a defendant's right to jury trial in complex fraud trials).

NB. In terms of statutory instruments in draft form, in December 2012 the Draft Legal Aid, Sentencing and Punishment of Offenders Act 2012 (Amendment of Schedule 1) Order 2012 was *not* approved by the House of Lords (*Hansard*, HL Vol 741, col 489).

Finally, regard should be had to the 2006 report of the Joint Committee on Conventions which was established to examine the practicality of codifying the constitutional conventions which regulate the relationship between the two Houses. Its report concluded that the term codification was unhelpful as it implied rule-making and an enforcement mechanism, whereas by their nature constitutional conventions were unenforceable. As a consequence, to codify a constitutional convention was a contradiction in terms:

QUOTATION

'Far from reducing the risk of conflict, codification might actually damage the relationship between the two Houses, making it more confrontational and less capable of moderation through the usual channels. This would benefit neither the Government nor Parliament (para 279). . . . However, we offer certain formulations for one or both Houses to adopt by resolution. In our view, both the debates on such resolutions, and the resolutions themselves, would improve the shared understanding which the Government seek (para 280) . . . all recommendations for the formulation or codification of conventions are subject to the current understanding that conventions as such are flexible and unenforceable, particularly in the self-regulating environment of the House of Lords (para 281).'

Joint Committee on Conventions, *Conventions of the UK Parliament*,
HL Paper 265-I, HC 1212-I (2006).

The formulation suggested by the Committee included the following:

- The primacy of the House of Commons over the House of Lords was a fact which did not require codification.
- The convention that a manifesto Bill should be accorded a second reading by the House of Lords (the Salisbury–Addison Convention – see above) should be described as a *Government Bill Convention*. The House of Lords could debate and set out the terms of this convention for the Commons subsequently to debate and note.
- The existing convention that the government should have its business considered in a reasonable time in the upper chamber could be adopted by the House of Lords by way of a resolution. In addition, a new symbol could appear on the Lords' order paper indicating a government Bill which had spent more than a certain period in the upper chamber (a period of 80 days was suggested).
- Although neither House rejects secondary legislation (statutory instruments) on a regular basis, in exceptional circumstances this may be appropriate and a statement to that effect could be adopted by both Houses (or either House):

QUOTATION

'There are situations in which it is consistent both with the Lords' role in Parliament as a revising chamber, and with Parliament's role in relation to delegated legislation, for the Lords to threaten to defeat an S.I.'

Joint Committee on Conventions, First Report of Session 2005–06, *Conventions of the UK Parliament*, HL Paper 265-I, HC 1212-I (2006), para 229.

The Committee noted that:

░ It was universally recognised that there was no need to *legislate* on these matters.
░ It was made very clear that the courts should have no role in relation to determining whether a parliamentary convention had been breached.

In December 2006 the then Labour government issued its Formal Reply to this report, in which it accepted the Committee's conclusions and recommendations (*Government Response to the Joint Committee on Conventions' Report of Session 2005–06: Conventions of the UK Parliament*, Cm 6997 (Crown Copyright, 2006)). In January 2007 both Houses (in separate resolutions) approved the Joint Committee's report.

Most recently, in October 2015 the House of Lords withheld its agreement (in effect, deferred its approval) to the Draft Tax Credits (Income Thresholds and Determination of Rates) (Amendment) Regulations 2015. Although the House of Commons had already approved them the month before, a major concern of peers in relation to these proposed cuts to the tax credits regime was that they were being made via secondary, rather than primary, legislation (ie an Act of Parliament). As a result of the actions of the House of Lords, the Conservative government asked Lord Strathclyde to undertake a review of the parliamentary passage of statutory instruments. The then Parliamentary Secretary (Cabinet Office), John Penrose MP, made the following written statement in November 2015:

QUOTATION

'By long-standing convention the House of Lords does not seek to challenge the primacy of the elected House on spending and taxation. It also does not reject statutory instruments, save in exceptional circumstances. Until last month, only five statutory instruments had been rejected by the House of Lords since World War II, none of which related only to a matter of public spending and taxation. The purpose of the review is to examine how to protect the ability of elected Governments to secure their business in Parliament in light of the operation of these conventions. The review will consider in particular how to secure the decisive role of the elected House of Commons in relation to its primacy on financial matters, and secondary legislation.'

Hansard, HC Vol 601, HCW S292.

In due course, Lord Strathclyde issued his report in December 2015: *Strathclyde Review: Secondary legislation and the primacy of the House of Commons*, Cm 9177 (Crown Copyright, 2015). In essence, the review suggested three options:

░ **Option one** – to remove altogether the House of Lords from the passage/procedure of statutory instruments.
░ **Option two** – to retain the current role of the House in respect of statutory instruments but codify the convention in a resolution or standing orders (with the 'restrictions' on how the House of Lords should use its powers in practice set out in a clear way).

Option three – to create a new statutory procedure which would allow the House of Lords to invite the House of Commons 'to think again', but ultimately the latter could insist upon its primacy. In this way the House of Commons would have primacy in respect of both primary and secondary legislation.

Lord Strathclyde recommended the third option above.

In December 2016 the Conservative government issued its response and stated that, although Strathclyde's third option would 'bring clarity and certainty', the government nevertheless had:

QUOTATION

'. . . decided not to take forward such legislation, because in our view it is not a priority for the session. However, the Government will introduce the legislation if it becomes necessary to intervene to maintain the primacy of the House of Commons, as the democratically elected chamber, on secondary legislation.' (para 2)

Government Response to the Strathclyde Review: Secondary legislation and the primacy of the House of Commons and the related select committee reports, Cm 9363 (Crown Copyright, 2016).

ACTIVITY

Exercise

Compare and contrast the legal and political powers of the House of Lords.

KEY FACTS

	Legal powers of the House of Lords

Parliament Acts 1911 and 1949	• No power to reject money Bills.
	• Only has the power to delay a public Bill for approximately one year.
	• Retains full legal power to veto:
	  (i) secondary legislation
	  (ii) a public Bill initiated in the House of Lords
	  (iii) a public Bill designed to extend the life of Parliament
	  (iv) a private Bill.
	  (v) a public Bill sent to the House of Lords less than a month
	     before the end of a session.

	Political powers of the House of Lords
Constitutional conventions	• The Salisbury–Addison Convention. • Government business to be considered within a reasonable time. • Does not reject secondary legislation.

10.12 The relationship between the House of Lords and the House of Commons

In general, the two Houses of Parliament co-operate with each other efficiently, otherwise parliamentary business would become unworkable. Indeed, in respect of

Lords' amendments made to government legislative proposals, in many cases these are accepted by the House of Commons (or, more specifically, the government). For its part, the House of Lords has traditionally accepted that it is the subordinate chamber, although on occasions it will force the Commons to reconsider issues/policies, thereby acting as a watchdog and protector of the constitution.

The Labour government of 1997–2010 suffered only a handful of defeats on government Bills in the House of Commons (for an example see section 6.7.5) whereas, in contrast, it suffered a significant number of defeats in the Lords (see *Government Defeats in the House of Lords*, SN/PC/03252 (House of Commons Library, 2009)). As indicated below, what does appear to be the case is that, since the removal of most of the hereditary peers in 1999, the House of Lords now sees itself as more constitutionally legitimate than before, and so appears more willing to challenge the wishes of the lower chamber (which is, of course, largely controlled by the government). In fact, the calendar year of 2005 appears to have been a watershed in terms of executive/House of Lords relations:

QUOTATION

'2005 witnessed the biggest row between the government and the peers since the start of the twentieth century, leading to the biggest defeats in the Lords since Labour came to power. . . . These and other events suggested that the chamber was growing increasingly assertive.'

M Russell and M Sciara, *The House of Lords in 2005: A More Representative and Assertive Chamber?* (The Constitution Unit, 2006), p 5.

The authors were referring to the major controversy of that year which was the passage of the Prevention of Terrorism Act 2005. This Bill had been introduced as a response to a ruling of the Appellate Committee of the House of Lords (*A and others v Secretary of State for the Home Department* [2004] UKHL 56, see section 6.7.4), which had declared that it was unlawful to detain terrorist suspects under the Anti-terrorism, Crime and Security Act 2001.

In respect of this Bill, as noted by Russell and Sciara, two particularly significant developments occurred due to the scrutiny in the House of Lords, as a result of which:

QUOTATION

'The final outcome was a compromise, whereby there was some judicial involvement in issuing all control orders, and the government promised to review the law within a year and bring in a more considered bill. Whilst not being written into the bill this was seen as a victory for its opponents.'

M Russell and M Sciara, *The House of Lords in 2005: A More Representative and Assertive Chamber?* (The Constitution Unit, 2006), p 10.

Three years later in the context of further terrorism legislation, the House of Lords defeated an attempt via the 2008 Counter-Terrorism Bill to extend the detention of terrorist suspects to 42 days. Although the then Labour government could have resorted to the Parliament Acts, this would have delayed the introduction of this legislation.

Detailed below are two more recent examples of the House of Lords affecting proposed legislation:

- **The Fixed-Term Parliaments Bill 2011** – in respect of this Bill the House of Lords acquiesced to a coalition government compromise which provided for post-legislative scrutiny of the Act by virtue of the Prime Minister setting up a committee in 2020. The House of Lords had previously inserted a clause which would have made the operation of the Act dependent upon future parliamentary approval – the government's compromise was in response to this clause and meant that the provision inserted by peers was excised.

■ **The Electoral Registration and Administration Bill 2013** – this Bill was amended in the House of Lords so as to delay the review of constituency boundaries until 2018, thereby postponing the reduction of MPs to 600. This amendment was accepted by the House of Commons by 334 votes to 292 (*Hansard*, HC Vol 557, col 840).

According to the Constitution Unit, during the (albeit extended) session of 2010–12 the coalition government was defeated 48 times in the House of Lords (*Government Defeats in the House of Lords* (www.ucl.ac.uk/constitution-unit/)).

Most recently in respect of the (albeit truncated) 2015–17 parliamentary term, the following three events are worth noting:

■ The Trade Union Bill 2015–16: In the House of Lords the Bill was amended, *inter alia*, to require the Secretary of State to commission a review of electronic balloting (the use of e-balloting should provide a practical way of achieving fuller participation in industrial action ballots).

■ The Housing and Planning Bill 2015–16: Amendments made in the House of Lords included, for example, providing protection to landlord and tenant money in the event of the property agent going into administration.

■ The European Union (Notification of Withdrawal) Bill 2017: The House of Lords amended the Bill to require ministers within three months of Art 50 being triggered (see Brexit, later at section 15.6.6) to bring forward proposals to protect (ie guarantee the rights of) EU nationals who were legally resident in the United Kingdom on the day the Act was passed. This amendment was rejected by the House of Commons, and on its return to the upper House peers agreed that the House of Lords should *not* insist on its amendment.

NB: in relation to the EVEL procedure introduced into the House of Commons in 2015 (see section 12.7.3), when an 'England-only Bill' is amended in the House of Lords, any subsequent vote by MPs on such amendments would be subject to a 'double majority' (ie a voting majority of both English MPs and MPs across the whole House).

ACTIVITY

Self-test questions

What is the constitutional relationship between the House of Lords and the House of Commons? Do you think that the House of Lords should ever obstruct the wishes of the lower (elected) chamber?

The differences between the House of Commons and the House of Lords		
	House of Commons	**House of Lords**
Composition	• Exclusively elected with constituency responsibilities.	• Unelected – although there are, in a very technical sense, 'elected' hereditary peers. • No constituents.
Type of member	• Elected politicians. • Few independents.	• Appointed and hereditary politicians. • Sizeable element of independents.

Expertise	• Full-time politicians.	• A wide range of experience and expertise. • Life peers specifically appointed for their expertise and experience. • Retired law lords possess legal expertise. • Bishops can provide expertise on religious matters. • Many members are part-time.
Payment	• Salaried.	• Unpaid except ministers and Bishops (but peers can claim expenses).
Size of chamber	• Statutorily capped at 650 MPs (but scheduled to be reduced to 600).	• No fixed cap.
Legislative procedure	• Committee stage taken in general (public Bill) committees. • Use of guillotine (see section 12.7.4). • (Largely) party political/partisan atmosphere.	• Committee stage on the Floor of the House. • No guillotine. • To some extent a less partisan/polemic atmosphere.
Relations with the government	• Responsible for both maintaining and removing the government (vote of no confidence).	• No direct responsibility for maintaining or removing a government.

Table 10.3

10.13 Reform since 1997

The 1997 Labour Party manifesto set out a commitment to reform the House of Lords by removing the hereditary peers and establishing a joint parliamentary committee to consider long-term reform. As indicated earlier (see section 10.6.3), the House of Lords Act 1999 removed all but 92 of the hereditary peers. In tandem with the introduction of the 1999 House of Lords Bill, the then Labour government issued a White Paper (*Modernising Parliament, Reforming the House of Lords* Cm 4183 (The Stationery Office, 1999)). This set out the various options for long-term reform to be considered by a Royal Commission. It also indicated the government's proposals for an Appointments Commission to select non-party political peers (a power previously exercised by the Prime Minister). This Appointments Commission was established in 2000 (see section 10.5.4) and has been operational ever since.

In January 2000 the Royal Commission under Lord Wakeham issued its report on future reform of the upper chamber (*A House for the Future* Cm 4534 (The Stationery Office, 2000)). In short, it recommended a mixed House with a largely appointed membership with a minority of members (65, 87 or 195) being elected as regional members.

In 2001 the government issued another White Paper on Lords reform (*The House of Lords – Completing the Reform*, Cm 5291 (2001)). This paper reaffirmed the government's commitment to remove the remaining hereditary peers and in terms of composition proposed a House of 600 members:

- One-fifth elected.
- One-fifth independents.
- The remainder being nominated by political parties.
- The law lords and bishops to remain.

This proposal proved unpopular and in 2002, in order to achieve parliamentary consensus on a reformed composition, a Joint Committee on House of Lords Reform was established. In 2003 both Houses voted on the different options put forward by the Committee:

- Wholly elected chamber.
- Wholly appointed.
- 80 per cent appointed.
- 80 per cent elected.
- 60 per cent appointed.
- 60 per cent elected.
- 50 per cent appointed/50 per cent elected.

The Commons did not approve any of these options, although they came closest (281 votes in favour to 284 against) to endorsing the option which proposed an 80 per cent elected House. The House of Lords, rather predictably, approved the fully appointed option. In addition to the above options, the House of Commons voted on, and rejected (by 390 to 172 votes), a further option of the abolition of the House of Lords (ie a unicameral Parliament). For an analysis of these votes see M Ryan, 'Parliament and the Joint Committee on House of Lords Reform' (2003) 37 *Law Teacher* 310.

In September 2003 the government issued a consultation paper (*Constitutional Reform: Next steps for the House of Lords*, CP 14/03 (DCA, 2003)), in which it stated that in the absence of consensus on composition it nevertheless proposed to:

- Remove the remaining hereditary peers.
- Place the Appointments Commission on a statutory basis.

These proposals were never legislated on. On this paper, see M Ryan, 'Reforming the House of Lords: A 2004 update' (2004) 38 *Law Teacher* 255.

In 2005 an all-party group of MPs published a paper in which it tried to show that party political consensus was possible and recommended a 70 per cent elected House (K Clarke, R Cook, P Tyler, T Wright and G Young, *Reforming the House of Lords: Breaking the deadlock* (Constitution Unit, 2005)). Thereafter, the 2005 Labour Party general election manifesto stated that it would:

- Remove the remaining hereditary peers.
- Legislate to place reasonable limits on the time the House of Lords could delay legislation.
- Seek agreement on codifying the conventions between the two Houses following a review.

In June 2006 a Cross-Party Working Group on Lords Reform, consisting of members from both Houses and the main political parties, began the first of a number of meetings to discuss the future of reform.

In the 2006 Queen's Speech the government stated that it would work towards cross-party consensus on Lords reform and remove the remaining hereditary peers. In February 2007 another White Paper was issued (*The House of Lords: Reform*, Cm 7027 (The Stationery Office, 2007)). For its part, the government in the White Paper suggested that the reformed House should be a partly elected/partly appointed chamber containing 540 members. Moreover, no political party should have a majority of party political members and at least 20 per cent of the chamber's membership should be made up of non-party political members. It also recommended retention of the spiritual element. In essence, the White Paper paved the way for the following debates and votes to take place in the House of Commons in March 2007:

- The retention of a bicameral Parliament (Yes 416 votes, No 163 votes).
- No 1 – wholly appointed chamber (Yes 196, No 375).
- No 2 – 20 per cent elected/80 per cent appointed (no vote).
- No 3 – 40 per cent elected/60 per cent appointed (no vote).
- No 4 – 50 per cent elected/50 per cent appointed (Yes 155, No 418).
- No 5 – 60 per cent elected/40 per cent appointed (Yes 178, No 392).
- No 6 – 80 per cent elected/20 per cent appointed (Yes 305, No 267).
- No 7 – wholly elected chamber (Yes 337, No 224).
- The removal of the remaining hereditary peers (Yes 391, No 111).

R Cracknell, *Commons Divisions on House of Lords Reform: March 2007*, SN/SG/4279 (House of Commons Library, 2007), p 2.

The overall result, therefore, was that the Commons supported the principle of retaining a second chamber, removing the remaining hereditary peers and having an Upper House which was either fully or overwhelmingly elected (the former having the support of a majority of 113 MPs and the latter 38). One week later, informed by the votes taken in the Commons, the House of Lords voted overwhelmingly in favour of (rather unsurprisingly) a fully appointed House by 361 votes to 121. All the other options were rejected, with the 50 per cent elected House being decisively dismissed by 409 votes to 46 (see *Hansard*, HL Vol 690, cols 741–759). On these votes, see M Ryan, 'A consensus on the reform of the House of Lords?' (2009) 60 NILQ 325.

In July 2008 the government issued a further White Paper aimed at completing the reform of the House of Lords (*An Elected Second Chamber: Further reform of the House of Lords* Cm 7438 (2008)). Following the votes in the Commons in March 2007, the White Paper confined the reform of the House of Lords to two options only: an 80 per cent or 100 per cent elected House (ie following the preferences of MPs in the 2007 votes). The paper left open which electoral system should be used. On the White Paper, see M Ryan 'The house that Jack built' (2008) 158 NLJ 1197.

In July 2009 the government unveiled the Constitutional Reform and Governance Bill which proposed the following:

- To abolish hereditary by-elections.
- To enable members to be removed (eg those convicted of serious criminal offences).
- To provide for the House to make standing orders whereby a member could be expelled/suspended.
- To allow a peer to resign from the House.
- To allow a member to disclaim their life peerage.

However, all of the above elements were removed from the Bill in the 'wash-up' before the measure became the Constitutional Reform and Governance Act 2010.

Part 4 of this Act did however make provision for members of the House of Lords to be deemed resident and domiciled in the UK for tax purposes. Section 42 enabled peers unwilling to be subject to the above to leave the House.

After the 2010 general election the new coalition government issued its *Coalition Agreement*, which stated that it would 'establish a committee to bring forward proposals for a wholly or mainly elected upper chamber on the basis of proportional representation' (*The Coalition: Our programme for Government* (Cabinet Office, 2010), p 27). In the event, in May 2011 a White Paper was issued which included a draft Bill: The House of Lords Reform Draft Bill, Cm 8077 (Cabinet Office, 2011). This draft Bill was, in turn, given pre-legislative scrutiny by a parliamentary Joint Committee, which reported in April 2012 (*Draft House of Lords Reform Bill*, Report Vol 1, HL Paper 284-I, HC 1313-I (The Stationery Office, 2012)). Following this scrutiny, the coalition government issued its fully fledged reform Bill: The House of Lords Reform Bill 2012, which received its second reading in July 2012 by the decisive margin of 462 votes to 124 (*Hansard*, HC Vol 548, col 274). However, as no accompanying programme motion could be agreed (without which the Bill would have endlessly eaten up parliamentary time), the Bill was abandoned. On the issue of whether there should be a referendum on the reform of the House of Lords, see M Ryan, 'A referendum on the reform of the House of Lords?' (2015) 66 NILQ 223.

Although long-term reform of the House of Lords appears to be in abeyance, smaller, more incremental reforms have been achieved in recent years. The House of Lords Reform Act 2014 enabled members to resign from the House (s 1), as well as to allow for expulsion for either non-attendance (s 2) or conviction for a serious criminal offence (s 3). According to figures extrapolated from the parliamentary website (www.parliament.uk), up until November 2017, 70 members had retired under the Act and six had ceased to be members through non-attendance. On this Act, see M Ryan, 'Bills of Steel: The House of Lords Reform Act 2014' [2015] PL 558.

In addition to the above, two other Acts were passed in 2015:

- The Lords Spiritual (Women) Act 2015 – which provided for the acceleration of female bishops to sit in the House of Lords (see earlier at section 10.3).
- The House of Lords (Expulsion and Suspension) Act 2015 – which expanded the circumstances in which a member could be expelled from the House beyond the narrow confines of the 2014 Act above. In addition, the Act provided for a member's suspension from the House to last beyond the end of a Parliament.

In terms of the burgeoning size of the chamber, in December 2016 a cross-party Lord Speaker's Committee under the Chair of Lord Burns was established to examine proposals to reduce the size of the House of Lords. This committee reported in October 2017 (Lord Speaker, *Report of the Lord Speaker's Committee on the Size of the House* (House of Lords, 2017)). In essence, this report proposed:

- Setting a cap on the size of the House of Lords at 600 members (this figure is currently lower than that for the House of Commons).
- In order to reduce the current size of the House to 600, the 'guiding principle' would be one of 'two-out' for every 'one-in'.
- Once the target of cap of 600 members had been met, in order to maintain this cap, vacancies would be filled by a system of 'one-out/one-in'.
- New peers would be appointed to the House on a non-renewable fixed term of 15 years.

See R Kelly, *House of Lords Reform in the 2017 Parliament*, Briefing Paper 08137 (House of Commons Library, 2017).

Finally, it is highly pertinent to record that during a debate in December 2017 on the above Burns report, the Leader of the House (Baroness Evans) confirmed that fundamental reform of the House of Lords required legislation and that was *not* a priority for this Parliament (*Hansard*, HL Vol 787, col 1969).

SUMMARY

- The House of Lords is the upper chamber of Parliament.
- Most of its members are appointed life peers who are appointed for life.
- The House is unusual in containing the following categories of members:
  - Spiritual Lords – bishops and archbishops of the Church of England.
  - Judicial peers – retired judges.
  - Hereditary peers – the rump of hereditary peers left after the major reforms of 1999.
- In terms of political composition no one political party controls the House. In addition, the chamber contains a significant number of crossbenchers.
- There are a number of factors which disqualify individuals from membership of the House (eg being under 21 years of age).
- The functions of the House include:
  - Making laws as part of the legislature.
  - Investigating policy issues.
  - Providing a forum for debate.
  - A protector of the constitution.
  - Disciplining its own membership.
- Its legal powers mean that it can delay a public Bill for approximately one year.
- Its political powers constrain it further by requiring that, for example, government business is considered in a reasonable time.
- The House of Lords has been subject to some reform in recent decades and there continues to be a lively political debate as to how this reform should be completed. It was clear, however, that at the start of 2018 long-term reform of the House of Lords had stalled and was very unlikely to be achieved in the near future.

SAMPLE ESSAY QUESTION

What function does the House of Lords serve and what is its importance to the British constitution?

Introduction:
- House of Lords is the second chamber in the UK bicameral Parliament.
- This historic chamber (it predates the Commons) has proved controversial owing to its distinct membership (see below).

Membership:
- Note the different categories of members:
- Spiritual Lords – Bishops and Archbishops of the Church of England.
- 'Ordinary' life peers – Appointed under the Life Peerages Act 1958.
- Hereditary peers – Now governed by the House of Lords Act 1999 (hereditary peers are a controversial element in a democratic chamber).
- Judicial life peers – Retired senior judges.

Functions:

- These blend with Parliament as a whole.
- Part of the legislative process by introducing Bills and revising those brought from the Commons (also involved in examining delegated as well as European legislation).
- Scrutinises the government (ie debates, questions, committees and in the context of the above).
- A guardian of the constitution (including the Select Committee on the Constitution).

Powers:

- Legal powers – regulated by the Parliament Acts 1911 and 1949.
- Political powers – regulated by constitutional convention (eg the Salisbury–Addison Convention).

Constitutional significance:

- It disperses power within Parliament between two chambers.
- It acts as a check on the executive/House of Commons.
- It improves legislation.
- It provides expert opinions on a wide range of issues and is a debating chamber.
- It is a constitutional safeguard (eg s 33 of the Constitutional Reform Act 2005 requires the consent of the House of Lords to remove Supreme Court justices).

Conclusion

Further reading

Books

Ballinger, C, *The House of Lords 1911–2011, A century of non-reform* (Hart Publishing, 2012).

Carroll, A, *Constitutional and Administrative Law* (9th edn, Pearson/Longman, 2017), Chapter 9.

Dickson, B and Carmichael, P (eds), *The House of Lords: Its parliamentary and judicial roles* (Hart Publishing, 1999).

Loveland, I, *Constitutional Law, Administrative Law, and Human Rights* (7th edn, Oxford University Press, 2015), Chapter 6.

Norton, P, *Reform of the House of Lords* (Manchester University Press, 2017).

Russell, M, *The Contemporary House of Lords: Westminster bicameralism revived* (Oxford University Press, 2013).

Articles

Lord Bingham, 'The House of Lords: Its future?' [2010] PL 261.

Ryan, M, 'A consensus on the reform of the House of Lords?' (2009) 60 NILQ 325.

Ryan, M, 'The house that Jack built' (2008) 158 NLJ 1197.

Ryan, M, 'A summary of the developments in the reform of the House of Lords since 2005' (2012) 21 *Nottingham Law Journal* 65.

Ryan, M, 'The latest attempt at reform of the House of Lords – one step forward and another one back' (2013) 22 *Nottingham Law Journal* 1.

Ryan, M, 'A referendum on the reform of the House of Lords?' (2015) 66 NILQ 223.

Ryan, M, 'Bills of Steel: The House of Lords Reform Act 2014' [2015] PL 558.

Papers

House of Lords Select Committee on the Constitution, *Constitutional Aspects of the Challenge to the Hunting Act 2004*, HL Paper 141 (2006), Appendix 3.

Royal Commission on the Reform of the House of Lords, *A House for the Future*, Cm 4534 (The Stationery Office, 2000).

Russell, M, and Sciara, M, *The House of Lords in 2005: A More Representative and Assertive Chamber?* (The Constitution Unit, 2006).

Work of the House of Lords 2015–16 (Parliamentary Copyright, House of Lords, 2016).

See also see the wide range of papers in the House of Lords Library.

Internet link

www.parliament.uk

11

The executive

At the end of this chapter you should be able to:

- Define the term executive
- Identify the different types of executive
- Explain the composition of the executive
- Identify the different functions of the executive
- Identify and explain the statutory and common law powers of the executive

11.1 Introduction and terminology

11.1.1 Definition of government

As indicated earlier (see section 5.3.2), the executive or governmental function is performed by 'Her Majesty's Government' or the administration. It is important to realise that the term 'government' can be used in the following senses:

- Firstly, government can be used in a very broad and general sense to indicate that an individual is being 'governed' (ie controlled and regulated) by the state and its *whole* apparatus including, for example, Parliament, the police, the armed forces and the courts.
- Secondly, government can be used in a much narrower sense to indicate government administration, namely Her Majesty's Government (ie *the government*).
- Thirdly, government can be used to denote local government whereby local authorities deliver services (such as housing and libraries) at a local level.

It is with the second definition that we will be particularly concerned.

11.1.2 The constitutional monarchy and the Crown

The United Kingdom has a constitutional monarchy with an unelected, hereditary sovereign as its head of state. In contrast, republican countries such as the United States and the Republic of Ireland have an elected President to act as their head of state. The Queen's role is to large extent symbolic, comprising ceremonial and formal responsibilities.

In the British constitution the executive is known as 'Her Majesty's Government' as in constitutional theory the monarch appoints and dismisses government ministers. In addition, civil servants are employed and dismissed by the Crown. Further, in terms of the executive in practice, in a technical sense, the Queen is the commander-in-chief of the armed forces.

At this point the term 'Crown' needs to be explained as in the British constitution it can be separated into two elements:

- Firstly, the Crown can be used to signify the monarch herself (ie the Sovereign/Queen),
- Secondly, the Crown can be used to refer to the government of the day or the administration.

In modern parlance, the Crown is typically used in the second sense in order to distinguish between the personal constitutional role of the monarch (who has a largely formal role) from her political government ministers (who make political and executive decisions). This distinction is important because we have a constitutional monarchy – the monarch and her constitutional role is constrained by the uncodified constitution. Indeed, Bagehot writing in the nineteenth century specifically distinguished between the '*dignified* parts' of the constitution (ie the monarchy) and the '*efficient* parts' (ie the Cabinet) – W Bagehot, *The English Constitution* (Oxford University Press, 2001), p 7.

The reality is that, although in strict law the sovereign enjoys considerable historic constitutional and legal powers, in practice these are either:

- regulated by constitutional convention, or
- are exercised by the Queen's ministers acting on her behalf in the name of the Crown/monarch.

Thus, today in a modern democracy it would be considered undemocratic (not to say morally unconstitutional – see section 4.16) for a monarch to personally exercise certain powers legally vested in her, as her predecessors would have done centuries before (eg to declare war).

11.1.3 The different forms of executive

The term executive embraces a number of elements and refers to those who administer and execute the law. A general distinction can be drawn between the following types of executive (drawing upon the terminology used by Heywood, *Politics* (Macmillan, 1997), Chapter 16):

- The political executive (Her Majesty's Government – see section 11.2).
- The non-political or bureaucratic executive (the Civil Service – see section 11.3).
- The executive in practical terms (the armed forces and various police forces – see section 11.4).
- Other executives (local authorities, the Scottish Government, the Northern Ireland Executive Committee, the Welsh Government, executive power in the European Union – see section 11.5).
- Public authorities/bodies. This is a public law term which we will return to in the context of judicial review (see section 19.3), but for present purposes it essentially refers to a public body performing public functions and so overlaps with the above elements. It would include, for example, the following:
  (i) Government ministers.
  (ii) Central government departments.
  (iii) Executive agencies and quangos.
  (iv) Local authorities.
  (v) Devolved executive institutions.

ACTIVITY

Quick quiz

What do the following terms mean?
- The Crown.
- The government.
- The executive.

11.2 The political executive/Her Majesty's Government

11.2.1 The monarch

The political executive is constitutionally Her Majesty's Government and ministers swear an oath of allegiance to the Crown. In practice, the monarch's role is largely formal.

On the monarchy, see A Hameed, 'The monarchy and politics' [2016] PL 401 and R Hazell and B Morris, *The Queen at 90: The changing role of the monarchy, and future challenges* (The Constitution Unit, 2016).

11.2.2 The Prime Minister

Although the monarch is the head of state and titular head of the executive, the Prime Minister is the effective head of government (contrast this with the position in the United States, where the elected President is both head of state and head of government). The constitutional office of the Prime Minister has developed historically by constitutional convention (contrast this with most other Prime Ministers/Presidents who owe their creation to a codified constitutional document) and is the head of the Cabinet (*primus inter pares* – first among equals). By constitutional convention the Prime Minister must be drawn from the House of Commons so that they can be held directly accountable to the elected representatives of the people (MPs).

The Prime Minister has *inter alia* the following constitutional functions/powers:

- To preside over Cabinet meetings (see section 11.2.3).
- To act as a conduit between the monarch and the government (in this way the Prime Minister can keep the monarch informed of ongoing political developments).
- To act as the Minister for the Civil Service (he also has the title of First Lord of the Treasury, although in practice the Chancellor of the Exchequer is the acting head of government finances).
- To determine certain appointments. For example, these include the appointment of government ministers as well as determining the number of non-party political peers to be appointed to the House of Lords (see section 10.5.4).
- To co-ordinate government policy.
- To establish certain non-statutory bodies (eg the House of Lords Appointments Commission in 2000 – see section 10.5.4).
- To issue and revise the ***Ministerial Code*** (Cabinet Office, revised January 2018), which is given to ministers on assuming office and details their responsibilities and expected standard of conduct. It is of interest to note that, if the United Kingdom were to ever adopt a codified constitution, the rules set out in this Code would undoubtedly form part of it.

NB. In 2011 the Prime Minister wrote the foreword to the first edition of *The Cabinet Manual – A guide to laws, conventions and rules on the operation of government* (Cabinet

---

Ministerial Code

a code of conduct issued by the Prime Minister which government ministers are required to follow

---

Office, Crown Copyright, 2011), which outlines 'the internal rules and procedures under which the Government operates'.

The Prime Minister is given advice by the Policy Unit and specialist advisers. In 2014 the House of Commons Select Committee on Political and Constitutional Reform published a useful report of suggested reforms to improve the accountability of the Prime Minister (*Role and Powers of the Prime Minister*, HC 351 (The Stationery Office, 2014)).

11.2.3 The Cabinet

This body, like that of the office of the Prime Minister, owes its existence to constitutional convention. In constitutional theory, the Cabinet is the most significant political decision-making body in the constitution. The Cabinet comprises the most senior ministers in the government (the head of each government department) who discuss, debate and collectively agree on government policy (eg in relation to crime or pensions). In this way, the British constitution is hallmarked by *Cabinet government*, with collective decision-making on major state and policy issues being made by senior government ministers. In recent decades, however, the dominance of the office and personality of the Prime Minister has prompted the question as to whether we have '*Prime Ministerial government*' instead, whereby the Prime Minister dominates and overshadows the Cabinet. After all, it is the Prime Minister who determines and co-ordinates Cabinet discussion, and 'sums up' the Cabinet opinion on a particular matter. Moreover, he determines who will be a minister and the government portfolio that they will hold (including when the Cabinet is periodically reshuffled). Ultimately, however, the Prime Minister needs the support and confidence of his Cabinet in order to maintain his position. Indeed, Margaret Thatcher lost the full support of her Cabinet (and party) at the end of her tenure as Prime Minister and resigned thereafter.

The Cabinet is supported by the Cabinet Office (a Department of State). In addition, the Cabinet Secretariat serves to ensure that Cabinet business is coordinated and efficient. It supports and serves Cabinet ministers (who chair Cabinet committees – see below) as well as the Prime Minister (and Deputy Prime Minister).

The Cabinet is regulated by the following conventions:

- As a general rule it is composed of around 20 ministers – the exact size of the Cabinet will vary over time as government departments are not static and will merge with each other from time to time (as determined by the Prime Minister).
- Its discussions remain secret (see section 12.2.3).
- Decisions are made collectively and once a decision has been reached all members of the Cabinet (together with all junior ministers) are bound, publicly, to support and endorse this policy. This is known as the constitutional convention of collective responsibility. In this way the Cabinet, together with the rest of the government ministers, presents a united front to Parliament and the public (see section 12.2.2).

The Cabinet is supplemented by a number of specialist sub-Cabinet meetings, which are composed of a number of ministers (known as Cabinet committees). According to *The Cabinet Manual:*

QUOTATION

'Cabinet Committees help to ensure that government business is processed more effectively by relieving pressure on Cabinet. The committee structure also supports the principle of collective responsibility, ensuring that policy proposals receive thorough consideration without an issue having to be referred to the whole Cabinet. Cabinet committee decisions have the same authority as Cabinet decisions.'

The Cabinet Manual – A guide to laws, conventions and rules on the operation of government (Cabinet Office, Crown Copyright, 2011), p 32.

Cabinet committees are established by the Prime Minister and in the autumn of 2017 they included, for example, committees on:

- Parliamentary Business and Legislation
- European Union Exit and Trade
- Social Reform.

Source: *Vacher's Quarterly* (Issue 1167, Dods, 2017), p 32.

According to Weir and Beetham:

QUOTATION

'The fact is that the cabinet is now the creature of its own cabinet committees. The cabinet committee structure is now the real "engine-house" of government policy-making and decision-making. It is there if anywhere, and not in Cabinet, that long-term strategies and policy changes, such as the poll tax, are developed.'

Political Power and Democratic Control in Britain (Routledge, 1999), p 128.

ACTIVITY

Self-test question
What is the constitutional difference between Cabinet government as opposed to Prime Ministerial government?

11.2.4 Junior ministers

The Cabinet comprises the most senior type of government ministers who head government departments (ie a Secretary of State). Most government ministers, however, are junior ministers (Ministers of State or Parliamentary Under-Secretaries of State) and do not form part of the Cabinet, although they are still bound by the convention of collective responsibility.

It is important to note that Her Majesty's Government is supported by a number of parliamentary private secretaries, who are not formally part of the government *per se* but who are each attached to, and support, a particular minister. The *Ministerial Code* states that they 'are expected to support the Government in divisions in the House' (*Ministerial Code* (Cabinet Office, revised January 2018), para 3.9).

ACTIVITY

Exercise

What is the distinction between a Secretary of State and a junior minister? Find out some examples to illustrate this distinction.

11.2.5 Central government departments headed by a government minister

Central government comprises a number of departments of state, each with a separate and specialist policy responsibility. In 2017 there were 24 government departments which included, for example:

- The Department for Work and Pensions.
- The Ministry of Justice.
- The Foreign and Commonwealth Office.
- HM Treasury.

Each department is headed by a senior government minister (typically a Secretary of State) who will be supported by a number of junior ministers. For example, in 2017 the Home Office comprised the following ministerial hierarchy:

Ministerial hierarchy in the Home Office
Secretary of State for the Home Department.
Four Ministers of State: • Minister of State (Immigration) • Minister of State (Security) • Minister of State (Policing and the Fire Service) • Minister of State (Countering Extremism).
One Parliamentary Under-Secretary of State (for Crime, Safeguarding and Vulnerability).

Table 11.1

Source: *Vacher's Quarterly* (Issue 1167, Dods, 2017), pp 19–20.

As indicated above, government departments are not static institutions, and ministerial policy responsibilities are subject to change, as the Ministers of the Crown Act 1975 enables (in effect) the Prime Minister to:

- Transfer policy responsibilities between ministers. In 2003 specified functions of the Lord Chancellor were transferred to the newly created post of Secretary of State for Constitutional Affairs – this was the case even though the same person held both offices – The Secretary of State for Constitutional Affairs Order 2003 (SI 2003/1887).
- Dissolve a government department and transfer its responsibilities to another minister.

The above are achieved through the passage of a (statutory) Order in Council under the aegis of the Ministers of the Crown Act 1975.

Central government departments can also be subdivided into the following two elements:

- **The political element (the temporary government ministers)** – most of whom will be elected politicians (although some will be unelected peers), who will determine the political direction of the department and the policies that it will administer.

■ **The non-political element (the permanent civil servants)** – who carry out and implement the policies as formulated by their government ministers (see section 11.3.1). It should be noted that, since the 1990s, aspects of government departments have been separated and reconstituted as 'Next Step Agencies', and these are considered at section 11.3.2.

ACTIVITY

Exercise

Explain the different aspects of a central government department. Identify one government department and explain what it does.

11.2.6 The Privy Council

The Privy Council was the precursor to the modern Cabinet and today the Council's executive responsibilities have effectively been eclipsed by it (on the Privy Council, also see section 5.7.7). Among other things, it enables the government of the day to pass Orders in Council. According to *The Cabinet Manual*:

QUOTATION

'The Privy Council advises the Sovereign on the exercise of the prerogative powers and certain functions assigned to the Sovereign and the Council by Act of Parliament. The Privy Council is established under the Royal Prerogative and is the mechanism through which interdepartmental agreement is reached on those items of government business which, for historical or other reasons, fall to ministers as Privy Counsellors rather than as departmental ministers.'

The Cabinet Manual – A guide to laws, conventions and rules on the operation of government (Cabinet Office, Crown Copyright, 2011), p 8.

KEY FACTS

Key facts on the political executive

The political executive is also known as Her Majesty's Government and consists of the following:

- The monarch, who is the titular head of HM Government. In practice, the monarch's role is largely formal.
- The Prime Minister, who is the practical head of government and of the Cabinet.
- The Cabinet, which is composed of Cabinet ministers who are senior government ministers who each head a particular government department of state. In theory it is the most important political decision-making body in the constitution.
- Junior ministers (eg Ministers of State or Parliamentary Under-Secretaries of State), who sit outside the Cabinet.
- Government departments each have a separate and specialist policy responsibility and are invariably headed by a Secretary of State. They are staffed by politically impartial civil servants who carry out and implement the policies as formulated by their government minister – see section 11.3.1 below.

11.3 The non-political or bureaucratic executive

11.3.1 The Civil Service

The *Civil Service Code* (Crown Copyright, 2015), which incorporated the core values of the Civil Service, states that:

QUOTATION

'Civil Service Values

'The Civil Service is an integral and key part of the government of the United Kingdom. It supports the Government of the day in developing and implementing its policies, and in delivering public services. Civil servants are accountable to ministers, who in turn are accountable to Parliament.

'As a civil servant, you are appointed on merit on the basis of fair and open competition and are expected to carry out your role with dedication and a commitment to the Civil Service and its core values: integrity, honesty, objectivity and impartiality.'

www.gov.uk/government/publications/civil-service-code.

Under s 5 of the Constitutional Reform and Governance Act 2010, the Minister for the Civil Service is required to publish a Code of Conduct for the Civil Service.

Civil servants can be broadly divided into two distinct groups:

■ **Senior civil servants** – They have been described as 'Whitehall mandarins' (see Weir and Beetham below), with the most senior civil servant in a department being the Permanent Secretary (not to be confused with political parliamentary private secretaries – see section 11.2.4). Senior civil servants provide information to their respective government minister (their political master) and offer expert advice on policy matters. Civil servants do not control public policy – that is the responsibility of government ministers, who are constitutionally accountable to Parliament. Civil servants account directly to their ministerial head and not to Parliament (see the Civil Service Code set out above). Instead, it is the minister (as the public face and head of the department) who accounts to Parliament for the actions and policies of his department and officials (this is by virtue of the constitutional convention of individual ministerial responsibility – see para 1.3(b) of the *Ministerial Code*). It should also be remembered that it is the case that the courts have sanctioned the practice whereby appropriately qualified civil servants can make decisions on behalf of their ministers (see sections 4.13.12 and 20.2.3).

In terms of determining policy, however, the dividing line between the senior graded civil servants and ministers is a fine one, as the latter necessarily make their policy judgments based (partly) on the information and advice provided by the former (but see also the role of special advisers below). Moreover, it should be pointed out that newly appointed Secretaries of State will inevitably lack experience and detailed knowledge of the area of administration that they have been assigned. This is in contrast to the permanent, professional and seasoned senior civil servant. In this way, although it is a partnership between the minister and senior civil servant, it is inevitable that the former will be heavily reliant upon the advice and information provided by the latter. It should also be pointed out that in addition to their ministerial duties, most government ministers are also elected MPs and so will also have constituency matters to attend to.

According to Weir and Beetham, the dynamics of the relationship between minister and civil servant is that:

QUOTATION

'It is the officials who draft the papers ministers see, who filter the information they receive, who define many of the problems, who suggest most of the solutions, who draft the legislation and who ultimately take the great majority of decisions.'

S Weir and D Beetham, *Political Power and Democratic Control in Britain* (Routledge, 1999), p 170.

More recently, a select committee report noted that 'Tensions exist between senior civil servants and the politicians they serve.' (The Public Administration and Constitutional Affairs Committee, *The work of the Civil Service: Key themes and preliminary findings* HC 253 (2017), p 11).

Senior civil servants must be distinguished from 'special advisers'. In addition to the advice proffered by senior civil servants, ministers may also be given advice by appointed special advisers who are technically temporary civil servants but who provide advice on a partisan and political basis. In this way they can provide a useful counterpoint to the advice of the senior civil servants. They are appointed by Cabinet ministers, having been sanctioned by the Prime Minister, and are governed by a code of conduct. Section 8 of the Constitutional Reform and Governance Act 2010 requires the Minister for the Civil Service to publish a Code of Conduct for Special Advisers (*Code of Conduct for Special Advisers* (Cabinet Office, December, 2016)). According to para 3.3 of the *Ministerial Code*, ministers are responsible for the decisions and actions of their special adviser. The number of special advisers has grown in the past decade or so. On special advisers, see M Everett and E Faulkner, *Special Advisers*, Briefing Paper 03813 (House of Commons Library, 2017).

- **Lower-ranking civil servants** (the vast majority of the Civil Service) who implement government policy and administration on a daily basis.

The constitutional characteristics of the Civil Service

Civil servants, historically, have been hallmarked by the following principles:

- **Permanence** – In the British constitution government ministers are temporary, whereas civil servants are permanent appointments. This means that a change in government after a general election does not result in a change in the composition of the Civil Service. Civil servants will serve and owe allegiance to the government of the day, irrespective of its political colour.
- **Impartiality** – Civil servants are politically impartial/neutral in the sense that they must serve all governments equally well (*Civil Service Code* – also see s 7 of the Constitutional Reform and Governance Act 2010). This means that, whatever their own personal political beliefs, civil servants must serve a government irrespective of its political persuasion. In addition, in terms of objectivity, the Code states that civil servants must not 'frustrate the implementation of policies once decisions are taken by declining to take, or abstaining from, action which flows from those decisions' (also see s 7 of the Constitutional Reform and Governance Act 2010). Moreover, s 1(1) (b) of the House of Commons Disqualification Act 1975 bars civil servants from becoming MPs. Furthermore, in light of their responsibilities to provide advice etc, the senior grades of the profession are barred from political activity at a national level. There are two categories below this politically restricted category: those who may engage in national and local political activity with permission and those in the lowest category who are free to be involved in such activities.

In terms of integrity, civil servants must not disclose official information without the requisite authorisation (*Civil Service Code* – also see s 7 of the 2010 Act, which makes reference to integrity). In the 1980s a senior civil servant disclosed to an Opposition MP information pertaining to the sinking of the Argentine ship the *General Belgrano*. He was subsequently prosecuted under the Official Secrets Act 1911, although at his trial he was acquitted by the jury (*R v Ponting* [1985] Crim LR 318).

Appointments to the Civil Service have historically been selected on merit and overseen by the Civil Service Commissioners, and is now carried out under the aegis of the Constitutional Reform and Governance Act 2010. Finally, it is pertinent to point out that the *Ministerial Code* imposes a duty on ministers to uphold the political impartiality of the Civil Service (*Ministerial Code*, para 5.1).

- **Anonymity** – As indicated above, government ministers must account to Parliament for the performance and actions of their department, thereby taking constitutional responsibility for their departmental civil servants. In this way the head of the government department (together with his junior ministers) represents the public face of the department with his permanent civil servants remaining anonymous. This in turn allows civil servants to give advice in confidence and enables them to serve successive different governments. The principle of anonymity has, however, been partly eroded by the fact that civil servants can appear before select committees to represent their minister (having been appropriately briefed in accordance with the 'Osmotherly Rules' – see section 12.6.5).

The management of the Civil Service

The minister responsible for the Civil Service (ie the Minister for the Civil Service) is the Prime Minister and the employment terms and conditions of civil servants have been historically regulated by Orders in Council (legislation made under the royal prerogative – see *GCHQ* (1985) at section 11.9.6). In recent years, however, there had been a call for a Civil Service Act to be enacted which would regulate civil servants on a statutory basis. In 2008 the then Labour government produced the Draft Constitutional Renewal Bill (Cm 7342-II), which proposed to place the Civil Service on a statutory footing. This Bill became the Constitutional Reform and Governance Act 2010, which provided for:

- a statutory basis for the Minister for the Civil Service to manage the Civil Service (Part 1) – s 3 states that 'The Minister for the Civil Service has the power to manage the Civil Service'.
- the creation of a statutory Civil Service Commission (s 2). The Commission has a role in relation to the selection of civil servant appointments and in dealing with conduct that breaches the *Civil Service Code of Conduct*.
- a requirement that the Minister publish a *Civil Service Code of Conduct* (s 5) as well as a code for special advisers (s 8).
- the setting out in statute that selections to the Civil Service 'must be on merit on the basis of fair and open competition' (s 10).

In terms of reform, in recent years there have been two 'Reform Plans':

- Civil Service Reform Plan (2012).
- Civil Service Workplace Plan (2016–20).

ACTIVITY

Self-test question

What do civil servants do? What is their constitutional significance?

11.3.2 Executive agencies/the 'Next Step Agencies'

According to *The Cabinet Manual* there are three types of 'arm's-length bodies', which are public bodies which carry out government functions at arm's length from government ministers. One such type are executive agencies:

QUOTATION

'Executive agencies are well-defined units with a focus on delivering specific outcomes. They are part of a department and are staffed by Civil Servants.'

The Cabinet Manual – A guide to laws, conventions and rules on the operation of government
(Cabinet Office, Crown Copyright, 2011), p 27.

It is important to note that today the vast majority of civil servants work not in central government departments *per se* but in executive agencies. The 'Next Step Agencies' (so-called because they were named after a Cabinet paper: *Improving Management in Government: the Next Steps* (Cabinet Office, February 1988)) were established in the 1990s in an attempt to make government administration more efficient. In essence, this meant that certain aspects of a government department were separated and reconstituted under a specified agency headed by a chief executive. The objectives to be obtained by each agency (thereby in theory ensuring administrative efficiency) would be determined by the relevant government minister. Three examples of executive agencies in 2017 will suffice:

- The Planning Inspectorate (with a chief executive), sponsored by the Department for Communities and Local Government – this agency is concerned with infrastructure and planning.
- The Driver and Vehicle Standards Agency (with a chief executive), sponsored by the Department for Transport – this agency is responsible for promoting road safety by improving driving standards, which includes the testing of putative drivers.
- HM Courts & Tribunals Service – this is an executive agency under the aegis of the Ministry of Justice (see section 21.1.6).

The parent government departmental minister remains constitutionally accountable for these *hived off* agencies (*Ministerial Code*, para 1.3(b)). There has nevertheless been some constitutional disquiet as to whether ministers in practice take political responsibility for the operation of them (they are, of course, each headed by a chief executive who is a specified office holder), leading to a gap in constitutional accountability. For example, in the mid-1990s when prisoners escaped from Parkhurst Prison, the Home Secretary argued that there was a distinction between operational responsibility (ie being responsible for the day-to-day security of prisons) and the responsibility for overall general policy. The prison escape was considered an operational matter and subsequently the Home Secretary announced that the director-general (chief executive) of the Prison Service agency had left his office. NB: today the HM Prison Service is an executive agency sponsored by the Ministry of Justice.

11.3.3 Non-ministerial departments

The second type of an 'arm's-length body' is the non-ministerial department:

QUOTATION

'Non-ministerial departments (NMDs) are central government departments staffed by Civil Servants. NMDs have a board and ministers do not have direct control over them. Instead, they have a sponsoring minister, who typically appoints the board.'

The Cabinet Manual – A guide to laws, conventions and rules on the operation of government (Cabinet Office, Crown Copyright, 2011), p 27.

Both the Crown Prosecution Service and HM Revenue & Customs are examples of non-ministerial departments.

11.3.4 Non-departmental public bodies

The third type of an 'arm's-length body' is non-departmental public bodies (NDPB), also variously called *quangos* (quasi-autonomous non-governmental organisations). The Cabinet Office has described them as follows:

QUOTATION

'An NDPB is defined as a "body which has a role in the process of national Government, but is not a Government Department or part of one, and which accordingly operates to a greater or lesser extent at arm's length from Ministers".'

Public bodies 2008. Making government work better (Cabinet Office, 2008), p 3.

For example, in 2017 the Parole Board was an executive non-departmental public body sponsored by the Ministry of Justice.

NB. Finally in terms of public bodies, Part 1 of the Public Bodies Act 2011 empowers a minister to abolish, merge, modify the constitutional/funding arrangements of or transfer/modify the functions of specified public bodies/offices set out in the Act.

KEY FACTS

The non-political or bureaucratic executive
(i) The Civil Service, which can be broadly divided into two distinct groups: • Senior civil servants who provide information to their respective government minister and offer expert advice on policy matters. • Lower-ranking civil servants who simply implement government policy and administration. • Civil servants account directly to their ministerial head and not to Parliament. The Civil Service is characterised by the following principles: • Impartiality – civil servants will serve and owe allegiance to the government of the day irrespective of its political colour. • Anonymity and permanence – as the departmental ministerial head represents the public face of the department, the permanent civil servants remain anonymous.
(ii) Executive agencies, which are aspects of a government department which, in order to promote efficiency; have been separated and reconstituted under a specified agency headed by a chief executive (eg the Driver and Vehicle Standards Agency).
(iii) Non-ministerial departments (eg the HM Revenue & Customs).
(iv) Non-departmental public bodies (eg the Parole Board).

11.4 The executive in practical terms

Both the armed forces and the various police forces (one for each area of the country) form part of the executive in a very general and practical sense. The police, for example, practically enforce the criminal law against those individuals who, *prima facie*, violate it. In short, they carry out and implement the law on a practical basis. They are barred from membership of the House of Commons (see section 11.6.3). Most recently, the Police Reform and Social Responsibility Act 2011 created a directly elected Police and Crime Commissioner for every police force area in England and Wales (excluding London). NB: one of the aims behind the recent Policing and Crime Act 2017 is to improve the efficiency, effectiveness and democratic accountability of police forces.

11.5 Other executive bodies in the British constitution

There are other executive bodies in the British constitution:

Local authorities

From a constitutional perspective, local authorities technically form part of the executive. Local councillors are elected by local residents and the political composition of local authorities will, in various parts of the country at any one time, be different to that of central government. Local authorities possess both legislative and executive powers (see section 14.2).

Devolution

As part of the devolved settlements, the following executives were established:

- **Scotland** – s 44 of the Scotland Act 1998 (as amended by s 12 of the Scotland Act 2012) established a Scottish Government (in effect, a Cabinet drawn from the Scottish Parliament). This section further provides that an individual cannot hold national ministerial office at Whitehall while being a member of the Scottish Government.
- **Northern Ireland** – Pt III of the Northern Ireland Act 1998 provided for the establishment of an Executive Committee (analogous to the Scottish Government).
- **Wales** – s 45 of the Government of Wales Act 2006 established a Welsh Assembly Government.

On all of the above executives see Chapter 14.

The European Union

Although there is no clear separation of powers within the institutional architecture of the European Union, historically the European Commission has been regarded as the executive and the Civil Service of Europe. However, both the Council and the European Council also perform executive functions by making executive decisions (see section 15.2.2).

11.6 The statistical breakdown of government ministers

11.6.1 The parliamentary executive

As the United Kingdom has a parliamentary executive system of government, government ministers are necessarily drawn from Parliament. The parliamentary executive in June 2017 can be illustrated by the following diagram:

Source: figures extrapolated from L Maer, *Ministers in the House of Lords*, Briefing Paper 05226 (House of Commons Library, 2017), p 5.

Figure 11.1 The parliamentary executive in June 2017

In terms of the statistical breakdown of the government in June 2017, of these 118 members, 23 were Cabinet ministers (including one peer – the Leader of the House of Lords). The United Kingdom Cabinet is smaller than in either Canada (36) or Australia (30), but larger than in Ireland (15) (S King, *Regulating the Behaviour of Ministers, Special Advisers and Civil Servants* (The Constitution Unit, 2003), p 10). In addition, it should be pointed out that no more than 20 Cabinet salaries, other than the Prime Minister and Lord Chancellor, are payable (Ministerial and Other Salaries Act 1975 as amended). In 2010 a report examined the number of ministers in modern government: House of Commons Public Administration Select Committee, *Too Many Ministers?* HC 457 (The Stationery Office, 2010).

11.6.2 Government ministers in the House of Lords

As is clear from the diagram above, the vast majority of ministers are MPs; however, a substantial minority (approximately one-fifth) are peers in the House of Lords. In fact, historically, the majority of Cabinet members in the nineteenth century were peers. Although in some countries ministers cannot form part of the upper chamber, the advantages of it are that:

- It ensures that the government has some representation in the upper House.
- The upper House has the opportunity to scrutinise directly some government ministers.
- Government ministers can pilot Bills through the upper House.

11.6.3 The executive and the separation of powers

The House of Commons Disqualification Act 1975 ensures that there is a degree of constitutional separation between certain elements of the executive and the House of Commons.

- Firstly, s 2(1) stipulates that no more than 95 persons can hold ministerial office in the House of Commons at any one time.
- Secondly, s 1 disqualifies the following members of the executive from membership of the House of Commons:

SECTION

....

s 1(1) (b) – those employed in the Civil Service
　　　(c) – members of the regular armed forces
　　　(d) – members of any police force.

ACTIVITY

....

Problem-solving

Explain the statistical breakdown of the parliamentary executive. What is the constitutional significance of such data?

11.7 The functions of the executive

The constitutional functions of the executive comprise the following:

- **To formulate domestic public policy.** In short, the constitutional function of the government is to govern the state. The essence of Cabinet government is that a group of senior ministers collectively debate, determine and co-ordinate policies (for example how to address the issues of Brexit, terrorism or pensions). These policies would thereafter be publicly supported by the government as a whole both in, and outside, Parliament.
- **To formulate and implement foreign policy.** This would include the deployment of troops overseas and responding to an international crisis.
- **To initiate legislative proposals.** Although Parliament is the legislature, it is the government of the day which drafts and introduces most Bills which are laid before Parliament to approve. Government ministers will have the constitutional responsibility to pilot these Bills through Parliament. These Bills will invariably embody certain government policy aims. For example, the Trade Union Act 2016 reformed the law in relation to industrial action by trade unions. For instance, s 2 introduced a minimum level of turnout of at least 50 per cent of all trade union members entitled to vote in order for it to constitute a valid ballot for industrial action.
- **To implement the law (and policy).** The executive 'executes' and carries out the law. Civil servants will implement the law in relation to their respective government department. As illustrated in the *Carltona* case (1943) (see section 4.13.12), senior civil servants can exercise legal powers on behalf of their minister thereby acting as their *alter ego*. In practical terms, the implementation and enforcement of the law is performed by the police and in emergencies, by the armed forces (thereby ensuring public order).

- **To provide political leadership.** This is performed by the government as a whole, but in recent years has typically focused on the Prime Minister (for example, in the context of summits of the European Council – see section 15.2.1).
- **To make appointments.** For example, the Lord Chancellor will (ultimately) determine appointments in respect of a range of judicial posts (see section 13.3).

NB. The Budget Responsibility and National Audit Act 2011 imposes duties on the Treasury in respect of fiscal policy.

ACTIVITY

Essay writing

Consider the different functions of the executive. Are some more important than others?

11.8 The powers of the executive

In order to perform its responsibilities, the executive enjoys both statutory and common law powers.

11.8.1 Statutory powers

Most powers which government exercises are statutory. For example, an Act may:

Confer a power on a minister to pass delegated legislation in order to achieve specified aims:

- Section 47(1) of the Prison Act 1952 empowers the Secretary of State to make rules in order to regulate and manage prisons (see *ex parte Leech* (1993) at section 20.2.2).

In addition, local authorities can pass delegated legislation in the form of byelaws in order to regulate local matters (eg local parks or the banning of the consumption of alcohol in specified areas).

Confer a power on a minister to achieve specified purposes:

- Section 1 of the Inquiries Act 2005 empowers a minister to establish a statutory inquiry (see section 21.2.3).
- Section 2 of the Terrorism Prevention and Investigation Measures Act 2011 empowers the Secretary of State to impose on an individual a specified Terrorism Prevention and Investigation Measure (ie a TPIM notice). This might, for example, impose restrictions on the individual in relation to their residence.

Confer a power on a minister to determine when primary legislative provisions should be brought into force:

- Section 148(4) of the Constitutional Reform Act 2005 authorised the Lord Chancellor to bring into operation the new Supreme Court (see the Constitutional Reform Act 2005 (Commencement No 11) Order 2009, which brought the new Supreme Court into effect in October 2009).
- Section 171 of the Criminal Justice Act 1988 gave the Home Secretary a power to decide when to bring the statutory Criminal Injuries Compensation Scheme into effect (*R v Secretary of State for the Home Department, ex parte Fire Brigades Union* [1995] 2 All ER 244 at section 6.7.10).

■ Under s 52(2) of the Constitutional Reform and Governance Act 2010, the Minister for the Cabinet Office made the following order to bring into force the provision to put the Civil Service on a statutory footing: The Constitutional Reform and Governance Act 2010 (Commencement No 3) Order 2010 SI 2010/2703.

Confer a power on a minister to pass delegated legislation which has the effect of amending primary legislation (known as a 'Henry VIII clause'):

■ Section 10 of the Human Rights Act 1998 authorises ministers to pass remedial orders in order to render a provision of primary legislation compatible with the European Convention (see section 17.7.3).

■ Section 2 of the European Communities Act 1972 empowers a minister to transpose a European directive into domestic law through secondary legislation – but now see Brexit later at section 15.6.6.

Impose a duty to achieve a specified purpose:

■ Section 7 of the Public Libraries and Museums Act 1964 imposes a statutory duty on all library authorities (in effect local authorities) 'to provide a comprehensive and efficient library service' (see *ex parte Times Newspapers Ltd* (1986) at section 20.2.4).

■ Section 149 of the Equality Act 2010 imposes a 'public sector equality duty' on public bodies when exercising their functions.

KEY FACTS

Key facts on HM Government's statutory powers

HM Government possesses a number of statutory powers to do the following:
- To pass delegated legislation in order to achieve specified aims (eg s 47 of the Prison Act 1952).
- To achieve specified purposes (eg s 1 of the Inquiries Act 2005).
- To determine when primary legislative provisions should be brought into force (eg s 171 of the Criminal Justice Act 1988).
- To pass delegated legislation which has the effect of amending primary legislation (eg s 10 of the Human Rights Act 1998).

11.8.2 Common law powers

In addition to statute, government also draws powers from the common law:

■ **A residual power to act** – There is a conception that public authorities enjoy a residual freedom to act as evidenced by *Malone v Metropolitan Police Commissioner* (1979) (see section 6.7.7) whereby Sir Robert Megarry VC made it clear that: 'England . . . is a country where everything is permitted except what is expressly forbidden'. As a result, Malone's telephone line could be tapped because there was no 'positive' law to forbid it (although today see the Human Rights Act 1998 – Chapter 17). According to Le Sueur, however, this residual freedom of action would not apply to public authorities established by statute (eg local authorities) whose specific powers would be stipulated in legislation ('The Nature, Powers and Accountability of Central Government' in D Feldman (ed), *English*

Public Law (2nd edn, Oxford University Press, 2009), p 187) – also see Laws LJ in *R v Somerset County Council, ex parte Fewings* [1995] 1 All ER 513. It is highly pertinent to note, however, that s 1 of the Localism Act 2011 has now conferred a broad statutory *general power of competence* on English local authorities (see section 14.2.2)

- **The royal prerogative** – (see directly below) this is an invaluable power which the government derives from the common law. A number of prerogative powers were abolished as part of the constitutional settlement which led to the Bill of Rights 1689, but a number still remain today.

11.9 The royal prerogative

11.9.1 Definition

QUOTATION

'A distinguishing feature of the British constitution is the extent to which government continues to exercise a number of powers which were not granted to it by a written constitution, nor by Parliament, but are, rather, ancient prerogatives of the Crown.'

The Governance of Britain, Cm 7170 (2007), p 16.

In its evidence to the House of Commons Public Administration Select Committee, the Treasury Solicitor's Department provided the following definition of the royal prerogative:

QUOTATION

'There is no single accepted definition of the prerogative. It is sometimes defined to mean all the common law, ie non-statutory powers, of the Crown. An alternative definition is that the prerogative consists of those common law powers and immunities which are peculiar to the Crown and go beyond the powers of a private individual eg the power to declare war as opposed to the normal common law power to enter a contract. . . . Whichever definition is used there is no exhaustive list of prerogative powers.'

Fourth Report of Session 2003–04, *Taming the Prerogative: Strengthening Ministerial Accountability to Parliament*, HC 422 (2004), Ev 13.

What is clear is that royal prerogative powers, historically, were exercised by successive monarchs over the centuries. Today, with a constitutional monarchy, the bulk of these powers have in effect passed in practice to the government of the day (of which the vast majority of its members will be elected, although some ministers do sit in the House of Lords).

11.9.2 The context of recent reform proposals

The 2007 Green Paper (*The Governance of Britain*, Cm 7170 (2007)) – in the context of limiting executive powers the then Labour government argued: ' . . . in general the prerogative powers should be put onto a statutory basis and brought under stronger parliamentary scrutiny and control' (para 24). In addition, the government proposed specified reforms (eg to the Civil Service) and 'to undertake a wider review of the remaining prerogative, executive powers' (see section 11.9.4). The Green Paper resulted in a number of consultation exercises.

- **The 2008 White Paper** (*The Governance of Britain – Constitutional Renewal*, Cm 7342–I (Crown Copyright, 2008)) – which set out the government's proposals for constitutional reform on, among other things, Treaties and war powers. The paper was published in conjunction with the following Bill below.
- **The 2008 Draft Constitutional Renewal Bill** (*The Governance of Britain – Draft Constitutional Renewal Bill*, Cm 7342–II (Crown Copyright, 2008)) – this Bill set out proposed legislative reforms on, among other things, the Civil Service and Treaties. This draft Bill (albeit greatly altered) became the Constitutional Reform and Governance Act 2010, which put on a statutory footing the management of the Civil Service, together with the scrutiny of Treaties (see below). On this Act, see M Ryan, 'The Constitutional Reform and Governance Act 2010: The evolution and development of a constitutional Act' (2014) 35 *Liverpool Law Review*, 233.
- In 2009 the then Labour government published its review of prerogative powers (see section 11.9.4).
- The 2014 House of Commons Political and Constitutional Reform Committee report on the Prime Minister (*Role and Powers of the Prime Minister*, HC 351 (The Stationery Office Limited, 2014)) proposed to place more prerogative powers exercised by the Prime Minister in statute.

11.9.3 The Public Administration Select Committee classification

In 2004 the House of Commons Public Administration Select Committee (see 11.9.1) divided the royal prerogative powers into three broad types:

- 'The Queen's constitutional prerogatives' (para 5).
- 'The legal prerogatives of the Crown' (para 7).
- 'Prerogative executive powers' (para 8).

In addition it is also possible to divide the prerogative powers broadly between:

- Those powers in the domestic sphere (eg the Royal Assent, mercy).
- Those powers relating to foreign affairs (eg declaring war, deploying armed forces abroad).

'The Queen's constitutional prerogatives'

The Public Administration Select Committee described these as 'the personal discretionary powers which remain in the Sovereign's hands' and would include the following:

To dissolve Parliament – Parliament must be dissolved prior to a general election and historically this was a prerogative act technically performed by the monarch, but by constitutional convention she acted on the advice of the Prime Minister. Today, however, the monarch no longer retains the prerogative power to dissolve Parliament as the arrangements for dissolution are now governed by the Fixed-Term Parliaments Act 2011. This Act set fixed dates of five years in between general elections – see section 8.1.1.

NB. The monarch, however, still summons a Parliament (albeit on the Prime Minister's advice).

To appoint the Prime Minister – Although under the prerogative it is the monarch who formally appoints the Prime Minister, the practical reality is that, following constitutional convention, she will appoint the party leader who has secured the majority of seats in the House of Commons (in other words, he who commands the support of the House). Problems could occur, however, following a general election when no one party has an overall majority of seats in a 'hung Parliament'. Following the inconclusive result of the 2010 general election the political parties engaged in negotiations which resulted in a coalition government being formed (comprising Conservative and Liberal Democrat members). According to *The Cabinet Manual*, the monarch would not expect to be involved in any negotiations between parties where a number of different governments could potentially be formed, 'although there are responsibilities on those involved in the process to keep the Palace informed' (p 15). But also see D Pannick 'The Queen becomes a kingmaker if no party is overall winner' *The Times* (London, 22 April 2010), p 67.

To appoint government ministers – Although the monarch formally appoints government ministers (it is Her Majesty's Government), by constitutional convention she will act on the advice of her Prime Minister, who will determine these appointments (eg after a reshuffle in the Cabinet).

To grant the Royal Assent – By constitutional convention the monarch will act on the advice of her ministers and grant Royal Assent to Bills. Such consent has not been refused for three centuries. In modern times the granting of the Royal Assent has not proved controversial.

The right to encourage, warn and advise her government ministers – Bagehot, writing in the nineteenth century, noted that a monarch had the constitutional right to encourage and warn her government ministers (by giving her opinion) as well as to be consulted by them, for example prior to the Budget (W Bagehot, *The English Constitution* (Oxford University Press, 2001), p 64). Indeed, the current monarch has considerable experience, particularly in relation to the Commonwealth, as she has been sovereign for over 60 years and has formally appointed a number of different Prime Ministers and numerous ministers over this time.

As noted by the Select Committee, although in normal circumstances the monarch would act on the advice of her ministers in terms of how these powers should be exercised, she also has the power: '(in grave constitutional crisis) to act contrary to or without Ministerial advice' (para 5).

ACTIVITY

Problem-solving

Do you think that it would be the monarch's constitutional duty to refuse to grant the Royal Assent (ignoring the advice of her ministers) to the (imaginary) 2020 Abolition of Elections Bill which proposed to abolish parliamentary elections for 30 years? (On acting constitutionally and unconstitutionally – see section 4.16).

'The legal prerogatives of the Crown'
As noted by the Select Committee these include, for example:

- '. . . the principle that the Crown (or the state) can do no wrong' – the monarch cannot be sued in her own courts (she is, of course, the font of all justice as implemented by Her Majesty's judges).

■ The Crown is only bound by Acts of Parliament through the use of express words or by necessary implication. For example, s 50 of the Inquiries Act 2005 states that the provisions of the Act bind the Crown.

ACTIVITY

Exercise

Compare and contrast the Queen's constitutional prerogatives with the legal prerogatives of the Crown.

'Prerogative executive powers'

The Select Committee suggested that the third type of prerogative power should be described as 'Ministerial executive' power, as in practice it is government ministers who exercise these powers in the name of the Crown (as detailed below).

Government ministers' main powers

The Select Committee identified the main 'royal prerogative, or Ministerial executive, powers exercised by Ministers' to be as follows:

■ **A declaration of war** – The decision to go to war is taken not by Parliament but by the government of the day (in effect, the Prime Minister) purporting to do so in the name of the Crown. In contrast, in the United States, Art 1, s 8 of the Constitution states that it is Congress which declares war. In 2005 Clare Short MP introduced (albeit ultimately unsuccessfully) a Private Members' Bill: the Armed Forces (Parliamentary Approval for Participation in Armed Conflict) Bill, clause 7 of which would have required that no declaration of war on behalf of the United Kingdom should be made unless the proposal had been laid before each House of Parliament and approved by them.

■ **The deployment and use of UK armed forces abroad** – Although the monarch is the titular commander-in-chief of the armed forces, as with the declaration of war it is the government of the day which in effect determines the disposition of troops overseas. In 2003 the Prime Minister allowed a vote in the House of Commons before the transfer of troops to Iraq, and this has in turn led to the question as to whether this is now a constitutional convention which must be followed in the future. It is clear that acting under the prerogative the Prime Minister could technically have ignored an adverse parliamentary vote in 2003; however, this would no doubt have raised the issue of whether such conduct would have been considered *morally* unconstitutional (see section 4.16). More recently, in March 2011 military action took place in Libya three days before Parliament had the opportunity to debate and vote on this (albeit it was clearly an emergency and exceptional situation which provided it with retrospective approval) – *Hansard*, HC Vol 525, col 807.

Following this, *The Cabinet Manual* issued later that year, pointed out that the coalition government had in 2011 'acknowledged that a convention had developed in Parliament that before troops were committed the House of Commons should have an opportunity to debate the matter . . . ' (para 5.38). Indeed, it is highly significant to point out that in August 2013 the House of Commons voted against military action in Syria. The Prime Minister accepted this decision and gave an assurance not to use military action under the royal prerogative in respect of Syria before another vote in the Commons (*Hansard*, HC, Vol 566, col 1556). In due course, MPs did vote to approve military action (ie air strikes) against ISIS in both Iraq (2014: *Hansard*, HC Vol 585, col 1361) and then in Syria (2015: *Hansard*, HC Vol 603, col 495).

In terms of *legal* reform, cl 1 of Clare Short's 2005 Armed Forces Bill (noted directly above) also proposed that parliamentary approval would be required for Her Majesty's armed forces to participate in armed conflict. In support of her Bill, she argued that the rationale behind it was that:

- It was democratically appropriate that Parliament should approve a declaration of war and the deployment of troops in an armed conflict.
- It would help to ensure that such decisions were more effectively scrutinised and informed (*Hansard*, HC Vol 437, cols 1085–90).

Similarly, clause 3 of Lord Lester's 2006 Constitutional Reform (Prerogative Powers and Civil Service etc) Bill would have enabled Parliament to approve the commitment of the armed forces to armed conflict or to war. Although neither Bill became law, in 2006 the House of Lords Select Committee on the Constitution issued a report on its review of the government's powers in this context and it concluded that:

QUOTATION

'The exercise of the Royal Prerogative by the Government to deploy armed force overseas is outdated and should not be allowed to continue as the basis for legitimate war-making in our 21st century democracy. Parliament's ability to challenge the executive must be protected and strengthened.'

House of Lords Select Committee on the Constitution, 15th Report of Session 2005–06, *Waging war: Parliament's role and responsibility*, HL Paper 236-I (2006), para 103.

It recommended that a constitutional convention should be developed which would require the government to seek parliamentary approval (except in emergency situations) prior to the deployment of troops in an armed conflict outside the United Kingdom.

In December 2006 another Private Members' Bill on this issue was published: Waging War (Parliament's Role and Responsibility) Bill. The Bill was sponsored by Michael Meacher MP and would have required the Secretary of State to lay before the House of Commons a mechanism to obtain the approval of MPs for the deployment of British troops for armed conflict. The then Labour government's 2007 Green Paper (see section 11.9.2) argued that the power of government under the prerogative to deploy the armed forces for conflict overseas in the absence of any formal parliamentary agreement was 'an outdated state of affairs in a modern democracy' (para 26). The subsequent 2008 White Paper *Constitutional Renewal* (see section 11.9.2) proposed that the best way forward was for the creation of a House of Commons resolution which would set out the parliamentary process which should be followed in order to approve the commitment of the armed forces to an armed conflict. More recently, in March 2011 the then Foreign Secretary stated that the coalition government would 'enshrine in law for the future the necessity of consulting Parliament on military action' (*Hansard*, HC, Vol 525, col 799). However, in April 2016 the then Secretary of State for Defence stated that:

QUOTATION

'After careful consideration, the Government have decided that it will not be codifying the convention in law or by resolution of the House in order to retain the ability of this and future Governments and the armed forces to protect the security and interests of the UK in circumstances that we cannot predict, and to avoid such decisions becoming subject to legal action. We will continue to ensure that Parliament is kept informed of significant major operations and deployments of the armed forces.'

Hansard, HC, Vol 608, col 10WS.

- **The deployment of the armed forces domestically** – As noted by the Select Committee this could involve maintaining the peace of the realm (an executive function) by supporting the police.
- **The making/ratification of international Treaties** – Treaties are typically signed by the Secretary of State for Foreign and Commonwealth Affairs or sometimes by the Prime Minister. Historically, there has been a constitutional convention (the 'Ponsonby rule') whereby the government laid the Treaty before Parliament for at least 21 days before ratification, thereby enabling Parliament to be informed and for the content of the Treaty to be scrutinised. The Constitutional Reform and Governance Act 2010 has now been passed, Part 2 of which placed the scrutiny of Treaties by Parliament on a statutory footing. In essence, s 20 provides that Treaties should be laid before Parliament before ratification and if the Commons resolved that a Treaty should not be ratified, the government could *not* proceed to ratify it. Section 22 provides for s 20 not to apply in exceptional cases.

Historically, the act of Treaty-making is a function of the executive and not susceptible to review by the courts:

JUDGMENT

'The treaty-making power of this country rests not in the courts, but in the Crown; that is, Her Majesty acting on the advice of her Ministers. When her Ministers negotiate and sign a treaty . . . they act on behalf of the country as a whole. They exercise the prerogative of the Crown. Their action in so doing cannot be challenged or questioned in these courts.'

Lord Denning MR in *Blackburn v Attorney General* [1971] 2 All ER 1380.

Similarly, the court dismissed Lord Rees-Mogg's judicial review application regarding the proposed ratification by the Secretary of State for Foreign and Commonwealth Affairs of the Maastricht Treaty (*R v Secretary of State for Foreign and Commonwealth Affairs, ex parte Rees-Mogg* [1994] QB 552).

In the context of *unmaking* Treaties, the seminal case in this area is the recent case of *Miller* (2017), which is considered in detail at section 15.6.6. In brief, the Supreme Court held that the government could not use royal prerogative power to notify the European Council (under Art 50) of the United Kingdom's withdrawal from the European Union, as this required parliamentary consent in the form of primary legislation. See also P Craig, 'Miller, structural constitutional review and the limits of prerogative power' [2017] PL 48.

■ **The issuing and revocation of passports** – this is determined by a government minister and has important implications as it affects an individual's freedom of movement. It is subject to legal supervision by the court:

CASE EXAMPLE

R v Secretary of State for Foreign and Commonwealth Affairs, ex parte Everett *[1989] 1 QB 811*

Everett, a British citizen in Spain, sought a new passport, but was refused one in pursuance of the Secretary of State's policy that passports were not issued where a warrant for arrest in the United Kingdom had been issued (Everett had not been given details of the warrant for his arrest). He sought judicial review of this refusal.

The Court of Appeal held that the judicial review of powers under the royal prerogative depended upon its subject matter. A decision in relation to whether or not a passport should be issued was an administrative one which affected the rights of an individual and was unlikely to have implications for foreign policy and so was reviewable by the courts. On the facts, however, Everett had suffered no injustice or prejudice (he had been given before the court hearing the information which should have been provided, ie the details of the warrant) and there was no suggestion that there were any special circumstances to justify an exception to the policy so as to issue him a passport.

Most recently, in *R (XH) v Secretary of State for the Home Department* [2017] EWCA Civ 41 the Court of Appeal confirmed that the prerogative power in respect of passports (ie their cancellation/withdrawal) had not been abrogated by the Terrorism Prevention and Investigation Measures Act 2011.

■ **The granting of pardons (the royal prerogative of mercy)** – This involves the Crown pardoning criminals or reducing their criminal sentences. The Home Secretary advised the monarch historically, but today it is the Secretary of State for Justice that does so. The exercise of this power is, to some extent, subject to review by the courts:

CASE EXAMPLE

R v Secretary of State for the Home Department, ex parte Bentley *[1994] QB 349*

The Divisional Court held that the failure of the Home Secretary to appreciate that the royal prerogative of mercy (which 'was a broad and flexible constitutional safeguard against mistakes') could be exercised other than by the issuing of a free pardon (ie a posthumous conditional pardon) was subject to review by the courts. The Home Secretary was, accordingly, required to consider afresh whether it was just to use his prerogative powers so as to recognise the commonly accepted view that Bentley's brother, Derek Bentley who had been executed in 1953, should have been reprieved.

The court stated that decisions taken under the royal prerogative were subject to judicial review where the nature and subject matter of the particular prerogative were amenable to judicial adjudication (ie where it did not necessitate the court reviewing questions of policy).

See more recently *R (Shields) v Secretary of State for Justice* [2008] EWHC 3102 (Admin).

- **The recommendations for honours** (eg by the Secretary of State for Defence).
- **The Prime Minister's ability to make appointments.**
- **The governance of territories (British) abroad.**
- **Diplomatic matters.**
- **The regulation of the Civil Service** – Historically, this was achieved under the royal prerogative, but Part 1 of the Constitutional Reform and Governance Act 2010 placed the power to manage the Civil Service on a statutory basis (see section 11.3.1).

11.9.4 The 2009 Review

In October 2009 the then Labour government published its report on its survey of prerogative powers (*Review of the Executive Royal Prerogative Powers: Final Report* (Crown Copyright, 2009)). The review identified four main categories (see Annex):

(i) **prerogative powers exercised by ministers**
   For example, these included:

   - the Civil Service (eg the regulation of civil servants – but now see the Constitutional Reform and Governance Act 2010)
   - the justice system (eg mercy)
   - foreign affairs (eg sending ambassadors)
   - war, times of emergency and the armed forces (eg deploying forces abroad)
   - miscellaneous (eg the power to hold non-statutory inquiries).

(ii) **executive 'constitutional/personal prerogative' powers exercised by the monarch**
   For example:

   - the Royal Assent
   - the granting of honours
   - the power to dismiss the government (but today, see the Fixed-Term Parliaments Act 2011)
   - the appointment and removal of ministers
   - to summon and dissolve Parliament (but today on the latter, see the Fixed-Term Parliaments Act 2011).

(iii) **'legal prerogatives of the Crown'**
   For example:

   - Crown immunities
   - the Crown as a preferred creditor.

(iv) **'archaic prerogative powers'**
   For example:

   - 'Right to sturgeon, (wild and unmarked) swans and whales as casual revenue'
   - 'Right to mine precious metals'.

11.9.5 The constitutional relationship between Parliament and the royal prerogative

In the hierarchy of legal sources, as statute law has a higher status than the common law, Parliament can pass Acts of Parliament which eclipse powers under the royal prerogative (see section 7.5.1). In fact, Parliament can:

- expressly limit or abolish prerogative powers (Bill of Rights 1689); or
- pass laws which supersede these powers.

CASE EXAMPLE

Attorney-General v De Keyser's Royal Hotel Limited *[1920] AC 508*

In 1916 the Crown took possession of De Keyser's Hotel to accommodate the headquarters personnel of the Royal Flying Corps. De Keyser sought compensation for this use and occupation of the hotel. The government argued that the occupation had been exercised under the royal prerogative (the defence of the realm) and so no compensation was payable. De Keyser argued that it was occupied in accordance with the Defence Act 1842 which made provision for compensation.

The House of Lords held that the government occupation of the hotel was under the terms of the Act (and so the powers under the royal prerogative were not available to the government) which necessitated compensation. In summary, the Crown could not purport to act under the royal prerogative where that power had been superseded by legislation. (The issue concerning compensation for taking property under the prerogative was decided later in *Burmah Oil* (1965), at section 4.9.)

More recently, Lord Browne-Wilkinson in *R v Secretary of State for the Home Department, ex parte Fire Brigades Union and others* [1995] 2 All ER 244, noted that royal prerogative powers continue:

JUDGMENT

'in existence to the extent that Parliament has not expressly or by implication extinguished them'.

In addition to displacing prerogative powers through legislation, Parliament can ensure through the convention of ministerial responsibility that ministers are constitutionally and politically accountable for the use of these powers. With respect to parliamentary questions, generally speaking they can be asked about the prerogative except, for example:

▪ The advice that the Prime Minister has given to the sovereign in respect of honours.
▪ The prerogative of mercy.

Reforms have been suggested to increase parliamentary control over the use of these powers.

▪ In March 2004 the House of Commons Public Administration Select Committee attached a draft Bill (supplied by Professor Brazier) to its report designed to ensure greater scrutiny of the prerogative. Clause 3 of the proposed Ministers of the Crown (Executive Powers) Bill would have imposed a duty on 'the Secretary of State' to lay a statement before Parliament setting out the nature, extent and safeguards in respect of all executive (royal prerogative) powers. Thereafter, a joint select committee would review these powers and indicate whether reforms (in the form of draft legislation) should be made for Parliament to consider (Fourth Report of Session 2003–04, *Taming the Prerogative: Strengthening Ministerial Accountability to Parliament* HC 422 (2004) App 1). The then Labour government, however, in response to this report remained unpersuaded 'that the Committee's proposal to replace prerogative powers with a statutory framework would improve the present position' (*Government Response to the Public Administration Select Committee's Fourth Report of the 2003–04 Session*, 2004). However, see the more recent reform proposals detailed at section 11.9.2.

Lord Lester's (albeit unsuccessful) 2006 Constitutional Reform (Prerogative Powers and Civil Service etc) Bill would have placed executive (prerogative) powers under the authority of Parliament. Clause 4 of the Bill would have established a Joint Committee of both Houses of Parliament to keep under review, and report to Parliament, the circumstances in which executive prerogative powers were being exercised.

11.9.6 The constitutional relationship between the judiciary and the royal prerogative

It is clear that, owing to their residual nature, new royal prerogative powers cannot be created, as noted by Diplock LJ in *BBC v Johns (Inspector of Taxes)* [1965] 1 CH 32:

JUDGMENT

'it is 350 years and a civil war too late for the Queen's courts to broaden the prerogative. The limits within which the executive government may impose obligations or restraints upon citizens of the United Kingdom without any statutory authority are now well settled and incapable of extension.'

Pre-existing prerogative powers such as keeping the Queen's peace can, however, adapt to the contemporary system of preserving the peace through modern-day police forces (*R v Secretary for the Home Department, ex parte Northumbria Police Authority* [1989] 1 QB 26).

In historic terms, the supervision of prerogative powers by the courts amounted to recognising and demarcating their scope and existence (*The Case of Proclamations* (1611) 12 Co Rep 74), rather than investigating the manner in which they were used. The *GCHQ* case (1985) (see below), however, made it clear that the courts could legally supervise executive use of the royal prerogative in the same way that they reviewed the manner in which statutory powers were exercised. The *GCHQ* decision followed on from the earlier cases of *R v Criminal Injuries Compensation Board, ex parte Lain* [1967] 2 QB 864 and *Laker Airways Ltd v Department of Trade and Industry* [1977] 1 QB 643.

CASE EXAMPLE

Council of Civil Service Unions v Minister for the Civil Service
[1985] 1 AC 374

This case is commonly known as the *GCHQ* case. In 1983 the Prime Minister (Minister for the Civil Service) issued an instruction pursuant to the Civil Service Order in Council 1982 that staff at Government Communications Headquarters (GCHQ) would no longer be permitted to be members of trade unions. No prior consultation had taken place before the instruction was issued and the workers' trade union sought judicial review of the Prime Minister's instruction on the basis that she had a duty to consult those affected by it before issuing it (ie the duty to act fairly).

The House of Lords held that government action was not immune from the jurisdiction of the courts merely because it derived from the royal prerogative. On the facts, the claimants would have had a legitimate expectation of being consulted prior to the issuing of the instruction, however, this was trumped by national security considerations (ie the risk of industrial unrest had prior consultation taken place). It was for the executive and not the judiciary to decide whether on the facts of the case the requirements of national security outweighed those of fairness.

non-justiciable

an issue not suitable for resolution by the courts

The *GCHQ* case (1985) represents a watershed in terms of the prerogative as the House of Lords made it clear that the manner in which these common law powers were used was, depending on the subject matter, subject to supervision by the courts. Thus, some uses of the prerogative would be *'justiciable'* (reviewable) while, according to Lord Roskill, others would be **'non-justiciable'**. For example, the latter would include:

- Ministerial appointments.
- Making Treaties (see *Blackburn v Attorney-General* (1971) at section 11.9.3).
- The defence of the realm.
- The granting of honours.
- Mercy (but now see *ex parte Bentley* (1994) at section 11.9.3).

This category of *'non-justiciable'* prerogatives attempts to ensure a constitutional demarcation between the separate roles of the judge and the politician. In other words, these politically sensitive powers are considered unsuitable for judicial/legal adjudication. However, the political and parliamentary supervision in respect of the use of these powers may well be considered insufficient.

Finally, the last Labour government in its 2009 review stated that the scope of prerogative power was 'notoriously difficult to determine', as, although the courts decide (ultimately) whether such a power exists:

QUOTATION

'The difficulty is that there are many prerogative powers for which there is no recent judicial authority and sometimes no judicial authority at all.'
Review of the Executive Royal Prerogative Powers: Final Report (Crown Copyright, 2009), p 7.

KEY FACTS

Key facts on the judicial supervision of the royal prerogative
Historically, the courts confined themselves to demarcating the scope and existence of royal prerogative powers.
In the *GCHQ* case (1985) the House of Lords made it clear that the courts could supervise the manner of the use of royal prerogative powers providing the subject matter was appropriate (ie *justiciable*).
According to Lord Roskill in the *GCHQ* case some uses of the prerogative were not amenable to judicial adjudication.

11.9.7 The constitutional significance of the royal prerogative

It is clear that government needs powers which are analogous to the royal prerogative (eg to deploy troops quickly and to respond to international crises). The question is whether there is sufficient constitutional control (legal or parliamentary) over the use of these powers. Royal prerogative powers raise the following issues:

- **The rule of law** – Brazier (the specialist adviser to the Public Administration Select Committee below) has stated that:

QUOTATION

'Governments should not have imprecise powers. As a matter of basic constitutional principle the user of a power should be able – and if asked should be obliged – to identify the source of that power and to describe its nature and extent. Ministers should be required to do just that.'

Fourth Report of Session 2003–04, *Taming the Prerogative: Strengthening Ministerial Accountability to Parliament*, HC 422 (2004), p 24.

Historically, the constitutional concern in relation to the royal prerogative has been that there was no definitive list of these powers and their precise extent was not always clear (but now see the 2009 review at section 11.9.4).

- **Democracy** – The government of the day can make major political and constitutional decisions without (in law) approval from the democratically elected House of Commons.
- **Legal accountability** – Although today the courts will review the manner in which prerogative powers are used, this is subject to the proviso that such powers are *justiciable* matters and so suitable for judicial supervision (ie they do not involve issues of political policy). Furthermore, s 21(1) of the Human Rights Act 1998 prescribes that an Order in Council made in exercise of Her Majesty's royal prerogative is treated as primary legislation and so cannot be invalidated by the courts under the Act. However, the House of Lords in *R (Bancoult) v Secretary of State for Foreign and Commonwealth Affairs* [2008] UKHL 61 held that prerogative legislation is subject to judicial review on the three traditional grounds (on the grounds of judicial review, see Chapter 20). Nevertheless, on the facts of the case the prerogative legislation (British Indian Ocean Territory (Constitution) Order 2004) was deemed lawful. Almost a decade later, the Supreme Court dismissed an attempt to set aside this decision in *R (Bancoult (No 2)) v Secretary of State for Foreign and Commonwealth Affairs* [2016] UKSC 35. On judicial review of Orders in Council, see also *R (Barclay) v Lord Chancellor and Secretary of State for Justice* [2014] UKSC 54.
- **The separation of powers** – The principle of *justiciability* is a judicial construction. It ensures that the judges act in a self-restrained manner and do not trespass onto the function of the executive which has been constitutionally charged with the responsibility for administering public policy and making executive/political decisions. *Justiciability*, therefore, on the one hand preserves the separation of powers between the executive and the judiciary, but on the other hand it leaves certain uses of the prerogative legally unaccountable to the courts.
- **Political accountability** – Although ministers can be asked to account for the use of the royal prerogative, some aspects are exempt. In addition, as with legal challenges, the 2004 Public Administration Select Committee has pointed out that accountability to Parliament will come *after* the event as ministers are not legally required to inform Parliament before such powers are exercised. The then Labour government's response to the Select Committee's report made the point that government ministers were accountable to Parliament for the use of

prerogative powers, in particular through departmental select committees and the Prime Minister appearing before the Liaison Committee (see section 12.6.7). It also noted that the Select Committee had itself recognised that Parliament could overrule a prerogative power with primary legislation and so 'Parliament is by no means powerless in the face of the prerogative' (*Government Response to the Public Administration Select Committee's Fourth Report of the 2003–04 Session* (2004)). More recently, however, the 2007 Green Paper emphasised the importance of putting prerogative powers on a statutory basis (see section 11.9.2).

SUMMARY

- The executive refers to those who administer and execute the law. In the British constitution it embraces the following:
  - The political executive (HM Government) – including the Prime Minister, Cabinet and junior ministers.
  - The non-political/bureaucratic executive (the Civil Service) – civil servants implement the policies of their respective government ministers.
  - The executive in practical terms – the armed forces and various police forces.
  - Other executives – local authorities and executive bodies in the devolution settlements.
- The British constitution is hallmarked by a parliamentary executive whereby the executive is drawn from the legislature.
- The functions of the executive include:
  - To formulate and implement policies.
  - To implement and carry out the law.
  - To make specified appointments.
- The executive enjoys statutory powers to, for example, pass delegated legislation or bring primary legislation into force.
- The executive enjoys powers under the common law known as the royal prerogative.
- Parliament can limit prerogative power and the courts can supervise the manner in which they are used providing these powers are considered *justiciable*.

SAMPLE ESSAY QUESTION

What is the royal prerogative and what is its significance to the British constitution?

Introduction:
- Definition – common law (non-statutory) powers enjoyed by the Crown.

Types and nature:
- Queen's constitutional prerogatives (eg to grant the Royal Assent).
- Legal prerogatives of the Crown (eg the Crown can do no wrong).
- Prerogative executive powers (eg the deployment of the armed forces).

- Also note the general distinction between prerogative powers in the domestic sphere (eg the Royal Assent) and those relating to foreign affairs (eg a declaration of war).
- See the recent 2009 classification by the then Labour government.

The constitutional relationship between the prerogative and Parliament:

- Parliament can pass laws which limit, abolish or supersede prerogative powers (*De Keyser's Royal Hotel* (1920)).
- Recent proposals and reforms to give Parliament more control and scrutiny over prerogative powers (*The Governance of Britain* (2007) and the Constitutional Reform and Governance Act 2010).

The constitutional relationship between the prerogative and the courts:

- Historically the courts would simply recognise the existence and scope of prerogative powers.
- The *GCHQ* (1985) case made it clear that the courts could legally supervise the exercise of prerogative powers (though there were some *non-justiciable* areas).

The royal prerogative and constitutional principles:

- The rule of law (consider whether these powers are sufficiently clear and precise).
- Democracy and political accountability (governmental decisions made without the approval of the elected House of Commons).
- Legal accountability (note some powers are *non-justiciable*).
- The separation of powers (consider the constitutional relationship between the executive and the judiciary).

Conclusion

Further reading

Books

Barnett, H, *Britain Unwrapped* (Penguin, 2002), Chapter 2.

Barnett, H, *Constitutional and Administrative Law* (12th edn, Routledge/Taylor & Francis Group, 2017), Chapters 5 and 9.

Benn, A, 'How Democratic Is Britain?' in Sutherland, K (ed), *The Rape of the Constitution?* (Imprint Academic, 2000), p 33.

Bradley, A, Ewing, K and Knight, C, *Constitutional and Administrative Law* (16th edn, Pearson, 2015), Chapters 10 and 11.

Drewry, G, 'The Executive: Towards Accountable Government and Effective Governance?' in Jowell, J and Oliver, D, *The Changing Constitution* (7th edn, Oxford University Press, 2011), p 187.

Fenwick, H, Phillipson, G and Williams, A, *Text, Cases and Materials on Public Law and Human Rights* (4th edn, Routledge, 2017), Chapter 11.

Lord Nolan, 'The Executive' in Lord Nolan and Sedley, S, *The Making and Remaking of the British Constitution* (Blackstone Press, 1997), p 33.

Weir, S and Beetham, D, *Political Power and Democratic Control in Britain* (Routledge, 1999), Chapters 6–8.

Articles

Ryan, M, 'Sum of constituent parts' (2008) 158 NLJ 739.

Ryan, M, 'The Constitutional Reform and Governance Act 2010: The evolution and development of a constitutional Act' (2014) 35 *Liverpool Law Review*, 233.

Samiloff, J, 'Who should declare war?' (2008) 158 NLJ 565.

Papers

Bartlett, G and Everett, M, *The Royal Prerogative*, Briefing Paper 03861 (House of Commons Library, 2017).

Eighth Report of Session 2008–09, *Good Government*, HC 97–1 (2009).

Fourth Report of Session 2003–04, *Taming the Prerogative: Strengthening ministerial accountability to Parliament*, HC 422 (2004).

Hazell, R and Morris, B, *The Queen at 90: The changing role of the monarchy, and future challenges* (The Constitution Unit, 2016).

Internet link

www.gov.uk

12

Executive/parliamentary relations

AIMS AND OBJECTIVES

At the end of this chapter you should be able to:

- Understand the nature and significance of the constitutional convention of ministerial responsibility
- Understand the role and effectiveness of parliamentary scrutiny of the executive through questioning, debates and committees

Introduction

One of the central constitutional relationships in the British constitution is that between the executive/government and the legislature. As we have a parliamentary executive, one of the constitutional functions of Parliament is to scrutinise government ministers in respect of their policy, administration and actions (whether individually or collectively). In constitutional theory, therefore, ministers are both collectively and individually responsible to Parliament. Government accountability to both Houses of Parliament is secured through various parliamentary mechanisms such as questioning, debates and select committees, all of which are considered below. In short, Parliament acts as a political and constitutional check on the government and this is crucial in the absence of a codified constitution constraining the activities of the executive. The balance between Parliament and the government was described in the following way by the late Charles Kennedy MP:

QUOTATION

'An effective Parliament should be neither excessively obstructive nor excessively subservient.'

Hansard, HC Vol 353, col 1109.

12.1 The constitutional convention of ministerial responsibility

12.1.1 Classification

The convention of ministerial responsibility is, arguably, the most important convention in our uncodified constitution, as it purports to hold the government accountable to Parliament (on constitutional conventions in general see section 4.13). In broad terms, the convention can be divided into:

- The convention of *collective* ministerial responsibility.
- The convention of *individual* ministerial responsibility.

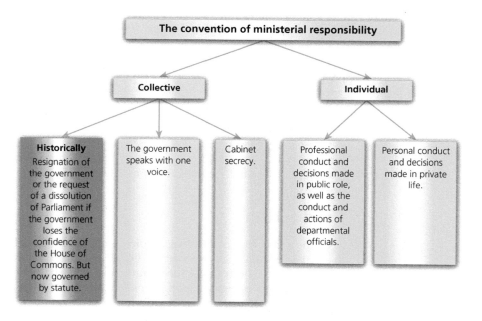

Figure 12.1 The convention of ministerial responsibility.

12.1.2 The *Ministerial Code*

The *Ministerial Code* sets out clearly the constitutional responsibility of government ministers in relation to the convention of ministerial responsibility:

QUOTATION

'b. Ministers have a duty to Parliament to account, and be held to account, for the policies, decisions and actions of their departments and agencies;

c. It is of paramount importance that Ministers give accurate and truthful information to Parliament, correcting any inadvertent error at the earliest opportunity. Ministers who knowingly mislead Parliament will be expected to offer their resignation to the Prime Minister;

d. Ministers should be as open as possible with Parliament and the public, refusing to provide information only when disclosure would not be in the public interest . . . '

Ministerial Code (Cabinet Office, revised January 2018), para 1.3.
Source: www.cabinetoffice.gov.uk.

The convention of ministerial responsibility should be seen in the context of the parliamentary mechanisms for holding the government to account (see sections 12.4 to 12.9).

It is worth noting that the convention of ministerial responsibility also applies to the devolved institutions. For example, in Scotland ministers in the Scottish Government are both collectively and individually responsible to the Scottish Parliament.

12.2 The constitutional convention of collective ministerial responsibility

In 1986 Geoffrey Marshall (*Constitutional Conventions* (Clarendon Press, 1986), pp 55–61) noted that in essence ministerial responsibility was composed of the following three elements:

- The government must resign or advise a dissolution of Parliament if the confidence of the House of Commons is lost (*the confidence rule*). NB: this element has now been overtaken by the passage of the Fixed-Term Parliaments Act 2011.
- The government is united and speaks with one single voice on policy (*the unanimity rule*).
- The discussions (and disagreements) within Cabinet should remain secret (*the confidentiality rule*).

12.2.1 The loss of the confidence of the House of Commons (now historical, as today this rule is governed by statute)

Historically, if the government lost a motion of no confidence, then by constitutional convention the Prime Minister would either recommend dissolution of Parliament in order that a general election could take place (which could, for example, result in a different government taking office as in 1979) or offer his resignation with that of the government. If the latter were to happen, it might have been possible for an alternative government to be cobbled together from the other existing parties in the House without the need for an election. The vote of no confidence was the only parliamentary mechanism for removing an unpopular government between general elections.

The practical reality of the convention however was that the motion of no confidence was rarely successful. In fact, in the past 100 years it has been successful only three times:

- 1979 Labour government.
- 1924 (January) Conservative government.
- 1924 (October) Labour government (the very first Labour government).

Three factors can explain why the vote of no confidence was rarely successful:

- The electoral system generally speaking (though not always) provided the government of the day with the support of the majority of seats in the House of Commons.

- Although recalcitrant government backbenchers may have been prepared to vote against the government on various legislative proposals, they would have been reluctant to vote against it on a vote of no confidence which would lead to the fall of that government.
- As an adjunct to the above, on a very cynical, but practical point, it is arguable that government backbench MPs may not have wished to trigger a general election mid-term, as there was no guarantee that they themselves would get re-elected.

NB. Today, this element of the convention of collective responsibility has now been placed in legal/statutory form by the enactment of the Fixed-Term Parliaments Act 2011 – see earlier at section 8.1.2.

12.2.2 The government speaks with one single voice

It is important that a government is seen to be confident and united over government policy. In contrast, a divided government which is split over major policies will be viewed as weak and lacking clear focus and direction. This principle, therefore, enhances the accountability of the government to Parliament because it avoids ministers disassociating themselves from policies with which they disagree or which have become deeply unpopular. Speaking with one voice (and voting the same way), therefore, requires individual ministers to defend publicly each other's broad departmental policies, as well as the overall strategy of governmental policy. Paragraph 1.3(a) of the 2018 *Ministerial Code* specifically requires all ministers to uphold the principle of collective responsibility.

The convention of presenting a united front raises the following issues:

- Although major governmental decisions will be taken in Cabinet, junior ministers not party to these decisions will still be expected to defend them publicly. Further, even Cabinet ministers themselves who were not party to a decision made in a Cabinet sub-committee (see section 11.2.3) will also be expected to support it.
- If a government minister disagrees personally with the policy adopted by the government, he must either:

  (i) resign from office. In 2003 Robin Cook MP resigned from the then Labour government over foreign policy in respect of Iraq and more recently, in 2014, Baroness Warsi resigned as Minister of State for Foreign and Commonwealth Affairs over the coalition government's policy in respect of Gaza; or

  (ii) accept the nature of collective Cabinet decision-making (ie that not all decisions made in Cabinet will be unanimous) and support that policy publicly, even though he has private reservations about it.

- Historically, the principle has been departed from in exceptional circumstances. For example, in 1932 it was set aside in respect of a national coalition government over the issue of tariffs. More recently, the convention was departed from in 1975 when the then Labour government was split over its attitude towards continuing membership of the European Economic Community (which the previous Conservative government had managed to secure). As a result, the incumbent Labour Prime Minister decided to set the convention aside for the purposes of an impending national referendum in 1975 on whether the United Kingdom should remain a member of the EEC. His justification was that this was a unique issue which divided the country as a whole (*Hansard*, HC Vol 884, col 1750). In addition to the above 'agreements to differ', ministers do not have to speak (or vote) the same way on free votes, for example on a moral/conscience matter such as the death penalty or the 2007 constitutional vote on the composition of a reformed

House of Lords (see section 10.13). Most recently, in 2016 in the context of the referendum on the question of remaining in the European Union, there was an agreement to differ whereby individual Conservative ministers were allowed to take a different position from that of the official policy of the Conservative government (which was to remain in the European Union).

The principle of collective responsibility can cause problems in the context of a coalition government composed of different political parties. For example, in January 2013 the then Leader of the House noted in relation to the debate and vote in the Commons on the amendment made by the House of Lords to the Electoral Registration and Administration Bill (the effect of which would be to postpone the review of constituency boundaries and so reduction of MPs to 600 – see section 9.2.1), that:

QUOTATION

'. . . the Prime Minister has responsibility for the Ministerial Code. Indeed, when ministerial collective responsibility is explicitly set aside, it is the Prime Minister who makes that decision. He is clearly doing it, as the House will understand, in the context of coalition government. As we know, that can give rise to occasions where there is not a collective view, and where by extension it is therefore not possible for a collective view to be the subject of collective ministerial responsibility.'

Hansard, HC Vol 557, cols 807–8.

In other words, there was no 'settled coalition view' on the issue of boundary reviews. In the event, the Lords' amendment was carried in the Commons with Liberal Democrat support (the Conservatives had opposed the amendment).

Finally, it has been recently suggested that:

QUOTATION

'The fact that collective responsibility can be set aside has led some academics to argue that it is as much a rule of political expediency – enforced by Prime Ministers when it suits them and discarded when it does not – as it is a convention of the constitution.'

M Everett, *Collective Responsibility*, Briefing Paper 7755
(House of Commons Library, 2016), p 3.

ACTIVITY

Exercise

Do you think that the Labour government acted unconstitutionally in departing from the convention in 1975, or does it just demonstrate that constitutional conventions can adapt to exceptional circumstances?

12.2.3 Cabinet discussions remain secret

It is a general principle that discussions within Cabinet remain secret. This enables all shades of opinion within Cabinet to be put forward freely (and without prejudice), safe in the knowledge that the nature and content of this discussion will not subsequently be disclosed publicly. The *Ministerial Code* is quite explicit on this point:

QUOTATION

'The principle of collective responsibility requires that Ministers should be able to express their views frankly in the expectation that they can argue freely in private while maintaining a united front when decisions have been reached. This in turn requires that the privacy of opinions expressed in Cabinet and Ministerial Committees including in correspondence, should be maintained.'

Ministerial Code (Cabinet Office, revised January 2018), para 2.1.

On the secrecy of Cabinet discussions see *Attorney General v Jonathan Cape Ltd* (1976) at section 4.13.12.

12.3 The constitutional convention of individual ministerial responsibility

At the outset, it is of interest to note that, in relation to the *Ministerial Code*, in 2011 Dr Liam Fox made the following personal statement in the House of Commons following his resignation as Secretary of State for Defence a few days earlier:

QUOTATION

'The Ministerial Code has been found to be breached, and for this I am sorry. I accept that it is not only the substance but perception that matters, and that is why I chose to resign.'

Hansard, HC Vol 533, col 923.

In essence the convention of individual ministerial responsibility is composed of two elements:

- Responsibility for conduct in a minister's public role as a minister of the Crown together with the actions of his departmental officials.
- Responsibility for conduct in a minister's private life.

NB. In two completely separate events within the space of a week or so in November 2017, two members of the Cabinet resigned: Sir Michael Fallon MP as Secretary of State for Defence and Priti Patel MP as Secretary of State for International Development.

12.3.1 Constitutional responsibility for professional conduct and departmental activity

Each Secretary of State will be head of a specific government department. As such, he will represent and defend that department in Parliament. Together with his ministerial team, he will answer questions during ministerial question time (see section 12.4.4) about the operation, policies and decisions made in respect of that department. In this way the Secretary of State will take the blame for errors or mismanagement that occur within his department and protect the anonymity of his officials (see section 11.3.1). Government ministers, therefore, are responsible not only for their own decisions and actions made as a minister but also for the actions of their departmental officials (see *Carltona Ltd* (1943) at sections 4.13.12 and 20.2.3).

12.3.2 Resignations due to ministerial decisions or actions made as a minister

Government ministers have to make executive and professional decisions for which they are responsible:

EXAMPLE

In 2002 Estelle Morris MP resigned from office as the Secretary of State for Education. She had previously, and publicly, committed herself to resigning if the government did not reach its literacy and numeracy targets by 2002. In addition, Morris also admitted that she was not as good a Secretary of State as she had been as an Under-Secretary of State.

In addition to the above:

- In 1988 the Minister of Health (Edwina Currie MP) resigned after her comments concerning salmonella in eggs.
- In 1990 the Secretary of State for Trade and Industry (Nicholas Ridley MP) resigned for inappropriate remarks made about Germany.
- In 1986 the Secretary of State for Trade and Industry (Leon Brittan MP) resigned following the leaking of a confidential letter from the Solicitor General.

12.3.3 Resignations due to the actions of departmental officials

The classic example traditionally cited in this context is the famous *Crichel Down* affair:

EXAMPLE

In 1954 Sir Thomas Dugdale MP resigned from office as the Minister of Agriculture. The issue concerned land ('Crichel Down') which had been acquired by the Air Ministry and then transferred to the Ministry of Agriculture (with the Crown Lands Commissioners subsequently administering it). Thereafter, a former landowner was refused permission to buy back the land and other landowners were not permitted to seek tenancies of it. An inquiry was established which criticised the handling by civil servants of this matter.

Dugdale subsequently resigned, stating:

QUOTATION

'I, as Minister, must accept full responsibility to Parliament for any mistakes and inefficiency of officials in my Department, just as, when my officials bring off any successes on my behalf, I take full credit for them. Any departure from this long-established rule is bound to bring the Civil Service right into the political arena, and that we should all, on both sides of the House, deprecate most vigorously.'

Hansard, HC Vol 530, col 1186.

Immediately following Dugdale's resignation, the Home Secretary (Sir David Maxwell Fyfe MP) reviewed the convention, which he stated comprised four categories:

■ Firstly, a minister must protect a civil servant who has carried out an explicit order.

■ Secondly, a minister must protect and defend a civil servant who has acted properly in accordance with a policy which has been set down by the minister.

■ Thirdly, '[w]here an official makes a mistake or causes some delay, but not on an important issue of policy and not where a claim to individual rights is seriously involved, the Minister acknowledges the mistake and he accepts the responsibility, although he is not personally involved. He states that he will take corrective action in the Department . . . he would not, in those circumstances, expose the official to public criticism.'

■ Fourthly, where a civil servant engages in actions which are reprehensible (of which the minister disapproves and had no prior knowledge), the minister is not obliged to defend what he believes to be wrong, or the errors of his officials. The minister is, however, still constitutionally required to 'account' (ie explain) to Parliament what had transpired 'and render an account of his stewardship'.

Hansard, HC Vol 530, cols 1286–1287.

Crichel Down, historically at least (although it has been subject to different interpretations), is regarded as the seminal example illustrating government ministers being responsible for the actions of their officials. However, since then it has been somewhat rare for ministers to resign in such circumstances.

12.3.4 Constitutional responsibility for conduct in a minister's private life

Government ministers are individually responsible to Parliament for personal conduct in their private lives (eg of a financial nature). As noted by the Nolan Committee:

QUOTATION

'The public is entitled to expect very high standards of behaviour from Ministers, as they have profound influence over the daily lives of us all. . . . Financial misbehaviour in particular matters to us all, because it strikes at the very heart of that confidence which people must have in Ministers and the motives behind their decisions. The same cannot normally be said of sexual misconduct. It is true that the private lives of Ministers may occasionally be relevant to the performance of their public duties, for example when their private conduct runs directly counter to some public policy, gives rise to embarrassing publicity, or involves a security risk.'

First Report of the Committee on Standards in Public Life, *Standards in Public Life*, Vol 1: Report, Cm 2850-I (1995), pp 47–48.

Following on from the Nolan Committee, the *Ministerial Code* states the following:

QUOTATION

'f. Ministers must ensure that no conflict arises, or appears to arise, between their public duties and their private interests;

g. Ministers should not accept any gift or hospitality which might, or might reasonably appear to, compromise their judgement or place them under an improper obligation.'

Ministerial Code (Cabinet Office, revised January 2018), para 1.3.

It could be argued that government ministers as individuals should enjoy absolute privacy in their private lives and that private activity should never be subject to public scrutiny. However, it can be argued more persuasively that a government minister's private affairs will be of public interest where these activities have an impact on his public role as a government minister.

Over the years there are a number of examples of government ministers resigning their office owing to actions in their private life. Most recently, in 2012 Chris Huhne resigned his position as Secretary of State for Energy and Climate Change immediately after he learned that he would be charged with perverting the course of justice.

Detailed below are two prominent examples of ministers resigning owing to actions in their private life:

In the context of financial activity

EXAMPLE

In December 1998 the following two ministers resigned:

- Peter Mandelson MP as Secretary of State for Trade and Industry.
- Geoffrey Robinson MP as Paymaster General (Treasury).

The latter had loaned the former money to help support the buying of a house. Mandelson later stated to the Committee on Standards and Privileges that the existence of the loan, which he had registered late, should have been made known to his Permanent Secretary 'so as to avoid the appearance of a conflict of interest' – which is why he resigned. Although he also argued that the House of Commons Register was not the only way to inform his Permanent Secretary (and others) of the loan.

In the context of sexual activity

EXAMPLE

In October 1983, Cecil Parkinson MP, the Secretary of State for Trade and Industry (he was also Conservative Party Chairman) resigned after it became known that he had made his former secretary pregnant. Parkinson was a married man.

ACTIVITY

Self-test question

Do you think that a minister's private life should always remain private?

KEY FACTS

Key facts on ministerial responsibility

Collective responsibility	• Government resignation or dissolution of Parliament if the confidence of the House of Commons is lost – now placed on a legal and statutory footing by the Fixed-Term Parliaments Act 2011.

	• The government is united and speaks with one voice on policy. • Cabinet discussions should remain secret.
Individual responsibility for professional conduct and actions of officials	• Actions as a minister (Estelle Morris). • Actions of officials (Sir Thomas Dugdale), but few resignations since.
Individual responsibility for private life	• In the context of financial activity (Peter Mandelson). • In the context of sexual activity (Cecil Parkinson).

12.3.5 Uncertain aspects of individual ministerial responsibility

The following four aspects of the convention are unclear:

▪ **The reality of modern government**

It is uncertain whether, practically, it is even possible for government ministers to be fully aware of what is going on inside their departments. Consider, for example:

● The size of modern government departments and complexity of modern-day administration.

● Frequent Cabinet reshuffles. Ministers tend to be transient as they will inevitably occupy their ministerial posts for relatively short periods before being moved elsewhere (either in or out of government).

▪ **Next Step Agencies**

The chain of accountability between government ministers and Parliament has in recent years been undermined somewhat by the emergence of the Next Step Agencies (see section 11.3.2), which are aspects of a department (like the Driver and Vehicle Standards Agency) which have been separated and reconstituted as an executive agency. These agencies have their own chief executives and are semi-autonomous in their affairs. In strict constitutional theory, however, according to para 1.2(b) of the *Ministerial Code,* ministers are to be held to account for the actions of their respective agencies.

▪ **Resignation**

When should a minister resign? Paragraph 1.3(c) of the *Ministerial Code* (and the parliamentary resolution which the Code incorporates) makes it clear that a minister who knowingly misleads Parliament should offer his resignation to the Prime Minister. In what other circumstances, however, is it an obligation?

Today this issue is not clear and it has been complicated by the distinctions made below in relation to accountability and responsibility. It seems from the pattern of resignations in recent decades that resignations tend to be concerned with personal misconduct in a minister's private sexual or financial life. In any event, the reality is that resignations are ultimately determined by extraneous factors (the unpopularity of the minister, the lack of support from the party and/or Prime Minister etc), rather than the actual event/decision in question. See also, S Finer, 'The individual responsibility of ministers' (1956) 34 *Public Administration* 377.

In fact, it is worth remarking that no ministers resigned in respect of the *Arms to Iraq affair* (which in turn led to the Scott Report). In short, this episode concerned the relaxation in the late 1980s of government restrictions in respect of export controls concerning the selling of equipment (which was indirectly militarily useful) to Iraq. Parliament, however, had not been informed of this change in policy by the government and the Scott Report concluded that Parliament had therefore been misled. In addition, the whole episode illustrated the limitations of parliamentary mechanisms of scrutiny as, for example, the House of Commons Trade and Industry Select Committee had had difficulty in getting full information from ministers.

In the wake of the *Arms to Iraq affair*, in 1997 the House of Commons passed a resolution (now incorporated within the *Ministerial Code*) setting out the responsibility of ministers to account fully to Parliament.

Two final points to note in relation to resignations are that:

- A minister may be reshuffled to another department before it becomes necessary to seek his resignation.
- Even if a minister does resign from government he may rejoin it at a later date. For example, although Peter Mandelson MP resigned in December 1998 (see section 12.3.4), less than a year later he had returned to the Cabinet as Secretary of State for Northern Ireland.

A distinction between accountability and responsibility?

In modern times the following distinction has been drawn (by ministers) between accountability and responsibility:

- Constitutional responsibility concerns ministers being personally at fault and culpable in some way (thereby being constitutionally *responsible* to Parliament).
- Constitutional accountability, in contrast, concerns ministers not being personally responsible (ie personally culpable), but remaining constitutionally *accountable* to Parliament to account for what has happened (also known as 'explanatory accountability').

Similarly, in recent years a distinction has also been drawn by ministers between:

- Being constitutionally responsible for general policy decisions.
- Not being constitutionally responsible (ie culpable) for their *operation* (ie the carrying out of that policy in a defective way).

For example, in 1984 James Prior MP as Secretary of State for Northern Ireland drew a distinction between being responsible for policy but not its implementation and so declined to resign for operational failures. Also, a decade later, Michael Howard MP as Home Secretary did not resign over prison escapes as these were considered operational matters in the Prison Service (see section 11.3.2).

This latter distinction is particularly controversial as it begs the question as to who is constitutionally responsible in such circumstances. It leads, arguably, to a gap in constitutional responsibility, with the relevant minister merely *accounting* to Parliament as to what has gone wrong.

Finally, it is worth noting that the House of Commons Liaison Committee made the following observation in 2012 about ministerial responsibility/accountability:

QUOTATION

'The old doctrine of ministerial accountability (by which ministers alone are accountable to Parliament for the conduct of their department) is being stretched to implausibility by the complexity of modern government and by the increasing devolution of responsibility to civil servants and to arm's length bodies. . . . The way ministerial accountability operates has on occasion been unacceptable, with ministers blaming officials for failures in their departments or in agencies for which they are responsible, but also with officials then refusing to answer questions which would indicate where responsibility for failure actually lies.'

Select committee effectiveness, resources and powers,
HC 697 (The Stationery Office, 2012), p 4.

ACTIVITY

Quick quiz

1. What is the difference between collective and individual responsibility?
2. What is the difference between individual responsibility for a minister's private life and individual responsibility for a minister's professional decisions?
3. In what circumstances is a minister responsible for the actions of his officials?
4. What factors militate against the operation of the convention (both collective and individual responsibility)?

12.4 Parliamentary questions

Introduction

Government ministers are asked parliamentary questions in both Houses and these questions can be either in written form (the overwhelming majority) or asked orally in either chamber:

QUOTATION

'The purpose of a question is to obtain information or press for action . . . '
E May, *Parliamentary Practice* (24th edn, LexisNexis Butterworths, 2011), p 358.

12.4.1 Oral questions in the House of Commons

Oral questions are questions set down for an oral answer on the Floor of the chamber. In essence, there are two types of oral questions:

- Oral questions to the Prime Minister.
- Oral questions to other government ministers.

12.4.2 Oral questions to the Prime Minister

Prime Minister's Question Time (PMQs) is the most visible and widely publicised manifestation of Parliament holding the government to account (whether it is actually effective is a moot point). It takes place each Wednesday for 30 minutes. The procedure at PMQs is that MPs can ask the Prime Minister an *open question* (eg 'If he will list his official engagements for that Wednesday'), but the real question is the *supplementary question* (which is asked without notice of the subject matter). For example, in May 2002 Charles Kennedy MP asked the following supplementary question:

'The Prime Minister acknowledged that the state of the railways today is worse than when he became Prime Minister. Will he address the obvious question: why is it that, five years after the shambles of privatisation, a Labour Government have not done more to redress the situation?'

Hansard, HC Vol 385, col 768.

NB. The 'engagements' question is only answered once (and at the start) by the Prime Minister at PMQs.

A good example of a question at PMQs was the one asked by the Labour MP William Bain in June 2013:

'In October 2010, the Prime Minister told the Conservative Party conference: "In five years' time, we will have balanced the books." That promise is going to be broken, is it not, Prime Minister?'

Hansard, HC Vol 565, col 298.

Questions about specific aspects of government departments (as opposed to the overall general tenor of government policy) should be directed to the relevant Secretary of State, rather than the Prime Minister.

12.4.3 The advantages and disadvantages of PMQs

Advantages

- Although the open questions have to be tabled a few days in advance, the supplementary questions do not require notice. In this way PMQs can be highly topical. In the absence of notice, a Prime Minister will be tested on their competence over a wide range of different governmental issues.
- On average the Prime Minister is questioned for two hours a month, in contrast to other government ministers, who are questioned on a rota for around one hour every five weeks.
- PMQs are a well-attended televised gladiatorial set piece at which the Prime Minister is visibly held to account by parliamentarians.
- A very poor performance by a Prime Minister in PMQs could affect their standing and perceived competence to govern both in and out of Parliament.

Disadvantages

- PMQs may be seen simply as a party point-scoring exercise where political comments are traded between party politicians. In this light they do not really achieve anything.
- The length of time available for questions is too short, the questions asked are too general and the answers are too brief (in contrast to written questions below).
- Sympathetic questions can be asked which draw attention to a positive aspect of government policy or achievements. For example, in October 2017 the following question was asked:

EXAMPLE

> Ranil Jayawardena (Conservative): 'May I commend my right hon. Friend for her pledge to build hundreds of new free schools? Does she agree that they are critical to drive up standards and increase parental choice, and is it not true that we are committed to creating a school system that works for everyone, while the Opposition want to hold everyone back?'
>
> Theresa May: 'My hon. Friend is absolutely right. Free schools have performed a very important function in raising standards . . . '
>
> *Hansard*, HC, Vol 629, col 332.

- Riddell (*Parliament under Blair* (Politico's, 2000), p 91) has suggested that the consolidation of two PMQ sessions to one (one of the first reforms undertaken by Tony Blair as Prime Minister) has resulted in a reduction in accountability. This is because the Leader of the Opposition can question/challenge the Prime Minister only once a week as opposed to twice (the overall time allocated, however, is still the same as previously).
- The Prime Minister will be fully briefed and informed by civil servants regarding possible and probable supplementary questions which may arise (eg an MP's particular interest).

ACTIVITY

Self-test question

Do you think that PMQs are an effective way of holding the Prime Minister to account?

12.4.4 Oral questions to other government ministers

All heads of government departments will be subjected to an oral question time session on a rota basis. For example, see the questioning of the Secretary of State for Health on 14 November 2017 (*Hansard*, HC, Vol 631, col 129). Oral answers can be shared between the team of ministers in the department (as in the above example). All government departments will be subjected to oral parliamentary questions approximately once every five weeks.

The procedure for asking oral questions is to submit them at least three days in advance. These are then shuffled and a number will be randomly selected to be asked. The answers to the main questions will be drafted by civil servants for ministers to approve. The Speaker of the House of Commons plays a pivotal role in oral questions as he determines the pace and the number of supplementary questions (which must be linked to the main one) that can be asked. In 2007, a part of ministerial question time was added allowing topical questions to be asked without notice of the subject (eg see the questions on 14 November 2017 above at col 146). Topical questions are somewhat analogous to PMQs (see section 12.4.2) in the sense that an MP will ask the minister an open question to make a statement on his departmental responsibilities, with the real question being the follow-up supplementary question.

12.4.5 The advantages and disadvantages of oral questions to ministers

Advantages

- It ensures that each government department (and so the government collectively) is publicly held to account for their actions or omissions approximately every five weeks. It is a direct way of holding the government to account as answers must be given.
- It enforces accountability as government ministers must demonstrate knowledge and competence in respect of their particular department and policies.
- Each oral answer (as with PMQs) is printed in *Hansard* and so is a printed public record which can be referred to in the future.

Disadvantages

- Ministers will be well briefed by their civil servants in respect of the main as well as the anticipated supplementary questions.
- Supplementary questions which are not sufficiently connected to the main question can be ruled out of order (also if they are *sub judice* etc).
- There is a lack of publicity concerning oral question time, other than for PMQs.
- Answers can be shared within a team of ministers and the rota ensures that they do not answer questions every week.

12.4.6 Written questions in the House of Commons

The vast majority of parliamentary questions are written rather than oral. This is due to the pressure of time on the parliamentary timetable as it would not be practical to expect ministers to provide oral answers to all, or even most, of the questions asked by MPs. The answers to written questions are printed in *Hansard*.

12.4.7 The advantages and disadvantages of written questions

Advantages

- MPs can be more persistent about a particular issue as MPs are permitted to ask more written questions than oral questions.
- Written answers to questions will tend to be more detailed, focused and informative (and arguably less elusive) than terse and somewhat general oral answers. For example, consider the highly detailed table of information provided on supply teachers to MP Sarah Teather's written question (*Hansard*, HC Vol 447, cols 2005W–2012W).
- It is arguable that written questions are more about seeking information than simply party point-scoring.
- Rogers and Walters (*How Parliament Works* (7th edn, Routledge, 2015), p 292) have noted that one advantage of written questions is that it permits MPs to ensure that a substantial amount of information is put into the public domain. In this way a valuable bank of public information is created (which we would not otherwise be

aware of). On this point it is worth recalling one of Parliament's functions as identified by Bagehot, that of educating and informing the public (see section 9.1.1).

- Government departments are monitored by Parliament to ensure that questions are answered in a timely fashion and are of the appropriate quality. For example, see the House of Commons Procedure Committee, *Written Parliamentary Questions: progress report for Session 2016–17, monitoring in the 2017 Parliament, and electronic tabling*, HC 661 (House of Commons, 2017).

Disadvantages

- Although answers are printed in *Hansard*, most people will be simply unaware of their existence.
- There are a number of ways in which an answer can be legitimately refused, for example if it concerns national security or commercial confidentiality or is simply too expensive to answer:

EXAMPLE

Chris Ruane MP: 'To ask the Minister of State, Department for Constitutional Affairs how many Orders in Council were passed in each of the past 30 years.'

Harriet Harman (The Minister): 'The information requested can only be provided at disproportionate cost.'

Hansard, HC Vol 443, col 1368W.

Similarly, in the House of Lords see the government's refusal to answer Lord Lester's written question concerning the pattern of compensation awards under the Human Rights Act 1998: *Hansard*, HL Vol 664, col WA191.

12.4.8 Oral and written questions in the House of Lords

As a number of government ministers sit in the House of Lords, questioning also takes place in the upper chamber. In this way the government is held to account in both Houses. Questions in the Lords are as follows:

- Oral questions – these consist of a minister answering oral questions together with supplementaries at the start of the day. Slots are reserved for 'topical questions'.
- Questions for short debate – this is in practice a mixture of a question and debate session whereby a minister answers the question in a speech. A pertinent example is where Lord Patten asked whether the then Labour government considered that Britain needed a written constitution (*Hansard*, HL Vol 664, col 1242). This was followed by an hour-long debate between members and was concluded by the Parliamentary Under-Secretary of State, Department for Constitutional Affairs. More recently, see the question and debate in relation to Brexit and an EU transitional deal (*Hansard*, HL, Vol 785, col 698).
- Written questions – as in the Commons, members of the Lords can request written answers to their questions. Members can ask up to six written questions per day and the answers are published in *Hansard*.

12.4.9 Urgent questions

Both Houses have procedures to enable urgent questions to be asked in exceptional circumstances on matters of public importance such as a major international incident. In the House of Commons the Speaker may allow such a question to be asked. For example, in March 2005 an urgent question was allowed regarding the nature of the Attorney General's legal advice to the government concerning military action in Iraq in 2003 – this resulted in the Foreign Secretary being asked a series of questions on this issue (*Hansard*, HC, Vol 432, col 1003). More recently, in April 2012 the Home Secretary was asked if she would make a statement in relation to the deportation of Abu Qatada. Following this statement, she was asked a series of questions on this issue (*Hansard*, HC Vol 543, col 507). At the time of writing, in November 2017 the then Foreign Secretary was asked an urgent question in respect of a British-Iranian national who was being held in jail in Iran. In his statement the Foreign Secretary said that:

EXAMPLE

'As I said in the House last week, my remarks on the subject before the Foreign Affairs Committee could and should have been clearer. I acknowledge that words I used were open to being misinterpreted, and I apologise to Mrs Zaghari-Ratcliffe and her family if I have inadvertently caused them any further anguish.'

Hansard, HC, Vol 631, col 23.

Urgent questions asked in the House of Lords are known as private notice questions.

KEY FACTS

Questions		
Type	**House of Commons**	**House of Lords**
Oral questions	• Oral questions to the Prime Minister (30 minutes weekly). • Oral questions to other government ministers (on a rota). • Urgent questions.	• Oral questions. • Questions for short debate. • Private notice questions (ie urgent questions).
Written questions	• Answers published in *Hansard*.	• Answers published in *Hansard*.

ACTIVITY

Essay writing

Do you think that parliamentary questions are effective in holding the government to account? Are written questions more effective than oral ones?

12.5 Parliamentary debates

Introduction

Debates concerning government policy, decisions and future intentions are a major way in which the executive is held to account by Parliament. The two Houses are, after all, debating chambers. In constitutional theory, debates allow members to probe and expose weaknesses in government policy as well as highlighting alternative policies/solutions. Ultimately, it forces the government to justify and explain itself in a more detailed way than through parliamentary questions.

12.5.1 Debates in the House of Commons

There are various ways in which debates can take place on government policy:

■ **Debate on a vote of no confidence** (see also section 12.2.1)

It is a key principle in our uncodified constitution that the government of the day must retain the confidence of the House of Commons. After all, elected MPs represent the people.

Historically if a government were to lose a vote of no confidence in it, a general election would generally be expected to follow as the House (as representative of the people) would have declared that it no longer had confidence in the government to govern the country. Not only would the government have morally lost the constitutional right to govern, but in practical terms it would be impossible for it to govern as it would be unable to secure the parliamentary passage for essential measures such as the Budget. The last government to lose a vote of no confidence was the Labour government in March 1979 (311 votes to 310 – *Hansard*, HC Vol 965, cols 461–590). This resulted in the May 1979 general election and the election of the Conservative government under Mrs Thatcher (who had tabled the motion of no confidence in the government as the Leader of the Opposition). Owing to the electoral system, which typically conferred a government with the support of a majority of seats in the Commons (together with the party machinery, which ultimately demands loyalty of MPs), such motions were rarely successful. Generally speaking, however, even though the vote of no confidence is arguably *the* most important constitutional check on the government – as it can remove a government during its term of office – it is rarely successful.

Today the Fixed-Term Parliaments Act 2011 has given legal effect to the loss by a government of a vote of no confidence in it – see section 8.1.2).

■ **Set piece debates on the Queen's Speech and the Budget**

The Queen's Speech heralds the start of a new parliamentary session and it will set out the government's proposed legislative programme. This will be followed by a debate of a few days in which the government's proposals in general (the precise details will generally not be available at this point) will be debated. Thereafter a vote will take place on the government's intentions and if this were to be lost it would represent a crisis of confidence in the government. The House of Lords also debates the Queen's Speech, but no vote is taken. In the context of the Budget (ie the tax proposals for the ensuing year) the Finance Bill will be debated and voted on by the Commons (as any other Bill) – see section 12.8.

■ **Opposition day debates**

Each parliamentary session, Her Majesty's Opposition is allocated 20 Opposition days (these were previously known as supply days) in which it can select the topic

Student mentor tip

'The best way to study this dense but interesting subject is to keep up with the news and watch some of the debates on BBC Parliament. Listen to *Parliament Today* on Radio 4 – it helps you relate theory to practice.'
Gayatri, University of Leicester.

of government policy for debate. In this way the Opposition can dictate the areas of government to be scrutinised and these debates are useful in exposing weaknesses in government policy. A highly pertinent use of one of these days was on 13 July 2000 (*Hansard*, HC Vol 353, col 1084), when the Opposition motion called for the introduction of reforms to reassert the authority of the House of Commons and reverse the undermining of Parliament. This echoes a prevalent theme in public law that in recent decades the constitutional balance between the executive and legislature has shifted far too much in favour of the former at the expense of Parliament (whose function is to supervise the government of the day).

A recent example of an Opposition day debate was on a proposed increase in the level of university tuition fees (*Hansard*, HC, Vol 628, col 849).

Debates in the context of an Early Day Motion

Early Day Motions (EDMs) enable a number of like-minded MPs to publicise and canvass support for specific issues. For example, in May 2013 a motion was tabled which deplored the coalition government's intention to award franchises for legal aid to a limited number of contractors (Reform of legal aid – No 36).

The parliamentary reality of EDMs is that they will not in general be debated but merely serve as a mechanism for expressing the views of groups of MPs of varying sizes (who can sign up to the EDMs) on a particular subject.

Other debates in the House of Commons

- General debates (including topical debates).
- Adjournment debates held daily.
- Debates on a substantive motion.
- Emergency debates (these are somewhat rare, but a recent example was in November 2017 on the issue of tax avoidance and evasion – *Hansard*, HC, Vol 631, col 157).
- Debates in the context of the scrutiny of legislation – see section 12.7.

(On debates in general see *Dods Handbook of House of Commons Procedure* (8th edn, Dods, 2011), Chapter 9.)

12.5.2 Debates in the House of Lords

Debates also take place in the House of Lords and it is often assumed that the quality and standard of these debates is higher than in the House of Commons owing to the existence of a wide range of (unelected) experts on various subjects. In addition, debates tend to be less partisan in the Lords because the party whips have less influence in the second chamber.

Debates in the House of Lords are as follows:

- Questions for short debate (see section 12.4.8) and also since 2013, topical questions for short debate.
- Motions for general debates (in effect in three types – on debates in general, see *Handbook of the House of Lords Procedure* (2nd edn, Dod's, 2006), Chapter 9):
  - (i) A 'motion to resolve' (ie to obtain the view of the House on a particular subject).
  - (ii) A 'motion for papers' (where a decision of the House on a subject is not required). NB: note the reform in 2011 for the House to discontinue debating 'motions for papers'.
  - (iii) A motion to 'take note' – for example, of the publication of a report:

EXAMPLE

Thereafter a two-and-half-hour debate followed on the report which was concerned with improving the legislative process.

- Debates in the context of the scrutiny of legislation (see section 12.7).
- Set piece debates on the Queen's Speech etc.

12.5.3 The advantages and disadvantages of parliamentary debates

Advantages

- They make the government justify their policies and explain their strategies, thereby enabling weaknesses to be exposed. They also provide backbenchers with the opportunity to challenge government ministers directly.
- Government ministers must retain the confidence of Parliament by demonstrating competence in their departmental area.
- They allow the Opposition to raise and explain alternative policies and provide an opportunity to influence government thinking or strategy.
- Debates become a matter of public record (they are printed in *Hansard*) and can inform and educate the public (see Bagehot at section 9.1.1).

Disadvantages

- Where a debate is followed by a vote (eg in the context of legislation, the Queen's Speech or a vote of no confidence), as the government of the day typically dominates the House of Commons it will inevitably win that vote. In this sense it could be argued that debates change nothing as, although the Opposition may 'morally' win a debate, it will invariably lose the subsequent vote.
- A number of debates, for example adjournment debates, may be sparsely attended. Although all debates will be printed verbatim in *Hansard*, many debates will not be widely reported by the media.
- In terms of information and resources, there is a clear imbalance of power between members (in both Houses) and government ministers. The latter have civil servants working for them providing them with invaluable information.
- There is limited time within the parliamentary timetable for full debates to take place (less so in the House of Lords, and the use of Westminster Hall has relieved some of the pressure in the Commons). Moreover, in the House of Commons the length of debate can be curtailed. For example, either a programme motion or a guillotine motion can be applied to the time which can be spent discussing and debating a Bill (see section 12.7.4).
- The question remains as to how influential parliamentary debates can be when it is arguable that the only political debate that really matters is the one in Cabinet (or more probably in a Cabinet committee) where government policy is being crystallised.
- Debates, particularly in the House of Commons, can assume a partisan party point-scoring exercise.

ACTIVITY

Exercise

Do you think parliamentary debates are effective in scrutinising the government?

KEY FACTS

Debates	
House of Commons	**House of Lords**
• Debate in context of legislation.	• Debate in context of legislation.
• Debate on a vote of no confidence.	• Questions for a short debate.
• Set piece debates on the Queen's Speech, the Budget etc.	• Debate on the Queen's Speech etc.
• Opposition day debates.	• Motions for general debates.
• EDMs.	
• Other debates in the House of Commons.	

12.6 The parliamentary committee system

12.6.1 Classification

Parliamentary committees are the key way in which Parliament can hold the executive to account. They can be divided into general and select committees (see Figure 12.2). In broad terms, public Bill committees (a type of general committee) scrutinise legislative proposals, whereas select committees are more investigative bodies which produce reports. It should be noted that, from the 2006–07 parliamentary session, standing committees were renamed general committees (with those standing committees scrutinising Bills being renamed public Bill committees).

12.6.2 Departmental select committees

Each government department is shadowed by a departmental select committee. In this way the range of government departments can be supervised:

Three examples of government departments and related select committees	
Government department	**Departmental select committee**
Ministry of Defence.	House of Commons Defence Committee.
Home Office.	House of Commons Home Affairs Committee.
Department of Health.	House of Commons Health Committee.

Table 12.1

Figure 12.2 The committee system in the House of Commons.

12.6.3 The function of select committees

QUOTATION

'Select committees shall be appointed to examine the expenditure, administration and policy of the principal government departments.'

Standing Order No 152. Source: www.publications.parliament.uk.

Select committees investigate issues (including collating evidence) and then issue reports on their findings. Their purpose is to supervise the activities, policies and decisions of their designated government department. In 2002 the Liaison Committee set out the following core tasks which select committees should seek to undertake (*Annual Report for 2002*, HC 558 (2003), p 9):

Core tasks of select committees

'Task 1: To examine policy proposals from the UK government and the European Commission in Green Papers, White Papers, draft Guidance etc, and to inquire further where the Committee considers it appropriate.

Task 2: To identify and examine areas of emerging policy, or where existing policy is deficient, and make proposals.

Task 3: To conduct scrutiny of any published draft Bill within the Committee's responsibilities.

Task 4: To examine specific output from the department expressed in documents or other decisions.

Task 5: To examine the expenditure plans and out-turn of the department, its agencies and principal NDPBs.

Task 6: To examine the department's Public Service Agreements, the associated targets and the statistical measurements employed, and report if appropriate.

Task 7: To monitor the work of the department's Executive Agencies, NDPBs, regulators and other associated public bodies.

Task 8: To scrutinise major appointments made by the department.

Task 9: To examine the implementation of legislation and major policy initiatives.

Task 10: To produce Reports which are suitable for debate in the House, including Westminster Hall, or debating committees.'

QUOTATION

'The overall effect of the core tasks has been to encourage select committees to carry out the full range of activities currently open to them.'

L Maer and M Sandford, *Select Committees under Scrutiny* (The Constitution Unit, 2004), para 22.

In 2012 the Liaison Committee revised the core tasks which they recommended committees take into account:

QUOTATION

'Overall aim: To hold Ministers and Departments to account for their policy and decision-making and to support the House in its control of the supply of public money and scrutiny of legislation

STRATEGY	
Task 1	To examine the strategy of the department, how it has identified its key objectives and priorities and whether it has the means to achieve them, in terms of plans, resources, skills, capabilities and management information.
POLICY	
Task 2	To examine policy proposals by the department, and areas of emerging policy, or where existing policy is deficient, and make proposals.

EXPENDITURE AND PERFORMANCE

Task 3   To examine the expenditure plans, outturn and performance of the department and its arm's length bodies, and the relationships between spending
and delivery of outcomes.

DRAFT BILLS

Task 4   To conduct scrutiny of draft bills within the committee's responsibilities.

BILLS AND DELEGATED LEGISLATION

Task 5   To assist the House in its consideration of bills and statutory instruments,
including draft orders under the Public Bodies Act.

POST LEGISLATIVE SCRUTINY

Task 6   To examine the implementation of legislation and scrutinise the department's
post-legislative assessments.

EUROPEAN SCRUTINY

Task 7   To scrutinise policy developments at the European level and EU legislative
proposals.

APPOINTMENTS

Task 8   To scrutinise major appointments made by the department and to hold
pre-appointment hearings where appropriate.

SUPPORT FOR THE HOUSE

Task 9   To produce timely reports to inform debate in the House, including Westminster
Hall, or debating committees, and to examine petitions tabled.

PUBLIC ENGAGEMENT

Task 10   To assist the House of Commons in better engaging with the public by
ensuring that the work of the committee is accessible to the public.'

Select Committee effectiveness, resources and powers, Second Report of session 2012–13,
HC 697 (The Stationery Office, 2012), p 11.

12.6.4 The composition of select committees

By constitutional convention membership is restricted to backbenchers and, historically, these members were proposed by a Committee of Selection. However, as a
result of recent reforms, they are now elected within their party groupings – these
names are then in turn proposed by the Committee of Selection (in 2017 renamed
the Selection Committee). As with public Bill committees, select committees will, by
constitutional convention, correspond with the party strengths on the Floor of the
House. As a result, the governing party will invariably have a majority of backbench
supporters on them. Each committee has historically elected its own Chair, but following recent reforms the Chair is now elected by the House as a whole. Over the
range of different select committees these positions as Chairs will be held by members of the main political parties. In terms of size, most of the departmental select
committees have a membership of 11.

12.6.5 The powers of select committees

■ **Specialist support** – Standing orders empower select committees 'to appoint specialist advisers to supply information which is not readily available or to elucidate matters of complexity'.

■ **Accessing information** (persons and documents) – In order to assist them in their work, standing orders enable select committees 'to send for persons, papers and records'. In essence, they have powers of investigation to:

(i) Request the attendance of a witness to provide oral evidence directly to the committee.

(ii) Request that documentary evidence be provided.

Although select committees can summon a witness to attend and give evidence (it would be contempt of Parliament to fail to do so), they cannot compel government ministers (or members of either House of Parliament for that matter) to attend. In essence, whether they attend is really a matter for Parliament as a whole to decide. Moreover, although technically a select committee can specify that a named civil servant attend, it is the government minister who will determine whether a civil servant will appear (and moreover, which one). Even then, the civil servant will be governed by the 'Osmotherly Rules' whereby:

QUOTATION

'Civil servants who give evidence to Select Committees do so on behalf of their Ministers and under their directions.'

Giving evidence to select committees, Guidance for Civil Servants
(Cabinet Office, 2014), p 4.

Furthermore, the above rules remind us that civil servants are directly accountable to ministers 'and that it is ministers who are accountable to Parliament' (p 4).

In general select committees tend to obtain the evidence (orally or in writing) that they seek. Two notable exceptions, however, include:

■ Edwina Currie MP (as Minister for Health) – she was initially reluctant to attend the Select Committee on Agriculture to explain her comments concerning the 'salmonella in eggs' issue. Although she did attend eventually, her attendance proved to be of little value.

■ The Maxwell brothers refused to give evidence to the Social Services Select Committee in respect of the alleged mismanagement of pension funds by their late father.

12.6.6 Select committee reports

Standing orders permit select committees 'to report from time to time'. The report is the essence of the select committee as it critically analyses the evidence before it and makes appropriate recommendations. These reports can be highly critical of government departments. By constitutional convention the government should reply to them within two months, however there have been concerns identified by the Liaison Committee about the timeliness of such replies (*Shifting the Balance: Unfinished business*, HC 321 (2001), paras 108–117).

In spite of the party political composition of select committees, it appears to be typically the case that their reports are unanimous. This makes a critical report of a government department all the more damaging as:

- It has been made on a cross-party basis.
- It is critical of the government notwithstanding that the governing party will ordinarily have a majority of support on the committee.

One problem with reports is that most are not debated on the Floor of the House. This is due to the pressure on the parliamentary timetable and a problem which is common to the other parliamentary mechanisms which aim to scrutinise the government. In each session a few days are set aside to debate select committee reports on the Floor of the House, while the rest of the debates take place in Westminster Hall.

12.6.7 Other select committees

There are a number of 'cross-cutting' non-departmental specialised select committees. For example:

- **Liaison Committee** – this comprises the Chairs of the select committees who meet to consider the work of the other select committees. Since 2002 the Prime Minister has agreed to attend this committee and answer questions (the current practice being three times a year).
- **Public Accounts Committee** – see section 12.8.
- **European Scrutiny Committee** – see section 12.9.
- **Public Administration and Constitutional Affairs Select Committee** – this considers reports of the Parliamentary Ombudsman (see section 21.3.4), issues concerning the Civil Service and constitutional matters.

12.6.8 Joint committees

There are also a number of joint committees which involve members from both Houses of Parliament. For example:

- **Joint Committee on Human Rights** – this considers, *inter alia*, remedial orders made by ministers under s 10 of the Human Rights Act 1998. In addition, it examines the nature and content of Bills with a view to highlighting any issues of human rights which their provisions raise (on the Human Rights Act 1998 see Chapter 17).
- **Joint Committee on Statutory Instruments** – this considers statutory instruments (see section 12.7.5).

12.6.9 Committees in the House of Lords

The House of Lords has its own separate system of committees. For the purpose of scrutinising the government the following are particularly important:

- **House of Lords Select Committee on the Constitution** – this committee is charged with the function of examining the constitutional implications of all public Bills (including, therefore, government Bills).
- **European Union Select Committee** – this committee considers European documents and other European Union matters (see section 12.9).
- **House of Lords Select Committee on Secondary Legislation Scrutiny** – (see section 12.7.5).

12.6.10 The advantages and disadvantages of select committees

Advantages

- They allow focused and in-depth examination of government departmental policy and activity in a way that is not possible through parliamentary questions or debates.
- As select committees are appointed for the duration of the parliamentary term (contrast with *ad hoc* public Bill committees), it enables their members to develop specialist knowledge in a specific area of government administration.
- They have discretion as to what they will investigate and how they will do so. Indeed, they can be very useful in investigating topical issues. For example, in August 2006 the Defence Select Committee issued a report on the situation in Iraq (13th Report of 2005–06, *UK Operations in Iraq*, HC 1241 (2006)).
- Select committees give backbenchers an enhanced role in holding the government to account and they tend to work on a non-partisan basis so that MPs of all political colours will work together as 'parliamentarians'. The cross-party political consensus of a report can prove particularly embarrassing for a government.
- Their reports, which contain written and oral evidence, provide useful public records of information on aspects of government policy (and other issues) which would otherwise not have been publicised. In addition, a report by the Constitution Unit has revealed that around 40 per cent of the recommendations of those select committees' studies were accepted by the government: M Russell and M Benton, *Selective Influence: The policy impact of House of Commons Select Committees* (The Constitution Unit, 2011), Executive summary).
- The reports of select committees can be used in the context of the legislative process to help inform and influence debate on the provisions of a Bill. For example, the House of Commons Public Administration Select Committee produced a useful and informative report on the Legislative and Regulatory Reform Bill as it was proceeding through Parliament (Third Report of Session 2005–06, *Legislative and Regulatory Reform Bill*, HC 1033 (2006)). Most recently, in November 2017 the House of Commons Exiting the European Union Select Committee published a report on the European Union (Withdrawal) Bill 2017–19 in order to inform MPs at the Bill's committee and report stages (*European Union (Withdrawal) Bill*, HC 373 (House of Commons, 2017). On the role of select committees in the legislative process, see M Russell and D Gover, *Legislation at Westminster* (Oxford University Press, 2017), Chapter 8.
- Their reports can inform and influence current political debate concerning, *inter alia*, the exercise of governmental powers and draw media attention to them. For example, in July 2006 the House of Lords Select Committee on the Constitution issued a report reviewing the government's use of the royal prerogative in times of war and put forward a number of recommendations (15th Report of Session 2005–06, *Waging War: Parliament's role and responsibility*, HL Paper 236-I (2006)). Also see the criticism of the government made by the Public Administration Select Committee for resisting the findings of the Ombudsman (see section 21.3.4).

- Governments, by constitutional convention, are expected to respond to reports, thereby forcing a government to explain itself in the wake of a highly critical report.
- Finally, according to the Select Committee on Modernisation of the House of Commons:

QUOTATION

'Our conclusion is that the select committees have served Parliament and the public well. They have enabled Members of Parliament to hold the Executive to account through more rigorous scrutiny than is possible on the floor of the House and they have brought before the public matters which otherwise might have remained concealed.'

First Report of Session 2001–02, HC 224 (2002), para 59.

Disadvantages

- In terms of their powers, select committees are the poor relation to the United States's Congressional Committees (Appropriation Committees) which can in effect withhold money from the administration if dissatisfied with departmental performance.
- On occasions select committees do not get access to the information that they seek. The *Arms to Iraq affair* illustrated the limitations of the select committee system to obtain information (see section 12.3.5).
- Its reports are mere recommendations, which a very confident government may be able to ignore. Select committees lack teeth because they cannot enforce their findings. Moreover, many select committee reports are not even debated, which results in a lack of publicity for their work.
- Although they are empowered to appoint specialist staff, it is arguable that select committees need more resources to assist them in their deliberations. In contrast, government ministers have the full support of their departments. In May 2002, however, the House of Commons did approve a resolution including extra resources for select committees (*Hansard*, HC Vol 385, col 648ff).

12.6.11 Recent reforms

In November 2009 the House of Commons Reform Committee published its report *Rebuilding the House* (First Report of Session 2008–09, HC 1117 (The Stationery Office 2009)). This in turn led the House of Commons, in February and March 2010, to agree to the following reforms:

- To provide for a reduction in the size of select committees to a standard maximum of 11 to make them more effective.
- To review the role, resources and tasks of select committees (see earlier at section 12.6.3).
- To allow Parliament to vote on September sittings.
- To engage the public more in relation to draft laws.
- To reform the petitioning system.
- To provide for the Chair (no longer Chairman) of select committees to be elected by the House.
- To provide for members of select committees to be elected (within their party groupings).

To provide for a Backbench Business Committee to schedule non-ministerial (ie backbench) business. An interesting example of a recent backbench debate was one on whether prisoners should have the legal right to vote at general elections (see section 9.6.3).

Although the creation of a House Business Committee was recommended by the above select committee, it has still not yet been established.

ACTIVITY

Quick quiz
1. What do select committees do?
2. What powers do select committees have?
3. What are the advantages and disadvantages of select committees in terms of holding the government to account?

12.7 Scrutiny during the legislative process

Introduction
The vast majority of Bills introduced in Parliament – which ultimately become law – are initiated by the executive (ie these are government Bills). These Bills will be subject to scrutiny by both Houses during the course of their various parliamentary stages. The consideration of a government Bill necessarily involves examining and scrutinising government policy as encapsulated within that Bill. Below is an overview of how the government is scrutinised during the law-making process.

It is worth noting at the outset that one of the criticisms made of primary legislation in recent years is not just the number of Bills which Parliament passes each year but the cumulative volume of these Bills. For example, the Constitutional Reform Act 2005 is over 300 pages long and contains 149 sections together with 18 Schedules. More recently, the Localism Act 2011 is almost 500 pages long, comprising 241 sections and 25 schedules. In addition, legislation can be passed expeditiously: see the Terrorist Asset-Freezing (Temporary Provisions) Act 2010, which passed *all* of its stages through both Houses in just five days. Most recently, the European Union (Notification of Withdrawal) Act 2017 completed all of its stages in both Houses in around seven weeks.

NB. On legislation, see the following useful guide: *Guide to Making Legislation* (Cabinet Office, revised July 2015).

12.7.1 Draft legislation
In recent years the government of the day has produced a number of Bills in draft in order that they can be subject to pre-legislative scrutiny. Although draft Bills have been published since the early 1990s, the practice of publishing Bills in draft has been slightly accelerated since 1997. It is argued that this produces better legislation as controversial or technical issues can be identified and discussed at this stage prior to the Bill being formally introduced into Parliament. Indeed, it offers a real opportunity to influence the government's stance on its proposed legislation before it takes final shape. One criticism levelled against the Constitutional Reform Bill in 2003 was that this highly significant Bill had not been subjected to pre-legislative scrutiny.

In contrast, parts of the July 2009 Constitutional Reform and Governance Bill had been issued previously in draft form (*Draft Constitutional Renewal Bill*, Cm 7342–II (2008)). More recently, in 2011 the coalition government issued its House of Lords Reform Bill in draft (albeit the fully fledged Bill was ultimately abandoned – see section 10.13). In fact, during the 2010–15 Parliament 35 Bills or clauses were published in draft (see R Kelly and S Priddy, *Pre-legislative Scrutiny under the 2015 and 2017 Conservative Governments*, Briefing Paper 07757 (House of Commons Library, 2017), p 4). In addition, the Investigatory Powers Act 2016 had also been issued in draft form during the 2015–16 session. In 2017 the House of Lords Select Committee on the Constitution produced a useful report on the preparation of legislation: *The Legislative Process: Preparing Legislation for Parliament*, HL Paper 27 (House of Lords, 2017).

12.7.2 The second reading

This permits the first opportunity for Parliament to reject a Bill with its general principles being debated and voted on (the first reading being a mere formality). Owing to executive dominance in the House of Commons, in general it is unlikely that a government would lose the vote on its Bill at second reading. One prominent exception was the Conservative government's defeat on the 1986 Shops Bill concerning Sunday trading. At this time Mrs Thatcher as Prime Minister had a commanding majority of support in the House and her defeat was due to a significant number of her own backbench MPs failing to vote in favour of the legislation. This illustrates that, no matter the number of seats a government has supporting it, ultimately it is the government's backbenchers who can thwart a government. This is the constitutional antidote to the 'elective dictatorship'.

12.7.3 The committee and subsequent stages

The committee stage

In the House of Commons the committee stage will typically take place in a public Bill committee which is composed of a small number of MPs (between 16 and 50). From the start of the 2006–07 parliamentary session the type of committees which were formerly known as standing committees were renamed 'general committees'. In particular, standing committees which were used to consider public Bills are now called 'public Bill committees' named after the Bill they are considering (eg the 2016 Digital Economy Bill Committee considered the Digital Economy Bill). The government minister sponsoring the Bill will be expected to defend it as it is considered in detail at this stage; however, a number of factors favour him:

- Firstly, by constitutional convention the committee will reflect the composition of the Floor of the House, inevitably, therefore, providing the governing party with a numerical advantage when voting takes place. At the time of writing, although the incumbent Conservative government was a minority administration, in September 2017 the House of Commons instructed the new Selection Committee to interpret Standing Order No 86 relating to general committees (ie public Bill and delegated legislation committees) to have the effect that, in the event that there is an odd number of committee members, the government should have a majority. The rationale behind this was to help the government to get its business through the Commons.

■ Secondly, the imbalance of power between the executive and the MP is illustrated by the fact that the minister will have a supporting team of civil servants to provide information. Indeed, historically, such committees, in contrast to select committees, were not ordinarily evidence-taking committees:

QUOTATION

'Consideration of a bill is confined to the words in the bill and members who wish to draw on the services of informed and affected bodies do so on a personal basis.'

14th Report of Session 2003–04, *Parliament and the Legislative Process*, Vol 1 Report, HL Paper 173-1 (2004), para 125.
But now see recent reforms below.

■ Thirdly, unlike their departmental select committee counterparts, public Bill committees are selected on an *ad hoc* basis and not for the duration of a parliamentary term. In contrast, permanent members of select committees develop subject specialised knowledge.
■ Fourthly, only members of the public Bill committee can make amendments at this stage.

As noted by the Select Committee on Modernisation of the House of Commons, standing committees (now public Bill committees) have been historically one of the most criticised aspects of the parliamentary law-making process. Indeed, in its written evidence to the above Committee, the Hansard Society stated that many people argue that standing committees:

QUOTATION

'. . . fall badly between several stools: they fail to deliver genuine and analytical scrutiny of the provisions involved, their political functions are neutered, dominated almost exclusively by government . . . they fail to engage with the public and the media (in contrast to select committees) and they do not adequately utilise the evidence of experts or interested parties.'

First Report of Session 2005–06, *The Legislative Process* HC 1097 (2006), Ev 108.

It should be noted that today, by virtue of House of Commons standing orders, a public Bill committee to which a Bill has been committed by a programme order/motion, 'shall have the power to send for persons, papers and records' (ie take oral and written evidence) Standing Order No 84A. This is analogous to the powers of a select committee – see section 12.6.5. Any evidence taken will help inform debate on the Bill in Committee. For example, see the oral evidence given on the Investigatory Powers Bill 2016 (*Hansard*, HC, Vol 607, PBC col 5). On improving public Bill committees, see M Russell, B Morris and P Larkin, *Fitting the Bill: Bringing Commons legislation committees into line with best practice* (The Constitution Unit, 2013).

In the House of Lords, the committee stage usually takes place on the Floor of the House, allowing all peers to be involved in scrutinising the Bill.

The committee stage and constitutional Bills

By constitutional convention, in the House of Commons a Bill of *first-class* constitutional importance would be committed to a Committee of the whole House, rather than to a smaller public Bill committee. Hazell ('Time for a new convention: Parliamentary scrutiny of constitutional Bills 1997–2005' [2006] PL 247) identified and examined the legislative process for 55 Bills considered to be constitutional between 1997 and 2005 (a period of dramatic reform of the constitution). He noted that there was a strong presumption that Bills of first-class constitutional importance (eg those dealing with devolution, referendums, Europe, Parliament and human rights) would be considered on the Floor of the House. In contrast, those Bills not counting as first-class (eg immigration, the court system and freedom of information) would be referred to standing committees. A second (intermediate) group of Bills (some first-class and some not) involving subjects such as elections, emergencies and Northern Ireland, would be considered by a mixture of standing committees and Committees of the whole House (with urgent Bills on these matters being taken on the Floor of the House).

As pointed out by Hazell, the advantages of consideration by a Committee of the whole House is that it allows more members (and a greater range of them) to contribute to the examination of the Bill. However, committee stages on the Floor tend to be shorter than those in a public Bill committee and as a result there is a limited number of amendments that can be moved and debated. Owing to its profound constitutional, legal and political significance, the European Union (Withdrawal) Bill 2017–19 was considered by a committee of the whole House.

NB. In 2011 a pilot 'public reading stage' was introduced in relation to the Protection of Freedoms Bill so as to allow the public to express its views on the Bill, which were then taken into account during the public Bill committee stage. The rationale behind this pilot scheme was to involve the general public in the legislative process. During the 2010–15 Parliament, two other government Bills received a pilot public reading stage.

Finally in relation to the committee stage, it is important to note that in 2015 in response to the 'West Lothian question' (see section 14.3.12), the standing orders of the House of Commons were altered to incorporate the new principle of EVEL (ie 'English Votes for English Laws'). In broad outline, where a government Bill will only affect and apply exclusively to England – and has been certified by the Speaker as an 'England-only Bill' – the committee stage will only involve MPs from England.

Report stage

This provides another opportunity to scrutinise the Bill and influence it by proposing amendments.

In terms of the EVEL procedure set out above, following the report stage on an 'England-only Bill', an English Legislative Grand Committee (composed of all MPs from England) must sit to approve it via 'consent motion' before the third reading (NB: in respect of an 'England and Wales-only Bill' the committee would be the English and Welsh Legislative Grand Committee). If approval of the Bill (or parts of it) is withheld, a 'reconsideration' stage of the whole House is held, which is followed by a second vote in the Legislative Grand Committee. If approval is still withheld, the Bill (or the disputed certified clause(s)) will fall. An example of the EVEL procedure being applied to legislation is the Telecommunications Infrastructure (Relief from Non-Domestic Rates) Bill 2017–19.

Third reading

This is typically a short session (although in the House of Lords amendments can be made). In the Commons only verbal amendments (ie to correct errors) can be made – although this is rare.

Royal assent

The final stage of legislation is where a Bill is converted into an Act of Parliament by virtue of the assent provided by the monarch.

Post-legislative scrutiny?

Although there have been improvements in terms of pre-legislative scrutiny of Bills in the Westminster system, the provision for post-legislative scrutiny of Acts of Parliament is much poorer. Two interesting exceptions are the post-legislative scrutiny afforded to the Mental Health Act 2007 (House of Commons Health Committee, *Post-legislative Scrutiny of the Mental Health Act 2007*, HC 584 (House of Commons, 2013)) and s 7 of the Fixed-Term Parliaments Act 2011, which provides for post-legislative scrutiny of the Act by a committee in 2020.

12.7.4 Procedural matters

The following factors favour the government in the legislative process:

- It controls the parliamentary timetable and the scheduling of Bills. In the House of Commons the government can use, for example, the guillotine motion (an allocation of time motion) to restrict debate and scrutiny of a Bill by providing that proceedings on the Bill end once a stated time has been reached. In the last decade, however, the guillotine has been overtaken by the introduction of 'programme motions' which are (theoretically) a more consensual and effective use of parliamentary time which formalises agreement on the timetable of a Bill between the frontbenches. Indeed, although the guillotine is still available, in practice today it is used when a Bill needs to complete all its stages in a single day in the Commons.
- As noted at section 10.10.1, under the Parliament Acts 1911 and 1949 the House of Commons (controlled by the executive), after it has sent a Bill to the Lords, can in any event ultimately reject any amendments made to it by the Upper House.
- A Bill which does not pass the requisite legislative stages within a parliamentary session will 'fall'. However, this has been mitigated in the past decade by the ' carry-over procedure', which allows a Bill to be carried over between parliamentary sessions, thus saving the Bill from abandonment. The Constitutional Reform Bill was an example of a high-profile Bill which was carried over (from the 2003–04 to the 2004–05 session).

There are some procedural differences in the way that the two Houses process legislation and these are indicated below:

- The committee stage in the House of Lords is (usually) taken on the Floor of the House, whereas in the Commons it usually takes place in a smaller public Bill committee.
- The government has control over the legislative timetable in the Commons, but not in the Lords.
- Unlike the Commons, in the Lords all amendments can (in theory and practice) be scrutinised.
- Unlike the Commons, debates in the House of Lords are not subject to the guillotine.

Overall, it would appear that the balance between the government of the day wishing to see its proposals enacted as law, and Parliament, whose role is to subject them to rigorous and detailed scrutiny, still clearly favours the executive. In short, if a government is determined enough, it can ensure that its proposals become law irrespective of the criticism levelled at it.

NB. In 2013 the House of Commons Political and Constitutional Reform Committee issued a report in which it argued that there was a need for improvement in the quality of legislation and put forward a number of recommendations including, *inter alia,* a set of standards for good-quality legislation which would be agreed between the government and Parliament – *Ensuring Standards in the Quality of Legislation,* HC 85 (The Stationery Office, 2013).

12.7.5 Delegated legislation

As indicated at section 5.7.2, when government ministers exercise a power to make delegated legislation they violate the principle of the separation of powers. As a consequence of this, there are a number of parliamentary controls over its use. Delegated legislation will typically be made in the form of a statutory instrument and so will be governed by the Statutory Instruments Act 1946. It should be pointed out that statutory instruments are now accompanied by an explanatory memorandum to explain their nature and aid understanding. This should be seen in the context of the rule of law at section 6.3.2, which requires that laws should be accessible and clear.

The enabling Act will indicate the type of scrutiny the delegated measure made under it is to receive from Parliament. In essence, the Act may state that the instrument:

- is *not* required to be laid before Parliament.
- is simply laid before Parliament. This means that Parliament's attention is simply drawn to it.
- is subject to a negative resolution, which means that it is laid before Parliament and is subject to annulment by it within 40 days. In other words, the instrument will become law *unless* Parliament objects to it.
- is subject to an affirmative resolution, which means that it is laid before Parliament, but will not come into force unless it is assented to. In other words, Parliament has to *approve* it in order for it to come into effect. A variant on this is that it is laid and comes into effect immediately, but requires positive approval (eg within 28 days) in order to carry on in force.
- is laid in draft form (with a positive or negative resolution).
- is subject to what has been termed a 'super affirmative' procedure (involving 60-day periods). For example, see the remedial orders made under s 10 of the Human Rights Act 1998 used in order to remedy an incompatibility with the European Convention on Human Rights (see section 17.7.3).

In addition, the following committees have a role to play in the scrutiny of delegated legislation:

The Joint Committee on Statutory Instruments

This Joint Committee, comprising members of both Houses, is responsible for scrutinising all statutory instruments. Under Standing Order 151 it can draw Parliament's attention to an instrument which, *inter alia*:

- Imposes a charge/tax.
- Purports to have a retrospective effect.
- Appears to be *ultra vires*.
- Exhibits defective drafting.

Those instruments which only have to be laid before the House of Commons are scrutinised by the House of Commons Select Committee on Statutory Instruments.

In essence, the Joint Committee examines the technical qualities of statutory instruments, rather than the merits or policy behind them.

The House of Lords Select Committee on Secondary Legislation Scrutiny

This was established in 2003 and it draws the attention of the House of Lords to a statutory instrument (subject to a positive or negative resolution) laid which, *inter alia,* raises issues of public policy or does not perfectly achieve its policy objectives. Unlike the Joint Committee above, this Committee considers the policy implications of statutory instruments.

The House of Lords Select Committee on Delegated Powers and Regulatory Reform

This committee considers whether:

- any enabling Bill proposes to delegate legislative power inappropriately (for a recent report, see earlier at section 5.7.2 in respect of the European Union (Withdrawal) Bill 2017–19), or
- the proposed parliamentary scrutiny of the delegated legislation to be made under the Act is inappropriate (ie it is insufficient). The Committee also reports on draft Legislative Reform Orders laid before Parliament under the aegis of the Legislative and Regulatory Reform Act 2006 (see section 7.5.7) and the Commons has a similar Committee (the Regulatory Reform Committee).

Delegated Legislation Committees

(see directly below)

The constitutional issues raised by delegated legislation

Firstly, each year statutory instruments statistically outnumber Acts of Parliament. For example, in 2015, 37 public general Acts gained Royal Assent, in contrast to the 2,059 statutory instruments which were made (V Apostolova, *Acts and Statutory Instruments: The volume of UK legislation 1950 to 2016,* Briefing Paper CBP7438 (House of Commons Library, 2017), p 7). Most domestic legislation, therefore, is not primary and so not directly made by the legislature (ie Parliament). Indeed, the House of Lords Select Committee on Delegated Powers and Regulatory Reform recently reiterated that 'Ministers already make considerably more law than Parliament' and that the European Union (Withdrawal) Bill 2017–19 was 'expected to generate another 800 to 1,000 statutory instruments in the near future' (*European Union (Withdrawal) Bill,* HL Paper 22 (House of Lords, 2017), para 5).

Secondly, it must be remembered that it is the government of the day which will draft the enabling Bill. This means that (unless the Bill is amended) it will determine the degree of parliamentary control and supervision that is to be exercised over government ministers making statutory instruments under the enabling legislation. It is, therefore, not surprising that the vast majority of statutory instruments subject to parliamentary supervision are *not* subject to a positive resolution.

Thirdly, parliamentary time is limited and negative resolutions rely on the willingness of parliamentarians to examine instruments subject to this procedure. This is another reason why positive resolutions are not used often.

Fourthly, debates in the Commons on statutory instruments may take place on the Floor of the House or, much more likely, in a delegated legislation committee – a type of general committee (formerly known as a standing committee). For an example, see the 2013 Fifth Delegated Legislation Committee, which considered the Draft Public Bodies (Abolition of Administrative Justice and Tribunals Council)

Order 2013, which proposed to abolish this advisory council. More recently, see the 2016 Second Delegated Legislation Committee which examined the Draft European Union Referendum (Conduct) Regulations 2016 which concerned the procedural framework of the administration of the impending referendum on the European Union (see Brexit at section 15.6.6).

Finally, as observed by the Select Committee on Modernisation of the House of Commons:

QUOTATION

Indeed, in the 2015–16 parliamentary session, whereas 757 statutory instruments were laid before the House of Commons, only 20 were considered in the House and 103 in committee (V Apostolova, *Acts and Statutory Instruments: The volume of UK legislation 1950 to 2016*, Briefing Paper CBP7438 (House of Commons Library, 2017), p 12).

NB. The EVEL procedure in the House of Commons, set out at section 12.7.3, also applies to secondary legislation.

KEY FACTS

Committees	
Departmental select committees	Appointed for each parliamentary term to supervise the activities, policies and decisions of their designated government department. Investigate issues, collate evidence and issue reports on their findings.
Public Bill committees	Appointed on an *ad hoc* basis to examine in detail the contents of proposed legislation.
Joint committees	Comprise members of both Houses to consider specific issues (eg the Joint Committee on Statutory Instruments).

ACTIVITY

Essay writing

Compare and contrast how primary and delegated legislation is scrutinised by Parliament. How effective is that scrutiny?

12.8 Scrutiny in the context of finance

Below is a very brief outline of how government is scrutinised in financial matters. It should be noted that financial matters are in essence determined by the House of Commons as it contains elected representatives.

Past expenditure

In terms of public money spent, government departments are monitored by the most important select committee in the House of Commons: the Public Accounts Committee. It scrutinises government expenditure (in terms of value for money) through the examination of audits/reports made by the Comptroller and Auditor General of the National Audit Office. This scrutiny involves assessing the efficiency of government spending and whether it has been used for the purposes authorised by Parliament. Each session Parliament will set aside a day to debate the reports made by the Public Accounts Committee.

Future taxation/expenditure

In particular, this will involve the raising of taxes in the form of the annual Budget (the Finance Bill), which will be debated and voted on in one of the major set piece debates in the parliamentary calendar. It should be remembered that under Art 4 of the Bill of Rights 1689 Parliament must authorise the raising of money/taxation. In addition, the government will supply estimates (requests for specified money) and these are approved annually by Parliament via a Supply and Appropriation (Main Estimates) Act. Finally, it is worth noting that the Budget Responsibility and National Audit Act 2011 provided for the establishment on a statutory footing, of the Office for Budget Responsibility to report on public finances/sustainability (including economic forecasts).

NB. The EVEL procedure in the House of Commons, set out at section 12.7.3, also applies to finance Bills.

12.9 Scrutiny in the context of Europe

Government ministers attend meetings of the Council (Council of Ministers – which is the legislature of the European Union) and can commit the United Kingdom to European legislative proposals. Parliament provides extensive provision for the consideration of these European legislative proposals. In brief, two parliamentary committees perform this function:

- **The House of Commons European Scrutiny Committee** – which examines the political and legal significance of European documents (ie proposals and draft European legislation) and the government's policy on them. In addition, it monitors the actions of British ministers in the Council and produces reports. There are three European Committees, A–C (types of general committees), which consider European documents recommended by the European Scrutiny Committee for debate. For example, Committee C considers, *inter alia*, business matters.
- **The House of Lords European Union Select Committee** – which scrutinises government actions/policies towards the European Union, together with examining European policies and draft legislation. The Committee has six sub-committees, for example the EU Justice Sub-Committee.

These two committees complement one another, with the House of Lords Committee being more selective and detailed in its treatment of European documents than its more wide-ranging counterpart in the Commons.

As noted by the Wakeham Commission:

QUOTATION

'The United Kingdom Parliament already has one of the most highly developed systems in the EU for considering proposed European legislation and other proposals and for ensuring that Ministers are aware of the balance of opinion within Parliament before they commit the United Kingdom to any significant new position.'

A House for the Future, Cm 4534 (2000), p 83.

In particular, the House of Commons European Scrutiny Committee will scrutinise government ministers (largely through written reports) before and after they attend sessions of the Council (Council of Ministers). In the Council, ministers are able to commit the United Kingdom to legislative proposals and so it is imperative that government ministers are scrutinised effectively. The House of Commons's 1998 *scrutiny reserve resolution* constrains a government minister from committing the United Kingdom in the Council, if the matter has *not* cleared scrutiny by the European Scrutiny Committee (or it is awaiting consideration by the Commons which has not yet agreed a resolution). The scrutiny reserve resolution also applies to the House of Lords European Union Select Committee. A minister can, however, give agreement where for example the proposal is 'trivial'.

NB. As a result of Brexit (see section 15.6.6), the House of Commons Select Committee on Exiting the European Union was established to shadow and monitor the Department for Exiting the European Union (including the newly created office of Secretary of State for Exiting the European Union).

SUMMARY

- One of the central relationships in the British constitution is that between the executive and the legislature.
- The government is held to account by Parliament by the conventions of individual and collective responsibility.
- Collective responsibility involves:
  - Historically, if a government lost a vote of no confidence in it, either Parliament was dissolved or the government resigned office – today this is governed under the legal arrangements of the Fixed-Term Parliaments Act 2011.
  - The government speaking with one voice.
  - Cabinet discussions remaining secret.
- Individual responsibility involves:
  - A minister being responsible for his public role/decisions and the actions of his officials.
  - A minister being responsible for his decisions/actions taken in his private life.
- Government is held to account through the following parliamentary mechanisms:
  - Ministers are asked parliamentary questions in both Houses, with the most famous type of questioning being Prime Minister's Question Time.
  - Debates are held in both Houses concerning government policy and decisions.
  - Departmental select committees shadow government departments and examine their actions, policies and decisions.
  - During the legislative process both Houses scrutinise Bills.
  - Scrutiny of financial (performed by the Commons) and European matters.

SAMPLE ESSAY QUESTION

How does the legislature hold the executive to account?

Introduction:
- Constitutional function of the legislature is to supervise the actions of, and hold to account, the executive/government.
- Link with the convention of ministerial responsibility.

Legislation:
- Primary (debates and votes during the various parliamentary stages in both Houses – though note the typical government dominance in the Commons and control of its timetable).
- Secondary (note the important committee work, eg the Joint Committee on Statutory Instruments).

Parliamentary committees:
- Departmental select committees attached to each government department and responsible for examining its administration and policies.
- Specialist committees (eg the Public Accounts Committee, which examines government expenditure).
- Public Bill committees examine proposed legislation.

Parliamentary debates and questions:
- Set piece (eg on the Budget or the Queen's Speech).
- Opposition days.
- Debates in the House of Lords.
- Vote of no confidence.
- Parliamentary questions (both oral and written).

Conclusion

Further reading

Books

Fox, R and Korris, M, *Making Better Law* (Hansard Society, 2010).

Horne, A and Le Sueur, A (eds), *Parliament: Legislation and Accountability* (Hart Publishing, 2016).

Marshall, G, *Constitutional Conventions* (Oxford, Clarendon Press, 1986), Chapters 4, 6, 13 and 14.

'Parliament and Executive Accountability' in Blick, A, *The Codes of the Constitution* (Hart Publishing, 2016), p 173.

Rogers, R and Walters, R, *How Parliament Works* (7th edn, Routledge, 2015).

Russell, M and Gover, D, *Legislation at Westminster* (Oxford University Press, 2017).

Weir, S and Beetham, D, *Political Power and Democratic Control in Britain* (Routledge, 1999), Chapters 12–14.

For a fascinating account of government mistakes, see King, A and Crewe, I, *The Blunders of our Governments* (Oneworld, 2014).

Articles

Greenberg, D, 'Dangerous trends in modern legislation' [2015] PL 96.

Lord Hailsham, 'Elective dictatorship', *The Listener* (1976), 21 October, p 496.

Hazell, R, 'Time for a New Convention: Parliamentary Scrutiny of Constitutional Bills 1997–2005' [2006] PL 247.

McEldowney, J, 'JAG Griffith: Parliament and legislation' [2014] PL 85.

Russell, M, Gover, D and Wollter, K, 'Does the executive dominate the Westminster legislative process? Six reasons for doubt' (2016) 69 *Parliamentary Affairs* 1.

Papers

Everett, M, *Collective Responsibility*, Briefing Paper 7755 (House of Commons Library, 2016).

Gay, O and Powell, T, *Individual Ministerial Responsibility – Issues and Examples*, 04/31 (House of Commons Library, 2004).

House of Commons Select Committee on Modernisation of the House of Commons, *The Legislative Process*, HC 1097 (The Stationery Office, 2006).

Maer, L and Sandford, M, *Select Committees under Scrutiny* (The Constitution Unit, 2004).

Maer, L, Gay, O and Kelly, R, *The Departmental Select Committee System*, 09/55 (House of Commons Library, 2009).

Sandford, M, *Parliamentary Questions: Recent issues*, Briefing Paper 04148 (House of Commons Library, 2015).

Scott, E, *Ministerial Collective Responsibility and Agreement to Differ: Recent developments*, LLN 2016/012 (House of Lords Library Note, 2016).

Winetrobe, B, *Shifting Control? Aspects of the executive–parliamentary relationship*, 00/92 (House of Commons Library, 2000).

Internet link

www.parliament.uk

13

The judiciary

At the end of this chapter you should be able to:

- Understand the principle of judicial independence and impartiality
- Appreciate the constitutional position of the judiciary

13.1 Introduction and definition

QUOTATION

'The public must have confidence in the impartiality, fairness and independence of the judiciary; otherwise they will be less likely to observe the law.'

Lord Woolf, *Shaping the Future*, www.dca.gov.uk (Crown Copyright, 13 October 2004).

JUDGMENT

'The rule of law requires that judicial tribunals established to resolve issues arising between citizen and citizen, or between the citizen and the state, should be independent and impartial. This means that such tribunals should be in a position to decide such issues on their legal and factual merits as they appear to the tribunal, uninfluenced by any interest, association or pressure extraneous to the case.'

Lord Bingham, *Davidson v Scottish Ministers* [2004] UKHL 34.

The independence and impartiality of the judiciary is a central element of any democratic constitution and, as noted at section 3.4.9, it is a key characteristic of Britain's uncodified constitution. The constitutional function of the judiciary is to provide for the resolution of constitutional/legal disputes and determine the law laid down in both statutory and common law sources. Although there is a close connection between the two terms and they are often used synonymously, it is common to draw a technical distinction between judicial independence and judicial impartiality:

■ Judicial independence means that the judges are structurally separate from both the legislature and executive. In this way they can perform their judicial function strictly in accordance with the law, free from any extraneous pressure from the executive or legislative to determine a case before them in a particular way.

■ Judicial impartiality means that judges perform their judicial function in a strictly impartial manner without any preconceptions or prejudgement based on class, sex, education, etc.

In this way judges can make independent and impartial decisions.

13.2   The constitutional dimension of the judiciary

The independence and impartiality of the judiciary must be viewed in the light of the following constitutional principles/concepts:

13.2.1   The separation of powers

JUDGMENT

'Just as the courts must apply Acts of Parliament whether they approve of them or not, and give effect to lawful official decisions whether they agree with them or not, so Parliament and the executive must respect judicial decisions, whether they approve of them or not, unless or until they are set aside.'

Lord Bingham, *Re McFarland* [2004] UKHL 17.

As indicated in Chapter 5, the British constitution does not follow a strict separation of powers. In terms of personnel, however, there has been a general separation between the judiciary on the one hand and the executive/legislative arms of the state on the other (s 1 of the House of Commons Disqualification Act 1975 prohibits full-time judges sitting in the House of Commons). Historically, however, there have been two prominent exceptions:

■ **The Lord Chancellor** (an overlap of the judiciary, executive and legislature).
Before 2003 the Lord Chancellor sat as a senior judge, was a member of the Cabinet as a senior ranking government minister and (by constitutional convention) was a member of the Upper House in Parliament where he performed the functions of both Speaker and a senior government spokesperson. As indicated at section 5.7.9, the Constitutional Reform Act 2005 has now reformed the office so that the Lord Chancellor no longer:
  (i) acts as a senior judge (in any event, in 2003 Lord Falconer as Lord Chancellor indicated that he would no longer sit as a judge); and
  (ii) acts as the head of the Judiciary of England and Wales. Under s 7 of the Constitutional Reform Act 2005 the Lord Chief Justice became President of the Courts of England and Wales as well as head of the judiciary and responsible, *inter alia*, for representing the views of the judiciary in England and Wales (s 5).

■ **The law lords** (an overlap of the judiciary and legislature).
Part 3 of the Constitutional Reform Act 2005 (which came into effect in 2009) barred serving law lords from the upper chamber of Parliament and reconstituted them in a constitutionally and physically separate Supreme Court (see section 5.7.10).

In terms of the judicial function, although historically this role has been performed by judges, the following points need to be noted:

- **Tribunals** – The strict, formalised court system is supplemented by a system of tribunals (see section 21.1). These tribunals were historically not staffed by judges *per se* (although some were), but they did perform an essentially judicial function in applying legal rules to factual disputes (sometimes highly specialised and technical, eg employment tribunals). The Tribunals, Courts and Enforcement Act 2007 which reformed the tribunal system now provides that legal members of tribunals (ie the legally qualified members) are designated as tribunal judges.
- **The executive performing judicial functions** – The executive, in the form of the Home Secretary, historically enjoyed the power to determine sentences (a judicial function) to be served by persons sentenced to life imprisonment:

CASE EXAMPLE

R (Anderson) v Secretary of State for Home Department *[2002] UKHL 46*

Section 29 of the Crime (Sentences) Act 1997 empowered the Home Secretary to determine the tariff (for punitive purposes) to be served by persons convicted of murder. Anderson sought judicial review of the tariff set by the minister under the Human Rights Act 1998.

The House of Lords made a declaration of incompatibility that s 29 of the 1997 Act was incompatible with Art 6 (the right to a fair trial). In brief, the determination of a prison sentence was a judicial function and Art 6 required such a sentence to be decided by an independent and impartial tribunal. The Home Secretary was not independent of the executive (in fact, he was a key member of the Cabinet). Referring to the jurisprudence of the European Court of Human Rights, Lord Bingham observed that:

JUDGMENT

'The European Court was right to describe the complete functional separation of the judiciary from the executive as "fundamental", since the rule of law depends on it.'

As a result of the declaration, the Criminal Justice Act 2003 now provides for the tariff (minimum) term for those sentenced to life imprisonment to be determined by the judiciary, and not the Home Secretary. This realigned the constitution so as to accord with a stricter separation of powers.

In discharging their judicial function, as indicated at section 5.7.4, inevitably judges will also exercise a *de facto* legislative function when they:

(i) develop the common law (which is after all *judge-made* law); and
(ii) construe ambiguous or unclear statutory provisions.

13.2.2 Parliamentary sovereignty

As noted in Chapter 7, it is a central element of the British constitution that the Queen in Parliament is the sovereign law-making body and that the judiciary is subordinate to the will of the legislature. In short, in interpreting and applying legislation, the judiciary must simply give effect to the will of Parliament. Indeed, Lord Diplock in *Duport Steels Ltd and others v Sirs and others* [1980] 1 All ER 529 (for the facts of the case, see section 5.8.3), made it very clear what the constitutional role of the courts is in relation to the provisions of a statute:

'Where the meaning of the statutory words is plain and unambiguous it is not for the judges to invent fancied ambiguities as an excuse for failing to give effect to its plain meaning because they themselves consider that the consequences of doing so would be inexpedient, or even unjust or immoral. . . . It endangers continued public confidence in the political impartiality of the judiciary, which is essential to the continuance of the rule of law, if judges, under the guise of interpretation, provide their own preferred amendments to statutes . . .'

Student mentor tip

'Try to get to grips with what the judges say re Parliamentary sovereignty, eg Dicey.'

Audrie, University of Dundee

It has been a hallmark of the British constitution that, unlike in other countries such as the United States of America and Ireland, the United Kingdom judiciary is constitutionally limited. In other words, historically they have been unable to invalidate or challenge Acts of Parliament (but see section 7.7). Indeed, even with the advent of the new United Kingdom Supreme Court, which came into operation in October 2009, it is not the constitutional equivalent of the United States Supreme Court, which can invalidate legislation which is inconsistent with the codified constitution (*Marbury v Madison* (1803) 1 Cranch 137). In recent years, however, the traditional judicial deference towards Acts of Parliament has to be revisited in light of European law:

European Union law

As we shall see at section 15.6.2, the Court of Justice of the EU has developed the principle of the primacy of European Union law, which states that Union law has primacy over, and is superior to, inconsistent national law. As a result, in *ex parte Factortame* (1991), the House of Lords disapplied provisions of an Act of Parliament as being in conflict with overriding European law (see section 15.6.4). The requirements of European law have also altered the technique of statutory interpretation in the United Kingdom, with the British judiciary adopting the legal reasoning applied by the judges in the European Court in Luxembourg (eg the teleological approach to interpreting legislation – see section 15.4.1). However, on Brexit see section 15.6.6.

European Convention law

In strict legal terms the Human Rights Act 1998 preserves parliamentary sovereignty. Section 4 does, however, authorise a court to issue a declaration of incompatibility (see section 17.7) which, at least in a moral sense, could be viewed as the courts *questioning* an Act of Parliament for being inconsistent with the provisions of European Convention law. The point must be remembered, however, that Parliament itself has specifically empowered the courts to make such a declaration. In any event, although there may be political pressure to reform the law as a result of a declaration, in law Parliament is free to accept or ignore such a declaration.

13.2.3 The rule of law and the protection of the individual

QUOTATION

'I think the independence of the judiciary and the rule of law are very difficult to sever. It is the role of the judiciary, in practice, to uphold the rule of law, to apply the rule of law, to enforce the rule of law, and to do that they have to be independent of outside influence.'

Lord Phillips (Lord Chief Justice), the House of Lords Select Committee on the Constitution, Fourteenth Report of Session 2005–06, *Meeting with the Lord Chief Justice*, HL 213 (2006), Q7.

JUDGMENT

'. . . the function of independent judges charged to interpret and apply the law is universally recognised as a cardinal feature of the modern democratic state, a cornerstone of the rule of law itself.'

Lord Bingham in *A and others v Secretary of State for the Home Department* [2004] UKHL 56.

The judicial arm of the constitution must be independent because, by judges ensuring that public bodies act under the law (thereby enforcing the rule of law), they will inevitably come into constitutional conflict with the executive. The independence and impartiality of the judiciary is also linked inextricably to the administration of justice and public confidence in the judicial system to resolve disputes fairly and impartially.

One aspect of the rule of law requires the judiciary to protect the individual. In the absence of a written codified constitution, historically the courts have done so by:

- developing common law remedies such as trespass (see *Entick v Carrington* (1765) at section 4.8.2); and
- interpreting statutory provisions in the light of certain constitutional principles which protect the individual (eg their access to the courts: *Chester v Bateson* (1920) at section 5.7.2).

Under the Human Rights Act 1998, the courts are charged specifically with applying and upholding the Convention rights of individuals (see Chapter 17).

13.2.4 Judicial review

Judicial review is linked inextricably with the principles of the rule of law (the courts holding the executive legally to account) and the separation of powers (the courts checking and balancing the actions of the executive – see section 19.2.3). It is of paramount importance, therefore, that the judiciary is independent of the executive. In the absence of a codified constitution limiting the actions of the executive, judicial review helps to fill the void by requiring government officials to exercise their executive powers legally, rationally and fairly (see Chapter 20).

QUOTATION

'The claim that the courts stand between the executive and the citizen, and control all abuse of executive power, has been reinvigorated and become a foundation of our modern democracy.'

J Steyn, 'The case for a Supreme Court' (2002) 118 LQR 382.

KEY FACTS

Constitutional principle	Role of the judiciary
The separation of powers	To interpret the law and resolve legal disputes.
Parliamentary sovereignty	To uphold the will of Parliament and give effect to its intention.

Constitutional principle	Role of the judiciary
Rule of law	To uphold and enforce the rule of law (particularly against the executive).
Protection of the individual	To protect the individual from state interference.
Judicial review	To hold the executive legally to account for the use of its powers.

13.3 The appointment of the judiciary

13.3.1 Judicial appointments

In historic terms, a member of the executive (whether the Lord Chancellor or the Prime Minister) has traditionally been involved in the appointment of the judiciary, with the appointment thereafter being confirmed formally by the monarch. Under the Constitutional Reform Act 2005 (s 61 and Sch 12) a new Judicial Appointments Commission was established (operational since 2006) to carry out the responsibility of recruiting and selecting candidates for judicial appointments in England and Wales. In addition, whenever a vacancy occurs in the Supreme Court, a Supreme Court Selection Commission will be convened by the Lord Chancellor. Although the process of appointment under the Act is somewhat complex, both the above Commissions would consider the suitability of individuals and put forward an appropriate candidate for consideration by the Lord Chancellor. It is of interest to note that there are no parliamentary affirmations of judges as the legislature does not take part in the appointment process. In 2008 the government in its White Paper on Constitutional Renewal (Cm 7342–I (Crown Copyright, 2008), p 30), argued that the role of the executive in judicial appointments should be reduced. Thereafter, the 2010 Constitutional Reform and Governance Bill proposed to remove the (albeit formal) role of the Prime Minister in appointments to the Supreme Court. However, this provision was removed from the Bill before the measure became the Constitutional Reform and Governance Act 2010.

NB. In 2012 the House of Lords Select Committee on the Constitution issued its report on the appointment of judges: *Judicial Appointments*, HL Paper 272 (The Stationery Office, 2012). A year later, the Crime and Courts Act 2013 made reforms to the judicial appointments process by transferring certain decisions from the Lord Chancellor to the Lord Chief Justice and Senior President of Tribunals. In brief, appointments below the High Court are to be made by the Lord Chief Justice and those to the First-Tier and Upper Tribunals by the Senior President of Tribunals (see Sch 13 of the Act).

13.3.2 Arguments against executive involvement in judicial appointments

The system of appointing judges is of immense constitutional importance because the individuals appointed must be considered to be constitutionally acceptable and legitimate. In fact, it is arguable as to whether the executive should have any involvement in this process at all. The arguments against executive participation include the fact that the judges appointed will inevitably be involved in reviewing the actions of government ministers at some point in the future (eg in the context of judicial review claims as well as actions under the Human Rights Act 1998). As a result, it could be suggested that conferring a member of the executive (here the Lord Chancellor, who is a Cabinet minister) with the power to determine who is appointed to the judiciary is manifestly inconsistent with the separation of powers.

In 2003 a Bar Working Party noted in the context of the appointment of High Court judges, that if the judiciary was 'to perform its proper role':

QUOTATION

'It must be protected by constitutional safeguards from the risk or even the perception that its independence might be threatened by the Executive. Put simply, it has become constitutionally unacceptable in our view that the judges should be appointed by the government of the day. We will stress that this is not an attack on the present or any past or future Lord Chancellor. It is a matter of public perception.'

Bar Council Working Party on Judicial Appointments and Silk Consultation Document (The Bar Council, 2003), p 66.

It should be remembered that the above point was made before the passage of the Constitutional Reform Act 2005.

13.3.3 Arguments in favour of executive involvement in judicial appointments

The arguments in favour of executive involvement include the following:

- It has been commonly argued that, if the judiciary were to appoint itself, this could amount to a self-appointing (and therefore constitutionally unaccountable) 'judicial oligarchy'.
- The executive (Lord Chancellor) is ultimately accountable to Parliament for any appointments made.
- In any event, the Commissions established under the Constitutional Reform Act 2005 necessarily fetter the discretion of the Lord Chancellor in the judicial appointments process. Indeed, in respect of the Supreme Court, the original version of the Constitutional Reform Bill envisaged the minister selecting a judge from a choice of between two and five candidates. The Bill was amended as it was felt that this conferred excessive discretion onto the minister/executive.
- Other democracies have executive involvement. For example, in the United States the President selects proposed Supreme Court justices (although these must be confirmed by the upper chamber of Congress: the Senate). In 2017 the President proposed, and the Senate confirmed, the appointment of Associate Justice Gorsuch.

ACTIVITY

Self-test question

Do you think that the executive should be involved in any way with the appointment of the judiciary? If so, why?

13.4 The independence of the judiciary

QUOTATION

'Judicial independence is sometimes mistakenly perceived as privilege enjoyed by judges, whereas it is in fact a cornerstone of our system of government in a democratic society and a safeguard of the freedom and rights of the citizen under the rule of law. The judiciary, whether viewed as an entity or by its individual membership, is and must be seen to be, independent of the legislative and executive arms of government.'

Guide to Judicial Conduct (Judiciary of England and Wales, March 2013), para 2.1.

In the absence of a codified constitutional provision explicitly safeguarding and protecting the judiciary, judicial independence in the British constitution is protected in the following ways:

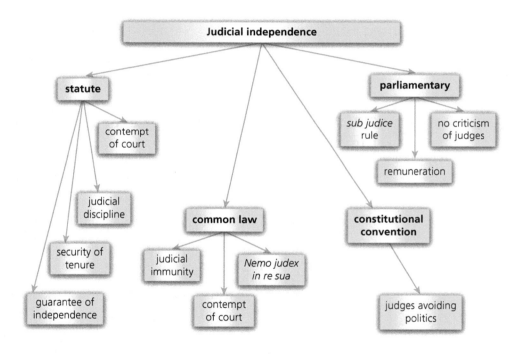

Figure 13.1 Judicial independence

13.4.1 Statutory protection

Guaranteed independence

Section 3(1) of the Constitutional Reform Act 2005 makes specific provision guaranteeing the independence of the judiciary:

SECTION

s 3
'Guarantee of continued judicial independence (1) The Lord Chancellor, other Ministers of the Crown and all with responsibility for matters relating to the judiciary or otherwise to the administration of justice must uphold the continued independence of the judiciary.'

NB. s 1 of the Tribunals, Courts and Enforcement Act 2007 extends this protection to the tribunal judiciary.

Section 3 of 2005 Act presupposes the existence of judicial independence in the British constitution as it refers explicitly to its 'continued' independence. Section 17 stipulates that the oath to be taken by a Lord Chancellor charges him to defend the independence of the judiciary (see section 5.7.9). In addition, s 3(5) aims to protect judicial decision-making from the influence of the executive as it states that:

SECTION

s 3(5)
'The Lord Chancellor and other Ministers of the Crown must not seek to influence particular judicial decisions through any special access to the judiciary.'

Security of tenure

Judicial independence is enhanced by giving senior judges security of tenure (during good behaviour), which means that their continued office is not dependent on the favour of the executive. In short, the political executive does not remove senior judges as this is achieved by the monarch following an address from both Houses of Parliament:

- Act of Settlement 1700 as amended by s 11 of the Senior Courts Act 1981 (formerly the Supreme Court Act) in terms of Court of Appeal/High Court judges.
- Section 33 of the Constitutional Reform Act 2005 in relation to justices of the new Supreme Court.

Moreover, as both Houses must act in concert, this serves to emphasise the constitutional significance of the modern House of Lords acting as a constitutional safeguard (see section 10.9.9) by protecting the senior judiciary from the executive.

Judicial discipline

Under Pt 4 of the Constitutional Reform Act 2005, the disciplining of judges (eg warnings, reprimands) involves the Lord Chief Justice acting with the agreement of the Lord Chancellor.

Contempt of court

The Contempt of Court Act 1981 preserves the integrity of the administration of justice and the right to a fair trial by prohibiting words which would prejudice court proceedings, for example a newspaper revealing the previous criminal convictions of a defendant so as to prejudice the jury against him.

13.4.2 Common law protection

▨ Judicial immunity

In order for judges and the administration of justice to perform effectively, it is a common law principle that judges are immune from legal liability for things said during the course of a trial in their judicial capacity (*Anderson v Gorries* [1895] 1 QB 668). If this were not the case, the judiciary would be unable to ensure that the administration of justice was carried out. As pointed out by Lord Denning MR in *Sirros v Moore* [1975] 1 QB 118:

JUDGMENT

'If the reason underlying this immunity is to ensure "that they may be free in thought and independent in judgment", it applies to every judge, whatever his rank. Each should be protected from liability to damages when he is acting judicially. Each should be able to do his work in complete independence and free from fear. He should not have to turn the pages of his books with trembling fingers, asking himself: "If I do this, shall I be liable in damages?" So long as he does his work in the honest belief that it is within his jurisdiction, then he is not liable to an action. . . . What he does may be outside his jurisdiction – in fact or in law – but so long as he honestly believes it to be within his jurisdiction, he should not be liable.'

Although the House of Lords subsequently overruled this majority decision in relation to magistrates (ie 'it applies to every judge') in *Re McC (A Minor)* [1985] AC 528, the Courts Act 2003 now protects them in terms of acting in or out of their jurisdiction (unless bad faith is shown in the latter).

▨ Common law contempt

Contempt laws protect the administration of justice and the integrity of court proceedings. It includes, for example, contempt in the face of the court, which could involve a refusal to answer questions in court. It is interesting to note that s 33 of the Crime and Courts Act 2013 abolished the common law offence of 'scandalising the judiciary' as a form of common law contempt.

▨ *Nemo judex in re sua*

This common law legal maxim means that no man should be a judge in his own cause (see section 20.5.3). It ensures that when the judiciary is hearing cases they remain independent and impartial so that people have confidence in the administration of justice.

JUDGMENT

'. . . a long line of cases shows that it is not merely of some importance but is of fundamental importance that justice should not only be done, but should manifestly and undoubtedly be seen to be done.'

Lord Hewart CJ, *The King v Sussex Justices* [1924] 1 KB 256.

In modern times the most important case concerning judicial independence is *ex parte Pinochet*:

CASE EXAMPLE

R v Bow Street Metropolitan Stipendiary Magistrate, ex parte Pinochet Ugarte (No 2) *[2000] 1 AC 119*

In *R v Bow Street Metropolitan Stipendiary Magistrate, ex parte Pinochet Ugarte* [2000] 1 AC 61, the House of Lords held that Pinochet (as the former head of state of Chile) did not enjoy immunity from extradition proceedings in respect of crimes against humanity allegedly committed during his period of office as head of state. The judgment was a three-to-two decision with Lord Hoffmann in the majority. Following the decision, Pinochet discovered that Lord Hoffmann was an unpaid director and Chairman of a charity controlled by Amnesty International, which had joined the action in order to seek Pinochet's extradition. As a result, it was alleged that this link gave the appearance that Hoffmann may have been biased against Pinochet.

In the ensuing hearing in the House of Lords, the court set aside its previous decision on the basis that the principle that a man should not be a judge in his own cause applied to the situation where a judge's decision would lead to promoting a cause in which he was involved together with one of the parties to the case. As with the *Dimes* case (see section 20.5.3), there was no suggestion that Hoffmann was actually biased, but instead it concerned a *presumption* of bias.

JUDGMENT

'If the absolute impartiality of the judiciary is to be maintained, there must be a rule which automatically disqualifies a judge who is involved, whether personally or as a director of a company, in promoting the same causes in the same organisation as is a party to the suit'

Lord Browne-Wilkinson.

'One of the cornerstones of our legal system is the impartiality of the trials by which justice is administered . . . everyone whom the prosecutor seeks to bring to justice is entitled to the protection of the law, however grave the offence or offences with which he is being prosecuted. Senator Pinochet is entitled to the judgment of an impartial and independent tribunal on the question which has been raised here as to his immunity'

Lord Hope.

Thereafter, a differently constituted House of Lords decided that Pinochet could be extradited, albeit on narrower grounds (*R v Bow Street Metropolitan Stipendiary Magistrate, ex parte Pinochet Ugarte (No 3)* [2000] 1 AC 147).

As a postscript to *ex parte Pinochet*, in *Meerabux v Attorney General of Belize* [2005] UKPC 12 the Privy Council distinguished *ex parte Pinochet* and held that the *mere* membership of a professional body did not require automatic disqualification. In this case the Chairman of the Belize Advisory Council who was also a member of the Bar Association (which was compulsory in this case) considered a complaint against a judge, but automatic disqualification did not apply as the Chairman had no financial or personal interest in the outcome of the case. Moreover, he had not taken part in the processing of the Bar Association's complaints against Meerabux.

In terms of apparent/appearance of bias see below and section 20.5.3. In *Locabail (UK) Ltd v Bayfield Properties Ltd* [2000] QB 451, the Court of Appeal (Lord Bingham CJ, Lord Woolf MR and Sir Richard Scott VC) joined together five cases alleging bias and requesting the disqualification of judges. It made clear that:

JUDGMENT

'It would be dangerous and futile to attempt to define or list the factors which may or may not give rise to a real danger of bias. Everything will depend on the facts, which may include the nature of the issue to be decided. We cannot, however, conceive of circumstances in which an objection could be soundly based on the religion, ethnic or national origin, gender, age, class, means or sexual orientation of the judge. Nor, at any rate ordinarily, could an objection be soundly based on the judge's social or educational or service or employment background or history, nor that of any member of the judge's family; or previous political associations or membership of social or sporting or charitable bodies; or Masonic associations; or previous judicial decisions; or extra-curricular utterances. . . . By contrast, a real danger of bias might well be thought to arise if there were personal friendship or animosity between the judge and any member of the public involved in the case, or if the judge were closely acquainted with any member of the public involved in the case.'

It should be noted that today the test for apparent bias is as follows:

JUDGMENT

'The question is whether the fair-minded and informed observer, having considered the facts, would conclude that there was a real possibility that the tribunal was biased.'

Lord Hope in *Porter v Magill* [2001] UKHL 67.

The following cases are also worth noting:

CASE EXAMPLE

Taylor v Lawrence *[2002] EWCA Civ 90*

The Court of Appeal held that no observer would consider it conceivable that a judge would favour a party to the case (where no relationship existed) simply because this party was represented in the case by solicitors whom the judge was using on a personal matter concerning a will.

CASE EXAMPLE

Lawal v Northern Spirit Ltd *[2003] UKHL 35*

The House of Lords held that an informed observer would conclude that there was a real possibility that a lay member of an Employment Appeal Tribunal might be biased (subconsciously) where counsel appearing before them had previously sat with them as a part-time judge. As a result, the court noted that this practice should be discontinued.

CASE EXAMPLE

AWG Group Ltd and another v Morrison and another *[2006] EWCA Civ 6*

The Court of Appeal held that a judge should have disqualified himself from presiding over a case where on the eve of the trial he discovered that he was a long-standing family acquaintance of a witness whom the claimant wished to call. The judge accepted the claimant's proposal not to call the witness but to call other witnesses instead and he was concerned about the disruption and cost in recusing himself from the case at this late stage. He had concluded that there was too small a risk that the case would change during the trial which would require him not to continue hearing it. In the Court of Appeal Mummery LJ, however, pointed out that:

JUDGMENT

'Inconvenience, costs and delay do not, however, count in a case where the principle of judicial impartiality is properly invoked. This is because it is *the* fundamental principle of justice, both at common law and under article 6 of the European Convention for the Protection of Human Rights. . . . If, on an assessment of all the relevant circumstances, the conclusion is that the principle either has been, or will be, breached, the judge is automatically disqualified from hearing the case. It is not a discretionary case management decision reached by weighing various relevant factors in the balance.'

Also see the case of *Howell v Lees Millais* [2007] EWCA Civ 720.

NB. Chapter 3 of the *Guide to Judicial Conduct* (Judiciary of England and Wales, March 2013), provides guidance in terms of judicial 'impartiality'.

13.4.3 Parliamentary protection

The *sub judice* resolution

It is a rule of Parliament that members of either House do not discuss or comment on matters which are 'active' in the court system (this includes both civil and criminal matters). This is known as the *sub judice* resolution, which was reaffirmed in 2001 in the House of Commons and 2000 in the Lords. This rule protects the integrity of the administration of justice and the independence of the judiciary.

Remuneration

Judicial salaries are relatively high, which ensures that appropriate candidates will apply (it also discourages bribery of judges). In addition, judicial salaries are drawn from the Consolidated Fund Services, which means that there is constant provision for them and so they are not subject to political debate. They are also not subject to reduction by the government, acting unilaterally.

No criticism of judges

By parliamentary practice the judiciary are not individually criticised in Parliament as this could lead to erosion in public respect for, and confidence in, judges. In short, there should be no reflection on the character or motive of a judge. An exception applies where the criticism of conduct is on a substantive motion for the dismissal of a judge.

13.4.4 Protection through constitutional convention

By constitutional convention, judges (though obviously having private political views) do not become overtly involved in politics. In addition, retiring full-time judges should not return to private practice.

ACTIVITY

Self-test question

Explain the different ways in which the independence of the judiciary is secured. Do you think that these methods achieve true independence?

13.5 Judicial accountability

Although judges are independent and impartial in our constitution, this does not mean that they are constitutionally unaccountable (this in itself would violate the rule of law). As indicated above, the senior judiciary can be removed by an address from both Houses of Parliament and they can be subject to disciplinary proceedings. In addition, judicial advancement is dependent upon merit and ability rather than favour. Moreover, as pointed out by Bradley ('The Constitutional Position of the Judiciary' in D Feldman (ed), *English Public Law*, p 291), judges are accountable in the following ways:

- The court process is in public and is typically adversarial (in general).
- Judges must take cognisance of the legal submissions made to them during the course of a case.
- In general, their decisions can be appealed against to a higher court (or possibly be subject to judicial review – see section 19.3.2).
- Judges give reasons for their decisions and deliver individual judgments which are a matter of public record.

13.6 The perception of judicial independence, neutrality and impartiality

13.6.1 The composition of the judiciary

The current composition of the judiciary is dominated by a narrow socio-economic group. Indeed, in April 2017 there was only one female Supreme Court justice and no heads of division were female. Moreover, only 24 and 22 per cent of Lords Justices of Appeal and High Court judges (respectively) were female. In addition, in April 2017, 7 per cent of court judges in general and 10 per cent of tribunal judges were black, Asian or minority ethnic (BAME) – see *Judicial Diversity Statistics 2017* (Crown Copyright, Ministry of Justice, 2017), pp 2–6. NB: since the publication of this report, a second female judge has been appointed to the Supreme Court, in addition to the appointment of the first BAME Lord Justice of Appeal. A significant proportion of the judiciary is female, however, if Justices of the Peace (magistrates) are included within the term (54 per cent of the 16,129 magistrates in England and Wales are women (source: *Judicial Diversity Statistics 2017* (Crown Copyright, Ministry of Justice, 2017), p 11). Moreover, magistrates' courts process the overwhelming majority of all criminal cases in the legal system.

For some commentators the unrepresentative nature of the judges in general raises concerns about the actual and perceived neutrality of the judiciary. The argument is that owing to their narrow composition there is an inevitability that subconsciously their judgments will favour the state and the status quo/establishment. According to Griffith:

QUOTATION

> '. . . judges in the United Kingdom cannot be politically neutral because they are placed in positions where they are required to make political choices which are sometimes presented to them, and often presented by them, as determinations of where the public interest lies; that their interpretation of what is in the public interest and therefore politically desirable is determined by the kind of people they are and the position they hold in our society; that this position is a part of established authority and so is necessarily conservative, not liberal . . .'
>
> JAG Griffith, *The Politics of the Judiciary* (5th edn, Fontana, 1997), p 336.

Some possible counter arguments to this are that:

- As professionals, when judges perform their judicial functions they leave behind them any bias/influences.
- The case law detailed in 13.6.2 indicates that the judiciary is prepared rigorously to hold the 'state' and executive to account.

Nonetheless, concern has been raised about composition of the judiciary:

- In 2003 a Bar Council Working Party report made clear the desirability of ensuring that there was greater diversity within the judiciary (*Bar Council Working Party on Judicial Appointments and Silk Consultation Document* (The Bar Council, 2003), pp 12–15).
- In 2003 the then Labour government indicated the need to do more to make the judiciary more reflective of the society that it serves (*Constitutional Reform: A new way of appointing judges* CP 10/03 (2003), p 45).
- In 2004 the Department for Constitutional Affairs issued a consultation paper into the current lack of diversity within the judiciary as a whole (*Increasing Diversity in the Judiciary* CP 25/04 (2004)).
- The first female member of the Supreme Court (and, at the time of writing, its President) has consistently argued for a more diverse judiciary (Lady Hale, 'Making a difference? Why we need a more diverse judiciary' (2005) 56 NILQ 281).
- The Constitutional Reform Bill was amended so that (although selection would continue to be on merit) the Judicial Appointments Commission would be required to:

SECTION

> '. . . have regard to the need to encourage diversity in the range of persons available for selection for appointments'.
>
> s 64 of the Constitutional Reform Act 2005.

Thereafter, Part 2 of the Tribunals, Courts and Enforcement Act 2007 amended the eligibility requirements for judicial appointments in an effort to increase the diversity of the judiciary.

- In 2009 an Advisory Panel on Judicial Diversity was established with the remit of making recommendations on how to make progress towards the goal of a more diverse judiciary.
- In 2012 the House of Lords Select Committee on the Constitution stated that:

QUOTATION

'A more diverse judiciary would not undermine the quality of our judges and would increase public trust and confidence in the judiciary.'

Judicial Appointments, HL Paper 272 (The Stationery Office, 2012), para 74.

Five years later the committee produced a follow-up report: *Judicial Appointments: follow-up*, HL Paper 32 (House of Lords, 2017).

NB. Sch 13 of the Crime and Courts Act 2013 now provides for measures designed to promote the consideration of diversity in the process of judicial appointments. Firstly, in cases where two candidates are of equal merit the selecting commission is not prevented from preferring one over the other in order to increase diversity within the relevant court/judiciary. Secondly, there is a duty on both the Lord Chancellor and Lord Chief Justice to take appropriate steps to encourage judicial diversity.

For a fascinating feminist approach to the issue of composition and judicial decisions, see R Hunter, C McGlynn and E Rackley (eds), *Feminist Judgments: From theory to practice* (Hart Publishing, 2010).

For others, however, there is no obligation to appoint judges reflective of the community; Sir Thomas Legg KCB, QC argued that:

QUOTATION

'It is no part of the professional judiciary's function to represent anybody or reflect anything. It is different for the lay magistrates, for whom one qualification is, and should be, to reflect the make-up of their local communities. The professional judges, on the other hand, have the unique property of being at once a powerful branch of government and at the same time a highly-skilled professional elite, whose contribution depends essentially on their learning, detachment and wisdom, and not who they are or where they come from in the community. We do not choose brain surgeons to reflect the community. They are chosen on professional merit. . . . It is, and should continue to be, the same with judges. "Reflection" should not in itself be an aim of the appointments system. Nor do I accept the view that public confidence is undermined by the present composition of the judiciary, or that it could be improved by intervening in appointments policy to change it.'

House of Commons Select Committee on Constitutional Affairs, First Report, *Written Evidence – Volume II* HC 48-II (2004), *Supplementary Written Evidence*, para 6.

ACTIVITY

Self-test question

Do you think that from a constitutional perspective the judiciary should be reflective of society or do you agree with the view of Sir Thomas Legg QC?

13.6.2 Judges and civil liberties

It is arguable that, from an historical perspective, the record of the judiciary in protecting civil liberties and holding the government to account has been variable at times (for example, see the historic cases of *ex parte Hosenball* (1977) and *Liversidge v Anderson* (1942), both at section 6.7.10). In more recent decades, however, there has been a measure of tension between the judiciary and the executive precisely because the courts have held government ministers to account.

During the course of this book we have already encountered the following decisions which indicate that the judiciary is prepared to subject the executive to rigorous scrutiny and/or protect individual rights (*Anderson* (2002) at section 13.2.1, *ex parte Venables and Thompson* (1997) at section 5.7.8 and *ex parte Fire Brigades Union* (1995) at section 6.7.10). In addition, the following three cases further illustrate this point:

CASE EXAMPLE

A and Others v Secretary of State for the Home Department (No 2) *[2005] UKHL 71*

This case concerned the Special Immigration Appeals Commission (SIAC), which was established under the Anti-terrorism, Crime and Security Act 2001. It processed appeals made by individuals against certification (and detention) by the Home Secretary, who reasonably believed them to be a risk to national security and reasonably suspected them of being terrorists. The House of Lords held that in hearing such appeals the SIAC could not receive evidence against these individuals where it had been obtained by torture.

CASE EXAMPLE

Secretary of State for the Home Department v JJ and Others *[2007] UKHL 45*

This case concerned the Home Secretary making (non-derogating) control orders under the Prevention of Terrorism Act 2005, in respect of six individuals suspected of being involved in terrorism-related activity. The orders, *inter alia*, permitted them to leave their residences (ie their one-bedroom flats) for six hours a day and restricted their movement to specified areas. The judge at first instance held that the cumulative effect of the orders was that they were contrary to Art 5 of the European Convention as being a deprivation of liberty and therefore these orders should be quashed. The Court of Appeal confirmed this decision and the House of Lords then dismissed an appeal by the Secretary of State.

CASE EXAMPLE

R (Mohamed) v Secretary of State for Foreign and Commonwealth Affairs *[2010] EWCA Civ 65*

In this case the Court of Appeal confirmed that sensitive information given by the American government to the British government under the 'control principle' (ie that this information would not be disclosed in the absence of the consent of the party that provided it) could be disclosed in an open version of the court's judgment. The claimant had issued proceedings against the Foreign Secretary to supply certain sensitive documents required to assist him in his defence in respect of legal proceedings which he anticipated the American government would bring against him (which were subsequently dismissed). The Foreign Secretary had declined to disclose this information.

JUDGMENT

'Justice must be done between the parties. The public must be able to enter any court to see that justice is being done in that court, by a tribunal conscientiously doing its best to do justice according to law . . . in my judgment the principles of freedom of expression, democratic accountability and the rule of law are integral to the principle of open justice and they are beyond question.'

Lord Judge CJ.

'. . . I have no doubt that there is a substantial and very strong public interest, as a matter of principle, in having the redacted paragraphs published. In any case where a judgment is being given, there is a significant public interest in the whole judgment being published, and it is undesirable that the executive should be seen to dictate to the judiciary what can and cannot go into an open judgment of the court. Where the judgment is concerned with such a fundamental and topical an issue as the mistreatment of detainees, and where it reveals involvement – or worse – on the part of the UK government in the mistreatment of a UK resident, there can be no doubt that the public interest is at the very top end of importance.'

Lord Neuberger MR.

13.6.3 Judges and 'difficult' cases

Listed below are five selected cases which illustrate where litigation before the courts has required the judiciary to face a number of difficult and controversial areas of law:

CASE EXAMPLE

Gillick v West Norfolk and Wisbech Area Health Authority and Department of Health and Social Security *[1986] AC 112*

The House of Lords held (by a three-to-two majority) that a girl under the age of 16 could be prescribed contraceptive treatment by a doctor – without the consent of her parents – provided the doctor was satisfied that the girl was sufficiently mature and intelligent to understand the nature of this treatment. This subsequently became known as the 'Gillick competency' test.

CASE EXAMPLE

R (Nicklinson) v Ministry of Justice *[2014] UKSC 38*

The Supreme Court held (by a majority) that, although the court would be within its 'institutional' power to make a declaration that s 2 of the Suicide Act 1961 (which prohibited assisted suicide) was incompatible with Art 8 of the European Convention on Human Rights, it would not be appropriate to make such a declaration in the instant case. As a result, in practice, therefore, the issue of assisted suicide would be left to Parliament (which is elected) to resolve.

CASE EXAMPLE

R (A) v Secretary of State for Health *[2017] UKSC 41*

The Supreme Court held (by a three-to-two majority decision) that the Secretary of State had not acted unlawfully when he refused to exercise a power under the National Health Service Act 2006 to provide Northern Irish women (not resident in England), travelling to England, with the same free abortion services in England which were available to women already resident there.

CASE EXAMPLE

Re X (A child) *[2017] EWHC 2036 (Fam)*

In this case the President of the Family Division made plain his concern at the lack of proper state provision for residential, clinical and other support services for young people/children with mental health difficulties:

JUDGMENT

'My judicial duty, as with every judge in this country, is "to do right to all manner of people after the laws and usages of this realm." There are occasions, and this is one, where doing "right" includes speaking truth to power.'

CASE EXAMPLE

R (Miller) v Secretary of State for Exiting the European Union *[2017] UKSC 5*

In this case the Supreme Court decided by a majority (eight to three) that the government could not use the royal prerogative to give formal notice to the European Union of the United Kingdom's withdrawal from it, but instead this required authorisation by an Act of Parliament. The President of the court, Lord Neuberger, made it clear at the outset that these court proceedings were concerned only with a question of law. In other words, the court judgment had nothing to do with the merits or otherwise of leaving the European Union (which of course is a political question). The facts and significance of this case are considered further at section 15.6.6.

KEY FACTS

Method of protection	Type of protection
Statute	<ul><li>Constitutional Reform Act 2005 requires government ministers to protect judicial independence.</li><li>Act of Settlement 1700/Constitutional Reform Act 2005 provide security of tenure for senior judges.</li><li>Contempt of Court Act 1981 protects the administration of justice and the right to a fair trial.</li></ul>
Common law	<ul><li>Judicial immunity for things said in a judicial capacity (*Anderson* (1895) and *Sirros* (1975)).</li><li>Contempt of court protects the administration of justice.</li><li>*Nemo judex in re sua* – no man should be a judge in his own cause.</li></ul>
Parliament	<ul><li>*Sub judice* resolution ensures active court cases are not commented on.</li><li>Character and motives of individual judges are not commented on.</li><li>Salaries drawn from the Consolidated Fund Services.</li></ul>
Constitutional convention	<ul><li>Judges are not overtly involved in politics.</li></ul>

SUMMARY

- The independence and impartiality of the judiciary is a key aspect of Britain's uncodified constitution.
- The independence of the judiciary is a fundamental principle as judges uphold the rule of law and protect the rights of individuals.
- In the context of the separation of powers the role of the judiciary is to interpret the law and resolve legal disputes.
- Judicial independence is secured through both law and constitutional convention.
- Judges are themselves accountable as proceedings exist to allow them to be removed and they can be subject to disciplinary proceedings.
- The current composition of the judiciary does not accurately reflect society at large (eg only two Supreme Court justices are female).

Further reading

Books

Barber, N, Ekins, R and Yowell, P (eds), *Lord Sumption and the Limits of the law* (Hart Publishing, 2016).

Bradley, A, Ewing, K and Knight, C, *Constitutional and Administrative Law* (16th edn, Pearson, 2015), Chapter 13.

Bradley, A, 'The Constitutional Position of the Judiciary' in Feldman, D (ed), *English Public Law* (2nd edn, Oxford University Press, 2009), p 281.

Darbyshire, P, *Sitting in Judgment* (Hart Publishing, 2011).

Ewing, K, 'Judiciary' in Flinders, M, Gamble, A, Hay, C and Kenny, M (eds), *The Oxford Handbook of British Politics* (Oxford University Press, 2011), p 262.

Gee, G, Hazell, R, Malleson, K and O'Brien, P, *The Politics of Judicial Independence in the UK's Changing Constitution* (Cambridge University Press, 2015).

Griffith, J, *The Politics of the Judiciary* (5th edn, Fontana, 1997).

Lee, H (ed), *Judiciaries in Comparative Perspective* (Cambridge University Press, 2011).

Lord Nolan, 'The Judiciary' in Lord Nolan and Sedley, S, *The Making and Remaking of the British Constitution* (Blackstone Press, 1997), p 67.

Stevens, R, *The English Judges: Their role in the changing constitution* (Hart Publishing, 2005).

Lord Woolf, *The Pursuit of Justice* (Oxford University Press, 2008).

Articles

Blom-Cooper, L, 'Bias: malfunction in judicial decision-making' [2009] PL 199.

Cahill-O'Callaghan, R, 'Reframing the judicial diversity debate: personal values and tacit diversity' (2015) 35 LS 1.

Devlin, P, 'Judges, government and politics' (1978) 41 MLR 501.

Dickson, B, 'Safe in their hands? Britain's Law Lords and human rights' (2006) 26 LS 329.

Flannery, L, 'In the eye of the beholder?' (2006) 156 NLJ 278.

Griffith, J, 'Judicial decision-making in public law' [1985] PL 564.

Lady Hale, 'Making a difference? Why we need a more diverse judiciary' (2005) 56 NILQ 281.

Hazell, R, 'Judicial independence and accountability in the UK have both emerged stronger as a result of the Constitutional Reform Act 2005' [2015] PL 198.

Sengupta, A, 'Judicial accountability: a taxonomy' [2014] PL 245.

Steyn, J, 'The weakest and least dangerous department of government' [1997] PL 84.

Lord Woolf, 'Judicial review – the tensions between the executive and the judiciary' (1998) 114 LQR 579.

Paper

Guide to Judicial Conduct (Judiciary of England and Wales, March 2013).

Internet links

www.judiciary.uk

www.supremecourt.uk

14

The decentralisation of public power

At the end of this chapter you should be able to:

- Understand the nature and constitutional significance of local government
- Understand the nature, type and constitutional significance of the devolved arrangements in Scotland, Wales and Northern Ireland
- Appreciate the position of England in terms of the overall devolution settlement in the United Kingdom

14.1 Introduction

QUOTATION

> '. . . unity is not uniformity. The different parts of the UK have different histories, distinctive cultures and differing aspirations. That is why the Government believes in devolution and decentralisation throughout the UK. In each part of the country that can and should take different forms.'
>
> *Scotland's Future in the United Kingdom: Building on ten years of Scottish devolution* Cm 7738 (Scotland Office, 2009), para 2.3.

The United Kingdom has a unitary state. In constitutional terms this means that power is focused and centralised in the apex of Parliament (which is generally controlled by central government). Notwithstanding this, for centuries power has been *decentralised* to local government (ie local authorities) to carry out governmental functions at a local level. In more recent years, power has also been *devolved* to regional bodies in Scotland, Wales, Northern Ireland and London. These different levels of government can be illustrated by the following two diagrams:

Figure 14.1 Tiers of government in the British constitution.

England				Wales	Scotland	Northern Ireland
NB: 9 'Combined Authorities' have been established outside London (see section 14.6.2)		NB: London has a strategic regional authority called The Greater London Authority (see section 14.6.3)		Power has been devolved to the National Assembly for Wales and the Welsh Assembly Government (see section 14.5)	Power has been devolved to the Scottish Parliament and the Scottish Government (see section 14.3)	Power has been devolved to the Northern Ireland Assembly and the Executive Committee (see section 14.4)
Outside London			**London**			
Non-metropolitan county councils	Metropolitan borough/ district councils (in major urban areas)	Unitary authorities/ councils	Borough councils	Unitary authorities	Unitary authorities	Single tier district councils
27 county councils ↓ *201 district councils*	*36 metropolitan borough/ district councils*	*55 unitary authorities/ councils (and the Isles of Scilly)*	*32 London borough councils and the City of London Corporation*	*22 unitary authorities*	*29 Unitary authorities and 3 Island councils*	*11 district councils*
A tier exists below known as parish/ town councils	Some parish/ town councils exist as a tier below	Some parish/ town councils exist as a tier below		A tier below of Welsh community councils/ meetings	A tier below of Scottish community councils	

Figures extrapolated from: D Wilson and C Game, *Local Government in the United Kingdom* (5th edn, Palgrave Macmillan, 2011), p 86; *Whitaker's Almanac 2017* (149th edn, Bloomsbury, 2016), pp 261–88 and M Sandford, *Local Government in England: Structures*, Briefing Paper 07104 (House of Commons Library, 2017), p 4.

Figure 14.2 The structure of local and regional government in the UK in 2016.

14.2 Local government

14.2.1 Introduction

QUOTATION

'Local government is a vital part of our democracy. The vast majority of interactions between citizens and the state take place through local government. It provides leadership for local areas and communities; democratic accountability for a wide range of public services; and is the key to effective partnership working at local level.'

Tony Blair, *Strong and Prosperous Communities, the Local Government White Paper*, Volume 1 Cm 6939-I (2006), Foreword p 2.

Local government is public power which has been decentralised and delegated to directly elected local authorities, which administer governmental functions at a local level. Local government has existed for centuries (and certainly precedes modern democracy in Britain). For example, during the nineteenth century local government boroughs exercised responsibility for the sanitation and education of their local inhabitants.

In modern times local government (now in the form of statutory local authorities, which, being creatures of statute, are at the mercy of Parliament) has been reorganised a number of times in the past few decades. Indeed, the result is that today the structure of local government is highly complex (not to say confusing for the public) and asymmetrical (ie some areas have different layers of government to others). This chapter provides a very basic outline of local government in England (as local government in Scotland, Wales and Northern Ireland are devolved responsibilities).

14.2.2 The functions of local government
What do local authorities do?

■ **The provision of services**
Local authorities, historically, have provided a wide range of different services. For example:

■ **Housing** – providing housing in the form of council housing and making provision for the homeless.

■ **Licensing** – regulating taxis, cinemas etc.

■ **Planning** – making decisions in respect of planning applications.

■ **Environmental health** – refuse collection, pollution control, food safety (through inspectors) and consumer protection (trading standards).

■ **Highways** – maintaining public roads, traffic management and the provision of street lighting.

■ **Social services** – care for the elderly/disabled and provision for the protection of children.

■ **Education** – providing and maintaining schools.

■ **Leisure** – providing libraries and museums.

Applying the law

Find out the type of local government that exists in your area and the various functions that it performs.

An administrative role

As indicated at section 5.3.2, local authorities are constitutionally part of the executive function of government (in a very broad sense of the term) and so therefore carry out government policy as expressed in primary legislation which has been passed at Westminster. In providing certain services, therefore, local authorities will be implementing government policy determined by the centre. For example, as a result of the National Curriculum being introduced in the Education Reform Act 1988, local education authorities were required to publish a general policy statement on the National Curriculum being adhered to by the schools in their area.

In terms of an administrative function, local authorities will make executive/administrative decisions, for example in the context of land planning or licensing (see *R v Liverpool Corporation, ex parte Liverpool Taxi Fleet Operators' Association* [1972] 2 QB 299).

A discretionary role

Local government has been traditionally characterised by the exercise of an element of discretion which allows them to adapt the provision of services to local needs. For example, the needs of an inner city area will not be the same as those of a largely rural area. Moreover, in this way local authorities can be innovative as schemes can be tested. For example, under the aegis of the Representation of the People Act 2000, pilot schemes were introduced by various authorities to test strategies aimed at combating voter apathy (eg all postal ballots, extended polling times, touch-screen voting). It is pertinent to note that the Localism Act 2011 provided local authorities in England with a 'general power of competence' as s 1(1) of the Act equips local authorities with the 'power to do anything that individuals generally may do.' Indeed, s 1(2) in effect provides that this power can be used innovatively including 'unlike anything that other public bodies may do' (s 1(2)(b)). In 2013 the Local Government Association issued a paper illustrating how councils are using the general power of competence: *Empowering councils to make a difference, Annex: case studies on how councils are using the general power of competence to bring about change and innovation* (Local Government Association, July 2013).

A legislative role

In order to carry out their roles, local authorities are empowered by statute to enact a form of delegated legislation in the form of **byelaws** which apply to local areas (eg a local byelaw concerned with banning alcohol consumption in a specified area). As local authorities are part of the executive, the enactment of such legislation is theoretically a breach of the separation of powers. However, the following controls do exist on their use:

(i) They will be subject to ministerial official confirmation from the Secretary of State from the relevant government department. However, s 129 of the Local Government and Public Involvement in Health Act 2007 provides that local authorities will be able to make certain byelaws without confirmation by the Secretary of State. For example, the Byelaws (Alternative Procedure) (England) Regulations 2016 (SI 2016/165) removes the requirement for the

byelaw

subordinate legislation made by local authorities

Secretary of State for Communities and Local Government to 'confirm' byel-aws in respect of the remit of the Department for Communities and Local Government.

(ii) If the byelaw is *ultra vires* it can be challenged in the courts by way of judicial review proceedings (see Chapters 19 and 20).

Two examples of local authorities exercising legislative power are:

• The Warwick District Council Off Street Parking Places Order 2006

Under the aegis of the Road Traffic Regulations Act 1984 (the primary/parent Act), Warwick District Council (part of Warwickshire County Council – an executive body) made the above delegated legislation, which updated the existing charges for local council car parks.

• Warwickshire County Council 2005 Byelaws

These were made under the aegis of s 19 of the Public Libraries and Museums Act 1964. For example, Byelaw No.8 prohibits any person destroying or damaging library property.

Raising of revenue

Local authorities acquire some of their revenue through taxation (formerly the rates, in modern times the council tax). Councils also raise money through charges for certain activities (car parks, swimming baths etc). In addition, revenue is collected through local business rates.

KEY FACTS

The role of local government	
Role	**Examples**
The provision of services.	• Social services. • Street lighting.
Making legislation.	• Byelaws.
A discretionary role.	• Pilot schemes (eg improving voter apathy).
Administrating government functions.	• Education.
Raising taxes.	• The council tax. • Charges for local services.

14.2.3 The advantages of local government

■ In constitutional terms it represents a decentralisation of power from the centre to local areas. In this way it acts as a constitutional counterbalance to central government and ensures that public power is not simply focused in central government departments.

■ Local government is an efficient way of administering governmental functions. Local authorities exist because central government could not operate without them. It would simply be impracticable for all services to be provided from the centre. As a result, local government prevents central government from being overburdened.

▢ It allows governmental functions to be specifically tailored to purely local needs and requirements.

▢ It promotes the constitutional principle of 'participatory democracy' whereby individuals can actively engage in the governmental process. Firstly, local authorities are directly elected and so they will be held directly accountable to local people for the public decisions that they make. This is equivalent to the European Union principle of 'subsidiarity', which is concerned with ensuring that decisions which affect people are taken at the lowest level nearest the people (this ensures greater accountability). Secondly, local government makes the democratic process and government in general more accessible to people in the sense that they have a far higher chance of becoming a local councillor than they ever would have of becoming a member of the government in Whitehall (or even an MP, for that matter). It therefore provides an opportunity for groups which are currently under-represented in politics (eg women, BAME) to become involved in political decision-making. Nevertheless, with 29 per cent of English councillors in 2004 being female and 3.5 per cent from a non-white background, the 2006 White Paper (*Strong and Prosperous Communities, The Local Government White Paper*, Volume 1, Cm 6939-I (2006), p 50) stressed that 'councillors are not representative of the population as a whole'. More recent figures indicate that, in 2013, 32 per cent of councillors in England were female (V Apostolova and R Cracknell, *Women in Parliament and Government*, Briefing Paper SN01250 (House of Commons Library, 2016), p 12).

▢ It allows a wider spread of political opinion to be represented, as some elected local councillors will not belong to the main political parties (eg they may belong to UKIP or the Green Party).

14.2.4 The disadvantages of local government

▢ The public appear to lack interest in voting at local government elections. Wilson and Game have stated that:

QUOTATION

'The one thing everyone thinks they know about local elections is that most people don't vote in them. They are right. . . . In almost all countries, fewer voters turn out for what are sometimes termed "second-order" elections, for local councils and the European Parliament, but in England the local-national gap is currently between, say, 38% and 65%, whereas in Western Europe generally it is between about 65% and 80%.'

Local Government in the United Kingdom (5th edn, Palgrave Macmillan, 2011), pp 251 & 253.

There are arguably a number of possibilities as to why there is such a low turnout in England. It could be that people are not interested in local affairs or that there is a perception that voting makes no real difference. Another explanation could be that as local authorities have been stripped of a number of their powers in recent decades, this has led to a misconception that local councils lack real powers. Finally, the cycles of elections can cause confusion, with some councils being elected as a whole, whereas other councils are elected one-half or one-third at a time. In any case, as a result of the very poor turnouts at local elections (although turnouts are higher in Scotland, Wales and Northern Ireland), it is possible to argue that local authorities may lack the constitutional or political legitimacy to make decisions. Indeed, a similar argument is used in respect of the European Parliament (see section 15.2.3). For example, in May 2012 it was estimated that the turnout at the local elections was only 32 per cent (F McGuinness and E Tetteh, *Local Elections 2012*, Research Paper 12/27 (House of Commons Library, 2012), p 1).

- Local government results in a variation in the provision of services around the country. This could lead to a perception of unfairness.
- Local government may actively encourage narrow local attitudes as well as providing a platform for political representatives with extreme political views.
- Local authorities may be viewed as wasteful public bodies. For example, in the 1980s the incumbent Conservative government perceived local government as not providing value for money (but see the reforms at section 14.2.5).
- Where the political colour of central government is different from that of local government (this will always be the case in terms of a number of councils at any one time) political friction may result. In particular, in the 1980s there was a clear ideological divide between the Conservative central government and a number of Labour-held councils, which led to deterioration in the constitutional and legal relationship between the two arms of the executive (see section 14.2.6).

ACTIVITY

Exercise

Do you think that the advantages of local government outweigh the disadvantages?

14.2.5 The control of local government

Local authorities are controlled in the following ways:

Democratically

Individual local councillors are subject to re-election every four years and so the actions, decisions and policies of local authorities are accountable directly to the local electorate. The electoral systems used for local government elections in the UK vary (for example, England and Wales use the 'first past the post' system, whereas Scotland and Northern Ireland use the single transferable vote). It is pertinent to point out that Part 5 of the Localism Act 2011, entitled: 'Community empowerment', provides for a local referendum in relation to any proposed 'excessive' increase in council tax. The local authority requires a yes vote in order to implement such an increase.

Legally

Local authorities, as public bodies, are subject to the law for their actions. They can be held to account in both public law (judicial review) and private law (contract, tort etc). For example, in relation to private law, in *Infolines Public Networks Ltd v Nottingham City Council* [2009] EWCA Civ 708 the Court of Appeal held that the council's disposal of Infolines's telephone kiosks was a wrongful interference with their goods. According to John Lambe (senior solicitor, then at DWF), who acted as Infolines' solicitor in this case, 'The case serves as a cautionary tale for local authorities and others who seek to exercise emergency powers and the restrictive interpretation which is likely to be adopted and applied when those powers concern dealing with the potential deprivation of another's property.'

In terms of public law, when a local authority enacts delegated legislation (ie byelaws) which is beyond its legal powers, it can be held accountable in the courts:

CASE EXAMPLE

Arlidge v Mayor, Aldermen, and Councillors of
the Metropolitan Borough of Islington *[1909] 2 KB 127*

A byelaw made by the council under the aegis of the Public Health (London) Act 1891 was
held to be unreasonable as it would have required a landlord to commit an act of trespass
in order to comply with it (ie to clean every part of a lodging house in the month of April,
May or June every year).

See also *Nicholls v Tavistock Urban District Council* [1923] 2 Ch 18.

For a recent case of a local authority being held to account in judicial review proceedings, see *R (BM) v Hackney London Borough Council* [2016] EWHC 3338 (Admin).
In addition, for the purposes of s 6 of the Human Rights Act 1998, local authorities
are public authorities and so must not act in a way which is incompatible with the
articles of the European Convention

From the centre

Local government is ultimately at the mercy of central government. In short,
it is central government (via its control of Parliament) which can set the legal,
political and financial context and parameters in which local government must
work (as well as providing advice in the form of circulars as to how its delegated powers should be exercised). A government minister will also approve and
confirm byelaws made by local government (but now see the reforms at section
14.2.2). Moreover, a government minister may well enjoy a 'default power' which
authorises him to step in and exercise the decentralised power instead, or transfer
it (see *R v Secretary of State for the Environment, ex parte Norwich City Council* [1982]
1 QB 808).

It must be remembered that local government, unlike in other countries with a
codified constitution, does not have any legally protected or 'constitutional status'.
Instead, local authorities are statutory bodies which owe their existence to Acts of
Parliament and therefore, in constitutional theory, could be extinguished by an Act
of Parliament (which has been forced through Parliament by a dominant executive).

Central government (by virtue of legislation being pushed through Parliament)
can remodel local government as it sees fit. For example:

(i)   In the 1980s the Conservative government reformed the nature of local government whereby, *inter alia*:

- Local government taxation was reformed (ie the poll tax – Local Government
Finance Act 1988).
- Local authorities became 'enabling authorities' regulating services provided
by private bodies, rather than directly themselves. This involved CCT (compulsory competitive tendering) whereby councils, which had traditionally
provided services, would have to compete with private contractors in order
to deliver that service in an effort to secure more efficient services. For example, it applied to:
  - Highways (Local Government Planning and Land Act 1980)
  - Refuse collection (Local Government Act 1988).

The subsequent Labour government under the Local Government Act 1999
replaced CCT with a 'best value duty'. Most recently see *Best Value Statutory
Guidance* (Department for Communities and Local Government, Crown
Copyright, 2011).

(ii) In terms of the constitutional arrangements of councils, the last Labour government introduced new executive arrangements in relation to how councillors operated (Local Government Act 2000). Historically, the committee system within councils made many decisions, but the new executive arrangements involved making a clear separation between executive councillors (who would make executive policy decisions) and non-executive councillors (who would supervise the executive councillors). The main councils in England were required to adopt one of the following types of executive models (following consultation with the local population – another example of participatory democracy):

- Leader (indirectly elected by the council) and Cabinet executive (appointed by either the leader or the council).
- Mayor (directly elected by local people) and Cabinet executive (appointed by the mayor).
- Mayor (directly elected by local people) and Council manager executive (appointed by the council).

Further reforms followed with the Local Government and Public Involvement in Health Act 2007, which provided for the discontinuance of the first and third executive models set out above. Section 62 of the Act required English councils to operate either a (new style) Leader and Cabinet Executive or the Mayor and Cabinet Executive. According to the then Labour government:

QUOTATION

'The 2007 Act strengthens leadership models with a choice for councils between a directly elected mayor with a four year term and an indirectly elected leader with a four year term.'
Strong and Prosperous Communities, The Local Government White Paper Implementation Plan: One Year On (Crown Copyright, 2007), para 49.

NB. The Localism Act 2011 made further changes to the governance arrangements for local government. In brief, the Local Government Act 2000 has been amended so that a local authority must operate one of the following:

- 'executive arrangements' (new s 9B(1)(a)), which consist of either a 'Mayor and Cabinet executive' (a directly elected Mayor who appoints two or more councillors to the executive) or a 'Leader and Cabinet executive' (an executive Leader is elected by the local authority, who in turn then appoints two or more councillors to the executive).
- a 'committee system' (s 9B(1)(b)), which in essence is the system which operated in councils before the 2000 Act reforms.
- 'prescribed arrangements' (s 9B (1) (c)), which enable the Secretary of State to make regulations which prescribe governance arrangements that councils can operate.

Finally, under the amendment made by the Localism Act 2011 to the Local Government Act 2000 (it inserted s 9N), the Secretary of State ordered specified cities to hold a local referendum in 2012 as to whether or not its governance arrangements should be changed to operate as a Mayor and Cabinet executive (in the event, the majority of which voted no). In total, in 2017 there were 16 directly elected mayors (outside London) holding office in local authorities (see L Audickas, O Hawkins and R Cracknell, *UK Election Statistics: 1918–2017*, Briefing Paper CBP7529 (House of Commons Library, 2017), p 66). NB: the Cities and Local Government Devolution Act 2016 provides for elected mayors for 'combined authorities' (see later at section 14.6.2).

Control is also exercised financially as a significant proportion of revenue (ie central government grants) which local government receives is, ultimately, determined by central government.

■ **Audits**

Local authorities were historically audited by the Audit Commission in terms of their financial efficiency. However, the Local Audit and Accountability Act 2014 abolished the Commission and replaced it with a local audit framework.

■ **Ombudsman**

Maladministration by English local authorities which results in injustice for individuals can be subject to investigation by the Commission for Local Administration (see section 21.3.7). The annual report of the Local Government Ombudsman indicated that during 2015–16 it had received 19,702 complaints and enquiries, upheld 51 per cent of detailed investigations and made 3,529 recommendations to 'put things right'. The most complained about area was Education and Children's Services (*Review of Local Government Complaints 2015–16* (Local Government Ombudsman, July 2016), pp 1–2).

maladmini-stration
poor administration

14.2.6 The relationship between central and local government

Relations between the two arms of the executive have historically been characterised by co-operation and an informal partnership (albeit with central government clearly being the dominant partner). Between the 1970s and the 1990s, however, this generally consensual relationship broke down. For example:

CASE EXAMPLE

Secretary of State for Education and Science v Tameside Metropolitan Borough Council *[1976] 3 WLR 641*

A Labour Secretary of State for Education and Science using powers under the Education Act 1944, tried to direct a Conservative council to fully implement a scheme in respect of comprehensive schooling which had been approved the year before by the previous Labour council administration and approved by the Labour Secretary of State. Thereafter, he unsuccessfully sought an order to compel the authority to comply with the previous Labour council's scheme.

Loughlin has referred to central–local relations since 1979 as having become 'politicised' and 'juridified' (ie legalised), with the courts being resorted to in order to determine the legal boundary of these relations (M Loughlin, 'Restructuring of Central–Local Government Relations' in J Jowell and D Oliver (eds), *The Changing Constitution* (4th edn, Oxford University Press, 2000), p 137). An example is detailed below:

CASE EXAMPLE

Nottinghamshire County Council v Secretary of State for the Environment *[1986] 1 AC 240*

Nottinghamshire County Council and the City of Bradford Metropolitan Council unsuccessfully sought judicial review of the Secretary of State's guidance determining expenditure targets for local authorities. The councils had contended that the expenditure targets were unfairly low. The House of Lords held that the courts would not intervene on a matter of 'unreasonableness' (in the absence of, for example, bad faith) in respect of public financial administration, which had been approved by the House of Commons.

In December 2007 a *Central–Local Concordat* was agreed between central government and the Local Government Association which established 'a framework of principles for how central and local government work together to serve the public'.

KEY FACTS

Controls on local government	
Control	**Example**
Democratic	• Local electors voting at local elections.
Legal	• Private law. • Public law (including under the Human Rights Act 1998).
Central government/ Parliament	• Setting the legal and political parameters in which local government must operate. • Financial control as significant revenue is secured from the centre. • Ministerial approval for byelaws etc.
Audit	• The auditing of local authority accounts.
Ombudsman	• Maladministration causing injustice to local individuals.

In May 2009 the House of Commons Communities and Local Government Select Committee issued a report analysing the relationship between local and central government (Sixth Report of Session 2008–09, *The Balance of Power: Central and Local Government*, HC 33-I (2009)). The conclusion it reached was that 'the balance of power between central and local government in England is currently in need of a tilt towards localities' (*Sic*) (para 146). More recently, in 2013 the House of Commons Political and Constitutional Reform Committee called for more autonomy for local government (*Prospects for Codifying the Relationship between Central and Local Government*, HC 656-I (The Stationery Office, 2013)).

NB. Local government, like other aspects of the constitution, will be affected by the United Kingdom's withdrawal from the European Union (see Brexit at section 15.6.6), and at the time of writing the House of Commons Communities and Local Government Select Committee had launched an investigation into the 'Impact of Brexit on local government'.

ACTIVITY

Quick quiz

1. What is the constitutional function of local government?
2. Give examples of what it does.
3. How is local government controlled?
4. Explain how central and local government relate to each other.

14.3 Scottish devolution

14.3.1 History

Until 1707 England and Scotland had their own separate parliaments. The Union with Scotland Act 1706 (passed by the then English Parliament) and the Union with England Act 1707 (passed by the then Scottish Parliament) united the two parliaments into one single legislature in Westminster (thereafter the Parliament of Great Britain). After this date the Westminster Parliament legislated for both England (and Wales) and Scotland.

Over the course of time, Scotland remained distinct from the rest of the Union (England, Wales and Northern Ireland), in particular in terms of its different systems of education and law. During the latter half of the twentieth century there was an increasing call from Scottish nationalist politicians for Scotland to be able to direct and govern its own affairs through the reestablishment of a Scottish Parliament. Indeed, in 1978 a Scotland Act was passed which would have provided Scotland with its own elected assembly. The Act, however, did not come into effect (and was repealed) because the Scots voting in the referendum to support devolution did not meet the threshold stipulated in the Act.

The election of the 1997 Labour government placed devolution back on the political agenda. In July 1997 the Labour government issued a White Paper which stated at the outset:

QUOTATION

'The Government are determined that the people of Scotland should have a greater say over their own affairs. With their agreement we will change the way Scotland is governed by legislating to create a Scottish Parliament with devolved powers within the United Kingdom.'

Scotland's Parliament, Cm 3658 (The Scottish Office, 1997), p 1.

Following this, a referendum was held in Scotland in September 1997 for the Scots to either endorse or reject the government's proposals. In constitutional theory this is an example of participatory democracy whereby individuals are given direct influence over proposals which will affect them. At the referendum the Scots were asked two questions:

▪ Do the Scottish people want a Scottish Parliament? (74 per cent voted yes).
▪ Should it have tax-raising powers? (64 per cent voted yes).

As a result of this endorsement, the Westminster Parliament duly passed the Scotland Act 1998.

The Scotland Act 1998

This Act devolved powers to Scotland so that for the first time in almost 300 years Scotland had its own Parliament to oversee its own affairs. In fact, the Scotland Act (like the corresponding legislation in relation to Wales and Northern Ireland) can be seen as a type of constitution for Scotland. Indeed, it has been described as 'a mini-constitution' by Lord Brodie in *Whaley v Lord Advocate* [2004] SC 78. It should be remembered that the purpose of a constitution (see Chapter 2) is to:

▪ Establish governmental institutions (eg the Scottish Parliament).
▪ Allocate them powers (eg the Scottish Parliament is empowered to legislate on health and criminal law etc).
▪ Limit their powers (eg the Scottish Parliament cannot pass legislation for international relations).

The Scotland Act 2012

This Act followed on from the Calman Commission (see section 14.3.2) and increased the powers of both the Scottish Parliament and the Scottish Government (ie ministers).

The Scotland Act 2016

The key elements of the Act are as follows:

- The permanence of the Scottish Parliament and Scottish Government (s 1) – see earlier at section 7.10.2.
- Statutory incorporation of the Sewel Convention (s 2) – see earlier at section 4.13.13.
- Elections – in particular, an election for the Scottish Parliament cannot take place on the date of a general election for the United Kingdom or a European parliamentary election (s 5).
- A 'supermajority' (ie two-thirds of the total number of seats) is required in the Scottish Parliament in order for it to pass specified electoral legislation (ie 'protected subject matter'). Such matters include modifying the law relating to, for example, elections to the Scottish Parliament, the electoral system, number of constituencies, etc (s 11).
- The power of the Scottish Parliament to modify the Scotland Act 1998 in relation to the operation of the Parliament and the Government (s 12).
- The power to set income tax rates (s 13) – see later at section 14.3.7. This then resulted in the standing orders of the House of Commons relating to EVEL (see section 12.7.3) being amended in 2017 to take this into account.

The 2012 and 2016 Scotland Acts illustrate that devolution, far from being a fixed state of affairs, is a somewhat (rolling) process.

14.3.2 Arguments for and against Scottish devolution

It should be noted that some of the arguments from 1997 set out below can, to a greater or lesser extent, apply equally to the other devolved settlements in Wales and Northern Ireland.

Arguments for Scottish devolution

- As Scotland was hallmarked by distinct characteristics (particularly its law), it required a local Parliament to oversee its affairs, rather than a distant Parliament hundreds of miles away.
- In political terms, devolution intensified between 1979 and 1997 when the majority of Scotland consistently returned non-Conservative MPs (largely Labour) to Westminster, but was governed by an 'English Conservative government'. In particular, it must be remembered that the controversial community charge (colloquially known as the poll tax) was first introduced in Scotland, *before* England.
- In constitutional terms, too much power was centralised in London and so devolution to Scotland (and elsewhere) was healthy in a democracy as a way of decentralising and dispersing power.

Arguments against Scottish devolution

- Devolving power would lead to the constitutional anomaly of the 'West Lothian question', whereby Scottish MPs would be able to vote on English legislative matters such as education and crime, but that English MPs would not be able to vote on corresponding Scottish education and crime matters, as these would be devolved to the Scottish Parliament to decide (see section 14.3.12).

- Devolving power to Scotland (and Wales and Northern Ireland for that matter), but not simultaneously establishing an 'English Parliament' to oversee and legislate on specifically English affairs, would lead to an imbalance in the constitution. In other words, devolution would be asymmetrical.
- Devolving power would inevitably widen the differences between Scotland and the rest of the Union. This would, therefore, lead to the eventual break-up of the Union of the United Kingdom. In short, once established, a Scottish Parliament would inevitably want more powers ceded to it from Westminster, eventually leading to Scotland becoming a completely separate and independent country. In response to this last point it was argued that providing the Scottish people with devolution – and so the ability to a large extent to regulate their own affairs – would actually stave off political support for complete independence. Indeed, according to the then Labour government in its 1997 White Paper:

QUOTATION

'The Government want a United Kingdom which everyone feels part of, can contribute to, and in whose future all have a stake. The Union will be strengthened by recognising the claims of Scotland, Wales and the regions to strong identities of their own. The Government's devolution proposals, by meeting these aspirations, will not only safeguard but also enhance the Union.'

Scotland's Parliament, Cm 3658 (The Scottish Office, 1997), p 10.

A decade later, in 2009, the Labour government reiterated that, by giving expression to diversity, devolution actually strengthened the Union (*Scotland's Future in the United Kingdom: Building on ten years of Scottish devolution*, Cm 7738 (Scotland Office, 2009), para 2.3). Earlier that year, the Commission on Scottish devolution (known as the Calman Commission) had issued its report (*Serving Scotland Better: Scotland and the United Kingdom in the 21st century*, Final Report – June 2009 (Commission on Scottish Devolution, 2009)), which noted that devolution had given Scotland clear benefits, but that the devolution settlement should be strengthened. Following the general election of 2010 the coalition government issued its paper: *Strengthening Scotland's Future*, Cm 7973 (Crown Copyright, 2010), which aimed to implement the Calman Commission's recommendations via the Scotland Bill (now the Scotland Act 2012).

Scottish independence?

In parallel events in Scotland, however, in 2007 the Scottish Executive/ Government issued a paper aimed at initiating a 'national conversation' about Scotland's constitutional future, including Scottish independence and other constitutional possibilities (*Scotland's Future, A National Conversation: Independence and responsibility in the modern world* (Crown Copyright, 2007)). In February 2010 a consultation paper setting out the proposals for a Referendum Bill was published (*Scotland's Future: Draft Referendum (Scotland) Bill Consultation Paper* (Crown Copyright, 2010)). However, the draft Bill was withdrawn owing to a lack of support (the Scottish National Party was a minority government in the 2007–11 parliament). After the Scottish 2011 election, at which the SNP won an overall majority of seats, the Scottish Government instituted a public consultation on its proposals for a referendum on Scottish independence (*Your Scotland, Your Referendum* (Crown Copyright, 2012)). In the foreword to this paper the First Minister stated that the referendum would be held in 2014 and in 2013 the Scottish Independence Referendum Act was passed providing for a referendum.

The referendum in Scotland took place in September 2014 and the turnout was high, at 85 per cent. In answer to the question of whether Scotland should be an independent country, 55 per cent answered 'No' (source: *Scottish Independence Referendum 2014, Analysis of Results*, Research Paper 14/50 (House of Commons Library, 2014)). Following the referendum a cross-party commission was set up (*The Smith Commission, Report of the Smith Commission for Further Devolution of Powers to the Scottish Parliament* (November 2014)). This was duly followed by the then coalition government's 2015 command paper taking forward the recommendations of the Smith Commission (*Scotland in the United Kingdom: An enduring settlement*, Cm 8990 (Crown Copyright, 2015)). In turn, this was implemented through the terms of the Scotland Act 2016 (see earlier at 14.3.1).

Notwithstanding the referendum result, Scottish independence *still* remains a live issue today, as illustrated by the recent 2017 debate in Westminster Hall in which two opposing e-petitions (180642 and 168781) were debated (*Hansard*, HC, Vol 631, col 1 WH). Indeed, as a result of Brexit, in March 2017 the Scottish Parliament approved a motion mandating the Scottish Government to discuss with the British government the details of an Order under s 30 of the Scotland Act 1998 to provide for the Scottish Parliament to legislate for a second Scottish referendum on independence. This was dismissed by the British government.

ACTIVITY

Self-test question

Do you think that the advantages of Scottish devolution (or devolution in general) outweigh the disadvantages?

14.3.3 The Scottish Parliament

Section 1 of the Scotland Act 1998 established a Scottish Parliament (it sits at Holyrood in Edinburgh). The Parliament is unicameral, consisting of one elected chamber.

Composition and elections

The Scottish Parliament consists of 129 members, known as Members of the Scottish Parliament (MSPs). They are elected on the following basis:

- 73 constituency MSPs elected under the simple majority system (s 1(2) – known as the constituency vote).
- 56 regional MSPs – 'additional members' – elected under the additional member system of proportional representation (s 1(3)– known as the regional vote).

Unlike the House of Commons, the Scottish Parliament is not elected solely on the basis of the 'first past the post' system. This is because this system can distort the wishes of the electorate (see section 9.4.4) and the then Labour government's 1997 White Paper made it clear that the 'electoral arrangements for the Scottish Parliament should reflect the will of the Scottish people' (p 27). Instead, there is a combination of MSPs elected by two different systems, with the majority being elected under the 'first past the post' system, thereby ensuring that there is a constituency link between MSPs and the Scottish people. These are supplemented by additional members (seven members elected from eight electoral regions, eg North East Scotland). According to the White Paper this would 'bring a closer relationship between votes cast and seats won' (p 27), thereby injecting greater proportionality (and so stability) into the overall devolution settlement. These new electoral arrangements indicated a willingness to move away in our constitution from the traditional 'first past the post' system.

The first elections took place in 1999 and the latest in May 2016, the results of which are detailed below. It produced a Parliament with the Scottish National Party (SNP) as the largest party, which formed the Scottish Government, albeit as a minority administration. As noted, voters are given two votes: one for a constituency MSP and one for a regional MSP (cast for a party).

The Scottish Parliament 2016			
Elections May 2016			
Political Parties	**Constituency MSPs**	**Regional MSPs**	**TOTAL**
SNP	59	4	63
Scottish Labour Party	3	21	24
Scottish Liberal Democrats	4	1	5
Scottish Conservative and Unionist Party	7	24	31
Scottish Green Party	0	6	6
TOTAL	73	56	129

Table 14.1

Source: O Hawkins, *Scottish Parliament Elections: 2016*, Briefing Paper CBP7599 (House of Commons Library, 2016), p 18.

The reason the above election took place in 2016 rather than 2015 (as originally scheduled), was as a result of s 4 of the Fixed-Term Parliaments Act 2011, which aimed to avoid a clash with elections at Westminster in May 2015. Moreover, the next scheduled Scottish election is due in 2021 (ie a five-year term) owing to the passage of the Scottish Elections (Dates) Act 2016. Although the 2016 Act was intended to avoid a clash with a national general election (ie in 2020), this has been rendered somewhat moot given that the 'snap' general election of 2017 means that the next scheduled Westminster election is in 2022 and not 2020.

The role of MSPs is similar to that of MPs in the Westminster Parliament:

- Representing constituents.
- Resolving complaints from constituents.
- Holding the Scottish Government to account.
- Raising issues of public concern.

- Asking parliamentary questions.
- Participating in parliamentary debates and the committee system.

The Presiding Officer

Section 19 provides for a Presiding Officer together with two deputies to be elected from the MSPs. In effect the Presiding Officer is the equivalent of the Speaker of the House of Commons as he chairs proceedings in the parliamentary chamber and is required to be impartial. MSPs are also governed by a *Code of Conduct (7th edn, The Scottish Parliament, August 2017)* and under the Scottish Parliamentary Standards Commissioner Act 2002 an independent Scottish Parliamentary Standards Commissioner was created to process complaints concerning MSPs.

The committee system

As in Westminster, the Scottish Parliament has a sophisticated committee system. These committees include:

- Subject committees allocated in respect of government departmental areas (analogous to departmental select committees). For example, the Justice Committee examines the Scottish Government's expenditure/policy in relation to justice.
- Mandatory committees for the parliamentary term (eg the Equalities and Human Rights Committee).
- Committees which consider Bills (eg the Referendum (Scotland) Bill Committee considered the 2013 Scottish Independence Referendum Bill).

14.3.4 The Scottish administration

Section 44 established the office of a Scottish Executive, known collectively as 'the Scottish Ministers'. In 2007 the Scottish Executive renamed itself the *Scottish Government* and following this, s 12 of the Scotland Act 2012 (legally) renamed the Executive the Scottish Government.

The Scottish Government consists of the following:

- The First Minister (analogous to the office of the Prime Minister).
- Ministers appointed by the First Minister (analogous to Cabinet ministers), but with the approval of Parliament.
- Lord Advocate and Solicitor General for Scotland (these law officers, *inter alia*, provide legal advice).

The Executive is the 'Scottish Government'/Cabinet. It is responsible for developing and implementing policies and assumes responsibility in devolved matters (it is governed by the principles of collective responsibility – see section 12.2). Scottish ministers are also governed by a code: *The Scottish Ministerial Code* (Revised 2016) and they can introduce Bills.

The constitutional arrangements in Scotland, therefore, involve a parliamentary executive (as in Westminster) whereby the Scottish Government is held to account by the Scottish Parliament. For example, as in Westminster, Scottish ministers can be asked oral or written questions, with the First Minister having a separate First Minister's Question Time (analogous to PMQs: see section 12.4.2). Furthermore, ss 45 and 47 require the resignation of the First Minister and individual ministers if it is resolved that the Scottish Government no longer enjoys the confidence of the Scottish Parliament (analogous with the Westminster vote of no confidence: see section 12.2.1).

Composition of the Scottish devolved institutions	
Parliament	129 MSPs • 73 constituency MSPs ('first past the post' system). • 56 regional MSPs (additional member system).
Government	• The First Minister/Deputy First Minister. • Other Scottish ministers. • Lord Advocate and Solicitor General for Scotland.

14.3.5 Legislation

Primary legislation

Scottish devolution involved 'legislative devolution' whereby the Scottish Parliament was empowered to pass primary legislation. Section 28 states that the Scottish Parliament can make laws, which are to be known as Acts of the Scottish Parliament. After a Bill has passed through the Scottish Parliament and has obtained the Royal Assent, it becomes an Act of the Scottish Parliament (s 28(2)).

The constitutional standing of these Acts, however, is worth noting as, although these Acts are analogous to primary legislation:

- For the purposes of the Human Rights Act 1998 (s 21), such legislation is treated as having the standing of, and classed as, subordinate legislation and so amenable to challenge and invalidation under the Human Rights Act 1998 (see Chapter 17).
- Under the Scotland Act, if the Scottish Parliament passes an Act of Parliament outside its legal jurisdiction (eg in respect of the British constitution), under s 29 it can be challenged as not being valid law. Contrast the position in respect of Westminster Acts (see Chapter 7).

Secondary legislation

The Scottish Government can pass delegated/secondary legislation (which is similar to British Cabinet ministers making statutory instruments). NB: the Scotland Act 2012 altered the competence of the Scottish Government/Ministers in relation to, for example, prescribing drink driving limits (s 20) and determining speed limits (s 21).

14.3.6 Devolved and reserved matters

Devolution involves devolving powers and responsibility from the centre (Westminster) to the regions (eg Scotland). The Scotland Act 1998 devolves powers to Scotland (devolved matters), while retaining specific powers in the centre (reserved matters).

Reserved matters

These are set out in Sch 5 of the Act and include, for example:

- International relations.
- National security.
- Matters affecting the United Kingdom constitution.

The then Labour government argued in its 1997 White Paper that these sorts of issues 'can be more effectively and beneficially handled on a United Kingdom basis' (p 10), thereby safeguarding the United Kingdom's integrity and the benefits of a consistent approach in such areas.

Devolved matters

The following are some of the matters over which the Scottish Parliament has legislative competence:

- Education (primary, secondary, further and higher).
- Health.
- Local government.
- Housing.
- Criminal law.
- Criminal justice and prosecution system.
- Civil and criminal courts.
- Economic development.

Since devolution the Scottish Parliament has not been reticent about exercising its legislative powers. Indeed, in its first parliamentary term (1999–2003, called Session 1) the Scottish Parliament passed 62 Bills:

- 50 were executive Bills (ie introduced by the Scottish Government – analogous to a Cabinet minister introducing a Bill in the Westminster Parliament).
- Eight were members' Bills (introduced by an MSP, analogous to Westminster private members' Bills).
- Three were committee Bills (introduced by a parliamentary committee).
- One was a private Bill (analogous to a Westminster private Bill).

Source: www.scottish.parliament.uk.

Some of these Bills proved to be controversial (for varying reasons) and actually served to widen the difference between Scotland and England. For example:

- The Protection of Wild Mammals (Scotland) Act 2002 (a member's Bill) ended mounted fox hunting and hare coursing in Scotland. This was two years before the Westminster Parliament passed the 2004 Hunting Act (see section 10.10.3).
- The Community Care and Health (Scotland) Act 2002 (an executive Bill). This Act set out the framework for providing, *inter alia*, free personal and nursing care for older people.

More recently, in Session 3 (2007–11) 53 Acts were made (*Scottish Parliament Fact Sheet, Scottish Parliament Legislation, Session 3* (Scottish Parliament, 2011), p 8). In the (albeit extended) last session of 2011–16 (Session 4), 79 Acts were passed (*Scottish Parliament Fact Sheet, Scottish Parliament Legislation, Session 4* (Scottish Parliament, 2016), p 9). A Bill of particular constitutional significance passed during this session was the Scottish Elections (Reduction of Voting Age) Act 2015, which reduced the voting age to 16 for elections to both the Scottish Parliament and local government.

14.3.7 Tax-varying powers

In the 1997 referendum the Scottish people endorsed the proposition that the Scottish Parliament should enjoy tax-raising powers. As a result, Pt 4 of the Scotland Act 1998 permitted the Scottish Parliament to vary central government taxation in

Scotland (ie to alter the basic rate of income tax by up to three pence in the pound). This provision (historically at least) set Scottish devolution apart from the devolution arrangements in both Wales and Northern Ireland. Part 3 of the Scotland Act 2012 replaced Pt 4 of the 1998 Act with a power to set a Scottish rate of income tax for taxpayers in Scotland on earnings, pensions and profits. More recently, Pt 2 of the Scotland Act 2016 conferred additional fiscal responsibility by providing the Scottish Parliament with the power to set income tax rates and thresholds on Scottish taxpayer's income from non-savings and non-dividends.

KEY FACTS

Scottish devolution powers	
Legislative	• Can pass primary legislation (Acts of the Scottish Parliament). • Can pass subordinate legislation.
Financial	• Tax-varying powers.

14.3.8 Legislative competence

In essence, the Scottish Parliament can legislate in respect of devolved matters and such Acts can modify existing primary legislation relating to Scotland. The Scottish Parliament, however, like other legislatures is a *limited* legislature (contrast the Westminster Parliament in Chapter 7). It cannot pass laws outside of its legislative competence (ie outside of its devolved powers):

SECTION

s 29(1) Scotland Act 1998
'An Act of the Scottish Parliament is not law so far as any provision of the Act is outside the legislative competence of the Parliament.'

Section 29(2) states that a provision will be outside the Scottish Parliament's legislative competence if it:

(a) Will form part of the law of another country/territory (eg England).
(b) Relates to reserved matters (eg national security).
(c) Breaches the restrictions in Sch 4 – this sets out certain legislation which is protected from being altered by an Act of the Scottish Parliament (eg the Human Rights Act 1998, etc).
(d) Is incompatible with the following:
  • European Convention rights (under the Human Rights Act 1998)
  • European Union law (under the European Communities Act 1972) – but now see Brexit later at section 15.6.6.
(e) Removes the Lord Advocate as the head of the systems of criminal prosecution and the investigation of deaths.

In this way the Scottish Parliament is not legislatively omnicompetent, as its Acts can be challenged as *ultra vires* if it legislates outside of its competence.

NB. The Scotland Act 2012 altered the legislative competence of the Scottish Parliament (eg s 10 gives the Scottish Parliament legislative competence in relation to the regulation of air weapons). The Scotland Act 2016 expanded its competence further in relation to, for example, disability, carer's benefits and industrial injuries (s 22) and abortion (s 53).

14.3.9 Ensuring the Scottish Parliament legislates within its powers

Scottish primary legislation can in effect be challenged at two stages to ensure that it is within its legislative competence:

▨ **The parliamentary stage**

Section 31 states that a person in charge of a Bill shall at the outset state that in his view the Bill is within Parliament's legislative competence. The Presiding Officer must also decide whether or not the Bill is within Parliament's legislative competence (ie whether it is *ultra vires* the Scotland Act 1998).

Under s 33 the Advocate General for Scotland, the Lord Advocate or the Attorney General may refer to the United Kingdom Supreme Court the question as to whether a Bill which has been passed by Parliament, but before Royal Assent has been granted, is within the chamber's legislative competence. Under s 32 if the Supreme Court determines that such a Bill is outside the Parliament's powers, the Presiding Officer is unable to submit it for Royal Assent in an unamended form.

Under s 35 the Secretary of State is empowered to prohibit the Presiding Officer from submitting a Bill for Royal Assent if, for example, he has reasonable grounds for believing it would be incompatible with international obligations, etc.

NB. s 11 of the Scotland Act 2016 also provides specific arrangements for Bills which relate to a 'protected subject matter'.

▨ **The court stage**

The legal validity of a Scottish Act of Parliament can be challenged in the courts if it is argued that the Act is outside the legal competence of the Scottish Parliament (ie *ultra vires* – contrast the Westminster Parliament in Chapter 7). This is known as *a devolution issue* and Scottish inferior courts may refer it to the Court of Session or the High Court of Justiciary. Ultimately, the issue may be determined by the Supreme Court in London.

Few attempts have been made to challenge Acts of the Scottish Parliament. In *Anderson v Scottish Ministers* [2002] SC (PC) 1, s 1 of the Mental Health (Public Safety and Appeals) (Scotland) Act 1999 was unsuccessfully challenged as being contrary to Art 5 of the European Convention. In *AXA General Insurance Ltd v Lord Advocate* [2011] UKSC 46 the Supreme Court held that the Damages (Asbestos-Related Conditions) (Scotland) Act 2009 was within the Scottish Parliament's legislative competence as it was compatible with Art 1 of the First Protocol of the European Convention. More recently, however, in *Salvesen v Riddell* [2013] UKSC 22 the Supreme Court held that s 72 of the Agricultural Holdings (Scotland) Act 2003 *was* outside the legislative competence of the Scottish Parliament by being incompatible with Art 1 of the First Protocol (ie the right to property) of the European Convention. In addition, in *Christian Institute v Lord Advocate* [2016] UKSC 51 the Supreme Court held that Pt 4 of the Children and Young People (Scotland) Act 2014 (ie the 'named person scheme') was incompatible with Art 8 (ie the right to a private and family life).

14.3.10 Challenging the actions of the Scottish Government

In relation to actions of members of the Scottish Government, s 58 authorises the Secretary of State to direct that such action is not taken if he has reasonable grounds to believe that it would be incompatible, for example, with any international obligations. Similarly, by order he can revoke subordinate legislation made by a member of the Scottish Government which contains provisions which he has reasonable grounds to believe are incompatible with, for example, the interests of defence or national security. Moreover, s 57 prohibits a member of the Scottish Government from acting or making subordinate legislation which is incompatible with European Convention rights or European Union law (on the latter now see Brexit at section 15.6.6).

In *RM v Scottish Ministers* [2012] UKSC 58 the Supreme Court held that the failure of Scottish Ministers to draft and lay a regulation before the Scottish Parliament under the aegis of the Mental Health (Care and Treatment) (Scotland) Act 2003 was unlawful.

14.3.11 The European Convention and devolution

The following cases raised devolution issues concerning claims that Convention rights had been violated in the context of Scottish criminal proceedings.

CASE EXAMPLE

Starrs v Ruxton *2000 SLT 42*

The High Court of Justiciary declared that temporary sheriffs were incompatible with the right to a fair trial (Art 6) as their appointments lacked security of tenure. As they held office at the pleasure, in effect, of the Lord Advocate (who was part of the Scottish Government), the appearance of independence was absent.

Following this case, the Scottish Parliament enacted the Bail, Judicial Appointments etc (Scotland) Act 2000 abolishing the office of temporary sheriffs.

CASE EXAMPLE

Brown v Stott (Procurator Fiscal) *[2003] 1 AC 681*

The Privy Council held that the prosecution could use evidence of Brown's compulsory admission to the police under the 1988 Road Traffic Act (that she had been the driver of a car) against her. Brown unsuccessfully argued that this infringed her right not to incriminate herself under Art 6 of the European Convention (the right to a fair trial).

In *Alvin Lee Sinclair v Her Majesty's Advocate* [2005] UKPC D2, the Privy Council quashed a conviction on the basis that a failure to disclose evidence to the defence violated Art 6 (the right to a fair hearing). Most recently, in *AB v HM Advocate* [2017] UKSC 25 the Supreme Court held that s 39 of the Sexual Offences (Scotland) Act 2009 was incompatible with the appellant's right to Art 8.

NB. In the context of Scottish criminal proceedings, however, it should be noted that the Scotland Act 2012 altered the meaning of a 'devolution issue'.

14.3.12 The relationship with Westminster

Even though Scotland has its own Parliament, this does not mean that it loses its MPs at Westminster (although the Scottish Parliament (Constituencies) Act 2004 did reduce the number of Scottish MPs from 72 to 59). Scottish MPs are still needed in Westminster to represent the people of Scotland in respect of reserved matters (ie issues which affect the whole of the United Kingdom). Historically, these Scottish MPs were entitled to (and did) vote on English matters, which raised the issue of the 'West Lothian question' (originally raised during the devolution debates in the 1970s by Tam Dalyell, MP for the constituency of West Lothian). In other words:

QUOTATION

'. . . MPs from outside England could help determine laws that apply in England, while MPs from England would have no reciprocal influence on laws outside England in policy fields for which the devolved institutions would now be responsible.'

The McKay Commission – *Report of the Commission on the consequences of devolution for the House of Commons* (March 2013).

One possible solution put forward to the 'West Lothian question' was proposed by Lord Baker's private member's Bill: The Parliament (Participation of Members of the House of Commons) Bill 2006 which would have enabled the Speaker of the House of Commons to certify the territorial extent of a Bill (eg a Bill affecting only England) on which only designated MPs could vote (ie English MPs voting on English legislation). Another solution was of course the creation of an 'English Parliament' (a parallel of the Scottish Parliament). According to the Justice Select Committee:

QUOTATION

'There is no consensus about solutions to the "English question", or the range of questions which arise under that heading. Each suggested answer has its own problems and limitations . . .'

Devolution: A Decade On, Fifth Report of Session 2008–09, HC 529-I (The Stationery Office, 2009), p 69.

In 2012 the McKay Commission was established with the remit 'to consider how the House of Commons might deal with legislation which affects only part of the United Kingdom, following the devolution of certain legislative powers to the Scottish Parliament, the Northern Ireland Assembly and the National Assembly for Wales' (The McKay Commission – *Report of the Commission on the consequences of devolution for the House of Commons* (March 2013)). It reported in 2013 and proposed the following constitutional principle be adopted by resolution of the House of Commons:

QUOTATION

'. . . decisions at the United Kingdom level with a separate and distinct effect for England (or for England – and – Wales) should normally be taken only with the consent of a majority of MPs for constituencies in England (or England – and – Wales).'

(para 12)

In 2015 the standing orders of the House of Commons were amended to provide for the EVEL ('English Votes for English Laws') procedure to – finally – address the 'West Lothian question' (see section 12.7.3) and this procedure now also applies to Scottish income tax provisions (see section 14.3.7).

Scotland is still represented in Cabinet by a Secretary of State and he represents a link between the Scottish Parliament, Westminster, Whitehall and the other devolved areas. In addition, a House of Commons Scottish Affairs Committee examines the administration and policy of the Scotland Office (including relations with the Scottish Parliament) and a Scottish Grand Committee (composed of all Scottish MPs) discusses and debates Scottish matters in general (although it has not met recently).

14.3.13 Parliamentary sovereignty and the Scottish Parliament

In strict constitutional theory, parliamentary sovereignty has not been affected by the establishment of the Scottish Parliament. Indeed, on this point the then Labour government in its 1997 White Paper made it very clear that:

QUOTATION

'The UK Parliament is and will remain sovereign in all matters. . . . Westminster will be choosing to exercise that sovereignty by devolving legislative responsibilities to a Scottish Parliament without in any way diminishing its own powers.'

Scotland's Parliament, Cm 3658 (The Scottish Office, 1997), p 12.

As a result, the United Kingdom Parliament (in legal theory) could choose:

■ To legislate for Scotland in respect of devolved matters without the consent of the Scottish Parliament:

SECTION

s 28(7) Scotland Act 1998
'This section does not affect the power of the Parliament of the United Kingdom to make laws for Scotland.'

Notwithstanding this, consequent upon devolution a constitutional convention had arisen known as the Sewel Convention (named after Lord Sewel, who piloted the Scotland Bill through the upper House), which regulated the relationship between the two parliaments. In essence the convention provided that the United Kingdom Parliament would not legislate for Scotland on a devolved matter (or where the competence of the Scottish Parliament or the responsibilities of the Government would be altered) without first obtaining the express consent of the Scottish Parliament. This consent was given in the form of a legislative consent motion (eg one was passed endorsing the principle of the putative Supreme Court, which of course would affect Scotland – Official Report, Session 2, 19 January 2005). Although the Sewel Convention was given statutory recognition in s 2 of the Scotland Act 2016, as pointed out earlier at section 4.13.13 this simply *recognised* the convention, rather than making it *justiciable* in the courts.

To revoke the Scotland Act 1998 itself, although Laws LJ indicated that this would have to be done expressly (see section 4.4.5). However, s 1 of the Scotland Act 2016 now provides for the 'permanence' of the Scottish Parliament and Scottish Government, which are *not* to be abolished without a referendum in Scotland. This raises the issue of the limitation of sovereignty through the (contested) redefinition theory – see section 7.10.2.

Finally, there has been some debate over whether parliamentary sovereignty has historically been fully accepted in Scotland in any event. This is on the basis that the principle was a purely English notion associated with the English, but not the Scottish Parliament, prior to the Union with Scotland Act 1706 (see Lord Cooper in *MacCormick v Lord Advocate* (1953) SC 396).

ACTIVITY

Quick quiz

1. What do the Scottish Parliament and Government do?
2. What is the difference between devolved and reserved matters?
3. How can the actions of the Scottish Parliament and Government be challenged?
4. What is the relationship between the Scottish and the Westminster parliaments?

14.4 Northern Irish devolution

14.4.1 History

England had exerted control over Ireland for centuries before the 1800 Act of Union unified the Parliament of Great Britain with that of Ireland. This Union created the Parliament of the United Kingdom of Great Britain (England, Wales and Scotland) and Ireland. By the beginning of the twentieth century the pressure from Irish nationalist politicians for home rule for the Irish to govern themselves led to the Government of Ireland Act 1914. This legislation aimed to establish an Irish Parliament, however it never came into effect owing to the outbreak of the First World War.

In 1920 the Government of Ireland Act was passed, which recognised the reality that two separate parliaments were needed in Ireland:

- One for the south (which was overwhelmingly Roman Catholic); and
- One for the north (a majority of which was Protestant).

Although the Northern Irish Parliament (Stormont) was established and operated until March 1972, in contrast the Southern Irish Parliament was repudiated by Sinn Fein. This in effect led to the creation in 1922 of the Irish Free State (with Dominion status), which thereafter became a Republic (1937) and then left the Commonwealth (1949). Northern Ireland with its Stormont Parliament remained part of the United Kingdom (now the United Kingdom of Great Britain and Northern Ireland).

Stormont

The Northern Irish Parliament functioned for five decades and was a bicameral legislature consisting of two chambers:

- House of Commons (directly elected).
- Senate (which was indirectly elected by the lower House).

The executive aspect of the arrangements involved a parliamentary executive comprising a Prime Minister together with a Northern Irish Cabinet. The Parliament was a limited legislature with certain areas (eg defence) excepted from its legislative competence.

The major problem with the Parliament was that in this divided community it continually had a unionist (effectively Protestant) majority. Civil unrest in the province, fuelled by the grievances of the Catholic minority community, led eventually in March 1972 to the suspension of Stormont (s 31 of the Northern Ireland Constitution Act 1973 abolished the Parliament of Northern Ireland) and direct rule being imposed by the United Kingdom government. Thereafter, a Secretary of State for Northern Ireland would make decisions for Northern Ireland and the legislative powers enjoyed by the defunct Stormont would be exercised through Orders in Council.

The 1998 Good Friday Agreement

During the period of direct rule there were various unsuccessful attempts at securing a solution to the 'Northern Ireland problem', but in 1998, in the aftermath of an IRA ceasefire, the Belfast Agreement (ie 'the Good Friday Agreement') was signed by all parties. It endorsed the resumption of devolution of power to Northern Ireland and the establishment of new institutional relationships between the United Kingdom, the Republic of Ireland and Ulster.

The Good Friday Agreement was subsequently endorsed in May 1998 by a vote north and south of the Irish border. Following this, the United Kingdom Parliament passed:

- The Northern Ireland (Elections) Act 1998 – to enable elections to take place for the new Northern Ireland Assembly.
- The Northern Ireland Act 1998 – to establish the institutional framework of devolution. NB: in *Robinson v Secretary of State for Northern Ireland* [2002] UKHL 32 Lord Bingham referred to this Act as effectively 'a constitution' for Northern Ireland.

Subsequent developments

Unfortunately, the actual operation of the devolved arrangements proved to be very problematic as it was not until December 1999 that power was finally devolved to the institutions, but then in October 2002 the Assembly was suspended. Notwithstanding the resumption of direct rule (with the Northern Ireland Office and Secretary of State exercising powers instead via Orders in Council), elections took place in November 2003 for a new Northern Ireland Assembly to revive devolution. Three years later, a 'transitional assembly' sat and was dissolved to pave the way for fresh elections to take place in March 2007. These elections were preceded by the *St Andrews Agreement*, made by the UK Prime Minister and the Irish Taoiseach – subsequently given effect by the Northern Ireland (St Andrews Agreement) Act 2006, which set out a timetable to revive devolution. Thereafter, devolution in Northern Ireland resumed in May 2007 with a functioning Executive Committee and Assembly. In early 2017, political division and the resignation of the Deputy First Minister led to fresh elections in March 2017 (see below at section 14.4.2). Unfortunately, despite these elections, no new Northern Ireland Executive Committee could be agreed to be formed, so in early 2018 Northern Ireland devolution was in abeyance.

14.4.2 The Northern Ireland Assembly

The Northern Ireland Assembly is a unicameral legislature which was initially elected on a four-yearly term (it is interesting to remember that Stormont had been bicameral). However, s 7 of the Northern Ireland (Miscellaneous Provisions) Act 2014 extended the term of the Assembly to five years.

Northern Irish devolution is distinctive in that certain decisions/votes have to be made on a cross-community basis. This involves obtaining the support of the majority of both community representatives (known as 'cross-community support'). Such parallel consent is seen as essential in a divided community.

Composition and elections

The Northern Ireland Assembly consists of 90 Members (MLAs), who are elected on the basis of STV (single transferable vote), with 18 constituencies returning five members each. The Assembly Members (Reduction of Numbers) Act (Northern Ireland) 2016 provided for each constituency to return five members, rather that six, as had previously been the case. The STV electoral system allows voters to indicate their varying preferences for different candidates, thereby maximising consensus among voters. The first elections took place in June 1998, with the latest taking place in March 2017.

The Northern Ireland Assembly 2017	
Northern Ireland Assembly Election, March 2017	
POLITICAL PARTY	**SEATS**
Ulster Unionist Party (UUP)	10
Democratic Unionist Party (DUP)	28
Social Democratic and Labour Party (SDLP)	12
Sinn Fein (SF)	27
Alliance	8
Green Party	2
Others	3
Total	90

Table 14.2

Source: L Audickas O Hawkins and R Cracknell, *UK Election Statistics: 1918–2017*, Briefing Paper CBP7529 (House of Commons Library, 2017), p 56.

All MLAs are governed by *The Code of Conduct and the Guide to the Rules Relating to the Conduct of Members* (2016), which details the standard of conduct expected of members.

Presiding Officer and committee system

Northern Irish devolution provides for the election from among its membership of a Presiding Officer (the Speaker) and two deputies (analogous with the Scottish

Parliament). As in Scotland, there is a committee system, with committees shadowing the different Northern Irish government departmental portfolios (eg the Committee for Justice scrutinises the Department of Justice). In addition, there are various standing committees (ie Public Accounts).

14.4.3 The Northern Ireland Executive Committee

Part III of the 1998 Act provides for the establishment of the following ministerial offices (the Executive Committee):

- First Minister and Deputy First Minister (one from the unionist and one from the nationalist community).
- Northern Ireland ministers – these are determined using the *d'Handt* political system (s 18) based on the proportion of Assembly seats each party has acquired. In this way Northern Ireland devolution is distinctive as its executive reflects the balance of opinion within the Assembly. In short, its *raison d'etre* is power-sharing between the two communities and the various political parties. Each Executive minister will head a government department (eg Department of Health). All ministers are governed by a *Ministerial Code of Conduct*. NB: it is interesting to note that, owing to the power-sharing composition of the Executive, the convention of collective responsibility seemingly does not apply (see section 12.2.2).

KEY FACTS

Composition of the Northern Irish devolved institutions	
Assembly	• 90 Members (single transferable vote system).
Executive	• First Minister and Deputy First Minister. • Northern Ireland ministers.

14.4.4 Legislation and legislative competence

Section 5 empowers the Assembly to make primary legislation, known as Acts of the Northern Ireland Assembly. During 2016, 30 Bills received the Royal Assent (source: V Apostolova, *Acts and Statutory Instruments: The volume of UK legislation 1950 to 2016*, Briefing Paper CBP7438 (House of Commons Library, 2017), Table 2). For an example of an Assembly Act, see the Commissioner for Older People Act (Northern Ireland) 2011, which established a Commissioner to safeguard and promote the interests of older people. As with Scotland, for the purposes of the Human Rights Act 1998 (s 21), such legislation is regarded as secondary and so subject to legal challenge. A more recent example is the Departments Act (Northern Ireland) 2016, which changed the nomenclature of the various Northern Irish government departments.

The Northern Ireland Assembly (like its 1972 predecessor and the Scottish Parliament) is a limited and subordinate legislature:

SECTION

s 6(1) Northern Ireland Act 1998
'A provision of an Act is not law if it is outside the legislative competence of the Assembly.'

Section 6(2) sets out the circumstances which will be outside of the Assembly's legislative competence. These are very similar to those already set out in relation to the Scottish Parliament (see section 14.3.8); however, one additional circumstance which applies specifically to the Northern Ireland Assembly is if its Acts discriminate on the ground of religious belief or political opinion (s 6(2)(e)). NB: in respect of European Union law, see Brexit later at section 15.6.6.

14.4.5 Reserved, excepted and transferred matters
Reserved matters
The Assembly cannot legislate in respect of reserved matters (Sch 3) unless they are allocated the specific responsibility to do so by the conversion of a reserved matter into a transferred one (under s 2 this would require an Order in Council). These areas include, for example, the Post Office.

Excepted matters
The Assembly cannot legislate in respect of excepted matters (Sch 2). Excepted matters include, for example, the defence of the realm.

Transferred matters
The Assembly can legislate in respect of transferred matters and these include, for example:
- The Arts.
- Education.
- Agriculture.

NB. The Northern Ireland Act 2009 paved the way for the transfer of policing and justice powers and following the *Hillsborough Castle Agreement* in February 2010 these powers were then devolved in April 2010.

14.4.6 Ensuring the Northern Ireland Assembly legislates within its powers
The Northern Ireland Assembly can be challenged at two stages:

The parliamentary (Assembly) stage
(i)   Section 9 of the Northern Ireland Act 1998 requires that a minister in charge of a Bill makes a statement at the outset that in his view it is compatible with the Assembly's legislative competence.
(ii) Section 10 states that a Bill will not be introduced if the Presiding Officer considers that it is not within the Assembly's legislative competence.
(iii) Section 11 empowers the Attorney General for Northern Ireland to refer a Bill (which has been passed by the Assembly) to the Supreme Court in London to determine whether it is within the Assembly's legislative competence. If it is not, the Secretary of State (not the Presiding Officer) cannot submit the Bill for Royal Assent in an unamended form (s 14). In addition, the Secretary of State may refuse to submit a Bill which he considers would breach international obligations.
(iv) Under s 13 the Human Rights Commission (see section 14.4.9) may be asked by the Assembly whether a Bill is compatible with human rights.

The court stage
The legal validity of an Act of the Northern Ireland Assembly can be challenged in the courts – ultimately before the Supreme Court – on the basis of a *devolution issue* (ie has the Northern Ireland Assembly acted within its powers?).

14.4.7 Challenging the actions of the Northern Ireland Executive Committee

Under s 24, a Northern Ireland minister or Northern Ireland department has no power to act or to make subordinate legislation which, *inter alia*:

- Is incompatible with European Convention rights.
- Is incompatible with European Union law (but see Brexit later at section 15.6.6).
- Discriminates on the ground of religious belief or political opinion.
- Modifies an entrenched enactment (eg modifies the Human Rights Act 1998 or European Communities Act 1972 – but on the latter, see Brexit later at section 15.6.6).

Moreover, if such legislation deals with an excepted or reserved matter the Secretary of State may revoke it by order (s 25). Similarly, he may do so where such legislation is incompatible, *inter alia*, with any international obligations (s 26).

KEY FACTS

Northern Irish devolution powers
• Primary legislation (Acts of the Northern Ireland Assembly).
• Subordinate legislation (passed by the Northern Ireland Executive Committee).

14.4.8 The relationship with Westminster and parliamentary sovereignty

As with Scotland, Northern Ireland returns MPs to Westminster (it returns 18 MPs). Northern Ireland also retains its Secretary of State. At Westminster, like Scotland at section 14.3.12, Northern Ireland has a House of Commons Northern Ireland Affairs Committee (in respect of the Northern Ireland Office) and a Northern Ireland Grand Committee (to debate and discuss the general affairs of Northern Ireland).

As with Scotland, the existence of a Northern Ireland Assembly does not in strict constitutional theory affect parliamentary sovereignty:

SECTION

s 5(6) Northern Ireland Act 1998
'This section does not affect the power of the Parliament of the United Kingdom to make laws for Northern Ireland.'

Further, the United Kingdom Parliament legally could revoke the Assembly. Indeed, as we have already seen, the previous Stormont Parliament was revoked by the Westminster Parliament in 1973.

In terms of sovereignty, however, the Act does make the following declaration at the outset:

SECTION

s 1(1) Northern Ireland Act 1998
'It is hereby declared that Northern Ireland in its entirety remains part of the United Kingdom and shall not cease to be so without the consent of a majority of the people of Northern Ireland voting in a poll held for the purposes of this section.'

ACTIVITY

Applying the law

Does s 1 of the Northern Ireland Act 1998 mean that the United Kingdom Parliament could not:
(a) legally
and/or
(b) politically
legislate to sever Northern Ireland from the rest of the United Kingdom without first obtaining the consent of the Northern Irish people? (See also section 7.10.2.)

14.4.9 Other strands to the Belfast Agreement

These included the following:

- **The North–South Ministerial Council** – composed of ministers from the Irish government (Republic of Ireland) and the Northern Ireland Executive Committee to consider matters of mutual interest.
- **The British–Irish Council** – composed of representatives from the British and Irish governments, together with those from the devolved institutions to agree common policies.

Human Rights Commission

Section 68 of the Northern Ireland Act 1998 established a Northern Ireland Human Rights Commission. Its functions include, for example:

- Keeping under review Northern Ireland's law and practice in respect of protecting human rights.
- Advising the Secretary of State and Executive Committee of legislative (and other) measures which ought to be taken to protect human rights.
- Advising the Assembly whether a Bill is compatible with human rights.

ACTIVITY

Quick quiz

1. What do the Northern Ireland Assembly and Executive Committee do?
2. What is the difference between transferred, reserved and excepted matters?
3. How can the actions of the Assembly and the Executive Committee be challenged?
4. How does Northern Irish devolution differ from that in Scotland?

14.5 Welsh devolution

14.5.1 History

For centuries Wales has been closely connected with England, as indicated by the 1536 Act of Union between the two countries. Today England and Wales are one single legal jurisdiction. By the second part of the twentieth century, however, there was a growing nationalist call in Wales for it to be able to govern itself. In 1978 the Wales Act was passed, which conferred a diluted form of devolution on Wales, but the legislation did not come into effect because only 12 per cent voted in favour of it in a Welsh referendum. The Labour Party election manifesto of 1997 was committed to the establishment of Welsh devolution and in July 1997 the then Labour government issued its White Paper detailing its proposals (*A Voice for Wales*, Cm 3718 (The Stationery Office, 1997)).

As in Scotland, these proposals were endorsed in a referendum in September 1997 (but only by the narrowest of margins: 50.3 per cent voted yes). Following this, the Government of Wales Act 1998 was passed, which devolved power to Wales. This Act has been superseded by the Government of Wales Act 2006, which re-enacts many of its provisions. The 2006 Act was enacted so as to strengthen and deepen the devolved arrangements in Wales and had been preceded by a White Paper, *Better Governance for Wales*, Cm 6582 (Wales Office, 2005). In recent years, two more Wales Acts have been passed (in 2014 and 2017), which have devolved further powers. It is significant to note that s 1 of the Wales Act 2017 explicitly recognises a body of 'Welsh law' which is made by the Welsh devolved institutions.

14.5.2 The National Assembly for Wales

Section 1 of the Government of Wales Act 2006 states that there is to be an Assembly known as the National Assembly for Wales (Cynulliad Cenedlaethol Cymru). Under s 1 of the 1998 Act the Assembly was a corporate body (with executive and legislative arms united), but this is no longer the case under the 2006 Act.

Composition and elections

The Assembly is composed of 60 Assembly Members (AMs). They are elected on the following basis:

- 40 Assembly constituency members – elected by the 'first past the post' system.
- 20 Assembly regional members – elected by the additional member system of proportional representation (four from each of the five regional electoral regions).

As in Scotland, the combination of electoral systems is designed to offset the disproportionate nature of the 'first past the post' system. Elections took place in 1999, 2003 and 2007 and 2011. The latest set of elections took place in May 2016:

The National Assembly for Wales			
2016 Assembly election			
POLITICAL PARTY	**CONSTITUENCY SEATS**	**REGIONAL SEATS**	**TOTAL**
Labour Party	27	2	29
Welsh Conservative Party	6	5	11
Plaid Cymru (Welsh Nationalist)	6	6	12
Welsh Liberal Democrats	1	0	1
UKIP	0	7	7
TOTAL	40	20	60

Table 14.3

Source: L Audickas, O Hawkins and R Cracknell, *UK Election Statistics: 1918–2017*, Briefing Paper CBP7529 (House of Commons Library, 2017), p 52.

Section 6 provides that voters have two votes:

- A constituency vote – a vote cast for a candidate in their constituency.
- An electoral regional vote – a vote cast for a political party or for an individual candidate.

Although elections were originally on a fixed-term basis of four years, s 1 of the Wales Act 2014 provided for a five-year term. All Assembly Members are required to adhere to the standards of conduct set out in the *National Assembly for Wales: Code of Conduct for Assembly Members and Associated Documents* (May 2016).

Presiding Officer and committees

Section 25 of the 2006 Act provides for the election by the Assembly of a Presiding Officer together with a Deputy Presiding Officer, similar to the Scottish Parliament. The Assembly operates through a variety of different committees. These include:

- The Health, Social Care and Sport Committee (which considers, *inter alia*, health matters)
- Other committees (eg the Public Accounts Committee, which scrutinises the expenditure of the Welsh Government).

14.5.3 The Welsh Government

Section 45 of the 2006 Act established a 'Welsh Assembly Government' (Llywodraeth Cynulliad Cymru), but this was renamed the Welsh Government (Llywodraeth Cymru) by s 4 of the Wales Act 2014. Following the 2016 election, the Welsh Government was Labour (albeit a minority administration). The Welsh Government comprises the following:

- The First Minister – nominated by the Assembly.
- The remaining Welsh Ministers – appointed by the First Minister from among the Assembly Members (the arrangements therefore are those of a parliamentary executive and under s 45 of the 2006 Act the First Minister and Welsh Ministers are collectively known as the 'Welsh Ministers').
- The Deputy Welsh Ministers – appointed by the First Minister to assist any of the above.
- The Counsel General to the Welsh Government – the government's legal adviser (a new office created by the 2006 Act).

Ministers are governed by the following code: *Ministerial Code* (Welsh Government, 2017), which is issued by the First Minister. Each minister will be allocated a particular governmental portfolio. For example, in 2017 these included, *inter alia*, the Cabinet Secretary for Finance and Cabinet Secretary for Economy and Transport.

One key change brought about by the 2006 Act was to formally/constitutionally separate the Welsh executive from the Welsh legislature. The 1998 legislation (unlike in Scotland or Northern Ireland) did not separate these constitutional functions as the Assembly was a corporate body exercising both. In 2005 the then Labour government's White Paper had proposed separating the legislative and executive aspects of the Assembly and this had followed a Commission Report by Lord Richard (*The Report of the Commission on the Powers and Electoral Arrangements of the National Assembly for Wales* (March 2004)), which had recommended that the *status quo* was no longer sustainable. As pointed out in the White Paper:

QUOTATION

'Often, decisions are made in the name of the Assembly which are in fact, quite properly, the responsibility of one Minister or official, making it hard to know who should be accountable to the public for them.'

Better Governance for Wales, Cm 6582 (Wales Office, 2005), p 3.

Under the 2006 Act the Welsh Government is a separate constitutional entity (although it sits in the Assembly and is directly accountable to it), thereby ensuring more transparent accountability for the use of its powers. In fact, under s 48 Welsh Ministers must resign if the Assembly resolves that they no longer enjoy the confidence of the Assembly (similar to a vote of no confidence in the House of Commons). Even before the 2006 Act, however, members of the executive were held accountable to the rest of the Assembly through the committee system, debates and questioning.

KEY FACTS

Composition of the Welsh devolved institutions	
Assembly	60 Assembly Members (AMs), comprising: • 40 Assembly constituency members (the 'first past the post' system). • 20 Assembly regional members (the additional member system).
Executive	• The First Minister. • Welsh Ministers (including deputies). • The Counsel General to the Welsh Government.

14.5.4 Powers and responsibilities

Detailed below is a brief outline of how the powers and responsibilities of the Assembly have developed over time (a demonstration of 'rolling' devolution):

▪ Under the aegis of the 1998 Act devolved powers included, for example, housing, environment, education and training, sport, transport and culture. Powers were conferred on the Assembly, which in turn in practice were typically delegated to the executive, which acted as the delegate of the Assembly. Today, under the 2006 Act, s 58 permits the transfer of functions directly onto the Welsh Ministers by way of an Order in Council. In this way, the Welsh Ministers exercise functions in their own constitutional right rather than as delegates of the Assembly. They will, therefore, make executive decisions, subordinate/secondary legislation, etc, albeit they will be scrutinised by the Assembly.

▪ Under the 1998 Act, the scheme of devolution as applied to Wales was termed *'executive devolution'* as the Assembly was not given powers to make primary legislation (contrast with Scotland and Northern Ireland). It was commonly argued that Wales did not need legislative devolution because its arrangements were not sufficiently distinctive (unlike Scotland). Indeed, it was partly this diluted form of devolution offered to the Welsh which explained the rather disappointing support for it at the 1997 referendum.

The Assembly could, however, make subordinate legislation (which the executive could propose for the Assembly to endorse).

As a result of the changes made under Pt 3 of the Government of Wales Act 2006, the Assembly was able to make laws known as Measures of the National Assembly for Wales within its specified legislative competence (ie in relation to a 'matter' in respect of one of 20 broad 'fields' in Sch 5 of the Act). According to the explanatory notes to the 2006 Act (Crown Copyright, 2006, p 51) this instrument was 'a type of subordinate legislation', although such Assembly Measures 'have the same effect as an Act of Parliament' as according to s 94(1) they '*may make any provision that could be made by an Act of Parliament*' (emphasis added). Amendments could be made to the content of Sch 5 by way of either:

- a 'framework provision' in a Westminster Bill, or
- a Legislative Competence Order (LCO). An LCO had to be approved in draft form by both the Assembly and both Houses of Parliament before an Order in Council was made by Her Majesty. For an example, see the National Assembly for Wales (Legislative Competence) (Social Welfare) Order 2008 SI 2008/1785, which extended the legislative competence of the Assembly in relation to Field 15 (social welfare).

In addition, the 2006 Act paved the way in the future for further legislative powers (to be known as Acts of the National Assembly for Wales) to be conferred subsequently onto the Assembly following the support of the Welsh people in a referendum (Pt 4 of the 2006 Act). Part 4 would then supersede Pt 3 and enable the Assembly to pass laws (Acts) on a broad range of subjects without having to have recourse to Parliament on the *ad hoc* basis of the LCO procedure above. Section 106 states that Pt 3 would cease to have effect when the Assembly Act (Pt 4) provisions came into force.

In 2007 the Welsh Government established the *All Wales Convention* to assess the law-making powers that the Assembly should enjoy. It reported in 2009 (*All Wales Convention Report* (Crown Copyright, 2009)) and concluded that there was solid support among the Welsh people for devolution (para 6.2.9). The Convention was convinced that Pt 4 of the Act offered 'substantial advantage' over the then current arrangements of Pt 3. Following a referendum in Wales in March 2011, which endorsed Pt 4 (primary legislative powers) being activated, the National Assembly can now pass Acts of the National Assembly for Wales. For example, the Local Government Byelaws (Wales) Act 2012 simplifies the procedure for making/enforcing local authority byelaws in Wales.

The Wales Act 2014 – although this Act made some changes to the constitutional arrangements of the Welsh devolved settlement (see earlier), the key aspect of the legislation concerned the devolution of tax-raising powers (Pt 2 – Finance). For an example of a use of these new fiscal powers, see the Land Transaction Tax and Anti-avoidance of Devolved Taxes (Wales) Act 2017.

The Wales Act 2017 – in broad terms this Act shifted the Welsh devolved settlement model more into line with the arrangements that pertain in Scotland. This 'reserved powers model' enables the National Assembly to legislate, with the exception on those matters which are 'reserved'. The Act also devolved further powers to both the National Assembly (eg s 16 power to authorise a change of name) and the Welsh Ministers (eg s 29 power in respect of Welsh harbours). Section 9 of the Act states that 'protected subject matter' (ie specified electoral legislation) must be passed by a supermajority of two-thirds of the total number of seats in the National Assembly.

The above two Acts had been proceeded by two Silk Commissions: *Empowerment and Responsibility: Financial Powers to Strengthen Wales* (Commission on Devolution in Wales, 2012) and *Empowerment and Responsibility: Legislative Powers to Strengthen Wales* (Commission on Devolution in Wales, 2014).

14.5.5 The competence of the institutions

The National Assembly for Wales

SECTION
....

> s 108 A Government of Wales Act 2006 (as amended by the 2017 Act)
> 'An Act of the Assembly is not law so far as any provision of the Act is outside the Assembly's legislative competence.'

Under s 108 A a provision will be outside the Assembly's legislative competence if, *inter alia*:

- ▪ It extends to a legal jurisdiction other than England and Wales (although England and Wales are historically a single jurisdiction, the Act will invariably apply *only* in Wales – albeit with specified exceptions).
- ▪ It is incompatible with European Convention rights or European Union law (but on the latter see Brexit later at section 15.6.6).
- ▪ It relates to a reserved matter.

In addition, the person in charge of a proposed Assembly Bill must state at the outset that in their view it is within the legislative competence of the Assembly, and the Presiding Officer must also decide if it is and state his decision (s 110). Further, under s 112 the Counsel General or the Attorney General can seek a decision of the Supreme Court as to whether a proposed Bill is within the Assembly's legislative competence. In 2015 the Supreme Court held that the Recovery of Medical Costs for Asbestos Diseases (Wales) Bill referred to it by the Counsel General was outside the legislative competence of the National Assembly (*Re Recovery of Medical Costs for Asbestos Diseases (Wales) Bill* [2015] UKSC 3). Under s 114 the Secretary of State also has the power to intervene to prohibit a Bill from being submitted to the Crown for Royal Assent where, for example, he has reasonable grounds that the Bill would, for example, be incompatible with the interests of national security or defence.

The actions of the Welsh Ministers

- ▪ Under the 2006 Act (as amended), Welsh Ministers have no power to make subordinate legislation or do any other act if it is incompatible with European Union law (s 80) or European Convention rights (s 81) – on the former, now see Brexit later at section 15.6.6.
- ▪ In addition, s 82 empowers the Secretary of State to direct that the Welsh Ministers do not take proposed action if it would be incompatible with any international obligation. Similarly, he can revoke subordinate legislation on the same basis.

A devolution issue

Schedule 9 of the 2006 Act (as amended) states that a devolution issue means:

1(1) (a) a question whether an Act of the Assembly is within the Assembly's legislative competence,

      (b) a question whether any function is exercisable by the Welsh Ministers, First Minister or Counsel General,

(c) a question whether an exercise of a function by the above (in b) is within their powers (including ss 80 and 81 – see above),

(d) a question whether the above (in b) have failed to comply with a duty imposed on them (including any obligation under European Union law under s 80) – but now see Brexit later at section 15.6.6,

(e) a question whether a failure to act by the above (in b) is incompatible with European Convention rights.

The court of last resort in relation to devolution issues, as with Scotland and Northern Ireland, is the Supreme Court in London.

KEY FACTS

	Welsh devolution powers
Legislative	• Passes laws (Assembly Acts) – Pt 4 of the Government of Wales Act 2006.
Financial	• Powers in relation to income tax.

14.5.6 The relationship with Westminster and parliamentary sovereignty

Wales returns 40 MPs to Westminster and the country is represented in central government by a Secretary of State. At Westminster, like Scotland and Northern Ireland, Wales has a House of Commons Welsh Affairs Committee (which considers matters within the Secretary of State for Wales's responsibility) and a Welsh Grand Committee.

As with the other devolution settlements, in legal theory parliamentary sovereignty is unaffected by Welsh devolution as these arrangements could simply be repealed by a Westminster statute. Moreover, the 2006 Act makes it clear that, notwithstanding the devolved arrangements, ultimately Parliament can legislate for Wales if it chooses to do so:

SECTION

s 107(5) Government of Wales Act 2006

'This Part does not affect the power of the Parliament of the United Kingdom to make laws for Wales.'

However, s 2 of the Wales Act 2017 provides an analogous provision to the statutory recognition of the Sewel Convention for Scotland (albeit in respect of the Welsh Assembly) – see earlier at section 14.3.13. Similarly, s 1 of the 2017 Act provides for the permanence of the National Assembly and Welsh Government, which 'are not to be abolished' without a referendum in Wales. This provision also mirrors the one in respect of Scotland (s 1 of the Scotland Act 2016) and raises issues concerning the (contested) redefinition theory of sovereignty (see section 7.10.2).

ACTIVITY

Quick quiz

1. What powers and responsibilities do the National Assembly and the Welsh Government have?
2. How can the actions of the National Assembly and the Welsh Government be challenged?
3. Does Welsh devolution differ from that in Scotland?

KEY FACTS

Links between the devolved settlements

- The British–Irish Council contains representatives from each of the devolved institutions together with the British and Irish governments.

- The Joint Ministerial Council contains representatives of all three executive administrations together with the British government.

- A *Memorandum of Understanding* has been agreed which promotes co-operation and communication between the devolved administrations and the United Kingdom government (see *Devolution, Memorandum of Understanding and Supplementary Agreements* (2012)).

14.6 The position of England

14.6.1 No English Parliament

The devolution arrangements in the British constitution are not symmetrical because, while Scotland, Wales and Northern Ireland have a tier of government between local government and central government/Parliament, there is no corresponding tier in England. In short, there is no English Parliament to regulate purely English affairs, which means that the vast majority of people in the United Kingdom, who are English, are not regulated by any form of devolved infrastructure (except for London – see below). Instead, England is regulated by the United Kingdom Parliament in Westminster. However, in 2015, in response to the 'West Lothian question', the EVEL ('English Votes for English Laws') procedure was adopted in the House of Commons (see section 12.7.3).

In addition, since 1998 England's regional constitutional arrangements have witnessed the following three developments (regional development agencies, combined authorities and the London Mayor and Assembly):

14.6.2 The English regions

Under the Regional Development Agencies Act 1998 a new level of strategic administration was inserted: the regional development agencies (RDAs). According to the Prime Minister in 2002:

QUOTATION

'We have already done a lot to decentralise decision-making to the English regions. Regional Development Agencies (RDAs) have been established to help strengthen the building blocks for economic growth in all regions, with a network of regional chambers to scrutinise them.'

Your Region, Your Choice: Revitalising the English Regions,
Cm 5511 (The Stationery Office, 2002), Preface.

In 2009, there were nine RDAs (West Midlands, North West etc). In essence they were strategic bodies whose remit included, *inter alia*:

- improving economic performance, development and regeneration
- promoting employment (and developing employment skills)
- assisting sustainable development.

In this way they provided a strategic and regional approach to these issues, which was specifically tailored for each particular region. However, the eight regional assemblies (voluntary bodies comprising representatives of local government, business and the wider community) had been abolished by 2010. Thereafter, the RDAs were abolished by virtue of s 30 of the Public Bodies Act 2011.

Notwithstanding the abolition of the RDAs, the Local Democracy, Economic Development and Construction Act 2009 provided for the establishment of 'combined authorities'. These enable two or more local authorities (outside London) to take joint and collective action in, for example, strategic economic development, with such powers being devolved from central government. Since 2009 nine combined authorities have been created. In May 2017 six of these had elections for directly elected regional mayors following *devolution deals* with central government (and so thereafter became 'mayoral combined authorities' under the aegis of the Cities and Local Government Devolution Act 2016). The rationale behind such mayors is to provide a focal point for democratic accountability. The 2016 Act also expanded the powers which could be devolved (ie beyond those stipulated in the previous 2009 Act).

14.6.3 The London Mayor and Assembly

In 1985 Parliament revoked the Greater London Council (Local Government Act 1985), which meant that London as a large capital city lacked an overall strategic body. The Labour government elected in 1997 implemented plans for a democratic city government for London by establishing the Greater London Authority under the Greater London Authority Act 1999, which comprises the following:

- A Mayor of London.
- A London Assembly.

As in Scotland, Wales and Northern Ireland, this legislation followed an endorsement of the government's proposals in a referendum of Londoners held in 1998.

The London Mayor

The Office of Mayor represents London. He has an executive role to, *inter alia*, develop transport, environment and planning strategies for London, and he also sets an annual Budget. He is supported by a mayoral team, which includes a statutory Deputy Mayor (a member of the Assembly).

The London Assembly

This is composed of 25 elected Assembly Members (AMs), whose role, *inter alia*, is to hold the Mayor to account by monitoring, debating and questioning his activities and decisions (eg at the *Mayor's Question Time* – analogous to PMQs at section 12.4.2). In addition, they investigate matters which are of significance to people living in London. The Assembly makes use of an investigative committee system (eg the Budget and Performance Assembly Committee) in carrying out its responsibilities. Both the Mayor and the Assembly Members are asked questions by Londoners in a bi-annual public 'People's *Question Time*'.

Elections

As a result of the last election in May 2016 the political make up of the Assembly was as follows:

The London Assembly 2016	
POLITICAL PARTY	Number of AMs
Labour Party	12
Conservative Party	8
Liberal Democrats	1
Green Party	2
UKIP	2
TOTAL	25

Table 14.4

Source: L Audickas, O Hawkins and R Cracknell, *UK Election Statistics: 1918–2017*, Briefing Paper CBP7529 (House of Commons Library, 2017), p 57.

The Mayor and each AM are elected for a term of four years (with the Mayor elected by the supplementary vote system and the AMs by the additional member system). The Greater London Authority Act 2007 provided the Mayor and Assembly with additional powers and further changes were made by the following two Acts: the Localism Act 2011 and the Police Reform and Social Responsibility Act 2011.

NB. In 2017 an agreement/memorandum on the next stage of devolution was published: *Memorandum of Understanding on further devolution to London* (Department for Communities and Local Government and Treasury, May 2017). On the GLA, see M Sandford, *The Greater London Authority*, Briefing Paper 05817 (House of Commons Library, 2017).

KEY FACTS

Key facts on the nomenclature, size and powers of the devolved institutions

	Scotland	**Wales**	**Northern Ireland**
Legislature	Scottish Parliament	National Assembly for Wales	Northern Ireland Assembly
Executive	Scottish Government	Welsh Government	Northern Ireland Executive Committee
Size of chamber and electoral systems	129 members in total • 73 constituency MSPs (simple majority system) • 56 regional MSPs (additional member system)	60 members in total • 40 constituency AMs (simple majority system) • 20 Regional AMs (additional member system)	90 members (MLAs) • (single transferable vote system)
Primary legislative powers	Yes	Yes	Yes
Subordinate legislative powers	Yes	Yes	Yes

SUMMARY

▦ Although the British constitution is hallmarked by being a unitary state, power has been decentralised to local government and to regional bodies in Scotland, Wales, Northern Ireland and London.

▦ Local government is public power which has been delegated to directly elected local authorities, which administer governmental functions at a local level and tailored to local needs.

▦ Local government performs a wide range of functions ranging from the delivery of services to passing byelaws. It also has the power to raise revenue through local taxation.

▦ The Scotland Act 1998 devolved power to Scotland and established the Scottish Parliament and Scottish Government.

▦ The Scottish Parliament is elected and has the power to pass Acts of the Scottish Parliament and also enjoys a tax-setting power.

▦ The Scottish Government is composed of the First Minister and Scottish Ministers together with the Lord Advocate and Solicitor General.

▦ Both the Scottish Parliament and Government must act within their powers as conferred by the Scotland Act 1998.

▢ As a consequence of the 1998 Good Friday Agreement, power was devolved to Northern Ireland (it had previously enjoyed devolved powers earlier in the twentieth century until being revoked in the 1970s).

▢ The Northern Ireland Assembly is elected and has the power to pass Acts of the Northern Ireland Assembly.

▢ The Northern Ireland Executive Committee comprises the First Minister, Deputy First Minister and remaining ministers. It is unique in the devolution settlements in the United Kingdom as it includes the principle of power-sharing, whereby ministers are allocated using the *d'Handt* political system of representation.

▢ Both the Northern Ireland Assembly and Executive Committee must act within their powers as conferred by the Northern Ireland Act 1998.

▢ The Government of Wales Act 1998 devolved power to Wales. Today under the Government of Wales Act 2006, Wales has a National Assembly for Wales and a Welsh Government (the latter comprising the First Minister, Welsh Ministers and the Counsel General to the Welsh Government).

▢ The National Assembly for Wales is elected and has the power to make laws known as Acts of the National Assembly for Wales.

▢ Both the National Assembly and Welsh Government must act within the powers conferred on them.

▢ Scotland, Northern Ireland and Wales all still send MPs to Westminster.

▢ England has no devolved equivalent of the Scottish Parliament, Northern Ireland Assembly or National Assembly for Wales, although the Greater London Authority Act 1999 established the Greater London Authority for London (including an elected Mayor).

▢ The 'West Lothian question' was finally addressed in 2015 by the alteration of standing orders in the House of Commons (ie EVEL).

▢ Local government in Wales, Scotland and Northern Ireland are devolved matters.

SAMPLE ESSAY QUESTION

What is local government, what are its functions and why is it considered an important aspect of the British constitution?

Introduction:
- Define the term local government (ie decentralised governmental powers).

Nature of local government:
- The UK is broken down into areas managed by local authorities.
- Local authorities/councils are statutory bodies.
- The structure and arrangement of local government varies across the four countries of the UK and within England itself (eg some areas have county councils, others have metropolitan borough/district councils).

Functions and powers of local government:

- Providers of the delivery of services (eg environmental health).
- Administers policies expressed in primary (Westminster) legislation (eg in relation to schools).
- Legislates on local issues (ie byelaws).
- Raises local revenue.
- Has a 'general power of competence' under s 1 of the Localism Act 2011.

Constitutional importance of local government:

- It disperses state power away from the centre so that public power is not all focused in the centre (ie Westminster/Whitehall).
- It gives expression to the constitutional and democratic principle of 'participatory government' which enables individuals to engage in the governmental process (eg by being elected as councillors). It allows local individuals to affect local decision-making (see the principle of subsidiarity).
- It is part of the executive, although the political complexion of local authorities may be different to that of central government (see the tension between the two and *juridification*).
- Local government can be innovative (ie piloting schemes) and allows a variation in the delivery of services.

Conclusion

THE DECENTRALISATION OF PUBLIC POWER

431

Further reading

Books

Barnett, H, *Constitutional and Administrative Law* (12th edn, Routledge/Taylor & Francis Group, 2017), Chapter 11.

Bogdanor, V, *The New British Constitution* (Hart Publishing, 2009), Chapter 4.

Chandler, J, *Explaining Local Government* (Manchester University Press, 2013).

Dalyell, T, 'Devolution: The End of Britain' in Sutherland, K (ed), *The Rape of the Constitution?* (Imprint Academic, 2000), p 257.

Dickson, B, 'Devolution' in Jowell, J, Oliver, D and O'Cinneide, C (eds), *The Changing Constitution* (8th edn, Oxford University Press, 2015), p 249.

Himsworth, C and O'Neill, C, Scotland's *Constitution: Law and Practice* (3rd edn, Bloomsbury Professional, 2015).

Leigh, I, 'The Changing Nature of the Local State' in Jowell, J, Oliver, D and O'Cinneide, C (eds), *The Changing Constitution* (8th edn, Oxford University Press, 2015), p 279.

Wicks, E, *The Evolution of a Constitution – Eight Key Moments in British Constitutional History* (Hart Publishing, 2006), Chapter 8.

Wilson, D, and Game, C, *Local Government in the United Kingdom* (5th edn, Palgrave Macmillan, 2011).

Articles

Himsworth, C, 'Prospects for codifying the relationship between central and local government' [2013] PL 702.

Leigh, I, 'Local government and political constitutionalism' [2014] PL 43.

Percival, R, 'How to do things with jurisdictions: Wales and the jurisdiction question' [2017] PL 249.

Rawlings, R, 'The strange reconstitution of Wales' [2018] PL 62.

Ryan, M, 'Central–local government relations' (2009) 14 *Coventry Law Journal* 18.

Papers

A Voice for Wales, Cm 3718 (The Stationery Office, 1997).

Act of Union Bill (Constitution Reform Group, July 2016).

Better Governance for Wales, Cm 6582 (Welsh Office, 2005).

Devolution Monitoring Programme (The Constitution Unit). These publications are produced continuously by the Constitution Unit (University of London) and cover all aspects of devolution.

Hazell, R (ed), *Devolution and the Future of the Union* (The Constitution Unit, 2015).

House of Commons Justice Committee, *Devolution: A Decade On*, Vol 1, HC 529-I (2009).

House of Lords European Union Select Committee, *Brexit: Devolution*, HL Paper 9 (House of Lords, 2017).

House of Lords Select Committee on the Constitution, *The Union and Devolution*, HL Paper 149 (House of Lords, 2016).

Scotland's Parliament, Cm 3658 (The Scottish Office, 1997).

Your Region, Your Choice: Revitalising the English Regions, Cm 5511 (The Stationery Office, 2002).

Internet links

www.parliament.scot

www.london.gov.uk

www.gov.wales

www.niassembly.gov.uk

15

The European Union

AIMS AND OBJECTIVES

At the end of this chapter you should be able to:

■ Understand the constitutional features of the European Union

■ Appreciate the impact that the European Union has had on Britain's uncodified constitutional arrangements

Introduction

In *Bulmer v Bollinger* [1974] Ch 401, Lord Denning MR observed that, in relation to European law:

JUDGMENT

'. . . The Treaty is like an incoming tide. It flows into the estuaries and up the rivers. It cannot be held back.'

The United Kingdom has been a member of the European Union (formerly the European Community) since January 1973 (European law became part of our legal system via the European Communities Act 1972). As a result, it is impossible to examine the modern British constitution without considering the impact of European Union law. In fact, membership of the Union has had a profound and wide-ranging effect on various different aspects of our constitutional arrangements. In particular, it has altered our understanding of the lynchpin of the British constitution: parliamentary sovereignty. In addition, it has also affected:

■ Individuals (by conferring European law rights on them).

■ Judges (by altering their approach to interpreting legislation).

■ Politicians/parliamentarians (who must now work within the constraints of European law).

■ The sources of law (the sources of the British constitution now embrace European Treaties, secondary legislation and case law decided by the Court of Justice of the EU).

As European Union law is considered in detail in *Unlocking EU Law*, this chapter will simply highlight the key constitutional aspects raised by joining the European Union. In 2016 the United Kingdom voted to leave the European Union and this is considered at the end of the chapter at section 15.6.6.

15.1 The Treaties

15.1.1 A *de facto* constitution?

The Treaty of Rome 1957 (technically the Treaty Establishing the European Economic Community) established the European Economic Community (called the European Community after 1993) and can be viewed as a *de facto* constitution. It should be remembered that in general terms a constitution will establish the apparatus of the state by creating institutions, allocating them specific responsibilities/powers and providing limitations on them (see Chapter 2). In this way the Treaty of Rome has many parallels with the constitution of a state. In particular, the Treaty:

- Set out aims and objectives, which included, *inter alia*, to establish a common market in goods, persons, capital and labour as well as to raise the standard of living. Similarly, state constitutions will set out their objectives (eg the protection of human rights). In fact, subsequent European Treaties (eg the Amsterdam Treaty of 1997) do explicitly refer to the protection of human rights, democracy and the rule of law.
- Established institutions (see section 15.2) – although it made use of the European Court and Assembly (the latter later renamed the European Parliament), which already existed having been established under the Treaty of Paris 1951 for the European Coal and Steel Community.
- Allocated these institutions specific roles. For example, one of the constitutional functions of the European Commission is to enforce European law by ensuring that Member States adhere to it (now Art 258). In addition, each institution is equipped with particular powers. For instance, under Art 263 (as it is now) the Court of Justice of the EU is authorised to review legislative acts of the other institutions. In this respect the Court of Justice is acting in a way which is analogous to a Supreme or Constitutional Court in a state constitution.
- Provided for the Court of Justice of the EU to issue the definitive interpretation of European law (now Art 267). This is also similar to state constitutions whereby a Constitutional or Supreme Court (eg the US Supreme Court) will act as the final arbiter as to the meaning of the provisions of the written/codified constitution.
- Has been interpreted by the European Court to be regarded as a form of higher and fundamental law which is superior to the law of Member States (see section 15.6.2). This is comparable with state constitutions where the law of the constitution has a special and fundamental legal status.

As indicated in Chapter 2, a codified constitution will usually set out the methods and procedures used to alter the content of the constitution. The procedure used to amend the original Treaty of Rome involved the unanimous agreement at a summit of the European Council (containing the respective Presidents/Prime Ministers of the Member States) and thereafter being ratified by each Member State. In fact, the Treaty of Rome has been revised by the following Treaties:

- 1986 Single European Act.
- 1992 Treaty on European Union (TEU).

- 1997 Treaty of Amsterdam.
- 2000 Treaty of Nice.

In particular, the 1992 Treaty created the European Union, which incorporated the (renamed) European Community as one of its three pillars. Moreover, each of the above Treaties has incrementally increased the powers of the European Parliament *vis-à-vis* the other institutions.

15.1.2 The European Constitution/Treaty of Lisbon

Although historically the British constitution has been described as unwritten or uncodified, by virtue of our membership of the European Community/Union one part of our constitution *is* now written and codified (namely, European law and principles). Moreover, European law is a fundamental law with a higher legal status than the law of Member States (including the UK). In this sense, whilst we remain a member of the Union, European law will continue to have a special status in our constitutional arrangements.

In 2004 at a European Summit the heads of state/government agreed a European Constitution (technically called the Treaty Establishing a Constitution for Europe), which was scheduled to be ratified by all Member States. However, in 2005 both France and the Netherlands rejected the Treaty in separate referendums. In any event, the term *European Constitution* was somewhat of a misnomer. The term European Constitution appears to suggest or presuppose that Europe does not *already* have a constitution of some description, whereas, as noted above, the original, founding Treaty of Rome performs many of the functions of a state constitution. Following the rejection of the European Constitution, in December 2007 the European Council signed the Treaty of Lisbon. Although the term 'constitution' is not used in the Treaty, much of its content is similar to that of the rejected European Constitution. After ratification by all 27 Member States, the Treaty of Lisbon came into force in December 2009 and its most interesting constitutional changes are as follows:

- References to the European Community were replaced with the European Union, thereby removing the technical distinction between the Community and the Union. This meant that the Treaty of Rome was renamed the Treaty on the Functioning of the European Union (TFEU).
- The European Union now has a legal personality.
- Member States can now voluntarily withdraw from the Union (on Brexit see section 15.6.6).
- The posts of President of the European Council and the High Representative of the Union for Foreign Affairs and Security Policy were created.
- The powers of national parliaments were increased in relation to the creation of European legislation.

The United Kingdom incorporated the Treaty via the European Union (Amendment) Act 2008. Although the then Labour government had earlier committed itself to holding a referendum in relation to the (aborted) European Constitution, it did not however give a similar commitment in respect of the Lisbon Treaty. This was on the basis that it was significantly different to the European Constitution. In other words, the Treaty of Lisbon was like other previous amending Treaties which had also not been endorsed by a referendum in the United Kingdom. In *R (Wheeler) v Office of the PM* [2008] EWHC 1409 (Admin) the court held that the government had not acted unlawfully in not holding a referendum on the Lisbon Treaty.

In 2013 the European Union expanded to 28 Member States with the accession of Croatia.

ACTIVITY

Applying the law

Revisit Chapter 2 and then consider whether the European Treaties represent a constitution for Europe and its institutions and citizens.

15.2 The institutions

15.2.1 An outline of the institutions

The European Union is a supranational body which comprises an institutional structure with each body having a designated role:

- **The European Council** – is composed of the heads of state/government, which make important decisions concerning the direction of the Union. They also agree new Treaties.
- **The Council (formerly known as the Council of Ministers)** – is composed of a government minister representing each Member State. It co-ordinates the economic policies of Member States and adopts secondary legislation.
- **The European Commission** – is composed of one nominee from each Member State but, once appointed, they are independent of their respective Member State. The Commission has many roles, which include drafting legislative proposals and enforcing European Union law.
- **The European Parliament** – is composed of elected MEPs (Members of the European Parliament) and, *inter alia*, is involved in the process of adopting legislation and acts in concert with the Council to agree the Union Budget.
- **The Court of Justice of the European Union** – is composed of one judge from each Member State. The court interprets European Union law (providing definitive interpretations under Art 267) and ensures both Member States and the other institutions follow it.

15.2.2 The separation of powers in Europe

We saw earlier in Chapter 5 that the British constitution is characterised by the fact that it does not adhere to a strict separation of powers. This is also true in relation to the institutional structure of the European Union as the three 'governmental' functions are distributed between the various institutions:

The legislative function is performed by:

- The Council in adopting secondary legislation (see section 15.3.2).
- The European Parliament in adopting legislation when the *ordinary legislative procedure* (formerly co-decision) is in use.
- The Court of Justice of the EU (in a *de facto* sense) when it develops principles of European Union law (eg the doctrine of direct effect – see section 15.5).
- The European Council when it agrees Treaty revisions (here it is performing effectively a *de facto* legislative role).

The executive function is performed by:

- The European Council in determining the direction of European policy.

- The Council in co-ordinating the national economies of Member States and making executive decisions.
- The European Commission in drafting the Union Budget.

The judicial function is performed by:

- The Court of Justice of the EU in providing definitive interpretations of European law and resolving legal disputes.
- The European Commission under Art 258 in determining that a Member State has breached European law and issuing a *reasoned* opinion (ie a non-binding opinion which sets out how the Commission believes that European Union law has been violated). In effect, it is performing a *de facto* quasi-judicial function.

Although there is no clear separation of powers in Europe, the institutional infrastructure has the following distinct checks and balances:

- Although the Council adopts legislation, under the *ordinary legislative procedure*, it has to work in concert (ie a joint adoption) with the European Parliament.
- Although the Council adopts legislation (analogous to the UK Parliament) it is dependent on the European Commission to draft proposals to put before it (analogous to the British government drafting a Bill).
- While the European Commission has a degree of discretion in drafting legislative proposals, ultimately it has to make them acceptable to the Council/European Parliament who have to agree to them.
- The European Parliament can dismiss the Commission *en bloc*.
- The European Parliament can block the Budget which has been drafted by the European Commission and approved by the Council.
- The Court of Justice of the EU can review the actions/legislation of the political institutions.
- The European Council can amend the Treaty to increase or decrease the power or responsibilities of any institution (including the Court of Justice of the EU).

15.2.3 Democracy and the European institutions

One charge which has historically been levelled at the European Community/Union has been its 'democratic deficit'. In other words, there was a deficit of democracy in its institutional framework as most of the institutions were not directly elected and so they lacked democratic legitimacy. Indeed, the body with the most democratic legitimacy (the European Parliament), historically had the least power.

- The European Council is composed of the various Presidents and Prime Ministers who may or may not be directly elected. For example, although the French President is elected by the people of France, neither the British Prime Minister nor the Irish Taoiseach is directly elected *per se*. Instead, they are drawn from their respective legislatures (United Kingdom Parliament and Irish Oireachtas, respectively), albeit they are drawn from the dominant political party within its lower House.
- British ministers who sit in the Council (which vary depending on the subject matter) are not directly elected *per se*, but rather they are drawn from the two Houses of Parliament, one of which is not even elected (see section 11.6.2). Both the European Council and the Council represent the interests of the Member States.
- The European Commission is composed of Commissioners who have been nominated by their respective national governments and approved by the (elected)

European Parliament. The European Commission represents the interests of the European Union, which is why, once appointed, Commissioners must be independent of their respective Member State.

- The European Parliament is the only wholly directly elected body in the European Union (and even then it has only been elected since 1979; prior to that representatives of each national Parliament would sit). The European Parliament represents the interests of the people of Europe. In order to address the 'democratic deficit', each revision of the Treaty of Rome has provided the European Parliament with more power. The point must be made, however, that the democratic legitimacy of the European Parliament itself has to be questioned given that the turnout at European elections (which take place every five years) is poor. For example, the average turnouts in Europe for the last three European elections were 43 per cent (2014), 43 per cent (2009) and 45 per cent (2004), with the corresponding turnout in the United Kingdom at 36 per cent, 35 per cent and 39 per cent, respectively (source: European Parliament website (www.europarl.europa.eu/elections2014-results/en/turnout)).
- The Court of Justice of the EU is composed of judges nominated from each Member State.

KEY FACTS

Institution	Composition	Role	Represents
European Council	Heads of state/government (composed of 28 heads of state/government and headed by the newly created office of the President of the European Council). The President of the European Commission also attends – the High Representative of the Union (see below) is also involved in the European Council's work.	• Provides general direction and impetus to the EU. • Makes political decisions. • Revises the Treaties.	Member States.
Council	Minister from each Member State (Council composed of 28 ministers).	• Adopts legislative proposals. • Makes executive decisions. • Co-ordinates national economies. • Confers powers on the Commission to make legislation. • Adopts the Budget.	Member States.

European Commission	Nominated from each Member State and approved/removed by the European Parliament (28 Commissioners headed by the President of the European Commission and now includes the newly created office of the High Representative of the Union for Foreign Affairs and Security Policy).	• Initiates and drafts legislative proposals. • Enforces EU law as a watchdog. • Exercises powers conferred by the Council. • Acts as a mediator. • Drafts the Budget.	European Union.
European Parliament	MEPs elected by the electorate in each of the 28 Member States (751 MEPs – 73 of these are from the UK). Parliament is headed by a President.	• Supervises the other institutions. • Involved in the legislative process. • Adopts the Budget with the Council.	European citizens.

ACTIVITY

Essay writing

To what extent does the institutional structure of the European Union depart from the separation of powers and do you consider that it is democratic?

15.3 Sources of law

Membership of the European Union has widened the legal sources of the British constitution. In broad terms, European Union law can be divided into primary and secondary sources:

15.3.1 Primary sources

These comprise the founding Treaty (Treaty of Rome 1957) together with its subsequent amendment over the years (eg the Single European Act 1986).

15.3.2 Secondary sources

These comprise the legislation known as legal Acts of the Union (see section 4.7.2) made by the Union institutions.

ARTICLE

'The institutions shall adopt regulations, directives, decisions, recommendations and opinions.'

Art 288, TFEU.

■ **Regulations** – these are self-executing and of general application (applying to all Member States). They ensure absolute uniformity and exactitude in all Member States. In constitutional terms they by-pass the legislatures of each Member State (including the UK Parliament) as they apply *automatically* in every Member State without the national legislature having to endorse them.

■ **Directives** – these are more flexible than regulations and are addressed to specific Member States in order to ensure an overall harmonisation of national laws. Directives are binding as to the result to be achieved but leave the Member State with a measure of discretion as to how to implement them.

■ **Decisions** – these are binding on those to whom they are addressed (Member States or companies).

These secondary sources enter the United Kingdom via s 2 of the European Communities Act 1972. In addition to the sources above, case law and preliminary rulings of the Court of Justice of the EU also represent a form of secondary source of law (see below).

15.4 The Court of Justice of the European Union

The Court of Justice of the European Union is the judicial arm of the European Union.

15.4.1 The distinctive nature of the court

The Court of Justice is distinctive in constitutional terms (at least from the perspective of a British public lawyer) in the following ways:

■ **Composition** – the court (like the European Court of Human Rights in Strasbourg) includes judges who are academics with no direct judicial experience.

■ **No public dissent** – the court (unlike the European Court of Human Rights) does not issue dissenting/minority judgments. All judges, whether or not they agreed with the decision, must sign the judgment.

■ **Advocates General** – the court is assisted by Advocates General, which have no parallel in the British court system. In brief, after the parties have delivered their submissions, an Advocate General will summarise the legal points in the case (even adding some that have been overlooked so that the court is fully conversant with all relevant information) and put forward a non-binding submission. The court often adopts these submissions.

■ **No *stare decisis*** – the court is, technically, not bound by precedent and so does not have to follow its own previous decisions. In practice, however, for legal certainty and practical reasons, the court generally follows its previous rulings.

■ **Legal reasoning** – the court's method of interpreting legislation is different from the traditional approach used by the British judiciary (ie the literal/ historical method). Instead, European Court judges adopt a more teleological/purposive technique. As a result of the inception of Union law into our constitution and legal system, the United Kingdom judiciary in applying European law must adopt the legal reasoning employed by the Court of Justice in Luxembourg. As indicated by Lord Denning MR in *Bulmer v Bollinger* [1974] Ch 401:

JUDGMENT

'Beyond doubt the English courts must follow the same principles as the European court. Otherwise there would be differences between the countries. . . . They must follow the European pattern. No longer must they examine the words in meticulous detail. No longer must they argue about the precise grammatical sense. They must look to the purpose or intent. To quote the words of the European Court in the *Da Costa* case . . . they must deduce "from the wording and the spirit of the Treaty the meaning of the community rules".'

15.4.2 The role of the Court of Justice of the EU

Application of European law

The Court of Justice ensures that the application of European Union law is observed by Member States (under Arts 258 and 259 enforcement proceedings are brought by the European Commission or another Member State, respectively) and the political institutions of the Union (under Arts 263 and 265).

Interpretation of European law

Student mentor tip

'Remember that all of the topics overlap and look for the links.'
Adil, Queen Mary University.

Article 267 provides that the Court of Justice shall have the jurisdiction to give preliminary rulings concerning, *inter alia*,

(a) the interpretation of the Treaties and
(b) the validity and interpretation of acts of the institutions of the Union (eg regulations, directives – see section 15.3.2).

In brief, where a national/domestic court or tribunal is faced with a provision of either a primary or secondary source of law which is unclear and requires interpretation, Art 267 provides a mechanism whereby that court/tribunal can make a reference directly to the Court of Justice requesting it to interpret and clarify that point of European law (ie to provide a preliminary ruling). National courts against which there is no appeal/review *must* make such a reference. The ruling issued by the Court of Justice is binding on the national court and represents *the* definitive interpretation of European law. In this way the Court of Justice is the final arbiter as to the meaning of European Union law.

The Art 267 procedure provides a direct link between the Court of Justice in Luxembourg and the national/domestic courts and tribunals of the Member States. It can be likened to a wheel, with the Court of Justice as the hub and the national courts and tribunals on the rim. In this way, all domestic courts and tribunals are directly connected to the Court of Justice and it links these European judges with the domestic judges of the Member States.

Article 267 is not an appellate system whereby national courts *appeal* to the Court of Justice. Instead, it is a reference system which involves a partnership between the judges of the Court of Justice and their counterpart judges in the Member States. In terms of the British constitution, the preliminary ruling procedure means that the UK Supreme Court is not the ultimate arbiter in respect of European Union law. This has been specifically authorised by s 3 of the European Communities Act 1972. In fact, as a court of last resort, our Supreme Court justices *must* refer ambiguous/unclear points of European Union law to the judges in Luxembourg. An interesting

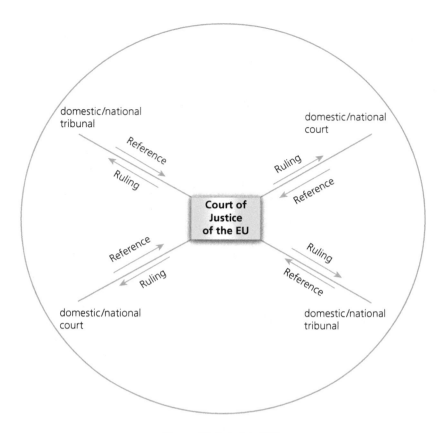

Figure 15.1 Article 267.

recent example of a reference was in the following case: *Secretary of State for the Home Department v Davis* [2015] EWCA Civ 1185. This case was in the context of the Data Retention and Investigatory Powers Act 2014 and its compliance with European Union law in terms of, *inter alia*, the lack of clear and precise rules governing access to communications data (see earlier at section 6.7.11).

KEY FACTS

Institution	Composition	Role
Court of Justice of the EU	One judge from each Member State.	• Interprets European Union law (Art 267). • Applies and enforces European Union law against European Union institutions (Arts 263 and 265) and Member States (Arts 258 and 259).

15.5 Individuals

Membership of the European Union has had a direct impact on individuals. Firstly, the Maastricht Treaty of 1992 conferred citizenship of the European Union on individuals in Member States. Secondly, European Union law has conferred European rights on individuals (eg not to be discriminated against on the grounds of sex), which can be enforced in their own domestic courts. This principle is known as the doctrine of direct effect which has been developed by the Court of Justice (as it was not explicitly set out in the original founding European Treaty).

CASE EXAMPLE

Marshall v Southampton and South-West Hampshire AHA (No 1)
Case 152/84 [1986] ECR 723

Ms Marshall was employed by Southampton and South-West Hampshire Area Health Authority and was forced to retire at 62 (the authority had a policy which required women to retire earlier than men – 60 rather than 65). She contended that the Sex Discrimination Act 1975 (which did not apply to retirement) contravened Directive 76/207 in terms of the equal treatment of men and women.

The Court of Appeal made a reference to the Court of Justice as to whether Marshall could rely on the directive (the doctrine of direct effect). The Court of Justice issued its preliminary ruling that a policy of different retirement ages contravened the directive and that Marshall could rely on the rights set out in the directive. Thereafter, the Court of Appeal applied the ruling to the facts of the case and held that in being dismissed, Marshall had been unlawfully discriminated against and so she obtained compensation. This case illustrates an individual using European law rights (eg the right not to be discriminated against) in a domestic court against a public body (the Area Health Authority being treated as a public body as an emanation of the state).

15.6 European Union law and parliamentary sovereignty

15.6.1 Introduction

Membership of the European Union has had a profound effect on parliamentary sovereignty. As noted in Chapter 7, the classic and historic doctrine of parliamentary sovereignty is that the Crown in Parliament can pass any law that it chooses. This absolute principle, however, is in direct opposition to the principle of the primacy of European Union law as developed and espoused by the Court of Justice of the EU. In short, according to the Court of Justice, where provisions of European Union law and national/domestic law conflict, the former *must* prevail (see *Costa* (1964) below).

15.6.2 The primacy of European Union law

The doctrine of the primacy (or supremacy) of European Union law, like the doctrine of direct effect, was not expressly set out in the original founding Treaty of Rome. Instead, it has been developed by the Court of Justice, thereby illustrating its quasi-legislative role in practice. The principle was first indicated in *Van Gend & Loos v Nederlandse administratie der belastingen* Case 26/62 [1963] ECR 1, where the European Court stated:

JUDGMENT

'. . . the Community constitutes a new legal order of international law for the benefit of which the states have limited their sovereign rights, albeit within limited fields, and the subjects of which comprise not only Member States but also their nationals.'

In the subsequent case of *Costa v ENEL* Case 6/64 [1964] ECR 585 the Court of Justice noted that:

JUDGMENT

'. . . the law stemming from the Treaty, an independent source of law, could not, because of its special and original nature, be overridden by domestic legal provisions, however framed, without being deprived of its character as Community law and without the legal basis of the Community itself being called into question.'

In short, if a provision of domestic law contravenes European law, the latter must prevail, thereby indicating the supreme and fundamental nature of European Union law. In the later case of *Internationale Handelsgesellschaft mbH v EVGF* Case 11/70 [1970] ECR 1125 the court made it clear that the principle extended to secondary sources of European law (eg a regulation) and that it prevailed over the constitutional rules of a Member State (ie its constitutional law):

JUDGMENT

'. . . the law stemming from the Treaty, an independent source of law, cannot because of its very nature be overridden by rules of national law. . . . Therefore the validity of a Community measure or its effect within a Member State cannot be affected by allegations that it runs counter to either fundamental rights as formulated by the constitution of that State or the principles of a national constitutional structure.'

See also *Simmenthal SpA v Amministrazione delle Finanze dello Stato* Case 70/77 [1978] ECR 1453 and *Commission v (French Republic)* Case 167/73 [1974] ECR 359. It is now pertinent to point out that a Declaration (No 17) in the Treaty of Lisbon states explicitly that the 'well settled case law of the Court of Justice of the European Union, the Treaties and the law adopted by the Union on the basis of the Treaties have primacy over the law of Member States'.

ACTIVITY

Self-test question
What is the nature and constitutional significance of the principle of the primacy of European Union law?

15.6.3 The reception of European Union law in the British constitution
The United Kingdom has a dualist constitution, which means that, even if a Treaty is agreed to in international law, its provisions do not become legally enforceable

in domestic law unless an Act of Parliament has formally incorporated the Treaty. In 1972 Parliament passed the European Communities Act, which provided for the reception of European law into our constitution and legal system. In constitutional terms, it is worth noting that this Act, in spite of its profound constitutional consequences, was passed in an ordinary parliamentary manner in the sense that no special majority was needed (although the committee stage was taken on the Floor of the House). In fact, the Bill only narrowly passed its third reading in the House of Commons. This indicates the flexibility of the British constitution. In contrast, the Republic of Ireland which joined the EEC (as it was then) at the same time, was required by its written constitution to hold a referendum.

By virtue of s 2(1) of the European Communities Act 1972, from 1 January 1973 European Union law (as it is called today) formally became part of the law of the United Kingdom. Section 2(4) is the most controversial aspect of the Act as it deals with the impact of European law on domestic law:

SECTION

Any such provision (of any such extent) as might be made by Act of Parliament, and any enactment passed or to be passed, other than one contained in this part of this Act, shall be construed and have effect subject to the foregoing provisions of this section.

In constitutional terms, s 2(4) means that United Kingdom statutes passed before and after 1972 must be construed and be held subject to European Union law:

CASE EXAMPLE

Macarthys Ltd v Smith *[1981] 1 QB 180*

Mrs Smith replaced a man to manage Macarthys' stockroom but was paid £10 a week less than he had been paid. She claimed equal pay under s 1 of the Equal Pay Act 1970 (although this appeared to be confined to contemporaneous employment) and this raised the issue of whether Art 119 (now Art 157 TFEU) of the Treaty of Rome (equal pay for equal work) applied to the situation where a woman replaced a man, but who had not worked contemporaneously alongside him. The Court of Appeal was uncertain on this point of European law and sent a reference to the Court of Justice asking whether Art 119 was confined to men and women working contemporaneously. The subsequent ruling stated that the principle of equal pay was not so confined but also applied where a woman replaced a man. The Court of Appeal then applied this ruling to the case and held for Mrs Smith. Lord Denning MR stated that:

JUDGMENT

'It is important now to declare – and it must be made plain – that the provisions of article 119 of the EEC Treaty take priority over anything in our English statute on equal pay which is inconsistent with article 119. That priority is given by our own law. It is given by the European Communities Act 1972 itself. Community law is now part of our law: and, whenever there is any inconsistency, Community law has priority.'

Similarly, in *Garland v British Rail Engineering Ltd* [1983] 2 AC 751, the House of Lords, following a preliminary ruling by the Court of Justice, construed the Sex

Discrimination Act 1975 in line with Art 119 (now Art 157) prohibiting discrimination. As a result the court held that British Rail had discriminated against Garland when it provided special travel facilities for the families of retired male employees but not female ones. The words of the 1975 Act could (without being unnecessarily strained) be interpreted so as to be consistent with Art 119.

In terms of United Kingdom secondary legislation, in *Lister and others v Forth Dry Dock and Engineering Co Ltd and Another* [1989] 1 All ER 1134, the House of Lords read and construed a domestic regulation (ie delegated legislation) so as to conform with a European directive which protected the rights of employees in circumstances when their employer changed. See also *Pickstone v Freemans plc* [1988] 2 All ER 803.

In terms of a conflict between European Union law and an Act of Parliament, Lord Denning MR, prior to the reference to the Court of Justice in *Macarthys Ltd v Smith* [1979] 3 All ER 325 (see above), made the following point (albeit as part of his dissenting judgment) concerning the constitutional impact of European law on United Kingdom statutes:

JUDGMENT

'Thus far I have assumed that our Parliament, whenever it passes legislation, intends to fulfil its obligations under the Treaty. If the time should come when our Parliament deliberately passes an Act with the intention of repudiating the Treaty or any provision in it or intentionally of acting inconsistently with it and says so in express terms then I should have thought that it would be the duty of our courts to follow the statute of our Parliament. . . . Unless there is such an intentional and express repudiation of the Treaty, it is our duty to give priority to the Treaty.'

In essence, Lord Denning was indicating that the domestic doctrine of implied repeal (see section 7.9.3) does not operate whenever European Union law applies. In other words, if domestic legislation passed after 1972 is inconsistent with European Union law (which forms part of our law through the European Communities Act 1972), European Union law (and so the 1972 Act) will prevail *unless* the later domestic legislation expressly and clearly intends to repudiate European Union law. If the domestic legislation violates European Union law, but does not do so intentionally, then the courts will apply European law over the statute. This appears to have been the approach taken by the House of Lords in *ex parte Factortame*, which involved a statute which was passed *after* 1972 (ie after the European Communities Act) but which was inconsistent with European Union law (ie which forms part of our law via s 2 of the 1972 Act).

15.6.4 The *Factortame* litigation

CASE EXAMPLE

R v Secretary of State for Transport, ex parte Factortame Ltd
and Others (No 2) *[1991] 1 AC 603*

Part II of the Merchant Shipping Act 1988 restricted the number of fishing vessels whose catch could form part of the United Kingdom fishing quota (the EEC – as it was then – had a policy to prevent over fishing of depleted fishing stocks). Under the authority of the Act, the Transport Secretary issued the Merchant Shipping (Registration of Fishing Vessels)

Regulations 1988, requiring vessels registered as British to re-register. Vessels would only qualify if their owners (or 75 per cent of their company shareholders) were British citizens or lived in Britain. Factortame and others were companies who before the Act had been registered as British but most of whose directors/shareholders were Spanish. As they could not meet the new registration requirements, they sought judicial review of the Act and the 1988 regulations on the basis that they breached European law, *inter alia* in terms of discrimination.

The Divisional Court faced with a provision of European law, which required interpretation made a reference to the Court of Justice (**the first reference**) and pending the receipt of this ruling provided Factortame with interim relief (thereby protecting their putative European Union law rights which had not yet been established) by disapplying Pt II of the Act and preventing the minister from enforcing the legislation against Factortame. The Court of Appeal set aside the order on the basis that the court had no jurisdiction to issue it. The House of Lords confirmed that the court had no power to issue the interim injunction in terms of either granting an injunction against the Crown or disapplying a statute prior to a ruling of the Court of Justice on a point of European Union law. Nevertheless, the House of Lords did refer to the Court of Justice the question (**the second reference**) as to whether it was a requirement of European Union law that a national court should provide an interim remedy in order to protect a party's putative European Union law rights while waiting for the Court of Justice to issue a ruling on the point.

In June 1990, in response to the second reference, the Court of Justice issued its ruling to the effect that a national court must set aside a rule of domestic law which impeded a national court from granting interim relief to protect European Union law rights (otherwise European law would be undermined).

Thereafter the House of Lords applied the ruling to the facts of the case and reinstated the interim injunction protecting Factortame's putative European Union law rights which had not yet been definitely established (ie in advance of the Court of Justice's ruling in respect of the first reference). Lord Bridge noted that:

JUDGMENT

'Some public comments on the decision of the European Court of Justice, affirming the jurisdiction of the courts of member states to override national legislation if necessary to enable interim relief to be granted in protection of rights under Community law, have suggested that this was a novel and dangerous invasion by a Community institution of the sovereignty of the United Kingdom Parliament. But such comments are based on a misconception. If the supremacy within the European Community of Community law over the national law of member states was not always inherent in the EEC Treaty . . . it was certainly well established in the jurisprudence of the European Court of Justice long before the United Kingdom joined the Community. Thus, whatever limitation of its sovereignty Parliament accepted when it enacted the European Communities Act 1972 was entirely voluntary. Under the terms of the Act of 1972 it has always been clear that it was the duty of a United Kingdom court, when delivering final judgment, to override any rule of national law found to be in conflict with any directly enforceable rule of Community law.'

Following the ruling of the Court of Justice in July 1991 in respect of the first reference (*R v Secretary of State for Transport, ex parte Factortame Ltd (No 3)* [1992] 1 QB 680), the Divisional Court applied this ruling to the facts of the case and declared that the Merchant Shipping Act breached European Union law. Thereafter, Parliament passed the Merchant Shipping (Registration) Act 1993, which amended and restated the law relating to the registering of shipping. In *R v Secretary of State for Transport, ex parte Factortame Ltd (No 5)* [2000] 1 AC 524 Factortame obtained compensation for the loss and expenses incurred as a consequence of the enforcement (albeit on a temporary basis) of the 1988 Act.

Similarly, in the later case of *Equal Opportunities Commission and another v Secretary of State for Employment* [1994] 1 All ER 910, the House of Lords issued a declaration that provisions of the Employment Protection (Consolidation) Act 1978 were contrary to European Union law (see section 19.4.2).

Also, in *Thoburn v Sunderland City Council* [2002] EWHC 195 (Admin), Laws LJ commented that the European Communities Act 1972 was one of a number of 'constitutional statutes' which were not subject to implied repeal (see section 4.4.5). On the facts of the case, however, the court held that there was no inconsistency between s 1 of the Weights and Measures Act 1985 and the earlier s 2(2) of the European Communities Act 1972.

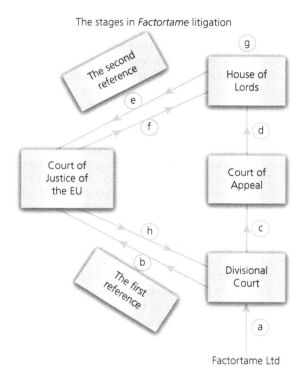

The stages in *Factortame* litigation

KEY FACTS

Key facts on European Union law and sovereignty

- Section 2(1) of the European Communities Act 1972 formally incorporated Community (now Union) law into the United Kingdom's legal system.

- Section 2(4) of the Act requires the courts to interpret all statutes – passed before and after the 1972 Act – in line with and subject to European Union law.

- In *Garland* (1983) the House of Lords interpreted the Sex Discrimination Act 1975 in line with Art 119, now Art 157 (prohibiting discrimination in retirement).

- In *Lister and others* (1989) the House of Lords interpreted domestic delegated legislation in line with a European directive.

- In *Factortame* (1991) the House of Lords suspended the operation of the Merchant Shipping Act 1988 as it conflicted with the putative European Union law rights of Factortame.

- In *Equal Opportunities Commission* (1994) the House of Lords issued a declaration that the Employment Protection (Consolidation) Act 1978 violated European Union law on the basis that it indirectly discriminated against women.

15.6.5 The constitutional impact of *Factortame*

The precise constitutional significance and impact of *Factortame* is not universally agreed upon by academics. Craig, however, has rather usefully summarised how the judgments in *Factortame* (1991), *Equal Opportunities Commission* (1994), *Thoburn* (2002) and *HS2* (2014) – see the last case at section 8.6.4 – can be conceptualised into three broad themes (P Craig, 'Britain in the European Union' in J Jowell, D Oliver and C O'Cinneide (eds), *The Changing Constitution* (8th edn, Oxford University Press, 2015), pp 121–123):

(i) **'statutory construction'**:

This approach is a rule of construction which requires any inconsistency between European law and a United Kingdom statute to be resolved in favour of the former. This is subject to the United Kingdom Parliament passing legislation which is clearly meant to depart from European law.

(ii) **'a technical legal revolution'**:

This approach regards the jurisprudence of the courts as revolutionary in the sense that it affected the traditional view of parliamentary sovereignty. In short, in *Factortame* the courts altered the rule of recognition in respect of statutes, with the result that the 1972 Parliament did something which Dicey (see section 7.9) had argued was not possible: it bound its successor. In other words, the 1972 Parliament (which passed the European Communities Act, which gave European law overriding force in our law) bound the later Parliament of 1988, because the legislation that it had passed (the Merchant Shipping Act 1988) had to be disapplied as being inconsistent with European law (see H Wade, 'Sovereignty – revolution or evolution?' (1996) 112 LQR 568).

(iii) **'arguments of legal principle'**:

Craig argues that the third conceptualisation (and his favoured view) of the above judgments concerning supremacy/sovereignty can be regarded 'as being based on *arguments of legal principle the content of which can and will vary across time*' *(Sic)*. In other words, the 'principled consequences' of membership of the European Union entail the United Kingdom being bound by European law (and so are reasoned constraints on Parliament's legislative omnipotence).

In any event, the following points are worth noting:

▪ It has been suggested that in the *Factortame* case the courts did something which Dicey had argued was impossible, namely the courts challenged and disapplied an Act of Parliament – the Merchant Shipping Act 1988. The constitutional/legal (and moral) authority for the courts to do this came from s 2(4) of the European Communities Act 1972. Indeed, as noted by Lord Bridge, it was Parliament which had voluntarily passed the 1972 Act. Moreover, by virtue of the jurisprudence of the Court of Justice (*Van Gend* (1963) and *Costa* (1964) – see section 15.6.2), in 1972 the United Kingdom would have been fully conversant with the principle of the primacy of European Union law. In fact, this was indicated in the then Labour government's 1967 White Paper (*Legal and Constitutional Implications of United Kingdom Membership of the European Communities*, Cm 3301 (1967)).

 It has also been suggested that the doctrine of implied repeal does not apply where European Union law operates. In other words, if, as a result of for example, a parliamentary oversight or misunderstanding of the requirements of European law, an Act of Parliament is passed which is inconsistent with European Union law, the UK courts will ensure that European Union law prevails over the statute. However, this would not be the case where the violation of European Union law is deliberate (see below). Notwithstanding this, Tomkins (*Public Law* (Oxford University Press, 2003), pp 118–119), along with others, has argued that the *Factortame* case did *not* engage the doctrine of implied repeal as, for one thing, there was no conflict in terms of substance between the Merchant Shipping Act 1988 (dealing with fishing registration) and the earlier European Communities Act 1972 (dealing with the relationship between European law and domestic law). In short, they were different statutes dealing with different subject matters.

In *Factortame,* although the House of Lords (and the Divisional Court in the earlier stage of the litigation) issued an interim injunction restraining the operation of the 1988 Act, it did not strike it down *per se*. This is not the same, therefore, as a Supreme or Constitutional Court striking down and permanently invalidating legislation.

It must be remembered that, whatever the impact of the decision on parliamentary sovereignty, European Union law does not govern every aspect of our lives and so in these non-European contexts the full force of parliamentary sovereignty will continue.

In the event of the United Kingdom passing legislation (whilst still a member of the EU) which violated or repudiated European Union law, an investigation would be mounted by the European Commission.

In conclusion, Hoffmann J in *Stoke-on-Trent City Council v B & Q* [1991] Ch 48 has provided a useful summary of the constitutional impact of our membership of the European Union:

JUDGMENT

'The EEC Treaty is the supreme law of this country, taking precedence over Acts of Parliament. Our entry into the European Economic Community meant that (subject to our undoubted but probably theoretical right to withdraw from the Community altogether) Parliament surrendered its sovereign right to legislate contrary to the provisions of the Treaty on the matters of social and economic policy which it regulated. The entry into the Community was in itself a high act of social and economic policy, by which the partial surrender of sovereignty was seen as more than compensated by the advantages of membership.'

Two important recent developments are worth noting in the context of the issue of sovereignty and the European Union:

Firstly, s 18 of the European Union Act 2011 confirms (by declaring the existing legal position) that directly applicable/effective European Union law is legally recognised in the United Kingdom by virtue of the European Communities Act 1972 (ie by virtue of the *will* of the United Kingdom Parliament).

Secondly, Pt 1 of the European Union Act 2011 provides that a domestic referendum would have to be held before the United Kingdom would be able to agree to an amendment to the Treaty on European Union or to the Treaty on the Functioning of the European Union, or agree to a decision if it would transfer power/competence to the European Union from the United Kingdom.

On this measure see: House of Commons European Scrutiny Committee, *The EU Bill and Parliamentary Sovereignty*, Volume 1, HC 633-I (The Stationery Office, 2010).

ACTIVITY

Exercise

Explain the *Factortame* litigation. What impact has this case had on the nature of the British constitution?

15.6.6 Brexit

The issue of Brexit and the United Kingdom leaving the European Union raises a host of issues relating to key elements of the British constitution. These include: individuals (direct democracy and rights post Brexit); the executive (scope of its powers post Brexit); Parliament (parliamentary sovereignty); the judiciary (litigation in the *Miller* (2017) case and the application of 'retained EU law' post Brexit); and sources (the conversion of existing EU law into domestic law).

Referendums and the British constitution

In 2015 the European Union Referendum Act was passed, which provided for a referendum to take place on the United Kingdom's continued membership of the European Union. It should be noted that referendums require statutory authority and the June 2016 referendum (held under the aegis of the 2015 Act) was only the third ever United Kingdom-wide referendum to be held. The first was in 1975 on whether to remain in the EEC (as it was known then) and the second was in 2011 on the electoral system for the House of Commons. In fact, up until the 1970s, the concept of referendums (ie direct democracy) in the United Kingdom was considered to be wholly inconsistent with, as it undermined, the principle of representative democracy, whereby MPs take decisions on behalf of their constituents (however, see the point on 'selective' referendums made by Dicey at section 7.2.2).

The 2016 referendum

As noted at section 12.2.2, during the referendum campaign the then Prime Minister set aside the convention of collective responsibility. At the referendum in June 2016 the majority (52 per cent) of those who voted (a 72 per cent turnout) did so in favour of leaving the European Union (as did the majority of voters in both England and Wales) – see E Uberoi, *European Union Referendum 2016*, Briefing Paper CBP7639 (House of Commons Library, 2016), p 5. In order to leave the EU, a Member State (according to its own internal constitutional arrangements) must trigger Art 50 of the Treaty of Lisbon (TEU), which is the mechanism by which the European Union is notified of an intention to withdraw. Following the referendum result, the then Conservative government announced its intention to trigger Art 50 under the royal prerogative, and this led to the litigation in the following case:

The Miller case

CASE EXAMPLE

R (Miller) v Secretary of State for Exiting the European Union
[2017] UKSC 5

Miller sought judicial review of the government's intention to trigger Art 50 under the prerogative. The Divisional Court upheld Miller's claim and held that Art 50 could not be lawfully triggered without prior statutory authorisation. NB: on the media criticism of the judges following this decision, see P O'Brien, '"Enemies of the people": Judges, the media, and the mythic Lord Chancellor' [2017] PL 135.

The Secretary of State appealed to the Supreme Court, which dismissed his appeal by a majority of eight to three and upheld the principle that primary legislation was necessary in order for the government to notify the United Kingdom's withdrawal from the European Union. The government had argued that under the prerogative it had the power to enter into (and pertinently) *withdraw* from EU Treaties. The court held, however, that the prerogative could not be used to alter domestic law (and withdrawal from the European Treaties would alter domestic law and existing rights under EU law). After interpretation of the European Communities Act 1972, the court concluded that this Act precluded the use of prerogative power to withdraw from the EU:

JUDGMENT

'. . . the prerogative could not be invoked by ministers to justify giving Notice: ministers require the authority of primary legislation before they can take that course.'

It also stated earlier that:

'We cannot accept that a major change to UK constitutional arrangements can be achieved by ministers alone; it must be effected in the only way that the UK constitution recognises, namely by Parliamentary legislation.'

The government had argued (unsuccessfully), that the 1972 Act had not expressly excluded the power to use the prerogative to withdraw from the Treaties.

The case also raised issues related to devolution, although the court held that the consent of the Northern Ireland Assembly (or the Scottish Parliament or the National Assembly for Wales) was not legally required before the Westminster Parliament passed the Act which would result in the withdrawal of the United Kingdom from the European Union.

NB. On the *Miller* case, see P Craig,' Epilogue: *Miller*, the Legislature and the Executive' in S Juss and M Sunkin (eds), *Landmark Cases in Public Law* (Hart Publishing, 2017), p 307. Indeed, such is the significance of this case that the journal *Public Law* devoted an entire issue to it November 2017.

The aftermath

Following the *Miller* case, Parliament passed (albeit fast-tracked) the European Union (Notification of Withdrawal) Act 2017, which authorised the Prime Minister to notify the European Union of the United Kingdom's intention to withdraw. This notification took place on 29 March 2017. The government also issued a White

Paper, *Legislating for the United Kingdom's Withdrawal from the European Union*, Cm 9446 (Crown Copyright, 2017). This foreshadowed a 'Great Repeal Bill' to repeal the European Communities Act 1972 but also to convert existing EU law into domestic law at the point of exit, in order to provide stability and a functioning statute book immediately following withdrawal.

The 'Great Repeal Bill'

In July 2017 the European Union (Withdrawal) Bill 2017–19 received its first reading in the House of Commons. At the time of writing, the key elements of the Bill were as follows:

- Clause 1 – repeals the European Communities Act 1972 on the day the United Kingdom exits the European Union and would end the supremacy of EU law in the United Kingdom (described by John Redwood MP as 'the most important constitutional matter to come before the House of Commons since the 1972 Act': *Hansard*, HC, Vol 631, col 242). Clause 14 provides that exit day means 29 March 2019, albeit the definition of exit day can be amended by a minister via regulations using the affirmative procedure.
- Clause 2 – provides that 'EU-derived domestic legislation', which at present implements EU law, would remain (ie remain in effect on the statute book).
- Clause 3 – provides that existing 'direct EU legislation' is converted/incorporated into domestic law.
- Clause 4 – provides that any existing EU rights/obligations not falling within cls 2 and 3 above would remain part of domestic law.
- Clause 5 – provides two exceptions to the 'savings and incorporation' provisions above, namely the principle of the primacy/supremacy of EU law and the Charter of Fundamental Rights.
- Clause 6 – provides that decisions of the Court of Justice of the EU after exit day will not be binding on the United Kingdom courts and that references for preliminary rulings to the Court of Justice will no longer be able to be made. However, the United Kingdom courts in interpreting 'retained EU law' will be able to have regard to post exit day case law of the Court of Justice where they consider 'it appropriate to do so'. Moreover, the interpretation of 'retained EU law' will *still* be determined according to the pre-exit day general principles and case law of the Court of Justice, albeit that neither the Supreme Court nor the High Court of Justiciary would be bound by any retained EU law case law/general principles.
- Clause 7 – provides for ministers via regulations to deal with 'deficiencies' of retained EU law after exit day.
- Clause 8 – provides for ministers via regulations to ensure the United Kingdom's compliance with its international obligations.
- Clause 9 – provides for ministers via regulations to implement the withdrawal agreement between the European Union and the United Kingdom. However, the government was defeated by MPs on an amendment at the committee stage which made this subject to the prior enactment of a statute approving the final terms of withdrawal (*Hansard*, HC, Vol 633, col 521).
- Clauses 10/11 – these deal with the impact withdrawal from the European Union will have on the devolved institutions. In particular, cl 10 provides that the devolved authorities will be able to deal with 'deficiencies' following withdrawal (this parallels the ministerial power in cl 7). Clause 11 provides that the Scottish Parliament, National Assembly for Wales and the Northern Ireland Assembly will be outside of their legislative competence if they modify retained EU law in

a way which would have been incompatible with EU law immediately prior to the United Kingdom's exit. NB: on the consequences of Brexit for the devolved settlements, see the House of Lords European Union Select Committee, *Brexit: Devolution*, HL Paper 9 (House of Lords, 2017).

At the time of writing, the Bill had passed its stages in the House of Commons and moved to the House of Lords – for detail on the Bill as it entered the second chamber, see the House of Lords Select Committee on the Constitution, *European Union (Withdrawal) Bill*, HL Paper 69 (House of Lords, 2018).

SUMMARY

- EU law became part of the United Kingdom's legal system via the European Communities Act 1972.
- Europe comprises a number of institutions (eg European Parliament), each of which have specified constitutional roles.
- EU law is a source of the British constitution and comprises primary sources (Treaties) and secondary sources (eg Regulations).
- The Court of Justice of the EU ensures that the application of EU law is observed by Member States and European institutions and it also provides definitive interpretations of EU law.
- Individuals in the United Kingdom enjoy rights under EU law which they can enforce in the domestic courts.
- The Court of Justice has developed the constitutional principle that European law takes primacy over inconsistent national law.
- Section 2(4) of the European Communities Act 1972 requires that British courts interpret all statutes passed before and after 1972 in line with, and subject to, European law.
- In *Factortame* the House of Lords disapplied the operation of the Merchant Shipping Act 1988 on the basis that it was inconsistent with the putative rights of Factortame under European law.
- Section 18 of the European Union Act 2011 confirms that EU law is recognised in the United Kingdom by virtue of the will of Parliament.
- In 2016 the United Kingdom voted to leave the European Union.
- The European Union (Withdrawal) Bill 2017–19 provides for the repeal of the European Communities Act 1972.

Further reading

Books

Alder, J and Syrett, K, *Constitutional and Administrative Law* (11th edn, Palgrave, 2017), Chapter 10.

Barnett, H, *Britain Unwrapped* (Penguin, 2002), Chapter 4.

Craig, P, 'Britain in the European Union' in Jowell, J, Oliver, D and O'Cinneide, C (eds), *The Changing Constitution* (8th edn, Oxford University Press, 2015), p 104.

Ellis, E, 'The Legislative Supremacy of Parliament and Its Limits' in Feldman, D (ed), *English Public Law* (2nd edn, Oxford University Press, 2009), p 127.

Jenkins, R, 'Britain and Europe: The Problem with Being Half Pregnant' in Sutherland, K (ed), *The Rape of the Constitution?* (Imprint Academic, 2000), p 277.

Tebbit, N, 'Britain and Europe: The Issue of Sovereignty' in Sutherland, K (ed), *The Rape of the Constitution?* (Imprint Academic, 2000), p 291.

Tomkins, A, *Public Law* (Oxford University Press, 2003), pp 108–120.

Wicks, E, *The Evolution of a Constitution – Eight Key Moments in British Constitutional History* (Hart Publishing, 2006), Chapter 7.

Articles

Phillipson, G, 'Parliamentary sovereignty, European Community law and Parliament's ability to bind future parliaments' (2003) 39 *Student Law Review* 11.

Wade, H, 'Sovereignty – revolution or evolution?' (1996) 112 LQR 568.

See *Public Law* (November 2017).

Internet link

http://europa.eu.

16

The European Convention on Human Rights

AIMS AND OBJECTIVES

At the end of this chapter you should be able to:

- Appreciate the significance of the European Convention on Human Rights both with respect to its contribution to the international protection of human rights and its effect on human rights in the United Kingdom

- Understand the machinery for the enforcement of human rights laid down in the Convention and administered by the European Court of Human Rights

- Be aware of the central rights contained in the Convention and how they have been interpreted and enforced by the European Court of Human Rights

- Appreciate the central principles applied by the European Court which determine the enforcement and restriction of human rights

- Appreciate the potential effect of the Convention and its case law on the protection of human rights in the United Kingdom including any proposals for the reform of the European Court and the (limited) effect of 'Brexit' on the Convention and the domestic protection of Convention rights

16.1 Introduction and background

The European Convention on Human Rights (1950) is central to the understanding and study of human rights and civil liberties. It is an international Treaty for the protection of individual human rights, containing such rights as the right to life (Art 2), freedom from torture (Art 3), liberty and security of the person (Art 5), the right to a fair trial (Art 6), the right to private life (Art 8) and freedom of expression (Art 10). The rights will be discussed in detail later in this chapter (see below).

1. The Convention has its own machinery for enforcing human rights and this machinery has been used on numerous occasions against the United Kingdom government, resulting in changes to domestic law and practice.
2. The Convention and its case law has informed the domestic law of human rights in the United Kingdom, being applied by the domestic courts as an indirect and persuasive source (see below).

3. More specifically, the Convention and its principles are now given effect by the Human Rights Act 1998, allowing the domestic courts to apply Convention principles and case law (see below).

The European Convention on Human Rights was devised by the Council of Europe, which was set up after the Second World War to achieve unity in matters such as the protection of fundamental human rights. It was drafted in the light of the atrocities that took place before and during the Second World War and was signed by the High Contracting Parties in 1950, entering into force in 1953. The United Kingdom ratified the Treaty in 1957, and in 1966 it accepted both the compulsory jurisdiction of the European Court and the power of the European Commission (now the Court) of Human Rights to receive alleged violations of Convention rights.

The Convention should not be confused with European Union (formerly Community) law:

- The Council of Europe is separate from the European Communities and has a larger composition than the latter. In 2010 there were 47 member states of the Council of Europe.
- The Convention is enforced by the European Court of Human Rights (ECtHR), whilst Union law is enforced by the Court of Justice of the EU.
- Whereas European Community law was incorporated via the European Communities Act 1972, the European Convention was given 'further effect' by the Human Rights Act 1998.
- European Union law has supremacy over domestic law via s 2 of the European Communities Act, whilst the Convention is still subordinate to clear contrary domestic law.
- Decisions of the Court of Justice have direct effect under s 3 of the 1972 Act, whilst the decisions of the ECtHR are binding in international law and can be taken into account by the domestic courts (under s 2 of the 1998 Act).
- The European Convention is not an EU Treaty, but the Court of Justice of the EU can take into consideration the decisions of the ECtHR, and *vice versa*.
- The European Convention on Human Rights should not be confused with the EC Charter of Fundamental Rights 2000, which seeks to protect a wide range of civil and political and social and economic rights within Union law. However, the EU will shortly accede to the European Convention on Human Rights, making the Convention an EU treaty.

* The UK's withdrawal from the European Union ('Brexit') will have an impact on the enforceability of EU rights but not the rights under the Convention (unless the government decides to replace the Human Rights Act 1998 with a domestic Bill of Rights).

The Convention has its own machinery for enforcement in the form of a European Court of Human Rights, possessing the power to make judicial decisions, which are then enforceable on the Member States (High Contracting Parties).

Although the Convention is now given effect by the Human Rights Act 1998, this machinery remains important:

- individuals can still petition the European Court of Human Rights if they do not receive a satisfactory remedy in domestic law;
- the domestic courts will apply the same principles and norms used by the European Court of Human Rights when adjudicating on human rights disputes;
- the case law (both former and current) will inform the domestic courts and law.

It should be noted that, under the Convention, the main obligation to protect human rights is placed on the member states.

ARTICLE

Art 1
The High Contracting Parties shall secure to everyone within their jurisdiction the rights and freedoms defined in Section I of this Convention.

- This imposes an obligation on the Member State to provide an effective procedure and remedy for protecting human rights, although it is not mandatory to formally incorporate the Convention; thus, repealing the Human Rights Act 1998 is possible without breaching Article 1 (although the present government has no plans to do that for the time being).
- Article 1 applies so as to impose a duty towards anyone within the state's jurisdiction, whether a citizen of that state or not.
- The Convention machinery is regarded as subsidiary to the national system for protecting rights and will only be used as a last resort.
- Individuals can only make a claim under the Convention machinery if they have exhausted all effective domestic remedies (Art 35).
- The European Court affords each Member State a certain discretion (a 'margin of appreciation') as to how they protect Convention rights (*Handyside v United Kingdom* (1976) 1 EHRR 737) and expects each state to interpret and apply the Convention in the context of its own system.

16.2 The European Court of Human Rights

Article 19 establishes a European Court of Human Rights to 'ensure the observance of the engagements undertaken by the High Contracting Parties in the Convention and the Protocols thereto'.

After the ratification of Protocol 11, the Court now functions on a permanent basis and has taken over any adjudicative role formerly carried out by the European Commission of Human Rights and the Committee of Ministers. The former body is now abolished but its decisions are persuasive authority for both the European Court and the domestic courts under s 2 of the Human Rights Act 1998. The Committee of Ministers (the foreign secretaries of each state) carry out a diplomatic role and ensure that the European Court's judgments are fully and effectively executed (Art 46).

16.2.1 The composition of the European Court of Human Rights

Under Art 20 the court consists of a number of judges equal to that of the High Contracting Parties, who are elected by the Parliamentary Assembly of the Council of Europe. The procedure of the court is regulated by the Rules of the European Court of Human Rights.

The European Court of Human Rights comprises:

- Committees, consisting of three judges who consider the admissibility of applications (Art 27(1)) and who possess the power (Art 28) to strike out cases from its list;

- Chambers of seven judges, who decide on the admissibility and merits of the application (Art 27(2)) combining the roles formerly carried out respectively by the Commission and the old European Court;
- The Grand Chamber, consisting of 17 judges who hear cases referred to them (Art 27(3)).

16.2.2 The Grand Chamber of the European Court

The Grand Chamber of the Court of Human Rights fulfils a number of roles:

- Under Art 31 it has the power to determine applications which, under Art 30, have been relinquished by a Chamber of the Court because the case raises a serious issue of interpretation of the Convention (for example, *A v United Kingdom* (2009) 49 EHRR 29 on the issue of detention in times of terrorist threats).
- It can act as an appeal court by considering referrals by the parties under Art 43 of the Convention (for example, *Hatton v United Kingdom* (2003) 37 EHRR 28, overruling the Chamber's decision on whether night flights violated the right to home and private life).
- It can consider requests for an advisory opinion under Art 47.
- It has the power to make 'pilot' judgments, which will make a judgment on an individual case which represents a multiple claim about a systematic breach of the Convention (*MT and Greens v United Kingdom* (2011) 53 EHRR 21, on prisoner enfranchisement).

Decisions of the Grand Chamber are final and binding (although whether they affect the domestic law depends on the legal system in question).

16.3 The role of the European Court of Human Rights

The European Court of Human Rights is the judicial arm of the Convention. In addition to considering the admissibility of claims under the Convention and striking out cases (below), the main role of the European Court of Human Rights is to interpret and apply the European Convention with respect to alleged violations brought before it and to make binding judgments. The court is bound to give reasons for its decisions, including its decisions on admissibility (Art 45).

In practice it must decide whether there has been a violation of one of the substantive rights in the Convention and whether there is any justification for any such violation. It will interpret and apply the Convention in the light of both the intention of the drafters and current philosophy on human rights protection (*Selmouni v France* (1999) 29 EHRR 403), and will use various human rights norms during that process – democracy, the rule of law, equality, the protection of human dignity etc.

16.3.1 The effect of the European Court of Human Rights' judgments and their domestic effect

Under Art 46 the decisions of the European Court (subject to any appeal to the Grand Chamber), are binding in international law against that state provided it has accepted the compulsory jurisdiction of the court. The judgment imposes an obligation on that state to comply with the judgment (including paying any 'just satisfaction') and to make any necessary changes to domestic law. For example, following the decision in *Malone v United Kingdom* (1984) 7 EHRR 14 Parliament passed the Interception of Communications Act 1985 to regulate telephone tapping; now contained in the Investigatory Powers Act 2016.

However, unlike the decisions of the Court of Justice of the EU, the decisions of the Court of Human Rights do not have an overriding force in our domestic law and do not automatically take precedence over inconsistent domestic law. For example, following the rulings of the European Court of Human Rights on prisoners' voting rights, in *Hirst v United Kingdom (No 2)* (2006) 42 EHRR 41 and *MT and Greens v United Kingdom* (2011) 53 EHRR 21, the government failed to repeal the offending legislation and UK law was thus not affected.

- The effect of the decision in domestic law will depend on how the Convention and its case law has been incorporated into that system.
- Under s 2 of the Human Rights Act 1998 domestic courts must take the decisions of the European Court into account, but any relevant domestic law remains in force until amended by Parliament.
- The courts can interpret and apply domestic law in the light of the Convention but decisions of the Court of Human Rights cannot override domestic law.

CASE EXAMPLE

R v Lyons and others *[2002] UKHL 44*

Following the decision of the European Court in *Saunders v United Kingdom* (1996) 23 EHRR 313, a number of individuals sought to have their convictions quashed as violating the rule against self-incrimination in breach of Art 6 of the Convention.

The House of Lords held that at the time the convictions were lawful under domestic law and that the decision of the European Court could not retrospectively overrule such convictions. Any remedy provided in *Saunders* imposed an obligation in international law and did not overturn domestic law. As the convictions took place before the Human Rights Act 1998 came into force the Act could not be applied to that case and the applicants needed to petition the European Court (*Lyons v United Kingdom* (2003) 37 EHRR 183 CD).

16.3.2 The power to award just satisfaction

Where the European Court finds a violation of the Convention it may under Art 41 award 'just satisfaction' to the injured party. The Member State then has an obligation under the Convention to abide by such a ruling and, for example, pay any compensation awarded by the court.

- The phrase 'just satisfaction' is also used in s 8 of the Human Rights Act 1998 and the domestic courts must ensure that any remedies awarded by them reflect the principles in Art 41 (see below).
- The European Court can award pecuniary damage to compensate for any direct financial loss, including loss or depreciation of property (*Lopez Ostra v Spain* (1994) 20 EHRR 277), or recovery of any fines or compensation (*Jersild v Denmark* (1994) 19 EHRR 1).
- The court may also award damages for non-pecuniary damage where the applicant has suffered things such as loss of liberty (*A v United Kingdom* (2009) 49 EHRR 29) or physical and/or mental distress from a violation of the European Convention (see *Smith and Grady v United Kingdom* (2000) 29 EHRR 493).

- The court can compensate for legal costs and expenses actually, necessarily and reasonably incurred by the applicant (*McCann v United Kingdom* (1996) 21 EHRR 97).
- In appropriate cases the court has the power to award no compensation other than costs and expenses (*McCann v United Kingdom* (above)), no compensation awarded for unlawful deaths of suspected terrorists (contrast with *A v United Kingdom* (above) where limited compensation was granted). In some cases, a finding of a violation, with an obligation to alter the law, will be regarded as just satisfaction – see *MT and Greens v United Kingdom* (above), where compensation for loss of voting rights was not awarded.

ACTIVITY

Self-test questions

1. Why was the European Convention on Human Rights devised and what does it generally contain?
2. How is the European Convention different from, and related to European Union law?
3. How do the Convention and its case law affect United Kingdom law and its practice?
4. How has the Convention been incorporated into domestic law? (Check your answer once you have studied Chapter 17.)
5. What is the role of the European Court of Human Rights, and what powers does the court have?

16.4 State and individual applications

The European Court receives applications from either Member States or from individual applicants claiming to be victims of a violation of the Convention.

16.4.1 Inter-state applications

Under Art 33 any High Contracting Party may refer to the court any alleged breach of the provisions of the Convention or the protocols by another High Contracting Party, including claims with respect to victims other than the state's own nationals.

CASE EXAMPLE

Ireland v United Kingdom *(1978) 2 EHRR 25*

The Irish government brought an inter-state case against the United Kingdom in relation to the treatment of suspected terrorists by British authorities detained in army barracks in Northern Ireland. The government claimed that such treatment constituted a violation of, *inter alia*, Art 3 of the European Convention, guaranteeing freedom from torture and inhuman and degrading treatment (the European Court held that there had been a violation of Art 3 in that the interrogation techniques constituted inhuman and degrading treatment, but not torture).

State applications must comply with Art 35, which requires the exhaustion of all domestic remedies and for claims to be brought within six months of the final decision.

16.4.2 Individual applications

Under Art 34 the court may receive applications from 'any person, non-governmental organisation or group of individuals' who claims to be a victim of a violation by one of the High Contracting Parties of the rights set forth in the Convention. The individual may bring an application against a state provided he or she was within that state's jurisdiction at the time (Art 1). Applications cannot be brought against another individual or a public authority, although the state can be liable for violations committed by state actors and individuals (*A v United Kingdom* (1999) 27 EHRR 611) and for the violations of another state if it exposes an individual to a risk of violation (*Soering v United Kingdom* (1989) 11 EHRR 439).

Individual applications are made to the Court Registry, which will register the complaint and the case will then be referred to the European Court for a determination on admissibility, below. High Contracting Parties must not hinder any individual petition (*McShane v United Kingdom* (2002) 35 EHRR 23).

16.4.3 The requirement to be a victim

Applications under Art 34 may only be brought by persons claiming to be a 'victim' of a breach of the Convention.

- The applicant must normally be directly affected by the alleged violation (*Klass v Germany* (1978) 2 EHRR 214).
- The law or practice must normally be applied to the applicant's disadvantage, although an individual might be directly affected by the mere existence of incompatible law or practice (*Dudgeon v United Kingdom* (1982) 4 EHRR 149 – existence of discriminatory law against homosexuals made the applicant a victim, even though he was never prosecuted).
- The court is also prepared to accept applications from family representatives of the actual victim, particularly in cases of potentially unlawful deaths (*McCann v United Kingdom* (1996) 21 EHRR 97).

The court thus takes a flexible approach to the issue where the applicant is a victim. In *Fairfield v United Kingdom* (Application No 24790/04) it held that the family of a person convicted for using insulting words and behaviour, and who subsequently died, were not victims under Art 34. The court noted that a different, more flexible, test applied in cases under Art 2 of the Convention, because of the importance of that right.

16.4.4 Admissibility of applications

Articles 34 and 35 of the Convention subject applications to an admissibility criteria and the initial role of the European Court is to rule on admissibility of the claim. This will filter out hopeless claims, or claims made in bad faith, and will ensure that the Convention machinery is only used as a last resort.

16.4.5 The admissibility criteria

Art 35, which applies to both inter-state and individual applications, provides that the court may only deal with the matter after all domestic remedies have been exhausted and within a period of six months from the date on which the final decision was taken.

- The six-month rule does not apply to continuing breaches of the Convention, or where the violation shows that there is no effective domestic remedy (*De Becker v Belgium* (1979–80)).
- The applicant is expected to exhaust all *effective* domestic remedies before applying to the court (*Spencer v United Kingdom* [1998] EHRLR 348 – failure to bring confidentiality proceedings for an alleged breach of Art 8).
- Since the passing of the Human Rights Act 1998, applicants would be expected to make full use of that Act in resolving their human rights dispute.
- The exhaustion rule does not apply to inter-state cases where the applicant state alleges widespread breaches (*Ireland v United Kingdom* (1978) 2 EHRR 25) or in individual applications where an administrative practice has rendered remedies ineffective (*Akdivar v Turkey* (1996) 1 BHRC 137).
- An applicant should normally pursue any effective appeal against an initial decision, unless such an appeal would be futile (*Handyside v United Kingdom* (1976) 1 EHRR 737), where the court held that appeal proceedings did not have to be exhausted when the initial court's finding was clearly within domestic law.

In addition to the above rules on time limits and exhaustion of remedies, the court may declare a case inadmissible under Art 35 on the following grounds:

- Where the application is anonymous.
- Where it is substantially the same as a matter that has already been examined by the court, or has already been submitted to another procedure of international investigation or settlement and contains no new information.
- Where the application is incompatible with the provisions of the Convention. In other words, where the claim does not engage a right protected by the Convention – *Bertrand Russell Peace Foundation v United Kingdom* 14 DR 117(1978), no right to diplomatic protection under the Convention.
- Where the application constitutes an abuse of the right of application. For example, where it is brought in bad faith for purely political or personal reasons (*M v United Kingdom* 54 DR 214 (1987)).
- Where the claim is manifestly ill-founded. In other words, where the applicant has failed to show a *prima facie* case against the respondent state, either because the relevant article is not engaged or where the violation is clearly justified (*Friend v United Kingdom; Countryside Alliance v United Kingdom* (2010) 50 EHRR SE6).

In addition, under Protocol No 14 cases can be declared inadmissible where the applicant has not suffered a serious disadvantage, and where respect for human rights does not require the court to examine the merits of the case (excluding cases where the dispute has not been considered by a domestic tribunal). Under that protocol, single judges may hear clear-cut applications and three person committees cases where the case law is settled.

With respect to proposals for reform of the European Court of Human Rights, in 2010 the Council of Europe agreed the Interlaken Declaration, which recognised the problem of the Court's increasing case load and called for an enhanced screening process for applications and for the Court to place greater reliance on the principle of 'subsidiarity'.

In addition, the UK held the Brighton Declaration in 2012 where it was suggested that the European Court should only deal with the most serious violations and that the Convention be amended to make specific reference to the principles of 'subsidiarity' and the 'margin of appreciation'.

16.4.6 Friendly settlements and striking out

Article 38 permits the European Court of Human Rights to effect a friendly settlement between the applicant and the defendant state after deciding on its admissibility. In such a situation the case will be struck out of the court's list (Art 40).

- Some settlements are effected on the basis that the state admits the violation and promises to change its law (*Sutherland v United Kingdom, The Times*, 13 April 2001 – friendly settlement agreed when the UK government agreed to amend incompatible legislation and to equalise the age of consent for heterosexual and homosexual sex (The Sexual Offences (Amendment) Act 2000)).
- Other settlements do not involve an admission of liability and are effected by a payment of compensation to the applicant (*Amekrane v United Kingdom* (1974) 44 CD 101 – payment of £30,000 compensation to a relative of a member of the Moroccan Armed Forces who had been sent back to his country to face the death penalty).

16.5 Lawful and permissible interferences with Convention rights

Many Convention rights may be interfered with in particular circumstances, provided that interference has certain qualities. In particular, the 'conditional rights' contained in Arts 8–11 of the Convention contain a particular mechanism for testing the legality of any interference:

- any such interference must be prescribed by, or in accordance with the law;
- it must relate to a legitimate aim listed in the qualifying part of the article;
- it must be necessary in a democratic society for the protection of one of a number of those aims.

This mechanism can also be used to test the legality of interferences with other rights, such as the right to a fair trial under Art 6 (*Osman v United Kingdom* (2000) 29 EHRR 245), the right to liberty of the person under Art 5 (*Steel v United Kingdom* (1998) 28 EHRR 603), and freedom from discrimination under Art 14 (*Pretty v United Kingdom* (2002) 35 EHRR 1).

The Human Rights Act 1998 adopts these principles and thus the domestic courts must subject any interference under domestic law to an equivalent test when adjudicating upon Convention rights.

16.5.1 Prescribed by law/in accordance with law

Any interference of Convention rights must comply with the rule of law and thus must derive from some legal provision.

- For example, under Art 2 of the Convention the death penalty is provided for, but only for a crime for which the penalty is *prescribed by law*.
- Art 5 of the Convention allows interference with a person's liberty, but only in accordance with a procedure *prescribed by law*.
- The 'conditional rights' contained in Arts 8 to 11 provide that any interference with those rights is '*prescribed by law*' or '*in accordance with law*'.

The meaning of 'in accordance with law' was considered in *Malone*, below, and the phrase 'prescribed by law' (used in Arts 9, 10 and 11), is interpreted and applied identically (*Silver v United Kingdom* (1983) 5 EHRR 347).

CASE EXAMPLE

Malone v United Kingdom *(1984) 7 EHRR 14*

The applicant's telephone had been tapped in the course of criminal investigation and the applicant claimed that the tapping was not authorised by law as the rules for interception were contained in administrative guidance.

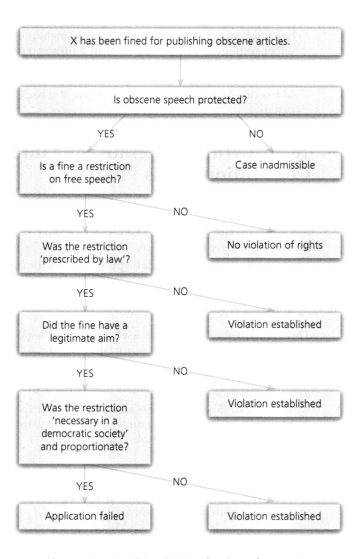

Figure 16.1 Conditional right – freedom of expression

The European Court held that, for a measure to be prescribed by law, it had to have a legal basis (the law must be identified and established), the rule had to be accessible, and should be formulated with sufficient certainty to enable people to understand it and to regulate their conduct by it.

The court concluded that it could not be said what elements of the power to intercept communications were incorporated in legal rules and what elements remained within the discretion of the executive. Accordingly the tapping was not in accordance with law and was thus in violation of Art 8.

In *Malone* the European Court insisted that there is a measure of legal protection against arbitrary interference by public authorities and that provisions must exist which are sufficiently independent of those who administer them. This law can be either in statutory or common law form (*Sunday Times v United Kingdom* (1979) 2 EHRR 245).

In addition, the rule has to be accessible, so that those who are likely to be affected by it can access and understand it (*Silver v United Kingdom* (1983) 5 EHRR 347 – the regulation of prisoners' correspondence via administrative guidance produced by the Secretary of State was not prescribed by law because such guidance was only available to the prison authorities).

Finally, the provision should be sufficiently clear to allow individuals to govern their future behaviour. This was explained by the European Court of Human Rights in *Sunday Times v United Kingdom* (1979) 2 EHRR 245:

JUDGMENT

'A law has to be formulated with sufficient precision to enable the citizen to regulate his conduct: that person must be able – if need be with appropriate advice – to foresee, to a degree that is reasonable in the circumstances, the consequences which a given action may entail. Those consequences need not, however, be foreseeable with absolute certainty. Whilst the Court noted that certainty is desirable, it also accepted that excessive rigidity should be avoided and that laws are inevitably couched in terms which, to some extent, are vague and whose interpretation and application are questions of practice. Similarly, although the law itself may be vague, its meaning and scope may become apparent after it has been construed and applied by the courts.'

The law's meaning and extent must, therefore, be capable of reasonable prediction, even though the European Court accepts that many laws are inevitably vague and open to flexible interpretation. For example, in *Hashman and Harrup v United Kingdom* (1999) 30 EHRR 241, when the applicants were ordered to desist in conduct that was *contra bonos mores* (conduct which is seen as wrong in the eyes of the majority of contemporary citizens), the court held that the offence failed to give sufficient guidance to the applicants as to what conduct they were not allowed to carry out in the future. See also *Gillan v United Kingdom* (2010) 50 EHRR 45, where it was held that stop and search powers under s 44 of the Terrorism Act 2000 were too arbitrary and uncertain to be prescribed by law as they provided too great an element of discretion to officers.

16.5.2 Legitimate aims

Any restriction of a Convention right must pursue a legitimate aim. These aims are expressly mentioned in the qualifying paragraphs of Arts 8–11 of the Convention, but also constitute implied restrictions of other articles, such as freedom from discrimination (Art 14), the right to marry (Art 12) and the right to vote (Art 3, Protocol 1).

For example, Art 10, guaranteeing the right to freedom of speech and expression, refers to a host of legitimate aims.

ARTICLE

Art 10(2)

'The exercise of these freedoms . . . may be subject to such . . . restrictions, conditions and formalities as are prescribed by law and necessary in a democratic society, in the interests of national security, territorial integrity, public safety, the prevention of disorder or crime, the protection of health or morals, the protection of the reputation and or rights of others, the prevention of the disclosure of information received in confidence and the maintenance of the authority and impartiality of the judiciary.'

The Member State must then satisfy the court that the restriction pursued one of those aims and was genuinely applied to the applicant in a particular case. Thus, in *Handyside v United Kingdom* (1976) 1 EHRR 737 the court accepted that the applicant had been prosecuted and convicted under the Obscene Publications Act 1959 for the legitimate purpose of protecting health and morals and the rights of others (the right of young, vulnerable individuals not to be corrupted).

16.5.3 Necessary in a democratic society

In addition to the restriction being legal and related to a legitimate aim, the Convention (and now the Human Rights Act 1998) guards against excessive or unnecessary interferences by insisting that a restriction is 'necessary in a democratic society' for achieving its legitimate aim.

The phrase 'necessary in a democratic society' was defined in *Handyside v United Kingdom* (1976) 1 EHRR 737:

JUDGMENT

'The word "necessary" does not mean "absolutely necessary" or "indispensable", but neither does it have the flexibility of terms such as "useful" or "convenient". Instead there must be a 'pressing social need' for the interference. The Court must ask whether there is a pressing social need for some restriction of the Convention and whether the particular restriction corresponds to that need, including whether it a proportionate response to that need, and whether the reasons advanced by the authorities are relevant and sufficient.'

The court is not faced with a choice between two conflicting principles but with a principle of, for example, freedom of expression subject to a number of exceptions, which must be narrowly interpreted (*Sunday Times v United Kingdom* (1979) 2 EHRR 245). However, the principles of necessity and proportionality are linked to the doctrine of the margin of appreciation (see below).

16.5.4 The doctrine of proportionality

The doctrine of proportionality (now part of domestic law after the Human Rights Act 1998 was passed – see Chapter 17) ensures that there is a fair balance between pursuing a legitimate aim and the protection of Convention rights.

Thus, any restriction should be strictly proportionate to the legitimate aim being pursued and the authorities must show that it does not go beyond what is strictly required to achieve that purpose (*Barthold v Germany* (1985) 7 EHRR 383). In doing so the court can consider the following factors:

margin of appreciation

A concept created by the European Court of Human Rights to allow a certain amount of freedom for each signatory state to regulate its own activities and its application of the European Convention on Human Rights

- The importance of the right that has been interfered with.
- The extent to which the right was violated, including the level of the sanction or penalty.
- The nature and importance of the legitimate aim (*Handyside v United Kingdom* (1976) 1 EHRR 737 – protection of morals best decided by national authorities).
- Whether there was a less restrictive alternative available to the domestic authorities (*Goodwin v United Kingdom* (1996) 22 EHRR 123 – disclosure of press source not necessary in addition to an injunction to prohibit disclosure of confidential information).
- Whether the restriction destroys the very essence of the Convention right in question (*Hirst v United Kingdom* (2006) 42 EHHR 41 – blanket prohibition of the prisoner's right to vote was disproportionate).

16.5.5 The margin of appreciation

In deciding whether there has been a violation of the Convention, and in determining whether the Member State has achieved a correct balance, the European Court is prepared to give the state a level of discretion – a '**margin of appreciation**'.

The doctrine was first used in the context of Art 15, allowing derogation in times of war or other emergency, and where the European Court gives the state a margin of error in deciding how to compromise Convention rights in such circumstances. The margin is offered by the European Court because it recognises that its role under the Convention is subsidiary to the system of rights protection adopted by each Member State (Art 1 of the Convention):

JUDGMENT

'The machinery of the Convention is subsidiary to the national systems safeguarding human rights, and consequently the Convention leaves to each state a margin of appreciation, given both to the domestic legislature and to the bodies called upon to interpret and apply the laws. This margin of appreciation goes hand in hand with the Court's power to give the final meaning on whether a restriction is compatible with the Convention right in question.'

Handyside v United Kingdom (1976)
1 EHRR 737.

The doctrine is flexible and the court will offer a wide or narrow margin depending on the circumstances. A wide margin will be offered in cases where free speech conflicts with public morality. Thus, in *Handyside v United Kingdom* (above) the European Court stated that it was not possible to find a uniform conception of morals within the Council of Europe, and that states were in a better position than the international judge to give an opinion on the exact content of the requirements of morals.

However, a narrower margin may be offered where the restriction in question impinges on the enjoyment of the individual's right to *private* life (*Dudgeon v United Kingdom* (1982) 4 EHRR 149).

CASE EXAMPLE

Smith and Grady v United Kingdom *(2000) 29 EHRR 493*

The applicants had been dismissed from the armed forces because of their homosexuality and claimed that their right to private life had been violated.

The court held that the restriction placed on homosexuals from remaining in the armed forces was not necessary for achieving national security and public order. The negative attitudes of heterosexuals towards homosexuals could not, of themselves, justify the interferences in question.

A similarly narrow margin may be offered in cases where the restriction impinges on press freedom. Thus, in *Sunday Times v United Kingdom* (1979) 2 EHRR 245 the court held that laws protecting contempt of court displayed a much more common European approach, allowing the court to more easily judge the necessity of any particular interference. In addition, the publication in question (an article on the ongoing thalidomide disaster) reported on a matter of great public interest, and an injunction should not be granted unless it was *absolutely certain* that the publication would hinder the due administration of justice.

The doctrine of margin of appreciation does not, theoretically, apply to domestic proceedings under the Human Rights Act 1998. However, it is clear that the domestic courts will show Parliament and public authorities a good deal of deference in cases where human rights have to be balanced with other rights and interests (see Chapter 17).

ACTIVITY

Problem-solving

Consider the following hypothetical case and answer the questions that follow it.

In June 2022 Parliament passes the (imaginary) Public Offices Act 2022, which regulates the conduct of those who hold public office and which encouraged responsible government. Under s 60 of the Act it is an offence for any person to use grossly offensive words either in describing a person who holds a public office, or to criticise such a person with respect either to the performance of his public duties or to the conducting of his or her private life; under s 60(4) 'grossly offensive words' are defined as those which relate to an individual's reputation or integrity and which a reasonable person would regard as highly indecent or improper'. The maximum fine for committing an offence under the Act is £2,000.

ACTIVITY

Applying the law

In August 2022, Lionel, a local councillor, was convicted under s 60 of the Act by Birdchester Magistrates when he distributed leaflets in Birdchester city centre which criticised the local Member of Parliament for his recent speech on immigration and asylum seekers. In the leaflet Lionel described the MP as 'a bloody Nazi and a hypocrite', stating that the MP and those who subscribed to his views were as dangerous as sex offenders. Lionel was fined £1,000 and the conviction and fine were upheld by the Court of Appeal.

Lionel now brings an application under the European Convention.

1. Have any of L's Convention rights been interfered with?
2. If so, is that restriction 'prescribed by law'?
3. Do the Act and the conviction pursue a legitimate aim?
4. In your view, was the conviction and fine necessary in a democratic society?
5. What level of margin of appreciation would the European Court give to the UK authorities in such a case?

16.6 Derogations and reservations

The Convention recognises that a state might not always be able to fully comply with its obligations under the Convention and allows it to compromise those rights in certain cases. Accordingly, Art 15 allows derogation in times of war or other emergency, and Art 57 permits the state to make a reservation with respect to a particular Convention right and its application within that jurisdiction.

16.6.1 Derogation in times of war or other public emergency
Article 15 of the Convention provides as follows:

ARTICLE

> Art 15
> 'In times of war or other public emergency threatening the life of the nation any High Contracting Party may take measures derogating from its obligations under this Convention to the extent strictly required by the exigencies of the situation, provided that such measures are not inconsistent with its other obligations under international law.'

This power was used in the 'war against terror' following the 9/11 attacks; see below. The right to derogate under Art 15 is qualified in a number of respects:

- The High Contracting Party can only take such measures as are *strictly required* by the exigencies of the situation.
- The measures must not be inconsistent with the state's other obligations under other Treaties.
- Article 15(2) provides that no derogation is allowed in respect of certain Convention rights: no derogation is possible in relation to Art 2 (the right to life) (excluding deaths resulting from lawful acts of war), Art 3 (prohibition of torture etc), Art 4(1) (prohibition of slavery or servitude) or Art 7 (prohibition of retrospective criminal law).
- The High Contracting Party must keep the Secretary General of the Council of Europe informed of the measures which it has taken and when such measures have ceased to operate, including the reasons for such action.

Derogation measures can be challenged under the European Convention and the court can adjudicate on their compatibility. In doing so, the court will provide the state with a wide margin of error.

CASE EXAMPLE

Lawless v Ireland (No 3) *(1961) 1 EHRR 15*

Although the court found that the detention of the applicant without trial for a period of five months was in violation of Art 5(3) of the Convention, it held that the Irish government was entitled to derogate from its obligations by virtue of the existence of a public emergency.

The court stressed that the measures governments can take when derogating are strictly limited to what is required by the exigencies of the situation and must not be in conflict with other international law obligations. However, the court was satisfied that those strict limitations were met in the present case. The court held that the respondent government should be afforded a certain margin of error or appreciation in deciding what measures were required by the situation, and it was not the court's function to substitute for the government's assessment any other assessment of what might be the most prudent or most expedient policy to combat terrorism.

Moreover, the court must arrive at its decision in the light of the conditions that existed at the time that the original decision was taken, rather than reviewing the matter retrospectively.

A similarly wide discretion had been given to the UK government with respect to provisions intended to deal with terrorism in Northern Ireland.

CASE EXAMPLE

Brannigan and McBride v United Kingdom *(1993) 17 EHRR 539*

The United Kingdom government lodged a derogation after the European Court's decision in *Brogan v United Kingdom* (1989) 11 EHRR 117, where it was held that detention provisions in the Prevention of Terrorism (Temporary Provisions) Act 1984 were in contravention of Art 5(3) of the Convention, guaranteeing the right to be brought promptly before a judge or other officer.

The European Court held that the derogation was lawful. The derogation was not invalid merely because the government had decided to keep open the possibility of finding a means in the future of ensuring greater conformity with Convention obligations. In addition there were effective measures in domestic law to challenge the use of the provisions and thus to safeguard against arbitrary action.

Note that the *domestic* courts have shown less deference with respect to the compatibility of more recent anti-terrorism measures: *A and others v Secretary of State*, where the House of Lords held that provisions allowing detention without trial were incompatible with Article 15 (see 17.11.1). That decision on derogation was subsequently upheld by the European Court of Human Rights (*A v United Kingdom* (2009) 49 EHRR 29), and *Lawless* should be read in the light of this new approach.

16.6.2 Reservations

Article 57 of the Convention allows a state to make reservations to specific provisions of the Convention when ratifying the Convention. The reservation must be in respect of laws in existence at the time of ratification and the article does not allow reservations of a general character. For example it would not be possible to make a reservation of an entire Convention right.

The United Kingdom made a reservation with regard to Art 2 of the First Protocol to the Convention, which imposes a duty on each state to respect the rights of parents to ensure education and teaching in conformity with their own religious and philosophical convictions. This duty is only accepted in so far as it is compatible with the provision of efficient instruction and training and the avoidance of unreasonable public expenditure. The reservation is contained in Sch 3 of the Human Rights Act 1998 and thus has effect in domestic law.

KEY FACTS

Principle	Legal authority
The European Convention imposes an obligation on each state to ensure the observance of Convention rights within its own jurisdiction.	Art 1, ECHR
The UK has given effect to the Convention via the Human Rights Act 1998 and thus the principles of the Convention and the court can be used in domestic proceedings.	s 2, HRA 1998
In addition, the Convention machinery can be used by victims who have exhausted all effective domestic remedies.	Art 34, ECHR
The European Court was set up to ensure the observance of the Convention and can receive inter-state or individual applications.	Arts 19, 33 and 34, ECHR
A full-time European Court decides on the admissibility and merits of all applications, which must be received within six months of the act and the applicant must have exhausted all effective domestic remedies.	Art 34, ECHR
A Grand Chamber of the European Court hears appeals and referrals from the European Court of Human Rights and its decisions are final.	Arts 43 and 44, ECHR
Individual applications are subject to further tests of admissibility and must not be manifestly ill-founded.	Art 35, ECHR
The court has the power to strike out cases and to secure friendly settlements between the parties.	Art 38, ECHR
The court has the power to make awards of 'just satisfaction', including granting pecuniary and non-pecuniary loss and costs and expenses.	Art 41, ECHR
Certain Convention rights can be interfered with provided the restriction is in accordance with or prescribed by law and necessary in a democratic society for the pursuance of a legitimate aim.	*Malone v United Kingdom* (1984) and *Handyside v United Kingdom* (1976)
The European Court adopts the concept of proportionality to judge the necessity of restrictions but also offers the state a margin of appreciation when it passes and maintain laws that interfere with Convention rights.	*Barthold v Germany* (1985) and *Handyside v United Kingdom* (1976)
The standard of review, and the width of the margin of appreciation, depends on the nature of the legitimate aim and the importance of the right.	*Handyside v United Kingdom* (1976) and *Smith and Grady v United Kingdom* (1999)
States can derogate from their Convention obligations and can make reservations under Art 57. Derogations are subject to regulation by the Council of Europe and the European Court, but the court offers a wide margin of error to the states.	Arts 15 and 57, ECHR and *Brannigan and McBride v United Kingdom* (1993)

16.7 The rights guaranteed under the European Convention on Human Rights

The substantive rights guaranteed under the European Convention are contained in section 1 of the Convention, in Arts 2–14 and a number of optional protocols. Most of these rights (excluding Art 13, guaranteeing an effective remedy in domestic law for violation of these rights) are contained in s 1 of the Human Rights Act 1998.

16.7.1 Absolute and conditional rights

Some Convention rights are absolute rights, whilst some are conditional. An absolute right is not capable of derogation under Art 15 and their violation cannot generally be justified. A conditional right, however, can be violated provided that interference is lawful and necessary.

For example, Art 2 (the right to life), Art 3 (prohibition of torture etc), Art 4(1) (freedom from slavery) and Art 7 (no punishment without law) cannot be derogated from under Art 15. Additionally, in the case of an absolute right such as freedom from torture, there can be no justification for a violation, whereas for conditional rights (such as freedom of expression) interference is allowed provided the restriction was prescribed by law and was necessary for the purpose of achieving a legitimate aim (see above).

The Convention also makes certain rights subject to express restrictions:

- Article 4 excludes work done in the course of detention from the term 'forced or compulsory labour'.
- Article 5 lays down a number of specific circumstances where it is permissible to interfere with liberty of the person.
- Article 2 provides that deprivation of life will not be unlawful where it results from the use of absolutely necessary force during, for example, a lawful arrest.
- Article 7(2) states that prohibition against retrospective criminal law does not apply to behaviour that is criminal according to the general principles of international law.

16.8 Article 2 – The right to life

The fundamental right to life is protected by Art 2 of the Convention, which seeks to protect a person's right to life under the law.

ARTICLE

Art 2
Law shall protect everyone's right to life. No one shall be deprived of his life intentionally save in the execution of a sentence of a court following his conviction of a crime for which the penalty is provided by law.

16.8.1 The scope of Article 2

The right to life cannot be derogated from even in times of war and other public emergency (apart from lawful acts of war), but intentional deprivation of life is allowed in exceptional cases listed in Art 2(2) (see directly below).

Article 2 imposes an obligation on the state to preserve life but does not extend to the right to die (*Pretty v United Kingdom* (2002) 35 EHRR 1). Neither does Art 2 extend to protect the right to life of the unborn child (*Vo v France* (2005) 40 EHRR 12).

Article 2 imposes a negative duty not to interfere with a person's right to life, but also places a positive duty on the state to ensure that an individual's life is not taken unnecessarily. The duty applies where the act is one of a state official (*McCann v United Kingdom* (1996) 21 EHRR 97) and the state can also be responsible where the death is caused by a private individual and the state has not taken due care to safeguard the victim's life.

CASE EXAMPLE

Osman v United Kingdom *(2000) 29 EHRR 245*

The applicants, the wife and son of the deceased, brought a claim under Art 2 after one of the son's teachers had killed the husband after forming an attachment to the son.

The European Court held that, under Art 2 the state must take appropriate steps to safeguard the lives of those within its jurisdiction, including the duty to put into place effective criminal law provisions backed up by law-enforcement machinery for preventing and sanctioning such deaths. This would also include a positive (although not an impossible or disproportionate) obligation on the authorities to take preventative operational measures to protect an individual whose life is at risk from the criminal acts of another individual. (On the facts, the court held the police could not be criticised for attaching greater weight to the presumption of the teacher's innocence, and accordingly there had been no violation of Art 2.)

That decision was followed in a domestic decision in *Van Colle v Chief Constable of Hertfordshire* [2008] UKHL 50, where the House of Lords held that there had been no violation of Art 2 when the police had in the circumstances taken adequate steps to safeguard the life of a prosecution witness from a real risk of attacks by suspects in a forthcoming trial. On appeal to the European Court (*Van Colle v United Kingdom* (2013) 56 EHRR 23), it upheld the decision of the domestic courts and held that the test was whether the police knew or ought reasonably to have known of a real and immediate risk.

The state will owe a specific positive duty to safeguard the lives of those in detention, from the actions of either fellow inmates or themselves (*Edwards v United Kingdom* (2002) 35 EHRR 19 – a cellmate posed a real and serious risk to the applicant's son and the prison authorities had not been properly informed of the cellmate's medical history and perceived dangerousness). Article 2 might also be engaged where the individual has taken his or her own life, provided there was a *clear risk* of such – *Keenan v United Kingdom* (2001) 33 EHRR 38, no breach of Art 2 when a vulnerable prisoner had committed suicide whilst under supervision by the prison authorities.

16.8.2 The duty to carry out an effective investigation

In addition to the substantive duty under Art 2, the article imposes a procedural duty on every Member State to carry out a proper investigation into any death that may be in violation of Art 2. In the case below, the court established some guidelines for establishing a violation of this procedural duty.

CASE EXAMPLE

Jordan and others v United Kingdom *(2003) 37 EHRR 2*

The court held that Art 2 required that there had to be some form of effective official investigation when individuals had been killed as a result of the use of force. The state must take the initiative in conducting the investigation and it should be carried out by someone independent from those involved in the events. It should lead to a determination of whether the force used in such circumstances was justified, and to the identification and punishment of those responsible. The authorities must take reasonable steps to secure the necessary evidence and the investigation should be carried out with reasonable promptness.

Article 2 also gives the victim's relatives the right to effectively participate in the investigation (*Edwards v United Kingdom* (above)) and, in conjunction with Art 13 of the Convention, the right to effective compensation, where appropriate (*Keenan v United Kingdom* (above)).

The procedural right has also been upheld by the domestic courts under the Human Rights Act 1998. In *R (Amin) v Secretary of State for the Home Department* [2003] UKHL 51 the House of Lords held that an internal investigation into the killing of a prisoner by his racist cellmate did not fulfil the requirements of Art 2, and that a full independent public investigation had to be held.

16.8.3 The exceptions under Article 2.2

Article 2(2) provides exceptions to the general right to life where the intentional deprivation of life will not constitute a violation of that right.

ARTICLE

Art 2(2)

The deprivation of life shall not be regarded as inflicted in contravention of Art 2 when it results from the use of force which is no more than absolutely necessary . . . in defence of any person from unlawful violence, in order to effect a lawful arrest or to prevent the escape of a person lawfully detained, or in action lawfully taken for the purpose of quelling a riot or insurrection.

For the exceptions in Art 2(2) to come into play the force used must be no more than absolutely necessary.

CASE EXAMPLE

McCann v United Kingdom *(1996) 21 EHRR 97*

Three suspected IRA terrorists were seen near a car. Members of the SAS, believing that the car contained a bomb and that it was to be detonated, shot them dead. The families brought a claim under Art 2 of the Convention.

The European Court held that, although the SAS members had used no more force than was necessary in the circumstances, there had been a violation of the right to life through the careless planning of the operation by the administrative authorities. The authorities had been negligent in the planning of the operation and the soldiers had been provided with misinformation.

Despite this decision, the court will normally afford the authorities and individual officers a wide area of discretion where they have acted in good faith and with reasonable diligence (*Bubbins v United Kingdom* (2005) 41 EHRR 24).

Note that in *Armani Da Silva v United Kingdom* (2016) 63 EHRR 12, the Grand Chamber held that the killing of Jean Charles de Menezes, who was mistaken as a terrorist in 2005, was lawful within Article 2 and that domestic law on the use of fatal force was compatible with the Convention

16.8.4 Article 2 and the death penalty

The first sentence of Art 2 provides for the death penalty, provided it takes the form of an execution of a sentence of a court following a person's conviction of a crime for which the penalty is provided by law. However the death penalty may be unlawful in a number of cases.

- Optional Protocol No 6 of the Convention provides that the death penalty shall be abolished in peacetime and that no one shall be condemned to such penalty or executed. In addition Optional Protocol No 13 abolishes it in all circumstances. The UK has ratified both protocols and thus any execution within its jurisdiction would be contrary to its Convention obligations. This would include executions in other jurisdictions where there was a real risk of such a penalty (*Soering v United Kingdom* (1989) 11 EHRR 439).
- In *Al-Saadoon and Mufhdi v United Kingdom* (2010) 59 EHRR 9 the European Court held that the second sentence in Art 2 should now be amended by state practice and that accordingly states would now regard it as an unacceptable form of punishment in peacetime and in violation of Art 3 (below).
- In any case, the circumstances of a death penalty may constitute a violation of Art 3 of the Convention (*Soering v United Kingdom* (1989) 11 EHRR 439), and any execution not preceded by a fair trial would breach Art 2(1).

16.9 Article 3 – Prohibition of torture and inhuman and degrading treatment and punishment

ARTICLE
....

Art 3
No one shall be subject to torture or to inhuman or degrading treatment or punishment

16.9.1 The scope of Article 3

The Article imposes an absolute prohibition on such treatment, even in times of war or other public emergency (see above). Thus, once a violation of Art 3 has been found, there can be no justification for that breach (*Chahal v United Kingdom* (1997) 23 EHRR 413).

The role of the European Court of Human Rights in such cases is, thus, to define the terms 'torture' and 'inhuman and degrading treatment or punishment' and to assess whether the applicant has been subjected to treatment in violation of the article.

Under Art 3 Member States owe a positive, yet limited, duty to ensure that a person does not suffer ill treatment at the hands of others, whether state actors or public or private individuals.

CASE EXAMPLE

A v United Kingdom *(1999) 27 EHRR 611*

The applicant, a young boy, had been beaten with a cane by his stepfather, who was then acquitted after relying on the defence of reasonable chastisement.

The European Court held that the United Kingdom government was held liable for the ill treatment of the applicant because domestic law provided him with inadequate protection against treatment which was contrary to Art 3 (see now s 58 of the Children Act 2004).

Also, in *Z v United Kingdom* (2002) 34 EHRR 3, the European Court held that the state (via social services) had a duty to take such measures to provide effective protection against long-term abuse and neglect in the home.

16.9.2 Definition of torture, inhuman and degrading treatment or punishment

The terms used in Art 3 were explored in the inter-state case of *Ireland v United Kingdom*.

CASE EXAMPLE

Ireland v United Kingdom *(1978) 2 EHRR 25*

The applicants had been the victims of the 'Five Techniques' interrogation measures, involving being subjected to intense noise, wall-standing and deprivation of food and sleep.

The European Court defined torture as treatment constituting deliberate inhuman treatment causing very serious and cruel suffering; inhuman treatment as causing if not bodily injury, at least intense physical and mental or psychiatric suffering; and degrading treatment as that which would arouse in victims feelings of fear, anguish and inferiority capable of humiliation, or taking away one's physical or moral resistance.

On the facts the court found that the techniques were inhuman and degrading, but were not severe enough to constitute torture.

A finding of torture is, therefore, reserved for treatment constituting an aggravated and deliberate form of inhuman treatment or punishment, although the court has stressed that Art 3 must be interpreted in the light of present-day conditions. As a result, certain acts (in this case, the deliberate, serious and prolonged assault of a detainee), which in the past had been classified as inhuman and degrading as opposed to torture, might now be classified as torture (*Selmouni v France* (1999) 29 EHRR 403). Note that in *Vinter, Moore and Bamber v United Kingdom* (2016) 63 EHRR 1 the Grand Chamber held that the imposition of whole-life sentences without review constituted inhuman punishment.

For a breach to take place the treatment or punishment must cross the threshold set by Art 3. Accordingly the humiliation or debasement must reach a particular level, and the European Court has stressed that such an assessment is relative and depends on all the circumstances of the case, including the victim's age (*Tyrer v United Kingdom* (1978) 2 EHRR 1).

16.9.3 Article 3 and corporal punishment

Not all forms of corporal punishment will necessarily be in violation of Art 3, although judicial corporal punishment appears to be outlawed by the European Court.

CASE EXAMPLE

Tyrer v United Kingdom *(1978) 2 EHRR 1*

A 15-year-old boy in the Isle of Man had been found guilty of assault and birched on his bare buttocks in accordance with Isle of Man law. The government argued that the punishment was an effective deterrent and that in all the circumstances was not inhuman or degrading.

The European Court described the punishment as institutionalised violence and held that the applicant had been subjected to an assault on his dignity and physical integrity and that it was immaterial that the punishment was an effective deterrent, or that the majority of society in the Isle of Man approved it as a punishment.

Corporal punishment in schools was abolished in the United Kingdom by the Schools Standard and Framework Act 1998, although the European Court has never outlawed the practice *per se* (*Costello-Roberts v United Kingdom* (1993) 19 EHRR 112). However, corporal punishment of a child against the parent's wishes would be in breach of Art 2 of the First Protocol, which gives them the right to have their children educated in conformity with their philosophical and religious convictions (*Campbell and Cosans v United Kingdom* (1982) 4 EHRR 293).

Whether parental chastisement is in breach of Art 3 depends on all the circumstances and the severity of the punishment. Thus, in *A v United Kingdom* (1999) 27 EHRR 611, when a nine-year-old boy had been repeatedly and severely beaten by his stepfather with a garden cane, it was held that the threshold in Art 3 of the Convention had been satisfied.

16.9.4 Article 3 and deportation and extradition

Deportation or extradition may expose a person to a real risk that they will face treatment or punishment in breach of Art 3. In such a case the state which deports or extradites may be liable for the violation committed by the receiving state.

CASE EXAMPLE

Soering v United Kingdom *(1989) 11 EHRR 439*

A young German national was to stand trial in the USA for the murder of his girlfriend's parents. The UK government agreed to his extradition, having been assured that the prosecutors would argue that he should not face the death penalty.

The European Court held that the UK government could be liable for a violation by the USA if it exposed the applicant to a real risk of a violation of Art 3. In this case, the death row phenomenon constituted a breach of Art 3 and extradition would constitute a violation of that article by the UK government as there was a real risk that he would be exposed to those conditions.

The *Soering* principle applies even though there may be good national or other security reasons for deportation. Thus, in *Chahal v United Kingdom* (1997) 23 EHRR 413 the

European Court held that the prohibition under Art 3 is absolute and the activities of the person, however undesirable, cannot be a material consideration in deciding whether Art 3 has been breached. This was upheld in *Saadi v Italy* (2009) 49 EHRR 30.

However, the court must be satisfied that the facts reveal a real risk of ill treatment in violation of Art 3, as opposed to a *mere possibility* (*Vilvarajah v United Kingdom* (1991) 14 EHRR 248).

The *Soering* principle can also apply even where the receiving state would not be in violation of Art 3 but nevertheless the applicant would be subjected to inhuman or degrading treatment (*D v United Kingdom* (1997) 24 EHRR 423 – return of applicant to the West Indies, where there would be inadequate medical treatment to deal with his condition (he had contracted AIDS), constituted a violation of Art 3 by the UK). However, the court stressed that the decision was based on the very exceptional facts of the case (see now *N v United Kingdom* (2008) 47 EHRR 39: the claim will fail unless the suffering is intense).

ACTIVITY

Self-test questions on the right to life and freedom from torture

1. What obligation does Art 2 impose on states with respect to the right to life?
2. Is the death penalty now in violation of Articles 2 and 3?
3. When is it lawful under Art 2 for life to be intentionally taken away?
4. How has the European Court defined the terms 'torture' and 'inhuman and degrading treatment'?
5. What is the *Soering* principle and what is its importance with respect to the protection of human rights?

16.10 Article 4 – Prohibition of slavery and forced labour

ARTICLE

Art 4(1)
No one shall be held in slavery or servitude.

Art 4(2)
No one shall be required to perform forced or compulsory labour.

Article 4(1) prohibits slavery and servitude in absolute terms and no derogation is allowed under Art 15.

16.10.1 The prohibition of slavery and servitude

CASE EXAMPLE

Siliadin v France *(2006) 43 EHRR 16*

The applicant had been used as unpaid help by a French couple for four years. She claimed that this constituted slavery and servitude under Art 4.

The European Court held that this did not amount to 'slavery'; although she had lost her autonomy, there was insufficient evidence that her employers had exercised a genuine right of ownership over her. However, the court found that as she was a vulnerable and unofficial immigrant entirely dependent on her employers for all assistance, she had been held in servitude. The failure of domestic law to create a specific criminal offence against slavery, and the failure to secure a criminal conviction against her abusers for wrongfully using the services of a dependent person meant that the state was in violation of its positive duty under Art 4.

16.10.2 Prohibition of forced or compulsory labour

Article 4(2) then guarantees freedom from forced or compulsory labour, which has been defined as unjust or oppressive work done against the will of the person, causing avoidable hardship (*X v FRG* (1974) 46 CD 22). This aspect of Art 4 can be derogated from and is subject to a number of exceptions listed in Art 4(3):

- 'forced or compulsory labour' does not include work required to be done in the ordinary course of detention or during conditional release from such detention.
- Article 4(3) excludes any service of a military character or, in the case of conscientious objectors, service instead of such service (*Johansen v Norway* (44 DR 155 (1985))).
- Article 4(3) exempts service exacted in the case of an emergency or calamity threatening the life or well-being of the community, and any work or service which forms part of normal civic obligations.

Note that s 71 of the Coroners and Justice Act 2009 makes it a criminal offence to hold someone in slavery or servitude or to require them to carry out forced labour.

16.11 Article 5 – Liberty and security of the person

ARTICLE

Art 5(1)

Everyone has the right to liberty and security of the person. No one shall be deprived of his liberty save in . . . accordance with a procedure prescribed by law.

16.11.1 Scope of the article

Article 5 is concerned with the protection of an individual's liberty, as opposed to a right of free movement, which is guaranteed under Art 2 of the Fourth Protocol (not ratified by the UK). Thus, in *Austin v United Kingdom* (2012) 55 EHRR 14 it was held that there had been no violation of Art 5 when the applicants had been detained as part of a containment and dispersal operation to deal with a serious outbreak of violence at a protest – given the seriousness of the actual and anticipated breach of the peace there had been no deprivation of liberty as opposed to a restriction on freedom of movement, despite the applicants being detained for seven hours.

However, a curfew or house arrest may amount to a deprivation of liberty (*Secretary of State for the Home Department v JJ and others* [2007] UKHL 45). Also, Art 5 is not engaged by a claim relating to the conditions of lawful detention (*Winterwerp v Germany* (1979) 2 EHRR 387).

The right under Art 5 is subject to a number of exceptions contained in Art 5(1) (a)–(f), below. Under Art 5(1) any interference will only be lawful if it is 'in accordance with a procedure prescribed by law' so must comply with principles of fairness and legality (see above at 16.5).

16.11.2 Lawful detention after conviction

Article 5(1)(a) provides for the lawful detention of a person after conviction by a competent court. Under this provision, any conviction must have a sufficient basis under domestic law (*Tsirlis and Kouloumpas v Greece* (1997) 25 EHRR 198) and there must be a sufficient connection between a finding of guilt by a competent *court* and any subsequent detention.

The European Court allows some exercise of administrative involvement in the detention process (*Van Droogenbroek v Belgium* (1982) 4 EHRR 443) provided there is a sufficient link with the original sentence.

CASE EXAMPLE

Stafford v United Kingdom *(2002) 35 EHRR 32*

The applicant had been sentenced to life imprisonment for murder and after release committed a number of property offences. The Home Secretary refused to release him on the grounds that there was a risk of him committing property offences in the future.

The European Court held that there was an insufficient connection between imposing a mandatory life sentence for murder, and the subsequent recall and detention of that prisoner on the basis of perceived fears that he would commit crimes of a non-violent nature. Accordingly, there was a violation of Art 5(1).

Such executive involvement may also constitute a violation of Arts 5(4) and 6, below.

16.11.3 Lawful arrest or detention for non-compliance of a lawful court order

Article 5(1)(b) permits the arrest or detention of a person who has not complied with a court order or when such arrest or detention is required for the fulfilment of an obligation that is prescribed by law.

This normally requires that a specific legal obligation has been, or is danger of being, breached (*Engel v Netherlands* (1976) 1 EHRR 647), although in *Steel v United Kingdom* (1998) 28 EHRR 603 the European Court held that the power to bind over an individual in order to keep the peace was compatible with Art 5, provided the applicant's conduct displayed some threat to the peace.

A detention by a court will not be unlawful simply because the decision to detain is overruled on appeal provided the initial court acted in good faith (*Benham v United Kingdom* (1996) 22 EHRR 293), unless it did not properly consider the law (*Beets and others v United Kingdom, The Times*, 10 March 2005).

16.11.4 Lawful detention following arrest

Article 5(1)(c) allows for the lawful arrest or detention of a person for bringing them before a competent legal authority, either on reasonable suspicion of them having committed an offence or when it is necessary to prevent them committing an offence or fleeing after having done so.

Any arrest or detention must be in accordance with clear domestic law (*K-F v Germany* (1997) 26 EHRR 390), and in particular any arrest must be made on *reasonable* suspicion. This does not require evidence that would justify a conviction at trial or the bringing of a criminal charge (*O'Hara v United Kingdom* (2002) 34 EHRR 32), but the European Court has laid down strict requirements in order to justify deprivation of liberty on such grounds.

CASE EXAMPLE

Fox, Campbell and Hartley v United Kingdom *(1990) 13 EHRR 157*

The applicants were arrested under s 1 of the Northern Ireland (Emergency Provisions) Act 1978 on suspicion of being terrorists and then released without charge.

The European Court held that 'reasonable suspicion' under Art 5(1)(c) presupposes the existence of facts that would satisfy an objective observer that the person might have committed the offence. However, in respect of terrorism the test differs from that involved in conventional crime, provided the essence of reasonableness is not impaired. The government must provide at least some facts or information which were capable of showing that the arrested person was reasonably suspected of having committed the offence. (In this case the only evidence was that they had committed offences seven years previously, which was insufficient for the purposes of Art 5.)

16.11.5 Other lawful restrictions

Article 5 also provides for lawful detention in the following cases:

- For the detention of a minor for the purpose of educational supervision or for the purpose of bringing him before a competent legal authority (Art 5(1)(d)).
- For the prevention of the spreading of infectious diseases, of persons of unsound mind, alcoholics or drug addicts or vagrants (Art 5(1)(e) and *Winterwerp v Germany* (1979) 2 EHRR 387).
- For the lawful arrest or detention of a person to prevent him from effecting an unauthorised entry into the country or to facilitate a person's deportation or extradition (Art 5(1)(f) and *Chahal v United Kingdom* (1997) 23 EHRR 413). In *A v United Kingdom* (2009) 49 EHRR 29 the European Court held that the detention of foreign terror suspects was not done for the purpose of eventual deportation and thus was in breach of Art 5.

16.11.6 Right to be informed of reasons for arrest and charge

Article 5(2) provides that everyone who is arrested shall be informed properly, in a language which he understands, of the reasons for his arrest and of any charge against him. An individual need not be supplied with full reasons for arrest at the actual time of that arrest provided it is done promptly in all the circumstances.

CASE EXAMPLE

Murray (Margaret) v United Kingdom *(1994) 19 EHRR 193*

The applicant was arrested under s 14 of the Northern Ireland (Emergency Provisions) Act 1978 on suspicion of having committed a terrorist offence and informed of the fact and reasons of arrest after two hours.

It was held that, although the reasons for her arrest had not been brought to her attention at the time of her arrest, she had been sufficiently notified during her subsequent interrogation and an interval of a few hours did not fall outside the definition of promptness as required by Art 5(2).

16.11.7 The right to be brought promptly before a judge for trial or release

Article 5(3) provides that everyone arrested or detained under Art 5 must be brought *promptly* before a judge or other officer authorised by law to exercise judicial power, that person then being entitled either to trial within a reasonable time, or to release (either absolutely or on conditions) pending trial.

The relevant 'officer' must be independent of the executive and of any parties to the action (*Assenov v Bulgaria* (1999) 28 EHRR 652), and the person must, in all the circumstances, be brought before the relevant judicial authority 'promptly'.

CASE EXAMPLE

Brogan v United Kingdom *(1989) 11 EHRR 117*

The applicants had been arrested on suspicion of terrorism and had been detained for periods between four and a half days and six days and eventually released without charge.

The European Court held that even the shortest of the periods in this case was inconsistent with the notion of promptness as required by Art 5(3). Even in the context of terrorism, such a period seriously weakened the essence of the procedural right guaranteed by that provision.

Article 5(3) does not preclude pre-trial detention provided there are sufficient safeguards (*Caballero v United Kingdom* (2000) 30 EHRR 643).

16.11.8 Right to challenge lawfulness of detention

Article 5(4) of the Convention provides that everyone deprived of their liberty by arrest or detention shall be entitled to take proceedings by which the lawfulness of their detention shall be decided speedily by a court and his release ordered if the detention is not lawful. This is the case even if the original detention was lawful, and for Art 5(4) to be complied with the original court order must be linked sufficiently with any subsequent detention (*De Wilde, Ooms and Versyp v Belgium* (1971) 1 EHRR 373).

Where a person is deprived of their liberty by the executive that person has a right of access to a court or court-like body in order to question the legality of that detention, including the evidence on which the decision was made (*Chahal v United Kingdom* (1997) 23 EHRR 413). Further, any review must not be limited to judging simple legality, and must assess the necessity and proportionality of the detention (*Winterwerp v Netherlands* (1979) 2 EHRR 387).

Article 5(4) has been used to challenge the legality of domestic law allowing the Home Secretary to determine the release of life sentence prisoners, and the European Court has held that such powers were incompatible with both the separation of powers and the Convention (*Thynne, Wilson and Gunnell v United Kingdom* (1990) 13 EHRR 666 (discretionary lifers) and *Stafford v United Kingdom* (2002) 35

EHRR 32 (mandatory lifers)). In addition, such prisoners are entitled to a review of their detention by a court-like body at reasonably regular intervals (*Oldham v United Kingdom* (2001) 31 EHRR 34).

In *A v United Kingdom* (2009) 49 EHRR 29 the European Court held that there had been a violation of Art 5(4) because the detainees had been deprived of their right to effectively challenge the legality of their detention because the closed evidence relied upon by the Secretary of State had not been made available to them.

16.11.9 Right to compensation for breach of Article 5

Article 5(5) provides that everyone who has been the victim of an arrest or detention in contravention of Art 5 shall have an enforceable right to compensation. The provision is contained within s 9(3) of the Human Rights Act 1998 (see Chapter 17).

The provision guarantees compensation whether the detention was lawful or otherwise under domestic law (*Brogan v United Kingdom* (1989) 11 EHRR 117 and *A v United Kingdom* (above)) and is supplemented by Art 13, which guarantees an effective remedy for violation of Convention rights (see below).

16.12 Article 6 – The right to a fair and public hearing

ARTICLE

Art 6(1)
In the determination of his civil rights and obligations or of any criminal charge against him, everyone is entitled to a fair and public hearing within a reasonable time by an independent and impartial tribunal established by law.

16.12.1 The scope of Article 6

Article 6 guarantees the right to a hearing before an impartial and unbiased court or tribunal, and specifically a number of procedural rights before and during the trial.

Article 6 applies to all proceedings where the applicant is either facing a 'criminal charge', or where that person's 'civil rights and obligations' are subject to determination.

With respect to the term 'civil rights and obligations', it is not necessary that both parties to the proceedings are private individuals (or that the proceedings are classed as public – for example judicial review proceedings), provided the result of the proceedings was decisive of private rights and obligations (*Ringeisen v Austria* (1971) 1 EHRR 455). For example, in *Tinnelly v United Kingdom* (1998) 27 EHRR 249 the European Court held that a right not to be discriminated against in the provision of contracts under domestic legislation was a 'civil right' even though the source of the right was statutory.

Whether the proceedings constitute a criminal charge will depend on how the offence has been classified in domestic law, the nature of the offence, and the severity of the punishment (*Engel v Netherlands* (1976) 1 EHRR 647). Prison disciplinary proceedings amount to a criminal charge where the penalty is sufficiently serious and the offence sufficiently criminal in nature (*Ezeh and Connors v United Kingdom* (2004) 39 EHRR 691).

16.12.2 The right of access to the courts

The European Court held in *Golder v United Kingdom* (1976) 1 EHRR 524 that the right of access to the courts is implicit in Art 6:

JUDGMENT

'Article 6(1) of the Convention was not limited to guaranteeing the right to a fair trial in legal proceedings that are already pending, but secures in addition a right of access to the courts to every person wishing to commence an action in order to have his civil rights and obligations determined . . . the Court could scarcely conceive of the rule of law without there being a possibility of having access to the courts.'

This includes the obligation of the state to provide facilities so to allow individuals to seek legal redress, for example legal aid (*Airey v Ireland* (1979) 2 EHRR 305). The right may be restricted to certain persons and on grounds of security (*Campbell v United Kingdom* (1992) 15 EHRR 137).

In addition, domestic law must not place procedural obstacles in the way of the parties, precluding claims irrespective of their merits.

CASE EXAMPLE

Osman v United Kingdom *(2000) 29 EHRR 245*

The applicants brought civil proceedings against the police in negligence but the domestic courts held that no action could lie against the police with respect to the investigation and suppression of crime.

The European Court held that the blanket application of that rule unjustifiably deprived the applicants of their right to have the merits of their civil action tried before a court. The application of the rule in this case constituted a disproportionate restriction on the applicants' rights under Art 6.

However, that case is now regarded as misguided and it is not now regarded as unlawful for *substantive* domestic law to limit the success of a particular legal action (*Z and others v United Kingdom* (2002) 34 EHRR 3 and *Smith v Chief Constable of Sussex* [2008] UKHL 50), although such a rule might violate Art 13 (see below).

16.12.3 The right to a public hearing before an impartial court or tribunal

Under Art 6 an individual is entitled to a trial before an impartial and unbiased court and this means a court that is free from the *appearance* of bias (*Findlay v United Kingdom* (1997) 24 EHRR 221). This includes freedom from the appearance of executive and political bias.

CASE EXAMPLE

McGonnell v United Kingdom *(2000) 30 EHRR 289*

The Deputy Bailiff of Guernsey, a senior judge and President of a number of state committees, adjudicated on the applicant's planning permission application.

It was held that there had been a violation of Art 6. That person's direct involvement in the passage of legislation or of executive rules was capable of casting doubt on his impartiality and thus was in violation of Art 6.

- Executive adjudication is not incompatible with Art 6 provided such decisions are subject to appropriate judicial review (*Bryan v United Kingdom* (1995) 21 EHRR 342).
- Article 6 is violated where there is evidence of bias from a jury (*Sander v United Kingdom* (2001) 31 EHRR 44).
- Article 6 guarantees the right to a fair sentence (*V and T v United Kingdom* (2000) 30 EHRR 121, and *R (Anderson) v Secretary of State for the Home Department* [2002] UKHL 46).
- Article 6 states that everyone is entitled to a fair and *public* hearing and that judgment shall be pronounced publicly, although it is lawful to limit the open and public nature of the proceedings in order to protect the rights of the participants, or justice in general (*V and T v United Kingdom* (2000) 30 EHRR 121).
- Article 6(1) guarantees that an individual receives a fair trial within a *reasonable time*. This applies to the length of the judicial proceedings, including appeals, and what amounts to a reasonable time depends on all the circumstances of the case (*Robins v United Kingdom* (1997) 26 EHRR 527).

16.12.4 The right to effective participation in the trial

Article 6(1) implicitly guarantees the right to put legal arguments before the court in support of one's case. This right is supplemented by the right of legal assistance, contained in Art 6(3)(c) (see directly below).

Any restriction of this right must be proportionate and necessary and ensure a basic right to a fair trial.

CASE EXAMPLE

P, C and S v United Kingdom *(2002) 35 EHRR 31*

The applicants (a mother and father of a child who was felt to be in danger from the mother) were not legally represented in the relevant care order or adoption proceedings.

The European Court held that, although courts had to strike a balance between the interests of the parents and the welfare of the child, the refusal of the domestic courts to defer the proceedings and to allow the applicants to obtain legal representation prevented the applicants from putting forward their case in a proper and effective manner.

Equally, *both* parties should be able to present any relevant evidence before the court in an equal manner (*Rowe and Davis v United Kingdom* (2000) 30 EHRR 1 – refusal to order disclosure of a document that the prosecution had provided to the court during a murder trial was in violation of Art 6). However, exclusionary rules are not unlawful provided they do not interfere with the basic right to a fair trial (*Jasper and Fitt v United Kingdom* (2000) 30 EHRR 97).

The use of unlawfully obtained evidence may lead to a violation of Art 6, but will not do so in all cases. Accordingly, in *Khan v United Kingdom* (2001) 31 EHRR 45 the European Court held that the admission of evidence obtained in breach of Art 8 did not violate the applicant's right to a fair trial within Art 6 because the applicant had been given an opportunity to question the admissibility of the evidence and the domestic courts had considered whether its inclusion would cause substantive unfairness. Note that the use of evidence obtained by torture will invalidate an individual's right to a fair trial as a flagrant denial of justice (*Othman (Abu Qatada) v United Kingdom* (2013) 55 EHRR 1).

For Art 6 to be complied with the individual should be aware of the nature of the charge or other proceedings and must be allowed to participate constructively in them (*V and T v United Kingdom* (2000) 30 EHRR 121 – subjection of 11-year-old defendants to an adult trial violated Art 6). Specifically, Art 6(3)(a) provides that every person has the right to be informed promptly, in a language which he understands and in detail, of the nature and cause of the accusation made against him (*Broziek v Italy* (1989) 12 EHRR 371), and Art 6(3)(e) guarantees the right to have the free legal assistance of an interpreter if he cannot understand or speak the language used in court.

16.12.5 The presumption of innocence and the rule against self-incrimination

Article 6(2) states that everyone charged with a criminal offence shall be presumed innocent until proved guilty according to law and in conjunction with Art 6(1) protects an individual from self-incrimination.

CASE EXAMPLE

Saunders v United Kingdom *(1996) 23 EHRR 313*

The applicant had been required to answer questions put to him by the Department of Trade and Industry in the course of their administrative investigations. The answers were used as evidence in a subsequent criminal trial, where he was found guilty.

The European Court held that the use of such evidence by the prosecution infringed the applicant's right against self-incrimination. In this case the prosecution had made use of these statements to question the applicant's honesty and integrity and it was irrelevant that the statements were not self-incriminating.

Although Art 6(2) implicitly recognises the right to silence, that right is not absolute (*Murray v United Kingdom* (1996) 22 EHRR 29), provided the applicant receives a fair hearing in all the circumstances (*Condron v United Kingdom* (2001) 31 EHRR 1 – violation of Art 6 when the trial judge had impliedly directed the jury to draw an adverse inference from the applicant's silence).

16.12.6 The right to legal assistance

Article 6(3)(c) states that everyone has the right to defend themselves against any criminal charge in person or through the legal assistance of one's own choosing. In addition, if the defendant has not got sufficient means to pay for such assistance, he has the right to be given it free where the interests of justice demand it. Whether the defendant is entitled to free legal assistance depends on all the circumstances, including the complexity of the case (*Steel and Morris v United Kingdom* (2005) 41 EHRR 22 – breach of Article 6 when protestors not able to effectively defend a lengthy defamation case brought by a multinational corporation).

CASE EXAMPLE

Granger v United Kingdom *(1990) 12 EHRR 469*

The applicant, a man of limited intelligence, had been charged with a criminal offence and had been refused legal aid and thus not provided with counsel on appeal. The applicant had notes from his solicitor but he clearly did not understand them when he read them out in court.

The European Court held that Art 6(1) and 6(3)(c) should be read together, and where it was apparent that a fair hearing could not take place without legal advice, then both provisions would be violated. In the present case, having regard to the applicant's intelligence and the complexity of the case he should have been given legal aid.

Article 6(3)(c) also guarantees the right to legal assistance during detention and interrogation where justice so requires (*Brennan v United Kingdom* (2002) 34 EHRR 18). But see the recent decision of the Court in in *Ibrahim v United Kingdom* (Application No. 50541/08), concerning the applicants' lack of access to a lawyer during police interviews regarding a failed terrorist attack in London.

16.12.7 The right to call and question witnesses

Article 6(3)(d) gives an individual the right to examine, or have examined, witnesses against him and to obtain the attendance and examination of witnesses on his behalf. This includes the right to confront witnesses (*Saidi v United Kingdom* (1993) 17 EHRR 251). Note that in *Al-Khawaja and Tahery v United Kingdom* (2012) 54 EHRR 23 the Grand Chamber held that the use of decisive hearsay evidence in a criminal trial was not necessarily in breach of Article 6 provided counterbalancing factors were in place to secure a right to a fair trial.

Article 6 does not guarantee an unlimited right to call and examine witnesses, the number of which remains within the discretion of the domestic courts provided the applicant receives a fair trial in the round (*Van Mechelen v The Netherlands* (1997) 25 EHRR 647).

16.13 Article 7 – Prohibition of retrospective criminal law and penalties

ARTICLE

Art 7(1)

No one shall be held guilty of any criminal offence on account of any act or omission which did not constitute a criminal offence under national or international law at the time when it was committed. Nor shall a heavier penalty be imposed than the one that was applicable at the time that the criminal offence was committed.

16.13.1 The scope of Article 7

Article 7 prohibits retrospective criminal law and penalties, and is fundamental to the rule of law and due process. Accordingly, under Art 15(2) a state cannot derogate from Art 7.

The article only applies where the applicant is found guilty of a criminal offence (see *Engel v Netherlands* (1976) 1 EHRR 706, discussed above), and lays down two basic principles:

- No person shall be guilty of an offence for an act which at the time of its commission was not an offence in domestic or international law.
- No person should be subjected to a heavier penalty than the one which existed at that time.

CASE EXAMPLE

Welch v United Kingdom *(1995) 20 EHRR 247*

The applicant was convicted of drug offences and as part of the sentence the trial judge imposed a confiscation order under the Drug Trafficking Act 1986, which came into force after the applicant's arrest but before his conviction.

The European Court held that the confiscation was clearly retrospective as it was made in respect of offences committed before the relevant provision came into force. Whether the confiscation proceedings constituted a 'penalty' depended on whether the measure was imposed following conviction for a criminal offence, the nature and purpose of the measure, its characterisation, and its severity. Taking into account a combination of punitive elements involved in this measure, the proceedings came within Art 7.

16.13.2 The exceptions to Article 7

Article 7 will not be violated where the relevant law has been developed in a foreseeable manner and then applied to the detriment of the defendant.

CASE EXAMPLE

SW and CR v United Kingdom *(1995) 21 EHRR 404*

The applicants had been convicted of rape as a result of the domestic courts' ruling that a husband could no longer rely on the defence of 'marital rape' (*R v R* [1991] 4 All ER 481).

The European Court held that there had been no violation of Art 7. The development of the law in this case, whereby such immunity was lost, had been foreseeable and consistent and the applicants must have foreseen that their act was unlawful at the time they committed it.

In addition, Art 7(2) states that Art 7 does not prejudice the trial and punishment of any person for any act or omission which, at the time it was committed, was criminal according to the general principles of law recognised by civilised nations (for example, torture or 'war crimes').

ACTIVITY

Self-test questions on due process rights

1. What rights does Art 5 of the Convention provide to the individual and what is the importance of those rights?
2. What exceptions to the right to liberty does Art 5 allow, and what are the restrictions on those exceptions?

3. What values does Art 6 of the Convention seek to uphold?
4. Name five specific rights that Art 6 bestows on the individual.
5. What does Art 7 of the Convention prohibit, and why?

16.14 Article 8 – Right to private and family life

ARTICLE

Art 8(1)

Everyone has the right to respect for his private and family life, his home and his correspondence.

16.14.1 The scope of Article 8

Article 8 provides the right to *respect* for private and family life, home and correspondence, including freedom from interference of those rights by both state actors and, in certain cases, private individuals (*X and Y v Netherlands* (1985) 8 EHRR 235). Thus, Art 8 can have a 'horizontal' effect, and the domestic courts have adopted this approach in developing the private law of confidentiality/misuse of private information (*Douglas v Hello! Ltd* ([2001] 2 WLR 992).

- Article 8 imposes a positive obligation on the state to ensure the enjoyment of those rights (*Marckx v Belgium* (1979) 2 EHRR 330).
- The right to private life includes the right to physical integrity, to private space, to communicate privately with others, to access personal information and to private sexual life.
- In particular Art 8 provides freedom from press and other intrusions into privacy (*Von Hannover v Germany* (2005) 40 EHRR 1 and *Peck v United Kingdom* (2003) 36 EHRR 31).
- Article 8 is a conditional right and interferences are permitted under Art 8(2) provided they are in accordance with law and necessary in a democratic society in the interests of national security, public safety or the economic well-being of the country, for the prevention of disorder or crime, for the protection of health or morals or for the protection of the rights and freedoms of others.
- Such restrictions will be invalid if they lack a proper legal basis (*Malone v United Kingdom* (1984) 7 EHRR 14).

16.14.2 The right to respect for private life

Article 8 covers privacy and confidentiality and the right to be let alone, but the European Court has also recognised the right to develop and establish relationships with others (*Niemietz v Germany* (1992) 16 EHRR 97). The court has also accepted that a private life can be enjoyed in the employment sphere (*Halford v United Kingdom* (1997) 24 EHRR 523).

Article 8 protects a person's right to physical and moral integrity, and a state owes a positive duty to protect those interests from attack from both state officials and other individuals (*X and Y v The Netherlands* (1985) 8 EHRR 235). Equally, the European Court has also held that the term private life protects an individual's health (*McGinley and Egan v United Kingdom* (1998) 27 EHRR 1).

The European Court will be reluctant to allow interference with private sexual life on the grounds of public morality or disapproval (*Dudgeon v United Kingdom* (1982)

4 EHRR 149 and *Smith and Grady v United Kingdom* (2000) 29 EHRR 493) but will permit it in cases where there is a sound reason for enforcing morality and protecting the rights of others (*Laskey, Jaggard and Brown v United Kingdom* (1997) 24 EHRR 39 – conviction of voluntary sado-masochistic acts permitted by Art 8(2)).

The court has also used Art 8 (and Art 12) to recognise the private rights of transsexuals (*Goodwin v United Kingdom* (2002) 35 EHRR 18), leading to the passing of the Gender Recognition Act 2004.

16.14.3 The right to respect for family life

Along with Art 12, guaranteeing the right to marry, Art 8 protects the right to *family* life and the European Court has extended the meaning of family beyond the marriage relationship (*X, Y and Z v United Kingdom* (1997) 24 EHRR 143 and *Goodwin v United Kingdom*, above). However, Art 8 does not guarantee the right to divorce (*Johnston v Ireland* (1986) 9 EHRR 203).

Although restrictions are permitted under Art 8(2), the European Court will have to be satisfied that there are pressing reasons for such interference and that such reasons are not arbitrary.

CASE EXAMPLE

Dickson v United Kingdom *(2008) 46 EHRR 41*

A prisoner had sought permission from the Home Secretary to allow his wife to be artificially inseminated by his sperm so as to found a family. The request was refused on policy reasons (that the interests of the child would not be furthered by such a birth as the relationship with his wife had not been tested outside prison).

The Grand Chamber held that Home Secretary's policy did not give sufficient weight to the right to family life of the prisoner and his wife and that it placed too much onus on the applicant to justify his request.

16.14.4 The right to respect for the home

Article 8 guarantees the right to respect for the home, protecting that right from intrusions by the state (*Akdivar v Turkey* (1996) 1 BHRC 137). The right is also related to Art 1 of the First Protocol (see below), protecting the right to property.

Such a right can be breached in the public interest, although the European Court will require a strong justification for any violation (*Gillow v United Kingdom* (1986) 11 EHRR 335). Thus any planning laws must strike a correct balance between the public interest and the enjoyment of private and family life (*Buckley v United Kingdom* (1996) 23 EHRR 101).

Despite the fundamental character of this right, the European Court will offer each state a wide margin of appreciation in balancing these respective rights.

CASE EXAMPLE

Hatton v United Kingdom *(2003) 37 EHRR 28*

Residents living on the flight path of Heathrow airport complained that the introduction of a scheme to regulate flights had increased night-time noise and interfered with their private and family lives and their homes.

The Grand Chamber of the European Court held that the authorities had achieved a proper balance between the rights of the residents to peaceful enjoyment of their homes and their family lives in allocating the number of night flights at Heathrow. Only a limited number of people were affected by the noise and house prices had not devalued, thus giving those people the opportunity to move.

16.14.5 The right to respect for correspondence

Article 8 protects the right to communicate with others, including correspondence with friends and family (*Silver v United Kingdom* (1983) 5 EHRR 347) and in a business context (*Halford v United Kingdom* (1997) 24 EHRR 523).

The European Court has afforded special protection with respect to legal correspondence, which also engages the right of access to the courts (*Golder v United Kingdom* (1976) 1 EHRR 524 – refusal of permission for prisoner to contact a solicitor for the purpose of bringing a civil action against a prison officer constituted a disproportionate interference with the prisoner's Art 8 rights and also constituted an impermissible breach of the his right of access to the courts under Art 6).

16.15 Article 9 – Freedom of thought, conscience and religion

ARTICLE

Art 9(1)

Everyone has the right to freedom of thought, conscience and religion; this right includes freedom to change his religion or belief and freedom, either alone or in community with others and in public or private, to manifest his religion or belief, in worship, teaching, practice and observance.

16.15.1 The scope of Article 9

The right to freedom of thought, conscience and religion is an absolute right in the sense that it is not subject to the restrictions laid down in para 2 of the article, which only apply to the manifestation of those beliefs.

Article 9 protects an individual from persecution on grounds of his beliefs and is not limited to religious beliefs or convictions (*Arrowsmith v United Kingdom* (1978) 3 EHRR 218 – pacifism was protected by Art 9). However Art 9 does not apply to every individually held opinion or conviction.

CASE EXAMPLE

Pretty v United Kingdom (2002) 35 EHRR 1

The applicant claimed that the state had interfered with her beliefs under Art 9 by denying her the right to die with the assistance of her husband.

The European Court held that the applicant's views on euthanasia did not involve a manifestation of a 'religion or belief, through worship, teaching, practice or observance'. The term 'practice' did not cover each act that was motivated or influenced by a religion or belief. (The applicant's views engaged her ideas of personal autonomy, under Art 8, but such a right was overtaken by the need to protect the rights of others.) Note that in *Purdy v Director of Public Prosecutions* [2009] UKHL 45 the House of Lords held that clear guidelines should be published with respect to the prosecution policy under the Suicide Act 1961.

Article 9 imposes a positive obligation on the state to allow individuals to enjoy their beliefs peacefully and without interference (*Dubowska and Skup v Poland* (1997) 24 EHRR CD 75), including enjoying these rights in employment, subject to necessary restrictions on the manifestation of such rights (*Ahmed v United Kingdom* (1981) 4 EHRR 126).

The European Court has not insisted that domestic law pass and maintain a law of blasphemy (*Choudhury v United Kingdom* (1991) 12 HRLJ 172). The English law of blasphemy was abolished by s 79 of the Criminal Justice and Immigration Act 2008.

16.15.2 Permissible restrictions

The right to manifest one's religion or beliefs is subject to limitations that are prescribed by law and necessary in a democratic society in the interests of public safety, for the protection of public order, health or morals, or for the protection of the rights and freedoms of others.

CASE EXAMPLE

Sahin v Turkey *(2004) 19 BHRC 590*

The applicant had been refused permission to wear a Muslim headscarf and was suspended from university for non-compliance with that order.

The Grand Chamber of the European Court held that the ban was proportionate to the protection of the rights of others and of public order, being necessary to preserve secularism in the country's educational institutions. Article 9 did not always guarantee the right to behave in a manner governed by religious beliefs and did not confer a right to disregard justifiable rules.

More recently, in *SAS v France* (2015) 60 EHRR 11, the Grand Chamber upheld a French law banning the covering of faces in public, which restricted the right of Muslim women to wear religious dress, even though it impacted on their Articles 9 and 14 rights. In the court's view the ban was necessary to accommodate the concept of 'living together' in French society.

See also *(R) Begum v Denbigh High School* [2006] UKHL 15, where the House of a Lords held that a school uniform policy banning full Muslim dress was not in breach of a schoolgirl's Convention rights. Contrast *Eweida and others v United Kingdom* (2013) 57 EHRR 8, where there had been a violation of Art 9 as a policy which forbade employees to wear religious crosses was not necessary and proportionate.

Further, in *McFarlane v UK and Ladele v United Kingdom* (2013) 57 EHRR 8, the court held that there had been no violation of Art 9 when employees had been dismissed for refusing to provide public services to homosexual couples (as a registrar and counsellor). Any interferences with religious and philosophical convictions were justified on behalf of the state's desire to protect homosexuals from discrimination.

16.16 Article 10 – Freedom of expression

ARTICLE

Art 10(1)

Everyone has the right to freedom of expression. This right shall include freedom to hold opinions and to receive and impart information and ideas without interference by public authority and regardless of frontiers.

16.16.1 The scope of Article 10

Article 10 guarantees the right to impart information and ideas, and the right of others to receive them. It is viewed as fundamental to both democracy and individual freedom by the European Court of Human Rights (*Handyside v United Kingdom* (1976) 1 EHRR 737).

Article 10 covers both commercial speech (*Markt Intern Velag GmbH and Klaus Beermann v Germany* (1989) 12 EHRR 161) and obscene and indecent speech (*Handyside* (above)), although the European Court has accepted that the state will be given a wider margin of appreciation to regulate such speech.

In contrast, the European Court places greater significance on the dissemination of information and ideas in the public interest (*Sunday Times v United Kingdom* (1979) 2 EHRR 245, protecting such speech in particular from prior restraint (*Observer and Guardian v United Kingdom* (1991) 14 EHRR 153)).

The European Court has also given greater weight to press and media freedom.

CASE EXAMPLE

Jersild v Denmark *(1994) 19 EHRR 1*

A broadcasting company had been fined for aiding and abetting the dissemination of unlawful racist speech by broadcasting their views as part of a documentary.

The European Court held that, although the views of the group were not protected by Art 10, punishing the applicant for statements made by that group during an interview was a serious restriction on the duty of the press to discuss matters of public interest.

Article 10 applies to restrictions on freedom of expression and does not provide a general right of freedom of information (*Leander v Sweden* (1987) 9 EHRR 343). However, refusal of access to private information could constitute a violation of Art 8.

16.16.2 Restrictions on freedom of expression – Article 10(2)

Article 10(2) provides that the exercise of the rights contained in para 1 carry with it duties and responsibilities and is therefore subject to restrictions and penalties that are 'prescribed by law' and necessary in a democratic society for the furtherance of a number of listed legitimate aims.

In such cases, therefore, the court has to consider whether the need for the legal restriction is sufficiently pressing and whether any penalty or condition is reasonable and proportionate.

CASE EXAMPLE

Von Hannover v Germany (2005) 40 EHRR 1

The former Princess Caroline of Monaco complained that persistent photographs taken of her by the 'paparazzi' were in violation of her rights under Art 8.

The European Court held that there had been an interference with the applicant's privacy rights and that there was no overriding public interest in the photographs so as to justify that violation on grounds of freedom of expression and the public right to know.

16.17 Article 11 – Freedom of assembly and association

ARTICLE

Art 11(1)

Everyone has the right to freedom of peaceful assembly and to freedom of association with others, including the right to form and to join trade unions for the protection of his interests.

16.17.1 The scope of Article 11

Article 11 of the European Convention provides that everyone has the right of association with others (including the right to join a trade union) and of *peaceful* assembly. The Article is conditional and subject to restrictions provided they are prescribed by law and necessary in a democratic society in the interests of national security or public safety, for the prevention of disorder or crime, for the protection of health or morals or for the protection of the rights and freedoms of others (Art 11(2)).

In addition, Art 11(2) allows lawful restrictions on members of the armed forces, of the police or of the administration of the state (*Council of Civil Service Unions and others v United Kingdom* (1987) 50 DR 228).

16.17.2 Freedom of association

The right of association specifically includes the right to form trade unions and the state has an obligation to ensure that this right is enjoyed by individuals even against private employers (*Swedish Engine Drivers' Union v Sweden* (1976) 1 EHRR 617). Although there is no right to insist on collective bargaining with employers, union members are entitled not to be discriminated against on grounds of their membership (*Wilson and others v United Kingdom* (2002) 35 EHRR 20).

Article 11, together with Art 9, also provides the negative right not to join a trade union (*Young Webster and James v United Kingdom* (1982) 4 EHRR 38), thus protecting non-unionists from discriminatory treatment.

The European Court has also held that the term 'association' covers various groups, including political parties (*United Communist Party of Turkey v Turkey* (1998) 26 EHRR 121). However, it does not include gatherings for entirely social purposes (*Anderson v United Kingdom* (1998) 25 EHRR CD 172).

The right of association is conditional and subject to lawful and necessary restrictions. However, proscription of a group would only be allowed in the most exceptional cases (*United Communist Party of Turkey v Turkey* (1998) 26 EHRR 121) – the banning of a group merely because it used the word communist in its name could not be justified in relation to any legitimate aim.

CASE EXAMPLE

Refha Partisi Erbakan Kazan and Tekdal v Turkey *(2003) 37 EHRR 1*

The applicant's party had been dissolved by the Turkish Constitutional Court on the ground that it had become a centre of activities against the principles of secularism.

The European Court held that political parties who incite others to use violence or support political aims that were inconsistent with democracy and the rights and freedoms of democracy could not rely on Art 11. In this case the measure was necessary and proportionate.

Such a finding may be strengthened by the state's reliance on Art 17 of the Convention, which provides that nothing in the Convention gives any person or group any right to engage in any activity or perform any act aimed at the destruction of any of the rights and freedoms in the Convention.

16.17.3 Freedom of peaceful assembly

Article 11 of the European Convention contains both a negative right not to have one's peaceful assembly interfered with, but also imposes a positive obligation on the state to ensure that everyone can enjoy that right (*Platform Arzte fur das Leben v Austria* (1988) 13 EHRR 204).

The Convention protects the right to *peaceful* assembly, excluding assemblies that use, advocate or incite violence. Such assemblies would also conflict with Art 17 of the Convention, above. Moreover, the alleged restriction must actually interfere with the right of assembly, as opposed to curtailing one of its activities (*R (Countryside Alliance) v Attorney-General* [2007] UKHL 52 – the ban on hunting did not stop the group assembling but simply outlawed a particular activity of that assembly).

As Art 11 is a conditional right, Art 11(2) also allows restrictions on peaceful assemblies, provided those restrictions are legal, necessary and proportionate to legitimate aims such as the preservation of public order, the protection of the rights of others and the prevention of crime. In this respect the European Court has given the domestic law and authorities a wide margin of appreciation in balancing the right of peaceful assembly with those aims, and may even permit the advance banning of meeting (*Rai, Allmond and Negotiate Now v United Kingdom* (1995) 19 EHRR CD 93).

The European Court will give the police authorities a wide discretion when dealing with alleged breaches of the peace (*Chorherr v Austria* (1993) 17 EHRR 358 and *Austin v United Kingdom* (2012) 55 EHRR 15), although interferences must not be disproportionate to achieving any legitimate aim (*Ollinger v Austria* (2008) 46 EHRR 38).

CASE EXAMPLE

Steel v United Kingdom *(1998) 28 EHRR 603*

Two demonstrators had been arrested and bound over for breach of the peace when handing out leaflets outside a conference.

The European Court held that on the evidence the police had no grounds for believing that the applicant's conduct would cause a breach of the peace. Consequently their arrest and subsequent restraint was an unlawful and disproportionate interference with their right to liberty and freedom of expression and assembly.

16.18 Article 12 – The right to marry

ARTICLE

Art 12
Men and women of marriageable age have the right to marry and found a family, according to the national laws governing the exercise of that right.

16.18.1 The scope of Article 12

Article 12 complements Art 8 of the Convention (the right to private and family life) and imposes a negative duty on the state not to interfere with the enjoyment of the right to marry. It does not guarantee the right to divorce (*Johnston v Ireland* (1986) 9 EHRR 203), but if national law does allow divorce it must not place unreasonable restrictions on a person's right to remarry (*F v Switzerland* (1987) 10 EHRR 411).

Although Art 12 leaves the right to marry and found a family at the discretion of national law, any conditions or restrictions on such a right must be necessary and proportionate (see below).

16.18.2 Restrictions on the right to marry

The European Court will offer Member States a reasonably wide margin of appreciation with respect to an individual's right to marry, although any restriction must not be arbitrary or destroy the essence of that right (*F v Switzerland* above).

CASE EXAMPLE

B and L v United Kingdom *(2006) 42 EHRR 11*

The applicants – former father and daughter-in law – were prohibited by domestic law from marrying unless both former spouses were deceased and claimed that this contravened Art 12.

The European Court held that the legal prohibition of such marriages was a disproportionate interference with the right to marry. Although there was a legitimate aim – the protection of family life and of children's interests – the fact that such relationships did not establish criminal liability suggested that there was no pressing need for such prohibition.

Domestic law prohibiting prisoners from marrying whilst incarcerated was held to destroy the essence of Art 12 (*Hamer v United Kingdom* (1982) 4 EHRR 139) and in *Goodwin v United Kingdom* (2002) 35 EHRR 18 the European Court recognised the right of transsexuals to marry in accordance with their new gender. Note now the Marriage (Same Sex Couples) Act 2013, allowing for the extension of marriage to same-sex couples.

16.19 Article 1 of the First Protocol – The right to property

ARTICLE

Art 1
Every natural or legal person is entitled to the peaceful enjoyment of his possessions. No one shall be deprived of his possessions except in the public interest and subject to conditions provided for by law and by the general principles of international law.

16.19.1 The scope of the right to property

This article guarantees the right to peaceful enjoyment of possessions (both real and personal property) and complements Art 8 of the Convention, guaranteeing respect for family life and the home.

The article makes the enjoyment of this right subject to the rules of domestic law and further states that it does not impair the right of a state to enforce such laws as it deems necessary to control the use of property in accordance with the general interest or to secure the payment of taxes or other contributions or penalties.

16.19.2 Lawful restrictions on the right to property

Any such restriction must be in accordance with law and constitute a necessary and proportionate measure, and the court will attempt to strike a fair balance between the interests of the community in general and the protection of the individual's property rights (*Sporrong and Lonnroth v Sweden* (1982) 5 EHRR 35).

The court will provide each state with a wide margin of appreciation in this respect (*James v United Kingdom* (1986) 6 EHRR 123; *National and Provincial Building Society v United Kingdom* (1997) 25 EHRR 127), but will protect the individual from arbitrary or unfair interferences.

CASE EXAMPLE

Pye (Oxford) Ltd v United Kingdom *(2008) 46 EHRR 45 (Grand Chamber)*

Landowners had lost possession of their land by virtue of the domestic rules on adverse possession.

The European Court (2008) 43 EHRR 3 held that the law at that time provided inadequate protection to the true owners, particularly as there was no statutory right for them to be notified of the possessor's intention to claim those rights. However, the Grand Chamber reversed that decision stating that the law achieved a proportionate balance between the conflicting interests.

16.20 Article 2 of the First Protocol – The right to education

ARTICLE

Art 2

No person shall be denied the right to education. In the exercise of any functions which it assumes in relation to education and to teaching, the State shall respect the right of parents to ensure such education and teaching in conformity with their own religious and philosophical convictions.

Article 2 of the First Protocol provides the individual with the right to enjoy the means of instruction that is provided by the state at any given time. The right is limited and there is no obligation on the part of the state to establish or fund any particular type of educational institution (*The Belgian Linguistic Case* (1968) 1 EHRR 252). The UK government has made a reservation with respect to guaranteeing parents' rights, restricting its obligations to the provision of efficient instruction and training and the avoidance of unreasonable public expenditure.

In addition, the Article complements the rights to private and family life (under Art 8) and the right to religion (under Art 9) by providing parents with the right to have their children taught in conformity with their religious and philosophical convictions.

CASE EXAMPLE

Campbell and Cosans v United Kingdom *(1982) 4 EHRR 293*

The applicants claimed that the threat of corporal punishment to their children constituted a violation of their Convention right to respect of their philosophical convictions.

The European Court held that, although there had been no breach of Art 3 (because the children had not been punished or threatened with punishment), there had been a violation of Art 2 of the First Protocol by subjecting the children to the regime of corporal punishment against the wishes of the parents.

(Note, there is no corresponding right to insist that one's child is subjected to corporal punishment (*R (Williamson) v Secretary of State for Employment* [2005] UKHL 15); see section 17.10.)

16.21 Article 3 – The right to free elections

ARTICLE

Art 3
The High Contracting Parties undertake to hold free elections at reasonable intervals by secret ballot, under conditions which will ensure the free expression of the people in the choice of the legislature.

16.21.1 The scope of the right to vote
The article imposes an obligation on each Member State to hold free elections, and thus provides a right to the general public to have such elections. Also, the European Court has held that the article provides individuals with the right to vote and the right to stand for election to the legislature (*Mathieu-Mohin and Clerfayt v Belgium* (1988) 10 EHRR 1).

An individual also has the right to vote in non-national elections (*Matthews v United Kingdom* (1999) 28 EHRR 361 – exclusion from voting in the elections to the European Parliament violated Art 3).

16.21.2 Limitations on the right to vote
The right to vote and stand for election is subject to implied limitations and domestic law can restrict it provided the very essence of the right to free elections is not undermined (*Mathieu-Mohin v Belgium* (1988)). The European Court has considered the legality of depriving prisoners of the right to vote (*Hirst v United Kingdom (No 2)* (2006) 42 EHRR 41 and *MT and Greens v United Kingdom* (2011) 53 EHRR 21 (see section 9.6.3)), and the government drafted a Bill proposing various possible reforms of the law to allow certain prisoners with shorter sentences the right to vote (Voting Eligibility (Prisoners) Draft Bill 2012. In 2017 the government announced

that it would pass a law to allow prisoners the right to vote if they were serving a sentence of less than one year, and where they had been released on temporary licence. This will affect only an estimated 100 prisoners but has been accepted by the Council of Europe. NB: see also section 9.6.3.

16.22 Articles 13 and 14 – The right to an effective remedy and freedom from discrimination

To facilitate the enjoyment of the above rights the European Convention guarantees the right an effective remedy for their breach (Art 13) and that the rights are enjoyed free from discrimination (Art 14).

16.22.1 The right to an effective remedy – Article 13

ARTICLE
....

> Art 13
> Everyone whose rights and freedoms as set forth in this Convention are violated shall have an effective remedy before a national authority notwithstanding that the violation has been committed by persons acting in an official capacity.

Article 13 complements Art 1 of the Convention, which places a duty on Member States to secure the rights and freedoms laid down in the Convention. Article 13 does not place a duty on the state to incorporate the Convention into domestic law, but domestic law should ensure that a person can enjoy his or her Convention rights in reality rather than theory. Article 13 is not 'incorporated' by the Human Rights Act 1998, but the government argues that the passing of the Act in itself satisfies Art 13.

In *Silver v United Kingdom* (1983) 5 EHRR 347 the European Court laid down the following principles with respect to Art 13:

- Where individuals have an arguable claim of a violation of their Convention rights, they should have a remedy before a national authority to have the claim decided and to obtain redress.
- The authority should normally be a judicial one, and if it is not then its powers and the guarantees should be as effective.
- The aggregate of remedies provided under domestic law must provide effective redress for the individual.

There will be a violation of Art 13 if domestic law fails to recognise a Convention right (*Malone v United Kingdom* (1984) 7 EHRR 14), or, if proceedings are struck out, precluding the court from determining whether there has been a violation, and if so what compensation should be granted (*Z v United Kingdom* (2002) 34 EHRR 3).

Domestic law should allow individuals to argue their case in accordance with principles such as proportionality (*Smith and Grady v United Kingdom* (2000) 29 EHRR 493), to air their complaint before a sufficiently independent body (*Khan v United Kingdom* (2001) 31 EHRR 45) and to be awarded compensation for breach of Convention rights in appropriate cases (*Edwards v United Kingdom* (2002) 35 EHRR 19).

16.22.2 Prohibition of discrimination – Article 14

> Art 14
> The enjoyment of the rights and freedoms set forth in this Convention shall be secured without discrimination on any ground such as sex, race, colour, language, religion, political or other opinion, national or social origin, association with a national minority, property, birth or other status.

As with Art 13, above, Art 14 complements the substantive Convention rights and prohibits discrimination in the enjoyment of such rights.

16.22.3 The scope of Article 14

Unlike Art 26 of the International Covenant on Civil and Political Rights 1966 – which ensures equality under the law – Art 14 does not provide a 'free-standing' right against discrimination. Thus, any complaint under Art 14 must be related to a violation of another Convention right. Note that Protocol No 12, as yet not ratified by the United Kingdom government, imposes a general prohibition on discrimination, thus establishing a general right of freedom from discrimination.

Thus, Art 14 is used in addition to (or in conjunction with) a claim under another article of the Convention (*Smith and Grady v United Kingdom* (2000) 29 EHRR 493 – dismissal from the armed forces on grounds of sexual orientation a breach of Arts 8 and 14; and *ADT v United Kingdom* (2001) 31 EHRR 33 – conviction of homosexual men for gross indecency a violation of Arts 8 and 14 as the law discriminated against homosexuals).

Accordingly the court cannot find a violation of Art 14 unless it establishes first that the Convention right in question is engaged.

Choudhury v United Kingdom *(1991) 12 HRLJ 172*

The applicants complained that the absence of a law of blasphemy to protect the Muslim faith was in breach of Art 9 and was discriminatory under Art 14.

The European Commission held that freedom to manifest one's religion under Art 9 of the Convention did not include a duty on the state to pass specific blasphemy laws. Accordingly, even though the domestic law discriminated in favour of the Anglican faith, the claim under Art 14 failed as Art 9 was not engaged.

However, the court may find a breach of a Convention right on the facts because of the evidence of discrimination (*Abdulaziz Cabales and Balkandali v United Kingdom* (1985) 7 EHRR 471).

16.22.4 Justifiable discrimination

Article 14 is not an absolute right and the European Court recognises that discrimination in the enjoyment of Convention rights is legitimate where there is objective or reasonable justification for such treatment. In such a case any difference must not only pursue a legitimate aim, but the measure must also be reasonably proportionate (*'Belgian Linguistic' case* (1968) 1 EHRR 252).

CASE EXAMPLE

Willis v United Kingdom *(2002) 35 EHRR 21*

The applicant applied for the equivalent of a widow's payment and Widowed Mother's Allowance when he was forced to leave his employment to care for his children after his wife died. No such payments were available to him as a widower.

The European Court held that there had been a violation of Art 14 taken in conjunction with Art 1 of the First Protocol to the Convention; the only reason for being refused the benefits was that he was a man; a female in the same position would have had a right to such payments, and the difference in treatment between men and women was not based on any objective and reasonable justification.

Similarly, in *PM v United Kingdom* (2006) 42 EHRR 45, where the applicant had been denied tax relief in respect of maintenance payments made to his daughter because he had not been married to the girl's mother, the European Court held that there was no justifiable reason to treat him differently from a married father, who would have been eligible for relief.

However, the European Court might be prepared to offer a wide margin of appreciation in some cases (*Pretty v United Kingdom* (2002), see section 16.15.1 – subjection of the applicant to a uniform law prohibiting assisted suicide was reasonably justifiable).

KEY FACTS

Key facts on the European Convention on Human Rights

The substantive Convention rights are contained in both Part One of the Convention and various protocols.	Arts 2–14 and Arts 1, 2 and 3 of the First Protocol, ECHR.
The rights (apart from Art 13) are 'incorporated' into domestic law via the Human Rights Acts 1998.	s 1 and Sch 1, HRA.
Some rights are absolute (for example, freedom from torture) and cannot be compromised, whilst others (for example, freedom of expression) are conditional and can be interfered with under specific conditions.	Arts 3 and 10, ECHR.
Under the Convention a state must protect life and must conduct effective investigations into deaths.	Art 2, ECHR, *Osman v United Kingdom* (2000) and *Jordan v United Kingdom* (2003).
The Convention prohibits torture and inhuman and degrading treatment or punishment in absolute terms and irrespective of any public good.	Art 3, ECHR, and *Chahal v United Kingdom* (1997).
States can be liable under Art 3 for violations committed by other states.	*Soering v United Kingdom* (1989).
The Convention guarantees due process by safeguarding liberty of the person and the right to a fair trial.	Arts 5 and 6, ECHR.

The Convention complements the above rights by prohibiting retrospective criminal law or penalties.	Art 7, ECHR.
The Convention rights of private and family life, freedom of religion, free speech, freedom of association and assembly, and the right to marry are conditional rights and can be restricted provided the interference is prescribed by law, has a legitimate aim, and is necessary in a democratic society.	Arts 8–12, ECHR.
The Convention protects the rights to property, education and the duty to hold free elections. These rights can be interfered with by legitimate and proportionate measures.	Arts 1, 2 and 3 of the First Protocol, ECHR (ratified by the UK and included in the 1998 Act).
The Convention guarantees access to an effective remedy when Convention rights have been violated.	Art 13, ECHR, and *Silver v United Kingdom* (1983).
The Convention guarantees the enjoyment of all Convention rights free from discrimination.	Art 14, ECHR.
Article 14 does not provide a 'free-standing' right against discrimination.	*Choudhury v United Kingdom* (1991).

SUMMARY

- The Convention is a product of the Council of Europe and was passed in order to enhance human rights and to achieve peace and stability in Europe.
- It contains a list of civil and political rights which are the basis of human dignity, individual liberty and the rule of law.
- The Convention contains its own enforcement machinery – the European Court of Human Rights – which hears state and individual applications and which has the power to make decisions which are binding on the states. There are various current proposals for reform of the Court to reduce its caseload and to ensure it plays a secondary role in protecting human rights in Europe.
- Decisions of the European Court of Human Rights do not automatically alter UK domestic law but can be followed by our courts and will generally be accepted by the government who will change relevant laws and practices.
- The Convention (in Article 1) encourages states to protect these rights via their own domestic law and the European Court's role is to supervise such enforcement.
- The Convention is 'given further effect' in the United Kingdom via the Human Rights Act 1998, where domestic courts must take into account Convention rights and interpret domestic law in line with such rights (see Chapter 17).
- The European Court uses principles of legality (prescribed by law) and reasonableness (legitimate aim, necessary in a democratic society, proportionality) to resolve applications and to achieve an appropriate balance. It also applies a 'margin of appreciation' to each state to allow them a discretion in protecting Convention rights within their own jurisdiction.
- The Convention rights are contained in Articles 2–14 of the Convention and in its additional protocols.

- Some of these rights are absolute (freedom from torture) and others conditional (freedom of expression).
- The Convention allows derogations of these rights during times of war or other emergencies (Article 15).

SAMPLE ESSAY QUESTION

What impact has the European Convention on Human Rights (1950) had on the protection of human rights, and, specifically, in the UK?

- Explain (briefly) the history of the Convention's passing and ratification, its central aims, and the nature of the rights contained in the Convention.

- Explain the 'dual' role of the Convention – to encourage domestic protection of human rights via 'incorporation' of the Convention, and to offer an international machinery for the resolution of human rights disputes brought by member states or individuals.

- Explain (briefly) the enforcement machinery of the Convention (the European Court) and the application process contained in Articles 34 and 35).

- By the use of cases, illustrate how the European Court has decided cases under the Convention and what impact those cases have had on specific rights and domestic law (*Golder v UK, Hirst v UK* (prisoners' rights); *Goodwin* (transsexual rights); *Sunday Times v UK* (freedom of the press); *A v United Kingdom* (detention without trial)).

- Explain the effect of European Court judgments on domestic case law and the 'incorporation' of the Convention via the Human Rights Act 1998.

- Explain, briefly, the controversy created by the Act and ongoing proposals to replace it with a British Bill of Rights.

Conclusion
- Summarise the effect of the Convention in both international and domestic law.

Further reading

Books

Amos, M, *Human Rights Law* (2nd edn, Hart, 2014), Pt II.

Fenwick, H, *Fenwick on Civil Liberties and Human Rights* (5th edn, Routledge, 2017).

Foster, S, *Human Rights and Civil Liberties* (3rd edn, Longman, 2011), ch 2.

Harris, D, O'Boyle, M and Warbrick, C, *The Law of the European Convention on Human Rights* (3rd edn, OUP, 2014).

Mowbray, A, *Cases and Materials on the European Convention on Human Rights* (3rd edn, Butterworths, 2012).

White, R and Ovey, C, *The European Convention on Human Rights* (7th edn, Oxford 2017).

Articles

Bratza, N, 'The relationship between UK courts and Strasbourg' [2011] EHRLR 505.

Cavanaugh, K, 'Policing the margins: Rights protection under the European Court of Human Rights' [2006] EHRLR 422.

Lester, A, 'The European Court of Human Rights after 50 years' [2010] EHRLR 461.

O'Boyle, K, 'On reforming the operation of the European Court of Human Rights' [2008] EHRLR 1.

17

The Human Rights Act 1998

AIMS AND OBJECTIVES

At the end of this chapter you should be able to:

- Appreciate the constitutional and legal significance of the Human Rights Act 1998 and why it was passed

- Appreciate the role of the law in protecting human rights before the Act was passed and how the Act has impacted on that role

- Understand the central provisions of the Act and appreciate how the Act impacts on the protection of human rights in the United Kingdom

- Be aware of the essential case law decided under the Act and appreciate whether and how such case law has achieved the Act's purpose

- Be aware of recent proposals for reform of the Act and its replacement with a domestic Bill of Rights; including any impact of 'Brexit' on the Act and any likely reform

17.1 Introduction

The Human Rights Act 1998 came into effect on 2 October 2000 and, while it does not strictly *incorporate* the European Convention into domestic law, it allows the courts to give 'further effect' to the Convention rights and to take Convention rights and case law into account when interpreting and developing domestic law. As a consequence individuals can now rely *directly* on Convention rights in the domestic courts.

Before the Act the courts could only give indirect effect to the Convention (eg where an Act of Parliament was ambiguous (*R v Home Secretary, ex parte Brind* [1991] 1 AC 696)), and they could not apply Convention rights where the domestic law did not recognise that right (*Malone v Metropolitan Police Commissioner* [1979] Ch 344 – an individual could not claim that telephone tapping was in violation of Art 8 of the Convention, guaranteeing the right to private life).

The Act builds on and enhances the traditional method of protecting civil liberties (see section 17.2). Thus, the courts can still apply traditional constitutional principles such as the presumption of innocence, the control of arbitrary power and the rules of natural justice. However, the doctrine of Parliamentary sovereignty is retained – the courts still cannot refuse to recognise an Act of Parliament and Parliament retains the right to pass incompatible legislation. Note, there have been proposals to repeal the 1998 Act and replace it with a domestic Bill of Rights (see below); those proposals have been shelved pending 'Brexit'

17.2 Pre-Human Rights Act 1998 position

In the absence of a written constitution and a Bill of Rights, individual human rights were protected by the courts, Parliament and the democratic process, including public support and opinion.

Dicey distinguished the British method from other countries by stating that our constitution was not the *source* but the *consequence* of the rights of individuals, as expounded by the common law courts (see Chapter 6). Thus, individual rights resulted from court decisions, applying the traditional private law to which all, including the government, were subject. For example, in *Entick v Carrington* (1765) 19 St Tr 1030 the court upheld the individual's right to property and person by applying the traditional law of trespass against government officials.

17.2.1 The role of the courts in protecting civil liberties

By the above methods and through the formal procedure of judicial review (see Chapters 19 and 20) the courts could safeguard against arbitrary and unreasonable interference with human rights. Thus the courts could:

- Interpret legislation in the light of constitutional fundamentals, ensuring a human rights-friendly interpretation (*Waddington v Miah* [1974] 2 All ER 377).
- Assume Parliament did not intend to interfere with fundamental rights (*Raymond v Honey* [1984] AC 1). Even in the post-Human Rights era the courts can have regard to these constitutional values in declaring secondary legislation *ultra vires*: *HM Treasury v Mohammed Jabar Ahmed and others* [2010] UKSC 2.
- Subject executive decisions to stricter review where human rights were violated (*R v Ministry of Defence, ex parte Smith* [1996] 1 All ER 257).
- Apply the principles of natural justice to ensure a fair and impartial hearing (*Ridge v Baldwin* [1964] AC 40 and *R v Bow Street Metropolitan Stipendiary Magistrate, ex parte Pinochet Ugarte (No 2)* [2000] 1 AC 119).

17.2.2 The role of Parliament in protecting civil liberties

In addition, Parliament could, and still can, pass legislation securing the rights and freedoms of its citizens.

- Statutes such as the Race Relations Act 1976 and the Sex Discrimination Act 1975 protect individuals from unlawful discrimination and safeguard the right to equality: see now the Equality Act 2010.
- The Police and Criminal Evidence Act 1984 provides safeguards against arbitrary police powers with respect to arrest, detention and search and entry.
- The Data Protection Acts 1984 and 1998 safeguard the right to privacy with respect to personal information.

However, Acts of Parliament could take away or interfere with rights without challenge from the courts on human rights grounds.

- The War Damage Act 1965 retrospectively took away the individual's right to compensation for war damage.
- The Public Order Act 1986 contains restrictions on the right of peaceful protest.
- Anti-terrorism legislation (for example the Terrorism Acts 2000 and 2006 and the recent Terrorism Prevention and Investigations Measures Act 2011) provided wide powers to the authorities to control terrorist activities and association.

17.2.3 The criticisms of the traditional system

The 'common law' method was subject to a number of criticisms:

- The common law courts did not recognise all rights, for example the right of privacy (*Malone v Metropolitan Police Commissioner* [1979] Ch 344).
- The courts were powerless to challenge primary legislation which clearly violated individual rights (*Rossminster Ltd* (1980) – see section 6.7.5).
- The courts were not willing to apply 'European' principles of necessity and proportionality when challenging executive actions (*R v Home Secretary, ex parte Brind* [1991] 1 AC 696).
- The courts could not take the European Convention on Human Rights into account as a direct source of rights (*Brind* (1991) and *Malone* (1979)).
- Acts of Parliament enjoyed sovereignty and could not be questioned by the courts.

As a consequence of these defects individuals very often had to take direct cases under the European Convention on Human Rights 1950. This resulted in a number of high-profile (and dozens of other) defeats for the United Kingdom government before the European Court of Human Rights:

- *Malone v United Kingdom* (1984) 7 EHRR 14 – where the European Court held that unregulated telephone tapping was contrary to the right to private life and correspondence under Art 8 of the Convention.
- *Sunday Times v United Kingdom* (1979) 2 EHRR 245 – where domestic contempt laws were held in violation of Art 10, guaranteeing freedom of expression and press freedom.
- *Smith and Grady v United Kingdom* (2000) 29 EHRR 493 – where the European Court held that the dismissal of homosexual armed forces personnel was both contrary to Art 8 and discriminatory under Art 14.
- *Chahal v United Kingdom* (1997) 23 EHRR 413 – where it was held that the deportation of the applicant on grounds of national security violated Arts 3 and 5 of the Convention (freedom from inhuman treatment and liberty of the person).

17.3 The passing of the Human Rights Act 1998

The passing of the Human Rights Act 1998 was intended to rectify these deficiencies and to allow the domestic courts to directly apply Convention principles and case law, thus improving our human rights record in Strasbourg and reducing the need for citizens to seek the assistance of the European Court.

17.3.1 Central aims and provisions of the Act

- To give effect to the rights contained in Part 1 of the European Convention (s 1).
- To allow victims of violations of human rights to rely on their Convention rights in domestic proceedings (ss 7–9).
- To make it unlawful for public authorities to violate Convention rights (s 6).
- To allow the domestic courts to take into account Convention case law when determining human rights cases (s 2).
- To give the courts greater powers to interpret legislation in line with the Convention (s 3).
- To allow the courts to declare domestic legislation incompatible with the Convention (s 4).
- To make provision for the government to initiate legislation repealing or amending incompatible legislative provisions (s 10).

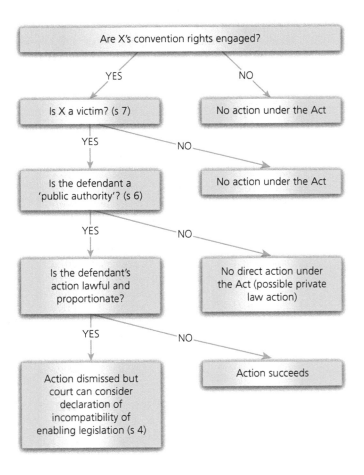

Figure 17.1 Actions under the Human Rights Act

- To make special provision for the protection of freedom of expression and freedom of religion (ss 12 and 13).
- To require the government to make statements of compatibility with respect to new legislation (s 19).

The basic aim of the Act is to bring the European Convention rights 'home' to domestic law and allow its provisions to be applied in the domestic courts, although the individual is still entitled to petition the European Court after exhausting domestic remedies (s 11).

17.3.2 Retrospective effect of the Act

The provisions of the Act generally only apply to acts or decisions of public authorities taking place after the coming into operation of the Act. Thus violations taking place before this time are subject to the general principles of judicial review and legality.

CASE EXAMPLE

Secretary of State for the Home Department v Wainwright *[2003] UKHL 53*

The claimants brought a case against the Prison Service alleging that they had been subjected to unlawful searches. Part of their claim was that this had violated their right to privacy under Art 8 of the Convention.

The House of Lords held that as the alleged violation took place before the Act came into force the claimants could not rely on the Act and the right to private life under Art 8. (Subsequently, the claimants were able to rely on Convention rights before the European Court: *Wainwright v United Kingdom* (2007) 44 EHRR 40.)

Neither does the Act apply to appeals against criminal convictions that took place before the Act, even where the appeal takes place after the Act's operation. Thus, in *R v Lambert, Ali and Jordan* [2001] UKHL 37 the House of Lords held that the Act does not have such retrospective effect and that such effect only applied to proceedings brought by a public authority. An unsuccessful appeal, brought by the defendant, was not to be treated as proceedings brought by or at the instigation of a public authority.

The decision in *Lambert* was reluctantly accepted by the House of Lords in *R v Kansal* [2001] UKHL 62, and the individual in such a case would need to petition the European Court: see now *Kansal v United Kingdom* (2004) 39 EHRR 31, finding a violation of Art 6.

Neither can the domestic courts overrule a court decision made before the Act, which has now become inconsistent with a decision of the European Court: see *R v Lyons and others* [2002] UKHL 44, explained in section 16.3.1. The individual in such a case would need to petition the European Court.

Also, the courts have not allowed the Act to have retrospective effect with respect to their powers of statutory interpretation (*R (Hurst) v HM Coroner for Northern District Council* [2007] UKHL 13).

17.3.3 The rights guaranteed under the Act

Section 1(1) of the Human Rights Act 1998 gives effect to the Convention rights contained in Arts 2 to 12 and 14 of the main Convention, Arts 1 to 3 of the First Protocol and Arts 1 and 2 of the Sixth Protocol (see Chapter 16 for details on the individual rights).

The rights that can be relied on are as follows:

- Article 2 – The right to life.
- Article 3 – Freedom from torture and inhuman and degrading treatment and punishment.
- Article 4 – Freedom from slavery, servitude and forced labour.
- Article 5 – Liberty and security of the person.
- Article 6 – The right to a fair trial.
- Article 7 – Prohibition on retrospective criminal law and penalties.
- Article 8 – The right to private and family life, home and correspondence.
- Article 9 – Freedom of religion, thought and conscience.
- Article 10 – Freedom of expression.
- Article 11 – Freedom of association and peaceful assembly.
- Article 12 – The right to marry.
- Article 1 of the First Protocol – The right to peaceful enjoyment of possessions.
- Article 2 of the First Protocol – The right to education.
- Article 3 of the First Protocol – The duty to hold free elections and the right to vote.

The Act omits Art 1 of the European Convention (Member States must ensure that the rights laid down in Part One of the Convention are guaranteed to everyone within the state's jurisdiction) and Art 13 of the Convention (which guarantees an effective remedy for breach of a person's Convention rights). This was because the government felt that the passing of the Human Rights Act 1998 in itself would provide the individual with a satisfactory remedy and thus comply with its obligations under the Convention. In any case, the Act can apply to acts committed outside the UK's geographical jurisdiction provided the UK is controlling that area: *Smith v Ministry of Defence* [2013] UKSC 41 – liability for safety of armed personnel serving in Iraq.

These rights are subject to any designated derogation or reservation made under ss 14 and 15 of the Act (see section 17.11).

17.4 Use of Convention case law by the domestic courts

Section 2 of the Act allows domestic courts to consider the relevant case law of the European Convention when determining disputes that raise Convention rights.

SECTION

S 2

When a court or tribunal is determining a question involving any Convention right, it must take into account any judgment, decision, declaratory or advisory opinion of the European Court of Human Rights, any opinion of the European Commission given in a report, any decision of the European Commission, and any decision of the Committee of Ministers whenever made or given, so far as, in the opinion of the court and tribunal, it is relevant to the proceedings in which that question has arisen.

The section does not state that the courts have to *apply* such decisions but, as the main aim of the Act is to avoid individuals having to petition the European Court, the domestic courts are unlikely to refuse to apply any case law favourable to the claimant. In addition, the courts are unlikely to depart from such case law and replace it by a more generous interpretation of the Convention, as seen in *Taylor and Anderson* (2001), below.

CASE EXAMPLE

R v Secretary of State for the Home Department, ex parte Taylor and Anderson *[2001] EWCA Civ 1698*

The Court of Appeal was asked to declare the Home Secretary's power to set tariffs for mandatory life sentence prisoners incompatible with Art 6, even though the European Court had stated that such powers were not in breach of the Convention.

The Court of Appeal held that it would be improper for the domestic courts to decide a case in a way that was contrary to the application currently being applied by the European Court of Human Rights. The Home Secretary's power to set tariffs for mandatory life sentence prisoners had clearly been accepted by the European Court of Human Rights (*Wynne v United Kingdom* (1995) 12 EHRR 333) and thus it would not be proper to act in a manner which was inconsistent with that approach.

NB. When the European Court overruled *Wynne* in the later case of *Stafford v United Kingdom* (2002) 35 EHRR 32, the House of Lords in *Anderson and Taylor* (2002) declared the Home Secretary's powers as incompatible with Art 6 and the government accordingly introduced new legislation in this area (see section 13.2.1).

Also, the courts may choose to follow binding domestic law where the European Court has not ruled directly on the legal issue. However, this approach is in danger of conflicting with Convention principles.

CASE EXAMPLE

Kay v Lambeth LBC; Price v Leeds County Council *[2006] UKHL 10*

Here the Court of Appeal ([2004] EWCA Civ 926) held that, when faced with a House of Lords decision that was inconsistent with a decision of the European Court of Human Rights, it should follow the decision of the House of Lords and refer the case to the House of Lords. As the domestic decision was on a particular statutory scheme it would subvert legal certainty if the European decision was followed.

In the House of Lords it was held that the European Court accorded a generous margin of appreciation to the national authorities, attaching much importance to the facts of the case. Thus, it was for the courts to decide how in the first instance the principles expounded in Strasbourg should be applied in the special context of national legislation, practice and social and other considerations. Subsequently, in *Manchester City Council v Pinnock* [2010] UKSC 45, the UK Supreme Court held that the domestic courts should follow clear principles laid down by the European Court in this area.

See also *R (Purdy) v Director of Public Prosecutions* [2009] UKHL 45, where the House of Lords followed the decision of the European Court in *Pretty v United Kingdom* (2002) 35 EHRR 1 in preference to the decision of the House of Lords in *R (Pretty) v DPP* [2002] 1 AC 800 with respect to whether Art 8 was engaged in decisions on the termination of life. Further, in *AF v Secretary of State for the Home Department* [2009] UKHL 28 the House of Lords chose to follow the decision of the European Court in *A v United Kingdom* (2009) 49 EHRR 29 rather than its own judgment in *MB v Secretary of State for the Home Department* [2007] UKHL 46 with respect to the use of closed evidence in control order proceedings.

See also *Re P and others* [2008] UKHL 38, where the House of Lords held that where the European Court has not laid down a definitive interpretation of the legal position the domestic courts were not bound to follow those decisions – the rights in the Human Rights Act were domestic and not international human rights and the domestic courts could give their own interpretation to them and apply the division between the decision-making powers of the courts and Parliament in a way which appeared appropriate for the UK.

The Supreme Court has made it clear that domestic courts must interpret the Convention rights in the Human Rights Act 1998 as domestic rights and are not totally bound to follow the European Court's approach and decisions: *R (Nicklinson) v Ministry of Justice)* [2015] UKSC 38.

Thus, our courts must follow the European Court where there is a clear and consistent line of authorities from Strasbourg on the related issue (*R (Ullah) v Special Adjudicator* [2004] UKHL 26). However, where the domestic courts feel that that line is not consistent it will refuse to follow it (*R (Animal Defenders International) v Secretary of State for Culture, Media and Sport* [2008] UKHL 15 – refusing to follow the European Court's decision in *VgT v Switzerland* (2001) 34 EHRR 159 on political advertising).

17.5 The doctrine of proportionality

Section 2 allows the courts to employ the doctrine of proportionality, which had been rejected by the domestic courts before the Act (*R v Home Secretary, ex parte Brind* [1991] 1 AC 696). Interference with a Convention right, such as freedom of expression, must correspond to a pressing social need and be proportionate to the aim that the restriction was seeking to achieve.

The effect of the doctrine on the court's review powers, and the distinction between proportionality and the traditional *Wednesbury* unreasonableness principles, were explained by Lord Steyn in *R v Secretary of State for the Home Department, ex parte Daly* [2001] UKHL 26:

JUDGMENT

'There is a material difference between the *Wednesbury and Smith* grounds of review and the approach of proportionality applicable in respect of review where Convention rights were at stake. Most cases would be decided in the same way whichever approach were adopted. But the intensity of review is somewhat greater under the proportionality approach. . . . First, the doctrine of proportionality may require the reviewing court to assess the balance which the decision-maker has struck, not merely whether it is within the range of rational or reasonable decisions. Secondly . . . it may require attention to be directed to the relevant weight accorded to interests and considerations. Thirdly, even the heightened scrutiny test developed in *R v Ministry of Defence, ex parte Smith* [1996] 1 All ER 257 is not necessarily appropriate to the protection of human rights. . . . The intensity of the review . . . is guaranteed by the twin requirements that the limitation of the right was necessary in a democratic society, in the sense of meeting a pressing social need, and the question whether the interference was really proportionate to the legitimate aim being pursued.'

After the Human Rights Act 1998 the courts do not have to show that the decision affecting the enjoyment of a Convention right was outrageous or irrational but can conduct a balancing exercise to see whether the interference was necessary and proportionate. This new power has been used in a number of high-profile cases.

CASE EXAMPLE

A and others v Secretary of State for the Home Department
[2004] UKHL 56.

In this case the House of Lords had to decide whether the detention of foreign nationals suspected of terrorism under s 21 of the Anti-terrorism, Crime and Security Act 2001 was a disproportionate response to the threat of terrorism and strictly required by the exigencies of the situation so as to allow the government's derogation under Art 15 of the Convention.

The court held that, while any decision of a representative democratic body commanded respect, the degree of respect would be conditioned by the nature of the decision made. The traditional *Wednesbury* approach was no longer appropriate and the domestic courts themselves had to form a judgment whether a Convention right was breached. Even in terrorist situations the Convention organs were not willing to relax their supervisory role. Given the importance of Art 5, judicial control of the executive's interference with individual liberty was essential; although the judiciary must keep to their proper limits, the courts possessed an express role under the Act to interpret legislation compatibly with Convention rights.

On the facts, the House of Lords held that the detention provisions contravened Arts 5 and 14 of the Convention (see section 17.11.1). This decision was upheld by the European Court of Human Rights in *A v United Kingdom* (2009) 49 EHRR 29.

The doctrine of proportionality increases the review powers of the courts (see *Huang v Secretary of State for the Home Department* [2007] UKHL 1) and raises concerns about whether it is proper for the courts to interfere with the decisions of government, or Parliament. In response the courts often show deference towards the executive and, in particular, to Parliament and in *Edore v Secretary of State for the Home Department* [2003] EWCA Civ 716 the Court of Appeal held that, given the margin of discretion available to decision-makers, there was often room for two possible proportionate outcomes in a particular situation. Within that margin, a decision-maker may, in some circumstances, fairly reach one of two opposite conclusions. However, both decisions would strike a fair balance between the competing claims and be proportionate.

The domestic courts will declare measures as disproportionate if it is arbitrary and inflexible. Thus, in *R (T) v Chief Constable of Greater Manchester* [2014] UKSC 35 it was held that statutory provisions were incompatible with Art 8 ECHR because they imposed a blanket statutory scheme requiring disclosure of cautions held on the police national computer. Such a regime was disproportionate and went beyond the legitimate aims of protecting employers and vulnerable individuals. It could not be justified on the basis that it created a 'bright line' rule which had the advantage of simplicity and ease of administration. The Supreme Court found that the disclosure could not in any event be regarded as necessary in a democratic society; the disclosure of T's warnings bore no rational relationship to the aim of protecting the safety of children with whom he might come into contact with as an adult.

However, in some cases the courts will show deference to the decision-maker and offer a wide margin of discretion to government and Parliament, either because the decision-maker has an area of expertise or because the issue is policy-based and sensitive.

CASE EXAMPLE

R (Countryside Alliance) v Attorney General [2007] UKHL 52

In this case the Hunting Act 2004, which made the hunting of live animals unlawful, was challenged as contrary to the hunters' and landowners' Convention rights. Dismissing the claims, the House of Lords held that the courts should show deference to Parliament with respect to its reasons to ban fox hunting because the matter had been subject to great parliamentary and public debate. It would thus be inappropriate for the claims to succeed legally when they had lost the moral and political arguments in Parliament. A subsequent application to the European Court of Human Rights was dismissed on similar grounds (*Countryside Alliance v United Kingdom* (2010) 50 EHRR SE6).

See also, *R (British American Tobacco and others) v Secretary of State for Health* [2004] EWHC 2493 (Admin), where the High Court upheld the proportionality of regulations banning the advertising of tobacco products and their compatibility with the applicant's right to commercial speech; there were areas in which the courts had to be particularly wary of imposing its own value judgments upon a legislative scheme.

More recently, in *R (Nicklinson) v Ministry of Justice* [2014] UKSC 38, the Supreme Court refused to declare the blanket ban on assisted suicide as a disproportionate interference with private and family life, or to create a defence of necessity to a charge of murder or assisting suicide: such a step must be taken by Parliament and not the courts. A subsequent challenge was also unsuccessful: *R (Conway) v Secretary of State for Justice* [2018] EWCA Civ 1431.

CASE EXAMPLE

R v Secretary of State for the Home Department, ex parte Farrakhan [2002] EWCA Civ 606

The Home Secretary had excluded F from entering the country because the claimant's presence would not be conducive to the public good and that he was likely to threaten public order and commit offences of racial hatred. The Court of Appeal held that the Secretary of State had struck a proportionate balance between the legitimate aim of the prevention of disorder and freedom of expression. The fact that the decision was personal to the Secretary, who was far better placed to reach an informed decision than the court, and that the Secretary was democratically accountable for his decision, made it appropriate to give him a particularly wide margin of discretion.

See also the more recent case of *R (Carlile) v Secretary of State for Home Department* [2014] UKSC 60, where the secretary's refusal to allow an Iranian political activist to visit the United Kingdom and address the House of Commons was upheld on the grounds that the secretary regarded that visit as damaging to diplomatic relations. The court recognised that the Secretary of State was better placed to make the judgement on the basis that she had access to necessary information on the relations between Iran and the UK.

See further *R (Catt) v Commissioner of the Police of the Metropolis; R (T) v Commissioner of the Police of the Metropolis* [2015] UKSC 9, where it was held that the retention by the police of records of an elderly and non-violent man's participation in demonstrations organised by an extremist protest group was proportionate for the purposes of Article 8 of the ECHR.

ACTIVITY

Self-test questions

1. Why was the Human Rights Act 1998 passed?
2. What were the deficiencies of the traditional method of protecting human rights in the UK and how does the Act address those issues?
3. What is the importance of s 2 of the Human Rights Act 1998?
4. What is the doctrine of proportionality and how important is it to the resolution of human rights disputes?
5. Do you think the decision in *A and others v Secretary of State* (2004) (above) displayed too much judicial power?

17.6 Interpreting statutory provisions in the light of the Convention

Under the Act the courts are given increased powers of statutory interpretation to allow them to reach a Convention-friendly result wherever that is possible. Even before, the courts could interpret legislation in the light of the European Convention when the statute was ambiguous (*Waddington v Miah* [1974] 2 All ER 377).

SECTION

Section 3 of the Act provides as follows:

(1) So far as it is possible to do so, primary legislation and subordinate legislation must be read and given effect in a way which is compatible with . . . Convention rights

(2) This section . . . (b) does not affect the validity, continuing operation or enforcement of any incompatible primary legislation; and (c) does not affect the validity, continuing operation and enforcement of any incompatible subordinate legislation if . . . primary legislation prevents removal of the incompatibility.

- Courts are now allowed to adopt a different interpretation to statutory provisions than applied by the courts before the Act and to disregard any previous interpretation of a higher court.
- The doctrine of parliamentary sovereignty is preserved because the section does not affect the validity etc of any incompatible primary legislation or any incompatible subordinate legislation where the parent Act clearly allows interference with Convention rights.
- Thus, the courts have no power to set aside an Act of Parliament and must follow it even where it is not possible to interpret it in a Convention-friendly manner.
- Under Section 3 the court does not have to find a true ambiguity in the statute, provided the Convention interpretation is 'possible'.

In addition, in *Wilson v First County Trust Ltd (No 2)* [2003] UKHL 40 the House of Lords held that courts were entitled to have regard to the policy objectives behind the legislation by looking at ministerial statements at the time the Bill was proceeding through Parliament.

17.6.1 The scope of Section 3

The scope of s 3 depends on the extent to which the courts are prepared to interpret legislation in the light of Convention rights – in other words, what the courts regard as a 'possible' interpretation.

CASE EXAMPLE

R v Offen [2001] 1 WLR 253

Section 2 of the Crime (Sentences) Act 1997 imposed a duty on the courts to grant an automatic life sentence to defendants who have committed two serious offences, unless there were 'exceptional circumstances'. The defendant was sentenced to life imprisonment despite the fact that the trial judge conceded that the offences were at the lower end of the scale and had been committed using a toy gun.

The Court of Appeal held that a court was entitled to decide that there existed exceptional circumstances if an offender did not constitute a significant risk to the public. An alternative interpretation would have made the sentence arbitrary and thus in violation of Art 5 of the European Convention on Human Rights. The word 'exceptional' must be given its ordinary meaning and Parliament could not have intended that the section apply to someone who did not pose a future risk.

A more radical approach was taken by the House of Lords in *R v A* (2001), below, and thus the courts were accused of legislating rather than interpreting existing legislation passed by the democratically elected Parliament.

CASE EXAMPLE

R v A (Complainant's sexual history) [2001] UKHL 25

Section 41 of the Youth Justice and Criminal Evidence Act 1999 provides that evidence of the complainant's sexual behaviour can only be allowed with leave of the court in express circumstances. The defendant wished to use the section in circumstances that appeared outside its terms.

The House of Lords held that the interpretative obligation placed on the courts under s 3 of the Human Rights Act 1998 applied even where there was no ambiguity and the court must strive to find a possible interpretation compatible with Convention rights. Section 3 required the courts to proceed on the basis that the legislature would not, if alerted to the problem, have wished to deny the right to an accused to put forward a full and complete defence by advancing truly probative evidence. Thus, the section should be read as being subject to the implied exclusion that evidence required to secure a fair trial under Art 6 of the Convention should not be inadmissible.

Section 3 thus allows the courts to depart from traditional principles of statutory interpretation and to assume, wherever possible, that legislation is not intended to conflict with the 1998 Act.

CASE EXAMPLE

Sheldrake v DPP: Attorney-General's Reference (No 4) [2004] UKHL 43

The House of Lords interpreted s 11(2) of the Terrorism Act 2000 as imposing an evidential rather than legal burden on the defendant so as to make that provision compatible with Art 6 of the Convention and to avoid a finding that that provision was disproportionate and incompatible.

The House of Lords held that even though Parliament had intended to impose a legal burden in such cases when passing the 2000 Act, having regard to its intention in passing s 3 of the Human Rights Act 1998 it was possible to read s 11(2) down in such a way as to avoid a legal burden.

See also *R (GC) v Commissioner of the Police of the Metropolis* [2011] UKSC 21, where the Supreme Court held that it was possible to read s 64 of the Police and Criminal Evidence Act 1984 so that it did not allow the indefinite retention of biometric data of all suspects. Such a power would be in breach of Art 8 ECHR, but it was possible to read s 64 so as not to allow such a power and thus to make police guidelines lawful.

However, s 3 does not allow the courts to read words into a statute that are clearly not there, and in *Poplar Housing and Regeneration Community Association Ltd v Donoghue* [2001] EWCA Civ 595 Lord Woolf CJ stressed that the courts must not radically alter a statute in order to achieve compatibility.

The House of Lords sounded a clear warning against 'judicial legislation' in the case below:

CASE EXAMPLE

In Re W and B (Children: Care Plan); In Re W (Child: Care Plan)
[2002] UKHL 10

The Court of Appeal ([2001] EWCA Civ 757) had authorised a system under the Children Act 1989 which allowed courts to star essential milestones in the care plan of a child so that action had to be taken by a local authority if they were not achieved within a reasonable time.

The House of Lords held that the 1998 Act maintained the constitutional boundary between the interpretation of statutes and the passing and repeal of legislation, and that a meaning that departed substantially from a fundamental feature of an Act of Parliament was likely to have crossed the boundary. Further, in using their powers of interpretation under s 3 the courts should be able to identify clearly the particular statutory provision or provisions whose interpretation led to that result.

Thus, in *R (Chester) v Secretary of State for Justice* [2010] EWCA Civ 1439, the Court of Appeal refused to read down the Representation of the People Act 1983 so as to give sentenced prisoners the right to vote. The court refused to distort the plain meaning of the statute in order to achieve possible compatibility. This was upheld by the Supreme Court on appeal: *R (Chester) v Secretary of State for Justice* [2013] UKSC 63.

The distinction between robust interpretation and judicial legislation is often difficult to make and will often depend on whether the courts are prepared to leave Parliament with the task of amending incompatible legislation. Thus, in *Bellinger v Bellinger* [2003] UKHL 21 the House of Lords held that it was not possible to use s 3 to interpret the words 'man and woman' to include a person who had undergone gender reassignment. However, in *Mendoza v Ghaidan* [2004] UKHL 40 the House of Lords held the words 'living together as husband and wife' could be interpreted to mean as if they were living together as husband and wife, so as to include same-sex couples. In *Mendoza* Lord Millett dissented on the grounds that it was for Parliament to change a law that was quite clearly not intended to cover same-sex relationships.

In some cases (such as *Bellinger*) the courts might feel that certain changes in the law should be carried out by Parliament rather than the courts: the decision in *Bellinger* was followed by the passing of the Gender Recognition Act 2004.

ACTIVITY

Self-test questions

1. How does s 3 of the Act change the courts' role with respect to statutory interpretation?
2. Does the Act threaten Parliamentary sovereignty in any respect?
3. What is the difference between statutory interpretation and 'judicial legislation'?
4. Do you think the House of Lords were guilty of 'judicial legislation' in *R v A* (2001), above?
5. Should the courts use s 3 to 'change' incompatible law, or should it make a declaration of incompatibility (below) instead?

17.7 Declarations of incompatibility

Under s 4 of the Act courts are allowed to declare both primary and secondary legislation incompatible with the substantive rights of the European Convention.

SECTION

Section 4(2) 'If the court is satisfied that the provision (of primary legislation) is incompatible with a Convention right, it may make a declaration of incompatibility'.

Section 4(4) 'If the court is satisfied that that the provision (of secondary legislation) is incompatible with a Convention right and that the primary legislation concerned prevents removal of the incompatibility it may make a declaration of incompatibility'.

Section 4(6) 'A declaration . . . does not affect the validity, continuing operation or enforcement of the provision in respect of which it is given and is not binding on the parties to the proceedings in which it is made'.

- Section 4 applies where the court has not been able to use its powers of interpretation under s 3 of the Act.
- Section 4 restricts the power to issue such declarations to courts including the High Court and above.
- Section 5 of the Act gives the Crown the power to intervene where a court is considering making a declaration of incompatibility.
- Section 4 does not include the right to strike down incompatible, but clear legislation.
- Incompatible legislation must be addressed and amended by Parliament, see s 10 of the Act, below.

Declarations cannot be granted in respect of violations of human rights caused by the application of incompatible legislation that took place before the Act came into operation: *Wilson v First County Trust Ltd (No 2)* [2003] UKHL 40 (see section 17.3.2).

It is not possible to use the powers under s 4 where the relevant legislation has not, or is not likely to, personally affect any particular person. Thus, the claimant must prove that they are a 'victim' of the violation.

CASE EXAMPLE

R v Attorney-General, ex parte Rusbridger and another *[2003] UKHL 38*

The House of Lords were asked to declare s 3 of the Treason Felony Act 1848 as incompatible with Art 10 of the European Convention.

It was held that the courts would refuse to make such a declaration without proof that there was any victim of the legislation. In this case there was no real risk of anyone being prosecuted under the legislation for non-violent conduct and thus no real risk of any interference with free speech. It was for the legislature and not the courts to keep the statute book up to date.

See also *R (Chester) v Secretary of State for Justice* [2010] EWCA Civ 1349, where the domestic court refused to grant a declaration of incompatibility with respect to the Representation of the People Act 1983 and the government's decision not to allow post-tariff life sentence prisoners the right to vote. The European Court had not made it clear that disenfranchisement of post-tariff prisoners was in breach of the Convention and the court would not consider granting a declaration until the statutory provision was in place, otherwise the parliamentary process would be interfered with. This decision was upheld by the Supreme Court: [2013] UKSC 63.

Courts will not issue a declaration of incompatibility merely because a statute contains a gap which, if included, would make it compatible with the Convention; *In Re S; Re W* (section 17.6.1). The relevant 'victim' would then have to pursue an action in Strasbourg. Following the decision of the House of Lords in *Re S; Re W* an application was lodged before the European Court of Human Rights, alleging a violation of Arts 6 and 8 of the Convention: *S v UK* (Application No 34407/02, 31 August 2004).

In *Wilson v First County Trust Ltd (No 2)* [2003] UKHL 40 (section 17.3.2 above) the House of Lords held that, in assessing the compatibility of primary legislation, a court was entitled to have regard to the policy objectives behind the legislation by looking at ministerial statements at the time the Bill was proceeding through Parliament. However, the content of parliamentary debates had no direct relevance to the issues the court was called upon to decide in compatibility matters and those matters were not a matter for investigation or consideration by the courts.

17.7.1 Declarations of incompatibility in practice

Since the Act has come into force, the courts have issued a number of declarations, some of which have resulted in legislative change. For example, in *R v Mental Health Tribunal ex parte H* [2001] EWCA Civ 415 the Court of Appeal held that ss 72 and 73 of the Mental Health Act 1983 were incompatible with Art 5 of the European Convention because they placed the burden of proof on a restricted patient to show that he no longer warranted detention. Following this decision the Mental Health Act 1983 (Remedial) Order 2001 amended the offending legislation.

The courts will declare legislation incompatible if it imposes excessive or unfair penalties.

CASE EXAMPLE

International Transport Roth GmbH and others v Secretary of State for the Home Department *[2002] EWCA Civ 158*

Drivers and owners of vehicles had all been subjected to penalties for effecting clandestine entrants to the United Kingdom contrary to s 32 of the Immigration and Asylum Act 1999. They claimed that the penalties were contrary to Arts 5 and 6 of the Convention and to the right of property under Art 1 of the First Protocol.

Held – the penalty regime did not adequately protect the rights of those alleged to be responsible for clandestine entrants. The scheme was unfair in imposing strict liability and in imposing so high a fixed penalty without the possibility of mitigation.

Also, a court is likely to declare legislation as incompatible if it is clearly out of line with the case law of the European Court of Human Rights.

CASE EXAMPLE

Bellinger v Bellinger *[2003] UKHL 21*

Here the House of Lords held that the refusal of domestic law to recognise a marriage celebrated between a man and a transsexual born a male was contrary to Arts 8 and 12 of the European Convention and in particular, the decision of the European Court of Human Rights in *Goodwin v United Kingdom* (2002) 35 EHRR 18.

Similarly, in *Anderson* (2002) (see section 13.2.1), the House of Lords declared the Home Secretary's sentencing powers incompatible with both Art 6 of the Convention and the decision of the European Court in *Stafford v United Kingdom* (2002) 35 EHRR 32.

The courts have issued a number of declarations of incompatibility where the relevant provisions are discriminatory:

CASE EXAMPLE

Re P and others *[2008] UKHL 38*

Here the House of Lords granted a declaration that a rule, contained in Article 14 of the Adoption (Northern Ireland) Order 1987 exempting unmarried couples from adopting, unjustifiably discriminated against unmarried couples. European Court case law pointed to the conclusion that such discrimination would be unlawful under Article 14 of the Convention (*EB v France* 2008 47 EHRR 21) and favoured the view that discrimination against persons on the grounds of marital status in this area was not acceptable.

See also the decision of the House of Lords in *A and others v Secretary of State* (2004) (see section 17.5) with respect to the detention without trial of foreign terrorist suspects. The decision in *A* also shows the courts' insistence that individual liberty and due process are not unduly interfered with. See also the case of *Re MB*, below.

CASE EXAMPLE

Re MB *[2007] UKHL 46*

Here the House of Lords held that the procedures in s 3 of the Prevention of Terrorism Act 2005 relating to the admissibility of closed evidence for supervision orders under that Act were compatible with Art 6 of the Convention, *provided* that the words 'except where to admit such evidence would be incompatible with the right of the controlled person to a fair trial' were added. (Note that these provisions have been replaced by the Terrorism Prevention and Investigation Measures Act 2011.)

On the other hand, the domestic courts are unlikely to interfere with legislation that appears consistent with European Convention case law and principles.

CASE EXAMPLE

R v Secretary of State for the Environment, Transport and the Regions, ex parte Barnes [2001] UKHL 23

The courts considered the compatibility with Art 6 of the Secretary of State's statutory power to decide planning applications that had not been determined by the local authority and to determine appeals against refusal of planning permission.

The House of Lords held that the planning laws were not incompatible with Art 6. Although the Secretary of State was not an independent and impartial tribunal, the power of the High Court in judicial review proceedings to review the legality of the decision and the procedures followed was sufficient to ensure compatibility with Art 6(1). Where the decision at issue was a matter of administrative policy, the European Court of Human Rights in *Bryan v United Kingdom* (1995) 21 EHRR 342 had accepted that the court's powers of appeal and review were sufficient to ensure that the decision-making process, as a whole, complied with Art 6.

The courts have also shown a good deal of deference to Parliament in deciding whether to grant a declaration of incompatibility.

CASE EXAMPLE

Brown v Stott (Procurator Fiscal) [2003] 1 AC 681

The Privy Council had to consider whether s 172(2)(a) of the Road Traffic Act 1988, which compelled a person to answer the question whether he or she had been driving a car, was compatible with the rule against self-incrimination as guaranteed by Art 6 of the Convention.

It was held that, although the right to a fair trial is an absolute right that cannot be compromised, there might be exceptional cases in which the defendant's procedural rights have to give way to the greater interests of the public that justice be done. Consequently, national courts should give weight to the decisions of the representative legislature and the democratic government within the discretionary area of judgment accorded to such bodies. In this case the provision was proportionate and compatible with Art 6. The reasoning behind this case was applied and upheld by the European Court of Human Rights in *O'Halloran and Francis v United Kingdom* (2008) 46 EHRR 21.

See also *R v Shayler* [2002] UKHL 11, where the House of Lords held that ss 1 and 4 of the Official Secrets Act 1989 were compatible with Art 10 of the European Convention. See section 18.3.6.

CASE EXAMPLE

R v DPP, ex parte Pretty and another [2001] UKHL 61

The House of Lords had to decide whether the DPP had the power to give an undertaking that the applicant's husband would not be prosecuted under s 2(1) of the Suicide Act 1961 if he assisted her in taking her own life, and whether that provision was incompatible with her rights under the European Convention.

The House of Lords held the right to life under Art 2 did not include the right to die. Further, although the case engaged the claimant's right to private and home life, and her right to enjoy her Convention rights free from discrimination, any interference with those rights was necessary and proportionate to meet the aims of the Suicide Act 1961. This decision was upheld by the European Court of Human Rights in *Pretty v United Kingdom* (2002) 35 EHRR 1 where it was held that it was within the state's discretion to impose a blanket ban on assisting suicide.

Note: in *Purdy v Director of Public Prosecutions* [2009] UKHL 45 the House of Lords held that as Article 8 rights were engaged the DPP must give sufficient guidance on his prosecution policies under the Suicide Act 1961. Subsequently, in *R (Nicklinson) v Ministry of Justice* [2013] EWCA Civ 961 the Court of Appeal held that the guidance was insufficiently clear in relation to healthcare professionals, and on appeal the Supreme Court upheld the compatibility of s 2(1) with articles 8 and 14: [2015] UKSC 38. A subsequent challenge to s 2, after Parliament had failed to change the law, was also successful: *R (Conway) v Secretary of State for Justice* [2018] EWCA Civ 1431.

17.7.2 Statements of compatibility

Under s 19(1) a minister of the Crown in charge of a Bill in either House must, before the Second Reading of the Bill, either make a statement of compatibility to the effect that in his view the provisions of the Bill are compatible with the Convention rights or make a statement to the effect that the government nevertheless wishes the House to proceed with the Bill.

- Because an Act of Parliament cannot bind future parliaments as to the manner in which legislation is passed, a Bill that did not contain such a declaration could not be invalidated by the courts.
- A declaration that a Bill is Convention-compliant would not bind the courts and prevent them from subsequently declaring legislation incompatible with Convention rights.

Thus far, only one statement of incompatibility has been made. This was in respect of s 321(2) of the Communications Act 2003, which makes political advertising unlawful. As the provision may be inconsistent with the European Court's decision in *VgT Verein gegen Tierfabriken v Switzerland* (2002) 34 EHRR 4, the responsible Minister made a declaration under s 19(1) that he intended to proceed with the Bill. Subsequently the provision was declared compatible with Art 10: *R (Animal Defenders International) v Secretary of State for Culture and Media and Sport* [2008] UKHL 15 and in *Animal Defenders International v United Kingdom, The Times*, 25 April 2013, the Grand Chamber held that there had been no violation of Art 10 as it accepted that the ban was proportionate and within the UK's margin of appreciation.

17.7.3 Remedial action

The Act leaves the ultimate power of deciding the compatibility of domestic legislation with Convention rights with the democratically elected legislature. Thus, where a court had declared a statutory provision incompatible with the Convention, it has no power to disapply the provision and the ultimate decision of whether the provision remains on the statute books rests with the lawmakers. Thus, Parliament can either leave the provision on the statute books, risking an application under the European Convention by a relevant victim, or alter that provision in line with the court's finding.

Specifically, s 10 of the Human Rights Act 1998 provides that where legislation has been declared incompatible under s 4 of the Act (or it appears to a minister of the Crown that a finding of the European Court of Human Rights against the United Kingdom makes such legislation appear to be incompatible with the Convention) the Minister may make such amendments to the legislation as he considers necessary to amend that incompatibility.

Under s 10(3) a similar power is created in the case of subordinate legislation, where a Minister considers it necessary to amend the primary legislation under which the subordinate legislation was made. This will allow an incompatibility between the provision and the Convention right to be removed. In such a case he may order such amendments to that primary legislation as he considers necessary.

- Under Sch 2, para 2 of the Act no remedial order can normally be made unless a draft of the order has been approved by a resolution of each House of Parliament made after the end of the period of 60 days beginning on the day that the draft was laid.
- Under para 3(1) of the Schedule no draft can be laid unless the person proposing to make the order has laid a document before Parliament containing a draft of the proposed order and the required information, explaining the reasons for the order, and a period of no less than 60 days has expired.
- In emergency cases where the order is made without being approved in draft, para 4 provides that the person making the order must lay it before Parliament, accompanied by the required information, after it is made.

KEY FACTS

Issue	Effect	Provision
European case law.	Domestic courts can now have direct reference to the articles, principles and case law of the European Convention on Human Rights.	s 2, HRA.
Convention principles.	Domestic courts must now inquire whether domestic law and decisions are prescribed by law, have a legitimate aim, and are necessary in a democratic society (including whether the measure is proportionate).	ss 2 and 6, HRA.
Following precedent.	The courts must merely take the case law of the European Convention into account when determining disputes raising Convention rights; it is not bound to follow it.	s 2, HRA.
Statutory interpretation.	Courts must interpret all legislation, wherever possible, in a way that is compatible with Convention rights.	s 3, HRA.
Parliamentary sovereignty.	Courts are not able to legislate or to strike down incompatible legislation.	ss 3 and 4, HRA.
Declarations of incompatibility.	Where it is not possible to achieve a Convention-friendly result, the higher courts can declare inconsistent legislation as incompatible, leaving the government to initiate any relevant legislative changes.	s 4, HRA.

Issue	Effect	Provision
Amending incompatible legislation.	Minister empowered to make remedial orders, amending incompatible legislation.	s 10, HRA.
Ministerial declarations of incompatibility.	Relevant Minister to make a statement of compatibility or incompatibility when introducing legislation before Parliament.	s 19, HRA.

ACTIVITY

Problem-solving

In 2022 Parliament passes the (imaginary) Public Order Act 2022. Section 1 of that Act allows the Home Secretary to pass such regulations as he thinks fit to secure public order. Acting under that provision, the Home Secretary passes a regulation in June 2022 that, provided that the Secretary of State is of the opinion that the formation of any group or society poses a serious threat to public order, he may order the proscription of that group, in which case it will be unlawful to join or take part in the activities of that group or society.

1. What Convention rights does s 1 potentially threaten?
2. Could the courts interpret s 1 in such a way that it would not conflict with any Convention rights?
3. In particular, could the courts interpret 'group or society' to exclude groups or societies who have a political message or mandate?
4. Do you think that the power of the Home Secretary under that section is compatible with those Convention rights?
5. How could the doctrine of proportionality be used to ensure that the section, and its use by the Minister, is not excessive?

17.8 Liability of public authorities under the Act

The Act applies principally with respect to violations committed by public authorities, although the Act can also operate in a 'horizontal' fashion and be applied in private proceedings.

Section 6 of the Act imposes an obligation on public authorities not to violate Convention rights.

SECTION

S 6(1)

It is unlawful for a public authority to act in a way that is inconsistent with a Convention right.

(2) Section 6(1) does not apply . . . if as the result of one or more provisions of primary legislation, it could not have acted differently, or in the case of a provision of, or made under, primary legislation which cannot be read or given effect in a way which is compatible with Convention rights, the authority was acting so as to give effect to or enforce those provisions.

Section 7 then provides a remedy to a person who claims that a public authority has acted (or proposes to act) in a way that is unlawful under s 6 (see section 17.9).

An act includes a failure to act but does not include a failure to introduce in, or lay before, Parliament a proposal for legislation, or make any primary legislation or remedial order (s 6(6)).

Section 6 retains parliamentary sovereignty by providing that the duty does not apply where the authority could not have acted differently having regard to the power granted by Parliament.

In such a case the court is limited to making a declaration of incompatibility under s 4 (see section 17.7).

17.8.1 Definition of 'public authority'

The term public authority is not defined under s 6. However:

it includes a court or tribunal, and does not include either House of Parliament or a person exercising functions in connection with proceedings in Parliament (s 6(3));

'public authority' includes any person certain whose functions are functions of a public nature (s 6(3)(b));

in relation to a particular act a person is not a public authority if the nature of the act is private (s 6(5));

the Act thus preserves the distinction between public and private bodies, and public and private law issues, employed in judicial review proceedings (see Chapter 19).

In the post-HRA era the courts have had to distinguish between public and private bodies and acts. Contrast the cases of *Heather* and *Poplar*, below.

CASE EXAMPLE

Heather, Ward and Callin v Leonard Cheshire Foundation *[2002] EWCA Civ 366*

A housing foundation had closed a care home, allegedly in violation of Article 8 of the Convention.

The Court of Appeal held that the housing foundation was not a public authority and did not exercise a public law function within the meaning of s 6. Before the 1998 Act it had been established that such bodies were not susceptible to judicial review, and the Human Rights Act had not done anything to alter that. The foundation was essentially private and carrying out private functions, despite the fact that it received public funding, was state regulated and, had it not existed, its functions would have been provided by the state.

However, note:

CASE EXAMPLE

Poplar Housing and Regeneration Community Association Ltd v Donoghue *[2001] EWCA Civ 595*

The applicant argued that a possession order executed by the defendants, an association set up by the local authority to take over its housing stock, was in breach of her Convention rights.

The Court of Appeal held that the defendant housing association was a public authority under s 6. The court held that the fact that the association provided a public service and was regulated by the local authority, which would have exercised its powers had the association not existed, were relevant, yet not decisive, factors. However, in this case the role of the association was so closely connected to that of the local authority that in this case it was performing public rather than private functions.

The decision in *Heather* was followed in *YL v Birmingham City Council* [2007] UKHL 27, but now s 145 of the Health and Social Care Act 2008 extends the protection of the Human Rights Act to people receiving publicly arranged care in independent sector homes.

Generally, the body in question has to have *sufficient* governmental links and public status.

CASE EXAMPLE

Parochial Church Council of the Parish of Aston Cantlow and others v Wallbank *[2003] UKHL 37*

The applicants had been required by the defendants to pay for the repair of the chancel of a church they had bought and claimed this was in violation of their right to property. The Court of Appeal held that the parochial church council was a public authority because it was created and empowered by the law and its notice to repair had statutory force.

On appeal the House of Lords held that a parochial church council was essentially a religious body and not a governmental one. It was not a 'core' public authority under the Act and its duty in this case was private rather than a public function. (The House also agreed that there was no violation of Article 1 of the First Protocol to the Convention simply because the owners of property acquired a very expensive duty to repair.)

17.8.2 The 'horizontal' effect of the Human Rights Act 1998

Although the Act applies directly to public authorities, it can, to a limited extent, impose obligations on private persons and thus be used in private proceedings. As courts are public authorities under s 6, and it is unlawful for them to act in a way that is incompatible with Convention rights, they will have a duty to develop the law, including the private law, consistently with Convention rights.

The Act will, therefore, have a 'horizontal' effect. This has been most evident in the area of the law of confidentiality, where that law has been applied and expanded so as to afford an individual a right of privacy consistent with Art 8 of the European Convention (see *Douglas and others v Hello! and others* [2001] 2 WLR 992 and *Venables and Thompson v Associated Newspapers* [2001] 1 WLR 1038 – where the courts accepted that confidentiality could be expanded to accommodate the claimants' Art 8 privacy rights).

The Act can also be applied to other areas of private law, such as the law of defamation (*Reynolds v Times Newspapers* [2001] 2 AC 127) and the law of employment, below:

CASE EXAMPLE

X v Y [2004] EWCA Civ 662

An employee claimed that his dismissal for receiving a caution for an indecency offence committed in a public toilet with another man was in breach of his Convention rights under Arts 8 and 14 of the Convention and that the test of unfairness should be interpreted in the light of those rights.

The Court of Appeal held that the 1998 Act might have an effect on unfair dismissals in the private sector in appropriate cases. It would not normally be fair to dismiss an employee in violation of the enjoyment of his Convention rights, although if there was a justifiable reason for his dismissal under the Employment Rights Act 1996 the tribunal should consider Art 8 in the context of the application of s 3 of the 1998 Act to the provisions of the 1996 Act (on the facts Arts 8 and 14 were not engaged because the act in question was not part of his private life and that the real reason for the dismissal was his failure to disclose the criminal caution).

The 1998 Act is thus used as a guiding principle for the main substantive law and the case below illustrates the courts' reluctance to give the Act full horizontal effect.

CASE EXAMPLE

Wainwright v Home Office [2003] UKHL 53

The applicants claimed that their search by a prison officer violated their right to privacy, even though it occurred before the 1998 Act came into force.

The House of Lords confirmed that there was no common law tort of invasion of privacy and that it was not necessary to develop such a general tort: the gap in the law had been filled by the passing of the Human Rights Act 1998, and it was not necessary to develop a law of privacy to apply to actions which occurred before the passing of the Act. The development of the law of privacy in accordance with Art 8 has been realised through the law of confidence and not by creating a separate tort of privacy: see *Campbell v Mirror Group Newspapers* [2004] UKHL 22.

17.9 Remedies under the Act

As we have seen, s 6 makes it unlawful for public authorities to act in a way that is incompatible with a person's Convention rights. Further, under s 7(1) a person who claims that a public authority has acted (or proposes to act) in a way which is made unlawful by s 6 may either bring proceedings against the authority under this Act in an appropriate court or tribunal or rely on the Convention right or rights concerned in *any legal proceedings* – such as during a criminal trial or in judicial review proceedings.

In the case of judicial review proceedings, the applicant may now take advantage of the 1998 Act where he is, or would be, a victim of that Act (s 7(3)). Thus, such an applicant could use the grounds of proportionality and breach of a Convention right, established under the 1998 Act. Other affected persons, such as representative groups, would bring proceedings on traditional grounds of review (*R v Secretary of State for the Environment, ex parte Greenpeace Ltd* [1994] 4 All ER 352).

Section 7(5) imposes a time limit and provides that proceedings must be brought before the end of the period of one year from the date on which the act complained of took place, or such longer period as the court or tribunal considers equitable having regard to all the circumstances. This provision is made subject to any rule imposing a stricter time limit in relation to the procedure in question, such as the time limit imposed under the Civil Procedure Rules 1998, where an application for judicial review must normally be brought within three months of the decision against which review is sought.

17.9.1 Victims of a Convention violation

Section 7(1) limits the Act to those who are 'victims' of a violation of Convention rights. Further, a person is only a victim of an unlawful act if he would be regarded as such for the purposes of Art 34 of the European Convention (s 7(7)) (see Chapter 16). This will cover anyone directly or potentially affected by the act as well as relatives and dependants of such persons (*R (Holub and another) v Secretary of State for the Home Department* [2002] EWHC 2388, and *R (Amin) v Home Secretary* [2003] UKHL 51).

However, for the person to be a victim there must be a real risk that the relevant legal provision be applied against them (*Rusbridger v Attorney-General* [2003] UKHL 38). The court will not thus decide a hypothetical case and will *generally* wait for a substantive decision.

CASE EXAMPLE

R (Hirst) v Parole Board *[2002] EWHC 1592 (Admin)*

Here it was held that a prisoner could not bring an application for a declaration that the Crime (Sentences) Act 1997 was incompatible with Art 5 of the European Convention until the Parole Board had considered his case for release. It would not be proper for it to rule on the question of compatibility until the Board had considered the claim, because until that time it would not be apparent that the statutory power was capable of impacting on the prisoner's case.

The Convention accepts that a person can be a victim if the individual is affected by the mere existence of the restriction (*Dudgeon v United Kingdom* (1982) 4 EHRR 149) and where there is an anticipated and real risk of a breach (*Soering v United Kingdom* (1989) 11 EHRR 439).

17.9.2 Power to award an appropriate remedy

Section 8 of the Act bestows on the courts the power to grant remedies for breach of the victim's Convention rights:

SECTION

Where a court finds that an act (or proposed act) of a public authority is (or would be) unlawful, it might grant such relief or remedy, or make such order, within its powers as it considers just and equitable.

Section 8 applies directly to violations committed by public authorities, but as that term includes courts and tribunals, victims will be able to rely on the principles and case law of the European Convention in all types of legal proceedings, including those taken against private individuals (see, for example, *Campbell v MGN Ltd* [2004] UKHL 22, where damages for breach of confidence included a claim for breach of the right to private life).

The courts' liability for violating Convention rights is limited and s 9(1) provides that the remedy for such a breach will be via judicial review or by appeal. Under s 9(3) of the Act damages are not generally awarded in respect of a judicial act done in good faith, although s 9(3) makes an exception in cases where there is a violation of Art 5(5) of the European Convention. This provision guarantees an effective remedy when a person's right to liberty has been violated.

17.9.3 Damages and the Human Rights Act 1998

The courts' power under s 8 includes the power to award damages, although only where the court has a power to award damages or order the payment of compensation in civil proceedings (s 8(2)).

Under s 8(3) no award of damages shall be made unless the court is satisfied in the circumstances that the award is necessary to afford 'just satisfaction' to the person in whose favour it is made. In deciding whether to award damages, or in deciding the amount of any award, the court must take into account the principles applied by the European Court of Human Rights in relation to the award of compensation under Art 41 of the Convention (s 8(4)) (see Chapter 16).

Note that the Act does not allow the courts to grant damages in respect of an act by a public authority that was clearly lawful under clear parliamentary legislation. Thus in *Tovey v Ministry of Justice* [2011] EWHC 271 the High Court refused to grant prisoners damages for the loss of their voting rights because such loss resulted from the clear provisions of the Representation of the People Act 1983. In such a case the prisoners would need to seek just satisfaction from the European Court of Human Rights.

The domestic courts have taken a flexible approach to the award of damages under the Act, taking into account factors such as the type of right that has been violated, the effect of the violation on the victim and the conduct of the public authority.

CASE EXAMPLE

R (Bernard and others) v Enfield LBC *[2002] EWHC 2282 (Admin)*

The local authority had failed to find suitable accommodation for the claimant (who was disabled) and her husband and six children.

The High Court held that damages for breach of human rights under the Act should be no lower than for a comparable tort and should, as far as possible, reflect the English level of damages. Also, awards recommended by the Local Government Ombudsman were a helpful guide. Awards should not be so minimal so as to diminish the policy that public authorities should respect Convention rights. Given the conduct of the authority and the humiliation suffered by the victim the award should be at the top end of the scale, in this case £10,000 (£8,000 to the wife and £2,000 to the husband).

CASE EXAMPLE

R (KB) v Mental Health Review Tribunal *[2003] EWHC 193 (Admin)*

The court held that damages would not be granted automatically for violation of Art 5, and that the courts should follow the principle of just satisfaction as practised by the European Court. Mental patients should not automatically receive damages for a violation of their rights, but the courts should recognise their vulnerability in assessing any damages. In this case the court awarded damages of between £750 and £1,000 to patients whose release had been delayed in breach of Art 5(4) of the Convention.

However, some cases have taken a more cautious approach and have limited the right to claim damages for breach of Convention rights.

CASE EXAMPLE

R (N) v Secretary of State for the Home Department; Anufrijeva v London Borough of Southwark *[2003] EWCA Civ 1406*

The High Court in *N* had granted damages when the Home Office had mishandled the claimant's asylum application, thus depriving him of income support and related benefits. On appeal the Court of Appeal held that although Art 8 of the Convention was capable of imposing a positive obligation to provide such support, maladministration on the part of an authority would only infringe Art 8 where the consequences were serious.

The Court of Appeal also held (in *A*) that damages for breach of Art 8 of the Convention were not recoverable automatically, and would only be awarded when necessary to give just satisfaction. Breach of a public law duty would not be sufficient on its own and for an award to be made there would have to be a degree of culpability together with foreseeable harm.

Also, in *Secretary of State for the Home Department v Wainwright* [2003] UKHL 53 the House of Lords held that it was doubtful whether damages could be claimed under the Human Rights Act 1998 for invasion of privacy by a public authority which had caused distress to a person, where that act was merely negligent.

In some cases a finding of a violation in itself is just satisfaction, especially if there is insufficient causal connection between any violation and the victim's loss.

CASE EXAMPLE

R (Greenfield) v Home Secretary *[2005] UKHL 14*

A prisoner had been refused legal representation during prison disciplinary proceedings, in violation of Art 6 of the European Convention.

The House of Lords held that when domestic courts are considering awarding compensation under s 8 of the Human Rights Act 1998 they should take into account the case law of the European Court, although they are not bound to follow such decisions. In particular, the courts should apply the principle applied by the European Court in cases where there has been held to be a breach of Art 6, to the effect that a finding of a violation of Art 6 is normally just satisfaction in itself, and that it was not appropriate for such awards to be comparable to tortious awards.

In the present case it would not be appropriate to speculate whether the procedural defect would have influenced the outcome of the proceedings and the prisoner's guilt or sanction.

KEY FACTS

Issue	Effect	Provision
Application to private law.	The Act has a limited horizontal effect, allowing the principles of the Act to be applied in proceedings of a private nature.	*Douglas v Hello!* (2001).
Who can use the Act and where?	The Act can be used in any proceedings by anyone who is a 'victim' of any alleged violation.	s 7, HRA.

Issue	Effect	Provision
Time limit for bringing proceedings.	Proceedings under the Act must be brought within one year, or via other proceedings in line with the appropriate time limit for such proceedings.	s 7, HRA.
Remedies.	The courts have the power to grant appropriate remedies to those whose Convention rights have been violated.	s 8, HRA.
Just satisfaction, including damages.	The courts may award 'just satisfaction' to the victim, in line with the principles applied by the European Court of Human Rights. 'Just satisfaction' includes the power to award damages to compensate for pecuniary and non-pecuniary loss suffered by the victim.	s 8, HRA.
Availability of damages.	The courts will not automatically grant damages for breach of Convention rights.	*Greenfield v Home Secretary* (2005).

17.10 Freedom of expression and freedom of religion

Because of fears that the Act might interfere unduly with free speech, press freedom and freedom of religious organisations, it makes specific provision to protect freedom of expression (s 12) and freedom of religion (s 13).

Section 12 applies whenever a court is considering granting relief which might affect the right of freedom of expression; see Chapter 18.

During the passage of the Human Rights Bill, church organisations were concerned that the right to employ suitable teachers in religious schools and to impose requirements for religious marriages would be threatened by actions under the 1998 Act. Under s 13, if a court's determination of any question arising under the Act might affect the exercise by a religious organisation of its right to freedom of thought, conscience and religion, it must have particular regard to the importance of that right. Thus, the courts will be obliged to take this right into account in developing the law in favour of the enjoyment of the rights contained in Art 9, including allowing interferences with other Convention rights.

Despite s 13, the right to religion may be outweighed by other interests and rights.

CASE EXAMPLE

R (Williamson) v Secretary of State for Employment *[2005] UKHL 15*

Teachers and parents claimed that the prohibition of corporal punishment in schools interfered with their Convention rights to have their children educated in conformity with their religious convictions (under Art 2 of the First Protocol) and was in violation of Art 9 of the European Convention, guaranteeing freedom to manifest religion.

The House of Lords held that, although the articles were engaged, Parliament was entitled to make an exception to those rights on the basis that they interfered with the child's rights not to be subject to inhuman and degrading treatment under Art 3. Parliament was entitled to have a broad blanket rule on prohibition and the domestic legislation was thus not incompatible.

CASE EXAMPLE

R (Begum) v Denbigh High School *[2006] UKHL 15*

A school had insisted that a student wear school uniform, which precluded the wearing of the full Muslim 'jilbab'. The student claimed that she had been excluded from the school in breach of her Convention rights to manifest her religion.

The House of Lords held that there had been no interference with her right to manifest her religion as she had chosen a school where such a policy existed; the two-year disruption to her schooling was the result of her unwillingness to comply with a rule to which the school was entitled to adhere. In any case the school was fully justified in acting in that manner as it had, after full consultation with parents and religious bodies, designed a flexible and fair uniform policy.

See also *Black v Wilkinson* [2013] EWCA Civ 820, where the Court of Appeal held that it was unlawful for a bed and breakfast owner to refuse accommodation to a homosexual couple because of her religious feelings. The right to be free from sexual orientation discrimination overrode such religious rights. See also *Bull v Hall* [2013] UKSC 73.

17.11 Derogations and reservations

Article 15 of the European Convention allows Member States to lodge a formal derogation in respect of a state of war or other public emergency. Article 16 also allows a state to place a reservation on its commitment to a specific Convention right.

17.11.1 Derogations

Article 15 allows a Member State to 'derogate' from its obligations under the Convention in times of war or other public emergency threatening the life of the nation (see Chapter 16), and under s 14 of the Human Rights Act United Kingdom derogations existing at the time of the Act's implementation are contained in Sch 3.

This included the government's derogation notices of 1988 and 1989, which were made after the European Court's decision in *Brogan v United Kingdom* (1989) 11 EHRR 117, where the court found that domestic provisions allowing extended detention of suspected terrorists were in violation of Art 5 of the Convention.

This derogation was withdrawn by an order made under the Human Rights Act (Human Rights Act (Amendment) Order 2001 SI 2001/1216) when the relevant statutory provisions were replaced by the Terrorism Act 2000. The Secretary of State then made the Human Rights Act 1998 (Amendment No. 2) Order 2001, derogating from Art 5(1) of the European Convention and providing for an extended power to arrest and detain foreign nationals whom it is intended to remove or deport from the United Kingdom but where such removal would be in violation of the Convention if a person were returned to that particular country (*Chahal v United Kingdom* (1997) 23 EHRR 413).

These powers were challenged in *A and others v Secretary of State for the Home Department* [2004] UKHL 56, where it was alleged that the detention provisions contained in s 23 of the Anti-terrorism, Crime and Security Act 2001 were in violation of Arts 5 and 14 of the Convention. The House of Lords held that the detention of foreign nationals suspected of terrorism under s 21 of the Anti-terrorism, Crime and Security Act 2001 was a disproportionate response to the threat of terrorism and not 'strictly required by the exigencies of the situation'. The fact that the provisions did not apply to British terrorists and failed to adequately safeguard against the threats from foreign terrorists (deported suspects could be deported and continue their activities) made those provisions discriminatory under Art 14 and a disproportionate interference with the liberty of the person. The decision in *A* was upheld by the Grand Chamber of the European Court of Human Rights: *A v United Kingdom* (2009) 49 EHRR 29.

17.11.2 Reservations

Article 57 of the European Convention on Human Rights allows each Member State to make reservations in connection with its obligations under the Convention (see Chapter 16), and s 15 of the Human Rights Act 1998 incorporates any designated reservation that has been lodged under the Convention. If a designated reservation is withdrawn wholly or in part it ceases to have effect (s 15(3)), and reservations cease to have effect five years after the Act came into force or five years after the designation order (s 16(1)). The Secretary may extend that period by a further five years, under s 16(2).

17.11.3 Proposals for reform of the Human Rights Act 1998

Recent governments have shown concern over the increased power of the European Court of Human Rights (see Chapter 16) and the domestic courts' increased power to use European Convention law to challenge government and Parliament.

- The coalition government set up an independent commission to inquire into the establishment of a Bill of Rights in the UK and to consider the curbing of the powers of the European Court of Human Rights.
- In August 2011 the Commission published a discussion paper, *Do We Need a UK Bill of Rights?* – seeking the public's views on a Bill of Rights and its content and application.
- In December 2012 the Commission published its findings on whether Britain should have a Bill of Rights: *A UK Bill of Rights? – The Choice Before Us*. The majority believed that there is a strong argument in favour of a UK Bill of Rights on the basis that such a Bill would incorporate and build on all of the UK's obligations under the European Convention on Human Rights, and that it would provide no less protection than is contained in the current Human Rights Act. It believed that the most powerful arguments for a new constitutional instrument were the lack of ownership by the public of the existing Human Rights Act and the European Convention on Human Rights, and the opportunity which a UK Bill of Rights would offer to provide greater protection against possible abuses of power.
- The Commission also agreed that a UK Bill of Rights should include the concept of responsibilities and should include additional rights beyond those contained in the Human Rights Act, and that the government should continue to pursue fundamental reform of the European Court of Human Rights.
- The Conservative Manifesto 2015 promised to repeal the Human Rights Act 1998:

QUOTATION

'We have stopped prisoners from having the vote, and have deported suspected terrorists such as Abu Qatada, despite all the problems created by Labour's human rights laws. The next Conservative Government will scrap the Human Rights Act, and introduce a British Bill of Rights. This will break the formal link between British courts and the European Court of Human Rights, and make our own Supreme Court the ultimate arbiter of human rights matters in the UK. . . . We will . . . introduce a British Bill of Rights which will restore common sense to the application of human rights in the UK. The Bill will remain faithful to the basic principles of human rights, which we signed up to in the original European Convention on Human Rights. It will protect basic rights, like the right to a fair trial, and the right to life, which are an essential part of a modern democratic society. But it will reverse the mission creep that has meant human rights law being used for more and more purposes, and often with little regard for the rights of wider society. Among other things the Bill will stop terrorists and other serious foreign criminals who pose a threat to our society from using spurious human rights arguments to prevent deportation.'

However the present government has stated that plans for repeal will be shelved to concentrate on the UK's withdrawal from the EU. Thus, despite 'Brexit' the UK will continue to be a party to the European Convention and the Human Rights Act will continue to use Convention rights and the jurisprudence of the European Court as the basis of protecting human rights in domestic law.

ACTIVITY

Self-test questions

1. What constitutes a 'public authority' under the Act, and how have the courts interpreted that term?
2. Who can claim to be a 'victim' under the Act? Give real and hypothetical examples.
3. Explain the term 'just satisfaction' with respect to the courts' powers to grant remedies under the 1998 Act.
4. In what circumstances may damages be granted by the courts and on what basis are they assessed?
5. How are freedom of expression and freedom of religion given specific protection under the 1998 Act?
6. Explain the powers of derogation under s 14 of the Act and explain how the government's derogation was successfully challenged in *A and others v Secretary of State* (2004).

SUMMARY

- Civil liberty was traditionally protected in the UK by the common law and by Parliament and the common law courts.
- Common law rights were subject to parliamentary sovereignty and the limited constitutional and review powers of the courts.
- Inconsistency of domestic law and protection with the European Convention on Human Rights, and a desire to strengthen human rights domestically, led to the passing of the Human Rights Act 1998.
- The Act came into force in October 2000, did not have retrospective effect for breaches before that date, and gave further effect to the rights contained in the Convention (Articles 2–12, 14 and subsequent protocols).

- The Act allows courts to employ Convention case law (including proportionality) when resolving Convention disputes (s 2), to interpret all legislation compatibly with such rights (wherever possible) (s 3) and to declare legislation incompatible with Convention rights (s 4).
- The Act does not affect the right of individual petition to the European Court of Human Rights (see Chapter 16).
- The Act does not allow the courts to question the validity of primary legislation, or secondary legislation that is consistent with clear primary legislation: thus parliamentary sovereignty is preserved.
- All public authorities must act compatibly with Convention rights, unless authorised otherwise clearly by primary legislation (s 6). Courts are public authorities and must apply all law (public and private) compatibly with Convention rights.
- The Act, thus, has some 'horizontal' effect (*Campbell v MGN*).
- Victims of Convention violations can bring actions (under s 7) in any legal proceedings against public authorities (and can use Convention rights 'horizontally' in private law against private individuals).
- Domestic courts can award just satisfaction to the victim against public authorities if they find a violation of their Convention rights (s 8).
- Ministers can fast-track legislative change when alerted to incompatibility of legislation (s 10), and must make a declaration of compatibility or otherwise of a Bill when introducing it to Parliament (s 19).
- The Act makes special provision for the protection of freedom of expression (s 12) and freedom of religion (s 13), although neither provision allows the courts to give added weight to those rights when in conflict with other Convention rights (*Re S (Publicity)* and *R (Williamson)*).
- The Act allows ministers to make Article 15 derogations of Convention rights (s 14) and Article 16 reservations (s 15).
- There have been constant discussions regarding the repeal of the Human Rights Act 1998 and its replacement with a UK Bill of Rights.

SAMPLE ESSAY QUESTION

How has the Human Rights Act 1998 changed the constitutional method of protecting human rights and civil liberties in the United Kingdom? Do you agree that it is in need of reform?

- Explain the particular features of the British Constitution with respect to the protection of fundamental human rights: no formal constitution or Bill of Rights, protection by the courts via the common law, parliamentary sovereignty and the limited role of the courts and the rule of law. Explain the advantages and defects of the 'traditional' method of rights protection, drawing on examples of protection (*Entick v Carrington*) and its limitations (*ex parte Brind*). Give examples of defeats before the European Court of Human Rights as a result of inconsistency with the Convention (*Golder v UK*; *Sunday Times v UK*; *Malone v UK* etc).
- Explain the purpose of passing the Human Rights Act 1998 and its effects: to give effect to Convention rights within domestic law; to allow domestic courts to achieve consistency of domestic law with Convention law by the process of interpretation and declarations of incompatibility; to provide a statutory list of positive fundamental rights as opposed to residual liberties.
- Explain and analyse the central provisions of the Act with respect to the courts' new powers (ss 2–4 and 6–8), together with provisions allowing Parliament and the government to achieve compatibility (ss 10 and 19).

- Critically explain relevant case law to examine whether the Act has, in practice, changed the constitutional method of protecting rights: has it provided the courts with greater powers of review and interpretation (*A*, *Daley*, *R v A*), and specifically has it changed the constitutional role of the courts and the British constitutional arrangements? Have we now got a bill of rights with a constitutional court? (assess the significance of the new Supreme Court in this respect).
- Examine recent proposals for the repeal of the 1998 Act and consider the advantages and disadvantages of such reforms.

Conclusion

- Summarise the effect of the Act on the protection of human rights in the UK and the effect on our constitutional arrangements for their protection, as well as the desirability of any reforms.

Further reading

Books
Amos, M, *Human Rights Law* (2nd edn Hart 2014), Pt I.
Fenwick, H, *Fenwick on Civil Liberties and Human Rights* (5th edn, Routledge 2017), Chapters 3 and 4.
Foster, S, *Human Rights and Civil Liberties* (3rd edn, Longman, 2011), Chapter 3.
Wadham, J and Mountfield, H, *Blackstone's Guide to the Human Rights Act 1998* (6th edn, Oxford University Press, 2011).

Articles
Blom-Cooper, L, 'The Commission on a Bill of Rights: an English approach to a UK Bill of Rights' [2013] PL 209.
Bowen, P, 'Does the renaissance of common law rights mean that the Human Rights Act 1998 is now unnecessary?' [2016] 4 EHRLR 361.
Feldman, D, 'The Human Rights Act and constitutional principles' (1999) 19 *Legal Studies* 165.
Fenwick, H and Masterman, R, 'The Conservative project to "break the link between British courts and Strasbourg" – rhetoric or reality?' (2017) 80 (6) MLR 1111.
Grieve, D, 'Can a Bill of Rights do better than the Human Rights Act?' [2016] PL 223.
Klug, F and Williams, A, 'The choice before us: the report of the Commission on a Bill of Rights' [2013] PL 460.
Klug, F, 'A Bill of Rights, do we need one or do we already have one?' [2007] PL 701.
Masterman, R, 'Interpretations, declarations and dialogues: rights protection under the Human Rights Act' [2009] PL 112.
O'Cinneide, C, 'Human Rights Law in the UK – is there a need for fundamental reform?' [2012] EHRLR 595.

18

Freedom of speech

AIMS AND OBJECTIVES

At the end of this chapter you should be able to:

- Appreciate the constitutional importance of freedom of expression and its position within the British constitution
- Appreciate the impact of the Human Rights Act 1998 on this right
- Explain some of the circumstances in which the criminal law can interfere with freedom of expression
- Explain some of the circumstances in which the civil law can interfere with freedom of expression

18.1 The constitutional importance of free speech

18.1.1 Introduction

Freedom of expression is a central aspect of all democratic states. In most countries this right is constitutionally ring-fenced and protected by being incorporated into a Bill or Charter of Rights. For example, the First Amendment of the United States constitution (ie the 1791 Bill of Rights) declares that:

ARTICLE

Congress shall make no law . . . abridging the freedom of speech, or of the press.

Similarly, Pt III, Art 19 of the Indian constitution states that:

ARTICLE

All citizens have the right to freedom of speech.

Freedom of speech, therefore, is one of the most important constitutional rights that an individual enjoys. The overriding constitutional significance of freedom of expression has been reaffirmed by the European Court of Human Rights in *Handyside v United Kingdom* (1976) 1 EHRR 737:

JUDGMENT

'. . . The Court's supervisory functions oblige it to pay the utmost attention to the principles characterising a "democratic society". Freedom of expression constitutes one of the essential foundations of such a society, one of the basic conditions for its progress and for the development of every man. Subject to paragraph 2 of Article 10 [see section 18.2.4], it is applicable not only to "information" or "ideas" that are favourably received or regarded as inoffensive or as a matter of indifference, but also to those that offend, shock or disturb the State or any sector of the population. Such are the demands of that pluralism, tolerance and broadmindedness without which there is no "democratic society".'

Two further points need to be made:

Firstly, although the terms freedom of expression and free speech are used interchangeably, the former is more inclusive than the latter. In short, whereas speech is typically associated with the written and spoken word, expression can be broader and includes artistic expression (eg a sculpture in an art gallery).

Secondly, the media have a particular role to play in a democracy in advancing freedom of expression interests and this function has been recognised by the European Court of Human Rights (*Lingens v Austria* (1986) 8 EHRR 407). In particular, the media can impart information which informs political debate and the political decision-making process.

18.1.2 The justification for the principle of free expression

Fenwick has drawn attention to four main justifications widely advanced in favour of free speech (H Fenwick, *Civil Liberties and Human Rights* (4th edn, Cavendish, 2007) at pp 300–06):

■ **Moral autonomy**

The argument under this heading is that freedom of expression supports an individual's moral autonomy by permitting him to make choices for himself as to what he reads, sees or hears. In other words, the individual chooses the information which he receives, rather than this being decided by the state.

■ **Self-fulfilment**

The argument in relation to self-fulfilment is based on the notion that freedom of expression advances the growth of an individual. In short, free access to information can stimulate and foster an individual's intellectual and moral growth.

■ **Democracy**

This argument is based on the inherent connection between free speech and the democratic process. In order for a democracy to function and flourish, it necessitates that individuals (and in particular the press) have the freedom to disseminate information concerning governmental and public affairs. In this way free speech informs political debate, discussion and the electoral process. Indeed, the European Court of Human Rights has repeatedly emphasised the importance of political speech. In *Castells v Spain* (1992) 14 EHRR 445:

JUDGMENT

'The limits of permissible criticism are wider with regard to the government than in relation to a private citizen, or even a politician. In the democratic system the actions or omissions of the government must be subject to the close scrutiny not only of the legislative and judicial authorities but also of the press and public opinion.'

Truth

The argument under this heading is that freedom of speech leads ultimately to the discovery of the truth. In other words, the danger with limiting free speech is the possibility that the truth could be suppressed.

ACTIVITY

Self-test question

Why do you think that freedom of expression is considered to be one of the most important human rights enjoyed by an individual?

18.2 Freedom of expression in the British constitution

18.2.1 The residual liberty of expression

Prior to the enactment of the Human Rights Act 1998, the British constitution was hallmarked by providing negative, residual liberties, rather than positive human rights (see at section 6.7.8 Dicey's views on the role of the judiciary being to protect the liberties of the individual). Historically, in the United Kingdom individuals did not (unlike as in the United States) enjoy a positive right to free speech *per se*; instead they had the residual liberty of expression. In other words, an individual could write or say whatever they liked provided they did not infringe a law (statute or common law) – see Sir Robert Megarry VC in *Malone v Metropolitan Police Commissioner* (1979) at section 6.7.7.

In this sense, therefore, provided an individual did not violate the laws of defamation, obscenity, indecency, contempt of court etc, everything else was permitted (ie the residue left when all the laws have been identified). This is illustrated by the figure below:

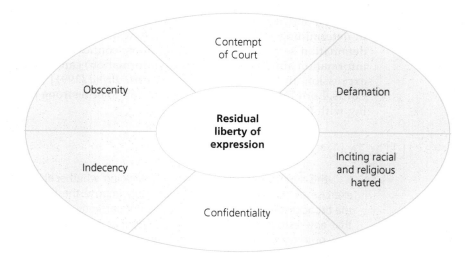

Figure 18.1 The residual liberty of expression

There were a number of difficulties with residual liberties:

- Firstly, it presupposed that an individual was aware of the laws (and their parameters) which restricted their liberty of expression.
- Secondly, Parliament (through the enactment of statutes), the executive (through the enactment of delegated legislation) and the courts (through the development of the common law) could incrementally reduce the residue of liberty. In this sense, residual liberties were vulnerable in a way that positive rights were not.

18.2.2 The interplay of freedom of speech with other competing interests

Notwithstanding the above, historically the courts, indirectly, have tried to protect residual liberties (such as the liberty of expression) from unnecessary interference. In other words, in interpreting, applying and determining the parameters of laws such as defamation and confidentiality, the courts could (indirectly) determine the extent to which these laws impinged on the residue of freedom of expression.

For example, in the context of the law of libel, the wider the defences to this tort are drawn the more difficult it will be for an individual to sue for libel. This in turn gives greater protection to freedom of expression. For example, in *Reynolds v Times Newspapers* [2001] 2 AC 127 the House of Lords developed the common law defence of qualified privilege to provide the press, in appropriate circumstances, with a defence (albeit restricted) of qualified privilege where the publication of information is in the public interest. This restricted defence depended on factors such as the seriousness of the allegation and public concern in respect of the subject matter, together with whether the claimant had been given an opportunity to explain or comment on the allegations. On the facts, however, the allegations made by the press were not considered to be information which the public had a right to know (*The Sunday Times* had failed to mention Reynolds's explanation). On defamation see section 18.4.1. Note: this common law *Reynolds* defence has now been replaced by s 4 of the Defamation Act 2013.

Conversely, the narrower these defences are drawn, the easier it is to sue for libel, and this necessarily impacts on free speech. In this way, the courts, in determining the parameters of laws which aim to protect other interests (eg defamation serves to protect reputations, confidentiality and misuse of private information aims to protect private information) can indirectly affect freedom of expression. In *R v Home Secretary, ex parte Brind* [1991] 1 AC 696 in the House of Lords, Lord Bridge stressed that there had to be a strong justification for interfering with free speech:

JUDGMENT

'. . . this surely does not mean that in deciding whether the Secretary of State, in the exercise of his discretion could reasonably impose the restriction he has imposed on the broadcasting organisations, we are not perfectly entitled to start from the premise that any restriction of the right to freedom of expression requires to be justified and that nothing less than an important competing public interest will be sufficient to justify it.'

At times, however, judges have disagreed with each other over the weight that should be attached to competing interests (eg the conflicting interests in balancing an individual's reputation with the principle of freedom of speech of the press). Another set of competing interests involve the freedom of speech of the press and the administration of justice/national security.

CASE EXAMPLE

Harman v Secretary of State for the Home Department *[1983] 1 AC 280*

Harman, a solicitor (legal officer of the National Council for Civil Liberties – now called LIBERTY), was acting for a person taking legal action against the Home Office. In the context of the litigation the latter disclosed documents and after the court hearing Harman allowed a journalist access to documents which had already been read out in court. The journalist then wrote an article and the Home Office sought an order against Harman for contempt of court. The House of Lords (dismissing Harman's appeal) held by three to two that a solicitor gave an implied undertaking not to use the information obtained on discovery during the course of litigation for a purpose other than for her client's action. The court confirmed that Harman had been guilty of a (civil) contempt of court.

Their Lordships, however, opined different views over whether the case engaged freedom of expression. Lord Diplock (in the majority) stated that:

JUDGMENT

'I start by saying what the case is not about. It is not about freedom of speech, freedom of the press, openness of justice or documents coming into "the public domain".'

Conversely, Lord Scarman (in the dissenting minority) commented that:

JUDGMENT

'A balance has to be struck between two interests of the law – on the one hand, the protection of a litigant's private right to keep his documents to himself notwithstanding his duty to disclose them to the other side in the litigation, and, on the other, the protection of the right, which the law recognises, subject to certain exceptions, as the right of everyone, to speak freely, and to impart information and ideas, upon matters of public knowledge.'

Lord Scarman's views are now representative of the present law – after the passing of the Human Rights Act 1998 judges must ensure that laws which impact on freedom of expression are necessary and proportionate.

Fenwick has stated that before the Human Rights Act 1998 'the judiciary did not seem to be united around a clear conception of their role' and 'that common practice as regards fundamental freedoms did not emerge'. In effect, the British courts, unlike other countries, lacked a Bill or Charter of Rights to 'anchor', and so help shape, their decisions (H Fenwick, *Fenwick on Civil Liberties and Human Rights* (5th edn, Routledge, 2017) p 134). The existence, however, of such a Charter or Bill of Rights which protects freedom of expression has not prevented judicial inconsistency in, for example, the Supreme Court of the United States.

Finally, it should be noted that the balancing of freedoms/rights/liberties is achieved sometimes by Parliament in enacting legislation. For example, the Obscene Publications Act 1959 makes it a criminal offence to publish an obscene article; however, s 4 of the Act protects freedom of expression where the article is in the interests of the public good (eg literature) (see section 18.3.3).

18.2.3 The Human Rights Act 1998

The passing of the Human Rights Act 1998 resulted in negative residual liberties being converted into positive rights which can be directly asserted in domestic courts. Moreover, the Human Rights Act 1998, together with the European Convention on Human Rights with its voluminous European Court of Human Rights case law, provides the modern British judiciary with an established set of principles concerning the protection of human rights and how they interrelate with other competing rights and interests. Indeed, s 2 of the Human Rights Act 1998 places a statutory obligation on our judges to have regard to the jurisprudence of the European Court in Strasbourg.

The 1998 Act attempts to give added protection to freedom of expression. Section 12 applies whenever a court is considering granting relief which might affect the right of freedom of expression. The section then lays down three rules:

- Any such relief should not normally be granted where the respondent is neither present or represented (s 12(2)).
- Where such relief would have the effect of restraining publication before trial, no such order should be given unless the applicant is likely to establish that publication should not be allowed (s 12(3) – see *Cream Holdings v Banerjee* [2004] UKHL 44).
- Where the proceedings relate to material which is journalistic, literary or artistic, the court must have regard to the extent to which the material has, or is about to become available to the public, whether it is, or would be, in the public interest for the material to be published, and any relevant privacy code (s 12(4)).

However the courts must not give added weight to Art 10 when it is in conflict with other rights (*Re S (Publicity)* [2005] UKHL 47) and must balance each right proportionately.

CASE EXAMPLE

PNM v Times Newspapers *[2017] UKSC 49*

In this case, where in assessing the competing rights of the press and the public against those of a man who had been arrested but not formally charged following an investigation into allegations of child sex grooming and prostitution, the court refused an interim non-disclosure order. In the circumstances, the court revoked an anonymity order made under the Contempt of Court Act 1981 s 4(2) and the appellant was to be referred to in the proceedings by his real name.

18.2.4 Article 10 of the European Convention on Human Rights (1950)

Article 10 of the European Convention states that:

ARTICLE

> Art 10(1)
>
> 'Everyone has the right to freedom of expression. This right shall include freedom to hold opinions and to receive and impart information and ideas without interference by public authority and regardless of frontiers . . .'

Article 10 is a conditional right and can be legitimately interfered with by other competing interests. This right also carries with it certain responsibilities and duties. The primary right of freedom of expression is thus not an absolute right (as it conflicts with other interests and carries with it responsibilities) and therefore can be restricted by the following wide range of interests as set out in Art 10(2):

ARTICLE

> 'national security, territorial integrity or public safety, for the prevention of disorder or crime, for the protection of health or morals, for the protection of the reputation or rights of others, for preventing the disclosure of information received in confidence, or for maintaining the authority and impartiality of the judiciary'.

Under the Human Rights Act 1998, if individuals contend that the state (ie a public authority) has, without lawful justification, interfered with their right to freedom of expression, they can petition a domestic court and seek a remedy. In such circumstances the court must follow the legal reasoning adopted by Strasbourg and will, therefore, have to determine:

- Whether there has been an interference with the primary right under Art 10.
- If so, whether this interference (ie the restriction) can be justified as:

  (i) being prescribed by law (ie being sufficiently clear and certain – see the case of *Sunday Times v United Kingdom* (1979) 2 EHRR 245 at section 16.5.1),
  (ii) having a legitimate aim (ie seeking to achieve one of the objectives set out in Art 10(2) above),
  (iii) being necessary in a democratic society (ie there is a pressing social need for it and it is not disproportionate).

Note: the courts, as public authorities, under s 6 of the Act, have to apply those principles in private law actions, eg the law of defamation and confidentiality, as those actions raise Convention rights (free speech and private life).

In this way the courts will balance competing interests, but will have the advantage of the jurisprudence of the European Court to assist them in determining this. In domestic law the Human Rights Act 1998 makes particular provision for Art 10 and freedom of expression: s 12 of the Act applies to a situation where a court is considering to grant relief that will impact on Art 10. In particular, a temporary injunction which restrains an article from being published pending the full trial on the matter will only be granted if the court is satisfied that the applicant (at the full trial) is likely to prove that the article should not be published. Section 12(2) also prevents *ex parte* applications (ie those where the other party is not present) being made, although they can be made in exceptional circumstances.

It should be noted that s 12 is peculiar to the Human Rights Act 1998 (ie the provision is not drawn from a corresponding European Convention article) and it is clear that the domestic judges have differed over its requirements (ie whether Art 10 should be given an elevated weighting – see *Re S (a child)* [2004] UKHL 47). In *Cream Holdings v Banerjee* [2004] UKHL 44, the House of Lords held that in applying s 12(3), when an applicant sought an interim injunction (which if granted would infringe Art 10), the test which the court should employ was to consider whether the applicant's prospect of success at the full trial was sufficiently favourable to justify the granting of the interim injunction.

ACTIVITY

Essay writing

Compare and contrast how freedom of expression was protected by the British courts before and after the passing of the Human Rights Act 1998.

KEY FACTS

Key facts on freedom of expression in the British constitution

Freedom of expression is one of the most important constitutional rights that an individual enjoys and it is recognised by all democratic states.
Article 10 of the European Convention states that everyone has the right to freedom of expression. This is, however, a conditional right which can be legitimately interfered with to secure a wide range of competing interests.
Under the Human Rights Act 1998 individuals can now raise Art 10 directly in domestic courts and the judiciary are required to take cognisance of the case law of the European Court of Human Rights and adopt the legal reasoning that it employs in determining whether Art 10 can be legitimately interfered with.

18.3 Free speech and the criminal law

Introduction

Although freedom of expression is of fundamental constitutional importance, as indicated above, it is not (and cannot be) an absolute right. As free speech comes into conflict with other competing interests (eg national security, public decency and the administration of justice), it is necessarily a conditional right which can be legitimately interfered with to protect these other interests. There are a wide variety of ways in which the criminal law (whether statutory or common law) can legitimately interfere with an individual's freedom of expression.

18.3.1 Protecting religious sensibilities

Article 9 of the European Convention guarantees freedom of thought, conscience and religion. This may be interfered with if the religious follower and their views are attacked, although there is no requirement under the Convention for the state to have a blasphemy law (*Choudhury v United Kingdom* (1991) 12 HRLJ 172).

Blasphemy was a common law criminal offence which in effect outlawed the scurrilous treatment and vilification of matters sacred to Christians which were likely to outrage and shock their feelings. The law was confined to the Anglican version of Christianity and did not apply to other religions (*R v Chief Metropolitan Stipendiary Magistrate, ex parte Choudhury* [1991] 1 All ER 306). Prosecutions for blasphemy were very rare, for example in *Lemon* – a private prosecution instigated by Mary Whitehouse: *Whitehouse v Lemon* [1979] AC 617.

Any law of blasphemy could be justified under Art 10(2) of the European Convention as a legitimate interference with free speech as protecting the *rights of others* (ie Christian believers not to be outraged, see *Wingrove v United Kingdom* (1996) 24 EHRR 1). In any event, the offence of blasphemy was abolished by s 79 of the Criminal Justice and Immigration Act 2008.

Note that, despite the absence of specific laws governing blasphemy, religious sensibilities and interests can be protected via racial and religious hatred laws (see below: section 18.3.4).

In addition, an offence can be committed under s 5 of the Public Order Act 1986 where abusive or threatening words are used which are likely to cause alarm, harassment or distress. Such offences can attract increased penalties where they are racially or religiously aggravated (ss 28–32 of the Crime and Disorder Act 1998). Thus, in *Norwood v DPP* [2003] EWHC 1564 it was held that such an offence had been committed when the defendant hung a poster out of his window which stated 'Islam out of Britain.'

18.3.2 Protecting the public from indecent material

Common law indecency

It is a common law offence to commit an act to outrage public decency (this is to protect the public from outrage). As with blasphemy above, there is no public good defence to this offence.

CASE EXAMPLE

R v Gibson and another *[1991] 1 All ER 439*

Sylveire ran an art gallery. In the gallery's catalogue was an exhibition entitled 'Human Earrings', which was a work (made by Gibson) which consisted of a model's head to which a freeze-dried human foetus had been attached to each ear lobe. Both Gibson and Sylveire were convicted of outraging public decency. The Court of Appeal dismissed their appeals against conviction on the ground, *inter alia*, that the prosecution did not have to prove that the appellants had intended to outrage public decency.

Statutory indecency

A number of statutory offences outlaw indecency. For example, s 1 of the Indecent Displays (Control) Act 1981 makes it a criminal offence (punishable by up to two years' imprisonment) to display an indecent matter publicly. The Act is essentially designed to deal with nuisance public displays and there is no public good defence.

The laws of indecency could be justified under Art 10(2) of the European Convention as a legitimate interference with free speech as serving the legitimate objective of protecting the *rights of others* (ie individuals not be offended by, or subject to, nuisance material) and the *protection of health or morals*.

Note: in addition to regulation via the criminal law, various broadcasting laws ensure that the authorities do not transgress standards of taste and decency.

CASE EXAMPLE

R (Gaunt) v OFCOM *(Liberty intervening) [2011] EWCA Civ 692*

In this case, the Court of Appeal upheld the decision of OFCOM, which found a breach of its code when a broadcaster repeatedly called an individual (a local officer who had suggested smokers should not be allowed to adopt children) a 'Nazi', a 'health Nazi' and an 'ignorant pig'. The Court held that the finding was not in breach of Art 10, as it was lawful and proportionate and in the circumstances it was difficult to find that G's freedom of expression had been interfered with. Note: it was found that the initial use of the words was justified in the context of political debate, but that their repeated use amounted to no more than ranting and abuse.

18.3.3 Controlling material which depraves and corrupts

The Obscene Publications Act 1959 (as amended in 1964) makes it a criminal offence, punishable by up to three years' imprisonment, for a person to publish an obscene article (or to have such an article in his possession for publication for gain).

The definition of obscenity is set out in s 1, namely that the effect of the article is such as (taken as a whole) to tend to deprave and corrupt those persons who are likely to see, read or hear the matter. In this context, therefore, the Act is not concerned with articles which shock or offend but instead with something much more pernicious: corruption. It should be recalled that Handyside (a publisher) was convicted under the Act for having in his possession for publication for gain an obscene article: copies of a reference book called *The Little Red Schoolbook* (see section 6.6.2). He was convicted and a forfeiture order was issued which resulted in the destruction of these books. Handyside subsequently unsuccessfully petitioned the European Court of Human Rights contending that this violated Art 10; however, the court held that it was a legitimate and proportionate interference with Handyside's right to freedom of expression.

The Obscene Publications Act 1959 aims to strike a balance between protecting the public from being depraved and corrupted and freedom of expression. Section 4 states that a person has a defence (the defence of public good):

SECTION

s 4(1)
'. . . if it is proved that publication of the article in question is justified as being for the public good on the ground that it is in the interests of science, literature, art or learning, or of other objects of general concern'.

In this context, it is of interest to note that Penguin Books were unsuccessfully prosecuted under the Act in relation to the publication of DH Lawrence's *Lady Chatterley's Lover* (*R v Penguin Books* [1961] Crim LR 176). The defence made use of expert witnesses to testify to the literary importance of the book and the jury acquitted, evidently on the basis that the book fell within s 4 as being justified in the interests of literature.

Note that s 63 of the Criminal Justice and Immigration Act 2008 created the offence of possessing extreme pornographic images – one which is both pornographic and which constitutes an extreme image (s 63(2)). An extreme image is one which is grossly offensive, disgusting or otherwise of an obscene nature (s 63(6)) and which portrays acts such as those which threaten a person's life, which results in serious injury to a person's anus, breasts or genitals, involves sexual interference with a human corpse or sexual acts with an animal.

The law of obscenity could be justified under Art 10(2) of the European Convention as a legitimate interference with free speech as serving the legitimate objective of *the protection of health or morals* (ie preventing the corruption of individuals) – see *Handyside* (1976).

ACTIVITY

Exercise

Do you think that the laws of indecency and obscenity are necessary in a democratic society and achieve a proper balance between free speech and public morality?

18.3.4 Protecting public order

There are a number of offences which restrict free speech in order to preserve public order. For example, s 18 of the Public Order Act 1986 makes it a criminal offence for a person to use threatening, abusive or insulting words and behaviour in order to intend to stir up racial hatred (or where it is likely to be stirred up). The Racial and Religious Hatred Act 2006 amended the Public Order Act 1986 and made it unlawful to stir up religious hatred. However, as a concession to free speech, s 29J (as incorporated into the 1986 Act) provides that:

SECTION

s 29J

'Nothing in this part shall be read or given effect in a way which prohibits or restricts discussion, criticism or expressions of antipathy, dislike, ridicule, insult or abuse of particular religions or the beliefs or practices of their adherents, or of any other belief system or the beliefs or practices of its adherents, or proselytising or urging adherents of a different religion or belief system to cease practising their religion or belief system.'

See also racially or religiously motivated public order offences under ss 28–32 of the Crime and Disorder Act 1998; see section 18.3.1 above.

The law of inciting racial hatred could be justified under Art 10(2) of the European Convention as a legitimate interference with free speech as serving to *prevent disorder or crime*.

18.3.5 Protecting the administration of justice

Under s 1 of the Perjury Act 1911 it is an offence for a person sworn in as a witness to make a statement during judicial proceedings which he knows to be false (or does not believe to be true). The law of perjury could be justified under Art 10(2) of the European Convention as a legitimate interference with free speech as serving to *maintain the authority and impartiality of the judiciary*. In addition, the Contempt of Court Act 1981 is designed to protect the integrity of court proceedings.

Section 2 of the 1981 Act provides that a person can be (strictly) liable for publications which cause a substantial risk that legal proceedings will be seriously impeded or prejudiced. Further, s 4 provides a public interest defence to cover discussions of public affairs or general public interest where any damage is merely incidental to that discussion (*Attorney-General v English* [1983] 1 AC 116).

The Act was introduced following the decision of the European Court of Human Rights in *Sunday Times v United Kingdom* (1979) 2 EHRR 245.

18.3.6 Protecting national security

Section 1 of the Official Secrets Act 1989 makes it a criminal offence for a member of the security and intelligence services to disclose information (without lawful authority) relating to security or intelligence:

CASE EXAMPLE

R v Shayler *[2002] UKHL 11*

Shayler had been charged with unlawfully disclosing information contrary to ss 1 and 4 of the 1989 Act. As the Human Rights Act 1998 was in force, he contended that the 1989 Act should be interpreted with a public interest defence (ie that Shayler was acting in the public interest in disclosing such information). The House of Lords dismissed Shayler's appeal and held that the Official Secrets Act 1989 was consistent with the requirements of Art 10 of the Convention. It was noted that Shayler could have sought internal authorisation for the disclosure of the information.

The Official Secrets Act could, therefore, be justified under Art 10(2) of the European Convention as a legitimate interference with free speech as serving the interests of *national security*.

18.4 Free speech and the civil law

In addition to the restrictions imposed by the criminal law, free speech can be legitimately interfered with by the civil law with the intention of protecting private interests such as reputation and confidential information.

18.4.1 The protection of reputation

The law of defamation serves to provide protection for a person's reputation from false statements which damage it, or which are capable of doing so. Under s 1 of the Defamation Act 2013 a publication must cause, or is likely to cause serious harm to the reputation of the claimant; serious financial loss if the claimant is a company.

In *Bruno Lachaux v Independent Print Ltd* [2015] EWHC 2242 (QB), the High Court stressed the liberalising effect of the Defamation Act on freedom of speech:

JUDGMENT

'In enacting the Defamation Act 2013 s 1(1), Parliament had intended that libel claimants should have to prove as a fact on the balance of probabilities that serious reputational harm had been caused by, or was likely to result from, the publication complained of.

'The court was entitled to have regard to all the relevant circumstances, including evidence of what actually happened after publication. Libel was no longer actionable without proof of damage, and the legal presumption of damage would cease to play any significant role.'

There are also a number of defences to an action for defamation which serve to protect free speech. These are:

- Justification – that the impugned statement was true (or substantially true). This is now known as the defence of truth (s 2 Defamation Act 2013).
- Fair comment – that the statement was simply a fair comment on an issue of public interest. This is now known as the defence of honest opinion (s 3 of the Defamation Act 2013).
- Absolute privilege – this provides immunity from legal liability for things said during the proceedings in court or Parliament (see section 8.6).
- Qualified privilege – this defence (providing there is no malice) is available in certain situations, for example, where one party has a duty to inform another who has a corresponding interest/duty to receive such information. In *Reynolds v Times Newspapers* (2001) (see section 18.2.2), the House of Lords had held that in certain circumstances the defence of qualified privilege might be available to the press to justify information published in the public interest. See also *Jameel v Wall Street Journal Europe Sprl* [2006] UKHL 44 and *Flood v Times Newspapers* [2012] UKSC 11. The *Reynolds* defence has now been replaced by s 4 of the Defamation Act 2013 where the statement is on a matter of public interest and the defendant reasonably believes that publishing the statement is in the public interest.
- Innocent dissemination – this is particularly relevant to broadcasters.

As noted above, the judges in interpreting and applying the law of defamation (and its defences) determine its impact on freedom of expression. For example, in *Derbyshire County Council v Times Newspapers Ltd* (1993) (for the facts see section 4.8.2) the House of Lords held that under the common law a local authority could not sue in defamation. Lord Keith stated that:

JUDGMENT

'It is of the highest public importance that a democratically elected governmental body, or indeed any governmental body, should be open to uninhibited public criticism. . . . I regard it as right for this House to lay down that not only is there no public interest favouring the right of organs of government, whether central or local, to sue for libel, but that it is contrary to the public interest that they should have it. It is contrary to the public interest because to admit such actions would place an undesirable fetter on freedom of speech.'

Note that individual members of such bodies can still sue in defamation, subject to the defences of truth, honest opinion and public interest, above – see *McLaughlin v Lambeth LBC* [2010] EWHC 2726 QB.

The law of defamation could be justified under Art 10(2) of the European Convention as a legitimate interference with free speech as serving to *protect the reputation of others*.

18.4.2 The protection of confidential and private information

The law of confidentiality seeks to protect the confidentiality of private/secret information (including information held by the state). There are a number of defences to an action for confidentiality which serve to protect free speech. One such defence is that such information is already in the public domain as demonstrated in the *'Spycatcher'* case:

CASE EXAMPLE

Attorney General v Observer Ltd and others *[1988] 3 WLR 776*

Peter Wright (a former member of MI5) wrote *Spycatcher*, a book which detailed alleged unlawful activities of members of MI5. In 1985 in Australia, the Attorney General sought to prevent the book being published on the ground of confidentiality (ie a duty to the Crown not to disclose information).

Thereafter, the Attorney General obtained interlocutory (temporary) injunctions against *The Guardian* and the *Observer* until trial from publishing any information from Peter Wright in his role as a member of MI5. The Attorney General also subsequently secured an interlocutory injunction restraining *The Sunday Times* from publishing further extracts from its serialisation of *Spycatcher*.

The House of Lords held that the worldwide publication of *Spycatcher* (it had been published in the United States) had destroyed the secrecy of its contents (hence its confidentiality) and as a consequence the injunctions against the newspapers were not necessary and should be discharged. In essence, for a public body to override freedom of expression in the context of confidentiality, a clear public interest of non-disclosure must be demonstrated.

The newspapers subsequently successfully petitioned the European Court of Human Rights on the basis that the continuation of the injunctions after the book was freely available (having been published in America) violated Art 10 (*Observer and Guardian v United Kingdom* (1991) 14 EHRR 153).

The law of confidentiality could be justified under Art 10(2) of the European Convention as a legitimate interference with free speech as serving to protect the *rights of others* (ie a private life/privacy).

In the post-Human Rights Act era, the law of confidentiality can also be used to protect privacy interests (Art 8 ECHR) and in such cases the action is known as misuse of private information. This is illustrated by the following case which involves a balance between privacy (private life) and the exercise of freedom of expression by the press:

CASE EXAMPLE

Campbell v MGN Ltd *[2004] UKHL 22*

Naomi Campbell (a model) sued MGN Ltd for breach of confidentiality for publishing details of her therapy for drug addiction at a self-help group meeting, together with photographs of her leaving a meeting.

The House of Lords held that the Convention right of Art 8 (the right of Campbell to a private life – including details of her therapy, which was private and confidential information) outweighed the competing right under Art 10 (the freedom of expression of the press). As a consequence Campbell was entitled to damages.

The press and other defendants can defend an action by claiming that, despite the claimant's legitimate expectation of privacy, publication was in the public interest and thus overrode the claimant's expectation.

- In this sense the law, and the European Court of Human Rights, draw a distinction between what is in the public interest – a matter of social, economic or political interest – and what the public are interested in, or curious about (see *Von Hannover v Germany* (2005) 40 EHRR 1).
- There is also a distinction between true public figures (politicians and public officers) and celebrities; although the law recognises that we sometimes expect a higher standard of behaviour from certain high-profile individuals, for example sportspersons: *Ferdinand v MGN Ltd* [2011] EWHC 2454. In this case the court accepted that publication of the ex-England football captain's affair was in the public interest as the public would expect a higher standard of conduct from him because of his position; note he had also publicly promised that he was a changed man after his last affair with the same woman.

Recently the Supreme Court made a controversial judgment with respect to the protection of private information that had already entered the public domain, which Is normally a defence to an action in breach of confidentiality (see 'Spycatcher' above).

CASE EXAMPLE

PJS v News Group Newspapers *[2016] UKSC 26*

The claimant, who was married with young children and well known in the entertainment industry, had allegedly engaged in extramarital sexual activities with a couple. The couple approached the defendant newspaper proposing a story about their sexual encounters with the claimant, who, although married, had an open relationship with his wife.

At first instance, the judge refused to grant interim relief restraining publication on the basis that the claimant and his wife had made many details of their relationship public, and that it was in the public interest to publish an account of the appellant's casual sexual exploits with others in order to correct a false image of monogamy. The claimant appealed and the Court of Appeal held that on balance the appellant's claims overrode those of the newspaper and granted the injunction, but following the publication of the information on several websites the Court of Appeal lifted the injunctions. The claimant appealed against that decision and the Supreme Court (Lord Toulson dissenting) upheld the interim injunction. In the Court's view, although the story and the celebrity's identity had been widely published overseas and online, the injunction served the purpose, pending a trial, of preserving the privacy interests of the celebrity, his partner and their young children. No genuine public interest in publication had been disclosed and without the interim injunction there would be further unrestricted and extensive coverage which would undermine the purpose of any trial.

The Supreme Court thus concluded that disclosure or publication of purely private sexual encounters would, on the face of it, constitute the tort of invasion of privacy, and that repetition of such disclosure or publication on further occasions was capable of constituting a further tort of invasion of privacy, especially if it occurred in a different medium.

KEY FACTS

Key facts on free speech

As a conditional right, freedom of expression can be legitimately interfered with by both the criminal and civil law.

The criminal law

Free speech can be infringed in order to secure the following legitimate objectives:

- Protection of religious interests (blasphemy – now abolished – inciting religious and racial hatred).
- The protection of national security (Official Secrets Act 1989).
- The protection of public order (Public Order Act 1986).
- The protection of the administration of justice (Perjury Act 1911/Contempt of Court Act 1981).
- The protection of the public from indecent material (common law and statutory indecency).
- The prevention of corruption (Obscene Publications Acts 1959 and 1964).

The civil law

Free speech can be infringed in order to secure the following legitimate objectives:

- The protection of reputation (defamation).
- The protection of private and confidential information (confidentiality/misuse of private information).

SUMMARY

- Freedom of expression/speech is a central aspect of all democratic states.
- In the United Kingdom, individuals historically enjoyed the residual liberty of expression, however this was overtaken with the advent of the Human Rights Act 1998, which allows individuals to raise Article 10 (the right to freedom of expression) directly before a British court.
- Freedom of expression is not an absolute right as it conflicts with other interests and so can be legitimately interfered with in specified situations. Article 10(2) sets out the wide range of circumstances when the primary right of expression (set out in Article 10(1)) can be lawfully restricted.
- Free speech can be legitimately interfered with by both the criminal law (eg to protect national security) as well as the civil law (eg to protect confidential information).

SAMPLE ESSAY QUESTION

How is it possible to balance the fundamental right of freedom of expression with other rights and interests it comes into conflict with?

- Explain (briefly) the fundamental importance of freedom of expression in a democratic society and the values that it upholds – moral autonomy, freedom of the press, democracy, the discovery of the truth etc.

- Explain the 'conditional' status of freedom of expression under Art 10 of the European Convention – that it is subject to duties and responsibilities and legal/necessary restrictions. Give examples of legitimate aims listed in Art 10(2) and try to link those aims to relevant laws – for example, 'the reputation or rights of others' refers to the laws of defamation and confidentiality.

- Explain the strict rules of legitimacy and necessity that any interference with free speech has to satisfy – that restrictions must be prescribed by law, have a legitimate aim and be necessary in a democratic society. Use cases such as *Sunday Times v United Kingdom* (1979) and *Observer and Guardian v United Kingdom* (1991) to illustrate. Also explain the constitutional status of free speech in the UK ('*Spycatcher*', *Attorney General v Observer Ltd* (1988) and *ex parte Brind* (1991)).

- Explain and analyse s 12 of the Human Rights Act 1998 with respect to the protection of free speech and the courts' role in upholding it.

- Critically analyse a number of domestic laws, for example obscenity, racial hatred, defamation, confidentiality, contempt etc, to consider the compatibility of such laws with Art 10 and the constitutional right of free speech in the UK.

Conclusion
- Summarise the current position of free speech protection with respect to the balance of free speech and other rights and interests.

Further reading

Books
Barendt, E, *Freedom of Speech* (2nd edn, Oxford University Press, 2005).
Bradley, A and Ewing, K, *Constitutional and Administrative Law* (17th edn, Pearson/ Longman, 2018), Chapter 23.
Fenwick, H, *Fenwick on Civil Liberties and Human Rights* (5th edn, Routledge, 2017), Pt II, pp 277–293 and Chapters 6–8.
Foster, S, *Human Rights and Civil Liberties* (3rd edn, Longman, 2011), Chapters 8 and 9.

Articles
Amos, M, 'Can we speak freely now?' [2002] EHRLR 750.
Bailin, A, 'Criminalising free speech' [2011] Crim. LR 705.

Foster, S, 'Tell us something that we don't know: celebrity privacy, interim injunctions and information in the public domain' (2016) Coventry Law Review 57.

Khan, A, 'A "right not to be offended" under Article 10(2)' [2012] EHRLR 191.

Korpisaari, P, 'Balancing freedom of expression and the right to private life in the European Court of Human Rights' (2017) Communications Law 39.

19

Judicial review I (rationale and procedure)

19.1 Administrative law

19.1.1 Introduction

As noted earlier at section 1.2.2, in broad terms administrative law concerns the principles relating to executive/governmental powers. Government officials and agencies are conferred with extensive powers (typically by statute) to provide public services (eg social security, housing). Administrative law focuses specifically on the powers and responsibilities exercised by governmental bodies and how they are regulated and controlled by both legal and non-judicial means. Although there is no clear demarcation between constitutional and administrative law (due largely to the absence of a codified constitution), the latter is particularly concerned with how the executive/administration uses and misuses its public law powers. In short, administrative law is concerned with ensuring that government and public law decision-makers are accountable for their actions.

Public lawyers are particularly interested in the following:

▪ The methods by which the exercise of public powers and duties may be controlled by the courts (via judicial review) or by non-judicial bodies (eg the Ombudsman).

▪ The ways in which the government/administration in exercising its public law powers and duties facilitate the constitutional principles of justice, participation in public affairs and open government.

An overview of the regulation of governmental power

Although administrative law primarily concerns the legal regulation of the exercise of public power by governmental bodies, it also embraces non-legal controls outside the strict court system. In general terms, government power is regulated in the following ways:

Figure 19.1 The regulation of public power

19.1.2 Political control

The government is *politically* controlled in the following ways:

(i) **Public pressure** – Government is influenced by public pressure and may therefore react to public opinion (for example, the replacement of the controversial community charge ('the poll tax') with the council tax by the vehicle of the Local Government Finance Act 1992). Sometimes by reacting to public opinion the government may act illegally (see *ex parte Venables and Thompson* (1997) at section 5.7.8, where the Home Secretary acted unlawfully in taking into account public concern regarding the length of Venables and Thompson's detention for killing James Bulger). Ultimately, of course, governments (or, more accurately, MPs in the government) need to seek re-election every five years and obtain the support of the electorate.

(ii) **Parliamentary pressure** – In constitutional theory, government ministers are controlled and regulated in Parliament through the following devices:

- Parliamentary questions (see section 12.4).
- Parliamentary debates (see section 12.5).
- Parliamentary committees (see section 12.6).

In fact, two of the most fundamental constitutional conventions underpinning the British constitution are the conventions of collective and individual responsibility (see sections 12.2 to 12.3).

19.1.3 Legal control

The government is *legally* controlled in the following ways:

- **Private law remedies** – In general terms, government bodies, like private individuals, are also subject to the private laws of tort, contract etc. In other words, should a local authority fail to fulfil its legal obligations under a contract made with a private citizen, the latter may sue for breach of contract. It should be noted however that the courts may apply constitutional principles of acting fairly (and not capriciously) to public bodies when they act in a purely private way.
- **Statutory appeal** – Appeals are statutory mechanisms which Parliament has specifically legislated for and so it may be possible, for example, to appeal against the decision of an administrative officer.
- **Judicial review** – This is the cornerstone of administrative law and will be considered in detail here and in Chapter 20. In essence, judicial review is the legal mechanism whereby a claimant in a court can seek to review the decision-making process of a public body.
- **Tribunals** – In essence, tribunals are a grievance mechanism which are an alternative to the strict formal court system. For example, an appeal concerning a social security officer's decision to refuse eligibility in respect of a particular benefit would proceed not to a court, but instead to a more informal (and cheaper) specialist tribunal (see section 21.1).

19.1.4 Other control/remedies

The government is also regulated by the following remedies:

- **Ombudsmen** – There are a number of different ombudsmen who supervise and regulate the activities of the administration (see section 21.3). The first, and most constitutionally significant, is the Parliamentary Commissioner for Administration who investigates complaints that government departments have engaged in maladministration (in effect, faulty administration) which has caused injustice to the complainant.
- **Inquiries** – There are a number of different types of inquiry which include, for example, a land inquiry concerning the decision of a local authority to refuse planning permission (see section 21.2.1).

19.2 Judicial review

19.2.1 Definition

QUOTATION

'Judicial review represents the means by which the courts control the exercise of governmental power. Government Departments, local authorities, tribunals, state agencies and agencies exercising powers which are governmental in nature must exercise their powers in a lawful manner.'

H Barnett, *Constitutional and Administrative Law*
(12th edn, Routledge/Taylor & Francis Group, 2017), p 612.

The High Court historically has exercised an inherent power to supervise the actions of public bodies, as well as inferior courts, to ensure that these bodies act strictly within their legal powers and thus act legally. For the purposes of judicial review, the part of the High Court which processes these cases is now known as the Administrative Court (see section 19.2.5). In addition, as a result of the Tribunals, Courts and Enforcement Act 2007, the Upper Tribunal has been conferred with a power of judicial review in relation to the First-Tier Tribunal. Moreover, s 22 of the Crime and Courts Act 2013 enabled immigration, asylum and nationality applications for judicial review to be transferred from the Administrative Court to the Upper Tribunal. In fact, since November 2013 the majority of asylum and immigration cases have commenced in the Upper Tribunal (Immigration and Asylum Chamber). The examples below illustrate the nature of judicial review acting as a check on the following bodies:

- **Government ministers** – In *R v Secretary of State for Foreign and Commonwealth Affairs, ex parte World Development Movement Ltd* [1995] 1 WLR 386 the pressure group World Development Movement successfully challenged the Foreign Secretary's decision to grant funding for the construction of a Malaysian hydro-electric power station on the Pergau river under the Overseas Development and Co-operation Act 1980 on the basis of it being economically unsound.

  In relation to delegated legislation, in *R v Secretary of State for Health, ex parte United States Tobacco International Inc* [1992] 1 QB 353 the court quashed the Oral Snuff (Safety) Regulations 1989 made by the Secretary of State for Health, on the basis that the claimants had not been given the opportunity to make representations before they were enacted.

- **Local authorities** – In *R v Wear Valley District Council, ex parte Binks* [1985] 2 All ER 699, a street trader successfully sought judicial review of the Wear Valley District Council's decision (made without prior notification or accompanying reasons) to give her notice to quit her hot food take-away caravan.

- **Parole Board** – In *R (West) v Parole Board* [2005] UKHL 1, prisoners successfully challenged the procedural fairness of the Parole Board in respect of revoking their licences (they had been released on licence) as they had not been offered oral hearings (see section 20.5.4).

- **Inferior courts** – In *R (DPP) v South East Surrey Youth Court* [2005] EWHC 2929 (Admin) the Director of Public Prosecutions sought judicial review of the decision of the South East Surrey Youth Court not to commit a defendant for trial at Crown Court. On the facts the court did not quash the decision of the Youth Court, but noted that its approach had been flawed when it had declined to consider certain statutory provisions.

These cases illustrate a number of points concerning judicial review:

- **(i)** Firstly, judicial review can be brought against a disparate number of public bodies (from a Secretary of State to a Parole Board). In fact, judicial review can be used against bodies which are not, in a strict sense, part of the government at all (see the *Panel on Take-Overs and Mergers* case at section 19.3.3).
- **(ii)** Judicial review can be sought by a number of different claimants (from individual street traders and pressure groups through to the DPP acting in the public interest).
- **(iii)** Judicial review is not confined to supervising the actions of government bodies, as it can include reviewing the decision-making process of judicial bodies (eg inferior courts, which are those ranking lower than the High/Administrative Court).

(iv) Judicial review is technically brought in the name of the Crown and as stated by Keene J in *R v Commissioner of Customs and Excise, ex parte Kay* [1996] STC 1500 '. . . it reflects the fact that this court is dealing with what are essentially issues of public law . . .'.

19.2.2 A review and not an appellate jurisdiction

In *Chief Constable of the North Wales Police v Evans* [1982] 1 WLR 1155, Lord Brightman stated that:

JUDGMENT

'Judicial review is concerned, not with the decision, but with the decision-making process. Unless that restriction on the power of the court is observed, the court will in my view under the guise of preventing the abuse of power, be itself guilty of usurping power.'

The constitutional function behind judicial review is to supervise the decision-making process of public bodies and not to act as an appellate court which questions the decision itself. In short, the Administrative Court is concerned with the legality and lawfulness of the actions taken by a public authority, rather than the merits of its decisions. Judicial review, therefore, is concerned with the nature of the decision-making process and with asking, for example, the following questions:

In reaching its decision (ie as part of the decision-making process) did the public body:

- Misinterpret its legal powers?
- Take into account an irrelevant matter?
- Ignore a relevant matter?
- Act for an improper purpose?
- Act in a procedurally unfair way by either ignoring a statutory requirement or by failing to follow the common law rules of natural justice?

By asking these sorts of questions, in constitutional theory, the court is in effect questioning the *process* of making the decision and not the *decision* itself. In other words, the reviewing court is not questioning the merits or quality of the decision made (eg was it qualitatively a good or bad decision?), which is an exercise carried out by an appellate court, but rather: was the process lawful? It is in this way that judicial review can be constitutionally justified. It must be remembered that this is an inherent legal remedy which the courts have developed. Appeals, on the other hand, are statutory, whereby Parliament has decided that in a particular set of circumstances, where a person disagrees with the decision made by a public body, it can be appealed against. As Lord Greene MR has made clear in *Associated Provincial Picture Houses Ltd v Wednesbury Corporation* [1948] 1 KB 223, the role of the court in judicial review proceedings (in respect of a local authority):

JUDGMENT

'is not as an appellate authority to override a decision of the local authority, but as a judicial authority which is concerned, and concerned only, to see whether the local authority have contravened the law by acting in excess of the powers which Parliament has confided in them'.

Similarly, in *R v Independent Television Commission, ex parte TSW Broadcasting Ltd* [1996] EMLR 291 Lord Templeman stated that:

JUDGMENT

'The courts have invented the remedies of judicial review not to provide an appeal machinery but to ensure that the decision-maker does not exceed or abuse his powers.'

Most recently, on the distinction between an appeal and judicial review, see the Supreme Court decision in *General Medical Council v Michalak* [2017] UKSC 71.

The following points need to be noted in this context:

(i) The constitutional theory set out above is more readily applicable to some grounds of judicial review than to others. For example, in relation to the ground of *irrationality*, the courts are, in effect, questioning the quality of the decision made (albeit, for the court to intervene the decision must be so irrational that no reasonable decision-maker could have arrived at it). Moreover, today in the context of the Human Rights Act 1998, the courts may have to consider whether an interference with human rights is proportionate (see Chapter 17).

(ii) The traditional view that a reviewing court has a supervisory role only (ie it does not *substitute* a decision for the decision in question) is now subject to Pt 54.19(2) of the Civil Procedure Rules and s 31(5A) of the Senior Courts Act 1981 (in relation to a decision involving an error of law made by a court or tribunal).

irrationality

a decision in law which no reasonable person could have come to

19.2.3 The constitutional dimension of judicial review

Judicial review is a central component of Britain's uncodified constitution and is inextricably linked with the following constitutional principles:

The rule of law

JUDGMENT

'The common law power of the judges to review the legality of administrative action is a cornerstone of the rule of law in this country and one that the judges guard jealously.'

Lord Phillips MR, *R (M) v Immigration Appeal Tribunal* [2004] EWCA Civ 1731.

Judicial review can be viewed as the rule of law in operation (see Chapter 6). In short, it ensures that public bodies act strictly within their legal powers and do not exceed them. As indicated earlier, the rule of law necessitates that government acts within the law and judicial review can provide a remedy if a public body misuses or exceeds its public law powers. In particular, the court will ensure that public decision-makers do not abuse their public law discretion. Although there is a clear public policy case for conferring discretion on government officials and administrators (see section 6.7.5), the process of judicial review aims to control and regulate the use of that discretion. In essence, judicial review underpins the rule of law in our uncodified constitution.

NB. See, however, the reform set out in s 84 of the Criminal Justice and Courts Act 2015 (detailed later at section 19.6.2).

The separation of powers

As noted at section 5.8.4, from one perspective judicial review can be seen as an illustration of the separation of powers with the judicial arm of the constitution (the Administrative Court) checking and balancing the actions of the executive (the government/administration). In this way the executive is held legally to account. Moreover, the courts have used the principle of the separation of powers as justifying their somewhat limited constitutional role as a reviewing court. Thus, in constitutional theory the judges confine themselves simply to reviewing the decision-making process of public bodies, while leaving the latter to make the actual decision themselves. After all, it is the public bodies which have been specifically charged with the responsibility to make the decision (a specialist executive/administrative role). In this way, the courts avoid trespassing on the constitutional role of the executive, which is to administer the law and take decisions. The courts will intervene via judicial review proceedings only when, for example, a public body misunderstands or misuses its powers, or adopts a faulty decision-making process.

Parliamentary sovereignty

As government derives most of its public law powers from Parliament, judicial review can be viewed as simply upholding parliamentary sovereignty by ensuring that public bodies act strictly within their allocated statutory powers. If these authorities were permitted to exceed their legal powers as conferred by Parliament, they would undermine the legal authority and status of Acts of Parliament. Judicial review, therefore, ensures that public decision-makers act within the legal parameters set by Parliament.

One difficulty with this point is that government also enjoys common law powers in the form of the royal prerogative and some uses of this power have been held subject to judicial review (see section 11.9.6). Clearly, in these cases, the justification for judicial review in this context *cannot* be to uphold the will of Parliament. A second problem concerns the judicial attitude to ouster clauses (see section 19.2.4).

The protection of human rights

Judicial review is a procedural remedy in the sense that it challenges the decision-making process, and in this way it is a somewhat limited remedy. In recent decades, however, the human rights context of a judicial review application has assumed increasing significance. In other words, the more a decision impacted adversely on human rights, the more justification was required by the court for the public body to be able to make it (see *ex parte Smith* (1996) at section 20.3.2). Today the Human Rights Act 1998 is in operation and the Convention rights can be upheld through an action in judicial review. Under s 6 of the Act, public authorities must act in accordance with the rights set out in the European Convention and if they do not, their actions can be subject to judicial review.

The control of the exercise of public law powers

QUOTATION

'Judicial Review is a critical check on the power of the State, providing an effective mechanism for challenging the decisions of public bodies to ensure that they are lawful.'

Judicial Review: proposals for reform, Cm 8515, CP 25/2012 (MOJ, The Stationery Office, 2012), p 4.

Judicial review can be constitutionally justified as a legal control on the misuse of public law powers (including both statutory and common law prerogative powers). In the absence of a formal codified constitution which constitutionally constrains the actions of the executive, judicial review provides a mechanism whereby the abuse of public law powers (which can affect millions of people) can be legally controlled. In fact, it could be observed that the dramatic growth of judicial review in the past 40 years has coincided with the overwhelming dominance of the executive in the legislature and so has, therefore to some extent, re-balanced the constitution. It is true to say that, although in the past 40 years there has been less *political* control over the executive, there has, however, been a significant increase in the *legal* control over it via judicial review proceedings.

19.2.4 The controversial nature of judicial review

Judicial review has a number of controversial and/or disputed elements.

An inherent and unelected jurisdiction

Judicial review is in effect a judge-driven process as it stems from the common law. In other words, it is the courts which have developed, expanded and refined the principles, grounds and remedies available in judicial review proceedings. In effect, the courts determine who can seek judicial review, against whom and on what grounds. The judges are, of course, unelected and largely unrepresentative of society (see Chapter 13) and therefore would appear to lack a democratic mandate for their actions in supervising the executive.

This common law basis of judicial review can, however, be justified as upholding the constitutional principles set out in section 19.2.3 and, in particular, controlling the abuse of public law powers. Moreover, it should also be remembered that the executive itself is not elected *per se*; it is merely drawn (largely, though not exclusively) from the elected House of Commons. In *ex parte Witham* (1997), for example, the courts declared secondary legislation passed by the *unelected* Lord Chancellor to be unlawful and *ultra vires* (see section 4.8.3). In a democracy it is paramount that the executive does not exceed its legal powers; therefore judicial review upholds the rule of law.

Controlling **ultra vires** *action?*

There is debate concerning the constitutional justification for judicial review, namely whether it is, in essence, concerned with questioning actions which are *ultra vires* (beyond the powers conferred). On the one hand, it has been argued that traditionally the courts are simply upholding the will of Parliament as by challenging *ultra vires* action they ensure that public bodies act *intra vires* (within the powers conferred). As noted earlier, however, judicial review also regulates the exercise of the royal prerogative, which is a common law power. In addition, the courts imply certain principles (eg the need to use powers rationally and fairly) into the statutory powers conferred on public bodies.

According to Barnett:

QUOTATION

'While judges continue to use the term *ultra vires,* it is nowadays too limited a term to encompass the whole ambit of judicial review. It may be preferable, therefore, to regard judicial review as the control of discretion and the regulation of the decision-making process by the courts.'

H Barnett, *Constitutional and Administrative Law*
(12th edn, Routledge/Taylor & Francis Group, 2017), p 648.

The ground of irrationality

As will be indicated below, irrationality (historically) is the second ground on which judicial review can be sought (see section 20.3). The difficulty with this ground is that it is difficult to reconcile with the principle that judicial review is concerned simply with review rather than appeal. When a court decides that a decision is irrational, in practice it is in effect questioning the *quality* of the decision made.

Ouster clauses

Ouster clauses are provisions in legislation which specifically exclude the jurisdiction of the courts. The judiciary has historically resisted such clauses, and it could be argued therefore, that in these circumstances, strictly speaking, the courts are not really upholding the plain will of Parliament. For example, in *Anisminic Ltd* (1969) at section 20.2.6, the relevant statutory provision stated explicitly that the determination of the Commission 'shall not be called in question in any court of law'. The court nevertheless held that this provision did *not* apply where the Commission had acted beyond its jurisdiction and so had not made a determination at all.

The controversial nature of total ouster clauses (which are arguably contrary to the principles underpinning the rule of law, as they aim specifically to exclude the supervisory remedy of judicial review) was demonstrated when the then Labour government was persuaded to drop such a clause from the Asylum and Immigration (Treatment of Claimants, etc) Bill in 2004.

The courts are, however, willing to accept provisions which restrict court jurisdiction to a limited time period (*Smith v East Elloe RDC* [1956] AC 736 and *R v Secretary of State for the Environment, ex parte Ostler* [1977] 1 QB 122). An example of such a provision is s 38 of the Inquiries Act 2005, which states that:

SECTION

S 38

An application for judicial review of a decision made –

(a) by the Minister in relation to an inquiry, or
(b) by a member of an inquiry panel,

    must be brought within 14 days after the day on which the applicant became aware of the decision, unless that time limit is extended by the court. [The rationale behind this provision is to prevent delays to inquiries. On inquiries, see later at section 21.2.3.]

Notwithstanding judicial suspicion of ouster clauses, in the recent case of *R (Privacy International) v Investigatory Powers Tribunal* [2017] EWHC 114 (Admin) the court held that s 67 of the Regulation of Investigatory Powers Act 2000 had established a valid ouster clause in terms of judicial review of the Investigatory Powers Tribunal's decisions. On this case, see P Scott, 'Ouster clauses and national security; judicial review of the Investigatory Powers Tribunal' [2017] PL 355.

An uneven remedy?

In some respects judicial review can be seen as lacking a clear overall uniform pattern. This is partly due to the fact that the court is a *reactive* body simply processing judicial review claims as and when they are brought before them. Thus, the ability to develop overarching judicial review principles is dependent upon the type and nature of the case brought before them at any given time.

In addition, as indicated at section 18.2.2, the courts historically have lacked an authoritative set of clear and agreed constitutional guidelines and so judicial review has developed in an *ad hoc* fashion. The modern courts do at least now enjoy the benefit of the principles espoused in the European Convention when processing human rights cases (see s 2 of the Human Rights Act 1998 at section 17.4).

The following points suggest judicial review lacks uniformity:

- The courts will determine, on a case by case basis, which bodies will be subject to judicial review. For example, in terms of two non-governmental bodies, the Panel on Take-Overs and Mergers and the Jockey Club, the former (in principle) was subject to judicial review while the latter was not (see section 19.3.3).
- Claimants seeking judicial review need to demonstrate that they have sufficient interest in the matter. For example, in terms of organisations/groups seeking review, Greenpeace was permitted to do so, while Rose Theatre Trust Co was not (see section 19.4.2).
- The courts will deem certain executive actions to be *non-justiciable* (ie owing to its subject matter, unsuitable for judicial resolution) and so not subject to judicial review. Historically, *non-justiciable* subjects have included national security and national finance. An example of a *non-justiciable* case in the context of international law/relations is *R (CND) v Prime Minister* [2002] EWHC 2777 (Admin).
- The remedies in judicial review are discretionary and so, even though an individual may succeed in demonstrating that a public body has acted illegally, the court may nevertheless decline to provide a remedy on the basis that if, for example, it quashed the decision in question, it could cause administrative chaos.

Conflict between the judicial and executive arms of the constitution

Judicial review has inevitably increased constitutional tension between the judiciary and government ministers (see for example, D Blunkett, 'I won't give in to the judges', *Evening Standard*, 12 May 2003). In the last two decades, this tension has been further heightened with the passage of the Human Rights Act 1998, which has provided a further ground of review, namely that a minister has breached the European Convention (see later at section 20.2.7). This was particularly ironic given that it was a Labour government that drafted and oversaw the passage of the Human Rights Bill through Parliament.

ACTIVITY

Self-test questions

1. What is the constitutional distinction between judicial review and an appeal?
2. To what extent do you think that judicial review is controversial? Revisit this question after you have completed Chapter 20.

19.2.5 A special 'administrative court'?

In the context of the rule of law (see section 6.7.6), it was pointed out that Dicey contrasted our constitution with that of France, where disputes between French citizens and government officials were processed in special tribunals (*tribunaux administratifs*), which were separate from the main court system. Instead, Dicey preferred our constitutional arrangements, whereby state officials were held to account before the ordinary courts like any other individual. This view, however, must be revised in the light of the modern development of judicial review proceedings, which in the following respects is similar to the French system of administrative law (*droit administratif*):

- In 2000, for the purposes of processing applications for judicial review proceedings, the Crown Office List was renamed the Administrative Court as it was recognised by Sir Jeffrey Bowman (Chairman of the Review of the Crown Office List) that there was a need for a specialist court to process public and administrative law cases. This court is staffed by specialist judges conversant with the principles of judicial review and administrative law. Judicial review is a highly specialist field of law.

- Under the **'exclusivity'** principle (see section 19.5.2), if a claimant wishes to challenge the misuse of public law powers by a public body, they must use the exclusive judicial review procedure set out in the Civil Procedure Rules and the Senior Courts Act 1981 (formerly the Supreme Court Act). In other words, a claimant will not be permitted to use the ordinary court system in order to assert public law rights.

- In judicial review proceedings judges apply special administrative principles (eg the responsibility of the public body to act rationally and follow the precepts of natural justice). These are principles which purely private bodies and individuals do not generally have to follow (but note section 19.3.4).

exclusivity

the principle that the enforcement of public law rights should be via the judicial review procedure

KEY FACTS

Constitutional concept	The connection with judicial review
The rule of law	It upholds the rule of law by ensuring that public bodies do not exceed their legal powers.
The separation of powers	It forms part of the checks and balances on the actions of the executive.
Parliamentary sovereignty	It upholds parliamentary sovereignty by ensuring that public bodies act within the powers allocated to them by Parliament.
The protection of human rights	Under the Human Rights Act 1998 public authorities can be subject to judicial review if they disregard Convention rights.
The control of the exercise of public law powers	It is a legal control on the misuse of public law powers.

19.2.6 The mechanics of judicial review

The basic mechanics of judicial review are illustrated by the following diagram:

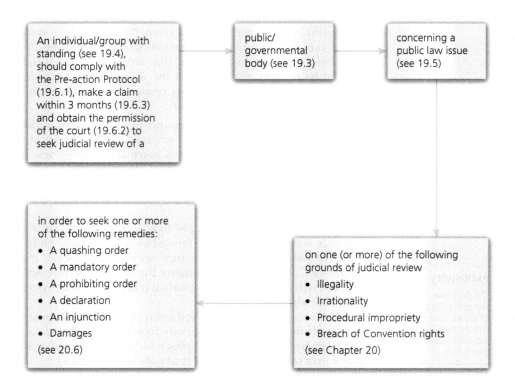

Figure 19.2 The mechanics of judicial review

19.3 Bodies subject to judicial review

Which bodies are subject to judicial review? In essence, judicial review is aimed chiefly at controlling government bodies/public authorities (public law bodies), although both non-governmental bodies and inferior courts are also subject to judicial review proceedings.

Figure 19.3 Bodies subject to judicial review

19.3.1 Government/public bodies

The following governmental/public bodies are subject to judicial review:

- **Government ministers/departments:** In *ex parte Venables and Thompson* (1997) (see section 5.7.8) the House of Lords held that the Home Secretary had acted illegally by misdirecting himself in law by considering an irrelevant consideration. In fact, government ministers are regularly subject to challenges in judicial review (eg see the recent case of *Miller* (2017) at section 15.6.6).
- **Local authorities:** In *ex parte Times Newspapers Ltd* (1986) (see section 20.2.4) the court held that the banning of *The Times* newspaper from the libraries of three councils was unlawful.
- **Parole Board:** For an example, see section 19.2.1.
- **Devolved institutions/bodies**: The devolved institutions set up under the various devolution settlements are subject to judicial review proceedings – see Chapter 14.

19.3.2 Judicial bodies

The following inferior courts and tribunals are also subject to judicial review by the higher Administrative Court:

- **The Crown Court:** providing the issue is unconnected with a trial on indictment.
- **The Magistrates' Court:** *R v Hereford Magistrates' Court, ex parte Rowlands* [1998] 1 QB 110 and more recently, *R (Woolcock) v Bridgend Magistrates' Court* [2017] EWHC 34 (Admin).
- **The Coroners' Court:** *R v Greater Manchester Coroner, ex parte Tal* [1985] 1 QB 67.
- **The Election Court:** *R (Woolas) v Parliamentary Election Court* [2010] EWHC 3169 (Admin).
- **Tribunals**: *R v Immigration Appeal Tribunal, ex parte Khan (Mahmud)* [1983] QB 790). It is important to remember that, as a result of the Tribunals, Courts and Enforcement Act 2007, the Upper Tribunal has been conferred with the power of judicial review of First-Tier Tribunals. Moreover, the Upper Tribunal itself is technically subject to judicial review (albeit in restricted circumstances) – see *R (Cart) v Upper Tribunal* [2011] UKSC 28 (see section 21.1.7).

NB. The High/Administrative Court and above are not subject to judicial review (*Re Racal Communications Ltd* [1981] AC 374).

19.3.3 Non-governmental bodies

Judicial review is also available to challenge certain non-governmental bodies. These are bodies which are not part of the government/administration *per se* but which exercise *de facto* public law powers. In practice, although such bodies have not been established by the government or Parliament, they do nevertheless exercise powers which are analogous to governmental powers. The courts, therefore, in determining what is subject to review do not merely confine themselves to looking at the source of power (ie statutory or royal prerogative) but also consider the nature of it (ie is the power *de facto* governmental in nature?).

CASE EXAMPLE

R v Panel on Take-Overs and Mergers, ex parte
Datafin plc *[1987] 1 QB 815*

Datafin plc sought judicial review of the actions of the Panel on Take-Overs and Mergers. The panel was not a government body and had not been established by an Act of Parliament or under the royal prerogative. In effect, it had been set up in the City of London in order to regulate the City Code on Take-Overs and Mergers of companies (a system of self-regulation).

The Court of Appeal held that judicial review was adaptable. Its jurisdiction could be extended to a body which operated as part of a system which performed public law duties. The panel, though not a government body, was a powerful body which made important decisions in regulating the financial activity in the City of London and so was treated as a *de facto* public body. In this case, Lloyd, LJ referred to a 'body' being subject to judicial review when it 'is exercising public law functions, or if the exercise of its functions have public law consequences . . .' On the facts of the case, however, there were no grounds for judicial review of the panel's actions.

Contrast *ex parte Datafin* with the following case:

CASE EXAMPLE

R v Disciplinary Committee of the Jockey Club, ex parte
Aga Khan *[1993] 2 All ER 853*

The Disciplinary Committee of the Jockey Club disqualified the Aga Khan's horse, which had won a major race. The latter sought judicial review of the Committee's decision.

The Court of Appeal held that, although the Jockey Club regulated horse racing in Britain, which affected the public (eg race meetings had to be licensed by the Jockey Club and people connected to racing had to be licensed by, or registered with it), nevertheless it was not subject to judicial review. According to the court, the club was not a public body (in terms of its history, constitution or membership) and the powers it exercised were not governmental in nature. In this case the powers of the Jockey Club derived from the agreement between the parties (ie with the Aga Khan), which gave rise to private rights which were enforceable by private law remedies. It should be noted that judicial review is a remedy of last resort, so the courts may decline judicial review where another legal remedy exists (see section 19.6.2).

See also *R v Football Association Ltd, ex parte Football League Ltd* [1993] 2 All ER 833, where the court held that the Football Association was not subject to judicial review.

CASE EXAMPLE

R v Chief Rabbi of the United Hebrew Congregations of Great
Britain and the Commonwealth, ex parte Wachmann *[1993]
2 All ER 249*

The High Court refused to subject the functions of the Chief Rabbi to the jurisdiction of judicial review. The court indicated that his functions were in essence spiritual and religious and were such that the government would not seek to discharge them in his absence.

A case in the context of the Human Rights Act 1998 is:

CASE EXAMPLE

R (West) v Lloyd's of London *[2004] EWCA Civ 506*

The Court of Appeal held that the actions of the Business Conduct Committee of Lloyd's were not amenable to judicial review. The decisions made by Lloyds were of a private nature and in terms of s 6 of the Human Rights Act 1998 it was not exercising public or governmental functions (contrast the *de facto* public law functions in *ex parte Datafin* (1987) above).

In short, if a non-governmental body exercises powers which are of a public nature and which are sufficiently governmental in essence (ie the government would have to exercise those powers if the body did not exist), then the court is more likely to declare that that body is susceptible to judicial review. Where, however, the relationship between the claimant and the non-governmental body is essentially a commercial one governed, for example, by contract law, the court may decline the claim for judicial review on the basis that an alternative remedy in private law is open to the claimant.

19.3.4 Private bodies and administrative principles

Even if a (powerful) private non-governmental body is not held to be subject to judicial review, there appears to be some evidence that the courts in the context of private law proceedings may nevertheless subject these bodies to certain administrative principles (eg to act fairly and not capriciously). This appears to be the case in the context of some sporting activities: *Nagle v Feilden* [1966] 2 QB 633.

NB. On fairness in respect of 'private law bodies', see further M Supperstone, J Goudie, P Walker and General Editor H Fenwick, *Judicial Review* (6th edn, LexisNexis, 2017), pp 382–4.

KEY FACTS

Bodies subject to judicial review
• **Government bodies** Government ministers, government departments, local authorities, devolved institutions, etc are subject in principle to judicial review.
• **Non-governmental bodies** These may be subject to judicial review providing their *de facto* powers are essentially governmental in nature and no other reasonable alternative remedy is available to the claimant (*ex parte Datafin* (1987)).
• **Purely private bodies/individuals** These are not subject to judicial review; however, some powerful private bodies *may* be subject to the administrative principles of acting fairly and not capriciously even in an area of private law (*Nagle v Feilden* (1966)).

19.4 Standing in judicial review

Who or what can seek judicial review? For a claimant (individual or group) to claim judicial review they must have sufficient interest (formerly known as *locus standi*) in the subject matter. In other words, there must be a connection between the claimant and the contested action of the public law body. From a constitutional perspective this ensures that those not affected by the action (ie 'mere busybodies') cannot seek judicial review as such claims would necessarily inflate the volume of claims before the Administrative Court. In doing so, these claims would interfere with the general process of administration.

The following have standing (ie sufficient interest) to seek judicial review:

Figure 19.4 Standing in judicial review

The following broad categories of standing draw upon (and adapt) those used in M Supperstone, J Goudie, P Walker and General Editor H Fenwick, *Judicial Review* (6th edn, LexisNexis, 2017), Chapter 18.

19.4.1 Individuals

Individuals directly affected by a public law decision

Individuals have standing to seek judicial review where they have been directly affected (financially or otherwise) by the actions of a public law body. For example, in *ex parte Binks* (1985) (see section 19.2.1), Binks was directly affected by the decision of the Wear Valley District Council to issue her with a notice to quit her take-away food caravan without prior notice or any accompanying reasons. In contrast, individual 'busybodies' (for example, a well-meaning citizen who was upset on Binks's behalf) would not have been able to apply for judicial review to challenge the District Council as they had not been directly affected.

An interesting recent case is *R (Hurley) v Secretary of State for Business, Innovation and Skills* [2012] EWHC 201 (Admin), where two lower sixth students sought judicial review in the context of regulations increasing university tuition fees (albeit the application to quash them was unsuccessful). Moreover, in the context of the action for judicial review of the government's intention to trigger Art 50 under the royal prerogative (see section 15.6.6), the Divisional Court in *R (Miller) v Secretary of State for Exiting the European Union* [2016] EWHC 2768 (Admin) stated that it was '. . . not difficult to identify people with standing to bring the challenge since virtually everyone in the UK or with British citizenship will . . . have their legal rights affected if notice is given under article 50'.

Individuals with a genuine public/constitutional interest

An exception to the 'mere busybody' rule above is that individuals who have a genuine constitutional interest in the actions of a public body may have standing to challenge it in judicial review:

CASE EXAMPLE

R v Secretary of State for Foreign and Commonwealth Affairs, ex parte Rees-Mogg *[1994] QB 552*

Lord Rees-Mogg (a peer in the House of Lords) unsuccessfully sought judicial review of the Foreign Secretary's decision to ratify the Maastricht Treaty. Although on the facts his claim failed, Lloyd LJ noted that there was no dispute as to standing: 'we accept without question that Lord Rees-Mogg brings the proceedings because of his sincere concern for constitutional issues'.

In the context of a public interest see the case of *R (Feakins) v Secretary of State for the Environment, Food and Rural Affairs* [2003] EWCA Civ 1546.

19.4.2 Groups/organisations

Acting on behalf of the public interest/in the public interest

Groups/pressure groups or organisations may seek judicial review if they are a recognised body acting in the interests of the wider public (analogous to *ex parte Rees-Mogg* (1994), above). In essence, they are not acting in their own interest *per se* but rather for the general public interest. As indicated at section 19.2.1, the pressure group World Development Movement Ltd successfully challenged the Foreign Secretary's decision to issue a grant to fund the building of the Pergau Dam.

An early (rather restrictive) case is the following:

CASE EXAMPLE

R v Secretary of State for the Environment, ex parte Rose Theatre Trust Co *[1990] 2 WLR 186*

A trust company (the Rose Theatre Trust Company) was established to preserve the remains of an historical theatre which were discovered during a development in London. They sought judicial review of the Secretary of State, who had declined to register the theatre in the schedule of monuments pursuant to the Ancient Monuments and Archaeological Areas Act 1979. The court held that the company did not have standing, as members of the public (in general) had insufficient interest to be entitled to apply for judicial review in respect of this particular matter (ie not to schedule the theatre).

The case of *ex parte Rose Theatre Trust Co* (1990) should be contrasted with the following two later cases:

Equal Opportunities Commission and another v Secretary of State for Employment *[1994] 1 All ER 910*

The Equal Opportunities Commission (a body established by statute) was successful in obtaining a declaration that provisions of the Employment Protection (Consolidation) Act 1978 were contrary to European Community law (as it was then known) as they indirectly discriminated against women. The House of Lords (by a majority) accepted that the EOC had standing as its statutory responsibility was to work towards eradicating sex discrimination.

R v Inspectorate of Pollution and another, ex parte Greenpeace Ltd (No 2) *[1994] 4 All ER 329*

Greenpeace (a pressure group on environmental issues) was granted standing to challenge the Inspectorate of Pollution's decision to vary authorisations concerning radioactive waste (although on the facts its claim failed). The court recognised that Greenpeace was a well-established and respected pressure group with concern for the environment. It is important to point out that Greenpeace was recognised as acting not only on behalf of the public interest but also on behalf of its members as a number of Greenpeace members lived in the Sellafield area.

▪ Acting on behalf of the interests of its members

These groups would include trade unions and professional bodies etc. For example, the Royal College of Nursing was granted standing in relation to a departmental circular in respect of abortion *Royal College of Nursing v Department of Health and Social Security* [1981] AC 800. In terms of associations, see *R (Montpeliers and Trevors Association and another) v Westminster City Council* [2005] EWHC 16 (Admin), where an Association representing the residents of two squares in London successfully challenged a traffic order made by Westminster City Council which affected their residential areas.

19.4.3 Local government/police

It must be remembered that judicial review can also be used by one branch of the executive against another. For example, in *Nottinghamshire County Council v Secretary of State for the Environment* (1986), Nottinghamshire County Council sought (albeit unsuccessfully on the facts) judicial review of the Secretary of State's guidance in respect of local authority expenditure targets (see section 14.2.6).

In terms of the police, in *R (Chief Constable of Greater Manchester Police) v Salford Magistrates' Court and Hookway* [2011] EWHC 1578 (Admin) the Chief Constable of Greater Manchester Police applied for judicial review of a decision of a Magistrates' Court (albeit unsuccessfully on the facts).

19.4.4 When should standing be determined?

CASE EXAMPLE

IRC v National Federation of Self-Employed and Small Businesses Ltd *[1982] AC 617*

The National Federation (representing small businesses and the self-employed) sought judicial review of the Inland Revenue in respect of its treatment of casual workers in Fleet Street (ie giving them an amnesty in terms of past tax which had not been paid). The National Federation sought a declaration that this was unlawful (as it differentiated between taxpayers) and an order of mandamus to compel the Inland Revenue to assess and collect this outstanding income tax.

The House of Lords held that the National Federation did not have standing (the Court of Appeal had held that they did) as it was merely a body of taxpayers. One taxpayer (or group of taxpayers like the Federation) did not have sufficient interest in asking the court to investigate the tax affairs of another.

The above case is notable as the House of Lords made it clear that, although in obvious ('simple') cases the issue of standing could be definitively decided at the leave stage (ie when permission is being sought from the court to bring a claim for judicial review – see section 19.6.2), in other more complex cases standing should be decided at the substantive hearing where full (factual and legal) information would be available. As a result, although standing may be granted initially, it may be subsequently reconsidered and refused at the main hearing in the context of the merits of the case as a whole. However, it has been noted that in modern times:

QUOTATION

'Notwithstanding the decision of the House of Lords in the Fleet Street casuals case, the courts now tend to adopt broadly the same approach to questions of standing whether it arises at the permission or the substantive stage.'

J Auburn, J Moffett and A Sharland, *Judicial Review*
(Oxford University Press, 2013), p 533.

ACTIVITY

Quick quiz

1. Who or what is subject to judicial review?
2. Who or what can seek judicial review?

19.5 A public law issue

19.5.1 Public law issues

JUDGMENT

'The boundary between public law and private law is not capable of precise definition, and whether a decision has a sufficient public law element to justify the intervention of the Administrative Court by judicial review is often as much a matter of feel as deciding whether any particular criteria are met.'

L J Scott Baker, *R (Tucker) v Director General of the National Crime Squad* [2003] EWCA Civ 57.

Judicial review is concerned with public law issues and the enforcement of public law rights. It is not concerned with private matters and private law rights (eg contract and tort).

Not every action of a public body falls within the ambit of judicial review. In order to seek judicial review a claimant must raise an issue of public law. In essence, this will relate to how public law powers have been misused, misunderstood or misapplied. The Civil Procedure Rules, Pt 54.1(2) (a), state that judicial review is concerned with 'the lawfulness of –

(i) an enactment; or

(ii) a decision, action or failure to act in relation to the exercise of a *public function'* (emphasis added).

For example, should a local authority breach its contract with an individual (eg it fails to pay a supplier for the supply of certain goods), the remedy lies in private contract law (ie a *private law* matter). Should the local authority, however, revoke a market licence without any prior notification or reasons etc, then the remedy for the complainant lies in asserting a public law right (namely that of the requirement in natural justice to be treated fairly) in judicial review proceedings (a *public law* matter). In other words, the mere fact that the defendant is a public body is not sufficient on its own to bring the matter within the ambit of judicial review. The issue at stake has to involve a public law issue.

19.5.2 Exclusive proceedings

If a claimant can demonstrate that a public law issue is at stake, in general terms he must use the special judicial review procedure (formerly under Order 53 and now governed by Pt 54 of the Civil Procedure Rules) to enforce this public law right. This procedure (see section 19.6) is hallmarked by certain characteristics, for example:

■ The requirement to obtain permission in order to bring an action for judicial review.

■ A short time limit to bring a claim.

These requirements limit the number of judicial review claims made and also prevent 'busybodies' from engaging in this process.

CASE EXAMPLE

O'Reilly v Mackman *[1983] 2 AC 237*

Four prisoners were charged with disciplinary offences in Hull Prison. The Board of Visitors found the charges proved and imposed penalties. The prisoners sought to challenge the Board alleging that it had breached the rules of natural justice; the fourth prisoner alleged bias. The prisoners did not use the judicial review procedure (ie then under RSC Ord 53), as they were outside the time limit, but instead used private law proceedings (writ and originating summons).

The House of Lords confirmed the order to strike out these proceedings as the prisoners had used the wrong procedure. It would be contrary to public policy as well as an abuse of the court process for an individual to seek redress by ordinary private law action when he contended that his public law rights (eg a breach of natural justice) had been violated. In other words, it would be contrary to public policy to evade the procedural protection given to public bodies under RSC Ord 53. Lord Diplock stated:

JUDGMENT

'My Lords, I have described this as a general rule . . . there may be exceptions, particularly where the invalidity of the decision arises as a collateral issue in a claim for infringement of a right of the plaintiff arising under private law, or where none of the parties objects to the adoption of the procedure by writ or originating summons.'

In essence, *O'Reilly* stands for the principle that the enforcement of public law rights (ie a grievance in public law) should be through the judicial review procedure which, of course, protects the administration. This is known as the *exclusivity* principle (for a more recent case, see *Carter Commercial Developments v Bedford BC* [2001] EWHC 669 (Admin)).

There are, however, some exceptions, which are illustrated in the diagram below:

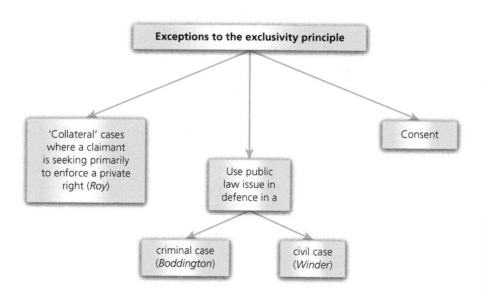

Figure 19.5 Exceptions to the exclusivity principle

19.5.3 Collateral cases

The judicial review procedure need not be used where the questioning of a public law decision is a collateral issue (ie incidental) to the enforcement of a private right.

CASE EXAMPLE

Roy v Kensington and Chelsea and Westminster Family
Practitioner Committee *[1992] 1 AC 624*

Roy was a general practitioner who brought a private action against the Family Practitioner Committee for withholding payment of part of his basic practice allowance. The Committee sought to have the action struck out as an abuse of process on the basis that the challenge should have been made by way of judicial review. The House of Lords held that the bringing of an ordinary action to enforce a private law right was not an abuse of the court, even though it would involve a challenge to a public law decision.

In this case, Roy's purpose was to enforce a private law right to compensation and it was merely collateral that this also involved considering the validity of a public law decision (ie the Committee's finding that Roy had failed to devote a substantial amount of his time to general practice).

It is important to point out that, as recognised by the Court of Appeal in *Clark v University of Linconshire and Humberside* [2000] 1 WLR 1988, today the Civil Procedure Rules have diminished in practice the differences between bringing an action under the *ordinary* court process as opposed to the *special* judicial review procedure.

19.5.4 The use of a public law issue in an individual's defence

In *Roy* (1992) above, the claimant had initiated legal action. Sometimes, however, an individual will be the defendant in legal proceedings commenced by another body. In these circumstances it appears that the questioning of the validity of a public law decision/act (a public law issue) can be used in defence.

■ **A criminal prosecution**

CASE EXAMPLE

Boddington v British Transport Police *[1999] 2 AC 143*

Boddington was prosecuted under byelaw 20 of the Railways Byelaws 1965 (made under the Transport Act 1962) for smoking in a train carriage. The House of Lords stated that he was not prevented from raising in his defence the contention that the byelaw was *ultra vires* and unlawful (on the facts it was held that the railway company had not acted unlawfully in bringing into operation the byelaw as it did).

■ **A civil case**

CASE EXAMPLE

Wandsworth London Borough Council v Winder *[1985] 1 AC 461*

Wandsworth Council commenced legal proceedings in the County Court against Winder (a council tenant) for arrears of rent and possession of his flat. Winder had considered recent rent increases excessive and refused to pay them. In his defence he argued that the resolutions to increase these rents were *ultra vires* and void.

The House of Lords stated that (in the absence of clear words to the contrary) an individual had a right to challenge a local authority's decision in their defence. Winder had not, after all, initiated the action.

19.5.5 Consent

This is where the parties to the case (ie the public body and the claimant) agree that a remedy can be sought via the 'ordinary' court procedure.

ACTIVITY

Quick quiz

1. What is a public law issue?
2. What is meant by the principle of exclusivity?
3. What is the purpose of this rule?

19.6 Procedure

In seeking judicial review special rules and principles apply. Formerly, judicial review was regulated by Order 53/Rules of the Supreme Court and the Senior Courts Act 1981 (formerly the Supreme Court Act). Order 53 has now been superseded by Part 54 of the Civil Procedure Rules 1998 which came into force in 2000 and added to in 2002 by the Pre-action Protocol.

The basic outline of the procedure for a claim for judicial review is as follows:

19.6.1 The Pre-action Protocol and claim

Before commencing proceedings the claimant (formerly the applicant) should write to the public body identifying the issues at stake to which the defendant public body should reply. The purpose of the Pre-action Protocol (which is a pre-trial code of practice) is to try to resolve the issue and so avoid litigation. One of the problems with judicial review in recent years has been its popularity, which in turn has lengthened the time the court takes to process a claim. For example, in 2011 there were 18,811 applications for permission to apply for judicial review before the Administrative Court of which 7,611 were considered that year (*Judicial and Court Statistics 2011* (MOJ, Crown Copyright, 2012), p 65). In this context, in *R (Cowl) v Plymouth City Council* [2001] EWCA Civ 1935, the Court of Appeal emphasised the importance of avoiding litigation whenever possible. It should be remembered, however, that the number of applications to the Administrative Court has fallen since 2013, when the majority of cases involving immigration and asylum were transferred to the

Upper Tribunal. Judicial review claims are brought before the Administrative Court (although as noted, a number are now brought before the Upper Tribunal). The claim form should state the action being challenged and the remedy sought.

19.6.2 Permission to apply for judicial review

Judicial review is not available as of right to a claimant, as the permission of the court (Pt 54.4) is required to commence the action (formerly known as seeking leave to apply). This is one way in which judicial review differs from private law actions. This acts as a filter system whereby the courts can weed out vexatious claims with no foundation. This protects public bodies and facilitates good administration whereby the government is not unnecessarily hampered by unrealistic claims. Judicial review is also a remedy of last resort (see Lord Templeman in *Re Preston* [1985] AC 835). This means that, if a claimant has an alternative remedy (eg a statutory appeal or a complaint procedure), he should avail himself of it instead. In terms of the availability of the former, see *R v Secretary of State for the Home Department, ex parte Swati* [1986] 1 WLR 477.

According to Underhill, LJ, permission is given where 'the application is "arguable" or has "a realistic prospect of success"' (*R (Wasif) v Secretary of State for the Home Department* [2016] EWCA Civ 82). Permission was formerly sought *ex parte* (in the absence of the other side), but today it is dealt with on a more *inter partes* basis. This enables the court to be better informed about the whole nature of the matter. If permission (which is determined by a judge on a consideration of the papers) is refused, the claimant can request a reconsideration at an 'oral renewal' (but see recent reforms below). If permission is refused at the 'oral renewal' the claimant can appeal to the Court of Appeal.

NB. Pt 4 of the Criminal Justice and Courts Act 2015 made further reforms to the process of judicial review. In particular, s 84 inserted a provision into the Senior Courts Act 1981 with the effect that, in determining whether or not to grant leave, the court may (and *must* if requested by the defendant) 'consider whether the outcome for the applicant would have been substantially different if the conduct complained of had not occurred' and must refuse to grant leave if it appears 'to be highly likely that the outcome for the applicant would not have been substantially different'. This requirement could be disregarded if 'it is appropriate to do so for reasons of exceptional public interest.'

19.6.3 The time limit

Claims for judicial review must be made *'promptly'* (Pt 54.5(1) (a)). In any event, they must be made 'not later than 3 months after the grounds to make the claim first arose' (Pt 54.5(1) (b)). However, statute may specify a shorter time period for making a claim (see s 38 of the Inquiries Act 2005 at section 19.2.4). This is another hallmark of judicial review which distinguishes it from private law actions as the time to make a claim is very short. The purpose of this is twofold:

▪ It protects public bodies (and the administrative process) as after three months such a body would know that its action/decision would not ordinarily be subject to judicial review. This provides some legal certainty in respect of public law actions/decisions.
▪ If a public body is acting illegally (and which has consequences for the public), then, in accordance with the rule of law, it is of paramount importance that it is legally constrained from doing so as soon as is possible.

The case of *R v Warwickshire CC, ex parte Collymore* [1995] ELR 217 is an example of a court accepting an out-of-time application for good reasons (ie the circumstances of the case).

In terms of acting 'promptly', see the case of *R (Harrow Community Support Ltd) v Secretary of State for Defence* [2012] EWHC 1921 (Admin), where it was held that proceedings were not brought promptly enough, even though technically *within* the time limit.

Recent reforms have taken place by virtue of the following measure (The Civil Procedure (Amendment No. 4) Rules 2013 SI 2013/1412):

- The time limit to file a claim for judicial review has been reduced to six weeks in relation to certain planning matters and to 30 days in respect of a decision in a procurement which is regulated by the Public Contracts Regulations 2006 (now 2015) – see Pts 54.5(5) and (6), respectively.
- At the permission stage, where an application is determined by the judge on the papers to be 'totally without merit', the claimant cannot request an oral reconsideration (ie an oral renewal) – see Pt 54.12(7). In *R (Grace) v Secretary of State for the Home Department* [2014] EWCA Civ 1091 the Court of Appeal confirmed that this phrase meant 'bound to fail'.

19.6.4 The substantive hearing

At the substantive hearing (ie a full hearing of the claim for judicial review) the court, typically involving one judge, will determine whether or not the defendant has infringed one or more of the grounds of judicial review (see Chapter 20 for the grounds). At this stage it can also reconsider whether the claimant has standing. The substantive hearing typically involves the consideration of documentary evidence, and the burden (civil burden of proof) rests on the claimant to prove unlawful action (cross-examination is rare in judicial review). If proven, the court may or may not issue a remedy (see section 20.6.2).

KEY FACTS

An overview of the judicial review procedure	
Pre-action Protocol	This should be complied with before a claim is made.
The claim	Is brought before the Administrative Court.
Permission required	Judicial review is not a remedy as of right.
Time limit	The claim must be made promptly (within three months – as a longstop position).
Standing	The claimant must have sufficient interest in the matter.
Public body	The claim must be sought against a public body.
Public law issue	The claim must concern a public law issue (ie public law rights).
Substantive hearing	The Administrative Court will determine whether a public body has acted unlawfully and if so, may provide a remedy (see Chapter 20).

SUMMARY

....

- Judicial review is the process whereby the Administrative Court supervises the actions of public bodies (and inferior courts) to ensure that they act strictly within their legal powers.
- Judicial review is a key aspect of the British constitution as it enables the executive to be held to account, thereby upholding the rule of law.
- Both individuals and groups can seek judicial review of a public body providing they have standing to do so and the claim involves a public law issue.
- Claimants must overcome certain procedural obstacles (eg a claim must be made promptly) in order to seek judicial review.

Further reading

Books

Auburn, J, Moffett, J and Sharland, A, *Judicial Review* (Oxford University Press, 2013), Pts I & VI.

Barnett, H, *Constitutional and Administrative Law* (12th edn, Routledge/Taylor & Francis Group, 2017), Chapter 23.

Budge, I, Crewe, I, McKay, D and Newton, K, *The New British Politics* (Addison Wesley Longman, 1998), Chapter 11.

Craig, P, *Administrative Law* (8th edn, Sweet & Maxwell, 2016), Chapters 25 and 27.

Craig, P, 'Access to Mechanisms of Administrative Law' in Feldman, D (ed), *English Public Law* (2nd edn, Oxford University Press, 2009), p 757.

Elliott, M, *The Constitutional Foundations of Judicial Review* (Hart Publishing, 2001).

Leyland, P and Anthony, G, *Textbook on Administrative Law* (8th edn, Oxford University Press, 2016), Chapters 8 and 9.

Supperstone, M, Goudie, J, Walker, P and General Editor Fenwick, H, Judicial *Review* (6th edn, LexisNexis, 2017), Chapters 18 and 19.

Weir, S and Beetham, D, *Political Power and Democratic Control in Britain* (Routledge, 1999), Chapter 15.

Articles

Adams, T, 'Ultra vires revisited' [2018] PL 31.

Duxbury, N, 'The outer limits of English judicial review' [2017] PL 235.

Forsyth, C, 'Of fig leaves and fairy tales: The ultra vires doctrine, the sovereignty of parliament and judicial review' (1996) 55 CLJ 122.

Laws, Sir J, 'Is the High Court the guardian of fundamental constitutional rights?' [1993] PL 59.

Lever, A, 'Is judicial review undemocratic?' [2007] PL 280.

Mills, A, 'Reforms to judicial review in the Criminal Justice and Courts Act 2015: promoting efficiency or weakening the rule of law?' [2015] PL 583.

Oliver, D, 'Is the ultra vires rule the basis of judicial review?' [1987] PL 543.

Woolf, Lord, 'Judicial review – the tensions between the executive and the judiciary' (1998) 114 LQR 579.

Paper

The Administrative Court: Judicial Review Guide 2017 (Judiciary for England and Wales, July 2017).

20

Judicial review II (grounds of review and remedies)

AIMS AND OBJECTIVES

At the end of this chapter you should be able to
- Identify and explain the different grounds of judicial review
- Distinguish between those grounds
- Identify those remedies that are available for a successful judicial review claim
- Assess the effectiveness of judicial review as a public law remedy

20.1 Grounds for judicial review

Judicial review can be sought on a number of different grounds. In *Council of Civil Service Unions v Minister for the Civil Service* [1985] 1 AC 374 (commonly known as the *GCHQ* case) Lord Diplock took the opportunity to reclassify the existing grounds of review in the following terms (in doing so he, in effect, provided a codification of them):

JUDGMENT

'Judicial review has I think developed to a stage today when without reiterating any analysis of the steps by which the development has come about, one can conveniently classify under three heads the grounds upon which administrative action is subject to control by judicial review. The first ground I would call "illegality", the second "irrationality" and the third "procedural impropriety".'

According to Lord Diplock, although there were essentially three different grounds of judicial review, he noted that proportionality might be developed at a later date (this has now been realised with the advent of the Human Rights Act 1998 – see section 20.4). It must be emphasised that these three grounds should not be viewed as rigid categories which are mutually exclusive of each other, as it is possible for a claimant to argue that the actions of a public law body involve more than one ground of review. It is also worth noting that another common division of the grounds of judicial review is between *substantive* judicial review (ie illegality and irrationality) and *procedural* judicial review (ie procedural impropriety).

In 2017, the different grounds of judicial review can be illustrated as follows:

Figure 20.1 Grounds of review

20.2 The ground of illegality

20.2.1 Definition and classification

The ground of illegality has a number of different aspects to it and was defined by Lord Diplock in *Council of Civil Service Unions v Minister for the Civil Service* [1985] 1 AC 374 in the following way.

JUDGMENT

'By "illegality" as a ground for judicial review I mean that the decision-maker must understand correctly the law that regulates his decision-making power and must give effect to it.'

Illegality can be further broken down into the following elements – the decision-maker has acted illegally because he has:

- Acted in an *ultra vires* way, that is beyond his powers (simple *ultra vires*).
- Misinterpreted his public law powers (excess of jurisdiction).
- Wrongly delegated his legal powers (wrongful delegation).
- Acted for an improper purpose (improper/ulterior purpose).
- Abused his discretion by failing to exercise it at all, or he has considered irrelevant factors and/or ignored relevant ones (an abuse of discretion).
- Acted in a way which is incompatible with the rights in the European Convention on Human Rights (the Human Rights Act 1998).

In essence, the ground of illegality is concerned with the misinterpretation or wrongful application of public law powers. These categories are not rigidly demarcated however; for example, a public body which takes into account an irrelevant factor may also act for an improper purpose at the same time.

20.2.2 Simple *ultra vires*

The principle of *ultra vires* means acting beyond and exceeding legal powers. For example, if A has been conferred with the legal power to do X, when he does X he acts *intra vires* (within his powers), but if he does Y instead, he acts *ultra vires*. The concept of *ultra vires* is associated with the intention of Parliament and so an action not authorised by the statute (eg Y above) is unlawful. However, as indicated previously at section 19.2.4, the concept of *ultra vires* alone cannot explain the ambit and nature of judicial review.

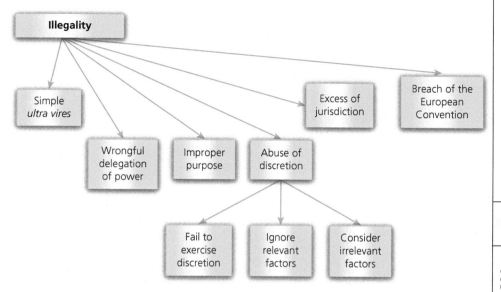

Figure 20.2 Illegality

CASE EXAMPLE

R v Secretary of State for the Home Department,
ex parte Leech *[1993] 4 All ER 539*

Under s 47(1) of the Prison Act 1952 the Secretary of State could make rules in order to regulate and manage prisons. Leech (a prisoner) successfully sought judicial review of r 33(3) of the Prison Rules 1964, which enabled a prison governor to read letters to and from a prisoner and stop any letter which was of inordinate length or objectionable. Leech argued that this rule allowed the reading and stopping of correspondence between a prisoner and his legal adviser where no legal proceedings were pending.

The Court of Appeal granted a declaration that r 33(3) was *ultra vires* the enabling Act (s 47(1) of the Prison Act 1952). It could not have been Parliament's intention to impede a prisoner's right of access to the courts (via his legal adviser).

CASE EXAMPLE

Attorney General v Fulham Corporation *[1921] 1 Ch 440*

Fulham Corporation, purporting to act under powers under the Baths and Wash-houses Acts 1846–78, established a laundry which involved customers bringing their clothes to the wash-house to be washed. These clothes were then washed by the employees of the Corporation and returned to the customers.

It was held that this scheme was *ultra vires* as it was not authorised by the Baths and Wash-houses Acts 1846–78. These Acts authorised the establishment of wash-houses whereby people could use the facilities to wash their own clothes. Instead, Fulham Corporation had created a laundry, which was an entirely different enterprise and not authorised by the 1846–78 legislation.

See also *London County Council v Attorney General* [1902] AC 165.

In addition, earlier examples of the use of *ultra vires* which we have already encountered in the text include the following:

- *Chester v Bateson* (1920) – where reg 2A (2) was held *ultra vires* the Defence of the Realm (Consolidation) Act 1914 for obstructing access to the courts (see section 5.7.2).
- *Commissioners of Customs and Excise v Cure & Deeley Ltd* (1962) – where reg 12 was held *ultra vires* the Finance (No 2) Act 1940 as it, in effect, purported to confer onto the Commissioners of Customs and Excise the powers of a judge and which ousted the jurisdiction of the courts (see section 6.7.5).
- *R v Lord Chancellor, ex parte Witham* (1997) – where the Supreme Court Fees (Amendment) Order 1996 was held *ultra vires* the Supreme Court Act 1981 (now known as the Senior Courts Act 1981) for precluding a person's access to the courts (see section 4.8.3).
- *Ahmed v HM Treasury* [2010] UKSC 2 – where the Supreme Court quashed the Terrorism (United Nations Measures) Order 2006 as being *ultra vires* s 1 of the United Nations Act 1946. In *HM Treasury v Ahmed* [2010] UKSC 5 the Supreme Court refused the Treasury's application to suspend the judgment of the court. Thereafter, the Terrorist Asset-Freezing (Temporary Provisions) Act 2010 was passed which specified that the 2006 Order was deemed to have been validly made under the 1946 Act (see section 6.7.11).

More recently, in *R (Public Law Project) v Lord Chancellor* [2016] UKSC 39 the Supreme Court held that the Lord Chancellor's proposal via a statutory instrument – that those who failed a residence test would be ineligible to receive civil legal aid – was *ultra vires* the power accorded to him to vary/omit services under s 9 of the Legal Aid, Sentencing and Punishment of Offenders Act 2012. Also see, *R (Detention Action) v First-Tier Tribunal* [2015] EWCA Civ 840 in terms of the *ultra vires* nature of the fast-track Tribunal Procedure (First-Tier Tribunal) (Immigration and Asylum Chamber) Rules 2014 in respect of s 22 of the Tribunals, Courts and Enforcement Act 2007.

The 'fairly incidental rule'

Although the *ultra vires* principle states that a public body may not do that which is not *expressly* authorised, in practice the courts have also permitted actions which are 'fairly incidental' to these expressly authorised powers.

CASE EXAMPLE

Attorney-General v Crayford Urban District Council *[1962] 2 All ER 147*

Crayford UDC made arrangements with an insurance company for council tenants to be able to insure their effects. This sum was collected at the same time as the council rent.

The Court of Appeal upheld the scheme as *intra vires* as acts of general management within s 111 of the Housing Act 1957. In short, if council tenants were uninsured, should they suffer loss (eg by virtue of fire or storm) then they were more likely to default on their council rent to make up the loss, than if they were insured against such loss. As a result, the council was helping to ensure the payment of council rents and so by implication were allowed to act as it did.

Furthermore, Parliament has (historically) recognised that local authorities should not be confined strictly to only those actions explicitly authorised – s 111 Local Government Act 1972 states that local authorities shall be empowered to do anything:

> S 111
>
> . . . which is calculated to facilitate, or is conducive or incidental to, the discharge of any of their functions.

CASE EXAMPLE

McCarthy & Stone Ltd v Richmond Upon Thames London Borough Council
[1992] 2 AC 48

Richmond Borough Council levied a charge on developers in respect of inquiries concerning speculative development proposals.

The House of Lords held that the above charge for pre-application advice was unlawful. In terms of s 111 of the Local Government Act 1972, the charge for such advice did not facilitate (nor was it conducive or incidental to) the council's functions of considering and determining applications for planning.

See also *Hazell v Hammersmith and Fulham London Borough Council* [1992] 2 AC 1.

NB. It is pertinent to note that s 1 of the Localism Act 2011 provided local authorities in England with a 'general power of competence' (see section 14.2.2).

20.2.3 Wrongful delegation of power

As a general constitutional principle, if public law powers are conferred on A (eg delegated to A by Parliament), they should not be delegated to B.

Figure 20.3 Wrongful delegation of power

The constitutional consequences of this are twofold:

- A does not fulfil his public law obligation to exercise the power conferred on him (he may well have been delegated that power because of his expertise).
- The wrong person in law (ie B) is exercising public law powers.

CASE EXAMPLE

Allingham and another v Minister of Agriculture and Fisheries *[1948] 1 KB 780*

A county war agricultural executive committee (which itself had been lawfully delegated powers by the Minister of Agriculture and Fisheries) decided that a number of acres of sugar beet should be grown by the owners of certain land. The committee, however, delegated to its executive officer the selection of the exact field on which to grow the sugar beet. It was held that the committee could not delegate its power to determine the land to be used and cultivated.

Whether a body can delegate powers is a matter of statutory construction for the court to determine. For example, the Act may expressly authorise delegation (eg s 101 of the Local Government Act 1972). Where, however, the Act is silent as to delegation, the courts will consider the nature, purpose and context of the powers. For example:

- Is the power a judicial or quasi-judicial one?
- Is the power purely administrative (eg involving simply the collation of information)?
- Has the power been conferred on a government minister?
- Would delegation be in the public interest and would it cause injustice?

A recent example of unauthorised delegation is *R (Austin) v Chief Constable of Surrey Police* [2010] EWHC 266 (Admin), in which it was held that a temporary Assistant Chief Constable's decision (a power wrongfully delegated to him by the Chief Constable) to dispense with the services of a probationer constable was *ultra vires*.

Judicial/quasi-judicial powers (including disciplinary powers)

Where the power is essentially a judicial or quasi-judicial power, the courts are reluctant to allow delegation. Lord Parker CJ, in *R v Governor of Brixton Prison, ex parte Enahoro* [1963] 2 QB 455, stated that:

JUDGMENT

'It is well settled that certainly no person made responsible for a judicial decision can delegate his responsibility.'

In relation to disciplinary powers, see the following case:

CASE EXAMPLE

Barnard and others v National Dock Labour Board and another *[1953] 1 All ER 1113*

The Dock Workers (Regulation of Employment) Order 1947 established the National Dock Labour Board. This Board was required to delegate specified disciplinary functions, including the power of suspension, to local dock boards (an example of an express authorisation to delegate). The Port Manager suspended Barnard and others with the power to do so being purportedly delegated by the local board. The Court of Appeal held that the power of suspension was a judicial/quasi-judicial function (it affected a person's rights) which could not be delegated by the local board. The suspensions were declared a nullity.

See also *Vine v National Dock Labour Board* [1957] AC 488, where a local dock labour board wrongfully delegated its disciplinary powers to a disciplinary committee of the board which had terminated Vine's employment. This dismissal was therefore invalid due to the delegation of a quasi-judicial function.

Administrative powers

Where a power is not judicial but merely consists of, for example, the collection of evidence or a preliminary investigation, then the courts have held delegation to be permissible (in this context see: *Jeffs v New Zealand Dairy Production and Marketing Board* [1967] AC 551 and *R v Race Relations Board, ex parte Selvarajan* [1975] 1 WLR 1686).

Government ministers

The courts have recognised the practical reality of government administration, that it is not practically possible for a government minister to exercise every single power conferred on him. Lord Greene MR, in *Carltona Ltd v Commissioners of Works* [1943] 2 All ER 560 (see section 4.13.12), stated that:

JUDGMENT

'The functions which are given to ministers . . . are functions so multifarious that no minister could ever personally attend to them. . . . The duties imposed upon ministers and the powers given to ministers are normally exercised under the authority of the ministers by responsible officials of the department. Public business could not be carried on if that were not the case.'

In fact, for the purposes of the decision the official becomes the *alter ego* of the minister and therefore in reality there is no real delegation (on this point see Widgery LJ in *R v Skinner* [1968] 2 QB 700). Moreover, the minister must select an appropriate official of sufficient experience and expertise:

CASE EXAMPLE

R v Secretary of State for the Home Department, ex parte Oladehinde *[1991] 1 AC 254*

The Home Secretary delegated to officials (of not less than inspector level) the power to make decisions, on his behalf, to deport persons under the Immigration Act 1971. Oladehinde was served with a notice of an intention to deport and he sought judicial review to quash the decision on the basis that the Home Secretary had wrongfully delegated his power under the Act to immigration inspectors.

The House of Lords held that the minister was entitled to authorise responsible officials to exercise his powers. The officials (immigration inspectors) were of suitable grading and experience to exercise these powers.

It should also be remembered that the minister will remain constitutionally account-able to Parliament for his decisions (whether or not he took them personally). In some cases, however, delegation will be prohibited where a statute specifically requires the minister personally (and no other person) to take the decision. For example, s 13(5) of the Immigration Act 1971 refers to directions having 'been given by the Secretary of State (and not by a person acting under his authority)'.

NB. In *R (King) v Secretary of State for Justice* [2015] UKSC 54 the Supreme Court held that the *Carltona* principle did not apply or extend to prison governors/prison officers.

ACTIVITY

Self-test questions
1. What is meant by action which is *ultra vires*?
2. What is meant by unlawful delegation of power?
3. When is it permissible to delegate a power?

20.2.4 Improper purpose/motive

According to Fordham, an improper motive is 'where the decision-maker was moti-vated by some aim or purpose regarded by the law as illegitimate' (M Fordham, *Judicial Review Handbook* (6th edn, Hart, 2012), p 531).

A public law power (or duty) therefore should be exercised for the purpose for which it has been conferred. If a power has been conferred in order for a public body to achieve purpose X, it will be unlawful for that power to be used to achieve pur-pose Y. In short, public power should not be used with an ulterior motive/purpose in mind, as this is an abuse of power (this area, therefore, could arguably also fall under section 20.2.5).

CASE EXAMPLE

Congreve v Home Office [1976] 1 All ER 697

In 1975 the cost of a colour television licence was increased from £12 to £18. In order to avoid paying this increase Congreve (along with others) renewed his licence early. The Home Office became aware of this and with the anticipated loss of revenue, Congreve and others were informed that unless they paid the £6 difference, their licences would be revoked.

The Court of Appeal held that the licence which Congreve had obtained lawfully was valid and the demand for payment was an unlawful exercise of power. Lord Denning MR held that the Home Secretary must use his statutory power to revoke licences under the Wireless Telegraphy Act 1949 in accordance with the law, that is to say not being influenced by ulterior/improper motives (eg want of money). It would be different if an individual had breached the conditions of the licence (this would be a proper purpose).

Similarly, in *Porter v Magill* [2001] UKHL 67 the House of Lords held that a local authority could dispose of land under s 32 of the Housing Act 1985 to achieve proper housing objectives, but not for promoting an electoral advantage of a party on the council (an improper purpose).

CASE EXAMPLE

R v Ealing London Borough Council, ex parte Times Newspapers Ltd and others *(1986) 85 LGR 316*

Under the Public Libraries and Museums Act 1964 it is the duty of a library authority to provide a comprehensive and efficient library service. As a result of an industrial dispute between *The Times* newspaper and their former employees, three councils banned copies of these newspapers in their library. *The Times* successfully sought judicial review of these decisions. The court held that the ban was imposed for an ulterior object (ie to be used as a weapon against *The Times* in their industrial dispute) and so declared it to be unlawful.

In *Wheeler v Leicester City Council* [1985] 1 AC 1054 Leicester City Council passed a resolution which prevented Leicester Football Club from using the council's recreational grounds for one year. The council considered that Leicester Football Club had failed to discourage three of its players from playing in an England rugby tour of South Africa during the apartheid era and should have condemned the tour. The House of Lords held that the council had, *inter alia*, misused its powers as, although under s 71 of the Race Relations Act 1976 it had a duty to make arrangements with a view to securing that its functions were carried out with due regard to the need to promote good race relations, Leicester Football Club had not acted improperly or broken any law. In this context also see *R v Lewisham London Borough Council, ex parte Shell UK Ltd* [1988] 1 All ER 938. One of the most significant cases in terms of improper purpose is the following case:

CASE EXAMPLE

Padfield v Minister of Agriculture, Fisheries and Food *[1968] AC 997*

Under the Agricultural Marketing Act 1958 the minister had a power/discretion to send (in any case he so directed) complaints arising out of the operation of the milk marketing scheme to a committee of investigation. Padfield (and others) asked the minister to appoint a committee to investigate their complaint (ie to refer their complaint to a committee of investigation) but the minister refused.

The House of Lords held that an order of mandamus should be made directing the minister to consider Padfield's complaint according to the law. The minister had argued that under the Act he had, in effect, a complete discretion in respect of whether or not to refer a complaint. The House of Lords held, however, that his discretion was not unlimited as it was conferred on him so that he could promote the object and policy of the Act (ie the investigation of substantial and genuine complaints). In other words, the minister could not frustrate the legislative purpose of the 1958 Act. Indeed, as stated by Lord Reid in the case 'Parliament must have conferred the discretion with the intention that it should be used to promote the policy and objects of the Act . . .'

NB. For a recent case of a regulation frustrating the purpose of an Act (*viz*, the Legal Aid, Sentencing and Punishment of Offenders Act 2012), see *R (Rights of Women) v Lord Chancellor and Secretary of State for Justice* [2016] EWCA Civ 91.

The *Padfield* case illustrates that the courts will not recognise an absolute (ie unfettered) discretion. It should be remembered that public decision-makers are exercising public law powers which can directly or indirectly affect millions of people. The *Padfield* case was, however, a somewhat pyrrhic victory as, although following the court case the complaint was referred, the minister concerned decided that it would not be in the public interest to implement the conclusions of the committee.

Aside from the ground of improper purpose, a decision-maker should also not act in bad faith.

20.2.5 Abuse of discretion

A public law discretion (the conferment of a power to act) should not be abused by a public law decision-maker. Abuse of discretion is a generic term which covers a number of unlawful actions, which include:

- Fettering a discretion.
- Ignoring relevant factors.
- Taking irrelevant factors into consideration.

In fact, it could also be argued that acting for an improper purpose (see section 20.2.4) is also an abuse of discretion. As indicated earlier, there are no rigid sub-categories within illegality. For example, it could be argued that by wrongfully delegating a power (section 20.2.3), a public decision-maker has failed to exercise his public law discretion (ie he fettered it) because he has divested himself of it altogether.

Although a statute may provide that a public body can make a decision as it thinks fit, the courts have adopted the approach that this does not mean that the public body can make literally *any* decision it thinks fit. Instead, the courts will imply certain limitations, as they do not accept the notion of an absolute or complete discretion. This is consistent with the rule of law (see section 6.7.5) as, although public law discretion is a valuable tool in public administration, if the use of the discretion is not controlled it is akin to an arbitrary power.

Fettering a discretion

If a public decision-maker has been conferred with a public law discretion, he should consider whether to exercise it.

Public law decision-makers can also abuse their discretion if they unnecessarily restrict the circumstances in which they will use it (eg they adopt an overly rigid or blanket policy which affects an individual). In this way the decision-maker is fettering his discretion by refusing to exercise it when new or exceptional circumstances arise. Lord Reid, in *British Oxygen Co Ltd v Minister of Technology* [1971] AC 610 stated that:

JUDGMENT

'What the authority must not do is to refuse to listen at all. But a Ministry or large authority may have had to deal already with a multitude of similar applications and then they will almost certainly have evolved a policy so precise that it could well be called a rule. There can be no objection to that, provided the authority is always willing to listen to anyone with something new to say.'

The point here is that it is common in public administration for administrators to adopt general guidelines or policies to assist them in making decision-making more efficient (on a 'structuring' of a discretion – see section 6.7.5). However, the adoption of an over-rigid/inflexible policy, excluding any exceptions in any circumstances, could be challenged by a claimant affected by it.

On a blanket ban/policy, see the cases of *R (Shutt) v Secretary of State for Justice* [2012] EWHC 851 (Admin) and *R (Lumba) v Secretary of State for the Home Department* [2011] UKSC 12. In contrast, however, in relation to a blanket policy under the royal prerogative, as opposed to statutory power, see *R (Sandiford) v Secretary of State for Foreign and Commonwealth Affairs* [2014] UKSC 44.

In addition, a discretion can be fettered if a public body *merely* acts 'under the dictation' of a third/other party.

Relevancy and irrelevancy

In making public law decisions a public decision-maker will necessarily have to consider a number of different factors/considerations. In public law a decision-maker must:

- Consider *relevant* factors and
- Disregard *irrelevant* factors.

Relevant factors

A decision-maker must consider relevant factors:

CASE EXAMPLE

R v Immigration Appeal Tribunal, ex parte Singh *[1986] 1 WLR 910*

The House of Lords held that an immigration adjudicator in deciding whether or not to deport Singh had ignored a relevant factor: that third party interests might be relevant. Singh was a talented musician who had performed the functions of a priest in the Sikh community and so his deportation would have had an impact upon the community.

Similarly, in *Bromley London Borough Council v GLC* [1983] AC 768 the House of Lords held *inter alia* that the Greater London Council (GLC) should have had regard to the interests of ratepayers (a fiduciary duty) in implementing its reduced fares scheme.

In *R (Forest Care Home Ltd) v Pembrokeshire County Council* [2010] EWHC 3514 (Admin) a local authority acted unlawfully by failing to take into account properly the potential adverse consequences of its decision on care home residents/providers. Most recently see the failure to take account of a material consideration (*R (Lucas) v Oldham MBC* [2017] EWHC 349 (Admin)).

Irrelevant factors

A decision-maker must ignore irrelevant factors:

In some respects the issue of a public body taking into account irrelevant factors can blur into the ground of acting for an improper purpose (see section 20.2.4). For example, if a public decision-maker in exercising a discretion has an ulterior motive in mind, he is also necessarily taking into account an irrelevant factor (ie the ulterior motive).

Below are two examples involving the consideration of irrelevant factors:

CASE EXAMPLE

R v Somerset County Council, ex parte Fewings *[1995] 3 All ER 20*

The council passed a resolution banning deer hunting over its land as the majority of councillors viewed the activity as morally repulsive. In the Divisional Court Laws J held that the council could not ban hunting on the basis that it was morally repugnant, as this was a free-standing moral perception and not an objective judgment as to what would 'conduce to the better management of the estate' as required by s 120 (1)(b) of the Local Government Act 1972. According to Laws J, the councillors' moral view on hunting had 'nothing whatever to do with such questions' (ie it was an irrelevant factor).

The Court of Appeal affirmed this decision that the hunting ban was unlawful (albeit on other grounds). The court held by a majority that the council had not exercised its power in order to promote the benefit of its area as, for one thing, it had not considered the statutory provision of s 120(1) (b). It is of interest to note that Sir Thomas Bingham MR indicated that it could not be said that the 'cruelty' argument was necessarily irrelevant to the question as to what is for the benefit of the area (see also Simon Brown LJ, albeit he dissented on the facts in the case).

In addition, as noted earlier in *ex parte Venables and Thompson* (1997) at section 5.7.8, the House of Lords held that the Home Secretary had misdirected himself in law by considering an irrelevant consideration (public protest concerning the sentences to be imposed in respect of these two particular individuals). Moreover, he had ignored relevant factors (ie the progress and development of Venables and Thompson while they were detained).

Permissible factors/considerations

There is a third category of considerations/factors: 'permissible considerations'. These are considerations/factors a public body/decision-maker *may* consider, albeit that it would not be unlawful for such a permissible consideration/factor to be disregarded – see further: J Auburn, J Moffett and A Sharland, *Judicial Review* (Oxford University Press, 2013), pp 339ff.

The ground of relevant/irrelevant factors in judicial review can be somewhat controversial as the judges are, in effect, determining which factors are relevant. As noted by Lord Collins in *R (Sainsbury's Supermarkets Ltd) v Wolverhampton City Council* [2010] UKSC 20, '. . . the question of what is a material (or relevant) consideration is a question of law, but the weight to be given to it is a matter for the decision-maker', although the point needs to be added that the latter judgment would still ultimately be subject to the test of irrationality (see section 20.3). The controversial nature of relevant and irrelevant factors is illustrated by the area of financial considerations concerning the 'duties' of local authorities to provide services:

CASE EXAMPLE

R v Gloucestershire County Council, ex parte Barry *[1997] AC 584*

Barry's cleaning and laundry services had been withdrawn because of financial resources. The House of Lords held (by a majority) that, in effect, financial considerations (ie the cost of care and the availability of resources) might be proper factors for a local authority to consider in assessing an individual's need for a service under the Chronically Sick and Disabled Persons Act 1970. (See also *R (KM) v Cambridgeshire CC* [2012] UKSC 23, which considered the above case.)

In contrast, however, see the following case: *R v East Sussex County Council, ex parte Tandy* [1998] 2 All ER 769. In this case the House of Lords distinguished *ex parte Barry* above and held that the availability of resources was *not* a consideration in determining what constituted suitable education (in the case – special educational needs) under the Education Act 1993. In particular see Lord Browne-Wilkinson's insistence that 'the courts should be slow to downgrade' statutory duties into discretionary powers.

Finally, a case concerning the relevance of considerations in the context of the rule of law is the following case:

CASE EXAMPLE

R v Coventry City Council, ex parte Phoenix Aviation
and others *[1995] 3 All ER 37*

Judicial review applications were sought against public authorities operating air and sea ports as to whether lawfully, they could ban the transportation of livestock so as to avoid the consequences of unlawful protests by animal rights protestors. It was held that the air and sea ports had to remain open to traffic and the trade in livestock.

In terms of their concern about the actions of the protestors, Simon Brown LJ commented:

JUDGMENT

'One thread runs consistently throughout all the case law; the recognition that public authorities must beware of surrendering to the dictates of unlawful pressure groups. The implications of such surrender for the rule of law can hardly be exaggerated. . . . Tempting though it may sometimes be for public authorities to yield too readily to threats of disruption, they must expect the courts to review any such decision with particular rigour – this is not an area where they can be permitted a wide measure of discretion.'

20.2.6 Excess of jurisdiction

Jurisdiction refers to the power of a body to act, for example if a local authority is empowered to provide a service or exercise a discretion. In terms of jurisdiction it is possible for a public body to make either a:

- Mistake of fact or
- Mistake of law.

NB. It is fascinating to note the following academic comment made in respect of the Supreme Court case of *R (Jones) v First-Tier Tribunal* [2013] UKSC 19:

QUOTATION

'In a surprisingly frank judgment, the Court indicated that whether something is to be characterised as an issue of law or fact may turn, in part, upon to what extent close judicial scrutiny is felt to be warranted.'

M Elliott and R Thomas, *Public Law* (3rd edn, Oxford University Press, 2017), p 503.

Mistake of fact

In broad terms the courts in judicial review proceedings will not interfere when a body makes a mistake of fact (ie it gets factual details wrong). This is because:

- They take the view that the specified public body has been conferred with the responsibility of determining facts.
- Judges are experts in law and not facts.
- judicial review would become overwhelmed with cases involving public bodies that had made factual errors.

▦ The nature of judicial review proceedings is not particularly amenable to investigating disputed facts (eg there is a limited use of cross-examination).

There are, however, some mistakes of fact that the courts will subject to review:

▦ Precedent facts.
▦ Facts which have no supporting evidence.

Precedent facts

The courts will interfere where the fact is a 'precedent fact' or 'jurisdictional fact' in that its existence is necessary in order for the public body to act. In other words, certain facts must be correctly established before the body can act, as these facts are central to the decision-maker's power.

CASE EXAMPLE

R v Secretary of State for the Home Department, ex parte Khawaja *[1984] 1 AC 74*

The House of Lords held that the existence of the power to detain Khawaja (with a view to deportation) under the Immigration Act 1971 depended upon him being an 'illegal entrant'. This was a precedent fact which had to be satisfied and it was the duty of the court to inquire whether there had been sufficient/adequate evidence to justify and support the immigration officer's belief that entry into the United Kingdom had been illegal. The executive/government had to prove to the court the facts that the immigration officer had relied upon.

In other words, the existence of some facts is so fundamental that they trigger the public law power of a public body to act. Similarly, in *White and Collins v Minister of Health* [1939] 2 KB 838 a local authority was not permitted to compulsorily purchase land which was part of a park. In this case the land was factually held to be part of a park and so the compulsory purchase order was quashed. See also *R (Maiden Outdoor Advertising) v Lambeth LBC* [2003] EWHC 1224 (Admin).

More recently, in *R (FZ) v Croydon London Borough Council* [2011] EWCA Civ 59 it was held that in terms of the word 'child' in respect of the Children Act 1989:

JUDGMENT

'. . . the question whether a person is or is not a child, which depends entirely on the objective fact of the person's age, is subject to the ultimate determination of the courts. It is a fact precedent to the exercise of the local authority's powers under the 1989 Act and on that ground also is a question for the courts. If such a decision remains in dispute after its initial determination by the local authority, it is for the court to decide by judicial review.'

Sir Anthony May.

Similarly, see *R (A) v Croydon London Borough Council* [2009] UKSC 8.

Facts which have no supporting evidence

This concerns the position whereby a public body makes a decision regarding a fact for which there is objectively no supporting evidence to support that factual finding. Lord Denning MR, in *Ashbridge Investments Ltd v Minister of Housing and Local Government* [1965] 3 All ER 371, stated that:

JUDGMENT

'The Minister must himself decide the question of "house or not a house", just as he must decide "fit or unfit". The legislature has entrusted it to the Minister for decision . . . it seems to me that the court can interfere with the Minister's decision if he has acted on no evidence; or if he has come to a conclusion to which, on the evidence, he could not reasonably come.'

See also *Coleen Properties Ltd v Minister of Housing and Local Government* [1971] 1 WLR 433.

Finally, in the context of errors of fact, note should be taken of the developing area of errors of material fact (causing unfairness to a person) – see P Leyland and G Anthony, *Textbook on Administrative Law* (8th edn, Oxford University Press, 2016), p 315. In this context see *E v Secretary of State for the Home Department* [2004] EWCA Civ 49 and the associated article of C Brasted and J Marlow, 'Matters of fact' (2010) 160 NLJ 609.

Mistake of law

The courts will review (and so correct) material errors of law. An error of law refers to a body misinterpreting its legal powers by misunderstanding the statutory provisions which enable it to act.

According to Barnett (*Constitutional and Administrative Law* (12th edn, Routledge/ Taylor & Francis Group, 2017), p 653), one example of an error of law is the wrongful interpretation of a word to which a legal meaning has been attributed. Historically, the issue of the court reviewing errors of law has generated some highly complex case law, with the seminal case being *Anisminic Ltd* (1969):

CASE EXAMPLE

Anisminic Ltd v Foreign Compensation Commission *[1969] 2 AC 147*

Under the Foreign Compensation Act 1950 the Foreign Compensation Commission was charged with the responsibility of determining claims of compensation in respect of British property which had been seized or destroyed during the Suez crisis in 1956. An Order in Council in 1962 (SI 1962/2187) set out the criteria for eligibility for compensation. Anisminic was a British company (whose property had been sequestrated by the Egyptian authorities) which appeared to satisfy the criteria required to claim compensation. In 1957 Anisminic sold the sequestrated property to an Egyptian organisation. The Commission rejected Anisminic's claim for compensation. Section 4 of the Act stated that a determination of the Commission could not be called into question by a court of law. In other words, this was an 'ouster clause' (which ousted the jurisdiction of the courts) which left the final decision with the Commission.

The House of Lords, however, held that the Commission had, in determining Anisminic's claim, asked itself in law the wrong question by misconstruing its responsibilities under the 1962 Order in Council. In short, the Commission had (wrongly) asked whether the successor in title to Anisminic's property was British. Thus, the court held that the Commission had gone outside its jurisdiction and as a result the ouster clause of s 4 did not apply as the Commission had not made a 'determination', but instead had merely purported to do so.

The case indicates the resistance of the courts to 'ouster clauses' (see section 19.2.4).

Following *Anisminic Ltd* (1969), a number of cases (eg *Pearlman v Keepers and Governors of Harrow School* [1979] 1 QB 56, *Re Racal Communications Ltd* [1981] AC 374 and *R v Lord President of the Privy Council, ex parte Page* [1992] 3 WLR 1112) clarified the position of the courts in respect of errors of law. Today the courts are concerned that public bodies properly interpret their public law powers. It may well be that a statutory appeal is available where a body commits an error of law, but, failing that, the courts will now review errors of law regarding them as 'jurisdictional errors of law'.

Mistake of law and fact

In terms of a mistake of mixed law and fact, the courts will be unlikely to interfere unless it is an aberrant interpretation. For example, in *South Yorkshire Transport Ltd* (below) the House of Lords held that the Monopolies Commission's interpretation of the term 'in a substantial part of the United Kingdom' in the context of s 64 of the Fair Trading Act 1973 (a mixture of law and fact) would be upheld as it was within the permissible field of judgement open to it. Lord Mustill in this case noted that:

JUDGMENT

'The criterion so established may itself be so imprecise that different decision-makers, each acting rationally, might reach differing conclusions when applying it to the facts of a given case. In such a case the court is entitled to substitute its own opinion for that of the person to whom the decision has been entrusted only if the decision is so aberrant that it cannot be classed as rational.'

South Yorkshire Transport Ltd and another v Monopolies and Mergers Commission and another [1993] 1 All ER 289.

ACTIVITY

Self-test questions

1. What is meant by a decision-maker abusing his discretion?
2. What is the difference between a mistake of:
   - fact
   - law or
   - a mixed question of fact and law?

20.2.7 Breach of the European Convention on Human Rights

As a result of the Human Rights Act 1998, it is now possible for a claimant to seek judicial review of a public law body on the basis that it has violated their rights set out in the European Convention. Under s 6 of the Act, a new statutory obligation is placed on public bodies that they must act consistently with Convention rights. Any discretion a public decision-maker has must now be exercised in line with the Convention (see Chapter 17). If a public body infringes these rights, the claimant (as a victim under s 7) can seek judicial review on the ground of illegality: namely, that the public body has acted illegally by infringing the European Convention. Although in general terms the Human Rights Act 1998 has added a new aspect of illegality, where however Art 6/the right to a fair hearing is raised, this will be subsumed under the third ground of review: procedural impropriety.

A case involving a violation of the Convention is *R (Purdy) v DPP* [2009] UKHL 45, in which the House of Lords held that Purdy's right to respect for private life under Art 8 had been breached by the DPP's failure to provide a specific policy as to the factors which would be taken into account in deciding whether a person would be prosecuted for aiding suicide contrary to s 2 of the Suicide Act 1961. In a more recent case, in *R (BBC) v Secretary of State for Justice* [2012] EWHC 13 (Admin) the BBC successfully obtained judicial review of the decision of the Secretary of State for Justice to refuse permission for a face-to-face interview with A (who was detained in prison) as being a violation of Art 10 – freedom of expression – and therefore unlawful by virtue of s 6 of the Human Rights Act 1998.

KEY FACTS

The ground of illegality	
Simple *ultra vires*	Acting beyond and exceeding legal powers (*Fulham Corporation* (1921), *ex parte Witham* (1997)).
Wrongful delegation of power	Public law powers should not be unlawfully delegated (*Vine* (1957)). Government ministers, however, typically confer power on officials to take decisions on their behalf (*Carltona Ltd* (1943)).
Improper purpose	Power should be used for its proper and lawful purpose (*Congreve* (1976)).
Abuse of discretion	A public law discretion should not be fettered (*British Oxygen Co Ltd* (1971)). Relevant factors must be considered (*ex parte Singh* (1986)). Irrelevant factors must not be taken into consideration (*ex parte Venables* (1997)).
Excess of jurisdiction	Generally the courts will not interfere with a mistake of fact unless it is a precedent fact (*White and Collins* (1939)) or it lacks supporting evidence (*Ashbridge Investments Ltd* (1965)). The courts will intervene in order to rectify a mistake of law (*Anisminic Ltd* (1969)).
Breach of the European Convention on Human Rights	Section 6 of the Human Rights Act 1998 requires public bodies to act in line with the European Convention on Human Rights (*Purdy* (2009)).

20.3 The ground of irrationality

20.3.1 Origins and definition

In general terms, an Act of Parliament will not state expressly that a statutory power conferred on a public law body must be exercised 'rationally'. The courts, however, imply that Parliament never intended such a power to be used unreasonably or in an irrational way. The ground of irrationality, therefore, is concerned with a public body acting strictly within its legal powers (ie within the four corners of its powers), but arriving at a decision which is totally unreasonable. In his reclassification of the grounds of review, Lord Diplock, in *Council of Civil Service Unions v Minister for the Civil Service* [1985] 1 AC 374, described irrationality as follows:

JUDGMENT

'By "irrationality" I mean what can by now be succinctly referred to as "Wednesbury unreasonableness". . . . It applies to a decision which is so outrageous in its defiance of logic or of accepted moral standards that no sensible person who had applied his mind to the question to be decided could have arrived at it.'

Lord Diplock's reference to *Wednesbury* unreasonableness is derived from the following case:

CASE EXAMPLE

Associated Provincial Picture Houses Limited v Wednesbury Corporation *[1948] 1 KB 223*

Under s 1 of the Sunday Entertainments Act 1932 a local authority had the power to grant licences for cinema performances on a Sunday 'subject to such conditions as the authority thinks fit to impose'. Wednesbury Corporation granted Associated Provincial Picture Houses Ltd a licence to provide Sunday performances subject to the condition that 'no children under the age of fifteen years shall be admitted to any entertainment whether accompanied by an adult or not'. The claimants sought a declaration that this condition was unreasonable and *ultra vires*.

The Court of Appeal held that Wednesbury Corporation had not acted *ultra vires* or unreasonably in setting this condition. Lord Greene MR noted that:

JUDGMENT

'It is true to say that, if a decision on a competent matter is so unreasonable that no reasonable authority could ever have come to it, then the courts can interfere. That, I think, is quite right; but to prove a case of that kind would require something overwhelming and, in this case, the facts do not come anywhere near anything of that kind.'

In other words, acting unreasonably (*Wednesbury* unreasonableness) means that a body has come to a decision which no reasonable body could have come to. In short this would have to: 'be something so absurd that no sensible person could ever dream that it lay within the powers of the authority' (Lord Greene MR). It is often forgotten in this case that the court held that the Wednesbury Corporation had imposed a condition which a reasonable corporation *could* have imposed. In the *GCHQ* case, Lord Diplock redefined this narrow form of unreasonableness (*Wednesbury* unreasonableness) as 'irrationality'. More recently, Lord Steyn in *Boddington v British Transport Police* [1999] 2 AC 143 stated that a rational decision was one 'within the range of reasonable decisions open to a decision-maker'.

ACTIVITY

Self-test question

Do you think that a modern court would hold the condition set by Wednesbury Corporation to be rational?

20.3.2 The controversial nature of irrationality

Irrationality is, historically, the most controversial ground of judicial review because, as indicated earlier at section 19.2.2, the nature of judicial review is that it concerns the decision-making process rather than the decision itself:

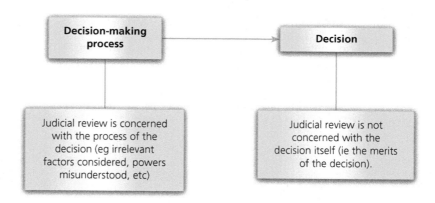

Figure 20.4 Judicial review and the decision-making process

The difficulty with irrationality, however, is that in essence it challenges the *decision* itself: namely *a decision which no reasonable decision-maker could have made*. Thus, it could be argued that this infringes the separation of powers as Parliament has conferred the power to make the decision on the public body and not the courts.

The justification for irrationality is on the following basis:

(i) For a decision to be irrational, by definition, the decision-making process is likely to have been faulty.

(ii) The courts set a very high threshold for irrationality. A court cannot interfere with a decision with which they simply disagree, but only if *no* reasonable body could have come to that decision. As an irrational decision needs to be, in effect, an absurd one, there are few examples of successful challenges on this ground.

(iii) The courts in interfering with an irrational decision, are only exercising a secondary judgment. The public body exercises the primary judgment and is only subject to a 'second look' (ie a secondary judgment) by the courts in the event that the decision is absurd.

It appears that the level of judicial intensity in looking at 'irrational decisions' depends on the context. In *R v Secretary of State for Education and Employment, ex parte Begbie* [2000] 1 WLR 1115 Laws LJ described it as 'a sliding scale of review, more or less intrusive according to the nature and gravity of what is at stake'. For example, in the context of politically controversial policy areas such as national security or national economic considerations, the courts are reluctant to interfere short of a minister taking leave of his political senses (known as *Super-Wednesbury*): *Nottinghamshire County Council v Secretary of State for the Environment* (1986) (see section 14.2.6). Indeed, as noted by Sir Thomas Bingham MR in *R v Ministry of Defence, ex parte Smith* [1996] 1 All ER 257:

JUDGMENT

'The greater the policy content of a decision, and the more remote the subject matter of a decision from ordinary judicial experience, the more hesitant the court must necessarily be in holding a decision to be irrational. . . . Where decisions of a policy-laden, esoteric or security-based nature are in issue even greater caution than normal must be shown in applying the test, but the test itself is sufficiently flexible to cover all situations.'

In contrast, in respect of human rights, the courts provide a more intensive look. Lord Bridge in *Bugdaycay v Secretary of State for the Home Department* [1987] 1 AC 514 pointed out that:

JUDGMENT

'The most fundamental of all human rights is the individual's right to life and when an administrative decision under challenge is said to be one which may put the applicant's life at risk, the basis of the decision must surely call for the most anxious scrutiny.'

Similarly, in *ex parte Smith* (see above and section 20.4.2) the Court of Appeal stated that the human rights context of a judicial review application was important and that the greater the interference with human rights, the more justification the court would require on the part of the decision-maker (see also *R v Secretary of State for the Home Department, ex parte McQuillan* [1995] 4 All ER 400).

In any event, according to Sir Thomas Bingham MR in *ex parte Smith*, the test of irrationality was sufficiently flexible to adapt to the context of the application (whether this involved a policy matter or fundamental human rights).

■ Today in the light of the operation of the Human Rights Act 1998 there is some academic debate over whether the ground of irrationality still exists as a separate free-standing ground of review, or whether it has been subsumed under the doctrine of proportionality (see section 20.4.5).

20.3.3 Irrationality in practice

Although the ground of irrationality has historically been raised by claimants, it is not usually successful. This is because the threshold which needs to be crossed is set at a very high level by the courts. Indeed, Lord Greene MR in *Associated Provincial Picture Houses Ltd* (1948) made reference to the example provided by an earlier judge which indicates the level of absurdity required. In *Short v Poole Corporation* [1926] 1 Ch 66 Warrington LJ commented that:

JUDGMENT

'I suppose that if the defendants were to dismiss a teacher because she had red hair, or for some equally frivolous and foolish reason, the Court would declare the attempted dismissal to be void.'

An unsuccessful example of the ground being raised is as follows:

R v Home Secretary, ex parte Brind *[1991] 1 AC 696*

The House of Lords held that the minister's decision to direct broadcasters to refrain from broadcasting words spoken by individuals representing organisations proscribed under terrorism legislation, was not unreasonable/irrational.

Similarly, the argument of irrationality failed in *ex parte Smith* (1996) (see section 20.4.2).

Detailed below, however, are some recent cases where the ground of irrationality was successful:

- In *R (Rogers) v Swindon NHS Primary Care Trust* [2006] EWCA Civ 392, the Court of Appeal held that the Trust's policy in relation to the funding of a drug was irrational.
- In *R (Technoprint Plc & Anor) v Leeds City Council* [2007] EWHC 638 (Admin), the granting of retrospective planning permission relating to industrial filters subject to the implementation of noise attenuation measures was deemed irrational by the Administrative Court.
- An interesting case in relation to the findings of the Ombudsman is *Bradley* (2008) (see section 21.3.4), in which the Court of Appeal held that the Secretary of State for Work and Pensions had acted irrationally in rejecting a finding of maladministration by the Ombudsman.
- In *Re Duffy* [2008] UKHL 4 the House of Lords held that two appointments made to the Northern Ireland Parades Commission were ones which a reasonable Secretary of State for Northern Ireland could not have made.
- In *R (Houchin) v Secretary of State for Justice* [2010] EWHC 454 (Admin) the Secretary of State's rejection of a Parole Board's recommendation was irrational.
- In *R (Litvinenko) v Secretary of State for the Home Department* [2014] EWHC 194 (Admin) it was held that the Secretary of State had provided no rational reasons for refusing to establish an inquiry under the Inquiries Act 2005 (see later at section 21.2.3).

NB. Most recently, in relation to a local authority, see the case of *R (OK) v Barking and Dagenham LBC* [2017] EWHC 2092 (Admin).

20.4 The ground of proportionality

20.4.1 Origins and definition

In 1984, when Lord Diplock reclassified the grounds of judicial review in *Council of Civil Service Unions v Minister for the Civil Service* [1985] 1 AC 374, he confined them to three grounds:

JUDGMENT

'That is not to say that further development on a case by case basis may not in course of time add further grounds. I have in mind particularly the possible adoption in the future of the principle of "proportionality".'

A test of proportionality is as follows:

QUOTATION

'Proportionality works on the assumption that administrative action ought not go beyond that which is necessary to achieve its desired result (in everyday terms, that one should not use a sledge-hammer to crack a nut) and, in contrast to irrationality, is often understood to bring courts much closer to reviewing the merits of a decision.'

P Leyland and G Anthony, *Textbook on Administrative Law*
(8th edn, Oxford University Press, 2016), p 334.

In other words, proportionality considers the aim of the decision-maker and whether the means to achieve that objective are proportionate.

For example, suppose with the aim of maintaining public order under the (imaginary) Public Order Act 2022 the Home Secretary chooses to ban *all* public demonstrations for two years. Although the government would inevitably succeed in securing the maintenance of public order (the objective), at what cost to human rights (eg the right to protest) has this been achieved? In short, the Home Secretary would be acting disproportionately (ie using a sledge-hammer to crack a nut).

Although historically proportionality has not been a ground of judicial review, it is a principle well known in other European countries (eg Germany) as well as in international law (both European Union and Convention laws – see Chapters 15 and 16, respectively). However, in *R (Lumsdon) v Legal Services Board* [2015] UKSC 41 the Supreme Court pointed out that the principle of proportionality is not applied or expressed in the same way under the laws of the European Convention and the European Union.

According to Michael Fordham proportionality is a contextual doctrine and that:

QUOTATION

'Its great virtue is as a structured approach, under which the State must convincingly demonstrate that the response in question is appropriate and necessary to achieve a legitimate aim, strikes a proper balance and avoids imposing excessive burdens.'

M Fordham, *Judicial Review Handbook* (6th edn, Hart, 2012), p 427.

20.4.2 Proportionality and irrationality compared

The tests of proportionality and irrationality are different legal tests. This is neatly illustrated in the *ex parte Smith* litigation:

CASE EXAMPLE

R v Ministry of Defence, ex parte Smith *[1996] 1 All ER 257*

The Ministry of Defence had a policy which prevented homosexual men and women from serving in the armed forces. This policy required the discharge of those of homosexual orientation. As a result, three gay men and a lesbian were discharged and they sought judicial review of the policy on, *inter alia*, the ground that it was irrational.

The Court of Appeal held that in terms of irrationality the greater the interference with human rights, the more justification would be required. Nevertheless, it could not be said that the policy was irrational – for one thing Parliament had supported the policy.

Although the claimants were unsuccessful domestically, subsequently they petitioned the European Court of Human Rights:

The claimants successfully contended that the MoD policy violated Art 8 – the right to a private sexual life. The European Court held in both cases that the blanket policy which required automatic discharge on the basis of sexual orientation could not be justified as it was a disproportionate interference with their right to a private life.

In short, the domestic and international tests were different:

▪ In the Court of Appeal the issue was one of irrationality: Could a reasonable body have devised that policy?
▪ In the European Court of Human Rights the issue was one of proportionality: Was the interference with the claimant's right to a private life justified and in proportion?

Thus, the proportionality test is much stricter and more exacting than the irrationality test. It is easier for a public body to show that its decision was rational (as an irrational decision needed to be effectively absurd), than it is to show that its decision was in proportion (ie it was a balanced one which was a proportionate method of achieving a lawful objective).

The test of proportionality, therefore, has a controversial element to it for the purposes of judicial review. It requires the court, in effect, to *assess the quality* of the decision made and to determine if the appropriate balance between means and objective has been achieved. It is for this reason, that Lords Ackner and Roskill were particularly averse to the introduction of proportionality as a ground of review in *ex parte Brind* (1991) (see section 20.3.3). Nevertheless, as a result of the Human Rights Act 1998, the principle of proportionality is now part of judicial review.

NB. In *R (H) v A City Council* [2011] EWCA Civ 403, Munby LJ stressed that proportionality and irrationality were 'fundamentally different'.

20.4.3 Proportionality pre-Human Rights Act?

Although historically the courts were unwilling to recognise a separate ground of review labelled proportionality, to some extent the concept was not unknown in our law *before* the advent of the Human Rights Act 1998.

▪ European Community law (now called European Union law) used the principle and so our judges were required to apply it in the context of European law:

R v Chief Constable of Sussex, ex parte International Trader's Ferry Ltd *[1999] 2 AC 418*

Animal rights groups protested against ferry operators carrying livestock cargo on their ferries. Due to resource implications, the Chief Constable of Sussex Police decided to reduce the level of policing provided. International Trader's Ferry Ltd sought judicial review on the ground, *inter alia*, that it violated European law (Art 34 of the Treaty of Rome – as it was then – as being a quantitative restriction on exports between Member States).

The House of Lords held that, assuming Art 34 could be enforced by the claimant, the actions of the Chief Constable were not disproportionate to the restrictions which they imposed. The actions were therefore within the public policy exemption of Art 36 (as it was then known).

It is interesting to note that a claim that the Chief Constable had acted irrationally also failed.

- In general, it was accepted by the courts that if a decision was lacking any proportionality at all, it was likely to be irrational in any event. Thus, in *R v Barnsley Metropolitan Borough Council, ex parte Hook* [1976] 3 All ER 452, the majority of the Court of Appeal held that the punishment imposed on a market trader (the loss of his licence) was altogether excessive and out of proportion.
- In *ex parte Leech* (1993) (see section 20.2.2) the Court of Appeal held that the more fundamental the right interfered with by a rule (in this case r 33) and the more drastic that interference, the stronger the justification would have to be. This is, in effect, a kind of proportionality in practice. Similarly, see *ex parte Smith* (1996) (section 20.4.2).

20.4.4 Proportionality and the Human Rights Act 1998

The Human Rights Act 1998 gave further effect to the rights of the European Convention in domestic law. This meant that the domestic courts must follow the legal reasoning adopted in Strasbourg, which includes the principle of proportionality. For example, as indicated earlier (sections 6.7.4, 17.5 and 17.11.1), in *A and others v Secretary of State for the Home Department* (2004), the House of Lords held that s 23 of the Anti-terrorism, Crime and Security Act 2001 was a disproportionate response and not strictly required by the exigencies of the situation.

In *R v Secretary of State for the Home Department ex parte Daly* [2001] UKHL 26 Lord Steyn made the following comments concerning proportionality:

JUDGMENT

'First, the doctrine of proportionality may require the reviewing court to assess the balance which the decision maker has struck, not merely whether it is within the range of rational or reasonable decisions. Secondly, the proportionality test may go further than the traditional grounds of review inasmuch as it may require attention to be directed to the relative weight accorded to interests and considerations.'

NB. For the full quotation see section 17.5.

ACTIVITY

Exercise

Define the terms irrationality and proportionality and explain the difference between them.

20.4.5 The demise of irrationality?

There is currently a debate over whether irrationality continues to exist as a ground of review, or whether with the establishment of the Human Rights Act 1998, it has been overtaken by (and subsumed under) proportionality. In *R (Association of British Civilian Internees: Far East Region) v Secretary of State for Defence* [2003] EWCA Civ 473 the Court of Appeal held that the principle of proportionality had *not* replaced irrationality where no European Community (now Union) or Convention issues were raised. In this context, however, Dyson LJ giving judgment for the court made the following comments:

JUDGMENT

'The *Wednesbury* test is moving closer to proportionality and in some cases it is not possible to see any daylight between the two tests. . . . Although we did not hear argument on the point, we have difficulty in seeing what justification there now is for retaining the *Wednesbury* test. But we consider that it is not for this court to perform its burial rites. The continuing existence of the *Wednesbury* test has been acknowledged by the House of Lords on more than one occasion.'

Although it appears that irrationality is still a free-standing ground of review, to what extent this will be the case in the future is debatable. According to Craig, writing in 2009:

QUOTATION

'It remains to be seen whether the *Wednesbury* test continues to exist together with proportionality, or whether the latter takes over as a general, independent head of review. It may be that the *Wednesbury* test will survive and continue to be used in cases where there is no link with EC law, and where this is no claim under the HRA. *Wednesbury* may however cease to operate as an independent test in its own right. It will be increasingly difficult, or impractical, for courts to apply different tests to different allegations made in an application for judicial review.'

'Grounds for Judicial Review: Substantive Control Over Discretion' in D Feldman (ed) *English Public Law* (2nd edn, Oxford University Press, 2009), p 729.

It is of interest to note that more recently Lord Mance in *Kennedy v Information Commission* [2014] UKSC 20 commented that there was no longer an insistence 'on the uniform application of the rigid test of irrationality'. On the principle of proportionality in English law, see Lord Sumption's observations in *Pham v Secretary of State for the Home Department* [2015] UKSC 19. In a decision later that year, Lord Neuberger in *R (Keyu) v Secretary of State for Foreign and Commonwealth Affairs* [2015] UKSC 69 (for the facts, see later at section 21.2.4) pointed out that the appellants had raised the argument as to whether Wednesbury rationality/irrationality of executive decisions should be replaced by proportionality:

JUDGMENT

'It would not be appropriate for a five-justice panel of this court to accept, or indeed to reject, this argument, which potentially has implications which are profound in constitutional terms and very wide in applicable scope. . . . The move from rationality to proportionality, as urged by the appellants, would appear to have potentially profound and far reaching consequences, because it would involve the court considering the merits of the decision at issue: in particular, it would require the courts to consider the balance which the decision-maker has struck between competing interests (often a public interest against a private interest) and the weight to be accorded to each such interest . . . However, it is important to emphasise that it is no part of the appellants' case that the court would thereby displace the relevant member of the executive as the primary decision-maker. . .'.

Nevertheless, he did recognise that in some cases 'the domestic law may already be moving away to some extent from the irrationality test'.

The ground of irrationality/proportionality	
Irrationality	A decision which no reasonable body could have come to: *Associated Provincial Picture Houses Limited* (1948). The test is flexible enough to involve: • a less intense review in the context of politically controversial policy areas (*Nottinghamshire County Council v Secretary of State for the Environment* (1986)) • a more intensive review in the context of human rights (*ex parte Smith* (1996)).
Proportionality	Proportionality considers the aim of the decision-maker and whether the means to achieve that objective are proportionate (see the Human Rights Act 1998 and European Union law).

20.5 The ground of procedural impropriety

20.5.1 Definition

Lord Diplock in *Council of Civil Service Unions v Minister for the Civil Service* [1985] 1 AC 374 stated:

JUDGMENT

'I have described the third head as "procedural impropriety" rather than failure to observe basic rules of natural justice or failure to act with procedural fairness towards the person who will be affected by the decision. This is because susceptibility to judicial review under this head covers also failure by an administrative tribunal to observe procedural rules that are expressly laid down in the legislative instrument by which its jurisdiction is conferred, even where such failure does not involve any denial of natural justice.'

Procedural impropriety can be subdivided into the following:

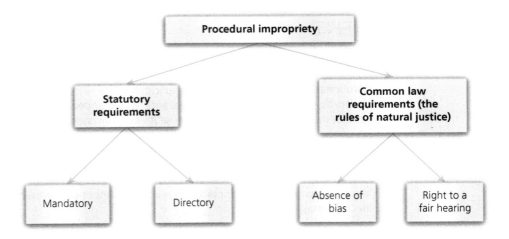

Figure 20.5 Procedural impropriety.

In other words, a public decision-maker will breach this ground of review if he ignores either the requirements of a statute or the principles of natural justice.

20.5.2 Statutory requirements

The courts can subject a public body to review if it has failed to comply with statutory procedural requirements (eg before X can take a decision, X must consult A, B and C). The point must be made at the outset, however, that not all breaches of statutory requirements are the same. Historically, therefore, the courts have distinguished between two types of statutory requirements:

- a mandatory requirement (an essential requirement which will invalidate the action if not followed);
- a directory requirement (a less important requirement which is not fatal, as it is a minor technical defect or a minor detail).

In a sense this is analogous to the classification of contractual terms into conditions (very important) and warranties (less important).

The above dichotomy begs the question as to which statutory requirements are mandatory and which are directory. This is essentially a question of statutory interpretation for the courts to determine using the following factors:

- The Act itself (rather unusually) may expressly state the consequences of a breach of a statutory requirement.
- In the absence of the above, what did Parliament intend to be the result in the event of a failure to follow a procedural requirement?
- Were obligatory terms such as 'must' used?
- What is the purpose of the Act and the requirement? Who or what is it intended to protect and for what reason?
- Does the requirement affect individual rights?

In *London & Clydeside Estates Ltd v Aberdeen District Council* [1980] 1 WLR 182 Lord Hailsham LC stated that, although the terms mandatory and directory may be helpful, he emphasised that the courts should not adopt an overly rigid set of legal categories in this regard.

JUDGMENT

'It may be that what the courts are faced with is not so much a stark choice of alternatives but a spectrum of possibilities in which one compartment or description fades gradually into another.'

In more recent years, Lord Woolf MR has noted that the question of whether a requirement was mandatory or directory was only at most a first step before, in the majority of cases, other questions have to be asked which are likely to be of greater use/assistance:

JUDGMENT

'The questions which are likely to arise are as follows:
   Is the statutory requirement fulfilled if there has been substantial compliance with the requirement and, if so, has there been substantial compliance in the case in issue even though there has not been strict compliance? (The substantial compliance question).

> Is the non-compliance capable of being waived, and if so, has it, or can it and should it be waived in this particular case? (The discretionary question) . . .
>
> If it is not capable of being waived or is not waived then what is the consequence of the non-compliance? (The consequences question).
>
> Which questions arise will depend upon the facts of the case and the nature of the particular requirement.'
>
> *R v Secretary of State for the Home Department, ex parte Jeyeanthan* [2000] 1 WLR 354.

Also see *R v Soneji* [2005] UKHL 49, in which Lord Steyn stated that the rigid mandatory/directory distinction had outlived its usefulness and instead 'the emphasis ought to be on the consequences of non-compliance, and posing the question whether Parliament can fairly be taken to have intended total invalidity.' In a more recent case (applying this approach), a failure in a notice – served by the Secretary of State on the claimant – to inform him that he was entitled to a right of appeal (in-country), rendered it invalid and so was quashed (*E 1/(OS Russia) v Secretary of State for the Home Department* [2012] EWCA Civ 357). In contrast, see *R (Garland) v Secretary of State for Justice* [2011] EWCA Civ 1335, where Hughes LJ stated that Parliament had not intended that *any* non-compliance with rule 53(1) of the Prison Rules 1999, 'however minimal and however devoid of prejudicial effect, should render invalid everything which follows.'

Historically the case law has indicated the following principles:

A requirement to consult

This is generally viewed as a mandatory and important requirement:

CASE EXAMPLE

Agricultural, Horticultural and Forestry Industry Training Board v Aylesbury Mushrooms Ltd *[1972] 1 WLR 190*

As the Industrial Training Act 1964 provided for prior consultation by the Ministry of Labour with interested organisations, and the Mushroom Growers Association had not actually been consulted, a 1966 Order (establishing a training board imposing a levy) had no application to them. Consultation was treated as a mandatory requirement in relation to the Mushroom Growers' Association.

CASE EXAMPLE

R (Moseley) v Haringey London Borough Council *[2014] UKSC 56*

The Local Government Finance Act 1992 (para 3(c) of Sch 1A) provided that before making a council tax reduction scheme a local authority must 'consult such other persons as it considers are likely to have an interest in the operation of the scheme'. In other words, this was a statutory obligation to consult. The Supreme Court held that the consultation exercise in this case was unlawful. In particular, Lord Reed stated that the purpose of this statutory duty of consultation must:

JUDGMENT

'be to ensure public participation in the local authority's decision-making process. . . . Meaningful public participation in this particular decision-making process, in a context

with which the general public cannot be expected to be familiar, requires that the con-
sultees should be provided not only with information about the draft scheme, but also
with an outline of the realistic alternatives, and an indication of the main reasons for the
authority's adoption of the draft scheme.'

However, although the Supreme Court held that the council's consultation had been
unlawful, it nevertheless declined to require it to carry out a fresh consultation exercise as this would not be in proportion given that the scheme had been in operation.

For another example of a breach of a statutory duty to consult, see *R (Smith) v
North Eastern Derbyshire Primary Care Trust* [2006] EWCA Civ 1291 in relation to s 11
of the Health and Social Care Act 2001.

▨ **A requirement to notify of the right to appeal**

CASE EXAMPLE

Agricultural, Horticultural and Forestry Industry Training
Board v Kent *[1970] 1 All 340*

The Court of Appeal held that the provisions of the Industrial Training Levy (Agricultural,
Horticultural and Forestry) Order 1967 were mandatory. As a consequence an assessment
notice (indicating a levy to be paid) must state clearly the address of the training board in
order that an individual (employer) may serve a notice of appeal.

See also the case of *London & Clydeside Estates Ltd* (1980) above.

▨ **Time limits**

According to Wade and Forsyth (*Administrative Law* (11th edn, Oxford University
Press, 2014), p 188), 'It has often been held that an act may be validly done after the
expiry of a statutory time limit', however time limits may be mandatory if they have
special importance or 'the rights of other persons depend on them'. For an example,
see *Howard v Bodington* (1877) 2 PD 203 concerning the Public Worship Regulation
Act 1874.

20.5.3 Common law requirements:
Nemo judex in re sua

JUDGMENT

'The rule against bias is one thing. The right to be heard is another. Those two rules are
the essential characteristics of what is often called natural justice. They are the twin pillars
supporting it.'

Lord Denning, *Kanda v Government of Malaya* [1962] AC 322.

Thus, the rules of natural justice (in modern times now known as the duty to act
fairly) can be subdivided into the following:

▨ *Nemo judex in re sua* (directly below).
▨ *Audi alteram partem* (see section 20.5.4).

Natural justice is a substantial area in its own right and accordingly below is a very
basic outline of the subject.

Nemo judex in re sua

(No man should be a judge in his own cause/the decision-maker must be unbiased.)

In essence, the rule against bias can be subdivided in the following way:

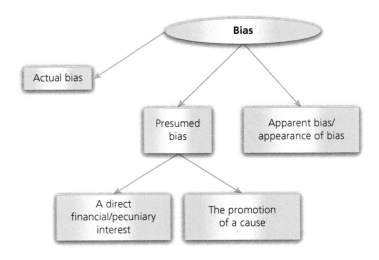

Figure 20.6 Bias.

Adapted from the categorisation used by J Auburn, J Moffett and A Sharland, *Judicial Review* (Oxford University Press, 2013), Chapter 8.

Actual bias

It is self-evidently a breach of natural justice/fairness if the decision-maker (administrative or judicial) is *actually* biased. For example, an immigration official deports X because he has taken a personal dislike to him. Cases of actual bias are, for obvious reasons, rare. Actual bias will result in automatic disqualification.

Presumed bias: a direct financial/pecuniary interest

As no man should be a judge in his own cause, if an administrative or judicial decision-maker has a direct financial/pecuniary interest in the outcome of the proceedings this leads to the automatic disqualification of the decision-maker:

CASE EXAMPLE

Dimes v The Proprietors of the Grand Junction Canal *(1852) 3 HLC 759*

In this case the Lord Chancellor (Lord Cottenham) affirmed on appeal the Vice-Chancellor's decree that Dimes could not obstruct the Grand Junction Canal's land. It transpired that the Lord Chancellor held shares in the Grand Junction Canal. The House of Lords reversed the Lord Chancellor's decree and Lord Campbell stated that:

JUDGMENT

'No one can suppose that Lord Cottenham could be, in the remotest degree, influenced by the interest that he had in this concern; but, my Lords, it is of the last importance that the maxim that no man is to be a judge in his own cause should be held sacred.'

In terms of a local councillor, see *R v Hendon RDC, ex parte Chorley* [1933] 2 KB 696.

Presumed bias: the promotion of a cause (ie non-financial interest)

The seminal case in this respect is *ex parte Pinochet Ugarte* (2000) (see section 13.4.2). This case concerned the connection between one of the judges in the case (Lord Hoffmann) and Amnesty International which had joined the case as a party seeking Pinochet's extradition for alleged human rights violations. The House of Lords held that Lord Hoffmann should have been automatically disqualified from the case and so set aside its own decision and reheard the matter. According to Ouseley J in *Bovis Homes Ltd v New Forest District Council* [2002] EWHC 483 (Admin), referring to the *Pinochet* case, he said 'automatic disqualification arising from a non-pecuniary interest is peculiar to those exercising judicial functions'.

Apparent bias/appearance of bias

The modern test for apparent bias (in respect of both administrative and judicial decision-makers) is set out by Lord Hope in *Porter v Magill* [2001] UKHL 67.

JUDGMENT

'The question is whether the fair-minded and informed observer, having considered the facts, would conclude that there was a real possibility that the tribunal was biased.'

This category involves various forms of interest and below are some cases in which apparent/appearance of bias was successfully raised:

CASE EXAMPLE

Metropolitan Properties Co (FGC) v Lannon *[1969] 1 QB 577*

In this case, landlords, Metropolitan Properties Co contended that the Chairman of a rent assessment committee should be disqualified on the ground of bias. In short, the Chairman had acted for and advised Regency Lodge tenants in a dispute with their landlords (who were a company in the same group as Metropolitan Properties). He had also advised his father, a Regency Lodge tenant, about a fair rent.

The Court of Appeal held that the decision of the committee must be quashed (and remitted to another committee) because of the connection between the Chairman and the Regency Lodge tenants. This connection was such as to give the reasonable impression that the Chairman was biased – though this was an appearance of bias as there was no actual bias.

CASE EXAMPLE

Hannam v Bradford City Council *[1970] 2 All ER 690*

Hannam was a schoolmaster who absented himself and refused to return to work. In December 1967 his employment was terminated by a meeting of the school governors. In January 1968 a council staff sub-committee met to consider whether the council should prohibit the dismissal. It decided not to do so. Three of the members of the sub-committee were governors, although they had not attended the meeting in December 1967.

The Court of Appeal held that as the three governors had sat on the staff sub-committee this gave rise to the possibility of bias. They did not cease to be part of the school governors when they sat on the sub-committee and it did not matter that they had not personally attended the meeting of the governors.

JUDGMENT

'No man can be a judge of his own cause. The governors did not, on donning their sub-committee hats, cease to be an integral part of the body whose action was being impugned, and it made no difference that they did not personally attend the governors' meeting.'

Sachs LJ.

CASE EXAMPLE

R (Gardner) v Harrogate Borough Council *[2008] EWHC 2942 (Admin)*

The court held that *a fair-minded and informed observer/person would conclude that there was a real possibility of bias* (ie the test in *Porter* above) when planning permission was granted where the Chairman of the planning committee had cast the deciding vote (contrary to the recommendation of the planning officers) in relation to a planning application made by a fellow councillor who was seen as an acquaintance. The grant of planning permission was quashed.

The issue of predetermination

QUOTATION

'Bias and predetermination are conceptually different. Bias is concerned with conflicts of interest, whereas predetermination concerns a decision-maker adjudicating on a matter in relation to which he or she does not have an open mind.'

J Auburn, J Moffett and A Sharland, *Judicial Review* (Oxford University Press, 2013), p 212.

In addition, they point out that the test to be applied to judicial and administrative decision-makers is:

QUOTATION

'would a fair-minded and informed observer, knowing the facts, think that there was a real possibility that the decision-maker had predetermined the matter to be decided' (para 8.90).

In the context of local authorities (ie administrative decision-makers), see the following two cases: *R (Lewis) v Redcar and Cleveland BC* [2008] EWCA Civ 746 and *R (Persimmon Homes Ltd) v Vale of Glamorgan Council* [2010] EWHC 535 (Admin).

In addition, the intention behind s 25 of the Localism Act 2011 was to 'clarify' the common law concept of predetermination in relation to councillors:

SECTION

s 25 Prior indications of view of a matter not to amount to predetermination etc
(2) A decision-maker is not to be taken to have had, or to have appeared to have had, a closed mind when making the decision just because –

(a) the decision-maker had previously done anything that directly or indirectly indicated what view the decision-maker took, or would or might take, in relation to a matter, and

(b) the matter was relevant to the decision.

NB. For something *not* amounting to 'predetermination' under the Act, see *R (IM Properties Development Ltd) v Lichfield DC* [2014] EWHC 2440 (Admin).

ACTIVITY

Self-test questions

1. What is the consequence of failing to follow the procedural requirements of a statute?
2. Explain the different ways in which a decision-maker could be biased.

20.5.4 Common law requirements: *Audi alteram partem*

Audi alteram partem
(Hear the other side/the right to a fair hearing.)

Natural justice (and now Art 6 of the European Convention) provides minimum standards of fairness in respect of public decision-making. Historically, *Ridge v Baldwin* (below) and the subsequent case of *In re HK (An Infant)* [1967] 2 QB 617 acted as a watershed in the development of the right to a fair hearing.

CASE EXAMPLE

Ridge v Baldwin *[1964] AC 40*

Ridge, a Chief Constable, had been dismissed from his office by a watch committee. The House of Lords held that this decision was null and void as the committee had not followed the rules of natural justice. They had not informed Ridge of the charges against him nor had they given him the opportunity to be heard.

It has been argued that this decision:

QUOTATION

'liberated natural justice from the constraints which had been imposed upon it by earlier cases, placing a renewed emphasis on the impact of administrative decisions on individuals' rights and interests.'

M Elliott and J Varuhas, *Administrative Law, Text and Materials*
(5th edn, Oxford University Press, 2017), p 375.

The exact requirements of natural justice (in modern parlance – the duty to act fairly/in fairness) will vary according to the context:

- the body involved
- the nature of the decision and
- the issue at stake.

NB. Art 6 of the European Convention applies only to 'criminal charges' or 'the determination of civil rights'.

In essence, the requirements of a fair hearing embody the following elements:

- The knowledge of the charge/allegations.
- An indication of adverse evidence.
- Notice of the hearing.
- The right to submit a defence (in writing or orally).
- The right to challenge/cross-examine adverse evidence (in writing or orally).
- The right to submit evidence.
- The right to legal representation.
- The right to reasons for a decision.

The right to a fair hearing (or fairness/the duty to act fairly) is variable depending upon the context and so its requirements may include all or a number of the features set out directly above. Indeed, as noted by Lord Bridge in *Lloyd v McMahon* [1987] 1 AC 625:

JUDGMENT

'. . . the so-called rules of natural justice are not engraved on tablets of stone. To use the phrase which better expresses the underlying concept, what the requirements of fairness demand when any body, domestic, administrative or judicial, has to make a decision which will affect the rights of individuals depends on the character of the decision-making body, the kind of decision it has to make and the statutory or other framework in which it operates.'

More recently, Lord Brown in *Permanent Secretary, Ministry of Foreign Affairs v Ramjohn* [2011] UKPC 20 stated that 'As is trite law, the requirements of fairness in any given case depend crucially upon the particular circumstances'. Nonetheless, in *R (L) v West London Mental Health NHS Trust* [2014] EWCA Civ 47, Beatson LJ noted the 'dangers in concentrating on a flexible notion of overarching fairness'.

The case law of natural justice/fairness is voluminous and below is a selection of some examples to suggest an outline of this area:

Legitimate expectation

In R (Bibi) v London Borough of Newham [2001] EWCA Civ 607 Schiemann LJ commented that:

JUDGMENT

'In all legitimate expectation cases, whether substantive or procedural, three practical questions arise. The first question is to what has the public authority, whether by practice or by promise, committed itself; the second is whether the authority has acted or proposes to act unlawfully in relation to its commitment; the third is what the court should do.'

There are various ways in which a legitimate expectation can arise. Indeed, Simon Brown LJ in *R v Devon County Council, ex parte Baker* [1995] 1 All ER 73 identified the following four 'broad categories' of legitimate expectation:

(i) '[A] substantive right', whereby the claimant asserts an entitlement which cannot be denied;

(ii) The claimant has an interest in an 'ultimate benefit which he hopes to retain';

(iii) A fair procedure (ie 'the public body will act fairly');

(iv) A procedure (not required by law) should be followed as a result of practice or a promise.

Below are a number of cases in which a legitimate expectation has been raised:

- *ex parte Liverpool Taxi Fleet Operators' Association* (1972) – taxi drivers had a legitimate expectation (based on past history and an undertaking given on behalf of the council) to make representations before more licences were issued (see section 20.6.1).
- *GCHQ* (1985) (see section 11.9.6) – Civil Service unions had a legitimate expectation based on previous practice to be consulted prior to their terms and conditions of service being changed (in the event trumped by national security).
- *R v North and East Devon Health Authority, ex parte Coughlan* [2001] 1 QB 213 – a number of disabled people had a legitimate expectation that a Heath Authority would keep the assurance that it had given to them that their move to an NHS facility would be for life.
- *Attorney General of Hong Kong v Ng Yuen Shiu* [1983] 2 All ER 346 – the Privy Council held that the Hong Kong government's announcement that the case of each illegal immigrant would be treated on its merits, created a legitimate expectation of a hearing before removal.
- *R (Bancoult) v Secretary of State for Foreign and Commonwealth Affairs* [2008] UKHL 61 – the House of Lords held that no legitimate expectation had been created by the government (ie there was no unambiguous and clear promise) that former inhabitants of the Chagos Islands would be allowed to return.
- *R (Bapio Action Ltd) v Secretary of State for the Home Department* [2008] UKHL 27 – informal guidance of the Secretary of State for Health was inconsistent with a legitimate expectation created by immigration rules and practice.
- *R (Patel) v General Medical Council* [2013] EWCA Civ 327 – the Court of Appeal held that the General Medical Council had to honour a clear assurance given to Patel that on completing his overseas primary medical qualification, that his qualification would be recognised.

In the context of legitimate expectations, see C Brasted and J Marlow 'Great expectations' (2008) 158 NLJ 1441. On the ambiguity of the doctrine, see J Bell, 'The doctrine of legitimate expectations: power-constraining or right- conferring legal standard?' [2016] PL 437.

Consultation

In the context of consultation, see the following case of *R (Harrow Community Support Ltd) v Secretary of State for Defence* [2012] EWHC 1921 (Admin) in which Haddon-Cave, J stated that a duty to consult did not arise in all circumstances otherwise '. . . the business of government would grind to a halt.' He then identified the following four main circumstances which require consultation:

(i) A statutory duty (see section 20.5.2);
(ii) A promise to consult;
(iii) An established practice of consulting (see above);
(iv) In exceptional cases, where the absence of consultation 'would lead to conspicuous unfairness'.

The right to know adverse evidence

Lord Denning in the Privy Council in *Kanda v Government of the Federation of Malaya* [1962] AC 322 commented that:

JUDGMENT

'If the right to be heard is to be a real right which is worth anything, it must carry with it a right in the accused man to know the case which is made against him. He must know what evidence has been given and what statements have been made affecting him.'

Although it may appear axiomatic that a person should know the exact particulars of the case against them, this principle has in the past been modified by national security. In *ex parte Hosenball* (1977) at section 6.7.10, Hosenball had a deportation order issued against him under the Immigration Act 1971. The Court of Appeal held there had been no breach of natural justice as the Secretary of State had considered personally Hosenball's request for further particulars of the allegations. Hosenball's request had been denied as it was not in the interests of national security to provide further information. The court noted that on occasions natural justice had to give way to considerations of national security. See also *R v Secretary of State for the Home Department, ex parte Cheblak* [1991] 1 WLR 890. More recently, however, now see the case of *Secretary of State for the Home Department v AF* (2009) at section 6.8.

■ **The right to have sufficient time to prepare a defence/answer the case against him** In order for an individual to defend himself, he must be given reasonable time to defend himself in answer to a charge:

CASE EXAMPLE

R v Thames Magistrates' Court, ex parte Polemis *[1974] 2 All ER 1219*

Polemis was served with a summons at 10.30am concerning an alleged breach of the Prevention of Oil Pollution Act 1971. At 4.00pm that day a stipendiary magistrate heard the case and convicted him. Polemis's conviction was quashed by an order of certiorari on the basis that natural justice required that a party should have a reasonable opportunity to prepare his case. Lord Widgery CJ stated that:

JUDGMENT

'Nothing is clearer today than that a breach of the rules of natural justice is said to occur if a party to proceedings, and more especially the defendant in a criminal case, is not given a reasonable chance to present his case . . . it necessarily extends to a reasonable opportunity to prepare your case before you are called on to present it.'

■ **The right to make representations**
The rationale behind the right to make representations is, of course, that it gives the individual/party who will be affected by a public law decision the opportunity to influence it *before* the decision is made.

In *ex parte Binks* (1985) (see section 19.2.1) the council's decision to issue Binks with a notice to quit was quashed. It was held that, as her livelihood was at stake (a street trader selling hot food under an informal arrangement), the council had denied her natural justice because:

(i) she had not been given prior notification before the issuing of its decision giving her notice to quit;
(ii) she had not been given an opportunity to be heard;
(iii) it had not given any reasons for its decision.

In *ex parte Doody* (1994) (see below) the House of Lords held that the Home Secretary was required to provide a mandatory life sentence prisoner with the opportunity to make written representations concerning the period he should serve (to satisfy deterrence and retribution) before the date was set by the Home Secretary for the first review of that prisoner's sentence. More recently, in *Bank Mellat v HM Treasury (No 2)* [2013] UKSC 39 the Supreme Court held that the Treasury should have afforded the claimant an opportunity to make representations before it imposed the Financial Restrictions (Iran) Order 2009 on it under the aegis of the Counter-Terrorism Act 2008. As an aside, this Order was also held to be irrational (see earlier at section 20.3.3).

The right to an oral hearing

The right to a hearing does not necessarily mean the right to an oral hearing, as (depending on the circumstances and what is at stake) the right to a hearing may only mean that written representations can be put forward. In any event, in a written hearing an individual can still submit evidence which he wishes the decision-making body to see.

CASE EXAMPLE

R (West) v Parole Board *[2005] UKHL 1*

The House of Lords held that an oral hearing before a Parole Board in respect of prisoners who had had their licences revoked, might be necessary where, for example, facts were at issue (ie were in dispute) which could affect the outcome. Such issues, of course, could be better resolved in person than on paper. Although the court held that whether an oral hearing was necessary depended on the circumstances of each particular case, on the facts it was held that the Parole Board had breached its common law duty of procedural fairness by failing to offer the prisoners an oral hearing.

Also see *Hopkins v Parole Board* [2008] EWHC 2312 (Admin), where the Parole Board had acted unfairly in not giving the prisoner an oral hearing allowing him to state his side of the case in relation to a parole application. More recently, see the following case:

CASE EXAMPLE

Osborn v Parole Board *[2013] UKSC 61*

The Supreme Court set out the circumstances in which oral hearings should be held by the Parole Board. In a single judgment delivered by Lord Reed, the court held that in order to ensure compliance with common law standards of procedural fairness, an oral hearing should be held before the Parole Board determined a prisoner's application for release or transfer 'whenever fairness to the prisoner requires such a hearing in the light of the facts of the case and the importance of what is at stake'. In so doing, it would be complying with its duty under Art 6 of the European Convention. The circumstances in which an oral hearing should be held (albeit not exhaustive) included the following factors:

- where important facts are disputed or an explanation/mitigation is required to be heard orally in order to assess its credibility;
- where an independent risk assessment cannot otherwise be made;
- when necessary in order to put the prisoner's case effectively;
- where it would be unfair for a single panel Board member's 'paper decision' to become final without permitting an oral hearing.

In *R v Army Board of the Defence Council, ex parte Anderson* [1992] 1 QB 169, the court held that the Army Board had been wrong to adopt an inflexible policy where it did not permit oral hearings before it.

The disadvantage of oral hearings is that they are much more time-consuming than paper hearings. The advantage of an oral hearing is, of course, the possibility of cross-examining evidence and witnesses (thereby allowing adverse evidence to be tested orally). Cross-examination is also another important aspect of the principles of natural justice. In *R v Hull Prison Board of Visitors, ex parte St Germain and others (No 2)* [1979] 3 All ER 545 the court noted that, in terms of hearsay evidence, a fair hearing might involve the Prison Board informing prisoners (accused of breaching Prison Rules) of the hearsay evidence against them and of allowing them the opportunity to cross-examine witnesses whose evidence was before it as hearsay. In addition, the Board had improperly failed to allow witnesses to be called in defence (ie the right to submit evidence). For a more recent case concerning hearing hearsay evidence, see *R (Bonhoeffer) v General Medical Council* [2011] EWHC 1585 (Admin).

The right to legal representation

When appearing before a criminal court a person will expect to enjoy legal representation; however, whether lawyers will be permitted in other (ie non-criminal) circumstances will depend on the facts/issue. For example, in *R (G) v Governors of X School* [2009] EWHC 504 (Admin) legal representation should have been permitted before disciplinary and appeal committee hearings given the serious nature of the consequences in the case. The advantage of legal representation is that it enables individuals lacking specialist knowledge or competence to present their case. The disadvantage of legal representation is that lawyers inevitably lengthen and complicate proceedings. Indeed, Lord Denning MR in *Enderby Town Football Club Ltd v Football Association Ltd* [1971] 1 Ch 591 noted that:

JUDGMENT

'In many cases it may be a good thing for the proceedings of a domestic tribunal to be conducted informally without legal representation. Justice can often be done in them better by a good layman than by a bad lawyer.'

In the context of prisoners see the following case:

CASE EXAMPLE

R v Secretary of State for the Home Department, ex parte Tarrant
[1985] 1 QB 251

The court held that the Board of Visitors had a discretion as to whether prisoners should be granted legal representation. In this case the two prisoners should have been allowed to have been legally represented (here the charge of mutiny was an especially grave offence).

In *R v Board of Visitors of HM Prison, The Maze, ex parte Hone* [1988] AC 379 the House of Lords held that natural justice did not require a Prison Board of Visitors to permit legal representation to a prisoner (who appeared before it on a disciplinary charge) in every case *as of right*. Whether legal representation was afforded was dependent on the circumstances of the case.

See also Art 6 of the European Convention on Human Rights, which specifically states that everyone charged with a criminal offence has, *inter alia*, the following rights:

ARTICLE

Art 6(3) (c)

To defend himself in person or through legal assistance of his own choosing or, if he has not sufficient means to pay for legal assistance, to be given it free when the interests of justice so require.

In *Ezeh and Connors v United Kingdom* (2004) 39 EHRR 691 the European Court of Human Rights held that the right to a fair trial had been breached when prisoners (who had been sentenced to additional days under Prison Rules) had been denied legal representation. For the purposes of Art 6, the court considered the charges against the prisoners under the Prison Rules criminal.

A duty to give reasons

In common law (historically) there has been no general duty for a decision-maker to provide reasons for a decision. In contrast, the judiciary gives reasons for decisions made in court (as do tribunals – see s 10 Tribunals and Inquiries Act 1992). In modern times, however, it is the hallmark of good administrative practice as, according to J Auburn, J Moffett and A Sharland, 'there is a clear trend towards requiring public bodies to give reasons for their decisions' (*Judicial Review* (Oxford University Press, 2013), p 248). Lord Mustill in *R v Secretary of State for the Home Department, ex parte Doody* [1994] 1 AC 531 stated that:

JUDGMENT

'The law does not at present recognise a general duty to give reasons for an administrative decision. Nevertheless, it is equally beyond question that such a duty may in appropriate circumstances be implied.'

Most recently, Elias, LJ commented that:

JUDGMENT

'the common law is moving to the position whilst there is no universal obligation to give reasons in all circumstances, in general they should be given unless there is a proper justification for not doing so.'

R (Oakley) v South Cambridgeshire District Council [2017] EWCA Civ 71.

The following case is interesting as it concerns the provision of information during the decision-making process:

CASE EXAMPLE

R v Secretary of State for the Home Department, ex parte
Al Fayed and another *[1997] 1 All ER 228*

The Fayed brothers applied for naturalisation as British citizens under the British Nationality Act 1981. Their applications were refused and no reasons were given for this refusal. They sought judicial review of the Home Secretary's failure to give reasons and claimed that there had been a breach of natural justice.

The Court of Appeal held that although the Home Secretary was not (owing to s 44 of the 1981 Act) required to give reasons when an application was refused, he still had to act fairly in arriving at a decision. As a result, the Home Secretary should have given the Fayeds information (ie the right to notice/adequate disclosure) in respect of the area of his concern. This, in turn, would then have allowed them to make representations on this issue to the Home Secretary before he made his decision. In the case, the decision of the Home Secretary was quashed. Lord Woolf MR, stated that:

JUDGMENT

'I appreciate that there is also anxiety as to the administrative burden involved in giving notice of areas of concern. Administrative convenience cannot justify unfairness but I would emphasise that my remarks are limited to cases where an applicant would be in real difficulty in doing himself justice unless the area of concern is identified by notice.'

The above case illustrates an example of Parliament legislating to exclude a requirement to give a reason for a decision. In contrast, a legislative (albeit delegated) requirement for reasons is illustrated by Article 22 of the Town and Country Planning (General Development Procedure) Order 1995, SI 1995/419. This required the 'full reasons' for any condition imposed by a local planning authority when it granted planning permission subject to conditions (see *R (Mid-Counties Co-operative Ltd) v Forest of Dean District Council* [2007] EWHC 1714 (Admin)).

Finally, in terms of what constitutes the adequacy of reasons, see the following comment of Lord Brown (made in the context of Town and County Planning law):

JUDGMENT

'The reasons for a decision must be intelligible and they must be adequate. They must enable the reader to understand why the matter was decided as it was and what conclusions were reached on the "principal important controversial issues", disclosing how any issue of law or fact was resolved. Reasons can be briefly stated, the degree of particularity required depending entirely on the nature of the issues falling for decision. The reasoning must not give rise to a substantial doubt as to whether the decision-maker erred in law.'

South Buckinghamshire District Council v Porter (No 2) [2004] UKHL 33.

ACTIVITY

Exercise

Explain the different aspects of *audi alteram partem*. Why do such rules exist?

KEY FACTS

	The ground of procedural impropriety
Statutory requirements	A failure to comply with statutory procedural requirements: • Historically, a mandatory requirement was an essential requirement which would invalidate an action if not followed (*Aylesbury Mushrooms Ltd* (1972)). • Historically, a directory requirement was a minor technical defect. • See now Lord Woolf's analysis (*ex parte Jeyeanthan* (2000)) and latterly Lord Steyn in *R v Soneji* (2005).
Nemo judex in re sua	• Actual bias where a decision-maker is actually biased. • Presumed bias where there is a direct financial interest (*Dimes* (1852)) or the promotion of a cause (*ex parte Pinochet Ugarte* (2000)). • Apparent bias (eg *Lannon* (1969)).

Audi alteram partem	Depending on the circumstances, decision-makers must respect all or most of the following requirements which protect the right to a fair hearing: • An awareness of the charge/allegations and notice of the hearing. • The right to submit a defence and evidence (in writing and/or orally). • An indication of adverse evidence and the right to challenge it (in writing and/or orally). • The right to legal representation. • The right to reasons for a decision.

20.6 Remedies

20.6.1 The different remedies available

If a claimant can demonstrate that a public body has breached one of the grounds of judicial review, he *may* obtain a remedy. There are six remedies available:

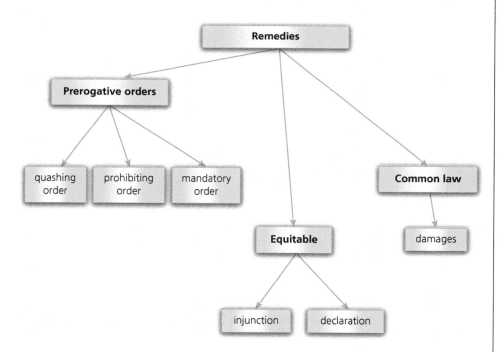

Figure 20.7 Remedies

It should be noted that a combination of remedies may be appropriate. For example, a quashing order combined with a mandatory order would compel a public body to take the decision again (after the original decision had been quashed by a quashing order), but this time in accordance with the law.

▨ **A quashing order**

This order (formerly known as *certiorari*) quashes an unlawful decision. For example, in *ex parte Binks* (1985) (see sections 19.2.1 and 20.5.4), Binks successfully obtained an order to quash an unlawful decision of Wear Valley District Council that she should cease trading. Similarly, in the context of delegated legislation see *R v Secretary of State for Health, ex parte United States Tobacco International Inc* [1992] 1 QB 353 at section 19.2.1.

A prohibiting order

This order (formerly known as *prohibition*) is pre-emptive in the sense that it prevents a body from acting unlawfully in the future (see *R v Liverpool Corporation, ex parte Liverpool Taxi Fleet Operators' Association* [1972] 2 QB 299 – preventing a council from granting further taxi licences without first hearing the representations of interested parties).

A mandatory order

This order (formerly known as *mandamus*) compels a body to act (eg to perform a statutory function). In *Padfield* (1968) (see section 20.2.4) the court directed the Minister of Agriculture to consider a complaint submitted to him according to the law.

An injunction

This equitable remedy can compel a body to perform an act or restrain it from doing so. In *ex parte Factortame Ltd* (1991), at section 15.6.4, the House of Lords issued an interim injunction which prevented the Secretary of State from enforcing provisions of the Merchant Shipping Act 1988. An injunction is a useful remedy because it can be obtained in a temporary form, as in the *Factortame* litigation.

A declaration

This equitable remedy is non-coercive as it represents a formal statement of the law by the courts. For example, in *Equal Opportunities Commission* (1994) (see section 19.4.2) a declaration was issued stating that provisions of domestic law indirectly discriminated against women and so were contrary to European law. This is also a remedy which can be obtained on an interim basis.

Damages

This common law remedy has historically not been a free-standing remedy as it had to be combined with another remedy. In practice, to claim damages a claimant was required to show that the unlawful public decision was also, for example, negligent.

Today a breach of the European Convention by a public body may result in compensation; however, the awards will usually be relatively modest as they will be in line with those made by the European Court in Strasbourg (see section 17.9.3).

20.6.2 The discretionary nature of remedies

Even though a claimant can demonstrate that a public body has acted unlawfully, the court may nevertheless decide to provide no remedy at all (or may provide a different one from the one sought). A remedy may be refused on the following basis:

- The behaviour of the claimant in the case (eg an ulterior motive in seeking judicial review).
- If the claimant has unduly delayed in making an application for judicial review and the court considers that the relief that is sought 'would be likely to cause substantial hardship to, or substantially prejudice the rights of, any person or would be detrimental to good administration' – s 31 (6) of the Senior Courts Act 1981.
- The remedy would provide no tangible benefit/use in practice. NB: s 84 of the Criminal Justice and Courts Act 2015 provided that the court must refuse to grant relief/remedy where 'it appears to the court to be highly likely that the outcome for the applicant would not have been substantially different if the conduct complained of had not occurred', albeit this could be disregarded 'for reasons of exceptional public interest'. For an example of denial of relief, see *R (H) v Secretary of State for Justice* [2015] EWHC 4093 (Admin).

20.7 The effectiveness of judicial review

How effective is judicial review?

20.7.1 Factors which support its effectiveness

Lord Scarman in *Nottinghamshire County Council v Secretary of State for the Environment* [1986] 1 AC 240 stated that:

JUDGMENT

'Judicial review is a great weapon in the hands of the judges: but the judges must observe the constitutional limits set by our parliamentary system upon their exercise of this beneficial power.'

- The existence of judicial review necessarily improves good administration. It encourages administrators and public decision-makers to exercise their powers in accordance with the law as they are aware that otherwise they will be subject to review. Indeed, government officials are issued with the booklet *The Judge Over Your Shoulder – A guide to good decision making* (5th edn, Government Legal Department, 2016), which reminds officials of their public law responsibilities. As a preventative measure, we will never know how many illegal public law decisions judicial review has prevented.

- Judicial review has caused friction between the courts and the executive in the past two decades, as successive ministers, of whatever political colour, have been subject to judicial review. In fact, it is arguable that it is actually healthy in a democracy for there to be some friction between the two arms of the constitution as it suggests that the courts are successfully holding the executive to account and restraining their actions. This is particularly important in the light of the modern executive's domination of the legislature.

- Judicial review claims can be used to highlight a particular issue (homelessness, prisoners' rights, etc). For instance, see the issue of the settlement of Gurkhas in the United Kingdom (*R (Limbu) v Secretary of State for the Home Department* [2008] EWHC 2261 (Admin)).

- An example of a successful case is *R (Brooke) v Parole Board* [2008] EWCA Civ 29, in which the Court of Appeal held that the Parole Board was insufficiently independent of the executive (for the purposes of Art 5 of the European Convention) owing to its sponsorship arrangements. Two months after this decision, the Secretary of State for Justice announced a change in the Parole Board's sponsorship, transferring it to the Access to Justice Group within the Ministry of Justice.

20.7.2 Factors which question its effectiveness

- It must be remembered that judicial review is in essence a procedural remedy whereby the courts have historically confined themselves to questioning the decision-making process, rather than the decision itself. The result of this is that judicial review may be in some cases a rather pyrrhic victory. Although the court may quash the offending decision of a public body, it will not replace it with another one but instead require the body to take the decision again (known as a 'remittal'), but this time in accordance with the law (eg this time by considering relevant factors that were previously ignored). This 'reconsideration' could still result in the decision-maker making the *same* decision and, provided it was taken legally, rationally and fairly, it will stand. In *R (Ali) v Secretary of State for the Home Department* [2003] EWHC 899 (Admin) Goldring J granted judicial review of the Secretary of State's decision refusing the claimant leave to remain in the country. He stated, however, that: 'Of course, dependent upon reconsideration on sufficient and proper evidence, the Secretary of State may reach exactly the same decision'.

- Some areas of public law decision-making such as national security and national economic considerations are not susceptible to judicial review (ie they are *non-justiciable*.

- The remedies available are discretionary and may be denied even though it has been demonstrated that a public body has acted unlawfully. In addition, note the recent legislative reform indicated at section 20.6.2, which set out the circumstances in which a court *must* refuse to grant a remedy.

- Judicial review is necessarily a reactive jurisdiction in which the ability of the courts to develop administrative principles is subject to claimants initiating actions.

- As noted by the Democratic Audit of the United Kingdom, in terms of the effectiveness of judicial review, it is clear that the few thousand judicial review claims made each year 'are infinitesimal when compared with the millions of decisions taken every year by public bodies' (S Weir and D Beetham, *Political Power and Democratic Control in Britain* (Routledge, 1999), p 446). Indeed, in 2011 a total of 7,611 applications for permission to apply for judicial review were considered by the Administrative Court (1,220 of these were granted) and, of the 396 substantive applications for judicial review decided that year, 174 were allowed (*Judicial and Court Statistics 2011* (MOJ, Crown Copyright, 2012), p 65). More recent figures are also very revealing. For example, in 2016 the Home Office had 1,832 applications lodged against it, 226 applications were granted permission with 12 being found in favour of the claimant (*Civil Justice Statistics Quarterly, England and Wales, January to March 2017 (provisional)* and *Royal Courts of Justice 2016* (Ministry of Justice, Crown Copyright, June 2017), p 6).

- Judicial review is a remedy of last resort to be used when there are no other (or reasonable) remedies available.

ACTIVITY

Exercise

Do you think that judicial review is effective?

20.8 Judicial review checklist

Judicial review examination questions are particularly amenable to problem-solving questions. One useful way of approaching such questions is to list each ground (and sub-division) of judicial review and work down this checklist in order to determine which issues are raised by the scenario:

Judicial review checklist
Procedural issues: Is the decision-maker a public body (or one which the courts would regard as performing governmental functions)? Is the decision/action complained about a public law issue? Does the claimant have standing? Has the claimant complied with the public law procedure required for judicial review?

Grounds of review:

Has the decision-maker acted illegally? Have they:

- Acted *ultra vires* the parent Act?
- Wrongfully delegated their public law powers?
- Acted for an improper purpose?
- Abused their discretion by (a) fettering their discretion (b) ignoring relevant factors (c) considering irrelevant factors?
- Acted in excess of their jurisdiction by misinterpreting their legal powers?
- Breached a European Convention right (and acted disproportionately)?

Has the decision-maker acted irrationally? Have they:

- Made a decision which no reasonable decision-maker would have made?

Has the decision-maker acted in a procedurally unfair manner? Have they:

- Breached a statutory requirement?
- Demonstrated bias, a presumption of bias or apparent bias?
- Ignored the rules concerning the right to a fair hearing?

Table 20.1

SUMMARY

- In *GCHQ* (1985) Lord Diplock reclassified the grounds of judicial review into illegality, irrationality and procedural impropriety.
- Illegality includes the following:
  - Simple *ultra vires* – exceeding specified legal powers.
  - Wrongful delegation – delegating power to another body.
  - Improper purpose – power is used for an improper purpose.
  - Abuse of discretion – discretion is fettered and/or relevant factors are ignored/irrelevant factors are considered.
  - Excess of jurisdiction – a mistake of law/fact.
  - Breach of the European Convention – a public body acts inconsistently with the Convention's articles.
- Irrationality is a decision which no reasonable body could have arrived at.
- In recent years the ground of proportionality has been developed which considers the aim of the decision-maker and whether the means to achieve that objective are proportionate.
- Procedural impropriety includes a failure to follow specified procedural requirements as laid out in legislation.
- Procedural impropriety also includes the common law requirements of fairness/natural justice:
  - The absence of bias (*nemo judex in re sua*).
  - The right to a fair hearing (*audi alteram partem*).
- There is a range of remedies available in judicial review, although they are issued at the discretion of the court.

Further reading

Books

Auburn, J, Moffett, J and Sharland, A, *Judicial Review* (Oxford University Press, 2013), Pts III & IV.

Bailey, S, 'Grounds for Judicial Review: Due Process, Natural Justice, and Fairness' in Feldman, D (ed), *English Public Law* (2nd edn, Oxford University Press, 2009), p 667.

Barnett, H, *Constitutional and Administrative Law* (12th edn, Routledge/Taylor & Francis Group, 2017), Chapters 24–25.

Bradley, A, Ewing, K and Knight, C, *Constitutional and Administrative Law* (16th edn, Pearson, 2015), Chapter 24.

Craig, P, 'Grounds for Judicial Review: Substantive Control over Discretion' in Feldman, D (ed), *English Public Law* (2nd edn, Oxford University Press, 2009), p 719.

Fordham, M, *Judicial Review Handbook* (6th edn, Hart, 2012), Part C.

Leyland, P and Anthony, G, *Textbook on Administrative Law* (8th edn, Oxford University Press, 2016), Chapters 11–17.

Sunkin, M, 'Grounds for Judicial Review: Illegality in the Strict Sense' in Feldman, D (ed), *English Public Law* (2nd edn, Oxford University Press, 2009), p 615.

Supperstone, M, Goudie, J, Walker, P and General Editor Fenwick H, Judicial *Review* (6th edn, LexisNexis, 2017), Chapters 6 to 12.

Weir, S and Beetham, D, *Political Power and Democratic Control in Britain* (Routledge, 1999), Chapter 15.

Articles

Craig, P, 'Judicial review and anxious scrutiny: foundations, evolution and application' [2015] PL 60.

Daly, P, 'Wednesbury's reason and structure' [2011] PL 238.

Lord Irvine, 'Judges and decision makers: the theory and practice of Wednesbury review' [1996] PL 59.

Kay, M, 'The developing role of judges in matters of public law' (2015) 128 *Graya* 19.

Turner, I, 'Judicial review, irrationality and the review of merits' (2006) 15 *Nottingham Law Journal* 37.

Walker, P, 'What's wrong with irrationality?' [1995] PL 556.

21

Grievance mechanisms

AIMS AND OBJECTIVES

At the end of this chapter you should be able to:

- Appreciate the role of grievance mechanisms (other than the courts) in the British constitution
- Understand the nature and constitutional role of the tribunal system
- Understand the nature and constitutional role of inquiries
- Appreciate the role, workings and constitutional importance of the system of Ombudsmen

Introduction

As government officials and agencies exercise disparate and wide-ranging powers to provide services and discharge responsibilities, it is inevitable that the actions and decisions of state officials will come into conflict with individuals. As a result, a number of different grievance mechanisms are available to individuals who feel aggrieved by the actions of the state. In brief, tribunals provide individuals with a legal form of redress which is an alternative to the strict formal court system. Inquiries are a grievance mechanism which permits individuals to challenge, for example, the decision of a local planning authority to refuse an application for planning permission. A further form of redress is the Ombudsman, which investigates an injustice caused to an individual by maladministration (ie faulty administration) by the state. This chapter will provide a very general overview of all three grievance mechanisms against the state.

21.1 Tribunals

21.1.1 Definition and history

In historical terms, the powers and responsibilities of the state have increasingly impacted on the lives of individuals (for example, whether it was the collection of taxes or the entitlement to a social security benefit). In the light of the millions of decisions made by state officials and administrators each year, mistakes and discrepancies are inevitably going to cause injustice to particular individuals. As a consequence, tribunals have been established on an *ad hoc* basis by Parliament to enable individuals to challenge the decisions of state officials in a forum which is outside the formal court system. In essence, tribunals are adjudicative bodies which apply laws and rules to a case in order to resolve disputes between the individual and the state.

In 1957 the Franks Committee (*Report of the Committee on Administrative Tribunals and Inquiries* Cm 218 (1957)) examined the network of tribunals. This in turn led to the passing of the Tribunals and Inquiries Act 1958 (as subsequently consolidated in the Tribunals and Inquiries Acts 1971 and 1992), which among other things established the Council on Tribunals. The Council's responsibility was to oversee and report on the operation and workings of tribunals (as well as inquiries). A further review of tribunals was undertaken by Sir Andrew Leggatt, whose report in 2001 (*Tribunals for Users: One System, One Service* (The Stationery Office, 2001)) stated that – at that point in time – there were 70 different types of administrative tribunals in England and Wales, which processed 1 million cases between them. The network of these tribunals, however, lacked co-ordination and needed to be rationalised. This in turn led the then Labour government to implement reforms to the organisation and system of tribunals (see section 21.1.6).

21.1.2 Types of tribunals

Today there are various different types of tribunals, ranging from tax (the Tax Chamber/Tribunal), mental health (the Mental Health Tribunal) and education (the Special Educational Needs & Disability Tribunal). In broad terms, however, a clear distinction can be drawn between:

- those which resolve disputes between the individual and the state (eg the Asylum Support Tribunal); and
- those which regulate disputes between private parties (eg employee and employer in the context of employment law issues such as redundancy (employment tribunals)).

Below are three brief examples of tribunals in operation:

- A has a dispute with the state concerning his entitlement to social security payments, to which social security officials have decided that he is no longer entitled. A can appeal against this decision to the Social Security and Child Support Tribunal (part of the Social Entitlement Chamber).
- B has made a claim under the Criminal Injuries Compensation Scheme but it was rejected by the Criminal Injuries Compensation Authority as being insufficiently serious. B can appeal against this decision to the Criminal Injuries Compensation Tribunal (part of the Social Entitlement Chamber).
- C claims that he has been unfairly dismissed by his employer. He can seek redress in an Employment Tribunal.

Examples adapted from the Tribunals Service website in 2010: www.tribunals.gov.uk (today see the following website: www.gov.uk).

21.1.3 The constitutional position of tribunals

Tribunals are fact-finding bodies which apply legal principles and administrative rules in order to adjudicate on legal disputes (largely between an aggrieved individual and the state). In constitutional terms, tribunals are impartial grievance mechanisms which are distinct from both the government as well as the ordinary court system.

Independent of the government/state

The existence of tribunals necessarily raises the constitutional question as to whether such bodies are part of the administration (executive) or the judicial arm of the state. In countries such as Australia, the tribunal system is considered to be part of the administration because, as noted by Leggatt in his 2001 report (para 2.5), they are specifically charged with administrative duties and 'putting themselves in the shoes of the relevant Government official'. In Britain, however, the 1957 Franks Committee plainly refuted the view that tribunals were part of the administration:

QUOTATION

'Tribunals are not ordinary courts, but neither are they appendages of Government Departments. . . . We consider that tribunals should properly be regarded as machinery provided by Parliament for adjudication rather than as part of the machinery for administration.'

Report of the Committee on Administrative Tribunals and Inquiries, Cm 218 (1957), para 40.

Notwithstanding this, historically there has always been a necessarily close connection between the tribunal and the arm of the state which it regulates. This is due to the fact that the government department concerned invariably provided the former with administrative support. As a result, there had been concern that, in terms of 'appearance', tribunals were not independent of the administration. Indeed, the Leggatt Report noted that there were significant doubts as to whether the (then) current arrangements of tribunals provided individuals with 'the necessary confidence in their independence and effectiveness' (para 2.3).

Moreover, the report commented that:

QUOTATION

'There is no question of the Government improperly attempting to influence individual decisions. In that sense, tribunal decisions seem to us clearly impartial. But it cannot be said with confidence that they are demonstrably independent. Indeed, the evidence is to the contrary. For most tribunals, the departments provide administrative support, pay the salaries of members, pay their expenses, provide accommodation, provide IT support . . . are responsible for some appointments, and promote the legislation which prescribes procedures to be followed. At best, such arrangements result in tribunals and their departments being, or appearing to be, common enterprises.'

Tribunals for Users: One System, One Service (The Stationery Office, 2001), para 2.20.

As a result of the Leggatt Report and the following 2004 government White Paper, the then Labour government, in an effort to enhance the independence of tribunals, implemented reforms in terms of their organisation (see section 21.1.6).

Distinct from the court system

Tribunals are part of the justice system but are outside the formal court structure. They are similar to courts in the sense that they act fairly, impartially, decide facts and apply legal rules to resolve legal disputes. Sometimes these are highly complex rules; for example, employment tribunals will apply convoluted European and employment law and principles. Tribunals, however, are broadly speaking less formal, less adversarial and less concerned with rules of precedent than the courts. Tribunals and courts are nevertheless connected in the sense that both are governed by an appellate system. Indeed, appeals from tribunals ultimately can end up being resolved in a court. For example, an appeal can progressively be made from the Employment Tribunal to the Employment Appeal Tribunal through to the Court of Appeal and the Supreme Court. In fact, the last Labour government also implemented reforms to rationalise the tribunal appellate system (see section 21.1.7). For example, under the Tribunals, Courts and Enforcement Act 2007, an appeal on a point of law can be made from the First-Tier Tribunal to the Upper Tribunal and thereafter to the Court of Appeal.

21.1.4 Advantages of tribunals

There are a number of distinct advantages to tribunals:

Volume of cases

State officials take millions of decisions annually and it is not practicable to process all challenges to official decisions in a court as this would overload the court system. For example, in 2003–04 the Appeals Service received 235,657 appeals and the Mental Health Review Tribunals 20,408 (*Transforming Public Services: Complaints, Redress and Tribunals*, Cm 6243 (DCA, 2004), para 3.28). As the Leggatt Report pointed out, in terms of their experience of the justice system, an individual is more likely to appear before a tribunal than a court. Indeed, 874,164 'receipts' (ie claims) were accepted during the financial year of 2012–13 and 740,605 were disposed of (*Tribunals Statistics Quarterly* (MOJ, 2013), pp 7–10). More recently, see the following report: *Senior President of Tribunals' Annual Report* (Senior President of Tribunals, 2017), which indicated, for instance, that in 2015–16 the Social Security and Child Support Tribunal had an intake of 157,145 cases (p 37).

Cost and efficiency

The court system involves lawyers and so is necessarily expensive. In contrast, tribunals are more efficient and cost-effective as typically they operate without paid legal representation and the awarding of costs (although the 2007 Act confers a discretion on tribunals to order costs and expenses). It should be noted, however, that in some tribunals such as Mental Health Tribunals, parties do use lawyers, with publicly funded legal assistance being available. Tribunals provide swifter resolution of disputes, which is consistent with the principle that *justice delayed is justice denied*.

Specialism

Tribunals are subject specific so that they process cases involving a highly specialist aspect of the administration (eg social security benefits) and so are staffed by experts in that particular area. For example, the panel on the Mental Health Tribunal will include a medical expert. Similarly, whenever a Social Security and Child Support Tribunal is processing an appeal involving a disability living allowance, in determining the case the Tribunal Judge will be supplemented by a medical practitioner and a disability expert. In contrast, where specialist knowledge is required in the court system, an (external) expert witness will be called.

Formalism and accessibility

Tribunals are intended to be more accessible and user-friendly than courts. As noted by the Leggatt Report, the procedure in tribunals (both pre and during hearings) is generally simpler and more informal than the court system. Not only are tribunals less formal than courts but they also tend to be less adversarial and so more inquisitorial.

■ **Good governance**

As pointed out in the Leggatt Report, in the light of the volume and variety of cases that they process, tribunals are in the invaluable position of being able to identify and highlight systematic administrative problems in departmental decision-making. In terms of good governance/administration, see the Ombudsman at section 21.3.5.

21.1.5 Disadvantages of tribunals

A number of problems are associated with tribunals:

■ **Historically, the organisation of tribunals was haphazard.**

The Leggatt Report described the then existing network of tribunals as incoherent and ineffectual with different procedures and rules applying to different tribunals. This was owing to tribunals having been established in an *ad hoc* fashion responding to specific needs at any given time. In fact, the report argued that in view of this lack of coherence: 'It is obvious that the term "tribunal system" is a misnomer' (para 3.2) – but now see the reforms at section 21.1.7.

■ **Independence**

As indicated at section 21.1.3, historically there had been concern that tribunals were not necessarily seen to be independent, however impartial they were. The Leggatt Report stated that: 'plainly they are not independent. Even in tribunals which are no longer paid for by "their" departments, there can be an unhealthy closeness' (para 1.19) – but now see the reforms detailed below at section 21.1.6.

■ **Legal representation**

Research conducted in this area has indicated that individuals are likely to be more successful in a tribunal if they are represented. The Leggatt Report recognised that, although legal representation can be beneficial, such representation inevitably drives up costs and works against tribunals being accessible. In any event, as suggested by the report, individuals could be better informed through the provision of more advice and assistance from the tribunal itself.

■ **Delay**

The Leggatt Report identified some unacceptable delays in processing cases, thereby mirroring the problems associated with the modern, overloaded court system.

ACTIVITY

Essay writing

Explain the constitutional and practical advantages and disadvantages of tribunals. Do the former outweigh the latter?

21.1.6 Reform

In 2001 the Leggatt Report made a number of recommendations, which included:

■ Rationalising the structure of the network of tribunals (bringing them together under one system) and its appellate system, thereby ensuring common structural arrangements.

■ Enhancing the position of 'users' of the tribunal system.

Following the report, the then Labour government issued its White Paper (*Transforming Public Services: Complaints, Redress and Tribunals* Cm 6243 (DCA, 2004)) in which it stated, *inter alia*, that it intended to:

- Place the system of tribunals on a unified and cohesive basis (including appeals).
- Rename the legal members of a tribunal 'tribunal judges'.
- Create the post of a Senior President of Tribunals.

In April 2006 the Tribunals Service became operational as an executive agency (from April 2011 it merged to create the HM Courts & Tribunals Service and is sponsored by the Ministry of Justice), providing common administrative support to the major tribunals of central government. At this time the Tribunals Service included the tribunals for which the then Department for Constitutional Affairs was responsible (eg asylum) and these were added to with other major central government tribunals such as the Social Security and Child Support Appeals Tribunal, the Criminal Injuries Compensation Appeals Panel and the Special Educational Needs and Disability Tribunal (others were scheduled to be added periodically). In this way, the independence of tribunals would be enhanced by removing them from their associated departments (eg the Mental Health Review Tribunal was transferred from the Department of Health, and the Social Security and Child Support Appeals Tribunal was moved from the Department for Work and Pensions).

Further reforms to the organisation of tribunals were achieved by the Tribunals, Courts and Enforcement Act 2007 (see below), which created a two-tier (flexible) system of tribunals which would allow other tribunals to be transferred in as well as enable new jurisdictional areas to be included. According to the Tribunals Service website in 2010 (then www.tribunals.gov.uk), the aim of these changes was to improve the service provided to customers by:

QUOTATION

- 'Making clear the complete independence of the judiciary, and their decision making, from Government;
- Speeding up the delivery of justice;
- Making processes easier for the public to understand;
- Bringing together the expertise from each Tribunal.'

21.1.7 The Tribunals, Courts and Enforcement Act 2007

The two-tiered tribunal system

The Act created a simplified two-tiered statutory framework of tribunals (composed of a First-Tier Tribunal and an Upper Tribunal) to which tribunals would be periodically transferred. The two generic tribunals (ie First-Tier and Upper) are organised into 'Chambers', each headed by a Chamber President so that similar jurisdictional areas can be grouped together. This allows for a more efficient organisational use of tribunal members and resources.

According to the Tribunals Service website in January 2018, the First-Tier Tribunal included, among others, the following Chambers:

- Social Entitlement Chamber (Asylum Support, Social Security and Child Support and Criminal Injuries Compensation)

- Health, Education and Social Care Chamber (Care Standards, Mental Health, Special Educational Needs & Disability and Primary Health Lists)

The Upper Tribunal contained the following four Chambers:
- Administrative Appeals
- Lands
- Tax and Chancery
- Immigration and Asylum

NB. Employment Tribunals are not part of this two-tier structure.

In general terms, the Upper Tribunal acts as an appellate tribunal (on a point of law) from the First-Tier Tribunal, thereby rationalising the appeals process. Thereafter, appeals are possible from the Upper Tribunal to the courts. In terms of judicial review of the Upper Tribunal's refusal to give permission to appeal to itself, in *R (Cart) v Upper Tribunal* [2011] UKSC 28 the Supreme Court adopted a restricted approach. It is of interest to note that the Act conferred on the Upper Tribunal a power of judicial review in respect of the First-Tier Tribunal in specified circumstances (s 18). In this jurisdiction, the Upper Tribunal has similar powers to those exercised by the existing Administrative Court (see Chapter 19).

Personnel

Under the Act the legal members of tribunals (ie those legally qualified) are designated as tribunal judges and the Constitutional Reform Act 2005 has been amended so as to provide for the independence of the tribunal judiciary (see section 13.4.1). In addition, a new statutory judicial office was created (the Senior President of Tribunals) to provide leadership to the tribunal judiciary and oversee the system of tribunals. The non-legal members of the panel are known as tribunal members. NB: Pt 3 of the Wales Act 2017 created the post of President of Welsh Tribunals (s 60) and enables the cross-deployment of tribunal members/judges. For example, under s 63 a member of a Welsh Tribunal can act as a member of the First-Tier Tribunal when asked to do so by the Senior President of Tribunals and with the agreement of the President of Welsh Tribunals.

The Administrative Justice and Tribunals Council

The Act replaced the Council on Tribunals (which oversaw tribunals and inquiries and made appropriate recommendations) with an Administrative Justice and Tribunals Council. This body not only would oversee and report on the new tribunal system but also had a wider remit to review the whole *Administrative Justice System* (including how government departments, the Ombudsman, etc, relate to the public). However, in 2013 The Public Bodies (Abolition of Administrative Justice and Tribunals Council) Order 2013 SI 2013/2042 abolished this advisory council. This vacuum has since been filled by the advisory Administrative Justice Forum, sponsored by the Ministry of Justice.

Procedures and rules

The rules and procedures which historically governed tribunals were generally composed by the Lord Chancellor or the relevant government minister. The Act created the Tribunal Procedure Committee, which has assumed responsibility for making these rules (Tribunal Procedure Rules), thereby providing greater consistency in the rules used in the tribunal system. For instance, see the Tribunal Procedure (First-Tier

Tribunal) (Social Entitlement Chamber) Rules 2008 SI 2008/2685 (L.13). In addition, the Senior President of Tribunals is able to issue Practice Directions (analogous to those in court). For example, see the Practice Direction, First-Tier Tribunal, Health Education and Social Care Chamber, Statements and Reports in mental health cases (October 2013, Tribunals Judiciary).

KEY FACTS

Tribunals
(i) Tribunals are a grievance remedy which enables individuals to challenge decisions made by state officials in a forum which is outside the formal court system.
(ii) Tribunals can be divided into those which resolve disputes between the individual and the state (eg the Social Security and Child Support Tribunal), and those which regulate legal disputes between the individual and a company/business/employer (ie employment tribunals).
(iii) A tribunal is an impartial decision-making body which is not part of the government department it oversees.
(iv) They are also separate and distinct from the formal court system.
(v) They are intended to be more accessible and user-friendly than the courts.
(vi) They typically do not involve paid legal representatives.

21.2 Inquiries

Introduction

In very broad terms inquiries can be divided into two types:

- Those which investigate and report on local land issues (eg the refusal of a local planning authority to grant planning permission) and these are known as 'routine administrative inquiries'. These concern an individual's dispute with the state.
- Those which investigate and report on specific events (eg the Bloody Sunday inquiry into the shooting of civilians in Londonderry).

21.2.1 Land inquiries

When a local planning authority refuses to grant planning permission under s 78 of the Town and County Planning Act 1990, an individual may seek to challenge such a decision by way of an appeal to the Secretary of State. In practice, however, this appeal will be determined by a planning inspector from the Planning Inspectorate which is an executive agency of the Department for Communities and Local Government. An appeal can be processed in one of the following three ways:

- **The (standard) written representations procedure** – this is the most basic of appeals and is appropriate for minor issues/works or alterations. The vast majority of appeals are dealt with by this procedure which involves the inspector considering the appeal on the basis of written representations. There is an expedited procedure for householder appeals.

- **The hearing procedure** – this is presided over by an inspector and is appropriate for more complicated cases than those discussed above, or where questions need to be asked. It is less formal than the public local inquiry procedure (detailed below).
- **The public local inquiry procedure** – this is the most formal of all the appeals and only occurs in a minority of cases. It considers the most complicated or largest appeals. The interested parties (ie the individual/appellant and the local planning authority) can call evidence and cross-examine witnesses and the procedure will usually involve legal representation (this is analogous to a court; however, the inquiry is *not* a court of law). The inspector will thereafter issue a report.

According to figures from the Planning Inspectorate, the following were received during 2015–16:

- 10,428 written representations
- 905 hearings
- 448 inquiries

Source: Planning Inspectorate, *s 78 Planning Appeals –
Received by procedure type*, Table 2.1 (www.gov.uk).

In the overwhelming majority of cases appeals in practice are determined by a planning inspector (acting in the name of the Secretary of State). However, a small number of appeals are decided (ie 'recovered' from the Planning Inspectorate under s 79 of the Town and Country Planning Act 1990) by the Secretary of State personally (eg in respect of major or contentious projects). In addition, under s 77 of the Act the Secretary of State has the power to 'call in' a planning application directly from the local planning authority and make the decision himself. In April 2012 the Minister of State, Department for Communities and Local Government set out the criteria used when a planning application is called in:

QUOTATION

'The Government believe that planning decisions should be taken in, and by, local communities, and so use their call-in powers sparingly. Essentially, the powers are used when matters are of national significance.'

Hansard, HC, Vol 543, col 1234.

The Secretary of State will make the decision following an inquiry at which a planning inspector has made recommendations – which can be accepted or rejected by the minister.

According to figures extrapolated from the Planning Inspectorate, during the calendar year of 2016, 16 'called in' planning applications were received and the Secretary of State received 75 'recovered' appeals (source: Planning Inspectorate, *Called in Planning Applications and recovered s 78 appeals*, Table 1.4 (www.gov.uk)).

On the powers of the Secretary of State to 'call in' applications or 'recover appeals' and their compatibility with Art 6 of the European Convention, see *R (Alconbury Developments Ltd) v Secretary of State for the Environment, Transport and the Regions* [2001] UKHL 23. In this case, the House of Lords held that the availability of judicial review in this context meant that these powers did not breach the Convention. In contrast, in *R (Moore) v Secretary of State for Communities and Local Government* [2015] EWHC 44 (Admin) the recovery of appeals in relation to caravan pitches in the Green Belt was contrary to the Equality Act 2010, and, owing to the delays caused, also a breach of Art 6 of the European Convention.

In addition, the National Infrastructure Planning Unit (under the aegis of the Planning Inspectorate) processes major infrastructure project applications which are of national importance, with the final decision resting with the Secretary of State.

Finally, it is of interest to note that the Growth and Infrastructure Act 2013 (which amended the Town and Country Planning Act 1990) allows a planning application in respect of a major development to be made directly to the Secretary of State in the event that the local planning authority is 'designated' under the Act (ie the authority is not performing adequately its function of determining applications).

21.2.2 Inquiries into national events/scandals

QUOTATION

'Inquiries into matters of major public concern are now an integral feature of the governance of this country. They establish disputed facts, determine accountability, restore public confidence, and make recommendations for preventing recurrence of events and taking forward public policy.'

House of Lords Select Committee on the Inquiries Act 2005, *The Inquiries Act 2005: post-legislative scrutiny*, HL Paper 143 (The Stationery Office, 2014), p 6.
NB: this report provided very useful post-legislative scrutiny of the Act.

The second type of inquiry investigates and makes recommendations in respect of a national event (eg the Scarman Report into the riots and disorder in Brixton in the early 1980s) or a public scandal (eg the Denning report into the Profumo affair). There are two categories of these types of inquiry:

- A statutory inquiry.
- A non-statutory inquiry.

In both cases these inquiries are not courts and their findings do not have legal effect:

QUOTATION

'Inquiries are designed to establish facts through an inquisitorial, investigatory process . . . inquiries are not courts and are not designed to determine criminal or civil liability or to settle disputes between parties.'

Department for Constitutional Affairs Consultation Paper, *Effective Inquiries* (DCA, 2004), para 81.

In the context of statutory inquiries, this point is reaffirmed by s 2 of the Inquiries Act 2005 (see below).

The constitutional purpose of both statutory and non-statutory inquiries is to investigate issues of national concern, evaluate the evidence and make recommendations. In doing so, as noted by the above government consultation paper, these inquiries can restore public confidence, provide some benefit for those affected by the event in question and identify lessons that can be learned.

21.2.3 Statutory inquiries into national events

Historically, there have been two types of statutory inquiry:

- A statutory inquiry under subject specific legislation, for example the Stephen Lawrence Inquiry established under s 49 of the Police Act 1996.
- A statutory inquiry under the Tribunals of Inquiry (Evidence) Act 1921, for example the (first) Bloody Sunday Inquiry under Lord Widgery. Under this Act inquiries were relatively rare, with only 24 in total, the last two being the Shipman Inquiry (into the deaths of a number of elderly women) and the (second) Bloody Sunday Inquiry under Lord Saville, which was established in 1998 and reported in 2010. Today, statutory inquiries are held under the Inquiries Act 2005. This Act repealed the Tribunals of Inquiry (Evidence) Act 1921, together with other statutory provisions authorising inquiries (eg s 49 of the Police Act 1996). Under the 2005 Act a government minister can establish an inquiry:

SECTION

S 1(1)

. . . where it appears to him that –

(a) particular events have caused, or are capable of causing, public concern, or

(b) there is public concern that particular events may have occurred.

Section 5 of the Act provides for the minister to set out the terms of reference of the inquiry and s 21 empowers the Chair of the inquiry to compel evidence (witnesses or documents). Under s 35 it is a criminal offence not to comply with a notice issued by the Chair under the Act.

The Act enables a minister to appoint a judicial figure to act as a panel member or Chair (though there would be consultation with, for example, the Lord Chief Justice). In constitutional terms the involvement of the judiciary in high-profile inquiries can raise questions as to whether participation (ultimately) undermines their constitutional independence. In short, as the subject matter of such inquiries can be overtly politically charged, it could be argued that whatever conclusions and recommendations are made, the judge involved will inevitably be subject to criticism from some quarters. The government, however, has defended the use of judges:

QUOTATION

'The Government believes that it can be appropriate for judges to chair inquiries, because their experience and position make them particularly well suited to the role. The judiciary has a great deal of experience in analysing evidence, determining facts and reaching conclusions. . . . The judiciary also has a long tradition of independence from politics, and judges are widely accepted to be free from any party political bias.'

Department for Constitutional Affairs Consultation Paper, *Effective Inquiries* (DCA, 2004), para 46.

Student mentor tip

'Keep up-to-date with current affairs – it really helps if you can mention hot topics in your exam.'

Adil, Queen Mary University

Under the 2005 Act a number of inquiries have been established, including:

- An inquiry into the death of Baha Mousa (an Iraqi citizen in British custody in Iraq) under Lord Justice Gage, which reported in 2011.
- An inquiry into the culture, practices and ethics of the press under Lord Justice Leveson, which reported in 2012.
- An inquiry set up in 2017 (with Sir Martin Moore-Bick as Chair) into the circumstances surrounding the fire at Grenfell Tower in London.

21.2.4 Non-statutory inquiries into national events

The government has regularly established non-statutory inquires to consider major national events. For example:

- The Hutton Inquiry into the circumstances surrounding the death of Dr David Kelly.
- The Scott Inquiry into the export of equipment to Iraq (see section 12.3.5).

Such inquiries are more flexible than statutory inquiries, although they lack enforcement powers to compel evidence (witnesses or documents). Under s 15 of the 2005 Act, however, a government minister can convert such an inquiry into a statutory one, for example where it is considered that enforcement powers are required.

Two relatively recent inquiries involving a committee of Privy Councillors (a variant of the non-statutory inquiry) were:

- The 2004 Butler Inquiry concerning the intelligence on WMD (weapons of mass destruction).
- The 2009 Iraq Inquiry. This was set up to establish what happened in Iraq and identify the lessons that could be learned from the Iraq conflict. Sir John Chilcot (an ex-civil servant) was the Chair of the inquiry, which began hearing evidence in late 2009. In respect of this inquiry, the Public Administration Select Committee made the following constitutional observation:

QUOTATION

'It is wrong in principle that the executive alone should determine the terms of this inquiry, when the conduct of the executive is a central part of what the inquiry will have to consider.'

Ninth Report of Session 2008–09, *The Iraq Inquiry*, HC 721 (2009), para 18.

The inquiry finally reported (albeit delayed) in July 2016. On the process of this inquiry, see Public Administration and Constitutional Affairs Committee, *Lessons still to be learned from the Chilcot Inquiry*, HC 656 (House of Commons, 2017).

Law and inquiries

In respect of Iraq, it is worth noting the case of *R (Gentle) v Prime Minister* [2008] UKHL 20. The House of Lords held that there was no duty on the part of the government under Art 2 of the European Convention to initiate a public inquiry in respect of whether there had been due diligence (in terms of being lawful under international law) regarding the decision to go to war in Iraq. More recently, in *R (Keyu) v Secretary of State for Foreign and Commonwealth Affairs and another* [2015] UKSC 69 the Supreme Court affirmed that there were no grounds for challenging the Secretaries of State's decisions when they exercised their discretion not to hold an inquiry under the Inquiries Act 2005 into the death of civilians in Malaya in 1948. In contrast, in *R (Litvinenko) v Secretary of State for the Home Department* [2014] EWHC 194 (Admin) the court held that the Secretary of State had provided no rational reasons for a refusal to set up an inquiry under the Inquiries Act 2005 into the circumstances surrounding the death of the claimant's husband. In the event, a few months after this case, the Home Secretary established an inquiry under the Chair of Sir Robert Owen and his report was delivered in 2016 (*The Litvinenko Inquiry, Report into the death of Alexander Litvinenko*, HC 695 (Crown Copyright, 2016)).

KEY FACTS

Inquiries

Land inquiries are a grievance mechanism which permits individuals to challenge, for example, the decision of a local planning authority to refuse planning permission.

A second type of inquiry investigates and reports on major public events. Such inquiries are either:

Statutory inquiries – historically these were established under statute:
- Stephen Lawrence Inquiry under the aegis of the Police Act 1996.
- The two Bloody Sunday inquiries under the aegis of the Tribunals of Inquiry (Evidence) Act 1921.

These have now been replaced by the Inquiries Act 2005. Under the 2005 Act a government minister can establish an inquiry into events which have, or are capable of, causing public concern. For example:
- The Gage Inquiry into the death of Baha Mousa.
- The Leveson Inquiry into the press.

Non-statutory inquiries
- The Hutton Inquiry.
- The Iraq Inquiry.

ACTIVITY

Essay writing

In terms of their nature and constitutional role, compare and contrast inquiries with tribunals.

21.3 Ombudsmen

Introduction

QUOTATION

'The activities of the Ombudsmen are concerned with holding public bodies to account and exposing maladministration where it has occurred. In so doing, part of their function is to encourage best practice in public administration.'

Reform of Public Sector Ombudsmen Services in England (Cabinet Office, 2005), para 45.

The British constitution has a number of different public sector ombudsmen, which cover central and local government, the National Health Service and the devolved administrations in Wales, Scotland and Northern Ireland. The function of these ombudsmen is to investigate complaints relating to maladministration – in other words, faulty government/administration. This part of the Chapter will focus on arguably the most constitutionally significant of the ombudsmen: the Parliamentary Commissioner for Administration (hereafter the Ombudsman):

'Our role

We consider complaints that government departments, a range of other public bodies in the UK, and the NHS in England, have not acted properly or fairly or have provided a poor service.'

> The Parliamentary and Health Service Ombudsman, *Moving Forward,*
> *Annual Report 2011–12*, HC 251 (The Stationery Office, 2012), p 4.

NB. By constitutional convention the same person occupies the office of Parliamentary Ombudsman as well as Health Service Commissioner (hence references to the Parliamentary and Health Service Ombudsman/PHSO).

21.3.1 Origins

Prior to the creation of the Ombudsman in 1967, there were essentially two remedies available to an individual who was aggrieved by the actions of the officials of government departments:

- **The parliamentary remedy** – individuals could consult their constituency MP in order to resolve their grievance. The effectiveness of this remedy depended upon the tenacity and ability of the MP to access governmental information.
- **The legal/judicial remedy** – individuals could seek justice before the courts by suing the government department concerned in public or private law. This was (as it is today) expensive and in any event, the action causing the grievance may not have even been illegal as not falling within a recognised legal category (eg negligence, breach of contract). Another legal remedy involved an appeal of a decision to a tribunal.

The Whyatt Report (*The Citizen and the Administration: the Redress of Grievances* (JUSTICE, 1961)) noted the limitations of the then 'existing means of seeking redress' and recommended the creation of an independent officer of Parliament to investigate such grievances against the state. In 1967 Parliament established the Parliamentary Commissioner for Administration under the Parliamentary Commissioner Act 1967 (as amended). Under s 1 the Ombudsman (currently Rob Behrens) is appointed by the Crown. The constitutional function of the Ombudsman is to independently investigate complaints of injustice caused by maladministration by government and public bodies. There had been concern that the creation of an Ombudsman, independently examining departmental issues, would undermine the constitutional convention of ministerial responsibility. It is clear, however, that the operation of the office over the decades has actively enhanced the convention by requiring ministers to account for maladministration found in their department.

21.3.2 Maladministration

Maladministration is referred to in the 1967 Act but it is not specifically defined. As a consequence, it has been apposite to refer to the famous *Crossman Catalogue* to indicate the type of behaviour that maladministration covers:

QUOTATION

'bias, neglect, inattention, delay, incompetence, inaptitude, perversity, turpitude, arbitrariness and so on. It would be a long and interesting list.'

Hansard, HC Vol 734, col 51.

Latterly the Ombudsman's website has indicated that maladministration also embraces, *inter alia,* the following types of behaviour:

- A faulty procedure.
- Rudeness.
- Avoidable delay.
- A refusal to answer reasonable questions.
- A failure to indicate a right of appeal.

Three points can be made in relation to maladministration.

Firstly, maladministration is concerned essentially with the procedure/behaviour of state officials, as opposed to the actual decision itself. In other words, it is concerned, for example, with how a person's claim for a social security benefit was processed by the department (eg was there an avoidable delay? Were forms lost? Were officials rude?), rather than whether they are legally entitled to a particular benefit (which is a legal question to be resolved, typically, in a tribunal). In this way maladministration focuses on the decision-making process rather than the actual decision itself. However, the select committee overseeing the Ombudsman has urged the office to infer maladministration where a decision is *bad* (as this presupposes an element of maladministration) – see the Second Report from the Select Committee for the Parliamentary Commissioner for Administration, HC 350 (1967–68). Indeed, as noted by Kirkham, the reading and implication of s 12(3) of the Act is 'that where a decision is taken *with* maladministration then the PO [Parliamentary Ombudsman] can legally consider the merits of the decision' (*The Parliamentary Ombudsman: Withstanding the Test of Time,* HC 421 (2007), p 7).

Secondly, although maladministration is broader than illegality, the precise dividing line between maladministration and illegality may on occasions be a very fine one. For example, avoidable delay or the provision of inadequate advice could well be considered to be legally actionable in negligence.

Thirdly, although the list above suggests behaviour which to an objective observer may appear to be somewhat trivial and unimportant (eg discourtesy by a public official), nonetheless, to the individual concerned, such behaviour will leave them feeling aggrieved against the state.

Under s 5 of the Act, individuals must claim 'to have sustained injustice in consequence of maladministration in connection with the action so taken'. The cases indicate that injustice can embrace financial hardship/loss or even distress/outrage.

21.3.3 Jurisdiction

The bodies subject to the investigations of the Ombudsman are set out in Sch 2 of the Act and include:

- Central government departments of state (eg the Home Office).
- Public bodies (eg the Arts Council of England).

As an illustration (albeit historical), the Ombudsman's Annual Report of 2011–12 identified the following five government departments, against which the most complaints were accepted for a formal investigation:

- Ministry of Justice.
- Home Office.
- Department for Work and Pensions.
- HM Revenue & Customs.
- Department for Communities and Local Government.

Moving Forward, Annual Report 2011–12, HC 251
(The Stationery Office, 2012), p 17.

It is not altogether surprising that these departments should have the most complaints against them given that the public have regular contact with them.

A number of matters are excluded from the Ombudsman's remit and these are detailed in Sch 3 and include, *inter alia,* investigations relating to:

- Foreign relations.
- Contractual/commercial matters.
- The investigation of crime.

In addition, the Ombudsman is precluded from investigating where the individual has a legal remedy available to them before a court or tribunal. This is subject to the proviso (s 5) that the Ombudsman *can* investigate such a compliant if satisfied that it would be unreasonable for that person to resort to such a remedy (eg it is too expensive or the law is unclear on the point). However, in the context of the *Debt of Honour case* (see below), the House of Commons Public Administration Select Committee made the following point:

QUOTATION

'The entire basis of the 1967 Parliamentary Commissioner for Administration Act is that it is possible for a measure to be legal, and yet to be maladministered. The fact that legality has been established through Judicial Review may be irrelevant to maladministration. There may even be circumstances where the Ombudsman feels it is appropriate to conduct an investigation while Judicial Review proceedings are taking place, so that she can subsequently report without delay. We would, in principle, support this.'

First Report of Session 2005–06, *A Debt of Honour*, HC 735 (2006), para 20.

In fact, the overlap between the Ombudsman and the courts can be illustrated by the *Congreve* case (see section 20.2.4), in which the court decided that the Home Secretary had acted illegally by threatening to revoke television licences purchased early in order to avoid paying an increased licence fee. This court ruling followed an earlier investigation by the Ombudsman which had held that maladministration had occurred, but had not recommended a remedy. According to the Law Commission:

QUOTATION

'Through the notion of maladministration, the ombudsmen are able to conduct a broad-brush assessment of the overall manner in which a public body has conducted itself, including instances of institutional failure. In this respect, it is a more holistic inquiry than judicial scrutiny, which tends to focus on isolated acts or omissions as being negligent or unlawful.'

Administrative Redress: Public Bodies and the Citizen, A Consultation Paper,
Law Commission, No 187, para 3.65.

21.3.4 The investigation process

In broad terms the three stages are as follows:

The first/screening stage

This is known as the filter or screening stage, whereby an aggrieved person must first send their complaint to an MP (generally their own, but other MPs can deal with it), who in turn may pass it on to the Ombudsman. The complaint must be given to the MP within 12 months of the individual having notice of the grievance. Although the Ombudsman has a discretion to accept a complaint outside the time limit, the limit is usually applied. In short, complainants cannot complain directly to the Ombudsman; instead, the MP referral system operates, which has proved controversial.

In fact, this filter system is unusual among the different public sector ombudsmen and can be seen to act as a barrier preventing access to the Ombudsman. On the other hand, the rationale behind the referral system was to protect the constitutional position of the MP, one of whose functions is to resolve the problems of constituents. A further problem with removing the filter is the argument that direct access would overwhelm the Ombudsman with complaints. In any event, over the years there have been attempts at removing this filter. In fact, in July 2001, the then Labour government indicated that it supported its removal. More recently, in 2009 the Public Administration Select Committee recommended the abolition of the filter as 'long overdue' (*Parliament and the Ombudsman*, HC, 107 (2009), p 4). Furthermore, the 2011–12 Annual Report indicated that the vast majority of respondents in the Ombudsman's public consultation supported removing the filter (p 7). Now see the draft Bill at later at section 21.3.8.

In terms of figures, during the period of 2016–17 the Ombudsman handled 31,249 new complaints (22,965 concerned the NHS and 6,909 related to government organisations, with the remainder related to bodies not within the Ombudsman's jurisdiction) (source: figures extrapolated from *The Ombudsman's Annual Report and Accounts 2016–17*, HC 207 (Parliamentary and Health Service Ombudsman Copyright, 2017), p 8).

The formal investigation stage

On receipt of a referral by an MP, under the Act the Ombudsman has discretion as to whether or not to investigate a complaint (s 5) and how an investigation is conducted (s 7). Moreover, the Ombudsman can discontinue an investigation once commenced. He has wide-ranging powers of investigation which enable him to require any government minister, officer or member of the department (or other person) to furnish information or documents apposite to the investigation. The Act states that for the purpose of the investigation the Ombudsman:

SECTION

s 8(2)
'shall have the same powers as the Court in respect of the attendance and examination of witnesses . . . and in respect of the production of documents.'

Furthermore, it will amount to contempt to obstruct the work of the Ombudsman (s 9). Although the Ombudsman has powerful investigatory powers, he operates in a more inquisitorial way than the courts, which employ an adversarial approach. Investigations are carried out in private and he can go directly to the heart of the government department or public body and obtain information. On completion of the investigation, a report will be issued.

The report stage

Under s 10 of the Act, on completion of the investigation a report is sent to the MP who referred the complaint, and to the principal officer of the government department. Where the report indicates a finding of maladministration resulting in injustice, generally speaking the department/authority concerned will comply with the recommendations for remedial action. In terms of figures (albeit historical), the *Annual Report 2011–12* provided some very revealing statistics about the process of complaints, as it indicated that the Ombudsman had resolved 23,889 enquiries (which included health statistics), as follows:

- 14 per cent of complaints were out of the remit of the Ombudsman.
- 38 per cent of complaints were not made properly (eg not referred by an MP).
- 23 per cent of complaints were premature (eg the complainant had not tried to resolve the complaint/issue with the relevant body).
- 18 per cent of complaints (in the exercise of the Ombudsman's discretion) were not accepted for a formal investigation.
- 6 per cent of complaints were withdrawn.
- 2 per cent of complaints (421) were accepted for a formal investigation (of these 328 were against the NHS and 93 were against government departments and agencies).

NB. The report noted that the percentages were rounded up and so do not add up to 100 per cent.

In addition, of the 4,732 enquiries 'looked at closely':

- 3,552 cases – there was found no case to answer.
- 759 cases – the complaint was put right without the need for a formal investigation, thereby showing the Ombudsman resolving complaints via 'informal means'.
- 421 cases – accepted the need for a formal investigation.

The report detailed that, during 2011–12, 410 formal investigations were conducted, with 60 per cent fully upheld, 20 per cent partly upheld and 20 per cent of complaints not upheld (*Moving Forward, Annual Report 2011–12*, HC 251 (The Stationery Office, 2012), pp 45 & 9).

More recently, during the period of 2016–17 the Ombudsman assessed 8,119 complaints and accepted 3,767 for investigation (3,297 in respect of the NHS in England and 470 of government departments/organisations). In addition, the Ombudsman completed 4,239 investigations (3,715 in respect of the NHS in England and 524 of government departments/organisations) in which the complaint was fully or partly upheld in 36 per cent of cases and not upheld in 52 per cent (the others were resolved or ended) (source: figures extrapolated from *The Ombudsman's Annual Report and Accounts 2016–17*, HC 207 (Parliamentary and Health Service Ombudsman Copyright, 2017), pp 8–12).

It should be noted, however, that, despite the Ombudsman's wide-ranging investigatory powers, his recommendations are not legally binding. In other words, although he can invite a department to, for example, award compensation, alter its administrative procedures or offer an apology, he cannot legally insist on it. Having said this, in general terms the Ombudsman's recommendations are accepted (although see below). Indeed, even in the Barlow Clowes affair of 1988 the government paid out *ex gratia* payments even though it did not accept the findings of maladministration. The 2016–17 Annual Report stated that 'In 99% of complaints the organisation agreed to act on our recommendations' (p 11). These recommendations included apologies, payments and service improvements. The work of the Ombudsman is overseen by a select committee:

the House of Commons Public Administration and Constitutional Affairs Select Committee.

Under s 10(3) of the Act, if after conducting an investigation the Ombudsman believes that the injustice he has identified will not be remedied, a special report can be issued which will draw the attention of Parliament (and the wider public) to this deficiency. The second of these reports to be issued occurred in 1995 in relation to the Channel Tunnel Rail Link, which resulted in the 'blighting' of houses which could not be sold while the exact route was being determined, and in the event the government proposed compensation. More recent examples of two special reports being issued are detailed below (these represent the third and fourth special reports issued by the Ombudsman in five decades):

CASE STUDY

'A Debt of Honour: The ex-gratia scheme for British groups interned by the Japanese during the Second World War', *HC 324 (July 2005)*

The Ombudsman held that injustice had been caused as a result of maladministration by the Ministry of Defence in respect of the operation of its *ex gratia* payments for British internees held by the Japanese during the Second World War. The government refused (at least initially) to accept two of the recommendations made: (a) to review the operation of the scheme and (b) to reconsider the position of those denied payment under the scheme. In January 2006 the Public Administration Select Committee published a report which was critical of the Ministry of Defence: First Report of Session 2005–06, *A Debt of Honour*, HC 735 (2006). Later, in a written answer in May 2006, Lord Drayson (the then Parliamentary Under-Secretary of State, Minister of Defence) confirmed that the Ministry of Defence had at that point in effect implemented all of the Ombudsman's recommendations (ie the eligibility under the scheme would be extended with an expectation of Professor Hayward thereby qualifying) (*Hansard*, HL Vol 681, col WA 87).

One interesting point to note about this case was that there was a delay in processing this complaint because the Association of British Internees Far Eastern Region challenged the Secretary of State in judicial review proceedings. They contended that the civilian eligibility criterion – which meant that for the purposes of the scheme being British meant being a civilian who had been born in Britain or whose parent or grandparent had been – was disproportionate and or/irrational and defeated a legitimate expectation. The Court of Appeal dismissed their appeal and held, *inter alia*, that it was not irrational for the Secretary of State to limit the application of the scheme to those individuals with close links to the United Kingdom at the time of their detention as an internee, or to introduce the birth criteria (*R (Association of British Civilian Internees: Far East Region) v Secretary of State for Defence* [2003] EWCA Civ 473).

CASE STUDY

'Trusting in the pensions promise: Government bodies and the security of final salary occupational pensions', *HC 984 (March 2006)*

The Ombudsman found injustice caused by maladministration *inter alia* in terms of official information provided by the government in respect of the security of members' final salary occupational pension schemes (the 'first' finding of maladministration). The government rejected the findings that maladministration had occurred and most of the Ombudsman's recommendations. In July 2006 the Public Administration Select Committee in support of the Ombudsman made the following constitutional point:

QUOTATION

'. . . this system will only work if the Parliamentary Ombudsman, the Government and Parliament share a broad common understanding of what maladministration might be and who should properly identify it [para 76]. . . . We share the Ombudsman's concern that the Government has been far too ready to dismiss her findings of maladministration. . . . It would be extremely damaging if Government became accustomed simply to reject findings of maladministration, especially if an investigation by this Committee proved there was indeed a case to answer. It would raise fundamental constitutional issues about the position of the Ombudsman and the relationship between Parliament and the Executive [para 78]. We trust that this Report will act as a warning to the Government. . . . The Parliamentary Commissioner is Parliament's Ombudsman: Government must respect her' (para 79).

Sixth Report of Session 2005–06, *The Ombudsman in Question: the Ombudsman's report on pensions and its constitutional implications*, HC 1081 (2006).

In December 2007 the Secretary of State for Work and Pensions made a ministerial statement outlining a 'Financial Assistance Scheme' (*Hansard,* HC Vol 469, col 100 WS).

As an interesting postscript to this case, in *R (Bradley and others) v Secretary of State for Work and Pensions* [2008] EWCA Civ 36, although the Court of Appeal made it clear that the Secretary of State was not required to accept findings of maladministration by virtue of the 1967 Act, the Secretary of State had, however, acted irrationally in rejecting the Ombudsman's first finding of maladministration and confirmed that this rejection should be quashed.

A fifth report was issued in May 2009:

CASE STUDY

'Injustice unremedied: The Government's response on Equitable Life', *HC 435 (Crown Copyright, 2009)*

In this report the Ombudsman stated that she was:

'. . . satisfied that the injustice I found in my report [ie *Equitable Life: A Decade of Regulatory Failure*, HC 815 (Crown Copyright 2008)], to have resulted from maladministration on the part of the public bodies responsible for the prudential regulation of the Society has not so far been remedied.'

(para 72)

In October 2009, the Administrative Court heard a (partly successful) action for judicial review: *R (Equitable Members Action Group) v HM Treasury* [2009] EWHC 2495 (Admin), brought by the Equitable Members Action Group of the HM Treasury's rejection of certain findings of the Ombudsman (the government had however accepted some of them). The court held, *inter alia*, that the government had failed to provide a cogent reason for rejecting certain findings of the Ombudsman. As a postscript to this matter, the Equitable Life (Payments) Act 2010 provided for payments to those affected by maladministration.

In December 2009 the Ombudsman laid a sixth report under s 10(3), this time concerning farmers and the Single Payment Scheme: *Cold Comfort: the Administration of the 2005 Single Payment Scheme by the Rural Payments Agency*, Second Report of Session 2009–10, HC 81 (Crown Copyright, 2009). Thereafter, the government agreed to provide compensation. The latest (and seventh) report issued under s 10(3) is *A Report by the Parliamentary Ombudsman on an Investigation into a Complaint about the Electoral Commission*, HC 540 (Parliamentary and Health Service Ombudsman Copyright, 2014).

In addition to the periodic special reports above, under s 10(4) the Ombudsman is required to provide an annual report detailing his activities. This subsection also enables the Ombudsman to lay before each parliamentary House 'such other reports with respect to those functions as he thinks fit'. For example, following on from the 2005 *A Debt of Honour* investigation, the Ombudsman then found injustice resulting from maladministration in the subsequent 'injury to feelings' scheme of payments (Mr A was treated unfairly and suffered distress). Although the Ministry of Defence accepted in full all of the recommendations, the Ombudsman nevertheless stated a report would be laid:

QUOTATION

'. . . first because of its connection with my earlier report; but primarily because it is the worst example I have seen, in nearly nine years as Parliamentary Ombudsman, of a government department getting things wrong and then repeatedly failing to put things right or learn from their mistakes.'

Defending the Indefensible, A report by the Parliamentary Ombudsman on an investigation of a complaint about the Ministry of Defence and the Service Personnel & Veterans Agency, Seventh report of session 2010–2012, HC 1462 (The Stationery Office, 2011), p 7.

More recently, the following two reports have also been laid under s 10(4):

- *Report on an Investigation into Complaints about High Speed Two Limited*, HC 620 (Parliamentary and Health Service Ombudsman Copyright, 2015).
- *Driven to Despair, How Drivers Have Been Let Down by the Driver and Vehicle Licensing Agency*, HC 660 (Parliamentary and Health Service Ombudsman Copyright, 2016).

21.3.5 Ombudsman or Ombudsmouse?

There has always been academic debate over the effectiveness of the Ombudsman. On the one hand the Ombudsman has wide-ranging investigatory powers, but on the other he has no legal powers of enforcement. However, as noted above by the Public Administration Select Committee in the context of the 2006 report on pensions, historically, even when government departments have denied maladministration found by the Ombudsman, 'they have ultimately been willing to offer some recompense out of respect for the Ombudsman's office' (para 67). Moreover, in her speech to the Constitution Unit in December 2006 the then Ombudsman made it clear that, in relation to the vast majority of complaints where maladministration is found, the government accepted these findings and then complied with her recommendations. As a consequence, she noted that she did not see the need for legal enforcement powers, although she added that this was subject to a proviso that if government departments systematically ignored her findings then she 'might begin to see some role for legal enforceability'.

In addition, it must be remembered that the Ombudsman also performs a *de facto* preventative role in that the very existence of the office acts to some extent as a deterrent to government departments to avoid engaging in behaviour which could be deemed as maladministration. In this way the Ombudsman promotes good governance. Indeed, according to the Ombudsman's 2005–06 Annual Report one of the aims for the 2006–09 period was: 'To contribute to improvements in public service delivery by being an influential organisation, sharing our knowledge and expertise' (p 59). Accordingly, in 2007 the Ombudsman produced a document on developing *Principles of Good Administration,* which set out in broad terms the Ombudsman's view as to what organisations and bodies should be doing in order to deliver good administration/customer service. The 2011–2012 Annual Report reiterated that part of the aim and vision of the Ombudsman was to drive 'improvements in public services' and to inform public policy (p 4).

Today, the *'Ombudsman's Principles'* embrace the following sets of principles:

- 'Good Administration'
- 'Good Complaint Handling'
- 'Remedy'

These are all governed by the following:

QUOTATION

'1. Getting it right
2. Being customer focused
3. Being open and accountable
4. Acting fairly and proportionately
5. Putting things right
6. Seeking continuous improvement'

www.ombudsman.org.uk.

A report, *The Parliamentary Ombudsman: Withstanding the Test of Time* (HC 421 (2007)), was published on the fortieth anniversary of the 1967 Act. Richard Kirkham, who wrote the report, commented that the Parliamentary Ombudsman 'has proved to be an effective addition to the system of administrative justice in the UK' (p 18) and concluded that: 'As well as improving the power of the citizen to gain redress, as was originally intended, Parliament itself has gained a valuable tool in the ongoing process of calling the government to account' (p 20).

21.3.6 Accountability

Under the rule of law all bodies are subject to the law. Although the Ombudsman is an independent officer of Parliament he is still accountable to:

- **The courts** – In *R v Parliamentary Commissioner for Administration, ex parte Dyer* [1994] 1 All ER 375 the court held that the Ombudsman was not outside the ambit of judicial review; however, the office did enjoy a broad discretion under the 1967 Act. In December 2006, in her speech to the Constitution Unit, the then Ombudsman noted that, although the number of applications for judicial review of the Ombudsman was increasing, they were generally rejected by the courts. The *2008–09 Annual Report* (*Every Complaint Matters,* HC 786 (2009)) noted that, of seven cases of judicial review issued against the Ombudsman during this period, six were refused permission to proceed, with one awaiting a decision. However, in a series of cases involving Balchin, the courts did review and quash the decisions of the Ombudsman: *R v Parliamentary Commissioner for Administration, ex parte Balchin* [1997] COD 146; *R v Parliamentary Commissioner for Administration, ex parte Balchin (No 2)* [2000] JPL 267; *R (Balchin) v Parliamentary Commissioner for Administration (No 3)* [2002] EWHC 1876 (Admin). NB: at the time of writing, the

Court of Appeal in *Miller v Health Service Commissioner for England* [2018] EWCA Civ 144 had quashed a decision of the Health Service Ombudsman.

■ **Parliament** – Under s 1 of the 1967 Act, the Ombudsman is removable by both Houses of Parliament (analogous to senior judges – see section 13.4.1). In addition, the Ombudsman is overseen by the Public Administration and Constitutional Affairs Select Committee and he also provides Parliament with an annual report of his workload.

KEY FACTS

The Ombudsman
The Ombudsman is a form of redress who investigates complaints of maladministration (eg poor government) against: • Central government departments of state (eg Home Office). • Public bodies (eg the Arts Council of England).
Individuals must have sustained injustice in consequence of maladministration and this can take the form of financial hardship or distress.
The Ombudsman (after being contacted by an MP) works in an inquisitorial manner and has wide investigatory powers to ascertain whether maladministration has occurred.
On conclusion of the investigation, a report will be issued detailing the maladministration found (or otherwise), together with any recommendations for remedial action.
Although the Ombudsman cannot legally enforce his recommendations, he can issue a special report where he considers that the maladministration will go unremedied.

21.3.7 Other ombudsmen

The system of public sector ombudsmen embraces the following:

■ **Health Service Commissioner** – This ombudsman was established under the National Health Service Reorganisation Act 1973 (as amended, but today his powers are drawn from the Health Service Commissioners Act 1993) and investigates complaints concerning a failure in services provided by the NHS in England. As noted, traditionally the office holder also operates as the Parliamentary Commissioner for Administration. The following legislation was recently passed to improve the handling of complaints: the Health Service Commissioner for England (Complaint Handling) Act 2015.

■ **Local government** (technically known as the Commission for Local Administration) – This ombudsman was established under the Local Government Act 1974 (as amended) to investigate complaints of maladministration in the context of local councils. It should be noted that in 2005 the then Labour government recommended streamlining the constitutional relationship of the parliamentary, health and local commissioners (*Reform of Public Sector Ombudsmen Services in England* (Cabinet Office: 2005)). In 2007 the Regulatory Reform (Collaboration etc between Ombudsmen) Order 2007/1889 was passed in order to increase the collaboration between the local government ombudsmen and the PHSO (ie in undertaking a joint investigation and sharing information). Also see reform below at section 21.3.8.

- **Scotland** – The Scottish Public Services Ombudsman Act 2002 rationalised the different ombudsmen under one organisation. The Scottish Public Service Ombudsman considers complaints in relation to, among others, the:
  - Scottish Government.
  - NHS in Scotland.
  - Councils and housing associations in Scotland.
- **Wales** – The Public Services Ombudsman for Wales was established under the Public Services Ombudsman (Wales) Act 2005. It considers complaints in the context of, for example:
  - Local government in Wales.
  - NHS in Wales.
  - Welsh Government.

NB. At the time of writing, the Public Services Ombudsman (Wales) Bill 2017 was being considered by the National Assembly for Wales.

- **Northern Ireland** – The Northern Ireland Public Services Ombudsman, established under the Public Services Ombudsman Act (Northern Ireland) 2016, considers complaints in respect of (among others):
  - Northern Ireland government departments and agencies.
  - District councils.
    (it should be noted that it has *initiative* powers in relation to investigations (s 8)).
- **Europe** – Under the Maastricht Treaty a European Ombudsman was established to investigate maladministration by the institutions of the EU (except the judicial bodies acting in their judicial capacity).
- **Judges** – Under s 62 of the Constitutional Reform Act 2005 a Judicial Appointments and Conduct Ombudsman has been created to investigate complaints in the context of the judicial appointments process and the handling of issues involving judicial conduct/discipline.

21.3.8 Recent reform proposals

Over the years there have been various proposals for reform of the Ombudsman. These have included removing the MP filter, expanding his jurisdiction and conferring the office with initiative and enforcement powers. In terms of recent proposals, in 2014 the Public Administration Select Committee recommended a number of reforms in order to create a more effective service for people (*Time for a People's Ombudsman Service,* HC 655 (The Stationery Office, 2014)). In response, the then coalition government commissioned a review by Robert Gordon CB, which reported later that year (*Better to Serve the Public: Proposals to Restructure, Reform, Renew and Reinvigorate Public Services Ombudsmen* (October 2014)). In essence, the report proposed the creation of a single Public Service Ombudsman (PSO). Following consultation, in December 2016 the Conservative government published the following draft Bill (together with explanatory notes): *Draft Public Service Ombudsman Bill,* Cm 9374 (Cabinet Office, Crown Copyright, 2016). Although this draft has to date not been transposed into a fully fledged Bill, its key elements were as follows:

- To establish a new single office of a Public Service Ombudsman (cl 2) to replace (and so abolish) the Parliamentary Commissioner for Administration, the Health Service Commissioner for England and the Commission for Local Administration in England.
- To establish a Board of the Public Service Ombudsman to provide the Ombudsman with resources and staff (cl 3).

- To abolish the MP filter, as cl 5 would allow a member of the public to make a complaint directly to the Ombudsman – it is noteworthy that at present the filter only applies to the Parliamentary Commissioner for Administration and *not* to the other ombudsmen.

SUMMARY

- There are a number of grievance mechanisms available to individuals who feel aggrieved by the actions of the state.
- Tribunals enable individuals to challenge decisions made by state officials in a forum which is outside the formal court system.
- Tribunals are more accessible and user-friendly than courts.
- Major structural reforms have taken place in recent years with the Tribunals, Courts and Enforcement Act 2007, which created a two-tiered system of tribunals (the First-Tier Tribunal and the Upper Tribunal).
- Inquiries come in different forms:
  - A local land inquiry into, for example, the refusal of a local planning authority to grant planning permission.
  - An inquiry into a national event or scandal. These can either be in the form of a non-statutory inquiry or a statutory inquiry under the Inquiries Act 2005.
- The Ombudsman is an officer who investigates injustice caused to individuals as a result of maladministration (faulty administration) by departments of state or bodies performing a public function.
- Complaints are referred by MPs. Thereafter the Ombudsman has wide-ranging powers of investigation in order to determine whether maladministration has occurred. On completion of the investigation a report will be issued.
- The finding of maladministration and any recommendations made are not legally binding, although (with some recent exceptions) they are generally accepted and followed.

SAMPLE ESSAY QUESTION

The Ombudsman is, in reality, an 'Ombudsmouse' and is in need of reform. Discuss.

Introduction:
- Definition – Parliamentary Commissioner for Administration (the Ombudsman) investigates complaints concerning maladministration.
- Established under the Parliamentary Commissioner Act 1967.

Purpose:
- Rationale for establishing the Ombudsman (see the Whyatt Report 1961) was due to the limitations of the existing parliamentary and legal avenues of redress for an aggrieved individual suffering at the hands of the administration.
- Investigates complaints of injustice due to maladministration caused by government departments and bodies performing a public function (Sch 2).

An Ombudsmouse:
- Jurisdiction is limited thereby excluding certain issues (eg commercial matters – Sch 3).
- In essence, concerned with the process of decision-making, rather than the actual decision itself (analogous to judicial review).
- Findings of maladministration and recommendations not legally enforceable so a government technically can disregard them, but note *Bradley* (2008).

An Ombudsman:
- Provides a remedy (which is free) when there is typically no other available.
- Considerable number of bodies subject to his jurisdiction.
- Strong powers of investigation – it is contempt to obstruct his work.
- Generally speaking the government accepts his findings and recommendations.
- In cases where the government does not accept maladministration, it may nevertheless provide a remedy (Barlow Clowes).
- In *A Debt of Honour*, although the government initially did not implement all the recommendations made, eventually it did.
- He acts in a *de facto* preventative capacity.
- He improves public administration/government (see the *Ombudsman's Principles*).
- The Ombudsman model has been extended to other contexts (eg local government).

Reform?
- Removal of the MP filter.
- Enforceable legal powers.
- Extended jurisdiction.
- Power to initiate an investigation.
- More publicity concerning his role.
- The 2016 Draft Public Service Ombudsman Bill.

Conclusion

Further reading

Books

Beer, J (ed), *Public Inquiries* (Oxford University Press, 2011).
Craig, P, *Administrative Law* (8th edn, Sweet & Maxwell, 2016), Chapters 8 and 9.

Leyland, P and Anthony, G, *Textbook on Administrative Law* (8th edn, Oxford University Press, 2016), Chapters 6 and 7.

Purdue, M, 'Investigations by the Public Sector Ombudsmen' in Feldman, D (ed), *English Public Law* (2nd edn, Oxford University Press, 2009), p 881.

Purdue, M, 'Public Inquiries as a Part of Public Administration' in Feldman, D (ed), *English Public Law* (2nd edn, Oxford University Press, 2009), p 919.

Richardson, G, 'Tribunals' in Feldman, D (ed), *English Public Law* (2nd edn, Oxford University Press, 2009), p 849.

Wade, H and Forsyth, C, *Administrative Law* (11th edn, Oxford University Press, 2014), Chapters 23 and 24.

Articles

Abraham, A, 'The Ombudsman and "paths to justice": a just alternative or just an alternative?' [2008] PL 1.

Abraham, A, 'The Ombudsman as part of the UK constitution: a contested role?' (2008) 61 *Parliamentary Affairs* 213.

Beatson, J, 'Should judges conduct public inquiries?' (2005) 121 LQR 221

Buck, T, Kirkham, R and Thompson, B, 'Time for a "Leggatt-style" review of the Ombudsman system?' [2011] PL 20.

Carnwath, R, 'Tribunal justice – a new start' [2009] PL 48.

Kirkham, R, Thompson, B and Buck, T, 'When putting things right goes wrong: Enforcing the recommendations of the Ombudsman' [2008] PL 511.

Scorer, R, 'Modern Inquiries and the public purse' (2005) 155 NLJ 60.

Lord Thomas, 'The future of public inquiries' [2015] PL 225.

Papers

Gay, O, *Investigatory inquiries and the Inquiries Act 2005*, SN/PC/02599 (House of Commons Library, 2009).

Kirkham, R, *The Parliamentary Ombudsman: Withstanding the test of time.* HC 421 (2007).

Internet links

www.ombudsman.org.uk
www.gov.uk

Glossary

Administrative Court
that part of the High Court which processes judicial review cases

bicameralism
a legislature composed of two chambers

Bill of Rights
document containing a list of basic and fundamental human rights

byelaw
subordinate legislation made by local authorities

by-election
an election which takes place in a constituency when an MP's seat becomes vacant

Cabinet
the collection of the most senior government ministers

Civil Service
the personnel who carry out and implement policies as determined by government ministers

constitution
the rules which govern the government which can be found in either a codified or uncodified form

constitutional convention
a binding political rule of the constitution

constitutionalism
the principle which requires a constitution to provide sufficient restraints on government/state power

declaration of incompatibility
a declaration by the courts under the Human Rights Act 1998 that legislation is inconsistent with the European Convention

delegated legislation
legislation made by the executive

devolution
power which has been delegated to regional bodies in Scotland, Wales and Northern Ireland

EU law
law and legal practices emanating from the European Union

electorate
individuals eligible to vote in an election

European Convention on Human Rights
originally formulated in 1950, this document aims to protect the human rights of all people in the member states of the Council of Europe

exclusivity
the principle that the enforcement of public law rights should be via the judicial review procedure

'first past the post'
the electoral system used to elect representatives in which the candidate with the most votes in a constituency wins the seat

freedom of expression
a right set out in Article 10 of the European Convention on Human Rights and now part of UK law as a consequence of the Human Rights Act 1998

human rights
rights and freedoms to which every human being is entitled

Human Rights Act
legislation enacted in 1998 that brought the European Convention on Human Rights into domestic law for the whole of the UK on 2 October 2000

intra vires
acting within specified powers

irrationality
a decision in law which no reasonable person could have come to

judicial independence
the principle that judges are independent of the other arms of the state

judicial review
the process whereby the courts review the legality of governmental actions

legislature
the law-making body in a constitution

life peers
persons appointed to the upper chamber of Parliament

local authorities
directly elected layer of government which administers functions at a local level and tailored to local needs

maladministration

poor administration

margin of appreciation

a concept created by the European Court of Human Rights to allow a certain amount of freedom for each signatory state to regulate its own activities and its application of the European Convention on Human Rights

Ministerial Code

a code of conduct issued by the Prime Minister which government ministers are required to follow

MP

a Member of Parliament, specifically in the House of Commons

natural justice/duty to act fairly

common law rules developed by the judiciary to ensure that public bodies exercise their powers and functions fairly

non-justiciable

an issue not suitable for resolution by the courts

Ombudsman

an officer who investigates complaints of maladministration

Parliament

composed of the House of Commons and the House of Lords

parliamentary executive

the constitutional arrangement whereby the executive/government is drawn from, and accountable to, the legislature/Parliament

parliamentary sovereignty

the legal principle that the Crown in Parliament can pass any law it chooses

peer

a person conferred with a peerage and a member of the upper chamber of Parliament, the House of Lords

private law

the law regulating the relationship between individuals

proportionality

the legal principle whereby the court considers the aims of the decision-maker and whether the means to achieve that objective is proportionate (ie the means used are not excessive)

public law

the law regulating the powers of the institutions of the state, how they relate to each other and how they relate to individuals

Royal Assent

the consent conferred on a Bill by the monarch in order to convert it into an Act of Parliament

royal prerogative

powers which the government draws from the common law

sub judice

the principle that there should be no discussion of matters proceeding through the courts

Supreme Court

the highest domestic court

ultra vires

acting beyond specified legal powers

Index